TEACHER EDUCATION MATTERS

TEACHER EDUCATION MATTERS

A Study of Middle School Mathematics Teacher Preparation in Six Countries

William H. Schmidt

Sigrid Blömeke

Maria Teresa Tatto

*With Feng-Jui Hsieh, Leland S. Cogan, Richard T. Houang,
Kiril Bankov, Marcela Santillan, Tenoch Cedillo, Shin-Il Han,
Martin Carnoy, Lynn Paine, and John Schwille*

TEACHERS
COLLEGE
PRESS

Teachers College, Columbia University
New York and London

The publisher wishes to acknowledge the following:

Figure 2.2. originally appeared in Blömeke, S., Herzig, G., & Tulodziecki, G. (2007). *Gestaltung von schule: Eine einführung in schultheorie und schulentwicklung [The formation of schools: An introduction to school theory and social development]*. Bad Heilbrunn/Obb, Germany: Klinkhardt. Copyright 2007. Used with permission of publisher.

Table 3.1. originally appeared in Blömeke, S., Felbrich, A., & Müller, C. (2008). Theoretischer rahmen und untersuchungsdesign [Theoretical framework and study design]. In S. Blömeke, G. Kaiser, & R. Lehmann (Eds.), *Professionelle kompetenz angehender lehrerinnen und Lehrer: Wissen, überzeugungen und lerngelegenheiten Deutscher mathematik-studierender und -referendare—erste ergebnisse zur wirksamkeit der lehrerausbildung [Professional competencies of future teachers: Knowledge, beliefs, and opportunities to learn for German mathematics teachers—First results about the effectiveness of teacher education]* (pp. 15–48). Münster, Germany: Waxmann. Copyright 2008. Used with permission of publisher.

Figure 3.1. originally appeared in Blömeke, S., Felbrich, A., Müller, C., Kaiser, G., & Lehmann, R. (2008). Effectiveness of teacher education: State of research, measurement issues, and consequences for future studies. *ZDM—The International Journal on Mathematics Education, 40*(5), 719–734. Copyright 2008. Used with permission of publisher.

Table 11.4. originally appeared in Carnoy, M., Brodziak, I., Loyalka, P., Reininger, M., & Luschei, T. (2006). *How much would it cost to attract individuals with more math knowledge into middle school (lower secondary) teaching: A seven-country comparison*. Palo Alto, CA: School of Education, Stanford University. Copyright 2006. Used with permission of publisher.

Published by Teachers College Press, 1234 Amsterdam Avenue, New York, NY 10027

Library of Congress Cataloging-in-Publication Data
Schmidt, William H.
     Teacher education matters : a study of middle school mathematics teacher preparation in six countries / William H. Schmidt, Sigrid Blömeke, Maria Teresa Tatto ; with Feng-Jui Hsieh . . . [et al.].
     p. cm.
     Includes bibliographical references and index.
     ISBN 978-0-8077-5162-6 (pbk. : alk. paper)
     1. Mathematics teachers—Training of. 2. Mathematics teachers—In-service training. 3. Middle school teachers—Training of. 4. Middle school teachers—In-service training
     I. Blömeke, Sigrid. II. Tatto, Maria Teresa. III. Title.
QA10.5.S36 2011
510.71—dc22   2010045274

ISBN 978-0-8077-5162-6 (paper)

Printed on acid-free paper
Manufactured in the United States of America
18   17   16   15   14   13   12   11   8   7   6   5   4   3   2   1

Contents

Preface

"Teachers make a difference" (National Research Council, 2010) is the opening statement of the recent report on teacher preparation published by the National Academy Press. Educators at all levels find validation in such a statement as well as heartfelt hope in the face of their everyday challenges. Interviews and biographies often mention a particular teacher who inspired a student to persevere and thus fulfill his or her personal potential and dreams. At the same time that great appreciation may be found in the popular press for individual teachers, the teaching profession in the United States does not enjoy the respect and economic rewards evidenced in some other societies. Thus it is only somewhat paradoxical that another recent report on teacher preparation programs notes that these "do not now, nor have they ever, enjoyed a particularly positive reputation" (National Council on Teacher Quality [NCTQ], 2010, p. 3).

International comparisons of student achievement at the primary or secondary level have frequently included some information on teachers in an effort to explain at least to some extent the observed differences in students' achievement. The Third International Mathematics and Science Study (TIMSS) conducted in 1995 by the International Association for the Evaluation of Educational Achievement included for the first time an in-depth comparison of the curriculum that was taught and intended to be learned by students. These curriculum-based analyses provided powerful explanations for country-level differences in student achievement both from a logical viewpoint and according to the standards of statistical research modeling (Schmidt, McKnight, Houang, Wang, Wiley, & Cogan, 2001).

Those curriculum analyses put a different light on how to think about teachers with respect to differences in student achievement. Given the important role that teachers have in selecting topics for classroom instruction, organizing and providing classroom learning opportunities, the issue of having a highly qualified teacher to do all of this becomes one of how such a teacher may be prepared. In other words, given the great range of student achievement differences observed in international comparative studies, how are teachers prepared in each country to teach the curriculum they will be required to teach? Although not conclusive, one might speculate that teachers in countries that have consistently highly performing students may be prepared somewhat differently than those in countries with lower levels of student performance.

Indeed, this question led to the present study and explains the set of countries that participated: Bulgaria, Germany, South Korea, Taiwan, Mexico, and the United States. The focus on middle school—lower-secondary, internationally—and mathematics stemmed from the TIMSS and the Programme for International Student Assessment (PISA) results and the recognition in the policy and education arenas of the importance of mathematics for societies' prosperity and competitiveness. Further details about the selection of these countries are provided in Chapter 3, but here we simply point out that these countries represent a range of industrialization, economic standing, and student performance on comparative assessments such as TIMSS and PISA.

Issues of teacher quality are a matter of concern and public policy in every society that sponsors public education. Thus the representatives from each country were very interested in learning what they could about teacher preparation and seeing how this compared to the practices found elsewhere. This sort of dialogue among colleagues from other contexts and cultures is always rewarding. However, even more rewarding is the opportunity to perhaps challenge some of the assumptions that may be held about teacher preparation and to therefore provide a different perspective on some of the policies and practices that relate to it. Without spoiling for the reader any of this book, we were all surprised by the many similarities shared by teacher preparation across the countries we analyzed. We were also surprised at times by those things that were different. These similarities seem particularly important to understand at this point in the U.S. context, where alternative paths to teaching seem to eclipse any discussion of the traditional paths found in colleges and universities. This book does provide an international context at least as represented by this select group of countries to explore many of the issues related to how quality teachers may be prepared. It is our hope that the book will challenge some of the assumptions of both educators and policy makers and provide a fresh perspective as we face the challenges of public education together in each of our cultural contexts.

Acknowledgments

The vision for this book came out of many international research meetings of the authors over several years. We began as tentative strangers at our first exploratory meeting, evolved into friends and colleagues through our work on the project, and produced a fulfilling body of work that surpassed even our expectations.

All 13 authors shared in the work presented in this book, but due to publisher limitations, only three are listed on the cover.

The authors are indebted to a number of individuals who worked with various aspects of the research throughout the project. We wish to acknowledge and thank the following individuals.

The staff at Michigan State University, particularly Jacqueline Babcock, for her management skills and for keeping everyone working in a cohesive and thriving environment; Jean Buhler, for her dedication and expertise in database management; Chris DeFouw, for her knowledge of the organization and for finding ways to stretch our resources to keep the research going; Neelam Kher, for her assistance with data analyses; Kathleen Wight, for her attention to detail in her work with the curriculum analysis; and Zhiwen Zou, for his expertise in writing programs and hours of performing data analysis.

We save our highest accolade for Jennifer Cady, for her countless hours of word processing and editing, her suggestions for improvements in style, and, especially, for her sharp eye for seeing, correcting, and managing every small detail of the final manuscript and all of the versions that came before.

We thank Richard Askey, Garbriele Kaiser, William McCallum, James Milgram, Paul Sally, and Hung Hsi Wu for their valuable time in reviewing, editing, and suggesting mathematics items used in the research surveys, and David Wiley for his expertise and ideas on data analysis issues.

There were a host of undergraduate and graduate students involved in the project who are too numerous to list, but the following students contributed in special ways: Minh Quang Duong, Jonghwan Lee, Yang Lu, Adam Maier,

Sungworn Ngudgratoke, Julia Ogg, Angela Pacheco, Kamila Rosolova, Tian Song, Saeeda Usman, and Anna Weiland.

We extend a heartfelt thank you to our colleagues who attended various meetings of the research team and provided important insights: Edward Britton, Hilary Constable, Anja Felbrich, Ee-Gyeong Kim, Glenda Lappan, Bruno Losito, David Plank, Ruth Vivero, and Hsing Chi von Bergmann.

We are grateful to the National Science Foundation (NSF) for providing funding under Award #0231886. We are especially indebted to Janice Earle at NSF for her encouragement and trust with this new area of research. NSF does not, however, assume responsibility for the findings or interpretations as expressed in this publication. We also thank the National Science Council of Taiwan, which funded a part of the Taiwanese project.

CHAPTER 1

Teaching Middle School Mathematics in Six Countries

This is a story about teaching lower-secondary (middle school) mathematics in six countries. To begin, we look at the professional lives of six teachers: Nedjalka Dimitrova in Bulgaria, Lukas Becker in Germany, Javier Lopez in Mexico, Eun-Young Choe in South Korea, Fong Wang in Chinese Taipei (Taiwan—throughout this book we will use the Taiwanese reference), and Judy Brazil in the United States. They all teach middle school mathematics, so their worlds are similar and yet very different. All teach mathematics to young adolescents, yet the nature of the mathematics they teach and the academic context in which the mathematics curriculum for the equivalent grade level is embedded can be quite different. Nonetheless, the issues and dilemmas with which they are confronted while teaching bear many striking similarities. Thus, in light of these similarities and in the face of many contextual and academic differences, the question becomes: How are these teachers prepared to teach the lower-secondary mathematics curriculum in their respective countries, and how is teacher preparation across these six countries similar or different?

This is an important story as it connects with yet another story that has already been told. The typical 8th-grade student being taught by these teachers in some of these countries will likely not perform as well as those in others (see, e.g., PISA, 2003, 2006, www.pisa.oecd.org; TIMSS, 2003, 2007, http://timss.bc.edu). Much research has shown how children around the world perform differently—especially in middle school mathematics—and we know how important such learning is to individual children and to a nation's growth. In fact, some studies suggest that this is strongly related to economic growth (see, e.g., Hanushek, 1997, 2009).

In addition, research has found that curricula vary substantially across some 50 countries and that this variability was related to the variation in student achievement. Furthermore, an analysis of the mathematics curriculum standards of the top-achieving countries (including South Korea) that participated in the

1995 Third International Mathematics and Science Study (TIMSS) at 8th grade found the curricular standards from these countries were quite unlike those of the United States (Schmidt, McKnight, & Raizen, 1996; Schmidt, Wang, & McKnight, 2005). More specifically, the curricular standards from these top-achieving countries exhibited three important characteristics: focus, coherence, and rigor—topics discussed in Chapter 2.

As important as quality, coherent content standards may be for an education system to provide all students with a challenging and world-class education, they represent an essential but not sufficient condition. Standards still must be translated into textbooks, workbooks, diagnostic tests for teacher use and other classroom materials, and translated by teachers into meaningful classroom learning experiences for students. Children do not just absorb a curriculum, however good it may be, by some osmotic process but rather are led to make sense of the curriculum by teachers like Nedjalka, Lukas, Javier, Eun-Young, Fong, and Judy.

This is where the importance of the story in our volume becomes apparent. The curriculum intended to be taught across the six countries in our study is different, so this raises an imperative question as to how the mathematics teachers that lead the learning in the classrooms in our different countries have been prepared. Some within-country research seems to suggest that the nature and quality of the preparation teachers are given makes a difference for their students, but this issue has not been examined across different educational systems as with the six countries studied here. Although many international studies of student mathematics achievement have included some information about their teachers' backgrounds, none have moved beyond cursory descriptions such as the number and type of degrees earned (see, e.g., PISA, 2003, 2006, www.pisa.oecd.org; TIMSS, 2003, 2007, http://timss.bc.edu). In this volume we examine in depth how middle school mathematics teachers in South Korea, Bulgaria, Germany, Mexico, Taiwan, and the United States are prepared and what level of professional knowledge they have as they finish their preparation programs.

Before turning to the study's detail, we first examine the professional lives of Nedjalka, Lukas, Javier, Eun-Young, Fong, and Judy—what is expected of them as they enter their classrooms each day and week. To understand the preparation each has had for their classroom teaching, we need to better understand what is expected of each of them as they step into their classrooms in each of their respective countries.

NEDJALKA DIMITROVA— A MIDDLE SCHOOL MATHEMATICS TEACHER IN BULGARIA

Nedjalka Dimitrova leaves her apartment by 6:50 A.M. to catch the bus to Plovdiv Secondary School, where she teaches mathematics and computer science.

It usually takes her at least half an hour to reach the school, in time for the first class at 7:30 in the morning. Plovdiv Secondary School covers grades 5 through 12. Nedjalka is pleased with her teaching schedule because this term she will be teaching the morning shift. Her students will be well rested and able to concentrate. Last term she had the afternoon shift that started right after lunch. Students, especially the younger ones, became increasingly tired as the day went on, creating an extra challenge. During the second term classes will be switched and the students in her current morning classes will be in the afternoon shift and vice versa.

Nedjalka teaches eighteen 45-minute class periods per week. Two of her classes this year are 7th grade, one in mathematics and one in computer science. The other classes are in 10th-grade mathematics. Three of the classes are on Curriculum Level I, which means that her students study basic mathematics for three class periods each week. On Friday, Nedjalka teaches two classes on Curriculum Level II grade 10, which is a more advanced level. Students receive two class periods of additional training on mathematics topics that are taught at Level I but in a more sophisticated way. Sometimes Nedjalka uses these class periods for solving problems that are considered hard for the Level I mathematics.

Nedjalka is also the form master of one of these classes. She meets with her students for 1 hour each week for administrative arrangements and to discuss moral or ethical issues. During this time Nedjalka discusses and resolves some organizational issues, such as conflicts between pupils and between pupils and teachers. She also discusses important topics with the students, such as: How do I learn effectively? How do I see my professional future? Why am I proud to be a Bulgarian citizen? As this is her third year with these students she knows all 19 very well and is looking forward to teaching them for one more year.

Typically, lessons begin by taking student attendance. Next is a short discussion and commentaries on the homework problems, which seem to be difficult for a majority of the students. The main part is either a presentation of a new topic or problem-solving exercises connected with a previously taught topic. In both cases Nedjalka first assesses the students' understanding of the main concepts, rules, and theorems that are needed for the lesson. At the end of the class Nedjalka makes a notation of those students who were especially active (or inactive) and summarizes the day's lesson.

Grade 7 is a stressful time for students because they must take a written exam if they want to go to a profile school. To be accepted at a so-called profile-oriented school (schools mainly for further study in mathematics or foreign language) students have to perform well on two exams: Bulgarian language and literature, and mathematics. Usually about 45% of the pupils graduating from grade 7 take the examinations, and about 95% of them pass. There is a quota for each profile school and students who pass both examinations are ranked and admitted to corresponding schools. Parents have high expectations regarding their children's admittance to these schools because it is believed that pupils at these schools get a better education. The students who do not pass the examinations or are not ranked high enough to be admitted to a profile-oriented school usually continue their education in grade 8 at their regular school.

Nedjalka has always admired the Plovdiv mathematics profile school for its well-equipped computer classrooms with Internet access. The school where she teaches has such rooms but older equipment and limited IT support and they are used only for computer classes. Given Nedjalka's limited financial resources, she consults materials from the library rather than purchasing additional resources on her own. The "teachers' room" has some computers with Internet access, a printer and a copier available for teachers, but the lack of regular support for malfunctioning equipment means teachers' access to these resources is either limited or completely lacking.

Nedjalka's classrooms are scattered across the school campus. The classroom for Class 7 is located in the school's oldest building, whereas her other classes meet in the new building. So, after teaching one class she must hurry during the 10-minute break to make it to her next class. During the 20-minute break moving between classrooms is less of an issue but she has to stop by her locker in the teachers' room to get the sandwich that she brought from home, eat, and informally catch up with the other teachers on school and student issues.

All teachers at the school are members of the teachers' council, which meets at least three times per academic year—at the beginning and end of the first term and at the end of the year. Less formal, discipline-specific organizations of teachers called "pedagogical unions" usually meet once a month to discuss curriculum issues, textbooks, teaching materials, and so forth. Nedjalka finds that recently, due to reduced school funds, there has been a lack of professional development opportunities.

At 1:30 P.M. she is done for the day and takes the bus home. Given her salary, which is below the average Bulgarian salary, Nedjalka cannot afford a car. The low salary does not concern her because she has job security and, besides, her love for mathematics and teaching led her to become a teacher. Nedjalka has been at Plovdiv Secondary School for 15 years now; the principal hired her after an intense selection process. Although the teaching profession is respected now in Bulgaria, when Nedjalka was hired this was not the case. Even so, there was more than one candidate for the teaching position in mathematics. Now, few young people want to become teachers. Consequently, there are vacancies for mathematics teachers throughout the school year, even in "good" schools in the centers of the big cities.

FIGURE 1.1. Typical weekly schedule for a teacher in Bulgaria.

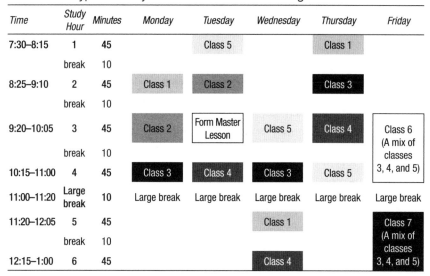

Time	Study Hour	Minutes	Monday	Tuesday	Wednesday	Thursday	Friday
7:30–8:15	1	45		Class 5		Class 1	
	break	10					
8:25–9:10	2	45	Class 1	Class 2		Class 3	
	break	10					
9:20–10:05	3	45	Class 2	Form Master Lesson	Class 5	Class 4	Class 6 (A mix of classes 3, 4, and 5)
	break	10					
10:15–11:00	4	45	Class 3	Class 4	Class 3	Class 5	
11:00–11:20	Large break	10	Large break	Large break	Large break	Large break	Large break
11:20–12:05	5	45			Class 1		Class 7 (A mix of classes 3, 4, and 5)
	break	10					
12:15–1:00	6	45				Class 4	

The next shift of teachers and students takes over the school while the morning shift prepares for the next day at home. There, Nedjalka also reviews student responses to a couple of intriguing problems she had assigned her classes on the mathematics topic that she taught in the last lesson, which came from the textbook she had chosen for this year. She also needs to finish grading an exam she had given to another class last week.

LUKAS BECKER—
A MIDDLE SCHOOL MATHEMATICS TEACHER IN GERMANY

Lukas Becker leaves home before 7 A.M. to catch the underground train from his home in a suburb to his school in southeast Dortmund. It is his second year of teaching in this Realschule. He completed his practical training for grades 5 through 10 at this school and the principal asked him to apply for one of the few open positions. Lukas immediately applied because he felt respected by his colleagues and loved living in the Ruhrgebiet area. Even given the general shortage of mathematics teachers in Germany, it is not always easy to find a position at a school of one's choosing.

Lukas teaches mathematics and English, so he has two subjects that require grading in addition to all of the typical teaching and preparation duties. He chose mathematics and English because he was interested in them and did not think much about the burdens associated with teaching them.

Lukas teaches 9 different groups of students, for a weekly total of 28 class periods of 45-minutes each. Since the average class size is 24 students, one of the great challenges is to learn 200 to 240 student names every year and then to provide the necessary attention to each student.

Lukas teaches in the intermediate track of middle school, in which students were evaluated by their primary teachers as being more intellectually talented than students who were sorted into the Hauptschule but not sufficiently qualified to go to a Gymnasium. Usually this means that the students had a weakness in one or two of the main subjects—mathematics or German—while demonstrating good achievement in all other subjects.

Since only the Gymnasium prepares students for university, those at the Realschule usually aim for white-collar jobs. The heterogeneity within classes is large because there is no tracking once students are sorted into the three-tiered middle school system.

Today, Lukas starts teaching class 6d. Four students are late this morning. Lukas documents this in the class book in which every teacher summarizes the main features of her[1] lesson (content, number of students present, disciplinary problems, etc.). He is also the head teacher and organizes extracurricular activities like participation in the annual 5K city run. Collecting permission slips and arranging activities take up a portion of his class time. At the beginning of each class, Lukas collects homework before he presents that day's mathematics problem. Sometimes students work on it in pairs and present their results at the end of the lesson. A short discussion follows in which the different groups' approaches are evaluated.

He is concerned about the level of anxiety and frustration felt by his grade 10 mathematics students. Many German federal states, including North Rhine-Westphalia, where Lukas's school is located, now have central exams. Lukas already knows many of his students will have trouble with this exam. Despite his efforts to accelerate their learning pace he will not make it through the whole curriculum.

Even though the German economy has improved, it is still difficult for students from the Realschule to find a high-quality vocational training position. It is even more difficult to transfer to the Gymnasium, since the gap between the knowledge of students who have attended the Hauptschule or the Realschule and those who have attended the Gymnasium increases substantially during the middle school years.

In the breaks between each class period Lukas tries to make it to the teachers' room because he likes to have the chance to talk to his colleagues and to

FIGURE 1.2. Typical weekly schedule for a teacher in Germany.

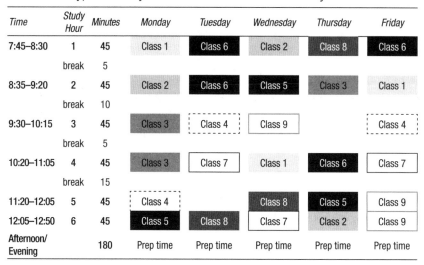

Time	Study Hour	Minutes	Monday	Tuesday	Wednesday	Thursday	Friday
7:45–8:30	1	45	Class 1	Class 6	Class 2	Class 8	Class 6
	break	5					
8:35–9:20	2	45	Class 2	Class 6	Class 5	Class 3	Class 1
	break	10					
9:30–10:15	3	45	Class 3	Class 4	Class 9		Class 4
	break	5					
10:20–11:05	4	45	Class 3	Class 7	Class 1	Class 6	Class 7
	break	15					
11:20–12:05	5	45	Class 4		Class 8	Class 5	Class 9
12:05–12:50	6	45	Class 5	Class 8	Class 7	Class 2	Class 9
Afternoon/ Evening		180	Prep time	Prep time	Prep time	Prep time	Prep time

stay in touch with what is going on at his school. He also uses this time to make phone calls to parents about disciplinary issues.

Lukas expects to be very busy this week. Thursday afternoon he has a conference for class 8a, where all teachers of this class will meet to discuss the unacceptable behavior of one group of students. On the same evening there will be another meeting with the parents of his 6d class for which he is the head teacher. The meeting will be well attended and will cover issues of curriculum, coursework trajectories, and increased homework load as well as planned out-of-school activities. On Friday there is one of the regular parent conferences about student achievement.

Right now there are many changes going on at the school. Although he likes some of the changes, Lukas is weary of all the developments because it seems as if his government is trying to make up for decades of no changes within a single election term. The changes reward teachers who work hard and support collaborative learning approaches. One of the topics of Thursday evening's conference will be to extend the length of class periods from 45 to 60 minutes. Teachers and students felt increasingly uncomfortable with working in 45-minute segments. Lukas had heard from another Realschule in the neighborhood that they plan to switch from half-day schooling to whole-day schooling. With the longer school day the school's administrators hope to give their students more informal learning opportunities so that they will be at less of a disadvantage compared to students from wealthier areas of the town or from a Gymnasium—which are often synonymous.

There is no lunch break during the school day, so at 1:15 P.M. Lukas goes home to eat lunch and start preparations for the next day. He takes home two large bags. In one he carries the assignments of classes 5a and 5b to review and in the other he carries the textbooks and hands-on materials he intends to use in preparing tomorrow's lessons. Before he starts his preparation and grading of homework assignments, however, he plans to take a break to do some grocery shopping and then go for a run. At about 10 P.M. Lukas has finished his preparation and heads to bed.

JAVIER LOPEZ—
A MIDDLE SCHOOL MATHEMATICS TEACHER IN MEXICO

Yucatán's largest middle school is located in Mérida. It houses grades 7 through 9, and Javier Lopez has been teaching there for 2 years. He simultaneously teaches in one other middle school. Both are public schools, so he is employed by the state. The teachers' union has extensive rights to participate in the selection process but, because Javier is a member of the union, he is unconcerned about this.

Javier has an employment contract for 42 hours per week. Of the 42 hours, 40 hours are spent in the classroom teaching and the remaining 2 hours are devoted to class preparation and grading. His day typically begins at 7:30 A.M. with the morning shift. He also teaches the late shift, which begins at 2:00, on four afternoons in one school and on Wednesday evening in the second middle school. There are no resources to build new schools and hire more teachers, so existing school buildings have to be used to their maximum capacity. Teaching in two shifts makes Javier's day long and exhausting because he not only teaches eight periods a day but must drive quite a distance from one school to the other. He doesn't particularly enjoy the late shifts as students are much less able to concentrate later in the day, but he needs the double shift to earn an adequate salary.

In the mornings, he teaches four 8th-grade classes in a row. He doesn't have to teach between 10:50 A.M. and noon, which is the lunch break, but there are other duties he needs to perform. Today he has to supervise the student cafeteria. After lunch, he teaches one more class of 8th graders. The class ends at 12:50 P.M. and then it is time for him to make the 30-minute drive to the second middle school for the afternoon shift that begins at 2 P.M.

In the afternoon, he teaches all three grades of the middle school. On most days, he is done at 4:30 P.M. except for Wednesdays, when his day doesn't finish until after 8 P.M. The last period each day is devoted to the 9th-grade students and that presents some additional challenges. As 9th grade is the last year of compulsory education, some students in this grade feel quite pressured to prepare for the national examination that will assess their achievement in Spanish and mathematics. Good results on the national examination are particularly important if students want to continue schooling, as this will determine whether they will attend general upper-secondary, vocational upper-secondary, or technical secondary school. About half the students plan to complete their schooling at the end of 9th grade and are not really concerned about the learning or the examination.

Javier's classes typically have over 30 students. These students were allocated to their groups based on the results of an entrance exam taken at the end of primary school. Because all his morning classes are in 8th grade, Javier

FIGURE 1.3. Typical weekly schedule for a teacher in Mexico.

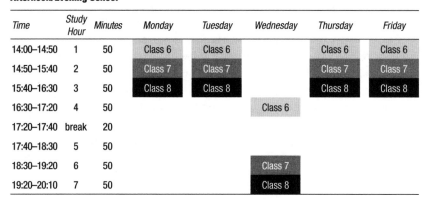

Morning School

Time	Study Hour	Minutes	Monday	Tuesday	Wednesday	Thursday	Friday
7:30–8:20	1	50	Class 1	Class 1	Class 1	Class 1	Class 1
8:20–9:10	2	50	Class 2	Class 2	Class 2	Class 2	Class 2
9:10–10:00	3	50	Class 3	Class 3	Class 3	Class 3	Class 3
10:00–10:50	4	50	Class 4	Class 4	Class 4	Class 4	Class 4
10:50–11:10	break	20		Prep time		Prep time	
11:10–12:00	break	50					
12:00–12:50	6	50	Class 5	Class 5	Class 5	Class 5	Class 5
12:50–13:40							

Afternoon/Evening School

Time	Study Hour	Minutes	Monday	Tuesday	Wednesday	Thursday	Friday
14:00–14:50	1	50	Class 6	Class 6		Class 6	Class 6
14:50–15:40	2	50	Class 7	Class 7		Class 7	Class 7
15:40–16:30	3	50	Class 8	Class 8		Class 8	Class 8
16:30–17:20	4	50			Class 6		
17:20–17:40	break	20					
17:40–18:30	5	50					
18:30–19:20	6	50			Class 7		
19:20–20:10	7	50			Class 8		

can prepare the same assignment for each of the five groups of 8th graders he teaches. Usually, he closely follows the textbook, which comes with additional materials and problems that can be assigned for homework. Fortunately, the textbooks are provided by the government and are often accompanied by teachers' guides that help to reduce preparation time. Consequently, teaching is very aligned to the textbooks but, considering the limited preparation time Javier has and how much he has to teach, it is the best he can do.

While Javier does not need to worry about textbooks, the availability of other school resources can vary considerably across schools. The first middle school where he teaches the morning shift is quite well equipped. The classroom has a computer, projector, and electronic white board and offers Internet access. Algebraic calculators and various types of manipulative materials are also available for each student. At the school where he teaches his late shift there are no electronic resources or Internet access, and other materials and supplies are also limited, so he sometimes incurs the cost of these.

Javier's busy schedule does not provide much time to share experiences with colleagues, although he tries to use the time between classes to talk to other mathematics teachers in the school. Every 2 months, there are staff meetings which offer more opportunities for information sharing and conversations with colleagues and school board members. Javier wishes he could have more interaction with colleagues but his crammed schedule limits these opportunities.

EUN-YOUNG CHOE—
A MIDDLE SCHOOL MATHEMATICS TEACHER IN SOUTH KOREA

The students in class 8b at Hangang's Middle School are already very busy when Eun-Young Choe enters the classroom. The 37 students, dressed in school uniforms, get up and recite the traditional morning greetings. It is Monday, 8:00 A.M., and Eun-Young's students spend the half hour before school finishing up yesterday's work from *hagwon*, academies for private education, which most of them attend. Eun-Young herself has done some administrative work in the teachers' room. She starts the class period with a 10-minute competition of mental calculation—first square roots, followed by linear equations. She then presents several challenging problems. Each student can choose one and work on it alone. At the end of the class period students have to demonstrate their work to the whole class.

During the break between classes Eun-Young heads back to her desk. There, during her free periods, she prepares for the next day and organizes her assignments. Her next class takes place in 7b next to the computer lab.

The proximity to the lab provides Eun-Young freedom to use the technology frequently. Last year Eun-Young decided to adopt a different textbook in this class to support greater use of the technology. Using a different textbook combined with technology necessitated additional preparation time for Eun-Young to make appropriate connections with the new themes. During one of her free periods, she has the opportunity to share her experiences with the new textbook and approach with colleagues who have adopted this textbook as well. Eun-Young and her colleagues have made several adjustments to their respective classes and are generally quite satisfied with the changes.

Eun-Young has been working at Hangang Middle School for 19 years. When she was selected into the teacher education program, her prospects for securing employment in teaching seemed assured as the government ensures that the number of available slots for mathematics teacher education are fairly balanced with the number of positions available for mathematics teachers. However, to secure employment in a good public school Eun-Young had to score in the uppermost percentiles on the Secondary School Teacher Selection Test.

Although the status of teachers has declined over the past decades, Eun-Young feels well respected and continues to enjoy her job. She earns a modest salary which, when combined with her husband's earnings, allows the family to live well.

Hangang Middle School houses grades 7 through 9. Admissions to the school are based on lottery assignments. The lottery system on admission helps eradicate distinctions between schools, and all elementary school graduates have equal access to all middle schools located in their respective school districts. Eun-Young teaches 20 mathematics class periods in 5 different classes per week; each class period is 45 minutes. She is also the head teacher of 9c, which includes many other responsibilities. These responsibilities include checking student grooming (uniforms and haircuts); supervising students at lunchtime, during self-study sessions, and in classroom cleaning; and organizing planned field experiences or class trips.

In addition, Eun-Young and her colleagues take turns supervising extracurricular activities in the afternoons and on Saturdays. Given these additional tasks, she usually does not get home before 6 P.M. Eun-Young knows that some of her students arrive home much later, especially students who intend to go to a top high school and subsequently to a top university. For these students the competition for the limited slots is fierce, so they receive extra instruction after school from private tutors.

Eun-Young prefers the Saturday work when she helps students to develop their reading skills or supervises a social service volunteer experience at an organization or facility. Sometimes she also offers activities related to mathematics, like

FIGURE 1.4. Typical weekly schedule for a teacher in South Korea.

Time	Study Hour	Minutes	Monday	Tuesday	Wednesday	Thursday	Friday	Saturday (every other week)
8:00–8:45	1	45	Class 5		Class 5		Class 2	Activity
	break	10						
8:55–9:40	2	45		Class 1	Class 3	Class 6		Activity
	break	10						
9:50–10:35	3	45	Class 6	Class 4		Class 1	Class 6	Activity
	break	10						
10:45–11:30	4	45	Class 4	Class 3	Class 4		Class 5	Activity
	Lunch break	70	Lunch break	Lunch break	Lunch break	Lunch break	Lunch break	
12:40–13:25	5	45	Class 3	Class 2	Class 1	Class 3	Class 1	
	break	10						
13:35–14:20	6	45	Class 2	Class 5		Class 2		
	break	10						
14:30–15:15	7	45					Class 4	

preparing for the Math Olympics. Eun-Young does get paid for the extra work, but having to work 55 to 60 hours each week is a burden. At her school there are some teachers who come early in the morning and stay longer than required. Such teacher behavior receives implicit principal support, so other teachers feel pressured to emulate it.

Eun-Young teaches in room 9f. The wide variability in student mathematics ability here is greater than in previous grades and may be attributed to the practice of moving students along to higher grade levels regardless of demonstrated achievement. To accommodate the needs of students at varying ability levels Eun-Young has prepared materials to maintain the interest and motivation of diverse groups of students. This class is a real challenge.

The 9th grade is where students experience the most pressure. Examination scores become very important for the top students hoping to gain entrance into the top high schools as well as for those in the middle hoping to get into an academic rather than a technical or vocational high school.

FONG WANG—
A MIDDLE SCHOOL MATHEMATICS TEACHER IN TAIWAN

Fong Wang arises at 6:45 A.M., gets ready for the day, and drives to his job at Lucky Middle School, which houses grades 7 to 9. Fong arrives in the 8th-grade teachers' office, where he has his own desk but shares the room with 15 teachers. Teachers arrive before 7:30 A.M. to check on their classes during students' morning self-study period. Upon entering the classroom Fong notes that all 34 students are present and the discipline office[2] is doing a good job keeping the class in order. He wanders through the class several times before returning to his desk in the teachers' homeroom.

During the self-study period, Fong is able to relax in the teachers' homeroom and go over the materials and progress of the math class he will teach later in the morning. He can also use this time to correspond with parents, answer student questions, and handle administrative tasks.

Fong moves to his next classroom at 8:20 A.M. After the bowing ceremony, he starts the 45-minute class at the chalkboard. Occasionally, he also uses teaching aides like posters, models, and manipulative teaching tools. His teaching typically involves lecturing and questioning. He asks students if they understood his teaching and, after he has taught the example questions, asks them to do one or two practice problems. Twice a month, he gives his students written tests.

During breaks, Fong rushes back to the teachers' homeroom to see if the principal or his colleagues have left him messages, then he moves to his next class. Students are assigned classrooms at the start of 7th grade and stay with the same group of classmates for the next 3 years. The group moves to a different classroom only for subjects that require specially designed spaces, such as physical education, music, and arts.

Designated teachers are not only responsible for the subject they are teaching but also for handling students' disciplinary and family issues. Sometimes they are even responsible for questions regarding subjects they do not teach. Mathematics is an emphasized subject in this school so mathematics teachers are more likely to become designated teachers. Fong takes on the role of a designated teacher almost every year. He thinks that even though it is mentally and physically draining, the benefits are worthwhile. Designated teachers teach four fewer periods per week than other subject teachers and receive an additional $70 USD every month. Designated teachers have a greater opportunity to build deeper relationships with students. Often, alumni come back to visit their designated teachers long after they graduate.

The third and fourth periods are free for Fong. During these periods, designated class teachers usually stay at school and use the time to correct homework and tests and review teacher-parent communication booklets. Some teachers prepare for the next class; others counsel students. If necessary, some teachers even hold teacher-parent conferences. Of course, teachers can also utilize this time to socialize. Every Friday, mathematics teachers meet in the conference room for 3 hours of professional development, with one of the teachers leading the meeting. The lead teacher prepares an intriguing question raised by students in a class or a classroom situation that was more difficult than expected. The teachers discuss the problems and situations together and try to come up with adequate solutions.

Fong will have lunch in the classroom with his students. The school lunch provider has already delivered today's lunches to each classroom. Afterward there is a 15-minute break during which students clean the classroom and the campus field. Fong stays for a short time to supervise his students' cleaning. After the cleaning break, it is time for a midday rest period. The students quietly lay their heads on the desk for 30 minutes and Fong can go back to his office.

The first period in the afternoon is a class meeting attended by the designated teacher. This is a period for student leaders to discuss class issues and activities. Class meeting is Fong's favorite period; this is the only class where he

FIGURE 1.5. Typical weekly schedule for a teacher in Taiwan.

Time	Study Hour	Minutes	Monday	Tuesday	Wednesday	Thursday	Friday
7:30–8:15	Self-study session	45					
	break	5					
8:20–9:05	1	45	Class 1	Class 2	Class 3	Class 3	
	break	10					
9:15–10:00	2	45	Class 3	Class 4	Class 4	Class 2	Class 1
	break	15					
10:15–11:00	3	45			Class 1		Class 2
	break	10					
11:10–11:55	4	45		Class 3			Class 4
11:55–13:15	Lunch, cleaning, noon nap break	80					
13:15–14:00	5	45				Class 2 meeting	Teacher professional meetings
	break	10					
14:10–14:55	6	45	Class 4				
	break	10					
15:05–15:50	7	45			Class 2	Class 1	

gets to see his students learn something other than mathematics. The last bell of the day sounds at 3:50 P.M.

While his 8th-grade students are dismissed, 9th-grade students are still in class. It is the beginning of the semester and the 9th-grade math teachers have already begun preparing their students for the national high school entrance exam at the end of the academic year. The pressure on the teachers and the students is tremendous, and they spend an extra period in school each day preparing for the exam. A small subset of students can be admitted to the high school of their choice through the recommendation of their schools. Most students are assigned to a high school or university based on the results of entrance exams, and great emphasis is placed on the subject of mathematics. Fong's students will be 9th graders next year. He has been teaching them since 7th grade and will stay with them until they graduate. This means that he will also be under pressure next year.

Fong has been teaching at Lucky Middle School for 15 years and has a good salary compared to the average income in Taiwan. The teaching profession is one of the best government jobs. Some of his colleagues tutor to bring in additional income. Tutoring is a profitable business; the hourly wage for tutoring is two to six times higher than the hourly school wage. About one third of the students in Fong's class have private tutors or attend the after-school classes at tutoring institutions. These students usually get home by 8 or 9 o'clock in the evening. While tutoring is not required, Lucky Middle School mandates that students attend school sessions 4 to 6 weeks during summer break and 1 to 2 weeks during winter break, increasing both teachers' teaching load and students' learning opportunities.

JUDY BRAZIL—
A MIDDLE SCHOOL MATHEMATICS TEACHER IN THE UNITED STATES

Northern Middle School is in a small urban school district. It houses grades 6 through 8. Judy Brazil has been working here for 7 years. She teaches five classes of 8th graders: four sections of algebra and one section of pre-algebra, a transition course targeted for students not yet ready for algebra.

Each class period lasts 50 minutes, with 5 minutes between classes for students to move from one classroom to another. Judy also has one "preparation" period and a 30-minute break for lunch. Since her classes have, on average, 27 students, she teaches about 135 students every day. For one of her algebra classes she also serves as homeroom teacher whereby, during a shortened period each day either before or after lunch, she takes attendance and oversees students working on homework or special activities.

Judy leaves home at 7:15 A.M. to drive to school as she likes to arrive early to prepare her room for the day and have time to focus on her first class before the bell at 8:15 A.M. Fortunately, she has her own room, unlike some of her friends at other schools nearby who have had to move between rooms, carrying all their materials on a cart from one room to the next.

She puts announcements for each class on a white board and sets up the computer and screen so that she can move into the lesson for the day immediately after her first period. Students turn in their monthly progress report—a tally of grades for homework, quizzes, and tests—signed by a parent. Judy planned lessons for each day over the weekend, although she knows even her best plans get altered, especially her second-period class, which really struggles.

At 8:15 A.M. her first class begins. She uses the side white board in her room to list the day's agenda. Although she teaches four sections of algebra, she has come to realize that they move at different paces, depending on the composition of the class. Her school, like many across the United States, has worked hard in recent years to strengthen the K–12 mathematics curriculum so that most students will take algebra in 8th grade. However, she feels that quite a few students are not yet ready for it. Student assignments are based on students'

FIGURE 1.6. Typical weekly schedule for a teacher in the United States.

Time	Study Hour	Minutes	Monday	Tuesday	Wednesday	Thursday	Friday
8:15–9:05	1	50	Class1	Class 1	Class 1	Class 1	Class 1
	break	5					
9:10–10:00	2	50	Preparation	Preparation	Preparation	Preparation	Preparation
	break	5					
10:05–10:55	3	50	Class 2	Class 2	Class 2	Class 2	Class 2
	break	5					
11:00–11:50	4	50	Class 3	Class 3	Class 3	Class 3	Class 3
	break	5					
11:55–12:25		30	Lunch	Lunch	Lunch	Lunch	Lunch
	break	5					
12:30–1:00		30	Homeroom	Homeroom	Homeroom	Homeroom	Homeroom
	break	5					
1:05–1:55	5	50	Class 4	Class 4	Class 4	Class 4	Class 4
	break	5					
2:00–2:50	6	50	Class 5	Class 5	Class 5	Class 5	Class 5

grades, teachers' recommendations and, to a lesser extent, results from standardized assessments given over the previous 2 years. However, parents sometimes urge school officials to place their children in such a class.

Once students are settled in the classroom, she asks them to review their homework. Judy uses a document camera to project the images from a student's paper or her own work onto a screen for all to see, asking students to mark their own papers and correct them. She then introduces the day's mathematics problem. At the end of the lesson Judy collects a random sample of students' math journals in order to assess student understanding. Students are expected to keep up with their work, and she uses quizzes as a way to enforce this. Once a year she and all the 8th-grade mathematics teachers in the building administer the state's standardized mathematics assessment, which has been required since passage of the 2001 No Child Left Behind federal legislation. The stakes of that test are high both for her and, possibly, her future students. Schools are ranked according to the percentage of their students who obtain passing scores. Consequences for schools failing to obtain satisfactory outcomes over several years vary across the nation but may range from reduced financial funding to mandated closure of the school.

Judy has had to develop good planning skills, as she has little time to plan during the day. She uses her planning period to review her lessons and explanations or consult with other teachers to discuss how to handle student difficulties. Some days her preparation time is devoted to school committee meetings or a meeting with other mathematics teachers. Otherwise her preparation time may include making copies of materials for her students, or contacting parents about classroom behavior or academic problems. Often, lunch is rushed because she is either wrapping up administrative business or preparing for her homeroom students.

Especially in the wake of the No Child Left Behind legislation, which requires schools to have "highly qualified teachers" who are certified in the subjects they teach, there is a shortage of teachers prepared to teach middle school mathematics and science. This helps account for why Judy teaches 8th grade exclusively. Having majored in mathematics in college, she is more qualified than many of her colleagues who are certified to teach mathematics but did not major in it.

Although classes end at 2:50 P.M., Judy usually leaves around 4:00 P.M. She often chats with students after school. Twice a week she offers a tutorial hour for any of her students. Some days only three or four students show up, others as many as 15 students come seeking additional help. Except on the days she offers the tutorial hour, she organizes her room for the next day, prepares handouts, and reviews student journals, special homework assignments, or quizzes. Even though she has to take work home, she is eager to leave by 4:00 P.M. to have time at home with her family.

Judy feels frustrated that many seem to think she earns a great salary. They tease her about having summers off. Judy is not at all convinced her salary matches her job demands, either during the school year or during her summer break. During the school year, she has little time to catch up, and given the demanding nature of each day's schedule, she has to take work home in the evenings and on weekends.

In the past, she valued the flexible summers and time with her young children. Nonetheless, the past two summers she has had to take online graduate courses to fulfill the continuing education required for her to maintain her state-issued teaching license. Balancing the demands of work, ongoing academic study and professional development meetings, and her family, Judy often thinks people who aren't teachers have little understanding of how hard it is to teach.

As is evident from these stories, there are many intersections in the professional lives of these teachers, yet there are also some differences in the structure and context in which they work and in the specific content they are expected to teach. Chapter 2 provides an overview of the various education systems, while Chapter 3 provides the theoretical framework as well as a description of the study. The remaining chapters tell what we have learned from our research in six countries about how teacher education prepares teachers like Nedjalka, Lukas, Javier, Eun-Young, Fong, and Judy to teach lower-secondary mathematics.

Middle school is one of the critical points in children's journey through school and teacher quality likely has some impact on whether a student succeeds or not. Therefore, in Mathematics Teaching in the 21st Century (MT21) we undertook the challenge to estimate what future teachers at the end of their teacher preparation know and believe about mathematics and the teaching of mathematics. We did this on a large scale and across countries, which is a new approach in teacher-education research.

CHAPTER 2

System Snapshots: K–12 Schooling, Teachers' Roles, and Teacher Preparation

The previous chapter introduced the stories of six teachers, all of whom teach lower-secondary mathematics. Imbedded in these stories is a sense that the educational systems in which they work are different. The stories suggest some major differences in what is expected of the teachers not only in terms of teaching but also in terms of other responsibilities, all of which likely influences how professional training is accomplished. This chapter provides a portrait of the professional context in which these teachers were trained and work.

For each country three areas are profiled:

- the organization of K–12 schooling;
- the role of mathematics teachers; and
- the organization of teacher education—for example, characteristic features with special emphasis on the role of mathematics.

The chapter concludes with a cross-country comparison of (1) the demographic background of future teachers, why they wanted to become teachers, and their perceptions of the teacher role; and (2) the lower-secondary mathematics topics they will be required to teach.

We provide this overview so readers may understand the big picture about middle school mathematics and the preparation of teachers for this important part of the school system before we go into the details of our data. The country context as represented by the first three bulleted issues is presented in a case-study format so that the cultural shaping becomes clear. The last two issues are presented by focusing on the similarities and differences among the six countries, which introduces the comparative approach employed throughout the book.

BULGARIA

K–12 Schooling

Bulgaria has three education levels: preschool (3 years old to 6 or 7 years old), school education, and higher education (see Figure 2.1). School education consists of basic and secondary education. Basic education includes primary school (grades 1 to 4) and pre-secondary or middle school (grades 5 to 8). After successful completion of grade 4, a Certificate of Primary Education is issued. A Certificate of Basic Education is issued after successful completion of grade 8. Education is compulsory up to age 16. The school year begins September 15 and ends in May/June, and it has two terms.

Secondary education is divided into general and vocational. Secondary general education can be obtained at secondary comprehensive schools (3 or 4 years) or profile-oriented schools (4 or 5 years). Students can enter the profile-oriented schools (mainly focused on mathematics and foreign languages) beginning in grade 8 (and sometimes, though rarely, in grade 9) after passing two

FIGURE 2.1. Structure of the educational system in Bulgaria.

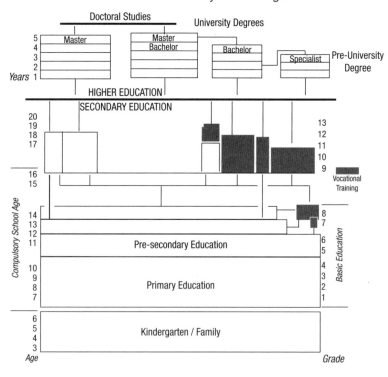

entrance examinations: one in Bulgarian language and literature, and another in mathematics or another subject according to the school's profile. Most of these schools offer intensive foreign language instruction.

Secondary vocational education can be obtained at technical schools beginning in grade 9 for a 4-year training period or in grade 8 for a duration of 5 years. Professional technical schools also provide intensive foreign language instruction. The professional qualification obtained provides access to the labor market. After successfully completing the last year of secondary school and passing the written examinations, a Diploma of Secondary Education is issued that identifies the chosen specialization.

Mathematics Teachers

In primary school students usually have one teacher for all subjects, including mathematics. This variety of tasks is reflected in their teacher preparation. During their university study, primary teachers take only one course of mathematics, delivered by a mathematician. The course covers topics concerning primary school mathematics and related teaching methods.

Beginning in grade 5, mathematics is taught by a teacher who is specifically prepared to teach mathematics. Typically, one mathematics teacher instructs the same cohort of students for the entire middle school education (from grade 5 to grade 8). Similarly, one mathematics teacher teaches all students in grades 9 to 12. In some schools, the same teacher instructs all students from grade 5 to the end of grade 12.

Organization of Mathematics Teacher Education

Secondary (middle school and high school) teachers are expected to have a strong background in mathematics. Therefore, their mathematics courses are taken in university departments of mathematics. Typically teachers are prepared to teach an additional subject which, most often, is computer science. To enter the teacher preparation program, one must have a diploma in secondary education and have successfully passed the university mathematics entrance exam. All students in mathematical fields, including teacher preparation, must take this exam. The exam takes 5 hours and consists of several open-ended, problem-solving items.[1] Based on its results, applicants are accepted into the teacher preparation track of the mathematics department. Each of the six Bulgarian universities has a quota for candidates that may be accepted for each year.

Teacher preparation in Bulgaria is subject-matter oriented. Future mathematics teachers receive their preparation in departments of mathematics. Courses in general pedagogy and psychology are taught by lecturers from departments of education. To finish the mathematics teacher preparation program, one must successfully pass all university exams on mathematics, mathematics pedagogy, and general pedagogy; pass the school-based practicum; and pass the required final exam. Those who finish the program receive a bachelor's degree, a teaching certificate allowing them to teach mathematics and, typically, computer science in middle and high school. No additional formal training is required.

Teacher preparation spans 4 years, with each year consisting of two 15-week semesters. The teacher preparation program is considered a difficult course of study in the mathematics department because students have more requirements than students in other programs. They must study all basic mathematics and informatics courses plus courses on subject matter pedagogy and general pedagogy.

Most courses consist of two parts: about one-half is theory (lectures), and the remaining part is practical (laboratory) work. The theoretical part is delivered by a senior professor (associate professor or higher), and the practical part is delivered by an assistant professor. All future teachers in one cohort (about 40 to 50) are together for the lecture part but are divided into groups of 12 to 15 for the practical work. Depending on the course, the practical work may consist of problem solving, investigation of documents, or presentation of students' work.

In the second to last semester future teachers participate once a week in school observations in a real school. The last semester students have a school-based practicum during which they are assigned to mathematics teachers for about 2 months and take on increasing levels of responsibility.

Students take an exam at the end of each course, which for most courses has two parts: practical and theoretical. In the practical examination students are asked to solve several problems, while on the theoretical part they must demonstrate their understanding of theory. Students first have to pass the practical part, but their final mathematics score is based on both parts.

At the end of the teacher preparation program state examinations are required. Students have to pass two school practicum examinations (one for teaching mathematics and one for teaching informatics) in a real school environment and one university examination. The university state exam is mostly on mathematics and some mathematics pedagogy and has both a practical and theoretical part.

GERMANY

K–12 Schooling

All students attend elementary school (grades 1 to 4, and 1 to 6 in a few federal states) except children with severe handicaps or learning disorders, who attend special needs schools (see Figure 2.2). After the 4th (or 6th) grade, students are placed into different kinds of middle schools on the basis of their ability. Classroom teachers recommend a certain school type according to each student's prospective academic competency. In some states, parents have the right to ignore this recommendation and to enroll their child in the school type of their preference. The process is expected to be based on ability, but strong socioeconomic and ethnic bias persists (Prenzel, Baumert, Blum et al., 2004).

The first 2 years at secondary school are considered an orientation phase wherein students, on principle, can change between the three school levels if their competencies are a mismatch with the chosen track. In reality, these changes are in the downward direction, very few in the opposite direction. Students whose abilities are more practical and less academic in nature attend the Hauptschule, which represents the lowest track. Education in this school type ends after 9th grade in most federal states. The Realschule (intermediate track) ends after 10th grade and prepares students for a middle-level career in trade and industry. The Gymnasium (highest track, with continuation to high school) offers the final examination called *Abitur* at the end of grade 12 or 13 (depending on the state) and qualifies students for university.

Comprehensive schools have been introduced in the last 30 years, and they have two manifestations: one integrates two or three of the aforementioned tracks

FIGURE 2.2. Structure of the educational system in Germany.

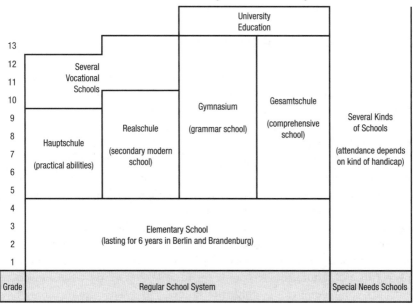

Note: Reprinted with permission from Blömeke, Herzig, & Tulodziecki, 2007.

(Hauptschule, Realschule, and Gymnasium) under one roof while the other offers student tracking by individual subjects. The prevalence of comprehensive schools differs widely among federal states. At lower-secondary, remarkable differences in the student body at each school type are evident (KMK, 2003). For instance, the Hauptschule in the state of Berlin represents a *leftover school*, with only the bottom 5% of students. In contrast, in Bavaria approximately 40% of students attend the Hauptschule and consequently student achievement is somewhat higher.

At the high school level a dual system of schools exists: the Gymnasium and comprehensive schools with an orientation toward general education offering the Abitur at the end and vocational schools preparing students for a vocational career without qualifying them for university study. Schooling is compulsory until the age of 18, which usually results in a total of 11 or 12 years of schooling.

Mathematics Teachers

In grades 1 to 4 students usually have one teacher for all subjects, including mathematics. The teacher usually stays with the same class through all four grades. Teachers are prepared as generalists and have to cover several subjects in teacher education. Starting in grade 5, teachers are prepared as subject-matter specialists, usually in two subjects that they choose out of the full range of school subjects. In lower-secondary, a mathematics teacher usually teaches the same group of students for 2 years, but there is a great deal of variation depending on the school's organization and philosophy.

Organization of Mathematics Teacher Education

Regulation of teacher education exists at three levels, which gives rise to considerable variation in requirements. The current transition of university programs to bachelor/master degrees has further contributed to the variability. Across federal states teacher education is under the regulation of the Kultusministerkonferenz (KMK), which is a committee of the 16 federal states' ministers of education. Here, basic guidelines for the arrangement of teacher education programs are negotiated to ensure comparability of licensure. These basic guidelines include the definition of teacher licenses types, minimum duration of study, licensing process, content areas, number and kind of practical experiences, and the duration of the second practical phase of teacher education.

Teacher education is divided into two phases: the academic study at a university (first phase) and the practical preparatory service (second). For all teaching certificates, future teachers must spend at least 3 years at the university and, after completion of the university studies, pass a state examination. They continue to a practical phase of at least 18 months, leading to the second state examination. The high school exit exam (the Abitur) is the minimal qualification required for entry into the first phase of all teacher education programs.

Institutions consider an applicant's performance based on the grade-point average in this exam. Other factors, such as the age of the candidate, the amount of time one has waited for admission, social hardship, and place of residence, may also play a role. Although there is no specific mathematics admission requirements, mathematics is a compulsory part of the Abitur.

Two types of lower-secondary mathematics teacher licenses exist (Bellenberg & Thierack, 2003):

1. One for either one or all middle schools *except* the Gymnasium (Hauptschule, Realschule, and comprehensive schools); in most federal states this license also qualifies for teaching of the primary grades.
2. Another for the highest track of middle school (Gymnasium and comprehensive schools) and high school, a license that explicitly excludes the primary grades.

The first phase for license A includes the study of general pedagogy, the study of up to three subjects including subject-related pedagogy, and practical components of general pedagogy and of specific subjects. German and/ or mathematics is compulsory for license A in those federal states that certify middle school teachers to teach in elementary grades.

The first phase of teacher education for the Gymnasium (license B) includes the study of two major subjects including subject-related pedagogy, the study of general pedagogy, and practical components related general pedagogy as well as the two subjects. Only subjects regularly taught at school may be chosen.

During the second phase of teacher education future teachers of both license types spend time in schools teaching their majors—part of the time as assistants to experienced teachers and the other time taking full responsibility for a class. Former teachers with extensive experience and high-quality teaching coordinate this aspect. The idea is to model successful teaching for the teacher candidates.

In most federal states the first phase lasts 3.5 (mainly license A) or 4.5 years (mainly license B), and the second phase lasts 1.5 (license A) or 2 years (license B). So, overall, mathematics teacher education for middle schools in Germany lasts between 5 and 6.5 years.

Within the KMK guidelines, considerable variation exists in the arrangement and requirements of programs among the 16 federal states. Every federal state has its own legislative framework for teacher education. For example, the prescribed number of study hours for subject-related pedagogy for license A varies from 8 to 52 hours, and variation in the number of study hours for general pedagogy ranges from 40 to 96 hours.

Before the so-called Bologna Process started, the implemented curriculum of future teachers in the MT21 sample was usually quite variable, as each student had a great deal of freedom in selecting courses. This was particularly true in the selection of general pedagogy courses, but also in mathematics pedagogy, where students were relatively free in their choice of courses and it was common to have no compulsory requirements regarding the specific content or the sequencing of content and courses. But even at that time and with respect to the MT21 sample, freedom of choice was usually less pronounced in mathematics, where a prescription of mandatory courses and their sequencing often existed, especially for the first 2 years.

Both phases of teacher education end with a high-stakes exit exam. The first state examination consists of several written and oral examinations related to the subjects studied. A thesis on a particular subject is part of the examination as well. This first examination is equivalent to a university degree like a diploma or master's. Passing this first examination is the entry requirement for the second phase of teacher education, which takes place at specialized teacher training institutions that are directly under the control of the federal states.

Second phase teacher education content is determined by the subjects a future teacher has chosen at the beginning of the first phase. For example, a future mathematics and English teacher is trained in these two areas and in general pedagogy. Future teachers must work part-time at schools and attend teacher training courses. The second state examination is taken at the end of the second phase. Future teachers must teach lessons that are observed and assessed by a board of examiners consisting of school staff, teacher educators, and state officials. Furthermore, an essay on a practical issue has to be written.

Reform initiatives are currently focusing on teacher education. Two important initiatives are the transition of university programs to bachelor/master degrees (BA/MA) modeled after English-speaking countries, and the implementation of a European-wide credit-point system known as European Credit Transfer System (ECTS). The goal is to make student achievement comparable across the European Union (Blömeke, 2001). The duration of study for bachelor programs is specified as ranging from 3 to 4 years with study loads of 180 ECTS. A final thesis (6 ECTS) is required. Master's programs range from 1 or 2 years with study loads of 60 or 120 ECTS, respectively. Furthermore, entrance to a master's program can be restricted and the selection of students based on their achievements in previous BA studies is possible. The curriculum of BA/MA programs has to be organized into modules, which can be finished by students within a semester or a year.

To make new BA/MA licenses comparable to traditional teacher education programs according to KMK regulations, the new programs have to incorporate the following criteria (KMK, 2005):

1. BA and MA programs for teachers must include two subjects—for example, mathematics and general and subject-specific pedagogy, as well as the practical phases already included in the BA program.
2. Study duration should range from 7 to 9 semesters (without practical phases), and lower-secondary programs are differentiated by school type.
3. The content of the MA exam has to be comparable to the former first state examination even if it is now solely a university responsibility.

Most federal states follow a consecutive model of teacher education in the first phase. A bachelor's *and* a master's degree must be acquired to become a teacher.

Accreditation of the new BA/MA teacher education programs by an independent council is required. The council consists of representatives of the 16 federal states, teacher education institutions, and students. Currently two thirds of the federal states have implemented programs of teacher education to be finished with a BA/MA degree, at least as model programs at single universities; the other federal states (except Bavaria and Baden-Württemberg) are planning to implement the programs as well (HRK, 2007).

MEXICO

K–12 Schooling

The Mexican educational system has three levels: basic education, upper-secondary, and higher education (see Figure 2.3). There is no tracking at any of these levels. Basic education includes preschool, primary (grades 1-6), and 3 years of lower-secondary education (grades 7-9). Lower-secondary education is offered in three main modes: general, technical, and tele-secondary (distance education). Over 50% of students attend the general mode; nearly 30% attend technical schools that are geared toward preparing students to work in industrial, agricultural, and other sectors; and around 20% of students live in communities that lack school infrastructure, so they receive their education via televised instruction. Compulsory education ends with lower-secondary but students may continue their education in upper-secondary

FIGURE 2.3. Structure of the educational system in Mexico.

Age		Grade		ISCED
17/18		12		
16/17	Upper-Secondary Education (Educación Media Superior)	11	Upper Secondary	3
15/16		10		
14/15		9		
13/14	Lower-Secondary Education (Educación Secundaria)	8	Lower Secondary	2
12/13		7		
11/12		6		
10/11		5		
9/10	Primary Education (Educación Primaria)	4	Primary	1
8/9		3		
7/8		2		
6/7		1		
5/6	Preschool Education (Educación Preescolar)	K	Preschool	0
4/5		PK		

schools (grades 10-12) either in general academic programs geared toward university preparation or in schools that are more technical in nature, serving students who may want vocational or technical training. Higher education includes university education, technical education, and teacher education.

At the end of primary school all students must take the entrance exam to lower-secondary level, which serves to allocate students in schools based on their test results. In urban districts lower-secondary classes may have up to 45 students while in rural districts they may have only 10 students. The high ratio of students to teachers in some schools raises important challenges for teachers who cannot always provide enough attention to individual students (OECD, 2008a). Small rural schools that do not have many students may teach children in multigrade classrooms where one teacher instructs more than one grade. Children's school experiences vary widely depending on the school they attend.

At the end of middle school all students who intend to enter the upper-secondary school must take the National Center for Educational Assessment examination. Upper-secondary school services are not compulsory. They are provided to students who are at least 15 years old. Class sizes are about the same as they are at the middle school level. Mexico continues to struggle with low enrollment rates for upper-secondary education (48.8%) that are significantly below OECD average (81.5%) although, since 2000, these rates have been on the rise (OECD, 2008a). At the end of upper-secondary school all students who want to enter the university level must take an exam designed by the correspondent institution.

Higher education is most commonly provided in public universities. Higher education institutions provide university education, technological education, and normal education. The purpose of normal education has been to train teachers for basic schools, including primary and lower-secondary schools.

Mathematics Teachers

Primary teachers work with a class throughout the entire academic year and teach all the subjects for that grade. Therefore, the program of studies for primary teacher education includes the teaching of mathematics and natural sciences.

At the middle school level, a mathematics teacher typically only teaches mathematics. Mexico has a national curriculum, and in lower-secondary schools mathematics occupies 14% of the curriculum, which is slightly above the Organization for Economic Cooperation and Development (OECD) average of 13% (see, www.oecd.org). However, Mexican students have produced dismal results in international comparative studies and part of the blame is ascribed to the poor quality of teachers.

School personnel in Mexico have little autonomy—the principal may propose candidates, but the hiring and firing of teachers is primarily done by state authorities in conjunction with the teachers' union. The teachers' union is very powerful, and no reform is likely to succeed without the union's engagement in the reform process. In May 2008, the Mexican president signed an agreement with the head of the teachers' union to launch a reform to strengthen the quality of teachers. This is another step in a succession of attempts to improve Mexican schooling. Teachers became the target of improvement initiatives in the early 1990s when Mexico implemented a reform "Carrera Magisterial" to provide economic incentives to teachers who participate in professional development and agree to be evaluated through teacher and student tests. The new initiative is expected to broaden the scope of the reform and allocate posts in public schools, not primarily through the union's interventions but according to how teachers perform on newly designed tests.

Organization of Mathematics Teacher Education

Teacher education in Mexico has been the purview of normal schools since the 19th century. For most of the 20th century, normal schools operated on the level of secondary education. In 1972, they were elevated to the status of senior high schools, and in 1984 they were incorporated into the network of higher education institutions with upper-secondary education required as a prerequisite for entry into a normal school. The purpose of normal schools is to prepare primary and lower-secondary teachers. Secondary teachers receive their training in universities. There are a total of 462 normal schools in Mexico, of which 61% belong to the public sector and 39% to the private sector.

The incorporation of normal schools into higher education meant that they had to adhere to a university-like model of academic organization and assume tasks and research activities they were historically unprepared to do. Since normal schools did not have the means to satisfy such expectations, they continued to operate within their existing structures and largely preserved their own identity, distinguished from other higher education institutions.

It became clear that if change was to be achieved, normal schools had to undergo a major transformation, including a renovation of their deteriorating infrastructure. Additionally, curricular reform in basic schools in 1993 also called for a change in how teachers were prepared for the teaching profession. In 1996, the Mexican Department of Public Education launched "The Program for the Academic Transformation and Strengthening of Normal Schools" and further extended it in 2004. The purpose was to ensure that the teacher education curriculum was aligned to the basic school curriculum and that normal schools undergo academic renovation as well as institutional transformation. Accordingly, a new national curriculum for teacher preparation was devised in 1999. Mexico has a highly centralized system of governance and although normal schools fall under the jurisdiction of individual states, they must follow the national curriculum.

The curriculum for normal schools draws on the future teachers' profile that identifies competencies that future teachers should achieve upon completing their studies. The profile includes five major areas: specific intellectual abilities, good command of the teaching contents, teaching competence, professional and ethical standards, and perceptive qualities and ability to respond to the social conditions of the school's environment. Elementary and middle-school teacher education are organized differently to accomplish future teachers' development in these areas.

To enter the program for lower-secondary mathematics teachers at a normal school, students must demonstrate knowledge of upper-secondary school mathematics on a national entrance examination. The entrance examination also has one part focusing on the assessment of general cultural knowledge and oral skills. The national normal school curriculum establishes the courses that future teachers need to take as well as their sequencing. The program of study for future teachers is thus set and there is virtually no allowance for electives or additional courses other than those prescribed. The teacher preparation programs in normal schools last eight semesters, cover 45 to 46 courses, and are organized into three main areas of activity:

1. classroom-based activities that include courses in educational theories and pedagogy;
2. activities that connect theory with practice, including classroom visits to different types of schools, observations, and initial teaching practice; and
3. intensive practice in lower-secondary schools.

The preparation of middle school mathematics teachers comprises 46 courses. Graduates of the program receive a bachelor's degree in lower-secondary education with specialization in mathematics. The 46 courses include courses in general pedagogy common to all teacher preparation programs (e.g., courses in history of education in Mexico, philosophy of education, etc.), courses related to mathematics and mathematics pedagogy, and courses in pedagogy. Most of the coursework during the first six semesters is theory-based, although each semester, future teachers also have classroom observations and preparatory work for school practice. The last two semesters are devoted solely to practice where future teachers, under supervision, spend around 10 hours a week teaching their subject specialization in a school.

SOUTH KOREA

K–12 Schooling

The school system in South Korea consists of 6 years of primary school, 3 years of middle school, 3 years of high school, and higher education that includes 2-year to 4-year colleges and universities as well as subsequent graduate studies (see Table 2.1). Prior to primary school, some children also attend preschools, although preschools are not part of the public school network and overall attendance is lower than in most OECD countries.

At the age of 6, children are automatically enrolled in primary schools. Progress from year to year is not affected by a student's achievement but is determined by age, at least until middle school. In primary schools, children

TABLE 2.1. Structure of the educational system in South Korea.

School System	Elementary School						Middle School			High School		
School Grades	1	2	3	4	5	6	7	8	9	10	11	12

typically have one teacher for all subjects, although for some specialized subjects like foreign languages (typically English starting at grade 3) or physical education they may have a different teacher. Primary education ends with grade 6 and students then move to middle schools.

Middle school (grades 7–9) admissions are determined by a lottery as well as by students' place of residence. The lottery system is in place to ensure a balance of students of various abilities in each school (Sorensen, 1994). Students stay with the same group of classmates and the whole class is taught the same subjects. However, the difference is that at this level each subject is taught by a subject specialist teacher. In contrast to primary schools, middle schools are more formalized. Students must wear uniforms, and there are also strict haircut policies. The stakes at this level grow and students' success begins to shape their future educational paths and success in life, which is closely tied to the prestige of the higher-education institutions they attend.

South Korea mandates 9 years of compulsory education, which ends with students completing middle school. However, almost all students (97%) continue to high schools, giving South Korea the highest upper-secondary education attainment rate among the OECD countries (OECD, 2008b). There are two types of secondary schools: general and vocational. General high schools prepare students for university education while vocational high schools train them to enter the job market in areas such as home economics and business, manufacturing, agriculture, fishery, and oceanography. Vocational high schools are less desirable because their graduates have lower earnings and a fairly low social status. The fact that 72% of students attend general high schools (OECD, 2008b) points to the importance that South Koreans place on general secondary education.

Which general high school students attend matters greatly because it may enhance or diminish their college entrance examinations performance. Upper-secondary schools include special-purpose schools that are geared toward the most talented students in various areas such as science, sports, and foreign language. Since general high schools serve as a filter to the best higher education institutions, the pressure on students to do well on entrance examinations and be accepted in the most prestigious high schools is high. The best high schools are public schools, which tend to be very competitive. South Korea also has a large number of private schools. High schools charge tuition but the difference between the tuition in public and private high schools is not significant because the fees are regulated by the state. Since private schools are limited in the tuition they may charge and also in the support they get from the state, they tend to have larger classes and are generally viewed as a second-rate option.

The importance of private institutions increases with each level of education as the stakes grow higher and students prepare for qualifying and entrance examinations from one level to the next. Most parents invest considerable amounts of money in tutoring and private after-school academies (so-called *hagwons*) that prepare students for the exams. A typical day for middle and high school students starts early in the morning at school and unfolds with afternoons and evenings in after-school academies where students receive extra instruction. The extra tutoring translates into very long and busy days with little time for sleep.

College education is practically a necessity in South Korea—an important prerequisite for obtaining a respectable job and for social recognition. In applying for entry to college or a university, students must take the College Scholastic Ability Test, which is similar to the SAT developed in the United States. The highly competitive environment demands that students achieve very high scores if they hope to be admitted into prestigious colleges and secure their life prospects.

Mathematics Teachers

In primary schools, one teacher typically teaches all subjects with a few exceptions—such as foreign language, physical education, and music education—that may be taught by a specialist teacher. In middle schools (grades 7–9) each subject is taught by a different teacher who is a subject specialist. Mathematics teachers are prepared to teach lower-secondary and secondary mathematics; typically, they do not teach other subjects. Middle school students take about 11 subjects every semester and may have about three class periods of mathematics per week, at different times of the day. The schedule for their mathematics teacher is thus different each day. Teachers do not have their own rooms but come to the classroom where they are assigned to teach. According to OECD (2008b), South Korean teachers' net teaching time in middle school amounts to 548 hours, which is lower than the OECD average of 672. However, the time they actually spend in schools—in preparation for their classes, tutoring, and other school-related activities—makes their work load rather heavy, with some teachers working as many as 80 hours a week.

Organization of Mathematics Teacher Education

Teaching mathematics is a high status job in South Korea—mathematics teachers enjoy social recognition as well as high salaries and lifetime job security. Accordingly, the profession is in high demand, attracting top candidates who have to compete for admission. People who want to become mathematics teachers obtain their teaching certificates through studies in teacher preparation programs at universities. The pool of future teachers includes both mathematics education and mathematics majors—the distinction between the two majors is blurred (Kang & Hong, 2008). Applicants to teacher education programs must demonstrate adequate performance at the upper-secondary level and undergo an interview that assesses their personality traits and suitability for the teaching profession. More importantly, they must have high scores on the national entrance examination, including the comprehensive mathematics assessment. Cut-off scores for future mathematics teachers tend to be set high in comparison to other programs such as pharmacy or medicine (Kang & Hong, 2008) so that only the highest achieving students get in to the teacher preparation program.

Upon completing the teacher preparation program, future teachers must take another examination (National Teacher Employment Test—NTET) to compete for public school jobs. NTET tests applicants' knowledge of mathematics (52–56% of total score), general pedagogy (20% of total score), and mathematics pedagogy (24–28% of total score) (Kang & Hong, 2008). There are many more applicants than jobs and the test is highly competitive, given that those who take it are already the top achieving students. Future teachers who do not succeed in being hired in a public school can become teachers at private secondary schools and after-school academies. Some may also get jobs related to mathematics in computation enterprises or research institutions.

Teacher preparation consists of four key areas: mathematics, mathematics pedagogy, general pedagogy, and liberal arts courses. Mathematics courses strive to prepare excellent professionals who are service oriented but who also possess research skills and can make contributions to humanity; they guide students to become good citizens. More specifically, the goal is to support future teachers to learn both mathematics theory and to gain the ability for personal growth and service to local community, country, and society. The goal of mathematics pedagogy is to teach the subject matter through experience and to study various kinds of situations for teaching mathematics to promote a better understanding. Consequently, the department of mathematics education teaches educational theories and teaching and learning theories related to general mathematics. General pedagogy is organized to prepare future teachers for theoretical research on evaluation methods connected to teaching and learning as well as to equip them with fundamentals in educational theories. Liberal education is designed to promote ethical and socially responsible conduct.

TAIWAN

K–12 Schooling

Kindergarten in Taiwan is not mandatory but about 30–40% of children attend public or private kindergartens at 4 or 5 years of age. Students between the ages of 6 and 15 are required to attend 9 years of compulsory education, which includes the elementary (grades 1–6) and lower-secondary (grades 7–9, see Figure 2.4).

FIGURE 2.4. Structure of the education system in Taiwan.

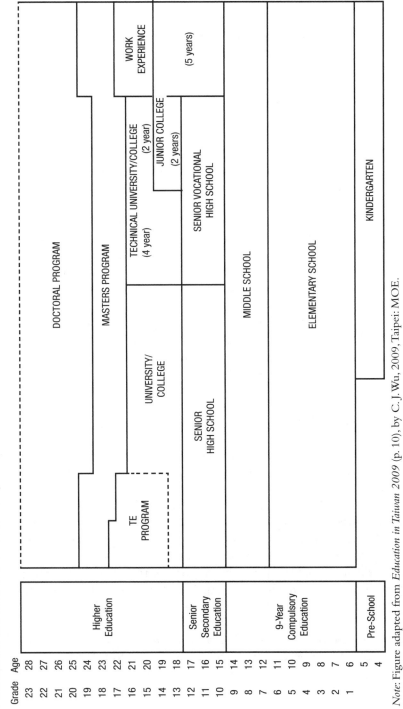

Note: Figure adapted from *Education in Taiwan 2009* (p. 10), by C. J. Wu, 2009, Taipei: MOE.

More than 90% of the students who graduated from middle schools will either go to the senior high schools (40%) or the senior vocational high schools (50%). An additional 5% will matriculate at a 5-year junior college. About 80 to 90% of senior high or vocational high school graduates continue on to college. Senior high school students must take national entrance examinations to enter universities/colleges. Senior vocational high school students choose between entering the job market or taking a joint entrance examination for technology universities and junior colleges. However, each track of students can cross over to the other track's route for advancing to the next education level.

Although the regulatory frameworks for schools are determined by the national government, most public schools are directly controlled by individual municipalities or county governments. In addition, there are schools governed by the central government as well as private schools. At the compulsory education level, about 99% of the primary and middle schools are municipal or county controlled and 1% are private. Only about 60% of senior (vocational) high schools are either national or municipal/county controlled; the rest are private.

About 70% of the senior high and senior vocational high schools have more than 1,000 students per school and only about 3% have fewer than 200 students in each school. The largest senior high school and senior vocational high school has about 6,500 and 9,500 students, respectively. Middle schools are a bit smaller: about 45% have more than 1,000 students each and 15% have fewer than 200 students each. Only about 20% of primary schools have more than 1,000 students and 40% that have fewer than 200 students.

Mathematics Teachers

Students are assigned to their classrooms in the 1st grade/year of that level. In grades 1–4 students usually have one teacher for all subjects, including mathematics. The teacher is regarded as the designated teacher of that class. A designated teacher also teaches most subjects in grades 5 and 6 but a few are taught by specialized teachers.

Lower-secondary students are assigned at 7th grade and stay with the same group of classmates for the next 3 years. The group takes all courses in the same room except for subjects that require specially designed classrooms such as physical education, music, and art. A mathematics teacher is assigned to a group/class and usually teaches them for 3 years. High schools are similar but since high school students must decide on an academic focus—liberal arts or science—in grade 11, some are likely to change mathematics teachers. Middle and high school teachers are all subject-matter specialists.

Given the high stakes nature of national entrance examinations and the important role of mathematics in the exam, mathematics teachers usually bear heavy responsibility for students' learning. This results in intensive work on planning lessons, making test items, and grading homework and tests. However, teachers do not need to teach all day. Middle school mathematics teachers typically teach twenty 45-minute class periods per week. Senior high teachers teach sixteen 50-minute class periods.

Most of Taiwan's schools are relatively large and have about 10 mathematics teachers. Thus the community of mathematics teachers has many opportunities for collegial discussions, which provides a strong basis for professional development.

Organization of Mathematics Teacher Education

Students experience a rigorous competition for admission to teacher education. Teachers enjoy a relatively high social status and better salaries than in other jobs—hence the teaching profession is highly attractive and popular. Four levels of teacher preparation exist: early childhood, elementary, secondary, and special education. Early childhood teachers teach preschool children age 4 to 6. Elementary teachers are generalists and teach grades 1–6. Secondary teachers teach either in middle schools or in senior high (vocational) schools as specialists in one subject unless they have studied an extra subject for teaching. Universities offer teacher education as an add-on to the bachelor's degree. Future teachers must obtain a bachelor's degree, complete the teacher education curriculum, finish the education practicum and pass the qualification assessment. They are allowed to complete the first two requirements simultaneously.

Students can apply for admission into a teacher education program in their second year of university study according to the 1994 Teacher Education Act. Students must also pass various program selection requirements specific to their own teacher education university. The screening and selection procedure and criteria for secondary and elementary teacher education programs are determined by each university, but they share many common features. Many base selection on an applicant's grades from their first year and may require tests such as general knowledge, language, attitude, or personality inventories. Some universities also consider student character, moral conduct, and extracurricular activities.

Usually, future teachers take 4 years to complete a bachelor's degree and to finish the teacher education curriculum. After this, students must complete a half-year on-site practicum in schools.[2] According to a national law and guideline, the focus of the educational practicum must include four parts: (1) a teaching internship—40%; (2) "homeroom" teaching (general class affairs) supervision—30%; (3) administrative work practice—20%; and (4) study and training activities—10%. Typically schools have interns practice all aspects

FIGURE 2.5. Differences between mathematics department–based and teacher education center–based teacher preparation models.

Courses	Mathematics Department–Based	Teacher Education Center–Based
General Pedagogical	Class is typically composed of future teachers (FTs) who will teach different subjects.	
Mathematics Pedagogical	1) A class usually only has FTs who are going to teach mathematics. 2) Lectures are often from the mathematics departments.	1) A class is usually composed of FTs who are going to teach different subjects. 2) Lectures are often from the teacher education centers or education departments
Mathematics	1) Most FTs are from the mathematics departments and they usually take more mathematics courses than are required by the teacher education program. 2) A class usually has many mathematics FTs who study together with some of their peers in the mathematics department.	1) FTs except those in the department of mathematics only need to take the required mathematics courses by the teacher education program. 2) A class usually has only a few FTs who study together with many other students in mathematics department.
On-site School Practicum	1) The university supervisors usually are professors in the fields of mathematics education or mathematics. 2) The university supervisors usually only supervise mathematics FTs.	1) The university supervisors usually are professors from the center, not majors in mathematics education or mathematics. 2) The university supervisors might supervise FTs in many different teaching subjects.

during the entire practicum but some equally divide the practicum into three periods, each having a different focus.

The homeroom teaching and supervision aspect provides experiences related to counseling or communicating with students, supervising a student's self-study period, conducting the flag-raising ceremony in the early morning, reviewing the teacher–parent communication booklets, supervising students in cleaning the classroom and campus, and guiding class meetings, among other such activities.

Regulations require teacher education universities and the schools to provide counseling systems to support future teachers during the practicum. Each practicum school has a team to counsel future teachers that includes teachers, internship supervisors, principals, and the school directors. Teacher education universities must visit and advise practicum schools as well as the interns, which includes providing counseling literature, setting up hotlines, and identifying Internet resources.

Although governed by national regulations implementation differs among different university types. Three kinds of teacher education universities exist:

(1) normal universities and universities of education, which prepare the largest number of teachers; (2) universities with teacher education departments (majors); and (3) universities with teacher education centers. The main differences between the last two preparation models are shown in Figure 2.5. Since the 1994 reform, normal universities and universities of education are no longer limited to only offering teacher education and related coursework.

UNITED STATES

K–12 Schooling

The U.S. educational system is complex and dynamic. Much of the complexity stems from a decentralized, locally controlled design. Public schools are taxpayer-funded with taxes typically based on property values. This leads to wide variation in school funding across districts and states. Individual states construct policies and regulations for the administration and operation of local schools. Recent legislation aims to require states to provide academic standards for each grade level.

Despite decentralized control some elements hold across all states. The traditional U.S. school experience consists of 12 years of compulsory schooling. Most states encourage students to enroll in kindergarten at age 5. While kindergarten is not mandatory, most states require enrollment in school by the age of 7. Most states also permit students to leave school before completing all 12 years of school but require students to remain in school until the age of 16.

Several levels exist in the K–12 grade-level breakdown (see Figure 2.6). Primary includes kindergarten through second grades; the intermediate elementary grades cover grades 3 through 6. Middle schools often include grade 6 and go up through either grade 8 or 9. High schools begin at grade 9 or 10 and go through 12th grade. Variations in these grade arrangements occur both between and within states. Some schools provide different tracks for students based upon ability, specialization, and need. The most common tracks in high school are vocational, general education, college prep, and special education. A growing number of high schools also provide different tracks for students based on ability.

After completing high school, students may continue schooling via several avenues. Ability, financial means, and the student's particular interests can significantly determine which avenue a student chooses. Two-year colleges (community colleges) and vocational training programs offer alternatives to traditional 4-year colleges and universities. Four-year colleges and universities exist as both

FIGURE 2.6. Structure of the schooling system in the United States, showing the International Standard Classification Education (ISCED).

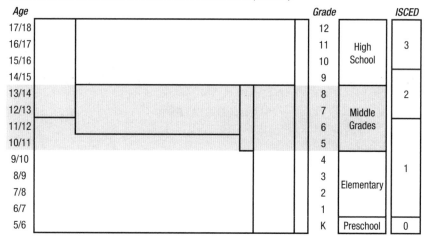

public and private institutions, all charging tuition. Tuition for 4-year institutions is higher than tuition for 2-year institutions and vocational training programs.

Mathematics Teachers

Since the 2001 No Child Left Behind federal legislation, all teachers are required to be highly qualified in the subjects they teach. For middle school mathematics teachers, this generally means that they should have a major or a minor in mathematics. As subject specialists, middle school teachers only teach the subjects in which they have certification, for example, mathematics, social studies, or physical science. In some states, such as California, teacher certification and the highly qualified designation is based on candidates' performance on state-sanctioned subject matter exams rather than whether they had a specific academic major or minor at a college or university. Teachers typically have their own classrooms, with students coming to the classroom only for the given lesson and then moving to another classroom for a lesson with another teacher.

Middle schools in the United States often assign students to mathematics classes according to ability. Thus all students do not take the same mathematics. Teachers typically do not stay with the same student group but teach only certain courses in mathematics, for example, pre-algebra or algebra. This means that every semester or every year, students may experience a different mathematics teacher as well as a different group of classmates. In addition, high school students beginning at grade 9 typically have a choice as to how many years they will take mathematics as well as which kind of mathematics courses they will take. The types of mathematics courses any student may take in high school is very much dependent on the mathematics that they have taken in middle school. Recently, a growing number of states have sought to reduce the variation in students' high school mathematics course choices by requiring more years of mathematics as well as specific courses for high school graduation.

Organization of Mathematics Teacher Education

Teacher education is not governed by national regulations or standards, although some have been developed by national professional associations. Most states have either adopted a set of nationally recognized standards or developed their own to provide a basic framework for the organization of teacher preparation in their higher education institutions. Nonetheless, there is great variation in how specific these state standards are. Several organizations, such as the National Council for Accreditation of Teacher Education (NCATE) and the Teacher Education Accreditation Council (TEAC), review the content and process of teacher preparation programs at institutions of higher learning and award accreditation or certification to institutions that meet their professional standards. Although all states require teacher preparation programs to be accredited through such an organization or through a similar state-sponsored accreditation process, institutions have a great deal of latitude in interpreting and implementing them.

Teacher preparation can be divided into two broad categories: traditional programs and alternative routes to teaching. Alternative programs serve those who already have a bachelor's degree in content area but lack a teacher license. Typically, the alternative program provides training opportunities in pedagogical areas while individuals serve as classroom teachers. Recent teacher shortages in subject areas such as mathematics and science have led to the development of alternative certification routes.

Traditional 4-year undergraduate programs combine preparation in general pedagogy, subject matter area, subject pedagogy, and field experiences. Future teachers apply to these programs in their second or third year at the university, after having completed the university's liberal arts requirements and other prerequisites. Admission criteria depend on individual institutions and, thus, vary greatly. Common requirements include: a minimum grade-point average in previous college coursework; completion of required liberal arts courses; a written essay to demonstrate communication skills; letters of recommendation; passing scores on basic skill tests in reading, writing, and mathematics (these tests differ from state to state); a criminal background check; and a specified performance on SAT or ACT (college entrance) exams. Admission decisions may reflect any combination or none of the various criteria listed.

Prospective middle school mathematics teachers can enroll in elementary or secondary education programs. Some institutions, reflecting the certification requirements of the state, have programs geared specifically toward middle school. Currently, those who study in elementary programs must have at least a minor in mathematics if they want to teach it at the middle school level and be considered highly qualified under the No Child Left Behind legislation. Elementary education programs are usually housed in colleges of education where future teachers take most courses. The content area courses tend to be offered in different departments and different colleges. Teacher preparation programs thus are not self-contained units and span several departments and colleges. Secondary education teachers are often primarily affiliated with mathematics departments, where they take content courses; for professional education, they go to the education department. These future teachers may obtain a degree in mathematics with teaching certification.

WHO CHOOSES TO BECOME
A MIDDLE SCHOOL MATHEMATICS TEACHER AND WHY

Given the differences among the national education systems just described one might expect differences among the countries in terms of who chooses to become a lower-secondary mathematics teacher. Individuals, in their final year of a lower-secondary mathematics teacher preparation program, are the focus of this book. Here we consider briefly their backgrounds, motivations for becoming teachers, and their perceptions of the role of a teacher in today's world. These descriptions come from the MT21 samples. These were not random samples of institutions within countries. On the contrary, much effort went into the institution selection criteria so that the purposeful samples drawn may reasonably be considered representative. More is said about this issue in the next chapter.

Future Teacher Backgrounds

As observed in Table 2.2, most sampled future teachers were 22–24 years old. The major exception is the German sample, in which none of the age categories characterized a majority and the two youngest age categories included less than 5% of all teachers. This is not surprising given that in the German sample those in their final year of teacher preparation were in the second insti-

TABLE 2.2. Estimated percentage of future teachers and the standard errors (se) in each age category for each country.

	Bulgaria	Germany	Mexico	South Korea	Taiwan	United States
18–21						
Percent	11.3	0.7	0.6	28.5	0.4	16.0
(se)	(3.2)	(0.5)	(0.8)	(3.7)	(0.4)	(2.5)
22–24						
Percent	82.8	3.5	57.4	40.3	64.4	53.2
(se)	(3.8)	(1.1)	(4.8)	(4.0)	(3.0)	(3.3)
25–27						
Percent	1.9	27.9	34.9	15.2	19.3	10.3
(se)	(1.4)	(2.7)	(4.7)	(2.9)	(2.4)	(2.0)
28–30						
Percent	0.8	24.6	6.6	4.8	11.1	5.0
(se)	(0.9)	(2.6)	(2.4)	(1.7)	(1.9)	(1.5)
31–35						
Percent	3.1	21.0	0.6	4.8	2.7	6.8
(se)	(1.7)	(2.4)	(0.8)	(1.7)	(1.0)	(1.7)
36–39						
Percent	0.0	11.9	0.0	3.6	0.7	5.7
(se)	(0.0)	(1.9)	(0.0)	(1.5)	(0.5)	(1.6)
40+						
Percent	0.0	10.5	0.0	2.9	1.5	3.0
(se)	(0.0)	(1.8)	(0.0)	(1.4)	(0.8)	(1.2)

tution (see the German case study), having already completed their university degree. Germany, Mexico, and the United States had the largest proportion of their final year future teachers who were at least 36 years old—22.4%, 6.5%, and 8.7%, respectively.

We also asked the future teachers to indicate in which year they began their teacher preparation program. In spite of the fact that many of the programs, with the exception of those in Germany and Taiwan, were designed to be completed in 4 years, the mean number of years students from the participating institutions had been in their programs exceeded 4 years with the sole exception of the United States (see Table 2.3). Students in teacher education programs sometimes need more time to finish their programs than other students because they take the teacher education courses in addition to, for example, liberal arts or subject-matter requirements. Furthermore, organizational or achievement problems may lead to additional years. For both Germany and the United States, means are presented for each type of program as described

TABLE 2.3. Means, standard errors (se), and standard deviations (SD) for the number of years future teachers have been in their teacher preparation program for each country.

Country	Mean	(se)	SD
Bulgaria	4.9	(0.1)	1.2
Germany	8.8	(0.1)	1.8
Primary	8.5	(0.2)	2.0
Secondary	9.0	(0.1)	1.6
Mexico	5.8	(0.1)	1.8
South Korea	4.6	(0.2)	1.5
Taiwan	5.7	(0.1)	1.2
United States	3.8	(0.1)	1.8
Primary	4.5	(0.2)	1.9
Middle Grades	3.6	(0.2)	1.9
Secondary	3.3	(0.2)	1.5

previously in this chapter. German future teachers indicated spending the most amount of time—over 8 years—in their teacher preparation programs. This is most likely related to the fact that German future teachers are older on average than the future teachers of the other countries, with 43% being over 30 years old. The mean number of years in teacher preparation for the other four countries was between 4.5 and 6 years.

Future teachers from each country indicated very different time frames within which they had made the decision to become teachers. As may be seen in Table 2.4, a majority of the future teachers from South Korea and Mexico indicated that they made this decision sometime while they were engaged in their own K–12 education. About one third of the future teachers from Germany, Taiwan, and the United States indicated a similar time frame for their decision. The largest percentage of the United States sampled future teachers—about 40%—indicated that they made up their minds about becoming teachers sometime after beginning their college or university education. This was also a popular decision time frame for those in Bulgaria and Taiwan, with over 21% of the future teachers in each of these countries indicating this option. Germany had the largest portion of sampled future teachers, indicating that the decision was made after they had finished college/university: over one quarter of the sampled future teachers (26.8%). This reflects the consecutive nature of German teacher education. The university degree (first state examination) includes two full subjects on a master's level. Indecision about being a teacher was not uncommon in the sample from any of the countries, but the largest portion of

TABLE 2.4. Estimated percentage of future teachers and standard errors (se) for each country indicating when they made the decision to become a mathematics teacher.

	Bulgaria	Germany	Mexico	South Korea	Taiwan	United States
Sometime During Primary/Secondary School						
Percent	16.2	32.8	75.4	53.1	26.2	34.2
(se)	(3.7)	(2.8)	(3.6)	(4.9)	(2.7)	(3.2)
Upon Applying to College						
Percent	27.0	10.1	6.0	20.8	34.9	3.7
(se)	(4.5)	(1.8)	(2.0)	(4.0)	(2.9)	(1.3)
After Being in College						
Percent	21.6	12.4	5.7	14.6	21.1	40.2
(se)	(4.1)	(2.0)	(1.9)	(3.5)	(2.5)	(3.3)
During/Following Military Service						
Percent	0.0	6.6	1.0	3.0	8.2	0.5
(se)	(0.0)	(1.5)	(0.8)	(1.7)	(1.7)	(0.5)
During/Following Post-Secondary Job						
Percent	1.6	8.0	1.7	0.0	2.3	1.7
(se)	(1.2)	(1.6)	(1.1)	(0.0)	(0.9)	(0.9)
After Finishing College						
Percent	0.0	26.8	7.4	3.0	0.7	10.4
(se)	(0.0)	(2.6)	(2.2)	(1.7)	(0.5)	(2.1)
Still Not Sure						
Percent	33.7	3.4	2.7	5.5	6.6	9.1
(se)	(4.8)	(1.1)	(1.3)	(2.2)	(1.5)	(1.9)

undecideds were in Bulgaria, where about one third of the sample remained undecided at the end of their teacher preparation program about actually entering the teaching profession.

Their Motivations for Becoming Teachers

Table 2.5 presents the data describing the reasons or motivations that future teachers gave for wanting to become mathematics teachers. They were asked to indicate to what extent various statements identified their reasons or motives for being a mathematics teacher. The statements included: intrinsic-pedagogical motives like "I like children"; extrinsic motives such as "a teacher's schedule"; and intrinsic-academic motives, for example, "I love mathematics" or "I couldn't think of anything else to do." These are the main motives of teachers to go into the profession, as indicated by other studies (Bodensohn,

Schneider, & Jäger, 2007; Eberle & Pollak, 2006; Herzog, Müller, Brunner, & Herzog, 2004; Ulich, 2000; Urhahne, 2006). The future teachers responded to the 20 statements on a 6-point scale ranging from 1 to 6 and were labeled from "not at all" to "to a great extent." Future teachers in every country were more motivated to become teachers by things other than the economic or structural characteristics of the teaching profession. Future teachers in Bulgaria, South Korea, and Taiwan indicated they were most motivated to become teachers because of their interest in and love of mathematics followed by their interest in and love of teaching students, and then the influence of an inspiring teacher that they had had during their own K–12 schooling. The priority of the first two motives was switched for those from Germany, Mexico, and the United States as they indicated they were most motivated to become teachers because of their interest in and love of teaching students, followed by their interest in and love of mathematics, and then the influence of an inspiring teacher that they had during their K–12 schooling. However, in the United States and Germany those who were prepared in secondary-focused programs exhibited the same motivation pattern as those from Bulgaria, South Korea, and Taiwan whose future middle school teachers are all prepared in secondary programs. Whether the motivation focuses on the content or the children seems related to the type of program ultimately chosen, at least in the two countries where choice is possible.

Their Perceptions About the Role of Teachers

Future teachers were asked to indicate the extent to which each of a series of ten statements described an essential part of the role of a teacher. For each of these statements, future teachers indicated their responses on a 6-point scale, from "not at all" to "to a great extent." Seven scales were created, each ranging in value from 1 to 6. The country means are also found in Table 2.5.

The means for pride expressed in the teaching profession are nearly at the top of the scale, that is, over 5, in every country except Bulgaria. Since 3.5 represents the midpoint of the scale, the Bulgarian average indicates that future teachers did not have a strong sense of professional pride.

The sampled future teachers from South Korea expressed a strong sense of teachers being responsible for providing knowledge to students and organizing and arranging learning experiences and opportunities for students (means of 4.3 and 4.7, respectively). The sampled future teachers in Taiwan expressed a similar endorsement for the teacher as a provider of learning opportunities (mean 4.5) but much less of an endorsement for the knowledge provider role (mean 3.4). Those in the Bulgarian sample also endorsed the role of teachers

TABLE 2.5. Country means and standard errors (se) related to reasons for becoming a teacher and the beliefs about the role of a teacher.

	Bulgaria		Germany		Mexico		S. Korea		Taiwan		U.S.	
	Mean	(se)	Mean	(se)	Mean	(se)	Mean	(se)	Mean	(se)	Mean	(se)
Why Be a Math Teacher?												
Position Characteristics	2.8	(0.1)	2.8	(0.0)	3.2	(0.1)	2.7	(0.1)	3.8	(0.1)	2.6	(0.1)
Like to Teach	4.1	(0.1)	4.9	(0.0)	4.1	(0.1)	5.1	(0.1)	4.7	(0.1)	5.1	(0.0)
Love Math	4.8	(0.1)	4.5	(0.1)	4.6	(0.1)	4.8	(0.1)	4.9	(0.1)	4.8	(0.1)
Teacher Inspired	2.9	(0.2)	2.8	(0.1)	3.8	(0.2)	4.1	(0.2)	4.5	(0.1)	4.0	(0.1)
Family Occupation	2.1	(0.2)	2.2	(0.1)	1.9	(0.1)	2.5	(0.2)	2.3	(0.1)	2.3	(0.1)
No Other Ideas	1.7	(0.2)	1.7	(0.1)	2.7	(0.2)	1.1	(0.0)	2.7	(0.1)	1.7	(0.1)
Teachers as												
Student Learning Observer	3.2	(0.2)	3.5	(0.1)	4.5	(0.1)	4.4	(0.1)	4.3	(0.1)	4.4	(0.1)
Knowledge Provider	4.9	(0.1)	3.8	(0.1)	5.3	(0.1)	3.6	(0.1)	4.4	(0.1)	4.2	(0.1)
OTL Provider	3.4	(0.2)	3.8	(0.1)	4.7	(0.1)	3.3	(0.2)	4.5	(0.1)	3.5	(0.2)
Teaching Profession Pride	3.0	(0.3)	5.4	(0.1)	5.2	(0.1)	5.6	(0.1)	5.3	(0.1)	5.3	(0.1)
Teaching Profession Perspective	3.4	(0.2)	3.6	(0.1)	4.0	(0.1)	3.7	(0.1)	3.8	(0.1)	3.7	(0.1)
Supervisor of Non-Academic Activities Role	2.1	(0.2)	1.5	(0.1)	3.5	(0.1)	1.4	(0.1)	2.5	(0.1)	1.3	(0.1)
Social Responsibility Role	3.5	(0.2)	3.7	(0.1)	4.3	(0.1)	4.1	(0.1)	3.9	(0.1)	3.4	(0.1)

as knowledge providers, although not as strongly as those from South Korea. Clearly, German and Mexican sampled future teachers did not endorse this role for teachers, with means below 3.0.

Future teachers from South Korea, Mexico, Taiwan, and the United States expressed a moderately strong endorsement of the perspective that one of the important roles a teacher has is to observe how students learn in the classroom. This perspective was only mildly supported by respondents from Bulgaria and Germany.

WHAT FUTURE MIDDLE SCHOOL TEACHERS WILL BE EXPECTED TO TEACH

Many, if not most, of these future teachers whose backgrounds, motivations, and perspectives on the role of the teacher we have just described will soon walk into their classrooms to teach mathematics. But which mathematics topics they will teach depends on the grade levels for which they will be responsible and also the country in which they will be teaching. The middle school curriculum is in general not the same across the world. The Third International Science Mathematics Study (TIMSS) has shown this to be true. So what will these future teachers in each of the six countries be required to teach? To address this issue we asked the question, What topics are intended to be taught in grades 1 through 8 in our six countries? To answer this we looked closely at the curriculum as specified in the national standards documents for each of the four countries with such national grade-level expectations. For the United States we developed data that are a composite of the state standards across the 50 states. For Germany, which has national standards that are specified only at grades 4 and 8, we analyzed the standards of one federal state which education experts agree represents the country fairly well.

Our rationale for incorporating curriculum analysis into this project was twofold. First, curriculum analysis helps to identify what our future teachers will be expected to teach in grades 6 through 8. Regardless of the structure and makeup of the teacher preparation program, the main question is, what content must the teacher master so as to appropriately instruct her future students? In the context of training, the overall objective is to blend what teachers will be teaching with the courses they have taken.

Prior training cannot be ignored in this context. Hence, our second rationale is that such a curriculum analysis provides a means to better understand what mathematics knowledge our future teachers brought to their teacher preparation programs. What was the future teacher's mathematics background before taking the first teacher preparation course? To get a complete picture, our analyses examined content intended in grades 9 through 12. Our approach, described below, enables us to easily identify curricular differences among the six countries.

The methodology was first used in the 1995 TIMSS (Robitaille, McKnight, Schmidt et al., 1993; Schmidt & Houang, 2007). The TIMSS analyzed both national standards and textbooks using systematic, well defined, and structured document-analysis coding procedures. The approach provides a low inference coding of the intended curriculum. The coding was based on a cross-nationally developed and tested framework that represented a comprehensive list of the topics covered in mathematics grades 1 through 12. The total list of over 200 content topics was aggregated to a much more manageable 32 topics for some of the analyses that follow.

From the data gathered in the TIMSS, a composite benchmark model for grades 1 through 8 was developed based on the national standards of the six countries whose students achieved the highest scores in the TIMSS 8th-grade assessment. Schmidt, Wang, and McKnight (2005) describe the procedure:

> The data used to develop the international benchmarks come from the curriculum component of TIMSS and derive from the procedure known as General Topic Trace Mapping (GTTM) . . . The respondents to the GTTM were educa-

tion officials (typically curriculum officers in the national ministry) of each nation who, using their national content standards or an aggregate of regional standards, indicated for each grade level whether or not a content topic was included in their country's intended curriculum. The result was a map reflecting the grade-level coverage of each topic for each country. . . .

Topic trace maps were available for each of the [top-achieving] countries. While none were identical they all bore strong similarities. The following procedures were followed to develop an international benchmark. First, the mean number of intended topics at each grade level was determined across all countries. Next, the topics were ordered at each grade level based on the percentage of [top-achieving] countries that included it in their curriculum. Those topics with the greatest percentage were chosen first, and only as many were chosen as were indicated by the mean number of intended topics at that grade level. (Schmidt et al., 2005, pp. 532–533)

The model for grades 1 to 8, developed from the TIMSS 95 analyses of intended curricula, is depicted in Figure 2.7 and serves as a framework, not to evaluate the curricular standards of the six countries in this study but to provide a measurement tool to help simplify the cross-country comparisons we wish to make in this section. The other approach would be to do all of the 15 paired comparisons between each pair of countries. This is cumbersome and the procedure followed here allows for each country to be compared to the benchmark and in that way to each other. The fact that the benchmark was derived from top-achieving countries makes it interesting from another, more normative point of view, but that is not our purpose here. We leave it to the reader to draw those kinds of conclusions.

In the tables that will be discussed in the next sections, the 32 topics are listed in rows. The grades appear in columns, allowing for any topic to be designated in the appropriate grade(s) according to the intended curriculum of that country. There are 99 shaded cells that identify the grades in which topics were included in the mathematics curricula in at least two thirds of the top-achieving countries (TAC). The figure lists topics in the same hierarchical sequence suggested by results from the TAC curricular studies, moving from elementary to more advanced topics. The progression of the topics over grades is logically consistent with the nature of mathematics. The idea is that once a topic has been fully developed, it is excluded from the curriculum and other, more complex topics are introduced. The topics taught in grades 1 through 5 build a foundation so that teachers in grades 6 through 8 are well positioned to move into algebra and geometry topics that must be taught in middle school to in turn prepare students for more advanced courses in geometry, trigonometry, pre-calculus, and calculus in high school.

FIGURE 2.7. Mathematics intended at each grade by top-achieving countries.

Topic	Grade							
	1	2	3	4	5	6	7	8
Whole Number: Meaning	•	•	•	•	•			
Whole Number: Operations	•	•	•	•	•			
Measurement Units	•	•	•	•	•	•	•	
Common Fractions			•	•	•	•		
Equations & Formulas			•	•	•	•	•	•
Data Representation & Analysis			•	•	•	•		•
2-D Geometry: Basics		•		•	•	•	•	•
2-D Geometry: Polygons & Circles				•	•	•	•	•
Measurement: Perimeter, Area, & Volume				•	•	•	•	•
Rounding & Significant Figures				•	•			
Estimating Computations				•	•	•		
Whole Numbers: Properties of Operations				•	•			
Estimating Quantity & Size				•	•			
Decimal Fractions				•	•	•		
Relation of Common & Decimal Fractions				•	•	•		
Properties of Common & Decimal Fractions					•	•		
Percentages					•	•		
Proportionality Concepts					•	•	•	•
Proportionality Problems					•	•	•	•
1D and 2-D Geometry: Coordinate Geometry					•	•	•	
Geometry: Transformations						•	•	•
Negative Numbers, Integers, & Their Properties						•	•	
Number Theory						•	•	
Exponents, Roots, & Radicals						•	•	
Exponents & Orders of Magnitude							•	•
Measurement: Estimation & Errors							•	
Constructions Using Straightedge & Compass							•	•
3-D Geometry							•	•
Geometry: Congruence & Similarity								•
Rational Numbers & Their Properties								•
Patterns, Relations, & Functions								•
Proportionality: Slope & Trigonometry								•

Key: |•| Topic intended by at least two-thirds of the top-achieving countries.

Figure 2.8 depicts results of the curriculum analyses that were completed for grades 1 through 8 in each of the participating countries. In Figure 2.8, the composite model depicted in Figure 2.7 (shaded region) is overlaid with the intended curriculum of the country in question.[3] Some observations about the similarities and differences in the content that middle school teachers will be expected to teach among the six countries are as follows:

- Nine topics were expected to be taught in each of grades 6 through 8 according to the composite model. These are: equations; data representation and analysis (only grades 6 and 9); two-dimensional basic geometry; polygons and circles; perimeter, area, and volume;

proportionality concepts; proportionality problems; two-dimensional coordinate geometry; and geometric transformations. For the most part the intended curricula of the six MT21 countries were consistent with the composite model for these topics. The least amount of agreement occurred with two of the topics: proportionality concepts and geometric transformations.

- During at least one of the lower-secondary grades (6–8) all countries except for Mexico intended coverage of the rational number system and its properties, functions, and congruence and similarity.

- The data suggest that lower-secondary teachers in Bulgaria were expected to teach the fewest number of topics and teachers in Mexico, South Korea, and the United States were expected to teach the greatest number of topics. In fact, only five topics were identified in the intended curriculum for Bulgaria's 7th-grade teachers. This compares with between 14 and 25 topics intended in the 7th grade by the remaining five countries.

- Although not a part of the model, Bulgaria was unique in expecting its teachers to teach mathematical reasoning, logical deduction, and proof across all of the middle school grades, introducing the logical connectives content as early as grade 5. The United States and Mexico were the only countries that did not expect their middle school teachers to teach such content at some point during grades 6–8.

- In Mexico, 7th- and 8th-grade teachers were expected to teach several topics that were taught earlier in the other countries. These include: estimating computations; decimal fractions; properties of common and decimals fractions; and percentages. On the other hand, they were not expected to teach other topics that were included in the other countries' curricula at these grades: rational numbers and their properties and functions.

- Middle school teachers in the United States were the only ones who were not expected to teach geometric constructions with a straightedge and compass.

The above describes the highlights of the similarities and differences in what middle school teachers will be expected to teach. There was, in fact, a great deal of overlap across five of the countries, with the exclusion of Mexico. But recall that the data portrayed for the 32 topics in Figure 2.8 were aggregated from data that were gathered initially for over 200 content topics. About a quarter of these content areas are typically covered in courses that focus on algebra—pre-algebra, basic algebra, or advanced algebra. Another 25 of these content areas are introduced in the upper-secondary grades in pre-calculus or

FIGURE 2.8. Mathematics intended at each grade in each of the six countries.

	Bulgaria Grade								Germany Grade								Mexico Grade							
Topic	1	2	3	4	5	6	7	8	1	2	3	4	5	6	7	8	1	2	3	4	5	6	7	8
Whole Number: Meaning	•	•	•	•					•	•	•	•	•				•	•	•	•	•	•	•	•
Whole Number: Operations	•	•	•	•					•	•	•	•	•				•	•	•	•	•	•	•	•
Measurement Units	•	•	•	•					•	•	•	•	•				•	•	•	•	•	•	•	•
Common Fractions		•		•	•	•					•	•	•	•									•	
Equations & Formulas											•	•	•	•	•	•							•	
Data Representation & Analysis	•	•	•	•	•	•	•	•	•	•	•	•	•	•	•	•	•	•	•	•	•	•	•	•
2-D Geometry: Basics	•	•	•	•	•	•	•	•	•	•	•	•	•	•	•	•	•	•	•	•	•	•	•	•
2-D Geometry: Polygons & Circles	•	•	•	•					•	•	•	•		•	•	•	•	•	•	•	•	•	•	•
Measurement: Perimeter, Area, & Volume	•	•	•	•					•	•	•	•								•	•		•	•
Rounding & Significant Figures		•	•	•					•		•													•
Estimating Computations	•	•																						
Whole Numbers: Properties of Operations	•	•																						•
Estimating Quantity & Size	•	•						•	•										•	•	•	•	•	•
Decimal Fractions					•	•					•	•	•	•									•	•
Relation of Common & Decimal Fractions					•						•	•	•										•	•
Properties of Common & Decimal Fractions					•						•	•											•	•
Percentages					•	•		•															•	•
Proportionality Concepts						•			•	•	•	•	•	•	•	•							•	•
Proportionality Problems						•			•	•	•	•	•	•	•	•							•	•
1D and 2-D Geometry: Coordinate Geometry								•						•	•	•							•	•
Geometry: Transformations						•	•																•	•
Negative Numbers, Integers, & Their Properties				•			•	•		•	•	•	•	•	•								•	•
Number Theory						•		•															•	•
Exponents, Roots, & Radicals																								•
Exponents & Orders of Magnitude													•		•	•								•
Measurement: Estimation & Errors						•						•	•			•								•
Constructions Using Straightedge & Compass													•											
3-D Geometry			•		•	•	•	•	•	•	•	•	•	•									•	•
Geometry: Congruence & Similarity												•		•	•	•						•	•	•
Rational Numbers & Their Properties															•	•							•	•
Patterns, Relations, & Functions		•		•		•	•	•		•	•	•	•	•	•	•		•					•	•
Proportionality: Slope & Trigonometry								•								•								•

Key: • Topic intended by country. ▓ Topic intended by more than half of the top-achieving countries.

52

FIGURE 2.8. (continued)

	South Korea								Taiwan								United States							
	Grade								Grade								Grade							
Topic	1	2	3	4	5	6	7	8	1	2	3	4	5	6	7	8	1	2	3	4	5	6	7	8
Whole Number: Meaning																								
Whole Number: Operations																								
Measurement Units																								
Common Fractions																								
Equations & Formulas																								
Data Representation & Analysis																								
2-D Geometry: Basics																								
2-D Geometry: Polygons & Circles																								
Measurement: Perimeter, Area, & Volume																								
Rounding & Significant Figures																								
Estimating Computations																								
Whole Numbers: Properties of Operations																								
Estimating Quantity & Size																								
Decimal Fractions																								
Relation of Common & Decimal Fractions																								
Properties of Common & Decimal Fractions																								
Percentages																								
Proportionality Concepts																								
Proportionality Problems																								
1D and 2-D Geometry: Coordinate Geometry																								
Geometry: Transformations																								
Negative Numbers, Integers, & Their Properties																								
Number Theory																								
Exponents, Roots, & Radicals																								
Exponents & Orders of Magnitude																								
Measurement: Estimation & Errors																								
Constructions Using Straightedge & Compass																								
3-D Geometry																								
Geometry: Congruence & Similarity																								
Rational Numbers & Their Properties																								
Patterns, Relations, & Functions																								
Proportionality: Slope & Trigonometry																								

Key: ● Topic intended by country. ▢ Topic intended by more than half of the top-achieving countries.

53

calculus courses or in a deductive geometry course that focuses largely on developing reasoning skills, particularly related to proving theorems.

In order to get a more specific description of the content middle school teachers will be teaching, lower-secondary data were examined at the level defined by the 200 topics. Given all of the content that a teacher was expected to teach, we calculated the percentage of the total that was related to pre-algebra, algebra, or a higher level algebra course.

The data suggest substantial variation among the countries in the percentage of algebra-related content that is expected to be taught, particularly in the 6th and 7th grades. A 6th-grade teacher in Germany or Mexico was not expected to teach any content related to algebra, yet in Bulgaria and Taiwan 20% or more of the content areas that a teacher was expected to cover were related to algebra. In grade 7 more than a third of the content was related to algebra in three of the six countries; in grade 8 a third or more of the content was related to algebra in four of the six countries. Bulgaria's teachers were expected to teach the greatest proportion of algebra content—two thirds in grade 7 and over half of the total content in grade 8. Teachers in Mexico were expected to teach a relatively low percentage of algebra content—3% in 7th grade and less than 20% in 8th grade were related to algebra. In the United States 15% was related to algebra in 7th grade and a third of the content was related to algebra in 8th grade. Clearly, algebra (including both equations and functions) played a more prominent role in middle school mathematics in Bulgaria, South Korea, and Taiwan.

This does not tell the entire story, however. The number of content topics covered in each grade varied across countries (from 18 to 58 content topics in any given school year). To fully capture the differences it is also necessary to examine the level of the algebra topics that were being taught not only in the three middle school grades but also in the elementary grades. Algebra content was classified into three categories: pre-algebra, basic algebra, and advanced algebra, including functions. The three content sub-areas were noted according to the grade in which they were first introduced.

The most noteworthy among the findings include:

- Though the other countries' teachers were expected to teach pre-algebra content as early as 1st grade, the first appearance of pre-algebra content in Mexico was in the 8th grade.
- Teachers in Mexico and Germany were not expected to introduce content related to basic algebra until 7th grade. The other four countries introduced basic algebra content as early as grades 4, 5, or 6.
- Teachers in Bulgaria, South Korea, and Taiwan began to introduce advanced algebra content as early as 7th grade.

- The United States is the only country whose teachers were not expected to introduce any advanced algebra content by 8th grade. Examples of the advanced algebra content include: solving systems of equations; solving systems of inequalities; and solving quadratic and polynomial equations.
- Teachers in Bulgaria, Germany, and Taiwan were expected to teach students mathematical reasoning, at least by 8th grade. As noted earlier, teachers in Bulgaria were expected to first introduce reasoning skills with discussion of logical connectives in the 5th grade.

The above discussion has highlighted the similarities and differences in the content that middle school teachers will be expected to teach. The next section discusses findings related to the second reason for including curriculum analysis in this project. It will provide information about the mathematics content knowledge that future teachers bring to their teacher preparation programs.

WHAT FUTURE TEACHERS BRING TO THEIR TEACHER PREPARATION PROGRAMS

Figure 2.9 depicts the topics intended in high school (upper-secondary) for each of the six countries. The same 32 topics described previously, plus nine additional ones typically covered at the secondary level, are depicted in the 41 rows. The grade columns are replaced with country names. A dot appears in a cell if the topic was intended to be covered in any of grades 9 through 12 by the country identified in the column.

Curricular data available for the secondary grades were not consistent across all countries. Data provided by Bulgaria, Germany, South Korea, and Taiwan were described for each of grades 9 through 12. Mexico's national standards do not include an intended curriculum for grades 10 through 12 and were eliminated from these comparisons. The U.S. data were derived from an analysis of documents from 47 states.[4] Some states had standards that specified a list of required topics for high school while others specified course requirements. Similar to the U.S. composite for grades 1 through 8, if more than half the 47 states intended coverage of a particular topic in upper-secondary, then it was considered as intended for coverage in the United States.

The data, though not grade specific, provide relevant information about topics that were intended during the secondary grades (9–12). These data must be viewed in light of the results in the previous section that indicated large differences among countries in what was intended to be taught in grades 6–9, only now viewed in terms of what could have been taken by the future teachers when

FIGURE 2.9. Mathematics topics intended in high school across five countries.

Topic	Bulgaria	Germany	South Korea	Taiwan	United States
Whole Number: Meaning					
Whole Number: Operations					
Measurement Units	•	•			•
Common Fractions					
Equations & Formulas	•	•	•	•	•
Data Representation & Analysis	•	•	•	•	•
2-D Geometry: Basics	•	•	•	•	•
2-D Geometry: Polygons & Circles	•	•	•	•	•
Measurement: Perimeter, Area, & Volume	•	•	•	•	•
Rounding & Significant Figures	•				
Estimating Computations		•			•
Whole Numbers: Properties of Operations					
Estimating Quantity & Size	•				
Decimal Fractions	•				
Relation of Common & Decimal Fractions	•				
Properties of Common & Decimal Fractions					
Percentages					
Proportionality Concepts			•		
Proportionality Problems	•	•		•	•
1D and 2-D Geometry: Coordinate Geometry		•	•	•	•
Geometry: Transformations	•	•	•	•	
Negative Numbers, Integers, & Their Properties			•		
Number Theory			•		
Exponents, Roots, & Radicals	•	•	•	•	•
Exponents & Orders of Magnitude					
Measurement: Estimation & Errors		•			•
Constructions Using Straightedge & Compass	•				
3-D Geometry	•	•	•	•	•
Geometry: Congruence & Similarity	•	•		•	•
Rational Numbers & Their Properties					
Patterns, Relations, & Functions	•	•	•	•	•
Proportionality: Slope & Trigonometry	•	•	•	•	•
Real Numbers, Their Subsets & Properties	•	•	•	•	•
Validation & Justification	•	•	•	•	•
Structuring & Abstracting	•		•	•	
Complex Numbers & Their Properties			•	•	
Uncertainty & Probability	•	•	•	•	•
Infinite Processes	•	•	•	•	
Change	•	•	•	•	
Vectors	•	•	•	•	•
Systematic Counting	•	•	•	•	

Key: • Topic intended by country. ▓ Topic intended by more than half of the top-achieving countries.

they were in these grades as students themselves. In other words, the results of the previous section address both issues of what future teachers will be expected to teach and what mathematics knowledge they bring to their teacher-preparation program. Most noteworthy is that the United States appears to be the only country in which topics covered in calculus (infinite processes and change) were not typically intended at least by grade 11 or 12. The data depicted in Figure 2.9 tell us that Bulgaria intended to cover infinite processes but not change. Bulgaria's upper-secondary program offers a regular level and an advanced level. Future teachers may receive instruction at either level, but only the curricular intentions of the regular level are depicted in Figure 2.9. Coverage of limits, series, and sequences was intended in Bulgaria at the regular level but not in the United States. Not depicted here is that change (differential calculus) was an intended topic for Bulgarian advanced-level students.

Some further observations are as follows:

- The previous section pointed out that teachers begin to teach reasoning skills as early as 5th, 7th, or 8th grade in Bulgaria, Taiwan, and Germany, respectively. Teachers in South Korea were expected to introduce this topic in 10th grade.
- Content related to trigonometry was introduced in: grade 9 in Germany and Taiwan; grade 10 in South Korea.
- Elementary analysis was first introduced in grade 10 in Germany and Taiwan, and in grade 11 in Bulgaria and South Korea.
- Less than 50% of U.S. states included elementary analysis content.
- Content related to infinite processes was included in 45% of states in the United States. These content areas include discussion of sequences, series, and limits. Only about a quarter of the states in the United States included content related to change. Many do not get much beyond teaching exponential growth and decay.

Across countries, future teachers come into teacher preparation with different backgrounds in mathematics. Those future teachers in Bulgaria, Taiwan, and South Korea have had substantially more advanced coursework in high school than in the other three countries. However, those from Germany have stronger backgrounds than the future teachers in Mexico and the United States. Not surprisingly, the future teachers from those countries with the more rigorous expectations will be expected to teach the same higher level of mathematics when they return to the classrooms from which they came. In this way, such advanced pre-teacher preparation is guaranteed for the next generation of future teachers and their future students. Unfortunately, the same is true in those countries where the expectations are not as high. In this way the last two sections of this chapter are inextricably intertwined.

CHAPTER 3

What We Studied and How We Did It

The previous chapter gave a brief overview of how K–12 schooling and teacher education are organized in the six countries we have studied. What follows in the next set of chapters examines what we have found from studying these six countries in the Mathematics Teaching in the 21st Century study (MT21).

TIMSS and PISA revealed extensive insight into the conditions for learning successes and failures of students in elementary and middle school. What is presently lacking is insight into the quality of their teachers. Several questions follow from this:

- What does the professional knowledge look like for these teachers and what beliefs do they hold?
- What is the effect of their teacher education?
- Which characteristics of teacher education are relevant for the professional competence of future teachers?

These issues were analyzed systematically and by international comparison for the first time for future middle school mathematics teachers. MT21 studies a group of future teachers that will be confronted with a central role in the preparation of future generations for an internationally driven and information-based economy. Mathematics not only belongs to the core academic subjects world wide (Mullis, Martin, Gonzalez et al., 2004, p. 365); to have mathematical competence is also a central need for meeting everyday occupational requirements (Freudenthal, 1983). Mathematical competence provides a tool for problem solving and is required to understand the world.

This chapter presents the conceptual framework on which the study is based and describes the study itself, including the sample we drew and the procedures we followed.

THEORETICAL FRAMEWORK

Teachers' Professional Competence

MT21 is based on the notion of professional competence as it is defined in general—for example, by Spencer and Spencer (1993), Eraut (1994), and Weinert (2001), and specifically with regard to teaching by Bromme (1997) and Taconis, Van der Plas, & Van der Sanden (2004). Competence in this tradition means to have the knowledge and the skills at one's disposal to successfully solve core, job-related problems. Weinert (1999) divides competence into cognitive abilities to solve certain problems, and into motivational and volitional predispositions to successfully and responsibly apply solutions in a variety of situations. In our case, cognitive abilities have been categorized as teachers' professional knowledge, and motivational and volitional predispositions as teachers' professional beliefs.

This definition of the outcomes of teacher education has a number of important implications for our study. First, we distinguish between the observed teacher performance that is measured by the test through the items dealing with professional tasks and the "true" underlying competence. Observed test performance is used as an indicator of teacher competence. The definition also takes into consideration that we do not observe actual classroom performance. There is still a chance, even for teachers who perform very well on our test, to fail in the classroom; but on average, with large groups of teachers and a large number of classroom situations presented in the test, teachers' professional competence should predict their actual classroom performance reasonably well.

Second, the notion of professional competence implies that this variable consists of several components which may not always be in line with each other. Since Weinert (1999) divides competence into cognitive and affective-motivational elements, it is certainly possible that a teacher would be willing to implement group work, for example, but that she does not have the knowledge to do it. Conversely, the intertwined structure of different components means that it is possible for a teacher to have the pedagogical knowledge of how to do it but does not possess the content knowledge for the specific topic being taught (or the willingness to do it). In order to be able to deal with this problem, we model teachers' professional competence as a multidimensional construct.

Another important implication of this construct definition is that competence is of a situated nature and characterized by applicability (Blumer, 1969; Schutz, 1967). Teacher knowledge is therefore only fully measured in our test if the items require the respondents to be able not only to reproduce it but also to apply it appropriately in different classroom situations. The problems and situations in the test to be dealt with by future teachers are set by constitutive features of the profession. To determine which features are in fact constitutive, we referred to existing standards in various national teacher education systems (KMK, 2004b; NCTM, 1991; NBPTS, 2003). Table 3.1 documents the tasks that lower-secondary mathematics teachers are expected to master in the six MT21 countries based on these standards. Our test focuses on A ("instruction") and B ("assessment")—tasks we identified as common across our countries.

Teachers' Professional Knowledge

As mentioned, we regard professional competence of future teachers as a multidimensional construct. We modeled its structure according to existing theories. The professional knowledge that future mathematics teachers need in order to accomplish tasks related to instruction and assessment can be divided into three general facets, which are frequently discussed in the literature: content knowledge, pedagogical content knowledge, and general pedagogical knowledge (Baumert & Kunter, 2006; Blömeke, 2002, 2005; Shulman, 1985).

Content knowledge here means knowledge of mathematics. The focus of the achievement items was on the mathematics underlying topics typically taught at the lower- and upper-secondary level across some 40 countries, including the six involved in MT21. The topics were identified through curriculum analysis done as part of TIMSS (Schmidt et al., 2001) and included number, algebra, functions, geometry, and data. The MT21 items were not designed to be at the advanced level of mathematics associated with an undergraduate mathematics

TABLE 3.1. Core tasks of lower-secondary teachers of mathematics.

Teacher Tasks	Situations
A: Choice of themes, methods; sequencing of learning processes	1. Selecting and justifying content of instruction 2. Designing and evaluating of lessons
B: Assessment of student achievement; counseling of students/parents	1. Diagnosing student achievement, learning processes, misconceptions, preconditions 2. Assessing students 3. Counseling students and parents 4. Dealing with errors, giving feedback
C: Support of students' social, moral, emotional development	1. Establishing teacher-student relationships 2. Fostering the development of morals and values 3. Dealing with student risks 4. Preventing, coping with discipline problems
D: School development	1. Initiating, facilitating cooperation 2. Understanding of school evaluation
E. Professional ethics	1. Accepting the responsibilities of a teacher

Source. Reprinted with permission from Blömeke, Felbrich, and Müller, 2008, pp. 15–48.

degree, although a small number of them do reach this level. Rather, they were at an advanced level that is necessary for a deep understanding of the topics taught in a challenging, rigorous, and coherent middle and high school mathematics curriculum (Valverde & Schmidt, 2000).

Pedagogical content knowledge means pedagogical knowledge related to mathematics. In MT21, it is subdivided into instructional planning knowledge, knowledge about student learning, and curricular knowledge:

- The instructional planning knowledge (planning) is needed before instruction begins. The mathematics content for students must be chosen appropriately, simplified, and prepared with the use of various representations (Krauthausen & Scherer, 2007; Vollrath, 2001).
- The knowledge about student learning (student) is related to the learning processes that occur during instruction. It focuses on teacher-student interactions. Such knowledge includes classifying student answers (verbal and written) in relation to the tasks or questions that stimulated them, asking questions at different levels of complexity, identifying common misconceptions, providing feedback, and reacting with appropriate intervention strategies. Such knowledge is assigned a prominent position, since it has been found relevant to the attainment of advanced student performance (Blum, Neubrand, Ehmke et al., 2004; Helmke, 2004; Klieme, Schümer, & Knoll, 2001).
- The curricular knowledge (curriculum) focuses on the development and progression of student competence in mathematics during the years of schooling. Teachers have to deal with questions such as: What would it mean for later lesson units if a classic subject area of school mathematics in the lower-secondary curriculum were removed or taught as a part of a different sequence?

General or *generic pedagogical knowledge* means the knowledge typically acquired in a teacher education program that is not subject-matter specific (Blömeke, Paine et al., 2008). Pedagogy is a significant component in all teacher-education programs we studied. The number of pedagogy classes as well as the content taught in these classes and the year in which pedagogical studies take place vary across and within countries. The classes are sometimes labeled not as *pedagogy* but as, for example, *educational foundations*. For that reason, it was a challenge to identify them. Another challenge was that the specific shape of pedagogy is highly influenced by cultural perspectives on the goals of schooling, the role of teachers, and the role of parents (Blömeke & Paine, 2008, Hopmann & Riquarts, 1995; Westbury, 1995). In MT21 we decided to focus on three areas of general pedagogical knowledge: lesson planning, assessment, and dealing with student heterogeneity, taking socio-economic differences as an example. Lesson planning and assessment are core tasks of teachers by their very nature. Dealing with heterogeneity is an issue school systems worldwide have to manage (Dupriez, Dumay, & Vause, 2008; LeTendre, Hofer, & Shimizu, 2003).

Teachers' Professional Beliefs

An understanding of *competence* as used in MT21 includes, in addition to the cognitive components, the instructional, professional, and personal beliefs held by the future teachers. In our understanding of beliefs we followed Richardson's definition of them as "psychologically held understandings, premises, or propositions about the world that are felt to be true" (1996). Teachers' beliefs are crucial to the perception of classroom situations and to the decision on how to act (Leder, Pekhonen, & Törner, 2002; Leinhardt & Greeno, 1986). If beliefs are operationalized specifically to include both the content taught and the challenges that a specific classroom situation presents, empirical evidence exists for a link between teacher beliefs and student achievement (Bromme, 1994, 2005). Beliefs have a vital function with respect to perspective as well as to action (Grigutsch, Raatz, & Törner, 1998). Therefore, they connect knowledge and action. In this sense, they are also an indicator for the type of instruction teachers will use in their future teaching (Brown & Rose, 1995; Nespor, 1987; Short & Short, 1989).

These findings require the inclusion of the measurement of beliefs into a study about future teachers' professional competence. As with regard to knowledge, we can distinguish between different types of teacher beliefs (Calderhead, 1996; Cooney, Barry, & Bridget, 1998; Ernest, 1991a):

- epistemological beliefs about the nature of the underlying academic discipline (Hofer & Pintrich, 2002)—in MT21 this means beliefs about mathematics;
- beliefs about teaching and learning in a subject (Thompson, 1992)—in MT21 this means beliefs about the teaching and learning of mathematics;
- pedagogical beliefs about the social context of schools and about teacher education and the process of professional development.

Epistemological beliefs refer to the structure and the origin of knowledge (Hofer & Pintrich, 2002; Schommer-Aikins, 2002). Epistemological beliefs about the nature of the underlying academic discipline are highly content-bound. Concerning mathematics teachers, Grigutsch, Raatz, and Törner (1998) categorize teachers' beliefs mainly by four aspects. Mathematics can be understood (1) as a science that mainly consists of creative problem-solving processes and discovery ("creative"); (2) as a science that is relevant for society and life ("usefulness"); (3) as an exact, formal, and logical science ("formalism"); or (4) as a collection of rules and formulae ("algorithmic"). In MT21 we use their scales in a shortened version to examine future teachers' beliefs.

With regard to beliefs on teaching and learning mathematics, research exists on a constructivist versus a transmission perspective (Peterson, Fennema, Carpenter, & Loef, 1989). Staub and Stern (2002) applied Peterson's instrument to teachers and linked their beliefs to student achievement. The study reveals that a constructivist perspective is related to higher student achievement as far as complex problem-solving abilities are tested. At the same time, teachers with constructivist approaches achieve a comparable level of students' algorithmic abilities compared with teachers with a transmission perspective. In addition to research about these broader beliefs on teaching and learning mathematics, comparative studies focusing on Chinese and American teachers describe different beliefs concerning the curricular structure of mathematics teaching and the source of success: Whereas Chinese teachers favor a more holistic view of central mathematical ideas, American teachers regard mathematics as more separated in smaller pieces (Ma, 1999). Chinese teachers view students' efforts as a reason for success, in contrast to American teachers, who believe in mathematical talent as the main determinant of student achievement (Stevenson, Lee, Chen et al., 1990).

In MT21, we also examine the objectives that future teachers hold for mathematics instruction as to whether and to what extent they want to support students' mathematical skills, mathematical reasoning, understanding of mathematics as a formal discipline, ability to communicate mathematics ideas, positive attitudes toward mathematics and better preparation to succeed in school, and taking further mathematics classes. Objectives provide teachers with a higher-order orientation for individual decisions in the course of their instructional planning, execution, and reflection.

In addition, we examine future teachers' beliefs about how students learn mathematics. These might predict the particular instructional strategies teachers would be inclined to use, whether it is the use of standard procedures, focusing on the right answer more than the procedure, learning and mastering skills and procedures, gaining understanding, or focusing on students being independent in their work.

We also ask for explanations for why children perform so differently on mathematics tests. This is an anthropological perspective on the origin of mathematical competence and deals with the question, "Are mathematical abilities learnable or do they stem primarily from deeply rooted talents?" In other words, what beliefs do future teachers hold about why some children do particularly well in mathematics while others struggle to achieve even the barest minimum accomplishment in mathematics? Whereas developmental differences could easily cause the achievement differences, we should be concerned if future teachers believe such differences simply reflect differences in natural ability or categorical differences, such as ethnicity and gender. Finally, beliefs regarding classroom management are considered since implementing objectives and instructional strategies depends significantly on the extent to which the available study time is effectively used.

Only very general findings exist about the *acquisition* of beliefs during teacher education. According to these, its mode of action can be specified as follows: Future teachers beginning in teacher education hold detailed beliefs about school and instruction, which only in a few cases outlast alterations made during their training, a phenomena known as *Konstanzer Wanne* (see, Dann, Müller-Fohrbrodt, & Cloetta, 1981). Beliefs can function as filters; thus, information that is incorporated is primarily information that fits into the existing system of beliefs (Kane, Sandretto, & Heath, 2002; Pajares, 1992; Richardson & Placier, 2001). The MT21 cohort design (explained in more detail later in this chapter) gives us the chance to examine to what extent beliefs actually may change according to instructional efforts during teacher education.

After having modeled professional competence as the criterion for effective teacher education and in this sense as the dependent variable of empirical studies on teacher-education outcomes, the question of which factors may influence the development of professional competence arises. Potentially influential factors can be divided into three categories:

- individual characteristics of future teachers,
- institutional characteristics of teacher education, and
- systemic characteristics of a country.

Individual Characteristics of Future Teachers

It is known from instructional research that student achievement at school is influenced by their prior knowledge and motivation (Brophy, 1999; Helmke, 2004). Such individual characteristics may also play a role in teacher education if one looks at findings about the development of learning motivation across age groups (Stuhlmann, 2005). A longitudinal survey of future teachers in Switzerland (Oser & Oelkers, 2001) showed that students who intended to become teachers right from the beginning did better in their classes, especially in general pedagogy, than students who were unsure about which occupation to follow in the future (Brühwiler, 2001). These influences on the acquisition of professional competence may also be cumulative, because empirical studies on mathematics education show that high performance appears together with a positive self concept and positive emotional attitude (Goetz, Pekrun, Zirngibl et al., 2004; Möller & Köller, 2004). We do not have empirical findings about this with regard to teacher education; however, we cannot rule out the possibility that these kinds of individual characteristics matter.

Prior knowledge is measured in MT21 by taking high school classes in mathematics as an indicator. Motivation is measured with several scales that distinguish between future teachers' intrinsic and extrinsic motivation to go into teaching, and between their subject-related and pedagogy-related intrinsic as well as between status-related and access-related extrinsic motivation.

Opportunity to Learn in Teacher Education

A central goal of this study is the connection of professional competence with the characteristics of teacher education. The present state of research regarding opportunities to learn for future mathematics teachers suffers from the fact that only crude data exist about the educational components of mathematics, mathematics pedagogy, general pedagogy, and practical experiences in teacher education. With respect to characteristics of teacher education programs that may influence the development of teachers' professional competence, one can think about a wide array of features: selectivity, program content, teaching methods, characteristics of teacher educators, accountability, location of teacher education, climate, and so on. It is difficult to make evidence-based choices out of this array to decide what to measure because only very few studies exist about the relationship of specific opportunities to learn (OTL) in teacher education and teacher education outcomes.

Many studies use the number of courses taken or the kind of teaching license to define OTL. So, not surprisingly, findings about the effects of content in teacher education on professional competence are inconsistent (Blömeke, 2004; Cochran-Smith & Zeichner, 2005; Wilson, Floden, & Ferrini-Mundy, 2001). A continuous, positive link between future teachers' opportunities to learn and their professional knowledge and beliefs could not be identified through analysis of the courses they take. This does not necessarily mean that content features can be left out in studies of teacher education. It merely points to the need for more sophisticated measures of OTL than are presently available. Regardless of how common it is to use indicators like degrees, majors, examination results, or the number of classes taken (see, e.g., Akiba, LeTendre, & Scribner, 2007; Goldhaber & Brewer, 2000; Monk & King, 1994), this approach is at high risk of washing out any kind of relationship between opportunities to learn in teacher education and the outcomes because there is unfortunately nothing in teacher education "that share[s] a relatively common meaning across various cultural contexts" (Akiba, LeTendre, & Scribner, 2007).

An example of this is the difference in the meaning of opportunities to learn general pedagogy. In comparison to a broad central European understanding of general pedagogy, the understanding in English-speaking countries is rather narrow since it is mainly operationalized as classes in teaching methods or classroom management (Hopmann & Riquarts, 1995). This methodological weakness results in a disturbing inconsistency of study results because differences due to cultural definitions of general pedagogy overlay differences between programs. In addition, because of the inconsistent findings, almost any inference can be drawn: teacher education may or may not matter, personality may or may not matter, and so on (see, e.g., Abell Foundation 2001a, b; vs. Darling-Hammond & Youngs, 2002). Thus, there is a need to develop less aggregated measures that capture the content of teacher education in a low-inference way.

This was attempted in the six-country study MT21. Future teachers were asked whether they encountered certain mathematics, mathematics pedagogy, and general pedagogy topics in one or more of the courses they took as a part of their teacher education program. What was listed represented the types of topics that may be studied in mathematics teacher education. The second set of questions asked the future teachers to rate the extent to which they had the opportunity in their teacher preparation program to study various topics or to be engaged in specific activities in mathematics, mathematics pedagogy, and general pedagogy.

The basic principle of these listings is to differentiate between knowledge delivered from the perspective of the formal discipline and that from the perspective of teachers' tasks. Despite all differences in conceptual detail and subsequently in classification, the collection of topics covered in mathematics is orientated toward an international definition of university basic courses in the baccalaureate education that are generally obligatory for all students (e.g., linear algebra or analysis). As an indicator of higher-level classes, advanced courses that are often designated as electives (e.g., topology) are also included.

The content of mathematics could be considered somewhat standardized, but finding an internationally comparable and at the same time nationally accurate representation of the topics in mathematics pedagogy and general pedagogy was especially difficult. A further difficulty arose in finding a common measure for the different kinds of practical experience in the MT21 countries. For example, while Germany assigns practical experience to a separate phase of education, Bulgaria and the United States include it as part of the university education.

MT21 goes beyond structural features into greater detail and records the actual content more precisely. In the tradition of other studies, especially those of the International Association for the Evaluation of Educational Achievement (IEA), MT21 additionally distinguishes between intended and implemented characteristics of teacher education at the institutional level and takes a multifaceted approach to describing learning opportunities in teacher education. The facets are the formally designated requirements as defined at the institutional level, a document analysis of a sample of the content, and the actual course offerings—that is, what the teacher educators as mediators of the educational offerings define the content to be, as well as what the future teachers define the opportunities to be. The individual instruments are largely organized in parallel to one another.

In the 1995 Third International Mathematics and Science Study (TIMSS), variation in the intended and implemented curriculum across countries was found to be related to achievement. The curricular expectations of a nation and the actual content exposure that was delivered to students by teachers were found to be among the most salient features of schooling related to academic performance. Countries with higher achievement gains from one year to the next had mathematics teachers who taught substantially different content than their counterparts in less accomplished countries (Schmidt, McKnight, Cogan et al., 1999; Schmidt, McKnight, Houang et al., 2001).

A basic assumption of MT21 is that this is the case in mathematics teacher education as well—that in countries with higher future teacher achievement, different content is taught than in other countries. Therefore, we measured the opportunities individuals had in their teacher preparation programs. We did this by surveying the students' experiences related to mathematics and pedagogy.

The *content* experienced in mathematics teacher education is differentiated according to the four main components of teacher education: mathematics, mathematics pedagogy, general pedagogy, and practical experiences. The areas listed in the survey were generated to be comprehensive for every one of them across all six countries. We believed that since the respondents were still students when asked to complete the survey, they would be able to remember accurately the courses and content areas they studied. For mathematics this included content categories such as linear algebra, abstract algebra, calculus, theory of complex functions, non-Euclidean geometry, and topology. Mathematics pedagogy included such categories as the history and psychology of mathematics, methods of teaching mathematics, and the principles and theory of various school mathematics topics such as geometry. The history, philosophy, and sociology of education were included under general pedagogy as was content related to assessment, curriculum theory, and principles and theory of instruction, among others.

Frequently discussed in teacher education is the question of how to implement *practical experiences*, so this was another area we wanted to examine as part of the OTL. A German-Swiss comparative study of future teachers shows that fewer experiences of school practice during the university study led to ideas about teaching with less theoretical and empirical foundation (Czerwenka & Nölle, 2000). Correspondingly, graduates who have been taught in theory-based classes about instructional issues show a more theory-based performance in their classroom practice (Niggli, 2004). However, it seems as if not only the amount of practical experiences but also their sequence is important. The pressure to act induces students to question the usefulness of scientific theories and unreflectively adopt traditional performance routines if the teaching load is too high in an early stage of their professional development (Jäger & Milbach, 1994; Oser & Oelkers, 2001). In MT21, we examine the amount of practical experiences as well as their sequence and how they are linked to theory.

Teaching methods used in teacher education may be an influential part of future teachers' opportunities to learn as well (Grossmann, 2005). Mayr (2003) shows that knowledge acquired during teacher education can be used more effectively if it is developed in practice-related class arrangements. Kotzschmar (2004) illustrates that classes based on exploratory and independent learning result in higher teacher knowledge. In turn, it becomes obvious that teacher educators may also be an element of opportunities to learn in teacher education, particularly because, in comparison with instruction in schools, there are usually fewer detailed guidelines in teacher education (Zaslavsky & Leikin, 2004) and much is up to the teacher educators themselves. Teaching methods and characteristics of teacher educators are therefore two further dimensions of the teacher education curriculum that we studied in MT21. Figure 3.1 summarizes the model that guided the work in MT21.

STUDY DESIGN

Sampling

MT21 was carried out in Bulgaria, Germany, Mexico, South Korea, Taiwan, and the United States. The selection of countries in MT21 was based on three criteria, using data from existing international comparisons:

- The set of countries had to cover the main types of teacher education (one-step concurrent university programs or two-step consecutive

FIGURE 3.1. Theoretical framework of MT21.

Broad Social Context	Cultural Context			
	Rationale of the society	Social status of the teaching profession		Social status of mathematics
	Education System			
	Rationale of the education system	Goals of schooling		Working conditions of teachers
	Teacher-Education System			
	Goals of teacher education	Content structure	Institutional structure	Relationship of theory and practice	Selectivity

Relevant Institution Context	Institutionally Intended Curriculum				
	Learning goals/content	Teaching methods	Accountability	Academic advising	Selectivity
	Institutionally Implemented Curriculum				
	Learning goals/content	Teaching methods	Selectivity	Accountability	Academic advising	FTs composition
	Teacher Educators				
	Knowledge	Beliefs	Demographics	Intended learning goals	Intended teaching methods

Individual/ Personal Context	Future Teachers' Competencies Prior to Teacher Preparation			
	Knowledge	Beliefs	Personality	Demographics
	Future Teachers' Use of Curriculum			
	Perception of learning goals and use of content	Experience of teaching methods	Accountability	Academic advising
	Selectivity	Emotions	Amount of learning time	Learning strategies/emotions
	Individual Future Teachers' Developed Competencies			
	Knowledge	Beliefs	Personality	Demographics

Note: Reprinted with permission from Blömeke, Felbrich, Müller, Kaiser, & Lehmann, 2008.

programs with university studies first, followed by extended practical experiences; specialized lower-secondary programs, combined elementary and lower-secondary programs, or combined lower- and upper-secondary programs; one-subject programs or multiple-subject programs; programs of different length).

- Middle school student performance as shown in TIMSS and PISA had to vary across the selected countries.
- The countries had to show at least a middle grade degree of industrialization in order to avoid serious bias through socioeconomic differences.

The number of countries for MT21 had to be restricted to six countries in order to make optimal use of the data and insights garnered through a discourse-oriented kind of project work (see Schmidt, McKnight, Raizen et al., 1996). Given these criteria, Bulgaria, Germany, South Korea, Taiwan, Mexico, and the United States were selected.

MT21 sampled at the institutional level within countries. The goal was to obtain a reasonably representative sample for each country that included the variation found across all teacher education institutions in the country. Four criteria were applied to accomplish this goal: type, size, location, and reputation of teacher education institutions. In the two largest countries, all four criteria were applied to select institutions; in the other four countries, those were applied that were regarded the most important according to the country representatives (see Table 3.2). The total number of institutions sampled across the six countries was 34.

The goal was to survey all eligible future teachers in each sampled institution. The total number of future teachers sampled was 2,628 (see Table 3.2). To ensure that samples were as representative as possible, the results were weighted according to the total number of lower-secondary teachers prepared in each university.

The future teachers sampled were subdivided into two or three cohorts, respectively: students at the beginning of their program (Cohort I), midterm students, and students at the end of teacher education (Cohort II). This was done to estimate what individuals actually gain in their teacher education program, at least as estimated by cohort longitudinal data (Keeves, 1992; Wiley & Wolfe, 1992). Identifying and comparing those at the end of their program was much easier operationally than identifying those who were just beginning their program. Definitions for the "beginners" differed across institutions according to program

TABLE 3.2. Sampling design and resulting sample sizes.

	Bulgaria	Germany	Mexico	South Korea	Taiwan	United States
Criteria for Selecting Institutions	Size & Reputation	Type, Size, Location, Reputation	Location	Reputation	Type, Size, Reputation, Location	Type, Size, Location, Reputation
Number of Institutions	3	4 (1st step) + 22 (2nd step)	5	4	5	12
Cohorts (1=beg., 2= mid., 3=end)	1 + 3	1 + 2 + 3	1 + 3	1 + 3	1 + 2 + 3	1 + 2 + 3
Number of Future Teachers	161	849	358	210	668	382
Program Levels	Lower/ Upper Sec.	Primary/Lower Sec., Lower/Upper Sec.	Lower Sec.	Lower/ Upper Sec.	Lower/ Upper Sec.	Prim./Lower Sec., Lower Sec., Lower/Upper Sec.
Length of Education (Years)	4	3.5 + 1.5, 4.5 + 2	4	4	4+1	4 +1

characteristics. Some programs limited enrollment and required students to apply for entry into the program after fulfilling certain prerequisites that might require 2 or 3 years at the university prior to entry into teacher preparation. Other programs were able to identify students upon their entry to the university. Thus, the length of time beginners had been at their institutions ranged from less than a year to nearly 3 years. But on average, our samples were very similar. Beginners in all MT21 countries except South Korea had between 2 and 3 years of university experience. Beginners in South Korea had about 1 year of such experience.

Four institutions were sampled in South Korea, with the sampling done so as to draw institutions with different levels of reputation. Within these four institutions, 210 future teachers were sampled, representing beginners and finishers of teacher education. The five Taiwanese sampled institutions included both normal and regular universities, representing a variety of institutions. The sampling included the largest and most prestigious university as well as others whose prestige varied, as well as some that produced larger numbers of future teachers. The 668 future teachers sampled were subdivided into three cohorts.

In Germany, four regions were sampled and all universities (first teacher-training phase) and surrounding state institutions (second teacher-training phase) in these regions were included. The regions cover the north, east, and west of Germany, and the sample cuts across important traditions of teacher education in Germany: Some institutions have a long history in teacher education and future teachers represent a significant proportion of all students, whereas other institutions are more research focused, have taken on the responsibility of teacher education only recently, and future teachers represent a small proportion of students. The institutions' selectivity as an indicator of reputation varies as well. Within institutions a complete census was taken, meaning that all eligible future teachers were sampled. This resulted in a sample size of 849 future teachers representing beginners, midterm students, and finishers.

In Mexico, five institutions were chosen to be regionally representative. This resulted in a sample size of 358 beginning and finishing future teachers. Twelve U.S. institutions were chosen in eight states so that they cut across some of the major categories that are considered important in understanding differences among institutions. Some were large institutions, which turn out very large numbers of future teachers, while others were smaller and more selective in their preparation. Within the institutions, 382 future teachers were sampled and subdivided into three cohorts.

In South Korea, lower-secondary teachers are prepared over the course of 4 years as part of a secondary teacher education program located at universities. The U.S. sample also reflects this model except for one institution where the program consists of two steps which last a total of 5 years. In addition, the U.S. sample provides one program in which lower-secondary teachers are prepared as part of a 4-year primary teacher education program, and one that focuses specifically on the preparation of lower-secondary teachers. At the five Mexican institutions, teacher preparation is designed specifically for lower-secondary teachers. Germany and Taiwan have a two-phase teacher education model. Future teachers enroll at university first and afterward have practical training. In Taiwan, the length of the university course is 4 years followed by a 1-year or a half-year practicum also associated with the university.[1] In Germany the same basic model applies both to lower-secondary teachers prepared as part of a primary program and lower-secondary teachers prepared as part of a secondary program; however, the second phase involves a second institution, not the university. The length varies from state to state but usually the primary program lasts for 3.5 years in its first phase and 1.5 years in its second phase; the secondary program lasts for 4.5 years in its first phase and 2 years in the second.

Instruments

MT21 sought to focus on policy-relevant variation in teacher education. Therefore, the study sought to measure what individuals learned in their teacher education programs. We did this by surveying students' knowledge and beliefs as well as their learning opportunities as they are structured and provided by educational institutions and by mathematics, mathematics pedagogy, and general pedagogy educators. Four main surveys were developed for this purpose:

1. *Expert Survey.* This instrument was lengthy and detailed. Here, we collected program-specific information including student recruitment, entry requirements, academic and practical course requirements, typical course topic electives, self-perceived program strengths, and recent or anticipated reforms, as well as qualifications that teacher educators should have (see Figure 3.1).
2. *Faculty Surveys.* Four types of surveys were developed—for faculty in mathematics, mathematics pedagogy, and general pedagogy as well as for school-based faculty—each intended for those who taught or supervised future teachers. The surveys paralleled a subset of issues, including questions about opportunities to learn which educators provide to future teachers in their classes; the type of learning activities employed in the courses taught; and questions about instructors' beliefs on mathematics and the teaching and learning of mathematics (see Figure 3.1).
3. *Future Teachers Surveys.* These had four main parts: Demographics and academic background; academic learning opportunities; beliefs and perspectives on schooling, mathematics teaching, and the learning of

mathematics of middle school students; and knowledge items related to the teaching of middle school mathematics (see Figure 3.1). All future teachers completed one of two forms. The demographics/background and academic opportunities portions were identical for both forms. The other two portions on beliefs and perspectives on schooling shared some common items between the two forms, but most of the questions were unique to a form.

4. Finally, we did a *syllabi analysis*. We sampled syllabi of required classes from all institutions and applied sophisticated rubrics we had developed according to the curriculum analysis of TIMSS 1995 (see Figure 3.1).

The process of item development for these four instruments can be described in five steps:

- Items were proposed by all participating countries.
- Each item was discussed intensely in group meetings in order to make sure that no cultural bias was evident in the instrument.
- Expert reviews were done.
- Several item pilots and a field study were carried out.
- Final decisions about the items were made based on the empirical data as well as on agreements between the six MT21 countries.

The mathematics assessment for MT21 consists mostly of multiple-choice items. The mathematics items cover number, algebra, functions, geometry, and statistics topics; the mathematics pedagogy items cover these topics as well, in addition to curricular, instructional, and student knowledge. These distinctions represented a heuristic for the test development (see Chapter 5).

This is the approach that has been typical for testing for many decades. However, to capture the sequentially organized structure of procedural knowledge in the field of pedagogy and its situated nature, step-wise considerations according to specific professional tasks are required. To achieve this goal with multiple-choice items is probably not possible (Baartman, Bastiaens, Kirschner et al., 2007; Birenbaum, 2003; Dierick & Dochy, 2001; Jonsson & Svingby, 2007). Since we wanted to take into account that teaching is a highly action-oriented and deliberative activity where teachers have to make long-term plans and produce ideas, we decided to use open-ended items in which we asked future teachers to deal with hypothetical classroom situations and to explain their reasoning in these situations. With this approach we also take into account the fact that there is a shift going on in measurement theory from a traditional testing culture focusing exclusively on multiple-choice items to a more complex assessment culture (Dochy, Gijbels, & Segers, 2006).

The open-ended items included three vignettes. The first simulates a situation in which the future teacher who is new to teaching is asked by a colleague to review her lesson plan for teaching the measurement of rectangular solids, including volume and surface area, to a class of average 8th-grade students (those who are not on the advanced or remedial tracks). Included is a description of the lesson's goals and the class composition as well as a detailed sequence of instructional activities. The future teacher is asked three questions: What are the criteria you would use to evaluate this plan? What would you praise about the proposed lesson plan? What would you criticize about it?

In the second vignette, socioeconomic differences in student achievement have to be explained and taken into account when it comes to teaching. The vignette recounts that tests on student achievement have shown that inequalities exist with regard to socioeconomic background. Two questions are related to this statement: How could one reasonably explain this phenomenon? What can a teacher do about this? The third vignette is about the assessment of student achievement. Future teachers are asked to describe methods and time points at which it is reasonable to evaluate the learning process for a specific topic. In addition, they need to give reasons for their decisions (see Chapter 6).

Challenges of the MT21 Study

A major challenge for comparative research in the field of education is the development of a shared understanding of terms. Teacher education is a cultural practice. As such, problems of language and meaning become important and are far more demanding to resolve than the "simple" translation of instruments or responses (Broadfoot & Osborn, 1991; National Research Council, 2003; Schmidt et al., 1996). Therefore, the country representatives met regularly over a period of 5 years in order to have face-to-face interactions, discussions, and so forth to foster a collaborative approach to study development.

Employing a discourse methodology (Schmidt et al., 1996), national experts of teacher education regularly presented features of their teacher preparation systems, which initiated a lively discussion among participants comparing aspects and probing policies and practices to ensure that the dynamics within each system were clearly understood by all participants. Participants needed to be ready to express their confusion or surprise as country representatives presented the features, as this procedure is essential for clarifying mutual understandings. The seminar-style, structured discussions took place during all meetings and culminated in a 16-hour session, distributed across 2 days during an MT21 meeting in Rome in June 2004.

There are widely used conventions for translation of the instruments (Hambleton, 2002). In MT21, two ways were applied in parallel to each other:

One translation was done within the countries participating; another translation was done in the United States. Differences between the two translations were discussed and solved by mutual agreement. This was one way to ensure the equivalence of the data across countries. However, since we have to rely on self-report data in some parts of the study (beliefs, OTL), another challenge was the well-known problem in comparative research of culturally different tendencies of study participants to agree or disagree with various statements (Byrne, 2003; Little, 1997). We have applied different statistical methods to check for this problem and, based on what we have found, we are reasonably confident about having invariance with respect to the factor loadings defining the scales. In this sense our instruments can be regarded as valid across countries. However, one must be careful in interpreting the means of self-reported data since there are no rules governing the extent of cultural differences that are tolerable (Schulz, 2009; van de Vijver & Tanzer, 1997). For this reason, we caution our readers.

In order to avoid the measurement of "idle knowledge" (Oser, 1997a, b), a special item format was used in MT21: open-ended teaching situations that can only be handled by using and linking several knowledge dimensions. However, it has to be acknowledged that even with such vignettes it is very difficult to measure professional competencies because it is still a paper-and-pencil format.

The use of open-ended items itself presented another challenge to ensure accuracy and consistency in the coding of the future teachers' responses. Coding rubrics help to ensure a sufficient reliability (Jonsson & Svingby, 2007). In MT21, complex coding rubrics were developed in a collaborative effort among the six countries' representatives. They capture declarative and procedural knowledge that is necessary to solve the problems presented, the technical vocabulary used by the future teachers, and the connectivity of their responses.

The codes were developed based on theory and data and were mainly intended to be low-inference with one exception within each vignette that is coded in a high-inference (or holistic) way. The exception is the connectivity of responses across subparts of a vignette. In this high-inference approach, raters have to judge a broader set of a person's responses and make inferences, whereas in the low-inference approach, every single response is coded with the least possible amount of inference. The first approach is much cheaper than the second one but loses the value of details (Jonsson & Svingby, 2007). Due to their different advantages we intended to make use of both in MT21.

Every country provided a comprehensive list of student responses, which would be accepted as correct according to the state of research within the country. This within-country approach was an important attempt to avoid cultural bias. In addition, a random sample of 20 tests from each country was drawn from which an additional list of responses was created.

CHAPTER 4

What Are the Components of Teacher Education? What Opportunities Are Offered, and What Do Future Teachers Take?

Teacher preparation programs intentionally provide specific structured learning experiences or opportunities to equip those who desire to become teachers with the knowledge and skills needed for classroom instruction and more generally to assume the professional role of a teacher. This chapter focuses on characterizing what these opportunities to learn (OTLs) were in our sample of 34 teacher preparation institutions by describing their academic or pedagogical content as well as the nature of their practical experiences.

As explained in Chapter 2, countries have different overall structures with regard to how teacher preparation is organized and accomplished, such as the amount of time that will typically be required to complete all that is expected. Most of the institutions in our six countries accomplished the preparation of teachers in programs future teachers were expected to complete in 4 years at either a college, university, or normal school.

In Taiwan and Germany there is a longer time frame associated with teacher preparation, which typically involves at least 5 years but may take some individuals in Germany as many as 8 years to complete. As was detailed in Chapter 2, the entire teacher preparation program in Germany involves experiences at two different types of institutions, including a specific second pedagogical training institution subsequent to the individual's university academic experience. In Taiwan the 5th year is a yearlong supervised practicum through the university.

Another departure from the general 4-year university program was found in one U.S. institution that also required a full year beyond an appropriate bachelor's degree, which typically requires 4 years. These structural features are briefly reviewed again here to emphasize that these set real limits—specifically in terms of time—as to how much academic work and how many practical experiences can be allocated to the preparation of future teachers.

However, given a specified number of years for a teacher preparation program, such as 4, the amount of actual coursework taken over those years can vary appreciably. Different institutions in different national contexts may have very different expectations as to the intensity and duration of the specified learning experiences. For example, the actual clock hours can vary as different institutions define a class session in terms of how often it meets and for what length of time the courses will meet. The reason this is important has to do with the focus of this chapter, opportunity to learn (OTL)—a central concept of our framework, as Chapter 3 makes clear. Opportunity to learn has been extensively studied in the context of K–12 schooling and the simple and fundamental generalization of that work is that opportunity is related to what students learn (Schmidt et al., 2001; Schmidt & Maier, 2009; Suter, 2000).

This would seem to be even truer at the university level as it is hard to imagine how one might learn about complex functions without having the opportunity to take a relevant course. There are, of course, exceptional students who would not fit this generalization, but the fact that they are outliers underscores the general principle. In this chapter in particular, as well as throughout the book, we explore and discuss OTL employing the historically central and foundational focus on the coverage of specific disciplinary or academic content.[1]

The same can be said about education or pedagogy-related courses. For example, it is hard to imagine how one would learn about the stages of cognitive development and the role these play in learning without having had a course that addressed these issues. There are some, at least in the popular press, who suggest that anyone can learn to teach simply by having been a student themselves and so pedagogy courses are not necessary. To most, at least those who have studied the issue, this is not the case, and so the same relationship of OTL to learning can be assumed.

We define OTL for four broad areas, including mathematics, general pedagogy, mathematics pedagogy, and practical knowledge as it may be gained through practical experiences in real schools. Mathematics pedagogy includes the study of *applied* mathematics specific to the topics covered in middle and high school (for further explanation, see below). The fourth area includes the practical knowledge and experiences related to teaching mathematics in the middle grades. This includes such things as serving as a teacher's aide, observing classes, and actually teaching in a middle-school setting. But it also includes other related knowledge and experiences. Here we differentiate between the more formal aspects of pedagogy, such as the cognitive theories of how children learn mathematics, and the practical aspects, such as how, during instruction, to ask questions that challenge students' mathematical thinking. The former is included in the section on mathematics pedagogy while the latter is discussed in the section on practical knowledge and experiences.

Two of the areas need further definition. What is applied mathematics? Many of the topics taught in schools become special cases of much more advanced mathematics and, as such, are not the focus of the more traditional advanced mathematics topics typically studied by mathematics majors at the university. This is similar in principle to the type of mathematics courses taken by engineering students. In addition to the formal mathematics coursework these students take, such as calculus and differential equations, often together with students who are majoring in mathematics, they also are required to study more applied mathematics specifically related to their professional needs. For mathematics teachers, similar applied mathematics coursework is appropriate and includes the elementary topics taught in school. Perhaps a good example is an understanding of the more formal locus-based definitions of various geometric objects so as to be more precise in explaining to middle school students what appear to be simple ideas such as an angle.

We begin this chapter first by examining the institutional course requirements associated with teacher preparation programs. The rest of the chapter is organized around the course-taking of future teachers in the four broad areas described above: mathematics, mathematics pedagogy (including applied mathematics related to teaching), general pedagogy, and practical experiences (including the practical aspects of both mathematics and general pedagogy). Within each of these four areas we characterize: (1) the type and amount of coursework taken, (2) the variability both across future teachers and institutions in such course-taking, including an indication of the relative amount of variation at each of these two levels, and (3) the pattern of course-taking for a relatively small number of specific but commonly taken courses. The chapter concludes with a section examining what is probably the main policy-relevant question that emerges, which is: What is the balance across these various areas given the limitation of the total time available in a typical future teacher preparation program?

HOW MUCH TIME IS AVAILABLE FOR TEACHER PREPARATION?

Before turning to the specific nature of the opportunities taken by the future teachers, we look at the quantity—the number of semester and clock hours required by the institutions during teacher preparation. Averaging data from the program questionnaires for each of the sampled institutions within each country gives an indication of the overall differences in course requirements across countries. The data are summarized in Table 4.1.[2]

The differences across the countries were large, especially with Taiwan in comparison to the elementary programs in Germany and the United States. The typical requirement for the sampled teacher preparation institutions in Taiwan was a total of 150 semester units,[3] resulting in over 2,300 clock hours. Keep in mind this was to be accomplished within a 4-year time frame because the 1-year practicum does not include formal coursework, implying an average of almost 19 semester units per term, or around 290 clock hours. In marked contrast, the ten U.S. sampled institutions (those with adequate data) averaged a total requirement of around 120 semester units. This accumulates to around 1,710 and 1,748 clock hours of course experiences for the two preparation programs, respectively. The amount of variation between elementary and secondary programs was 40 more clock hours required by the secondary preparation programs. For the typical U.S. institution that we sampled and averaging over the two types of programs, the requirement amounts to about 16 semester units per term or 216 clock hours per term. The resulting difference between the United States and Taiwan was around 560—which is 600 fewer clock hours of formal instruction or required classroom-related experiences over the entire preparation program. Put simply and using typical United States definitions, Taiwanese future teachers would probably end up taking 12 more 3-hour courses.

TABLE 4.1. Total instructional time, total mathematics and mathematics pedagogy instructional time, and total instructional time in general pedagogy expressed as average clock hours for sampled institutions in each country.

	Mathematics	Mathematics Pedagogy	Second Specialization	General Pedagogy	Other	Total Clock Hours
Bulgaria	1037	76	483	98	116	1810
Germany						
Elementary	220.5	370.5	591	516		1698
Secondary	588	234	822	516		2160
Mexico		896[b]		2688		3584[a]
South Korea	741	53		210	722	1726
Taiwan	1286	165		225	634	2310
United States						
Elementary	346	57	195	458	662	1710
Secondary	518	114	139	505	471	1748

Note: [a] See endnote 4. [b] Instruction time is in mathematics pedagogy only; no formal mathematics.

The German programs that prepare teachers as a part of an elementary program have requirements similar to those in the United States. For the middle school teachers who are prepared as part of a secondary preparation program, the requirements are similar to those of Taiwanese programs in terms of the number of semester units but still less (150 hours) for the total number of clock hours.

By far the country with the most clock hours of preparation time was Mexico. The typical total number of semester units required for the five sampled normal schools was 224 semester units spread over 46 courses. This number seems extremely large compared to the other five countries. The total number of clock hours (3,584 hours) is almost twice that of some U.S., German, and Bulgarian institutions. These requirements are nationally dictated by the Ministry of Education.[4] This implies the typical load for a Mexican future teacher was between five and six courses covering 28 semester units per term but, most spectacularly, resulting in almost 450 clock hours per term—234 more than the United States and 160 more than Taiwan. However, it is important to bear in mind here that these hours in Mexico include practical experiences since they are counted as classes, which they are not in Germany and Taiwan.

These results are an important context for looking at the specific requirements associated with the four broad areas as they represent what is the upper limit of what is possible. Several notable observations are worth making about the number of hours allocated to the four areas, although the issue of how the total clock hours are apportioned across the four areas is further discussed later in this chapter. Taiwanese-sampled institutions allocated almost 1,300 clock hours to the study of mathematics, which is over half of the total hours in the preparation program. At the other extreme, Mexican institutions allocated almost 2,700 clock hours to the study of general pedagogy. Clearly different conceptions of what constitutes the preparation of middle school teachers exist across the six countries. In addition, these numbers spell out the total effort required to become a future teacher, at least in terms of their formal preparation, and what we find are very large differences in that upper limit, which has profound implications for OTL.

The foregoing describes the course or semester-hour requirements for future teachers to complete their preparation programs, which includes coursework outside of the four broad areas related specifically to their preparation to be middle school mathematics teachers. For example, in the German institutions future middle school teachers are required to have a second specialization and in Bulgaria they also take coursework in information technology. It also includes university general requirements, which in the United States is called liberal arts. In German institutions there are no such requirements, as such coursework is taken in the secondary school before matriculating to the university. Also, there are no such requirements in Mexican normal schools. In Bulgaria the only coursework of this type required includes one to two semesters of foreign language and one sports class. It is in this area where South Korean and U.S. elementary preparation program requirements are larger than in other countries, representing about 40% of the total clock hour requirements.

WHAT AMOUNT OF COURSEWORK DID FUTURE TEACHERS TAKE?

What is the nature of the opportunities most directly related to their preparation as future teachers? To answer this question we turn to the data provided by the future teachers. Future teachers were asked to indicate from a list of topics that could have been covered in their preparation programs which of them they had experienced in their particular coursework.[5] The list was organized into three sets covering three of the broad areas: mathematics, mathematics pedagogy, and general pedagogy. The area of applied mathematics was included as a part of mathematics pedagogy for these analyses. The list describes topics in each of these broad areas but at a fairly large grain size. In fact, for most of the countries these were topics that would typically define a course. We will refer to them in this way for simplicity in presentation, recognizing that in some cases they actually were topics included in one or more courses that covered other topics as well.[6] We do the same for mathematics pedagogy. For general pedagogy the opposite is generally true—many of those listed are topics covered in one or more courses and in many cases are not courses themselves. For that reason we refer to them as *topics* in the following discussion, rather than as *courses,* as we do in both mathematics and mathematics pedagogy.

We tabulated the total number of courses (topics) taken in each of the three areas (with applied mathematics being included in mathematics pedagogy) for each future teacher. Table 4.2 presents the results. The mean values were averaged over all future teachers at the end of their program within an institution and then a weighted average was taken over all sampled institutions. The resulting means were rounded to a whole number.[7]

What follows is a discussion of those results. In each case we present the country means followed by a discussion of the within-country variation across future teachers. The discussion of the variance includes an examination of the variance components to determine the source of the variation—whether it is mainly driven by individual future teacher choices or by cross-institutional variation likely reflecting course offerings and requirements. This structure is reflected throughout this chapter and in others as well.

Table 4.2. Mean number of courses (topics)[a] in mathematics, mathematics pedagogy, and general pedagogy (including the standard errors[8] and standard deviations) taken by the sampled future teachers in each country.

	Mathematics			Mathematics Pedagogy			General Pedagogy		
	Mean	*(se)*	*SD*	*Mean*	*(se)*	*SD*	*Mean*	*(se)*	*SD*
Bulgaria	14	(0.3)	2.8	5	(0.2)	2.2	4	(0.3)	2.9
Germany	10	(0.3)	4.1	3	(0.2)	2.8	5	(0.2)	3.5
Mexico	8[b]	(0.3)	4.1	8	(0.3)	3.1	8	(0.3)	4.1
South Korea	16	(0.2)	2.5	5	(0.4)	3.6	8	(0.3)	3.5
Taiwan	16	(0.2)	2.8	5	(0.2)	3.3	7	(0.1)	2.1
United States	11	(0.3)	4.1	4	(0.2)	3.2	8	(0.3)	4.0

Note.[a] Generally, the topics listed in the survey are broad enough to constitute a single semester course at many colleges and universities. This would most likely be the case for the mathematics topics but is probably less likely to be true for the list of general pedagogy topics. The link between topics and courses is particularly problematic in Germany as universities are organized around lectures rather than courses. As such, one series of lectures might well address numerous topics while other lectures might address any one of these same topics either alone or in conjunction with other topics.

[b] All mathematics instruction occurs in the context of mathematics pedagogy instruction, which are courses focused on how to teach middle grades mathematics topics. No formal college-level mathematics was required. The eight courses listed here were denoted by the Mexican future teachers as mathematics courses but actually would have been mathematics pedagogy courses.

We first included all 47 topics/courses defining the three broad areas. This would be comparable to what was described previously as the overall requirement but is limited only to the coursework directly related to the teaching of mathematics in the middle grades. It therefore does not include general university-related coursework such as liberal arts requirements or work related to a second major emphasis (as is required for the future teachers in German and Bulgarian institutions) or optional courses unrelated to mathematics or the teaching of mathematics. Future teachers in the Taiwanese and South Korean sampled institutions took on average between 28 and 29 of the 47 courses (or covered this many of the topics). For the Bulgarian, Mexican, and U.S. institutions, future teachers reported covering typically around four or five fewer courses. But especially surprising were the German future teachers, who indicated they covered around eight or nine fewer topics (for Germany the term *topic* or *lecture* comes closer to a more appropriate description than does the term *course*).

Several things about these results are important to note, and in some cases are quite surprising. Some of the differences could result from well-known, culturally different tendencies to endorse statements, in this case to label a topic as "covered" or "not covered" (Little, 1997; Schulz, 2009). However, the differences seem too large to be explained only by this limitation, specifically in our case, since the response format was dichotomous and fact-oriented and not based on a Likert-type scale focusing on beliefs. The fact that Taiwanese sampled future teachers took on average four more courses than U.S. future teachers is consistent with the previously described analysis of course requirements. That analysis suggested some 13 more courses were available, given formal degree requirements, and it would appear that four of these were directly related to formal coursework in teacher preparation-related areas. The fact that Mexican future teachers on average took fewer courses is likely related to the fact that they were not required to take formal mathematics courses. It is possible that the difference was made up in terms of practical experiences that were not included in the course/topic total reported here.

Finally, the lower total for Germany's sampled future teachers is surprising because their teacher preparation program stretches over 5 to 6½ years but, again, the last 18 months to 2 years is mostly made up of practical teaching experience. Even though there are definitional differences in terms of the German *lecture* versus a *course* the result is the same: fewer content areas were covered in Germany over more years of teacher preparation. However, it should also be noted here that Germany is the only one of the six countries that requires future teachers to be fully prepared to teach two school subjects—that is, the number of required hours for preparing to teach mathematics is also required for being prepared to teach a second subject (see Table 4.1).

Table 4.2 also describes the typical number of courses taken in each category of mathematics, mathematics pedagogy, and general pedagogy. For mathematics the number of courses taken ranges from 16 courses for Taiwanese and South Korean future teachers to no courses in Mexico. The only mathematics taught to Mexican future teachers is that which was contained in their mathematics pedagogy courses. As a result (considering the eight mathematics courses in Table 4.2 as pedagogy courses as well), Mexican future teachers in the sampled institutions had 1½ to 2 times as many the number of mathematics pedagogy courses as the other countries' future teachers. The German future teachers in our sample took the smallest number of mathematics pedagogy courses (four), while all the other future teachers took on average around five such courses.

In general pedagogy the typical number of courses taken for South Korean, Mexican, and Taiwanese future teachers was seven or eight. The future teachers in the Bulgarian and German institutions took only four or six courses. U.S. future teachers took on average the largest number of general pedagogy courses—eight. The above description focuses on the weighted means across the sampled institutions within each country. There is variation in terms of the number of courses taken both among future teachers within institutions and also among the sampled institutions. The variation in course-taking related to individuals within an institution likely reflects choices available within the program's structure. If there were no requirements or limited requirements then the variation could be relatively large depending on the number of available offerings. In the United States and Germany, variation among individuals within an institution could also reflect differences between the various types of programs within the same institution.

On the other hand, variation across institutions would likely be related to differences in course requirements or course offerings if there were no requirements or only limited requirements. Such variation could also result from a combination of differences in both requirements and course offerings or differences in only one of these with the other in common across institutions. These variations would simply influence the size of the cross-institutional variation. Such variation in both cases reflects differences in institutional definitions or at least expectations of what is important for teacher preparation. Using statistical techniques we estimated the percentage of variation attributable to each of these two sources.[9] The smaller the proportion that is attributable to institutions, the more likely the requirements and optional course offerings—or the course offerings if there are no requirements—are fairly common across institutions within a country.

In terms of the overall total amount of coursework taken that is related to the teaching of middle school mathematics, the percentage related to institutional variation was relatively small (equal to or less than 6%) for the Bulgarian, German, and U.S. sampled institutions. The sampled institutions in both South Korea and Taiwan accounted for a larger proportion of the total variation—between 29% and 33%. However, the total amount of variation across all future teachers in Taiwan was not large compared to Bulgaria and Germany, but a substantial amount of the variation that did emerge was related to differences in institutional requirements and/or course offerings. South Korea, on the other hand, had substantial total variation in total course-taking across all sampled future teachers.

The country with the largest total variation, however, was the United States, with a variance about double that of Taiwan, Germany, and Bulgaria. The countries close to that large amount of variation in total number of courses taken were Mexico and South Korea. However, in Mexico all but 10% of it was attributable to variation across individual future teachers within the institutions.

For the total number of mathematics courses taken, the total variation was relatively small, the standard deviations reflecting that variation ranging across the six countries from 2.8 to 4.1 (against an overall mean of 12.3) with around 85% to 95% of that variation reflecting individual choices among the future teachers within their institutions.[10] The one exception was for the sampled Taiwanese institutions, where over half (53.5%) of the total variation was at the institution level, likely reflecting different course requirements or at least different course-taking at the sampled institutions.

Course-taking in the area of mathematics pedagogy presents a different story. Although the total variation is comparable to that of mathematics, the relative contribution of course requirements versus individual future teacher choice of courses varies more across the countries. The percentage related to institutional variation ranged from zero in Bulgaria to almost 58% for South Korea. The difference between the estimated variance components for the institutions in these two countries suggests that in Bulgaria (and Germany, where the estimated value was 0.4%) the course requirements don't vary across the sampled institutions, whereas in South Korea (and Taiwan, with 29% institutional variation) there is a fairly large amount of variation across institutions in what is required in terms of mathematics pedagogy courses. The countries in which the overall variation is the greatest include the United States, South Korea, and Mexico. It is in Taiwan where there is little variation in OTL across future teachers with respect to general pedagogy, but once again, over one fourth of that is attributable to cross-institutional differences.

What follows in the rest of this chapter is a description of course-taking or opportunity to learn. This, we argued in Chapter 3, defines the core of teacher preparation as it is the set of courses and practical experiences that the institutions have defined as the means by which to develop the professional competencies of the future teachers. What ensues in a preparation program is not a set of chance experiences but a planned sequence reflecting an institution's vision of what it takes to prepare a quality teacher. Analyzing those experiences as aggregated from our sample of future teachers within the institution is to characterize the heart and core of teacher preparation, which is what we use in a later chapter to explore its relationship to the measured competencies of the future teachers.

MATHEMATICS COURSE-TAKING

All of the sampled institutions in five of the countries required mathematics (Mexico, as described previously, only offered instruction in mathematics as part of mathematics pedagogy courses), but as indicated previously, the amount varied. Here we look at the specific mathematics topics included in the various teacher preparation programs. There were 20 distinct mathematics courses or topics listed in the questionnaire. These were then grouped into eight broader categories: linear algebra; number theory; geometry (including non-Euclidean geometry); probability and statistics; the history of mathematics; advanced mathematics, which includes topology, differential geometry, multivariate calculus, differential equations, and the theory of real and complex functions; abstract algebra; and a basic calculus sequence. The means, standard errors, and standard deviations are presented in Table 4.3. The mean values indicate the estimated number of courses taken in each of the eight areas averaged over all sampled future teachers in each country. Also included is the percentage of courses or topics taken in each of the eight aggregate areas. Some of the eight areas are defined by only a single course—linear algebra, number theory, and the history of mathematics. The mean percentage in this case is the percentage of future teachers having taken the course. For the other areas the average is an indication of the typical percentage of courses in an area that have been taken.

An analysis of the results indicates some important differences in the types of mathematics covered. With regard to all future teachers and all course types, the typical (median) percentage of courses taken in a topic area is around 70%.[11] At the country level the future teachers sampled in Mexico and Germany typically covered only around 55% of the potential courses in each of the areas, with some specific exceptions. For example, German future teachers took more linear algebra and basic calculus than would be expected given their typical pattern and given what was taken in these two areas more generally across all countries combined. This result clearly reflects the typical tradition of lower-secondary school mathematics and teacher training (Blömeke, Kaiser, & Lehmann, 2008).

This kind of statistical analysis essentially identifies country effects, course type effects, and interaction effects. The interaction effects are anomalies or deviations from the pattern of means created by taking into account both the median over countries for a course type and the median over course types for a country. We will use this approach for summarizing findings throughout the book and simply refer to these as interaction effects.

For Mexican sampled future teachers an exceptionally large percentage of future teachers covered the history of mathematics but covered on average few advanced mathematics topics. We report what topics the sampled Mexican future teachers said they covered but keep in mind that these were not covered in formal mathematics courses but in mathematics pedagogy courses. The U.S. and Bulgarian sampled future teachers covered around the typical 70% of courses in each area with the one exception being course-taking in the history of mathematics. In Bulgaria the percentage who took that course was only 14%. Taiwanese

TABLE 4.3. Country means, standard errors (se), and standard deviations (SD) for the percentage of courses taken in formal mathematics from the sampled future teachers in each country.

	Bulgaria	Germany	Mexico	South Korea	Taiwan	United States
Linear Algebra						
Mean	98.0	88.1	60.7	98.5	99.7	79.5
(se)	(1.4)	(2.0)	(4.0)	(1.2)	(0.4)	(2.7)
SD	14.0	32.4	49.1	12.2	5.8	40.4
Number Theory						
Mean	98.0	63.5	83.8	82.8	80.5	78.4
(se)	(1.4)	(3.0)	(3.0)	(3.7)	(2.4)	(2.8)
SD	14.0	48.2	37.0	37.9	39.7	41.3
Geometry						
Mean	76.8	40.9	43.9	76.8	63.1	59.8
(se)	(2.8)	(2.0)	(2.4)	(2.9)	(2.2)	(2.3)
SD	27.7	32.5	29.5	29.2	35.6	34.1
Probability & Statistics						
Mean	80.3	51.8	74.3	76.1	94.2	81.7
(se)	(3.1)	(2.4)	(3.0)	(3.3)	(1.1)	(2.1)
SD	31.1	39.3	36.7	33.6	18.0	30.7
History of Mathematics						
Mean	14.2	38.6	70.5	31.0	81.1	36.0
(se)	(3.6)	(3.0)	(3.8)	(4.6)	(2.4)	(3.2)
SD	35.2	48.7	45.8	46.5	39.2	48.1
Advanced Mathematics						
Mean	58.7	37.1	17.2	84.0	72.9	35.8
(se)	(1.8)	(1.9)	(1.7)	(1.8)	(1.1)	(1.7)
SD	18.2	30.3	20.2	18.3	17.5	25.0
Abstract Algebra						
Mean	44.6	36.7	33.6	86.7	78.2	42.4
(se)	(3.2)	(2.0)	(2.8)	(2.2)	(1.9)	(2.4)
SD	32.1	31.9	34.5	22.0	30.4	35.9
Basic Calculus						
Mean	85.2	87.3	63.5	95.5	99.5	78.3
(se)	(3.2)	(1.9)	(3.5)	(1.5)	(0.4)	(2.5)
SD	31.5	31.1	42.8	15.3	6.4	37.1

sampled future teachers were some 15 percentage points higher than the median of all countries in terms of course-taking across all areas, with no notable exceptions other than a slightly lower percentage of future teachers who took courses in number theory and geometry. South Korean future teachers were similar to the Taiwanese but with many fewer future teachers taking the history of mathematics (31% vs. 81%) and a larger percentage taking abstract algebra.

With the exception of the history of mathematics, the future teachers from South Korea and Taiwan typically took around 80% of the available courses in each of the eight areas, which is in marked contrast with U.S. sampled future teachers who took around 60% of those available courses. For example, Taiwanese as well as South Korean sampled future teachers took on average four or five courses in advanced mathematics, which was more than any other country's future teachers. By contrast, U.S. sampled future teachers only took on average two courses in this area. Even in terms of the basic calculus sequence there were differences. Virtually all Taiwanese and South Korean sampled future teachers took both courses (the mean number of the two possible courses taken equaled 1.99 and 2.0, respectively). The U.S. future teachers again had the lowest mean, indicating coverage of between one and two courses (a mean of 1.6).

From the perspective of the types of courses, those which were taken, averaged across countries, paints an interesting portrait of what in the aggregate future middle school teachers have studied. Linear algebra and number theory are courses taken by around 80–90% of the future teachers in all sampled institutions combined. Of the two basic calculus courses, 83.2% of the future teachers took both. By contrast, much less is taken in the areas of advanced mathematics, where what was taken on average is only around half of the available courses. Only around half of the sampled future teachers took the abstract algebra and the history of mathematics courses. Although not as extreme, less coursework was also taken in geometry (60.9%). An examination of the 20 individual courses reveals few anomalies from the general conclusions.

However, the important question of which courses are taken by all sampled future teachers across all institutions in all six countries can be examined with these data. The answer is simple: there is no one mathematics course that all sampled future teachers reported having taken. This is true even if we *only* consider those future teachers prepared in programs devoted to secondary-school teacher preparation. If we change the criterion to require that sampled institutions have at least 90% of their responding future teachers to have taken a particular course, we find that in 20 out of the 23 institutions that have secondary programs that prepare middle school teachers, linear algebra is the most commonly covered course. Doing it in this way, by institution and requiring 90% or more agreement, comes close to suggesting this course is required by nearly all secondary program institutions. Two other courses meet the criterion in at least 20 of the 23 institutions; they are the two basic calculus courses. Only two other courses meet this criterion in at least half of the institutions: number theory (15 institutions) and probability (14 institutions).

Variation in Course-Taking

The standard deviations (reflecting the total variation across all sampled future teachers in each country) are also listed in Table 4.3 and were quite large. For example, on average across the eight categories, U.S., Mexican, and German sampled future teachers exhibited larger variation in course-taking (ranging from 35% to 38%) than for those future teachers sampled in Bulgaria, South Korea, and Taiwan (26% to 27%). This is not inconsistent with the first section of this chapter, which talked about course-taking requirements in mathematics. These were defined in terms of the number of courses required, and from these data, apparently, which particular courses make up the total number may not be so easily specified.

Typically across the six countries the estimated median standard deviations for each of the eight areas separately is also relatively large—ranging from 23% to 46%—indicating substantial variation in mathematics course-taking as the estimated overall mean percentage of courses taken plus or minus one standard deviation ranges from 36% to 100%. The two areas where this overall variation was the largest included course-taking related to number theory and the history of mathematics, while the two areas with the smallest variation were linear algebra (which had the highest percentage of students taking this course) and advanced mathematics (which had the smallest mean percentage covered of the six possible courses). The country which overall had the greatest variation across all topic areas was the United States.

A key question to understanding this relatively large amount of variation in course-taking in mathematics is: What proportion of this is attributable to variation across institutions likely reflecting differences in the definition of what mathematics is central to teacher preparation? Those cross-institutional differences in preparation likely reflect either differences in formal course requirements or differences in terms of what courses are offered and hence available to be taken. Such differences could also occur due to informal expectations of what future teachers should take even though it is not formally required of them. In two of our countries—Germany and the United States—variation within institutions may also to some extent reflect the different emphases of the two types of programs that prepare middle grades teachers, as was evidenced in Table 4.1. To examine this issue we estimated the proportion of the total variance in course-taking that is attributable to cross-institutional variation for the eight areas of mathematics (see Figure 4.1).

FIGURE 4.1. Percentage of the total variation attributable to variation both between and within institutions by course and by country. The area of the circle represents the size of the total variation.

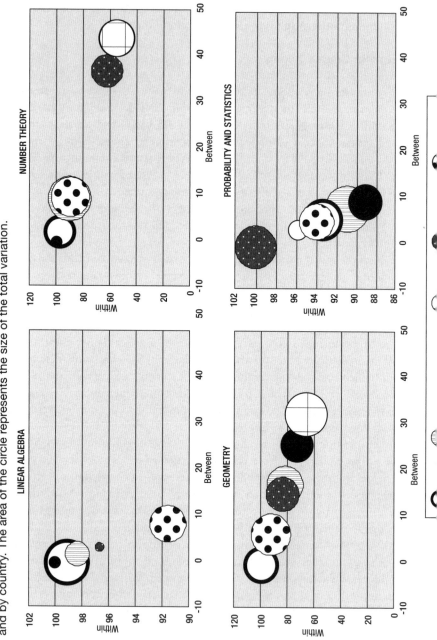

FIGURE 4.1. (continued)

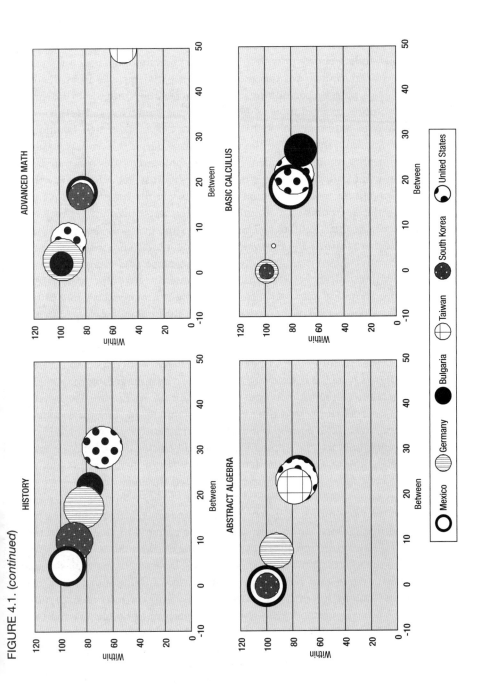

In general, the vast majority of variation in course-taking in formal mathematics was found within institutions—around 85%—most likely reflecting individual student choice or within-institution program differences (see Figure 4.1). This would imply two things: (1) that what students take in mathematics as part of their preparation to become teachers does not vary that much from institution to institution within each of the countries; and (2) that the relatively large variation, coupled with the fact that most of that variation is within-institution, implies that the mathematics courses that are taken allow for a substantial amount of student choice. To some extent this relatively large variation within institutions suggests the possibility that students may have had some difficulty in making the connection between the list of topics/courses found in the questionnaire with the various learning opportunities they had experienced at their institution. This also raises the question about what students may have learned. In other words, if a student took a linear algebra course but doesn't recognize it among a list of topics/courses, did this student really learn any linear algebra? Given that every institution has some requirements and expectations for what students should study, it is rather surprising to find such a large percentage of the variation within institutions. However, in comparing the percentage of variation, one must bear in mind the amount of total variation found within each country, which in some cases is quite small.

Nonetheless, one country is substantially different with respect to this general pattern. Overall and relatively, the greatest variation among the sampled institutions in mathematics course-taking occurred in Taiwan. The average percentage of variation across the eight scales among the Taiwanese sampled institutions was 32%, but for some areas of mathematics it was much larger, including number (45%), the history of mathematics (65%), and advanced mathematics (50%). One reason for the large variation is that in some of the sampled institutions future teachers are prepared through a mathematics department while others are prepared through a teacher education center. This is described more fully in Chapter 2. The consequence is that future teachers prepared through mathematics departments are required to take more mathematics. This illustrates how different organizational structures can influence the nature of the OTL that future teachers receive. However, for linear algebra and basic calculus there was virtually no variation across institutions and very little within institutions. Essentially, it is safe to say that with virtually no exceptions, all sampled future teachers in Taiwan took courses in linear algebra and basic calculus. This results from the fact that basic calculus and linear algebra are the introductory courses in the areas of algebra and analysis—two areas in which future teachers are required to take coursework.

The U.S.-sampled institutions had the more typical pattern of 14% or less institutional variation in all but three of the areas. For the history of mathematics, abstract algebra, and basic calculus, the percentage of variation across institutions ranged between 20% and 31%. The fact that abstract algebra and especially calculus are basic mathematics courses means they would almost certainly be offered at all of the sampled institutions, implying that these differences in course-taking are likely the result of different institutional or program-level requirements. Apparently, different U.S. colleges and universities or the programs within them have different perceptions about the importance of these courses for preparing future middle school teachers. This is especially the case for a basic two-course sequence in calculus, but the difference in elementary and secondary preparation program requirements becomes important here. Those future teachers prepared in an elementary program took on average between one and two of the calculus courses, while virtually all those prepared in a secondary program took the two-course sequence.

Across the sampled institutions in the six countries and across the eight topic areas there are few general patterns. Many of these results are specific to a particular topic in a particular country.[12] South Korea, for example, has substantial variation (37%) across its sampled institutions only for course-taking in number theory. For Germany, the largest relative amount of variation across institutions (18%) was in the area of geometry. This likely reflects to some extent the different ideological traditions institutions have had with respect to the study of geometry as well as the different traditions of future teachers following the two different program types available in Germany. Bulgaria shows the greatest differences across topic areas in the percentage of cross-university variation. Three areas show essentially no such variation—linear algebra, number theory, and advanced mathematics—while around 20–27% cross-institutional variation was demonstrated for geometry, history of mathematics, and abstract algebra. For the three areas with virtually no cross-institutional variation, there was also smaller total variation compared to the other countries, implying that many future teachers in the sampled Bulgarian institutions took linear algebra, number theory, and a similar amount of advanced mathematics—that is, around four of the six possible courses, especially differential equations and the theory of complex functions, both of which were taken by 95% or more of the sampled future teachers.

FORMAL MATHEMATICS PEDAGOGY

Teacher preparation programs across the institutions we studied all included preparation in mathematics pedagogy. That preparation included both the theoretical or more formal aspects of mathematics pedagogy, such as the psychology of mathematics; and the more practical aspects related to classroom practices, such as how to ask questions that challenge mathematical thinking. We turn to the more formal aspects of mathematics pedagogy in this section and to the more practical aspects in a later section.

To characterize the opportunities to learn the formal aspects of mathematics pedagogy we use the course-taking items from the future teacher questionnaire. The 12 courses divide into two broad groups. The first refers to courses that focus on the advanced treatment (theory and principles) of various elementary mathematics topics that are encountered in the middle school mathematics curriculum. These include the following topics: school algebra, school arithmetic, school geometry, school probability, and school calculus. The latter is, in some countries, not typically a topic in middle school curricula but is in the secondary curriculum, and the preparation of middle school teachers is often in secondary preparation programs (see Chapter 2). The second group of courses deals with such aspects of mathematics pedagogy as history, curriculum, psychology, and methods, including assessment.

For analysis purposes the 12 courses or topics were combined to form five scales. The first scale includes courses on the mathematics curricula of schools, the psychology of mathematics, methods for teaching mathematics, and assessment in mathematics instruction. We label this scale *general mathematics pedagogy*. The second scale focuses on courses related to the principles and theories of the five school mathematics topics (school topics) described previously. The last three scales include only one item each: the history of school mathematics, methods for solving school mathematics problems, and practical teaching experiences related to mathematics. The latter course has students teaching peers or middle school students but is not a part of formal student teaching.

The means and standard errors for each of the five scales are listed in Table 4.4. The mean values for the first two scales estimate the percentage of courses taken averaged over all future middle school teachers in the sampled institutions within each country. For scales three through five the estimate is the percentage of future teachers who took each of the courses in each country. Over five scales and six countries, the future teachers in general took about 45% of the available courses (or topics). The South Korean sampled future teachers on average covered around two thirds of the possible topics in general mathematics pedagogy and around 70% of the school topics. By contrast, with the exception of Mexico, the other countries all took around half or fewer of the available courses. The course which on average was taken less frequently across future teachers in all six countries was the history of school mathematics.

There were several anomalies to these general patterns. Given the general level of opportunity experienced by South Korean future teachers in all five of the formal mathematics pedagogy scales, and the typical coverage of the scale of general mathematics pedagogy across all countries, South Korean future teach-

TABLE 4.4. Country means and standard errors (se) for the percentage of courses taken in the formal areas of mathematics pedagogy.

	General Mathematics Pedagogy		School Mathematics Topics		History of School Mathematics		Methods of Solving School Mathematics Problems		Opportunity to Practice Teaching Peers or Students	
	Mean	(se)	Mean	(se)	Mean	(se)	Mean	(se)	Mean	(se)
Bulgaria	37.0	(3.1)	46.4	(1.8)	13.8	(3.5)	58.5	(5.0)	39.6	(5.0)
Germany	24.2	(1.7)	23.5	(2.0)	6.6	(1.5)	18.6	(2.4)	45.3	(3.1)
Mexico	67.7	(2.5)	33.0	(4.5)	67.7	(3.9)	44.6	(4.9)	42.1	(4.1)
South Korea	62.7	(3.0)	72.4	(2.3)	17.0	(3.7)	63.1	(4.0)	59.3	(4.8)
Taiwan	54.2	(1.8)	29.1	(2.6)	29.4	(2.8)	58.9	(3.0)	87.3	(2.1)
United States	42.2	(2.3)	24.8	(2.3)	19.2	(2.6)	56.7	(3.3)	65.4	(3.2)

ers typically took a large number of the available courses in this area—three (2.51) of the four possible courses. This was second only to Mexican future teachers. Similarly, more Mexican future teachers took the history of school mathematics than would be expected—68%.[13] Again, employing the same analytical logic, two anomalies indicated the opposite type of result, whereby a smaller percentage than would be expected had certain opportunities. This included the coverage of school mathematics topics in Taiwan, as described previously, and the opportunity for practice teaching in Mexico.

An examination of the 12 separate courses or topics that make up the scales described above reveals a few additional insights. South Korean future teachers were unusual in the large percentage (81%) that took the course entitled psychology of mathematics, which looks at the application of cognitive science to mathematics as well as cognitive developmental perspectives on learning mathematics. Related to school topics, a large percentage of Bulgarian sampled future teachers covered the topics of algebra and geometry (over 93%) but very few (less than 26%) covered the other three school topics. This was in contrast to Mexico, where over 75% of the future teachers covered each of algebra, arithmetic, geometry, and probability but only one third took the calculus-related course. Remember, in Mexico they do not take any formal mathematics courses in their preparation to become teachers. It is in these mathematics education courses that they have their opportunities to learn mathematics.

Variation in Course-Taking

The variation in opportunity for the mathematics education topics is also quite large, with a mean standard deviation of 39%, larger than was the case for mathematics (31%). The two scales where there was a substantially larger variation than the overall average were methods for solving school mathematics problems and practical teaching experiences, where both average standard deviations were around 50%. But the next question is how much it varies across the institutions within each country. If that is small, this would suggest that the noted, large total variation is mostly attributable to student choice in course-taking. Similar to formal mathematics coursework, the typical percentage of the variation among institutions is around 14% (see Table 4.5). However, that varies appreciably across the six countries.

The two countries which by far had the largest percentage of variation among sampled institutions were South Korea and Taiwan, where across the five scales the average relative amount of variation was between 25% and 30%. This is an interesting contrast for South Korea, which had only 10% cross-institutional variation in mathematics course-taking, but for Taiwan is similar to what was observed for mathematics pedagogy. These results are somewhat surprising given that for the K–12 system these countries have common standards related to education. The concept of common standards appears to be less applicable for teacher preparation, at least in the area of mathematics pedagogy in South Korea, and for Taiwan in both formal mathematics and mathematics pedagogy.

In contrast, in Mexico, where the Ministry defines the normal school curriculum for all normal schools, more consistency across institutions is observed, given that only 3% of the total variation is related to institutional differences. This is the opposite of Taiwan and South Korea, where the sampled institutions are virtually the same, implying a common view of what teacher preparation should look like, at least from the point of view of mathematics pedagogy and, by implication, formal mathematics. This probably reflects the presence of a

TABLE 4.5. Standard deviations and the percentage of the total variation in the five areas of formal mathematics pedagogy course-taking that is attributable to cross-institutional variation.

	General Mathematics Pedagogy		School Mathematics Topics		History of School Mathematics		Methods of Solving School Mathematics Problems		Opportunity to Practice Teaching Peers or Students	
	SD	Percent Between	SD	Percent Between	SD	Percent Between	SD	Percent Between	SD	Percent Between
Bulgaria	30.5	7.0	17.7	9.6	34.8	3.8	49.7	16.5	49.3	6.1
Germany	27.9	16.4	31.8	9.8	24.8	0.0	39.0	0.3	49.9	14.1
Mexico	30.7	2.9	28.5	8.2	47.0	0.0	48.5	0.0	49.6	3.9
South Korea	30.9	24.8	45.5	17.7	37.8	16.2	50.0	46.1	49.4	44.5
Taiwan	28.8	36.5	42.9	7.3	45.6	9.8	49.3	57.9	33.4	15.3
United States	34.4	11.6	34.3	4.3	39.4	13.4	49.6	0.0	47.6	9.9

national policy. Two of the five topics within mathematics pedagogy have especially small cross-institutional variation typically across the six countries. These two are the history of school mathematics and the theory and principles of school mathematics topics, where the percentage of variation across institutions for both is only around 7% to 9%.

General anomalies to these patterns arise. The Taiwanese sampled institutions' relative amount of variation is extremely large for the general mathematics pedagogy scale (37%) and even larger for methods of solving school mathematics problems (58%). It seems evident that course-taking in these two areas varies across the sampled Taiwanese institutions, suggesting differences in institutional definitions (reflecting the two types of teacher preparation models, as discussed in Chapter 2) of what constitutes important opportunities to learn for future middle school mathematics teachers or, perhaps, that certain institutions do not even offer such courses.

By contrast, course-taking related to the principles and theory of school mathematics topics is more commonly done across the sampled institutions, with only 7% of the relatively large total variation attributable to cross-institutional variation. The course on the methods for solving school mathematics problems was also quite variable across institutions in South Korea (46%) but less so in the United States, where the percentage of total variation attributable to institutional variation was essentially zero. For the United States, where the total variation was large and on average 61% of future teachers took such a course, this implies that although it is not likely a requirement, there is a fairly common expectation across institutions that this course or topic should be taken.

Patterns of Course-Taking

Looking at course-taking one by one (the marginals) tells only part of the story as one attempts to characterize what is typically taken across the six countries and perhaps idiosyncratically within each of the six countries. This analysis characterizes the set of mathematics pedagogy courses taken by future teachers—what might be called the program of study. In this section we look at the sets of courses that were taken together to see if there were any particular sequences of courses that were common across all future middle school mathematics teachers. We attempted to do this with all of the 12 individual courses in mathematics pedagogy but without success, as the number of distinct patterns was overwhelming and defied simple summarization. Most of the course patterns accounted for no more than 5% of those taken by the future teachers. This finding itself tells an interesting story. There does not seem to be a worldwide agreement on what constitutes mathematics pedagogy. Interestingly and in contrast to our expectations, this applied to mathematics as well. We tried the same approach in formal mathematics but were not successful.

However, feeling this to be an important issue, we collapsed the 12 courses into two separate sets, each set to be analyzed separately. The first set includes those courses taken in mathematics pedagogy and included mathematics curricula in schools, psychology of mathematics, methods of teaching mathematics, and teaching practice in mathematics. The topic/course related to classroom assessment should have been included here as well but was too infrequently encountered to be included in this table. The second set included the five courses focusing on the theory and principles of school mathematics topics, including algebra, geometry, arithmetic, probability, and calculus. Left out of these analyses—because we would not have been able to accomplish our goal of identifying patterns with them included—were the history of school mathematics, methods for solving school mathematics problems and, as mentioned, assessment in mathematics instruction.

The first set considered here relates to general mathematics pedagogy. Over all six countries, six patterns accounted for slightly more than two thirds of the future teachers. These are summarized in Table 4.6. There were ten other patterns represented in the course-taking, accounting for the remaining sampled future teachers. The most common pattern included taking all four of the courses. It accounted for only 15% of course-taking of all sampled future teachers. The next most common included all except for the psychology of mathematics course, while the third most common pattern excluded the curriculum course as well. In the end the single most often taken course across all sampled future teachers was the methods course, taken by 70%.

The three most common patterns for each country separately were not the same across countries and did not necessarily match the overall pattern just described. Taking all four courses was the fourth most common pattern (10%) for Bulgarian sampled future teachers but was only the ninth (4%) most common in Germany, most common in South Korea (30%) and Mexico (26%), third most common in Taiwan (18%), and fourth most common in the United States (14%). In Germany, the five most common patterns all included practical experiences, which clearly reflects the importance of the second step of teacher education. The most common pattern in the United States included taking only the methods course and the practical experience course or part of a course.

For the study of school mathematics, five patterns accounted for 78% of the course-taking over all countries and overwhelmingly the most common pattern (40%) included covering none of the topics. By contrast, the next most common pattern (16%) included taking one or more courses covering all five school topics. These two patterns were repeated in all countries with the exception of Bulgaria and Mexico. In Mexico's case only calculus was not covered in

TABLE 4.6. Course-taking patterns for selected formal mathematics pedagogy courses/topics across countries and within each country (percentage and cumulative percentage for each course-taking pattern).

Country	Mathematics Curricula in Schools	Psychology of Mathematics	Methods of Teaching Mathematics	Teaching Practices in Mathematics	Percent	Cumulative Percent
ALL	1	1	1	1	14.9	14.9
ALL	1		1	1	14.6	29.5
ALL			1	1	14.2	43.8
ALL				1	8.8	52.6
ALL			1		7.5	60.2
ALL					7.1	67.2
Bulgaria					22.9	22.9
Bulgaria			1		16.3	39.2
Bulgaria			1	1	11.7	50.9
Bulgaria	1	1	1	1	9.8	60.7
Bulgaria				1	6.3	67.0
Bulgaria	1		1	1	1.5	68.5
Germany	1		1	1	19.4	19.4
Germany				1	15.5	34.8
Germany	1			1	13.5	48.3
Germany					10.1	58.4
Germany			1	1	7.7	66.1
Germany	1	1	1	1	4.0	70.1
Mexico	1	1	1	1	26.2	26.2
Mexico	1	1	1		15.4	41.6
Mexico	1		1		13.1	54.7
Mexico	1		1	1	7.7	62.4
Mexico			1	1	3.3	65.8
Mexico				1	1.1	66.8
South Korea	1	1	1	1	29.5	29.5
South Korea	1		1	1	4.9	34.4
South Korea			1		2.7	37.1
South Korea			1	1	0.6	37.7
South Korea		1	1		15.0	52.7
South Korea		1			11.0	63.7
Taiwan			1	1	31.8	31.8
Taiwan	1		1	1	22.3	54.1
Taiwan	1	1	1	1	17.7	71.8
Taiwan		1	1	1	9.0	80.8
Taiwan			1		7.8	88.6
Taiwan				1	4.9	93.5
United States			1	1	16.5	16.5
United States				1	14.3	30.9
United States	1		1	1	14.3	45.2
United States	1	1	1	1	13.6	58.8
United States					10.2	69.0
United States			1		6.9	75.9

Note. "1" indicates that the course was taken by the future teacher. The absence of a "1" indicates the course was not taken.

the most common pattern, with the second pattern involving all courses being taken—the two accounting for 71%. In Bulgaria, the two most common patterns accounted for a combined 72% of all course-taking and included studying algebra and geometry or algebra, geometry, and arithmetic. In summary, the most common pattern, which represented only 15% of sampled future teachers, was taking all four courses in mathematics pedagogy, yet none of these courses covered the theory and principles of school mathematics topics.[14]

Even more generally, what seems a reasonable summary is that there appears to be little agreement over which opportunities to learn future teachers should have in the area of mathematics pedagogy. This stands in marked contrast to what we found to be the case in mathematics. Underscoring this point even more strongly is the fact that in performing the analysis parallel to what was done for mathematics, in which a criterion of 90% of future teachers reported taking the same course (linear algebra in 20 of 23 institutions), we found no such course being taken in mathematics pedagogy. In fact, the only courses (topics) receiving any concentration across institutions were methods of teaching mathematics and teaching practice, but that was the case in only four of the 23 institutions that prepared future middle school mathematics teachers at the secondary level.

GENERAL PEDAGOGY

Pedagogy not only includes that which is specific to the teaching of mathematics—the focus of the previous section—but it also deals with understanding the psychology of learning and the dynamics of the social context from which the students come, as well as the micro social system of the classroom, the organization and history of schooling, the theory of instruction, and curriculum theory, including assessment, lesson planning, and classroom management, among other issues. It is in this area that there is often much debate about just how much of the myriad of such issues teachers really need to know in a theoretical way as opposed to learning them through practical experience in real classrooms in real schools. To address this there were 15 specific topic areas included in the student questionnaire. These included such formal topics as the history, philosophy, and sociology of education; educational psychology; theory of instruction; general methods of teaching; classroom management; and curriculum theory. Again, future teachers were asked to indicate which of these topics they had taken as a part of their preparation.[15]

We formed two general pedagogy indices. One, termed General Pedagogy, reflects the percentage of all listed courses/topics related to the theories that provide the rationale and academic background of schooling: educational psychology, student diversity, curriculum theory, and so on. The second of these was specific to the organization and operation of the classroom. This included not only classroom management but also coursework in general methods of teaching, including lesson planning and motivating students. These topics all deal with the theory and organizational issues involved with accomplishing the central goal of schooling—organization of the instructional flow toward setting up an environment in which students can learn. This second index is called Instructional Planning and Classroom Management. The means and standard errors across the sampled institutions for the six countries for these two indices are listed in Table 4.7.

Large differences exist in the percentage of topics that are taken related to general pedagogy. Of the 13 possible topics, the typical future teacher in the sampled institutions in the United States took about 55% of them—nearly eight topics (7.7)—during their teacher preparation. This was the most among the six nations, although the sampled future teachers in Mexico and South Korea also studied around half of the topics—about seven courses. By contrast, Bulgarian future teachers studied only around four of the topics (3.7).

For the coursework related to managing the classroom learning environment, different patterns emerged. Sizeable differences in the two indices were evidenced in the South Korean and Taiwanese samples. South Korean sampled future teachers studied on average about one fourth of the topics compared with half for the general pedagogy coursework. German future teachers studied on average about 40% of both types of topics. In the area of instructional and classroom management, which is more directly related to the actual classroom situation, Taiwanese sampled future teachers took an average 56% of the coursework compared to 44% for the general pedagogy courses.

In the area of classroom/instructional management, U.S. future teachers had by far the largest value of the index—68%. Thus, in both areas of general

TABLE 4.7. Country means and standard errors (se) for the percentage of topics covered in two formal general pedagogy areas.

	General Pedagogy		Instructional Planning and Classroom Management	
	Mean	*(se)*	*Mean*	*(se)*
Bulgaria	23.7	(1.9)	22.8	(3.2)
Germany	32.9	(1.5)	33.4	(2.3)
Mexico	51.1	(2.3)	43.9	(3.0)
South Korea	51.6	(2.4)	25.2	(3.5)
Taiwan	43.9	(0.9)	56.1	(1.8)
United States	54.6	(1.9)	67.7	(2.6)

pedagogy, the sampled U.S. future teachers took on average the largest amount of coursework across the six countries—over two thirds of the possible topics, representing on average nine topics. Recall that in the United States for mathematics pedagogy they took on average five courses when rounded to the nearest whole number, implying a total of 18 courses/topics. This contrasts with formal mathematics, where they took a total of 11 courses/topics.

The general pedagogy index is based on 13 different courses or topics. The question is, Are there any particular differences in opportunity to learn related to those specific areas, such as, for example, educational psychology? The courses/topics that were much more frequently covered across all countries (79% or more) in the programs of the future teachers were introduction to education and educational psychology. Five other topics were studied by over 50% of the sampled future teachers. These include classroom assessment, technology, and general methods of teaching. The topics least typically studied included student diversity, educational research, principles of counseling, comparative education, and curriculum theory. The remaining courses were taken by between 40% and 50% of the future teachers.

Most interesting, however, are the anomalies to these general patterns. There were only a few such interaction effects, and these were large. More Taiwanese sampled future teachers had opportunities to learn classroom management and the principles of counseling than was generally the case—85%. Typically across the other countries, less than 30% had such opportunities. The only exception to that was in the United States, where 68% of the sampled future teachers took the opportunity to study classroom management—but only 8% studied the principles of counseling, the lowest among the six countries.

Another interesting anomaly was for the South Korean sampled future teachers, who had fewer opportunities than would be expected, given their general course-taking in these areas, in the general principles and theory of instruction, general methods of teaching, and classroom management—all of which are related to the actual delivery of instruction. A higher percentage of Mexican future teachers typically had opportunities to learn most of the courses in general education, second only to the United States. The one big exception to this was in the introduction to education course. Only 54% indicated that they took that course, while for the other five countries, on average 70% or more of future teachers indicated having had this.

Variation in Course-Taking

The typical country variance for opportunities to learn related to general pedagogy is smaller than what was found for both mathematics and mathematics pedagogy—a standard deviation of 22%. However, for opportunities related to instructional planning and classroom management the variation was more similar to the other two areas—35%. This seems an important difference in that one could imagine that there would be less variation for the area most closely tied to the central role of schooling—namely, instruction—yet the opposite is the case.

Less variation occurs for the more formal disciplinary base of teaching, suggesting that within countries there is more agreement as to what should be taken even though, as cited previously, there was some large variation among the countries. This suggests somewhat of a cultural position related to the opportunity needed for quality teacher preparation in general pedagogy. Sampled South Korean and Mexican future teachers have the largest variation in general pedagogy course-taking and over half of it (58%) is between institutions, suggesting a counterpoint to the argument of a cultural position, at least for South Korea (see Table 4.8). Taiwanese institutions are also more variable in that 32% of the variance is attributed to cross-institutional variation. However, the total variance for the sampled future teacher is quite small—in fact, the smallest of all countries—with a standard deviation of 16%.

For all other countries most of variation in opportunity related to general pedagogy was mainly individual future teacher-driven—around 90% or more. Actually, for both the United States and Bulgaria the estimated percentage of variation was zero. This implies that for the United States, across the 12 sampled institutions, there was little difference in terms of course-taking in general pedagogy. The variation around opportunities related to instructional planning and classroom management was mostly related to individual future teacher choice (85% to 99%). Interestingly, it is again South Korea that has the largest relative amount of variation between its sampled institutions.

TABLE 4.8. Standard deviations and the percentage of the total variation in the two areas of formal general pedagogy course-taking that is attributable to cross-institutional variation.

	General Pedagogy		Instructional Planning and Classroom Management	
	SD	Percent Between	SD	Percent Between
Bulgaria	19.2	0.0	31.5	0.0
Germany	23.7	0.2	37.6	0.6
Mexico	28.3	7.3	36.8	0.8
South Korea	24.3	57.8	35.9	18.4
Taiwan	14.9	32.1	28.6	5.9
United States	27.8	0.0	38.3	7.9

Patterns of Course- or Topic-Taking

Among the main disciplinary areas supporting the practice of teaching—introduction to education, history, philosophy, sociology, and psychology of education—the most common patterns are for future teachers from all countries to take only the introduction to education course or to study all five of the topic areas either as courses or as topics in one or more courses. These two patterns account for 38% of the sampled future teachers, about evenly split between the two. In South Korea half of the future teachers studied all five areas. In both Mexico and the U.S., 31% studied all five. The most common pattern in Bulgaria and Germany was taking only the introduction to education course—38% and 31%, respectively.

For classroom-related topics/courses including general principles and theory of instruction, general methods of teaching, and classroom management, the three most common patterns were: covering all three topics, covering none of them, or covering the theory of instruction and general methods of teaching, including lesson planning and student motivation. These accounted for 58% of all sampled future teachers (Table 4.9). In the United States, taking all three courses was true for 38% of the sampled future teachers, while taking none of the three courses was true for only 16%.

Other notable differences include the fact that almost two thirds of the South Korean sampled future teachers studied none of the three topics on classroom-related management, including instructional management; whereas in Taiwan it was 2% and in the United States, 16%. In the German case this most likely reflects the traditional focus of university education on topics designed to be more academic and the focus of the second phase of teacher education on practical issues without the need to give them a research basis. For Taiwanese sampled future teachers the most common pattern included all three topics. Looking at the 90% criterion, as we did for both mathematics and mathematics pedagogy, leads again to the same conclusion, as only a course in educational psychology was taken by the sampled future teachers in 11 of the 23 institutions preparing secondary teachers. Sociology of education was the closest, with 6 of 23 institutions meeting the 90% criterion. In both areas of pedagogy there appears to be little agreement as to what all future middle school mathematics teachers should study; what little agreement there is focuses on methods of teaching and educational psychology.

PRACTICE-RELATED OPPORTUNITIES

The three previous sections focused on the more formal coursework related to the preparation of future teachers. Clearly, country differences exist regarding

TABLE 4.9. Course-taking patterns for selected formal general pedagogy courses/topics across countries and within each country (percentage and cumulative percentage for each course-taking pattern).

	General Principles of Instruction	General Methods of Teaching	Classroom Management	Percent	Cumulative Percent
ALL				26.8	26.8
ALL	1	1	1	18.9	45.7
ALL	1	1		12.3	58.0
Bulgaria				56.1	56.1
Bulgaria	1	1		13.4	69.5
Bulgaria	1	1	1	7.1	76.7
Germany				38.2	38.2
Germany	1	1		16.4	54.7
Germany	1	1	1	12.4	67.0
Mexico	1	1		28.4	28.4
Mexico				25.7	54.1
Mexico	1	1	1	17.1	71.2
South Korea				56.5	56.5
South Korea	1	1		11.6	68.1
South Korea	1	1	1	6.9	75.0
Taiwan	1	1	1	20.1	20.1
Taiwan	1	1		3.2	23.3
Taiwan				2.3	25.6
United States	1	1	1	37.8	37.8
United States				15.9	53.7
United States	1	1		7.3	61.0

how the limited time available at teacher preparation institutions (universities or colleges for five of the countries) is allocated.

There is, however, another aspect to the learning opportunities provided. This has to do with the more practical aspects of how teaching is accomplished and practiced. Two types of items asked on the future teacher questionnaire are used to characterize what follows. First, questions were asked about the nature of the school-based experiences the teachers gained while they were in teacher preparation. They were asked about the types of practical experiences they had in K–12 schools. We identified five different experience types that they had in addition to practice teaching, or what in the United States is usually referred to as student teaching. These experience types included: observing mathematics instruction, being a teacher aide or assistant for mathematics, teaching practice lessons under supervision, teaching practice lessons without supervision, and general in-school observations not specifically related to mathematics. These were not necessarily courses, but often related experiences that were required as a part of courses in their programs. We formed a six-point scale ranging from zero—having had no practical experiences of the sort described—to five—having had all five types of experiences.

The second index was the number of weeks of practice teaching where they had the full responsibility for teaching more than one class per week. The means for the number of different types of practical experiences is presented in Table 4.10. For the number of weeks of student teaching we used the median that is also presented in Table 4.10.

The mean number of different types of practical experiences in K–12 schools gained as a part of their teacher preparation programs across all six countries was 3.4 out of the possible 6 types listed in the questionnaire. Thus, only about half of the possible types were encountered by the typical future teacher across the six countries. Only Bulgarian sampled future teachers were different on average from those in the other five countries. For them the typical number of different types of opportunities was only 2.3. When it comes to the actual number of weeks of practice teaching defined in terms of having full responsibility for teaching a mathematics class for more than one day a week, the differences across countries were more pronounced.[16]

Over the entire sample, the typical number of weeks of practice teaching was almost five. However, some future teachers reported having had only 1 week of such experiences while others had over 25 weeks. As would be expected given the German system of two-stage preparation, where in the second institution they spend around 1 to 2 years in a situation where one of their major responsibilities is teaching, the typical future teacher in the German sampled institutions had more than double (26 weeks) the number of weeks compared

TABLE 4.10. Means and standard errors (se) for the extent of opportunity related to in-school practical experiences for future teachers in each country.

	Number of Practical Experiences		Number of Weeks of Practice Teaching	
	Mean	*(se)*	*Mean*	*(se)*
Bulgaria	2.3	(0.2)	4.6	(0.3)
Germany	4.0	(0.1)	25.9	(1.8)
Mexico	3.5	(0.2)	10.7	(0.9)
South Korea	3.4	(0.2)	3.8	(0.4)
Taiwan	3.6	(0.1)	8.1	(0.7)
United States	3.8	(0.1)	11.5	(1.3)

with those in Mexico and the United States (11–12 weeks) and five times that of the Bulgarian future teachers (5 weeks).[17] In Germany, the estimate of 26 weeks is probably low as the nature of the sampling design took students in the Phase 2 institution but was not able to distinguish between those in their first year from those in their second year. This implies that the mean would be even higher if we had only sampled students in their last year of Phase 2 preparation.

The types of K–12 experiences that future teachers had varied across countries. For example, around 85% or higher of the future teachers in each country observed mathematics classes and taught a single lesson under supervision. However, the United States sampled future teachers were somewhat less likely to have had this type of experience (73%). Fewer of the sampled future teachers had the other three types of practical experiences—but this also varied by country. For example, teaching a single lesson without supervision was done by 70% to 85% of the sampled future teachers in all of the countries except for Bulgaria and the United States (only around 40%). However, an overall view of the numbers reveals that there might be, in fact, some cultural differences in responding to our questions. Take Germany as an example. As pointed out before, teachers in that country have by far the most weeks of practical experience. The kinds of responsibilities that the future teachers might assume are quite regulated. Yet when they are asked to evaluate their practical experiences, the German mean is the lowest. This most likely reflects the future teachers' high expectations and their annoyance about the fragmented German teacher-education system that requires them to study at the university level for many years before they can go into schools. This is precisely what Heine and colleagues (2002) call "the reference group effect."

Were these types of practical K–12 experiences relatively common within a country or did they vary appreciably, likely reflecting institutional differences with respect to how they viewed the importance of these types of activities in the preparation of future teachers? The total variation across future teachers was large in each country in terms of the number of types of K–12 practical experiences. The standard deviations ranged from around 2 (United States) to 2.5 (Mexico). There was little to no variation within countries across institutions for South Korea, Taiwan, and Mexico. Apparently in these countries there is a common view of what should be included in the teacher preparation programs related to such practical experiences.

In the United States, where the total variation is the smallest of all countries, a little more than one quarter (27%) of that variation was across the sampled institutions—implying substantial institutional differences. However, other than the United States, the variation that was reasonably large given a six-point scale derived mainly from within institutional variation. This occurs in the same countries where there is no such large variation for taking courses in areas of mathematics such as calculus or the study of functions—namely, in Taiwan and South Korea.

Pulling all these data together suggests a lack of stringent requirements in the area for all but the United States. However, in the United States there is institutional variation, which likely reflects differences in requirements, or at least in recommended K–12 experiences. The variation with respect to the number of weeks of practice teaching with full responsibility for the class on 2 or more days a week was very large in all countries except for Bulgaria, with the standard deviations ranging from about 10 to 20 weeks. Part of the problem here, in terms of interpreting these data, is the future teachers' interpretation of the phrase *full responsibility*. Some, we speculate, assumed that since it was a supervised practicum they couldn't have had full responsibility, while to others it meant teaching mathematics for the whole day on their own. This, unfortunately, cannot be resolved from the data we have.

The second question asked of the future teachers was to what extent they had experienced 29 different types of opportunities related to the more practical aspects associated with classroom instruction. Some examples include trying out new approaches to teaching mathematics; learning how to teach students to use algorithms; learning how to probe student understandings; preparing mathematics lessons; learning about student misconceptions; learning about the country's or state's curriculum standards; learning about middle school teaching materials; incorporating classroom management into teaching; and gaining a deep understanding about middle school number, geometry, algebra, function, and data/probability topics, among others. For each of these topics the future teacher was asked to indicate the extent of their opportunity to learn that topic, ranging from "not at all" (coded 1) through "to a great extent" (coded 6), with four unlabeled gradations in between.

These experiences and learnings could have been gained in any of the pedagogy courses the future teachers took, although most of them would have likely occurred in mathematics pedagogy courses, given that almost all of them are defined specifically in terms of teaching middle school mathematics. Such experiences and learnings could also have been gained in their practice teaching or in other activities related to observing or assisting in K–12 schools as a part of their teacher preparation. The 29 separate items were combined into seven indices: classroom management and professional practice (not mathematics-specific); instructional interaction around mathematics; methods of teaching algorithms, proofs, and nonroutine problems (abbreviated as proofs); general methods of teaching middle school (methods); understanding how students learn (learning); deep understanding of middle school mathematics topics (mathematics topics); and planning, preparing, and practicing mathematics lessons (practice).[18] For these seven opportunity variables, means of 3 to 4 were taken to suggest a midlevel of opportunity—adequate—for the typical future teacher, while means less than 3 indicate that the typical future teacher believed he or she had had relatively little (inadequate) opportunity in that area.

However, means greater than 4 indicate an extensive amount of opportunity to learn, at least in the judgment of the sampled future teachers. This, at least, is our interpretive frame—the actual means are presented in Table 4.11 and the reader certainly can use other interpretive frames. Over the six countries and across the seven scales on practical pedagogy the mean was 3.9, indicating a midlevel of the opportunity to learn.

Upon closer examination, however, there are significant differences among countries and across the seven indices as well as various interactions that produce important anomalies in terms of the opportunities to learn for the future middle school mathematics teachers. For example, Germany's sampled future teachers reported that they had not received adequate opportunities to learn in six of the seven areas for which the mean ratings were all less than 3, ranging from 2.3 to 2.8. Only the opportunities related to gaining a deeper understanding of various middle school mathematics topics—what we have termed "the advanced study of elementary mathematics"—were rated as being adequate but not extensive. That mean was, however, still low (3.4), indicating significantly lower opportunities than is typical across all countries (a mean of 4.1).

In contrast, in Mexico and Taiwan the sampled future teachers indicated extensive opportunities in general across the seven areas—means ranging from 4.1 to 4.8. This was especially true for the Mexican future teachers. For example,

TABLE 4.11. Means and standard errors (se) for the extent of opportunity related to attaining practical knowledge for classroom instruction for each country.

	School Mathematics Topics		Teaching Including Classroom Management		Instructional Interaction Around Mathematics		Methods of Teaching Algorithms, Nonroutine Problems, and Proofs		Teaching Mathematics in the Lower-Secondary Level		Understanding How Students Learn Mathematics		Working With and Understanding Lower-Secondary Math Topics	
	Mean	*(se)*	*Mean*	*(se)*	*Mean*	*(se)*	*Mean*	*(se)*	*Mean*	*(se)*	*Mean*	*(se)*	*Mean*	*(se)*
Bulgaria	3.3	(0.1)	3.6	(0.2)	3.9	(0.1)	3.7	(0.1)	4.0	(0.2)	3.9	(0.2)	4.2	(0.1)
Germany	2.2	(0.1)	2.3	(0.1)	2.6	(0.1)	2.6	(0.1)	2.8	(0.1)	2.6	(0.1)	3.4	(0.1)
Mexico	4.6	(0.1)	4.8	(0.1)	4.5	(0.1)	4.1	(0.1)	4.6	(0.1)	4.4	(0.1)	4.4	(0.1)
South Korea	2.7	(0.2)	3.0	(0.1)	3.5	(0.1)	3.6	(0.1)	4.3	(0.1)	4.3	(0.1)	4.5	(0.1)
Taiwan	2.5	(0.1)	4.2	(0.1)	4.5	(0.1)	4.1	(0.1)	4.8	(0.1)	4.5	(0.1)	4.4	(0.1)
United States	2.2	(0.1)	3.6	(0.1)	3.8	(0.1)	3.3	(0.1)	4.2	(0.1)	3.6	(0.1)	3.8	(0.1)

related to classroom management, the reported extent of OTL for the typical future teacher was 4.8. This is especially significant given that the mean for the other five countries was only 3.3. From the previously described patterns for countries and for the seven areas, the only other significant deviation centers mainly around the South Korean future teachers. These future teachers do not fit the general pattern at all. They were provided with many fewer opportunities to learn in the areas of classroom management; instructional interaction around mathematics; and planning, preparing, and practicing mathematics lessons than would be expected given their general level of OTL in practical pedagogy and the general level of OTL for these areas across countries. But the future teachers reported extensive OTL with respect to understanding the middle school mathematics topics. In fact, the self-reported mean of 4.5 was the highest across all countries. The U.S. future teachers reported the second lowest amount of opportunity (a mean of 3.7) in general across the seven areas (second only to Germany) and reported the second lowest extent of OTL for the study of methods related to teaching algorithms, nonroutine problems, and proofs (3.3).

Given the particular practical relevance of each of the items from the questionnaire that make up the seven scales, we examined each of them to determine if there were any particular idiosyncrasies worth noting that weren't captured by the seven scales. We do this since each of the 29 items deals with some specific aspect related to what these future teachers will need to do as future middle school mathematics teachers.[19] In terms of individual items, the three following generally received significantly larger amounts of opportunity across all countries: understanding middle school algebra topics; planning and preparing mathematics lessons; and learning general methods of teaching mathematics. In contrast, the following received very little emphasis: learning how to teach students how to do mathematical proofs, learning how to teach students how to solve nonroutine problems, planning mathematics lessons that are sensitive to the learning needs of students, and learning how to contribute to school development.

Within that context and the patterns across countries in terms of the provision of general OTL across all 29 items (which was the same as described for the seven indices that we reported on previously), we noted the following important interaction-type effects. There were exceptions to the above patterns related to those areas which in general received little coverage in the teacher preparation programs. For example, OTL related to learning how to teach students to do mathematical proofs was reported by the future teachers in Bulgaria and South Korea as being more extensive than in general, but for U.S. teachers the reported extent of OTL was exceptionally low. Similarly for OTL related to learning how to teach students how to solve nonroutine problems, the noteworthy exception to the general pattern was for the German sampled future teachers, who reported more extensive coverage related to this aspect of teaching than they tended to in general on practical issues.

Mexican future teachers were given greater opportunities related to learning how to plan mathematics lessons that are sensitive to the learning needs of students with diverse social, cultural, and ethnic backgrounds. Future teachers in both Germany and the United States reported having had extensive training related to learning about their country's or state's curriculum standards in mathematics. The sampled future teachers in South Korea indicated that they had had little opportunity to learn how to incorporate classroom management strategies into their teaching compared to other countries' future teachers. Finally, the U.S. sampled future teachers indicated exceptionally low OTL related both to learning about mathematics textbooks and teaching materials and how to give feedback to middle school students about their mathematics learning.

The different amounts of emphasis future teachers reported for their OTL for particular practical areas related to teaching middle school mathematics suggest differences among the sampled institutions regarding what they found important enough to provide such opportunities as a part of their formal program. Here again, we remind the reader that these are the future teachers' own assessments about the extent of the opportunities they received while in their teacher preparation programs. This requires their judgments on what the varying amounts are. We would argue that in spite of the subjective nature of that judgment with regard to how much counts (e.g., as "a great extent"), it is still relevant as these individuals about to enter the field of teaching reflect on what they know about these issues and how much OTL they received related to them. Certainly the aggregate measure is likely to be more valid. Such a judgment, at its very least, reflects how comfortably they envision themselves in each of these areas. Furthermore, given the mean level differences across countries, these probably reflect not only differences across institutions in definitions related to what is necessary to produce good middle school mathematics teachers but also country-level differences related, if not to official policy prescriptions, at least to the zeitgeist created by the scholars who study these issues in the country and those who are directly involved in designing teacher preparation programs.

Variation in Practical Experiences

This leads to examining the variation related to six of the seven scales (excluding school mathematics topics, as an alternative measure of this was discussed in the mathematics section) and the degree to which that variation in OTL is mostly individually or institutionally driven (see Table 4.12). The total variation across all future teachers within each of the countries is relatively small—much smaller than was the case for course-taking indices discussed in this chapter. The mean value of the standard deviations averaged across all countries and all the scales was 2.2, which is relatively small for a six-point scale. In general, across the six scales the variation was the largest in Germany and the smallest in South Korea and Taiwan but, again, the differences are relatively small in absolute values, even though the variation in Germany is one and a half times as large as that in Taiwan. Clearly, sampled future teachers in Taiwan report more similar amounts of OTL related to these six scales than do the future teachers in Germany. The one scale to have substantially more variation across all countries is developing an understanding of how students learn middle school mathematics.

A few notable exceptions to these general patterns related to country and area of OTL emerged. The area of methods of teaching algorithms, nonroutine problems, and proofs had the most anomalies. The future teachers in both Germany and the U.S. exhibited substantially less variation in this area than would be expected given their general variation on these scales. This, coupled with the U.S. mean, tells an important story. The sampled U.S. future teachers had the second lowest mean for OTL in this area and also one of the smallest amounts of variation, meaning the typical sampled future teacher in the United States indicated having received the low end of adequate OTL in this area; and what is true for the typical future teacher holds for most of them. The same was true for sampled German future teachers if we assume that the mean tendency of the two groups of German future teachers endorsed the statements in the same way.

TABLE 4.12. Standard deviations and the percentage of the total variation on the extent of opportunity related to attaining practical knowledge for classroom instruction that is attributable to cross-institutional variation.

	Teaching Including Classroom Management		Instructional Interaction Around Mathematics		Methods of Teaching Algorithms, Nonroutine Problems, and Proofs		Teaching Mathematics in the Lower-Secondary Level		Understanding How Students Learn Mathematics		Working With and Understanding Lower-Secondary Mathematics Topics	
	SD	% Between	SD	% Between	SD	% Between	SD	% Between	SD	% Between	SD	% Between
Bulgaria	1.5	15.0	1.2	11.2	1.3	10.3	1.4	3.8	1.6	12.7	1.2	0.0
Germany	1.4	14.9	1.3	17.5	1.2	8.0	1.4	16.2	1.6	9.4	1.6	10.4
Mexico	1.0	1.4	1.0	9.8	1.2	0.0	1.1	2.3	1.2	3.9	1.0	0.0
South Korea	1.0	7.1	1.0	9.1	0.9	5.3	1.0	18.7	1.1	3.8	0.9	0.0
Taiwan	1.0	2.0	0.8	5.9	0.9	6.4	0.9	4.1	1.1	2.8	1.1	11.3
United States	1.3	1.0	1.1	10.2	1.0	0.0	1.2	8.8	1.4	11.6	1.3	12.9

Little opportunity, related to this area, seems to be the case for most sampled U.S. future teachers, likely reflecting that this is not generally viewed by teacher preparation institutions as a key area in which to prepare future middle school mathematics teachers, at least as reported by the future teachers themselves. This hypothesis is supported by the fact that the variation among U.S. future teachers in this area of study is 100% the result of individual choices: none of the variation is attributable to institutional differences.

Most of the variation in OTL related to any of these practical experiences was found to be at the individual level, with less than 10% typically attributable to institutional differences. The exceptions to that story are Germany and Taiwan, but in different ways. Across the seven practical areas, Germany typically exhibits a larger percentage (13%) of the variation at the institutional level, which is likely a reflection of different definitions of teacher preparation at different sampled institutions.

Conversely, Taiwan and Mexico have the opposite pattern, whereby most of the total variation is individual in nature, likely reflecting individual future teacher choice. This is not surprising given the very practical nature of these types of learning experiences; there are many exceptions to the general pattern described previously. For example, in Germany some 10% to 18% of the variation in OTL is related to cross-institutional differences for all the areas except two. The exceptions are methods of teaching algorithms, nonroutine problems and proofs, and understanding how students learn middle school mathematics where only 8–9% of the variation is at the institutional level.

By contrast, in Taiwan the proportion of variation at the individual level ranges from 94–100% for all the areas with the exception of gaining an understanding of middle school topics, where it is 89%. In South Korea most of the variation in OTL related to practical experiences is found at the individual level. The only exception is general teaching methods in mathematics, where the between-institutional variation accounts for almost 20% of the total variation. This must be an area where the different institutions have varying notions of the importance of practical experiences related to this area. In the United States the source of variation for these seven areas varies itself, with four topic areas having 10 or more percent of the variation at the institutional level, and three having less than 10—in fact, two of these three have virtually no variation at the institutional level. Those two are classroom management and methods of teaching algorithms, nonroutine problems, and proofs. For the latter the total variation in OTL is very small, as is the mean. All this points in the direction that providing OTL related to this area is not a high priority for any of the sampled institutions and there is very little variation; what little does exist is due to self-selection. Perhaps the reason OTL is so small in this area in general is because few institutions even offer the possibility of such an area of study.

HOW DO ALL THESE OPPORTUNITIES FIT TOGETHER?

In the previous sections we described the types of course experiences and opportunities future teachers reported they had received in relation to key areas associated with teacher preparation. For each of these areas we reported the average percentage of content topics covered in one or more of the courses taken by the sampled future middle school teachers in each of the six countries. The topics represented all the types of content included in teacher preparation programs in any of the six countries. For most countries each of these content areas typically represented a course. We have already mentioned anomalies based on median polishes. In this section we look at the three areas of mathematics, mathematics pedagogy, and general pedagogy in concert to gain an understanding of the teacher preparation program as a whole. In focusing on such profiles we also remove some of the possible cultural bias resulting from differences in response tendencies across the countries.

We began this chapter with an indication of the size of the whole program—the total number of hours involved in the preparation of mathematics middle school teachers. We now look at how those total times are allocated to the three areas. We first examine the institutional data to determine what program staff and documents at those institutions told us were the official requirements. These were then averaged across the sampled institutions within

TABLE 4.13. Mean percentage of total instructional clock hours in each country required for mathematics, mathematics pedagogy, second specialization study, general pedagogy, and other areas.

	Mathematics	Mathematics Pedagogy	Second Specialization	General Pedagogy	Other
Bulgaria	58%	4%	27%	5%	6%
Germany					
Elementary	13%	22%	35%	30%	
Secondary	27%	11%	38%	24%	
Mexico		25%		75%	
South Korea	43%	3%		12%	42%
Taiwan	56%	7%		10%	27%
United States					
Elementary	20%	3%	11%	27%	39%
Secondary	30%	7%	8%	29%	27%

each of the six countries. Table 4.13 presents these results. The data characterize the percentage of the total clock hours that are designated for the different areas associated with teacher preparation.

Coursework associated with general university requirements such as liberal arts is listed as "other." Keep in mind that as Table 4.1 indicated, the total number of clock hours varied substantially across the six countries' sampled institutions, ranging from around 1,700 to 2,300 hours for five of the countries; but for Mexican institutions the total number of hours was approximately 3,600. In Table 4.13, as was the case in Table 4.1, the subprograms by which middle school teachers are prepared are listed separately. For the United States only the elementary and secondary programs are listed, given inadequate data for the middle school preparation programs.

Again the variation was substantial. For mathematics instruction the required hours in Bulgarian and Taiwanese sampled institutions was over half of the total number of hours involved in teacher preparation and more than 40% for the South Korean institutions. Furthermore, there were no formal mathematics course requirements other than the mathematics that was a part of the mathematics pedagogy courses in Mexico, and only around 10% to 20% for both German and U.S. institutions, where the preparation was done as a part of an elementary program. The sampled secondary preparation programs in the United States and Germany required around 30% of the total hours of preparation to center on formal mathematics. These differences are even more pronounced when one considers the fact that the Taiwanese institutions required at least 150 more semester units of total instruction than did all of the other countries, with the exception of Mexico. This difference between Taiwan and the other five countries translates to a difference in actual clock hours of mathematics instruction to 500 hours more than in Bulgaria and up to 600 hours more than in the United States, where the middle school teachers are prepared as a part of the elementary school program. Yet all of these future teachers are being prepared to teach middle school mathematics.

In the United States, even the secondary preparation program falls short of Taiwan by some 768 clock hours of mathematics. The differences in general pedagogy were pronounced, ranging from around 10% of the total hours of preparation in Taiwan and South Korea to around 25% to 30% in the United States and Germany, and up to 75% of the clock hours in Mexico. Mathematics pedagogy, on the other hand, varied from around 11% or less in Germany (secondary preparation), to about 4% or less in South Korea, Bulgaria, and the United States (elementary preparation program). The Bulgarian institutions were the least involved in pedagogy, as only 9% was required in the two areas of pedagogy. The relative amounts of clock hours for each country can be summarized graphically, as shown in Figure 4.2.

FIGURE 4.2. Relative emphases associated with four aspects of mathematics teacher preparation for the six countries. The area of the circle is proportional to the total clock hours associated with teacher preparation.

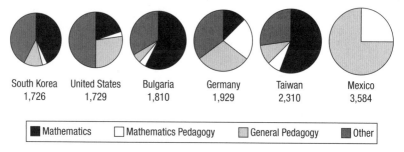

| South Korea | United States | Bulgaria | Germany | Taiwan | Mexico |
| 1,726 | 1,729 | 1,810 | 1,929 | 2,310 | 3,584 |

■ Mathematics   □ Mathematics Pedagogy   ▨ General Pedagogy   ■ Other

Since these results are in terms of averages across the sampled institutions, the standard deviations indicate the degree to which these are more like country-level requirements. In fact, for the pedagogy requirements these were common for both Mexico and Taiwan as the standard deviation was zero. In all of the other countries except the United States the estimated standard deviations were relatively small. In the United States, however, the estimated standard deviations for both types of preparation programs were some four to five times larger than the largest standard deviation for any of the other five countries.

Apparently, across the sampled U.S. institutions there was little agreement as to how much pedagogy should be required in the preparation of middle school mathematics teachers. In fact, among elementary programs involved in middle school teacher preparation, the estimated standard deviation was almost 200 against a mean of 515. Such uniformity of requirements in terms of clock hours, which was characteristic of all countries except the United States, was not the case for the number of hours required in mathematics. Taiwan, South Korea, and Bulgaria, which on average across the sampled institutions required many more hours than was required in the other countries' sampled institutions, had the largest estimated standard deviations and the United States had the smallest amount of variation around the smallest mean value. This implies that there is general agreement that future middle school teachers prepared in those programs only need a low number of hours of mathematics, which is also the case for future elementary teachers.

Another way to characterize the issue of balance is to look specifically at the ratio of mathematics required hours to pedagogy required hours. Mexico is left out of this calculation since all mathematics instruction is integrated with mathematics pedagogy instruction and thus the amount of time devoted to mathematics instruction may not be uniquely estimated. Statements related to proportions of hours using the mean values are important even though they do not characterize the actual differences in number of required hours (given the fact that the total number of clock hours varies across institutions). These statements reflect the conception—no matter how many total hours are available—of how those hours are to be traded off against each other given that the total, whatever it is, is limited. We argue that it reflects the institution's sense of value of which is more important or how the valuable, limited time available for teacher preparation should be divided between content knowledge and pedagogy.

The value of the ratio can be less than one (indicating more pedagogy course requirements than mathematics course requirements), one (an equal allocation of the clock hours to the two areas), or more than one (indicating relatively more coursework in mathematics than pedagogy). In effect, we argue that values less than one imply the conception that pedagogy is more important than content. When the ratio is greater than one, content is viewed as more important than pedagogy, and when equal to one there is an even balance between the two. On the other hand, the total number of clock hours reflects the country's or institution's definition of how much time overall is required to prepare a high-quality, middle school mathematics teacher. We argue that both are important.

In Bulgaria, South Korea, and Taiwan the estimated ratios are greater than one. In Germany and the United States the ratios for both types of preparation programs vary between .25 and .83. In the two Asian countries the ratio is around 3 and in Bulgaria, around 6. Clearly, in Bulgaria pedagogical preparation is relegated to a very minor role, while in South Korea and Taiwan it is about a three-to-one ratio of content to pedagogy.

The big exception is for the U.S. and German sampled institutions, where the estimated ratios are slightly less than one for secondary teacher preparation but only around .25 for German elementary teacher preparation. In this case one can conclude that pedagogy is more important in the preparation of middle school mathematics teachers, reflecting the fact that these teachers are being prepared to teach not only grades 5 through 10 but also elementary grades 1 through 4. In the case of the German elementary preparation programs sampled, pedagogy is viewed as about four times more important than content. These are important differences and, as will be seen in Chapter 5, are consistent with the patterns of knowledge across the countries.

All of the above is in terms of formal requirements at the institutional level, but how that plays out in terms of specific courses and topics that are actually taken is what was described in the previous sections. However, those indications in terms of courses or content areas were examined separately for each of the mathematics and two pedagogy areas. Here we look at what number of courses (or, at the least, what number of content areas) were actually taken in each of the three broad areas within the requirements just discussed in terms of total clock hours. When characterizing the preparation of future teachers using these data, we have no way of differentiating required from elective courses, so what is true here in terms of the number of courses or topics in each area could be different from what was just described, which was defined only in terms of requirements.

Table 4.14 indicates the proportion of the number of courses taken in each of the three areas as calculated from Table 4.2. Comparable to the results for the required courses as derived from Table 4.1, the ratio of the number of mathematics courses to the number of pedagogy courses (mathematics pedagogy and general pedagogy) taken is greater than one in all countries except the United States (.92).[20] In Germany and the United States, where future middle school teachers are prepared in different programs, the sampled future teachers reported major differences between the primary (elementary) and secondary programs. In both countries the sampled future teachers prepared in secondary programs had ratios more similar to the other countries but the ratios for the elementary were less than one.

The percentage of the pedagogy topics that are related to mathematics pedagogy for each of the countries is also discernible from Table 4.14. For each country, the sum of the percentages across the three areas is 100, which represents the total mathematics teacher preparation (ignoring coursework unrelated to being prepared as a middle school mathematics teacher). We defined a ratio of the proportion of teacher preparation time related to mathematics pedagogy

TABLE 4.14. Mean percentage of total courses taken (or topics studied) in each country related to mathematics, mathematics pedagogy, and general pedagogy as reported by future mathematics teachers.

	Proportion of Teacher Preparation Devoted to Mathematics	Proportion of Teacher Preparation Devoted to Mathematics Pedagogy	Proportion of Teacher Preparation Devoted to General Pedagogy
Bulgaria	61%	22%	17%
Germany	56%	17%	27%
Primary	45%	24%	31%
Secondary	53%	18%	29%
Mexico	0%	50%	50%
South Korea	55%	17%	28%
Taiwan	57%	18%	25%
United States	48%	17%	35%
Primary	42%	20%	37%
Middle	44%	20%	37%
Secondary	50%	18%	32%

versus general pedagogy. These ratios are all less than one, except for Bulgaria and Mexico, indicating that, typically, future teachers took more coursework in general pedagogy than they did in mathematics pedagogy. The ratios ranged from .54 in the United States to 1.2 in Bulgaria. For the United States this indicates that although the typical future teacher takes a large number of pedagogy-related courses, only about half of them are related to mathematics. It is also true that they take a relatively small number of mathematics courses.

The last way we approach this issue is to trichotomize the course-taking or topic coverage in each of the three areas. For mathematics the three groups were taking (a) less than 9 courses (topics), (b) 9–13 courses, and (c) more than 13. In mathematics education the cut-off points were (a) less than 2, (b) 2–3 courses, and (c) more than 3. Finally, general pedagogy was split based on (a) less than 3, (b) 3–4, and (c) more than 4. Over all sampled future teachers without regard to country identification, five patterns accounted for over two thirds of the cases. Figure 4.3 gives those results as well as the country-specific results.

Slightly more than one fourth of all future teachers in the sample took the highest category in each of the three areas. This implies that typically one fourth of sampled future teachers in the six countries took more than 13 mathematics courses, more than 3 mathematics pedagogy courses, and more than 4 general pedagogy courses. Interestingly, the next two course-taking patterns—which, when combined with the first one, account for 52.1% of the future teachers—take less only of mathematics and mathematics pedagogy. This suggests that mathematics pedagogy is not as important as general pedagogy, at least as reported by the course-taking reported to us by the future teachers.

The combination of the highest category for each of the three broad areas was the most commonly taken among the sampled future teachers in Bulgaria (21%), South Korea (49%), and Taiwan (56%). It accounted for only 7% in Germany. The most common pattern, accounting for more than one fifth of the sample in Germany, is a lower number of mathematics topics but the highest categories of mathematics pedagogy and general pedagogy topics. This pattern clearly reflects the lower-secondary teachers being trained together with elementary teachers. In contrast, the remaining three patterns reflect typical secondary programs with a substantial variation in the amount of mathematics pedagogy topics, which is reality given the big differences between federal states in this respect. Only 21% of sampled U.S. teachers took the pattern with the most coursework in each of the three areas. More took the pattern that included the second highest level of course-taking in mathematics (24%). In Taiwan only three patterns were needed to account for 80% of the sampled future teachers (in South Korea almost the same percentage was reached with four patterns). The final concluding thought for this chapter concerns the amount of variation across the institutions within the countries in terms of the self-reported course-taking.

FIGURE 4.3. Course-taking patterns in three areas—mathematics, mathematics pedagogy, and general pedagogy—as reported by future mathematics teachers in each country (percent and cumulative percent).

| | Number of Courses/Topics | | | | |
	Mathematics	Mathematics Pedagogy	General Pedagogy	Percent	Cumulative Percent
ALL	■	●	◆	26.4	26.4
ALL	□	●	◆	18.7	45.1
ALL	■	◉	◆	7.0	52.1
ALL	■	○	◆	1.4	53.5
ALL	■	○	◇	0.2	53.7
Bulgaria	■	●	◆	21.3	21.3
Bulgaria	□	●	◆	12.4	33.7
Bulgaria	■	◉	◆	1.2	34.9
Germany	□	●	◆	21.0	21.0
Germany	■	●	◆	6.9	27.9
Germany	■	◉	◆	5.3	33.2
Germany	■	○	◆	0.7	33.9
Mexico	□	●	◆	39.4	39.4
Mexico	■	●	◆	6.4	45.8
South Korea	■	●	◆	49.3	49.3
South Korea	□	●	◆	13.3	62.6
South Korea	■	◉	◆	5.5	68.1
South Korea	■	○	◆	4.0	72.1
South Korea	■	○	◇	1.9	74.0
Taiwan	■	●	◆	56.2	56.2
Taiwan	■	◉	◆	18.6	74.8
Taiwan	□	●	◆	4.6	79.4
Taiwan	■	○	◆	3.1	82.5
United States	□	●	◆	24.0	24.0
United States	■	●	◆	21.0	45.0
United States	■	◉	◆	3.6	48.6

Mathematics Key: ■ > 13 courses   ▣ 9–13 courses   □ < 9 courses
Mathematics Pedagogy Key: ● > 3 courses   ◉ 2–3 courses   ○ < 2 courses
General Pedagogy Key: ◆ > 4 courses   ◈ 3–4 courses   ◇ < 3 courses

Overall, the average percentage of the total variation among future teachers that was attributable to institutional variation was around 10–13%. This implies that most of the differences in course-taking occurred among students within institutions, likely reflecting individual choice or program difference where more than one existed within the institution. For Taiwan that average percentage was nearly double—32% for mathematics course-taking, 25% for mathematics pedagogy course-taking, and 19% for general pedagogy. However, for the extent of OTL obtained in the program related to practical knowledge and experiences, it was only 5%. For South Korea the difference among institutions was greatest for the general pedagogy course-taking (38%)—almost four times larger than what was the case for formal mathematics course-taking. German and Mexican sampled institutions varied very little across institutions in all of these areas—less than 10% of the total variation.

SOME GENERAL CONCLUSIONS

In this concluding section we make some observations about the nature of the opportunities provided for the preparation of future lower-secondary (middle grades) mathematics teachers. Bringing together several elements from the preceding descriptions reveals an important story about each country's sampled institutions and future mathematics teachers. The following overall profiles demonstrate particularly sharp contrasts for the sampled institutions in the United States.

The story for the Bulgarian part of the sample is rather straightforward: Lower-secondary teacher preparation focused mainly on mathematics with little pedagogy (a ratio of 6 to 1), and what pedagogy existed was split between mathematics and general pedagogy. Mexican sampled institutions presented a very different profile, in which the number of required clock hours exceeded all other countries by at least 1,274 hours and exceeded what was done by most of the other five countries by around 1,700 hours. Almost all of that time was spent on studying pedagogy with no formal mathematics instruction, and any coverage of mathematics topics only occurred in mathematics pedagogy courses.

For the sampled U.S. institutions, the total number of clock hours required was not that different from the sampled South Korean, German, and Bulgarian institutions. However, it was quite different from the Taiwanese institutions as well as those in Mexico. Yet in terms of required clock hours in mathematics, the United States was very different from all of the other countries except Germany. The required U.S. clock hours in mathematics were substantially below that of the other countries (this was especially true for Taiwan); only Mexico and Germany were lower. Within the United States, middle school teachers who prepared in an elementary or middle school preparation program had around 600 clock hours less of required mathematics. In short, U.S. future teachers, at least those sampled, were required to take substantially less formal mathematics courses than future teachers in the other countries, with the exception of Mexico and the elementary program in Germany.

Using the data provided by the future teachers leads to much the same conclusion about the emphasis on mathematics in their mathematics teacher preparation programs. On the other hand, these same U.S. future teachers covered more general pedagogy topics than all of the other countries except Mexico and South Korea. Using a ratio of mathematics to pedagogy, we found that all of the countries' future teachers took more coursework in mathematics than they did in pedagogy. For the United States it was the opposite. More specifically, they took about twice as many general pedagogy courses as they did mathematics pedagogy courses. In fact, the future teachers took less mathematics pedagogy hours than all other countries except Germany, which trains teachers in two full subjects like the United States does, naturally leaving less time for each of them. Simply stated, sampled U.S. future middle school mathematics teachers covered one of the smallest number of mathematics topics (excluding Mexico), as well as the second lowest number of mathematics pedagogy topics, but covered the most general pedagogy topics (tied with two other countries). German future elementary mathematics teachers reported a similar pattern of emphasis in their preparation, but with fewer topics covered in general pedagogy.

By way of contrast, the Taiwanese and South Korean future mathematics teachers covered more formal mathematics topics and mathematics pedagogy topics as well as a high number of general pedagogy topics. When asked specifically about the coverage of advanced school topics and the coverage of methods of teaching algorithms, nonroutine problems, and proofs, U.S. sampled future teachers as well as their German counterparts indicated less extensive coverage of these two topics than was the case in the other four countries.

All this suggests very strongly that the U.S. pattern of course-taking across the three areas shows a weakness in the coverage of mathematics, whether this coverage is considered in terms of the formal discipline itself or how it relates to schooling. Yet much more emphasis on general pedagogy is found in the U.S. sample. This pattern is similar to Germany, although more coursework is taken in mathematics, especially for those future teachers prepared in a secondary program, and all teachers are trained in two subjects, which gives the advantage of avoiding out-of-field teaching. The lack of strong preparation in the United States on issues of substance and pedagogy with respect to mathematics is made even more starkly when we consider aspects of both that are especially germane to middle school curriculum. The smallest percentage of future teachers in the sample took linear algebra as well as fewer courses in advanced mathematics, many of which deal with functions, abstract algebra, and calculus, which also is a foundation area for functions. On top of that they also took less school-related mathematics—including algebra—and indicated fewer opportunities to learn how to teach algorithms, proofs, and solving nonroutine problems. All of these topics are covered to a much greater extent in Taiwan and South Korea.

CHAPTER 5

What Do Future Teachers Know?

In the previous chapters we described in great detail the types of opportunities future teachers had to learn formal mathematics, mathematics pedagogy, and general pedagogy and to gain practical experience. Mathematics pedagogy includes understanding the mathematical theory underlying typical lower- and upper-secondary school topics. No institution in the study excluded these types of experiences in their teacher preparation programs. Even the sampled Mexican institutions that do not include formal mathematics courses taught by mathematicians had students study some formal mathematics, but as a part of their mathematics pedagogy courses.

This chapter focuses on what content knowledge and pedagogical content knowledge these future teachers knew as they finished their programs, essentially ready to teach middle school mathematics. What they knew by the end of their program was most likely influenced by the coursework they took at the university as well as the mathematics they had studied before entering the university. This is important, as it represents the knowledge of mathematics they possess as they become eligible to teach lower-secondary mathematics.

From a different point of view, we are also interested in knowing what role the teacher preparation program played in their acquisition of that knowledge. For this purpose we are interested in learning itself—the gain in knowledge. The difficulties in estimating such gain from this type of study, as well as some interesting but more exploratory and tentative findings, are presented in Chapter 9. The more formal findings are presented in Chapter 10.

ASSESSING FUTURE TEACHER COMPETENCIES

To measure these important outcomes of teacher preparation we developed a Mathematics Knowledge test consisting of five sub-areas: algebra, functions, number, geometry, and data; and a Mathematics Pedagogy test consisting of three areas—curriculum, instructional practices (teaching), and student learning. We refer to the last mathematics knowledge area as a test of data or data analysis rather than the more conventionally identified area of statistics because the items are focused mostly on interpreting data and not on formal statistical theory.

The focus of the achievement items used in these eight areas was on the mathematics content typically taught at the lower- and upper-secondary level across some 40 countries, including the six involved in MT21 (Schmidt et al., 2001). The MT21 mathematics knowledge items were in general not designed to be at the knowledge level typically associated with advanced undergraduate mathematics courses such as the theory of complex functions (however, a few such items were included). Rather, they were designed for the advanced level of mathematics knowledge that was necessary for a deep understanding of the topics typically taught in a challenging, rigorous, and coherent middle and high school mathematics curriculum (Valverde & Schmidt, 2000). The items were also developed to represent different types of cognitive demand ranging from using algorithms and modeling real-world situations to problem solving, including nonroutine problems and mathematical reasoning (including proof).

The resulting three dimensions were used as a blueprint for developing the mathematics and mathematics pedagogy items. The first dimension—formal mathematics—had five levels, while the mathematics pedagogy dimension had

FIGURE 5.1. Examples of mathematics content knowledge items.

For each of the statements below, indicate the largest set from which the exponents can come to make the statement true for all $x > 0$

Check one box in each row

	Natural Numbers	Integers	Rational Numbers	Real Numbers
1. $x^a x^b = x^{a+b}$	☐	☐	☐	☐
2. $\dfrac{x^a}{x^b} = x^{a-b}$	☐	☐	☐	☐
3. $\dfrac{x^a}{x^a} = 1$	☐	☐	☐	☐
4. $\sqrt[q]{x^p} = x^{\frac{p}{q}}, q \neq 0$	☐	☐	☐	☐

145. Which of the following is a correct definition for a continuous function at point x_0 contained in domain of f:

Check one box in each row

	Yes	No	Not Sure
1. For every $\varepsilon > 0$ there is $\delta > 0$ such that for every x if $|x - x_0| < \delta$ then $|f(x) - f(x_0)| < \varepsilon$	☐	☐	☐
2. For every $\delta > 0$ there is $\varepsilon > 0$ such that for every x if $|x - x_0| < \delta$ then $|f(x) - f(x_0)| < \varepsilon$	☐	☐	☐
3. If $|x - x_0| < \delta$ then $|f(x) - f(x_0)| < \varepsilon$	☐	☐	☐
4. $\lim\limits_{x \to \infty} f(x) = f(x_0)$	☐	☐	☐
5. For every sequence $x_1, x_2, \ldots, x_n, \ldots$ converging to x_0, (x_n contained in domain of f) the sequence, $f(x_1), f(x_2), \ldots, f(x_n), \ldots$ converges to $f(x_0)$	☐	☐	☐
6. There is a sequence, $f(x_1), f(x_2), \ldots, f(x_n), \ldots$ converging to $f(x_0)$	☐	☐	☐

three. Both of these dimensions were crossed with the four previously described levels of cognitive demand. Not all combinations of cognitive demand and content were used, but across the two test forms all dimensions were represented.

All of the test items were designed to include mathematics content, and as a result could be classified according to that dimension, but not all items were developed to include pedagogical content. This approach represents our belief that mathematics pedagogy includes, by definition, mathematics content. This results in two types of items: those with mathematics content only and those with both mathematics and pedagogical content. Items with pedagogy content alone are properly classified as general pedagogy and are described in Chapter 6. The first type is represented by the two items found in Figure 5.1. An example of two items containing both types of content is given in Figure 5.2.

FIGURE 5.2. Examples of mathematics pedagogy knowledge items.

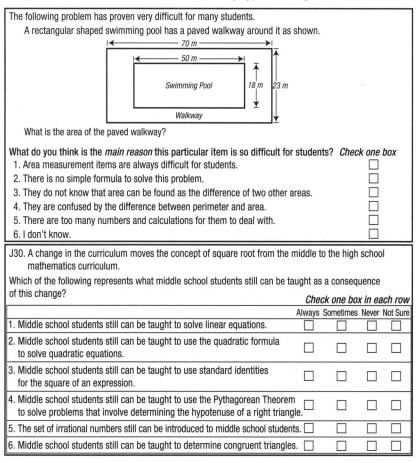

The following problem has proven very difficult for many students.

A rectangular shaped swimming pool has a paved walkway around it as shown.

Swimming Pool — 50 m wide, 18 m; outer 70 m, 23 m. Walkway.

What is the area of the paved walkway?

What do you think is the *main reason* this particular item is so difficult for students? *Check one box*

1. Area measurement items are always difficult for students. ☐
2. There is no simple formula to solve this problem. ☐
3. They do not know that area can be found as the difference of two other areas. ☐
4. They are confused by the difference between perimeter and area. ☐
5. There are too many numbers and calculations for them to deal with. ☐
6. I don't know. ☐

J30. A change in the curriculum moves the concept of square root from the middle to the high school mathematics curriculum.

Which of the following represents what middle school students still can be taught as a consequence of this change? *Check one box in each row*

	Always	Sometimes	Never	Not Sure
1. Middle school students still can be taught to solve linear equations.	☐	☐	☐	☐
2. Middle school students still can be taught to use the quadratic formula to solve quadratic equations.	☐	☐	☐	☐
3. Middle school students still can be taught to use standard identities for the square of an expression.	☐	☐	☐	☐
4. Middle school students still can be taught to use the Pythagorean Theorem to solve problems that involve determining the hypotenuse of a right triangle.	☐	☐	☐	☐
5. The set of irrational numbers still can be introduced to middle school students.	☐	☐	☐	☐
6. Middle school students still can be taught to determine congruent triangles.	☐	☐	☐	☐

Multiple-choice items were used for both the Mathematics and the Mathematics Pedagogy test. This portion of the future teacher survey was developed for a 1-hour administration. In order to incorporate enough items to develop the desired eight scales, matrix sampling was employed with two rotated forms. The two forms were randomly assigned to future teachers in each institution. The test items were administered to the future teachers in the native language of each country. There were 22, 17, 22, 18, and 13 score points, respectively, for the Number, Geometry, Algebra, Function, and Data scales. In addition, of these 92 items (score points), 57 also focused on the pedagogical aspects of mathematics in each of the five areas.

Since the items were distributed over two forms, the Rasch model was used to obtain scale scores based on the item classifications. There were several sub-areas—combinations of five levels of mathematics knowledge alone or in combination with mathematics pedagogy—available from the design blueprint. Each set of items pertaining to one of the sub-areas, as well as their marginals, was scaled in a separate Rasch analysis. The scaled scores for the five mathematics knowledge areas and the three mathematics pedagogy areas were computed from these Rasch scores. The scaling was done combining the data from the two cohorts (as defined in Chapter 3). A covariance structure model was used in which some of the pattern weights defining the relationships between the sub-areas and the eight scales were fixed to known values. The remaining parameters were estimated by maximum likelihood procedures and used to derive estimates of the scales.[1] The resulting eight scales were re-scaled so that each had an international mean of 500 and a standard deviation of around 10 for Cohort II.

FORMAL MATHEMATICS KNOWLEDGE

What Do Future Teachers Know?

Before examining the country differences, we first turn to the general level of mathematics knowledge exhibited by the 1,124 future teachers tested in MT21 at the end of their preparation programs. Figure 5.3 presents the distribution of scores over the sampled future teachers from all six countries combined for each of the five tests. For each of the five tests, scale scores ranged from around 325 to 650, with means of around 500. They are all above 500, as these are the distributions for Cohort II and not Cohort I future teachers. Both were included in the original scaling. Throughout this chapter as well as throughout all but Chapter 9, we present results related to the future teachers at the end of their preparation programs—Cohort II. When we use the term *future teachers* the reader should assume we are talking only about those future teachers and not about those

FIGURE 5.3. Future teacher scale score distributions for each of the five areas of mathematics knowledge for all future teachers from the six countries.

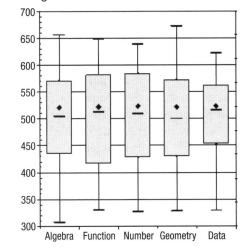

beginning their programs. When we refer to the beginning cohort, an explicit designation will be made so as to differentiate the two cohorts.

There was substantial variation across future teachers on all five scales. Scores ranged over +2 standard deviations, and the five distributions are reasonably well approximated by the normal distribution. The correlations among the five mathematics knowledge scales ranged between .47 (between Algebra and Geometry) and .75 (between Number and Function). Most of the remaining correlations were around .5, suggesting that the five tests, although related, are measuring different aspects of future teachers' competencies in mathematics knowledge. See Table 5.1 for the estimated correlation matrix defined at the future teacher level. The reliability of each the mathematics knowledge scales ranged from .79 to .85 (see Note 1 for details).

TABLE 5.1. Individual level correlations among the five mathematics knowledge scales.

	Algebra	Function	Number	Geometry	Data
Algebra	1.00				
Functions	0.68	1.00			
Number	0.54	0.75	1.00		
Geometry	0.47	0.65	0.54	1.00	
Data	0.49	0.51	0.50	0.53	1.00

Note: All correlations are significant (p < .0001).

Figure 5.4 shows the distributions for sampled male and female future teachers separately. Small differences are the general pattern except in Germany, where males outperformed female future teachers by about one-half a standard deviation in the areas of Number and Function; and in Bulgaria, where differences occurred in Algebra and Function, with the female future teachers outperforming the males.

As described in Chapter 1, Germany and the United States have future teachers prepared in different programs. Germany prepares their future lower-secondary teachers in both a primary and a secondary program, while the United States additionally prepares future teachers in a specific middle grades–only program. Figure 5.5 shows the five distributions separately for future teachers prepared in each of the different programs in Germany and the United States.

In Germany the future teachers who prepared in secondary programs statistically significantly outperformed those who prepared in primary programs ($p < .001$) in all areas, with the differences being the largest in Function and Algebra.

The United States had a similar pattern, with the future teachers prepared in the primary and middle school programs being outperformed by those prepared in the secondary program. The difference was most pronounced for the Function test and the least pronounced for the Data test. Unfortunately, the largest differences in both countries were found for Function—one of the two areas central to the lower-secondary curriculum. For Germany, the area of Algebra also demonstrates a significant difference. Interestingly, if one compares male and female future teachers within each of the two program types in Germany, the before-mentioned differences favoring the male future teachers is eliminated. The gender difference noted previously has to do with the fact that future teachers prepared in primary programs are predominantly female and that program has a lower average performance than does the secondary program. Similarly, in the United States males are more likely to be prepared in a secondary program; very few males are prepared in elementary programs. This result confirms the growing body of findings on the school level that gender differences are more a function of course choices than of differences between the sexes (Blömeke & Kaiser, 2010; Köller & Klieme, 2000).

Country Differences in Performance

The means and standard errors for each of the five scales in each of the six countries are included in Figure 5.6. On average, South Korean and Taiwanese sampled future teachers each scored somewhere from around one third to over a full standard deviation-and-a-half above the means of each of the other four

FIGURE 5.4. The five mathematics knowledge score distributions by country and gender.

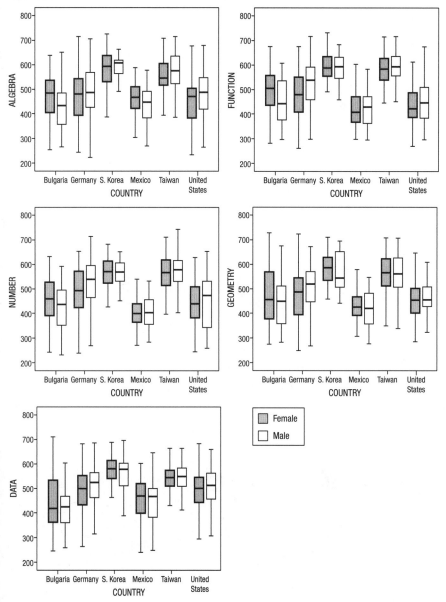

FIGURE 5.5. The five mathematics knowledge score distributions by preparation program in Germany and the United States.

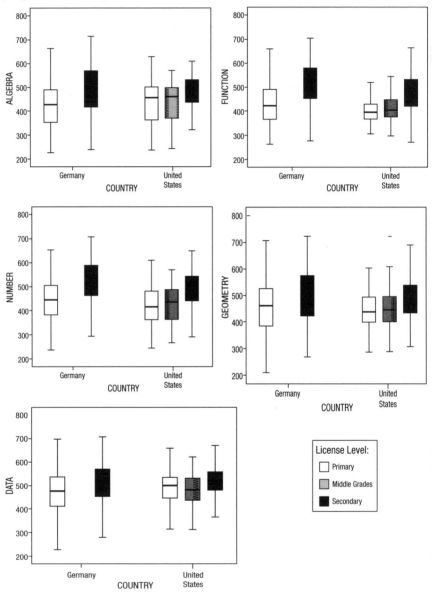

FIGURE 5.6. The five mathematics knowledge score distributions by country.

Country	Mathematics Knowledge	Mn	(se)	Scale
South Korea		586	(6.6)	Algebra
Taiwan		567	(4.4)	
Germany		476	(6.4)	
United States		457	(5.8)	
Bulgaria		456	(10.0)	
Mexico		452	(5.9)	
South Korea		584	(5.5)	Function
Taiwan		582	(3.7)	
Germany		495	(5.9)	
Bulgaria		477	(9.0)	
United States		433	(5.1)	
Mexico		418	(5.7)	
Taiwan		570	(4.0)	Number
South Korea		570	(6.0)	
Germany		511	(5.6)	
Bulgaria		461	(9.4)	
United States		451	(5.8)	
Mexico		415	(5.6)	
South Korea		577	(8.1)	Geometry
Taiwan		564	(5.1)	
Germany		494	(6.0)	
Bulgaria		469	(11.3)	
United States		459	(5.3)	
Mexico		430	(5.5)	
South Korea		567	(5.7)	Data
Taiwan		540	(3.6)	
Germany		497	(5.4)	
United States		490	(5.7)	
Mexico		453	(6.6)	
Bulgaria		433	(10.3)	

200   300   400   500   600   700

Percentiles of Performance
5th ▪▪ ▪▪ 95th
95% Confidence Interval for Average (±2SE)

countries on all five of the mathematics scales. Germany was typically in the middle of the international distribution while Mexico was well below the international mean on most scales. Bulgaria and the United States varied in their performance depending on the scale—the United States was between one-half and one-and-a-half standard deviations below the average performance in South Korea and Taiwan. In general they scored anywhere from the middle of the distribution to almost one full standard deviation (.8) below the six-country mean. What is clear from this description is that the 34 institutions, when aggregated to the country level, provide distinctly different patterns of performance. However, we remind the reader of the following caveat—that these sampled institutions were not drawn randomly and, therefore, there are no assurances that the mean patterns are representative of the countries as a whole.

From the point of view of the almost 50 countries from around the world that were studied in the 1995 TIMSS, the middle grade curriculum centers mostly on algebra (which includes elementary functions). As a result, how well the future teachers in each of these countries performed on the Algebra and Function tests is particularly important. The U.S. future teachers' performance was at its worst in Function. The mean U.S. future teachers' performance was essentially at the bottom of the six-country international distribution (along with Mexico and Bulgaria) in the area of algebra.

Within Country Differences

Although not technically accurate, we view the institutions as a random sample since we are not interested in the specific institutions in each country but only insofar as they represent the population of institutions that prepare future teachers in that country. As such, in this section we look at the total variation in test scores and partition it into two components, one of which represents cross-institutional differences within each country.

The achievement variation derives not only from individual differences in performance across different future teachers but also from institutional differences in achievement that could reflect the influence of program differences. The analyses summarized in Table 5.2 indicate the percentage of the total variation (as portrayed in Figure 5.6) that is attributable to cross-institutional differences, indicating at least the possibility of program differences (if there were no cross-institutional variation other than that created through an unequal distribution of students across institutions, there would be little or no possibility of program differences). However, the presence of cross-institutional differences does not in and of itself imply program preparation differences; only the possibility thereof. Program differences are explored more fully in Chapters 9 and 10.

Table 5.2 also indicates the estimated variances for both between and within institutions—the latter characterizing individual differences in future teacher performance. These variance components were estimated by standard statistical procedures.[2] Focusing on the percentages across the five areas indicates that only Bulgaria had a consistently high relative amount of cross-institutional variation, ranging from 23% to 42%. This would imply that students and/or programs differed substantially across the three sampled Bulgarian institutions. None of the other countries had such a large component of variance for between-institution differences.

TABLE 5.2. Percentage of the total variance in the five mathematics content scale scores attributable to cross-institutional variation.

		Algebra		Function		Number		Geometry		Data	
	Source	*Estimate*	*%*	*Estimate*	*%*	*Estimate*	*%*	*Estimate*	*%*	*Estimate*	*%*
Bulgaria	Institution	4805.0	42.0	3680.9	39.9	3205.1	32.9	5330.0	37.6	2667.6	23.4
	Individual	6646.3	58.0	5550.8	60.1	6549.0	67.1	8833.4	62.4	8719.5	76.6
Germany	Institution	1044.3	8.5	624.2	6.2	229.0	2.5	154.5	1.5	123.2	1.5
	Individual	11173.6	91.5	9439.3	93.8	8884.8	97.5	10011.7	98.5	8269.0	98.5
Mexico	Institution	265.0	5.2	593.5	11.9	319.2	6.8	18.9	0.4	337.8	5.2
	Individual	4812.4	94.8	4389.2	88.1	4376.4	93.2	4486.9	99.6	6161.4	94.8
South Korea	Institution	0	0	152.2	4.8	0	0	124.7	1.8	0	0
	Individual	4570.5	100.0	2995.0	95.2	3772.3	100.0	6772.1	98.2	3323.1	100.0
Taiwan	Institution	716.7	13.5	165.3	4.4	0	0	227.4	3.3	10.0	0.3
	Individual	4588.7	86.5	3584.5	95.6	4194.4	100.0	6630.9	96.7	3451.0	99.7
United States	Institution	218.6	2.9	1010.5	16.9	770.0	10.1	540.9	8.6	962.5	13.2
	Individual	7345.0	97.1	4978.7	83.1	6883.7	89.9	5720.3	91.4	6351.0	86.8

However, for each of the other countries the percentage of between-variation itself varied across the five test areas. For South Korean, Taiwanese, and German institutions very little cross-institutional variation was present. In fact, in South Korea the between-variance component was 0 for Algebra, Number, and Data and less than 5% for the other two areas. In Taiwan this was true for Number (0) and Data (.3%).

The United States had the second largest relative amount of cross-institutional variation, averaging 9% over the five test areas, with the largest being in Function (16.9%) and Data (13.2%). It is also important that although the standard deviations of the five scales all center around 100, the total variance can differ for the six countries individually. In general, the largest total variation was found in Bulgaria. Sampled German future teachers exhibited the largest variation for the Algebra and Function tests. South Korea and Taiwan, however, had the lowest total variation in all areas except for Geometry. The total variance for the sampled U.S. future teachers was on the high end in most of the five areas.

MATHEMATICS PEDAGOGICAL KNOWLEDGE

The theoretical concepts that guided item development for the assessment were identified in the previous section. As previously noted, the distinction between mathematics and mathematics pedagogy is a matter of ongoing discussion among mathematicians and mathematics educators. Well aware of the ongoing discussion and research around pedagogical mathematics knowledge or the mathematics knowledge related to the teaching of mathematics, we identified three aspects of classroom mathematics instruction to serve as heuristics in the development of items. One aspect centered around knowledge of the school mathematics curriculum. More specifically, these items sought to tap into the knowledge teachers have of the trajectory specific mathematics topics have in the school mathematics curriculum—that is, how a topic may be related to other topics in the curriculum and why. Items developed for this area explored the role of the concept of square root, the role of proof, and the role of graphing in the school curriculum. This group of items is represented by the Curriculum scale.

Another group of items centered around understanding and making sense of student work during the process of teaching. Items developed for this purpose addressed issues such as evaluating the adequacy of specific story problems for teaching a specific concept and evaluating the mathematical adequacy of students' work. This group of items is represented by the Teaching scale. A third group of items centered around knowledge teachers may have of specific mathematical misconceptions students may have, how they may think about specific problems, or how students might perform on various types of problems. This group of items is represented by the Students scale.

What Do Future Teachers Know?

The overall performance of those future teachers in their final year of teacher preparation on these three scales may be seen in Figure 5.7. The distributions for these scales are very similar to one another as well as to the math-

FIGURE 5.7. Future teacher scale distributions for each of three areas of mathematics pedagogy knowledge.

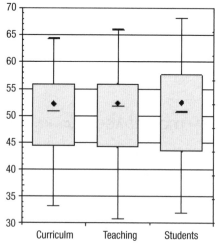

ematics knowledge scales distributions: their range is nearly plus two standard deviations and they approximate a normal distribution reasonably well.

At the individual level, the correlations among these three scales appear to be somewhat smaller than the correlations among the five mathematics knowledge scales. Table 5.3 illustrates the correlations among these scales (see Endnote 1 for data on the reliability of each these three scales—they range from .66 to .83). These correlations do not necessarily provide evidence for the validity of the mathematics pedagogy construct but they do suggest that the three different groups of items are different from one another.

All of the correlations are significant at the $p < .001$ level. The largest correlation was observed between Curriculum and Students. Both of these scales addressed knowledge that teachers may have whether or not they have any classroom experience. In contrast, the Teaching scale had items that attempted to tap into the sort of knowledge teachers might need to evaluate situations on the fly, making decisions or evaluations of instructional options or student work during the course of classroom instruction. This may explain the somewhat lower correlation between this scale and the other two.

Figure 5.8 contains the distributions by country for each of the three scales by gender. As was the case for the mathematics knowledge scales, there are essentially no gender differences; males and females in most countries perform relatively the same. The exceptions would be in Bulgaria on the Teaching and Students scales, in Taiwan and Germany on the Teaching scale, and in the United States on the Students scale.

As was the case for the mathematics knowledge scales, the slight apparent differences in performance by gender that may be seen in Germany and the United States in Figure 5.8 turn out to be performance differences according to the type of program in which future teachers have been enrolled, which may be seen in Figure 5.9. This is true because in both countries males are more prominent in secondary programs than in primary programs. Thus, the differences that first appear to be gender differences actually reflect the differential enrollment in the different types of teacher preparation programs.

TABLE 5.3. Individual level correlations among the three mathematics pedagogy knowledge scales.

	Curriculum	Teaching	Students
Curriculum	1.00		
Teaching	0.36	1.00	
Students	0.52	0.43	1.00

Note: All correlations are significant ($p < .0001$).

FIGURE 5.8. The three mathematics pedagogy score distributions by country and gender.

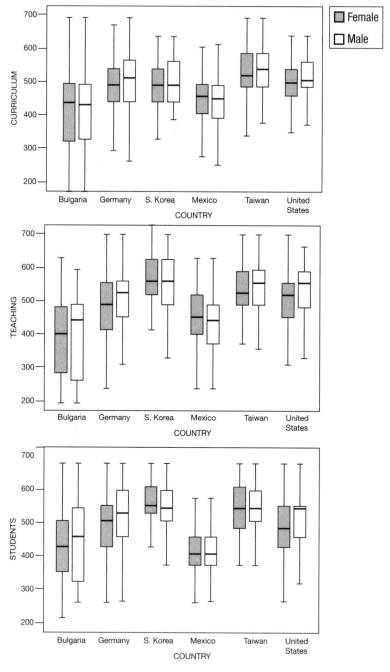

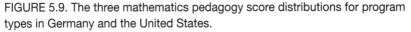

FIGURE 5.9. The three mathematics pedagogy score distributions for program types in Germany and the United States.

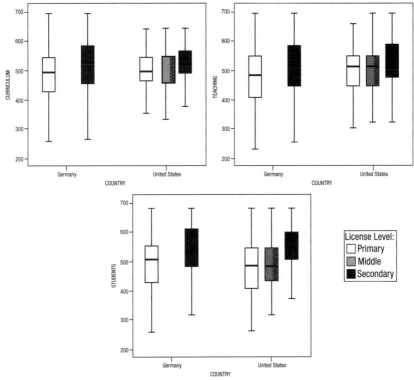

In Germany, future teachers who prepared in secondary programs consistently outperformed those prepared in primary programs. Performance differences were a little more than one quarter of a standard deviation for the Curriculum and Teaching scales (p < .01) and about one half of a standard deviation for the Students scale (p < .001). In the United States, those prepared in secondary programs generally outperformed those prepared in either of the other two types of programs. Future teachers who prepared in primary programs did not perform statistically significantly differently from those who prepared in a middle grades–focused program on any of these three scales. Thus, program performance difference contrasts were evident between those from secondary programs and those from primary programs. Similar to the case of Germany, these differences in the United States were a little over one quarter of a standard deviation for the Teaching scale (p < .01) and over one half of a standard deviation for the Students scale (p < .001). There were no program performance differences on the Curriculum scale.

Country Differences in Performance

Means, standard errors, and distributions for the three mathematics pedagogy scales are presented in Figure 5.10 for future teachers in each country. Typical or average performance in each country demonstrated large cross-country variation. Future teachers in Taiwan tended to score at least one quarter to over one standard deviation higher on the curriculum scale than the means of those from other countries. Future teachers in South Korea scored over a third of a standard deviation higher than those in Taiwan on the Teaching scale and about a 10th of a standard deviation on the Students scale.

For the most part, the average future teachers' performance in each country was fairly consistent across the three scales. There were two notable deviations from this general pattern. In South Korea, average performance on the Curriculum scale was over three quarters of a standard deviation below the average on the Teaching scale, and in Bulgaria, average performance on the Teaching scale was about one half of a standard deviation lower than the average on the Students scale.

Figure 5.10. The three mathematics pedagogy knowledge score distributions by country.

	Mathematics Pedagogy Knowledge Distribution	Mn	(se)	Scale
Taiwan		540	(4.5)	Curriculum
Germany		514	(5.6)	
United States		507	(5.1)	
South Korea		486	(8.0)	
Mexico		459	(7.7)	
Bulgaria		422	(15.3)	
South Korea		572	(7.1)	Teaching
Taiwan		538	(4.7)	
United States		508	(6.1)	
Germany		504	(5.5)	
Mexico		438	(7.1)	
Bulgaria		400	(11.5)	
South Korea		555	(6.7)	Students
Taiwan		543	(4.7)	
Germany		518	(6.1)	
United States		498	(6.0)	
Bulgaria		447	(11.5)	
Mexico		413	(6.7)	

0   100   200   300   400   500   600   700

Percentiles of Performance
5th   95th
95% Confidence Interval for Average ($\pm 2SE$)

Within-Country Differences

Within-country variation on these three scales exists almost entirely at the individual level. Table 5.4 provides estimates of the variation of each scale at the individual and at the institution level in each country. These were estimated using the same procedure described for the mathematics knowledge scaled scores. Bulgaria again demonstrates the most variation between teacher preparation institutions, with closely 20% to almost 30% of scale variation occurring at this level. Again, differences between programs are more fully addressed in later chapters. Here we simply note that there appears to be very little difference in the performance of students from different programs within each of the countries except for Bulgaria.

WHAT IS MATHEMATICS PEDAGOGICAL KNOWLEDGE?

In the preceding discussion we defined mathematics pedagogical knowledge by scaling items that we designed to measure the pedagogical aspects of teaching and learning mathematics and not just straight mathematics knowledge. However, to focus on the pedagogical aspect of the teaching as content-related and not as general pedagogy, mathematical content was included in the item as well. Thus, the scaled pedagogical scores reported on in the previous sections draw on both competencies—formal mathematics knowledge and mathematics pedagogical

TABLE 5.4. Percentage of the total variance in the three mathematics pedagogy scale scores attributable to cross-institutional variation.

		Curriculum		Teaching		Students	
	Source	*Estimate*	*Percent*	*Estimate*	*Percent*	*Estimate*	*Percent*
Bulgaria	Institution	7175.7	28.1	4102.7	28.6	2688.9	19.0
	Individual	18345.7	71.9	10222.3	71.4	11431.7	81.0
Germany	Institution	94.6	1.1	324.6	3.1	22.5	0.3
	Individual	8815.7	98.9	10214.3	96.9	8675.1	99.7
Mexico	Institution	40.2	0.5	196.7	3.0	335.6	4.4
	Individual	8708.6	99.5	6434.2	97.0	7219.6	95.6
South Korea	Institution	389.1	5.8	96.7	2.1	0	0
	Individual	6301.1	94.2	4582.8	97.9	5247.0	100.0
Taiwan	Institution	221.0	4.1	586.6	9.8	48.5	0.8
	Individual	5227.5	95.9	5385.1	90.2	5821.6	99.2
United States	Institution	163.3	2.8	1063.6	13.4	605.9	7.4
	Individual	5720.3	97.2	6874.2	86.6	7603.6	92.6

knowledge. The notion of what mathematics pedagogical knowledge is has not been firmly agreed upon. Ball and colleagues (Ball, Hill, & Bass, 2002, 2005; Hill & Ball, 2004; Hill, Schilling, & Ball, 2004) have devised a set of items that they claim measure this construct. In support of this they cite evidence that mathematicians cannot always do these types of problems.

This line of inquiry has been sparked to a great extent by Shulman's 1986 AERA Presidential Address in which he suggested a distinction between three types of content knowledge for those who teach: (1) subject matter content, (2) pedagogical content, and (3) curricular content (Shulman, 1986). He notes that historically no such distinctions were necessary. Indeed, pointing to Aristotle, he makes the argument that what it has meant to know something well was the ability to teach it to others. Nonetheless, the distinctions make explicit different aspects of the types of knowledge teachers need for teaching. Our three mathematics pedagogy scores were an attempt to contribute to the developing academic inquiry around teachers' pedagogical knowledge. Whether these aspects can, indeed, be distinguished and how they might relate to one another is a matter of ongoing debate and study.

The correlations of the mathematics pedagogical scaled scores (reported on in the previous section) and the mathematics scaled scores at the individual future teacher level are given in Table 5.5.

The correlations range in value from .22 between Number and Curriculum up to .75 between Data and Teaching. Most of the other correlations are all around .3 to .4, indicating a relatively modest degree of relationship. Overall, collapsing across all five areas of mathematics and three areas of mathematics pedagogy, the correlation between the two sets is .54, supporting the above indication of a moderate relationship.

At the country level the Taiwanese and South Korean future teachers performed among the best across the six countries on both mathematics and mathematics pedagogy scaled scores. For mathematics knowledge South Korean and Taiwanese sampled future teachers ranked first or second across all five areas. On the three pedagogical scales they were first or second in all three areas,

TABLE 5.5. Individual level correlations between mathematics content knowledge scales and mathematics pedagogy knowledge scales.

	Algebra	Function	Number	Geometry	Data
Curriculum	0.34	0.29	0.22	0.42	0.26
Teaching	0.38	0.36	0.38	0.37	0.75
Students	0.39	0.46	0.40	0.58	0.37

with one exception—South Korean future teachers in Curriculum, where they ranked fourth. The question is, does this mean that they are the best in both areas, or does that result imply that the two tests are measuring much the same thing, at least at the aggregate or country level?

Furthermore, at the institutional level the correlations between the two sets of scores are higher, ranging from .50 to .95 with most around .6 to .7, leading to a similar question. We explore this issue somewhat further in this section not to give a definitive answer but to at least raise the question of how to define mathematics pedagogy. We conceptualize the issue as follows: Mathematics pedagogy is the intersection between general pedagogy—especially issues of curriculum teaching and learning—and mathematics, including the subset of formal mathematics, school mathematics (see Figure 5.11).

Looking at it in this way, one possibility is to define mathematics pedagogy in a way that controls for mathematics knowledge, thereby minimizing its influence. In effect, this is recognizing that the substantive content of the pedagogical items other than pedagogical content itself must be mathematics by definition, but that once the response is elicited one could in effect define mathematics pedagogical knowledge as the knowledge level of pedagogy for a given level of mathematics knowledge. Put another way, future teachers who do better on the mathematics pedagogy scale than others, given that they have the same mathematics knowledge, could be considered to have more pedagogical knowledge related to mathematics. One could think of this as having a large number of future teachers all of whom have the same general level of formal mathematics knowledge, and defining variation on the mathematics pedagogical items as reflecting variation in pedagogical knowledge related to mathematics—in effect, holding constant formal mathematics knowledge.

FIGURE 5.11. Hypothesized relationship between mathematics knowledge and knowledge of pedagogy.

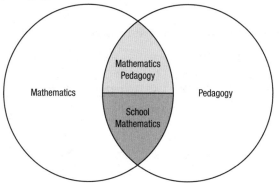

One direction this conception has led us is to condition out mathematics knowledge from the pedagogical scale statistically.[3] Table 5.6 shows the country means on both measures of mathematics pedagogical knowledge, which reveals large differences. Taiwan and South Korea are no longer the highest performing countries on the conditional mathematics pedagogical scale as they were on the unconditioned scales and in fact rank no higher than third. By contrast, the United States, which ranked no higher than third on the non-conditioned measures, now ranked number one or two of the three conditioned pedagogical scales and very near the top on the third one.

This seems reasonable given that the sampled U.S. institutions provided the largest amount of coverage associated with pedagogy as compared with the other five countries (see Chapter 4). Germany is the only country where the difference between the two approaches is negligible. Its future teachers always show about medium performance.

As can be seen from the above discussion, it isn't entirely clear exactly what has been tapped by our mathematics pedagogy scales. It may well be that mathematics pedagogical knowledge is something that teachers need and something that is likely to deepen as they continue to grow in their own mathematics understandings and insights, prodded through classroom interactions. However, while we have statistically partitioned the pedagogical insights from the mathematics in which the items were presented, their fundamental inextricability is in evidence. From our data it seems reasonable that a deep *understanding* of mathematics may provide important insights for teaching. Conversely, an awareness of the pedagogical demands and tools for teaching may spark one to plumb mathematics for greater insight and understanding, all toward the end of helping students learn mathematics. Better yet, maybe opportunities for future teachers to think deeply about the mathematics in the curriculum they will be required to teach and to consider how best to form and sequence the mathematics learning experience of their future students will produce the best results.

TABLE 5.6. Country means for two types of mathematics pedagogy scale scores.

	Curriculum		Teaching		Students	
	Math Conditioned Out	*Math Included*	*Math Conditioned Out*	*Math Included*	*Math Conditioned Out*	*Math Included*
Bulgaria	435	422	457	400	464	447
Germany	519	514	511	504	513	518
Mexico	503	459	502	438	446	412
South Korea	452	486	475	572	520	555
Taiwan	482	540	484	538	518	543
United States	551	507	538	508	516	498

Measuring and Characterizing the General Pedagogical Knowledge of Future Teachers

Teachers' professional competence is a hypothetical construct consisting of several knowledge and belief components (Blömeke, Felbrich, Müller, Kaiser, Lehmann, 2008; Weinert, 2001). Regarding the knowledge components, we have pointed out in the previous chapters that three core domains have been frequently identified in the literature: content knowledge, pedagogical content knowledge, and general pedagogical knowledge (Bromme, 1997; Grossman, 1990; Shulman, 1987). A teacher has to develop all three of them in order to be able to deal successfully with her various professional challenges: instruction, assessment, nurturing students' social and moral development, counseling, and school development. Correspondingly, most teacher education programs offer opportunities to acquire content knowledge, pedagogical content knowledge, and general pedagogical knowledge.

The present chapter describes the difficult task of measuring general pedagogical knowledge. MT21 is the first attempt to measure this knowledge domain on a large scale and across countries. During this effort we faced many conceptual challenges, especially with the intertwining of pedagogical knowledge and beliefs, and with large international differences in what constitutes pedagogical knowledge. In the first section we lay out the conceptual frame of how we dealt with these challenges. In the next section the methods used to measure general pedagogical knowledge in MT21 are introduced in detail. In the last section the main findings of the study are presented.

THEORETICAL FRAMEWORK

Why Measure General Pedagogical Knowledge?

One might argue that, when looking at mathematics teacher education, it is sufficient to measure the content knowledge and eventually the pedagogical content knowledge of future mathematics teachers because that is all that matters. In fact, we do find a number of studies that are done this way (see, e.g., Hill, Ball, Sleep et al., 2007; Krauss, Kunter, Brunner et al., 2004). We are convinced that there are important conceptual reasons to include general pedagogical knowledge in a measurement of teacher competence.

First, to leave out a measure of general pedagogical knowledge would mean to miss the goal of assessing the outcomes of opportunities to learn in teacher education. General pedagogy represents a significant part of all the programs studied for MT21. The number of pedagogy classes varies across countries as does the content taught and the year in which these studies take place. For example, the classes are not always labeled as *general pedagogy* but sometimes as *educational foundations*. However, every single teacher-education program has these kinds of classes. So, if we want to measure outcomes of opportunities to learn in teacher education, the measurement of general pedagogical knowledge is a vital part of such a study.

Second, the professional competence of teachers consists of several components that are intertwined, and one of these components is general pedagogical knowledge. In MT21, we took seriously the fact that, if one really wants to examine the complex structure of competence, the measurement has to include all its components. According to Shulman (1987), general pedagogical knowledge involves "broad principles and strategies of classroom management and organization that appear to transcend subject matter" (p. 8), as well as knowledge about learners and learning, assessment, and educational contexts and purposes. Future teachers of mathematics need to draw on this range of knowledge and weave it into coherent understandings and skills if they are to become competent to deal with what McDonald (1992) calls the "wild triangle" that connects learner, subject matter, and teacher in the classroom. Lampert (2001) stresses the need for teachers to have intellectual resources and repertoires that bridge different domains. As she explains:

> When I am teaching fifth-grade mathematics, for example, I teach a mathematical idea or procedure to a student while also teaching that student to be civil to class-mates and to me, to complete the tasks assigned, and to think of herself or himself and everyone in the class as capable of learning, no matter what their gender, race, or parents' income. (p. 2)

Consistent successful performance in solving corresponding, typical professional problems is an indicator of competence and requires the intertwined structure of the knowledge (and beliefs) dimensions mentioned. The above quote demonstrates that it is not sufficient to dispose of the single elements of professional competence separately, nor is it sufficient to dispose only of some of the elements. To leave one measure out, for example, general pedagogy, would mean not to be able to determine the reason for a teacher's strengths or weaknesses. Is it due to her content knowledge, her pedagogical content knowledge, or her general pedagogical knowledge, or is it because they are not sufficiently connected to one another? An answer to these questions is only possible if the separate areas are measured, otherwise one can never exclude the effect of a not-measured variable.

Definition of "General Pedagogy"

Whereas mathematics is a fairly uniform construct all over the world (Bishop, 1991; Clarke, 2003; Mullis, Martin, Smith et al., 2003), this does not apply to general pedagogy. Its specific shape is highly influenced by cultural perspectives on the goals of schooling, the role of teachers, and the role of parents (Blömeke & Paine, 2008; Hopmann & Riquarts, 1995; Westbury, 1995).

In a German *Didaktik* tradition, for example, *Allgemeinbildung*—insufficiently translated as "all-around education"—is highly valued, and this goal goes along with a strong focus on the process of learning and instruction instead of its products only. Standardized controlling of outcomes has been widely unknown for a long time; corresponding discussions have only recently started after Germany's disappointing performance in the PISA and TIMSS studies. Teachers do have relatively broad autonomy to design their lessons within general state guidelines, and this autonomy goes along with the necessity and the freedom to combine the state guidelines with ideas of their own. Against this background, high-quality teaching is regarded as teacher performance according to didactical models of lessons. Lesson plans serve as frames of reference, and Didaktik—classes in teacher education—include a highly theorized set of ideas about how to structure a lesson plan.

In contrast, a U.S. tradition of what works is much more focused on student achievement as the outcome of instructional efforts. Teachers carry out what is prescribed by the state; they put curriculum into action. In this sense, lesson plans are regarded as courses of action. Recent increased efforts at state accountability and the introduction or expansion of measures of accountability and backward mapping to curriculum frameworks, pacing guides, and other state and district directives have strengthened this tendency. Because textbooks are widely used, teaching methods are to some extent prescribed, too, and they tend to be discussed at a highly practical level. The result of these long-standing and more recent trends is that U.S. traditions and conventional practice in general pedagogy have emphasized the practical.

Again, in contrast to these two Western countries, comparative work shows that high-achieving Asian countries focus much more on student cognition. Not only in mathematics education but also in general pedagogy, understanding student thinking and development are key domains. Correspondingly, generic psychological approaches to instruction are of high relevance during teacher education. Especially in Taiwan, classes in cognitive psychology as well as in developmental psychology and educational psychology influence the shape of general pedagogy much more than in the other countries.

In addition to these cultural differences in the shape of general pedagogy due to different educational traditions, there are countries in which not only education but also other academic disciplines are part of this program component (e.g., sociology). Of course, this influences the shape of general pedagogy, as well. Furthermore, there are countries that offer noncontent-related components in their teacher education, such as national history, religion, or native language. Is this general pedagogy as well?

In MT21 we decided to focus on three areas of general pedagogical knowledge: lesson planning, assessment, and dealing with heterogeneity—taking socioeconomic differences as an example. Several conceptual considerations led to this decision:

- First, lesson planning and assessment are core tasks of teachers by their very nature. This means our test would cover important aspects of teachers' professional competence as it is defined, for example, by Spencer and Spencer (1993), Eraut (1994) and Weinert (2001) in general and with regard to teaching by Bromme (1997) and Taconis, Van der Plas, & Van der Sanden (2004). Competence in this tradition implies having the knowledge and the skills at one's disposal to successfully solve core job-related problems.

  An important implication of this construct definition is that competence is of a situated nature (Blumer, 1969; Schutz, 1967). The past 2 decades of research in teaching and teacher learning have demonstrated the importance of recognizing the situated nature of teaching as well as of teacher knowledge (Putnam & Borko, 2000). Moreover, as Lampert's discussion of "teaching problems and the problems of teaching" (2001) reminds us (see the preceding quote), the complexity of teaching requires recognizing the simultaneity of the problems teachers must deal with. Therefore, we designed our instrument in ways that the knowledge falling within general pedagogy could be assessed within a classroom or school situation through a vignette or a task. Our goal was to tap into what we realized would be contextualized understandings (Ham, Kim, & Tanner, 2008).

In turn, being situated implies that generic teaching knowledge partly manifests itself in content areas. For instance, there is a general ability to plan lessons. A teacher has to know general criteria of what a lesson plan looks like, why it looks as it does, and what it means to specify the single elements of a lesson plan. However, the application of this generic knowledge to a specific teaching unit necessarily takes place with respect to mathematics (in case of mathematics teachers), history, or other content areas. Thus, an assessment of general pedagogical knowledge is by its nature never only a generic measure but includes content-related issues. The line between general pedagogy and mathematics pedagogy—which is important for analytical and heuristic reasons—is in practice, therefore, a very fine line and partly artificial.

- Second, MT21 is a comparative study, which means that we have to cover aspects common in the countries participating in the study. In fact, we can find teaching standards about lesson planning and assessment explicitly or implicitly in Bulgaria, Germany, Mexico, South Korea, Taiwan, and the United States. So we measure knowledge that is relevant and comparable from a curriculum point of view in all countries. Furthermore, the knowledge necessary for lesson planning and assessment is covered in methods classes or in educational psychology classes, respectively—courses which are usually not elective but required. This means in turn that we capture core opportunities to learn.

However, we must point out that the amount to which this is done in general pedagogy varies. In some countries—such as in Germany—these issues are the main domain of general pedagogy. In other countries, such as the United States, some of the issues—like dealing with heterogeneity, especially with socioeconomic differences—certainly are part of more generic components of teacher education. In contrast, lesson planning and assessment are sometimes treated in general pedagogy and in mathematics pedagogy in parallel (and sometimes competing) ways. In Taiwan most of these issues are the exclusive domain of mathematics pedagogy. Our hypothesis is that the location largely determines the number of subjects to be studied and the range of grade levels to be taught. The more subjects there are to be studied in teacher education, the more it makes sense to include generic instructional classes in order to avoid having to cover these questions in every single subject. Similarly, the broader the range of grade levels a lower-secondary teacher has to teach, the more it makes sense to include generic instructional classes. To have a component labeled as general pedagogy may therefore be a matter of efficiency. Germany, for example, does not have single-subject or single-grade teachers. Every future teacher has to acquire at least two full majors and every future teacher— for example, at the lower-secondary level—teaches at least six grade levels (grades 5 through 10, with only a few exceptions in some federal states, in which lower-secondary starts in grade 7 or ends in grade 9).

- Third, we intended to develop the general pedagogy test in an evidence-based way. Areas of teachers' knowledge to be covered had to be proven to contribute to higher student achievement in instructional research as well as in school effectiveness research (see especially Brophy, 1999; Fraser, Walberg, Welch et al., 1987; Scheerens & Bosker, 1997; Seidel & Shavelson, 2007; Slavin, 1994). Besides content-specific characteristics, in this research the very same generic teaching components continuously emerge as effective. This is with regard to elementary as well as to secondary grades and to reading as well as to mathematics and science achievement—the structure and organization of the lesson, the evaluation of student achievement, adaptive instruction, time on task, and reinforcement. Only when teachers are able to diagnose precisely the students' learning process and adjust their teaching methods to the results of these assessments, with a specific effort to consider the students' heterogeneity, does instruction lead to higher student achievement. The general pedagogy part of MT21 precisely covers these aspects.

- Finally, recent discourses should be considered as well. Dealing with heterogeneity is an issue school systems worldwide must manage, and they do it in very different ways. Tracking, streaming, geographical differentiation, ability grouping, retention, and individualized teaching are common strategies (Dupriez, Dumay, & Vause, 2008; LeTendre, Hofer, & Shimizu, 2003). Socioeconomic inequalities increasingly worry many countries and in some cases have done so for decades (Dahrendorf, 1965; Hanushek & Wößmann, 2006; Kozol, 2006; Picht, 1964; Postlethwaite, 1967; Wiggan, 2007). In a democratic society it does not seem defensible to have the kind of inequalities that derive not from individual effort but from a child's background. In this context, both within countries and across countries, the role of the teacher to recognize, make sense of, address, and/or challenge inequality is a pertinent issue, one that can be seen by some as relating to the moral and social purposes of education and the role of the teacher. It can also be seen as one that touches on teachers' abilities to understand contexts, recognize the relationship of education to society and broader social forces, and understand their learners—all aspects that fundamentally connect to general pedagogy.

By including the issue of socioeconomic differences, MT21 also takes on a more sociological perspective on teaching (Broadfoot, 1996) besides the didactical and psychological perspectives covered by lesson planning and assessment. So the range of the most prominent academic disciplines in this part of teacher education is covered as well.

To sum up, lesson planning, assessment, and dealing with socioeconomic differences in student achievement presented a reasonable choice of knowledge areas to be measured, and this from an outcome point of view—the underlying knowledge of dealing with typical job situations as an indicator of professional competence—as well as from a cross-national curriculum point of view.

Measurement of Different Types of Knowledge

In addition to this definition of knowledge, a distinction can be made between types of knowledge, especially between declarative and procedural knowledge (Anderson, Krathwohl, Airasian et al., 2001). Declarative knowledge is factual knowledge in the sense of "knowing that." It means the knowledge of basic elements of a discipline, including specific details, but also conceptual knowledge about the relationship of these elements, including knowledge of classifications and structures. In contrast, procedural knowledge means knowing how to do something, including knowledge of criteria for determining when it is appropriate to use certain techniques. Procedural knowledge is therefore situated knowledge, and it is organized sequentially in the form of cognitive schemes. Regarding teachers, this means that they perceive and carry out classroom actions stepwise according to typical instructional sequences experienced earlier (Aebli, 1983; Putnam & Borko, 2000). Declarative knowledge is a necessary precondition to action, but procedural knowledge is especially relevant to it. If a teacher has command only of declarative knowledge, she will have problems with its application in practice (Ausubel, 1968; Stark & Mandl, 2000). Thus, in MT21 we intend to measure both types of knowledge.

The distinction between declarative and procedural knowledge has consequences for the item format. The mathematics-related part of MT21 consists mostly of multiple-choice items. This approach has been typical of testing for many decades. Declarative knowledge can certainly be measured this way. However, measuring procedural knowledge is more difficult. In order to capture the sequentially organized structure of this type of knowledge and its situated nature, stepwise considerations according to specific professional tasks are required (Birenbaum, 2003; Dierick & Dochy, 2001). Since we in MT21 definitely wanted to take into account that teaching is a highly action-oriented and deliberative activity where teachers must create long-term plans, think ahead, and produce ideas, we decided to use open-ended items in which we asked future teachers to deal with hypothetical classroom situations and to explain their reasoning in these situations. In doing so, we followed those recent discussions in measurement theory that are based on cognitive theories in which learning is regarded as an active and individual process of constructing cognitive schemes (Baartman et al., 2007). However, even if the sequential and situated nature of teaching recommends itself to using open-ended, task-based tests, with this decision another issue arises that is very much prevalent in performance measurements, namely, cross-task reliability (Shavelson, Gao, & Baxter, 1996). It is not certain that there is consistency in a teacher's performance across the tasks with which she has to contend.

Another challenge is that classroom situations develop at high speed and may pose different tasks at the same time (Sabers, Cushing, & Berliner, 1991), so a teacher's knowledge must not only be procedural but also quickly accessible and well connected. Research shows that in the long run a teacher perceives more precisely and faster what is going on in the classroom when she has a sophisticated repertoire of technical terms at her disposal to describe what is going on (Berliner, 2004). To develop a rich and meaningful vocabulary and to insist on clear expressions is especially important when developing concepts in mathematics (Buckley, 1982; Capps, & Pickreign, 1993).

METHODS

Instrument Development

Since MT21 was the first study ever to measure general pedagogical knowledge on a large scale, it was not possible to look at exemplary studies in order to learn from them. Instead, this MT21 test had to be developed from scratch. The closest we could get to our test intention were the instruments of the Educational Testing Service (ETS, 2005) and the PACT Consortium (2005) for licensure in teacher education. They gave us initial ideas on how to measure pedagogical knowledge, but we could not follow their conceptualization as they were not created for international comparisons and a large-scale assessment of competence.

The final instrument consisted of three complex hypothetical teaching situations. In the vignette covering the area of lesson planning, a colleague who teaches mathematics in grade 8 presents a lesson to another and asks for help. The future teacher's task is to develop criteria with which to review this lesson plan and then to apply these criteria in praising and criticizing the plan. The vignette captures declarative knowledge (criteria for evaluating the lesson plan) as well as procedural knowledge (application of the criteria to the specific lesson plan in order to be able to give advice to the colleague). Since open-ended items require a lot of testing time, a rotated test design was used with two test forms. Lesson planning was part of both of them.

In the second vignette, socioeconomic differences in student achievement have to be explained and taken into account as part of a class's heterogeneity. The vignette covers one third of a page, including the space for providing the answers. It first explains that tests on student achievement have shown that inequalities exist with regard to socioeconomic background, then poses two questions related to that statement: How can one reasonably explain this phenomenon, and what can a teacher do about it? The first question is supposed to assess declarative knowledge, the second to assess procedural knowledge.

The vignette that covers the knowledge of assessment consists of three parts in which future teachers had to give time points, methods, and reasons for a continuous evaluation of student achievement in a unit about data and probability in grade 8. Future teachers were asked to describe how and when they would assess their students. They had the chance to evaluate student achievement up to four times.

The use of open-ended items presents a specific challenge in large-scale assessments where this item format is not often used. It is not only a question of costs, because the coding requires a lot of work, but also one of accuracy and consistency in the measurement in view of the openness of the future teachers' responses. Coding rubrics help to ensure a sufficient reliability (Jonsson & Svingby, 2007). As a result, we decided collaboratively to develop complex coding rubrics to deal with this challenge. The rubrics were created to capture the *criteria*, their *application* to a specific lesson plan, including praise and criticism, and the *professional vocabulary* used by the future teachers with respect to the lesson-plan vignette. With respect to the vignette about dealing with heterogeneity, the coding rubrics covered the *explanations* given for socioeconomic differences in student achievement, *strategies* on how to consider these in teaching, and the *professional vocabulary* used. Regarding the assessment vignette, *reasons* for using specific evaluation approaches, *time points* and *methods* were covered by the codes as well as the use of *professional vocabulary* (see Figure 6.1).

The MT21 rubrics we developed were both theoretical and data-based and were designed to be low-inference codes. The one exception was the code describing the connectivity of responses across subparts of a vignette. In the latter approach, raters had to make inferences using responses from different questions to judge the adequacy of the logical connections. Every country provided a comprehensive list of student responses that would be accepted to be correct due to the state of research within the country. This within-country approach was an important attempt to avoid cultural bias. In addition, a random sample of 20 tests from

FIGURE 6.1. Conceptual framework for the measurement of general pedagogical knowledge.

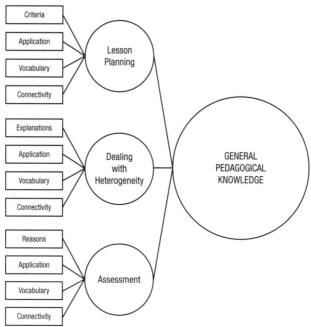

each country was drawn from which an additional list of responses was created. In the lesson-plan area we developed about 60 codes that were to be exhaustive.

Graduate students were trained to reliably apply the complex coding scheme. Taking Germany as an example, a daylong training for the coding of the lesson planning was done. As a measure of consensus and internal consistency, Cohen's Kappa was estimated. Again using Germany as an example, the within-country reliability was about .7 on average, with a range from .5 to .9. In comparison to other studies this is adequate, especially if one considers that we calculated Kappa for which values above .4 represent agreement beyond chance instead of a simple percentage of consensus agreement (Jonsson & Svingby, 2007).

Scoring and Scaling

The codes represented the basis for the scoring of future teachers' level of knowledge based on cognitive complexity theories (Anderson, 1992; Eye, 1999; Kline, Pelias, & Delia, 1991). According to these, a higher level of cognitive abilities is indicated by a higher number of analytical perspectives on a phenomenon or a higher number of solution strategies. Therefore, we valued breadth and depth in the students' declarative and procedural responses instead of expecting a specific response—provided that the perspectives and options were part of the nationally created lists of acceptable responses.

As an indicator of cognitive breadth, we counted the number of perspectives a future teacher indicated in planning a lesson or dealing with heterogeneity. For example, regarding explanations of socioeconomic differences in student achievement, it was an advantage to consider a student's family background and instructional quality at school instead of only one of the two aspects. As an indicator of cognitive depth, the number of ideas mentioned within each broader category was taken. For example, regarding family background it was an advantage to come up with several different characteristics that were relevant instead of only one.

In addition to breadth and depth in the declarative and procedural knowledge, the use of professional language was evaluated, since technical terms allow for a faster and more precise perception of classroom situations. For example, in the context of explaining socioeconomic differences, the professional-language score awarded future teachers for using expressions like "self-fulfilling prophecy" in contrast with future teachers who just described with everyday terms the phenomenon that teachers sometimes expect less from some groups of students because of their belonging to ethnic minorities or lower social classes.

The connectivity of responses across the different questions within a vignette was also evaluated. Connectivity is regarded as one of the most important characteristics of cognitive complexity and is used in the sense of seeing relationships, making comparisons, relating causes to effects, applying abstract reasoning to a specific behavior, or extrapolating (Adey, Csapo, Demetriou et al., 2007; Spearman, 1927). If a future teacher's responses in the second or third part of an item matched her responses to the first part, up to two points were given.

The cognitive breadth measures were created by counting how many of the internationally accepted responses were used by the future teachers as described above. The final set of measures we developed used the same logic but first subdivided the acceptable responses into smaller subsets or categories according to the substantive nature of the different perspectives. These are specific to each of the three tasks and will be described in each section detailing the results of the analyses. The measures resulting from these procedures remain as counts but only of subsets of the acceptable responses. The next sections present results using these five types of measures for each of the three teaching situations or vignettes.

LESSON PLANNING

The coding scheme for the lesson plan vignette includes four perspectives: lesson structure, instructional interactions, instructional materials, and motivational issues. The international team agreed on a comprehensive coding rubric for the criteria and application codes as well as for the professional vocabulary. Two examples for each are given in Table 6.1, which documents the range of codes. In addition, there was a code "other." Since the coding rubric was thought to be reasonably exhaustive, the proportion of responses coded into this category was to be as low as possible. In some sense, this would be an indicator of how well the rubric worked. In fact, only 7.6% of the future teachers gave a response that had to be classified as "other." This was the third lowest use of any of the codes.

Figure 6.2 gives the means, standard errors, and distributions for each of the six countries for the four scales related to lesson planning, which build on the rubrics according to the methods explained in the section above. Following the general scheme outlined in the previous section, the scales were counts of the number of different analytical perspectives brought to bear on the issue, a measure of connectivity, and a measure of the extent to which technical language was used in evaluating the lesson plans. Specifically, the first scale is a count of the number of criteria stated by the future teacher with regard to how she would evaluate the proposed lesson plan. There were 23 criteria designated as acceptable by the international team.

After listing the criteria they would use as an approach to measure their declarative knowledge about lesson planning, future teachers were asked to apply these and to indicate what they would praise and what they would criticize about the lesson plan. Scale 2 gives the total number of acceptable praises or criticisms mentioned by the future teacher. Scale 3 indicates whether there is a connection between what was praised or criticized and the criteria listed in the first scale. The scale ranges from zero (no match) to two, indicating a strong connection between evaluation criteria listed as part of scale one and what

TABLE 6.1. Coding structure (breadth of perspectives) and examples for the criteria and application codes (depth of perspectives) as well as for the professional vocabulary of the lesson plan vignette.

	Depth of Perspectives	
Breadth of Perspectives	*Criteria and Application Codes*	*Professional Vocabulary*
Lesson Structure	Lesson Goals Lesson Sequence	Conceptual Understanding Advanced Organizer
Instructional Interactions	Teaching Methods Student Cognition	Seat Work Preconditions
Instructional Materials	Mathematics Content Textbook	Density Hands-On Materials
Motivational Issues	Class Climate Consideration of Diverse Needs	Maslow Interest

was then praised or criticized. Thus, it is a measure of the connectivity of their responses—that is, whether the suggested changes in the form of praise or criticism logically flow from the stated criteria. Finally, the use of technical language is evaluated by the fourth scale, which counts the number of professional terms used in developing the criteria and in their evaluation of the actual plan.

FIGURE 6.2. Country means for the four scales related to the lesson plan vignette.

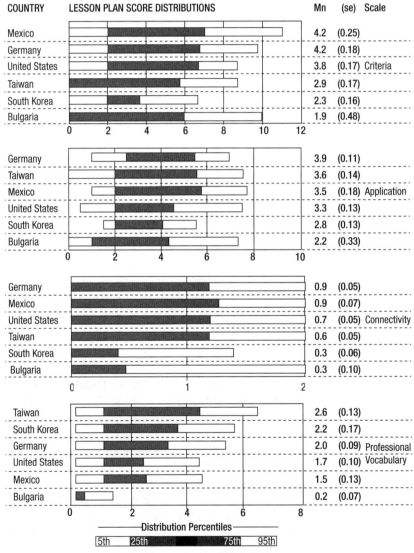

The country means reveal some interesting patterns. Clearly Bulgarian future teachers did not do well on any of the subscales for the lesson plan item. This is not surprising as the data in Chapter 4 revealed that they did not have much coursework related to pedagogy, especially general pedagogy. One clear manifestation of this revolves around the measure describing the number of technical terms used by the future teachers in their responses. For Bulgarian future teachers, the mean number employed (.2) indicates on average either none or only one being used. This probably reflects the absence of formal coursework in this area that would provide them with the relevant terminology.

By contrast, German and Mexican sampled future teachers performed quite well, especially for the first three scales. This reflects the structure of their teacher education quite well as both countries provide future teachers with a great deal of practical experiences, either as part of their courses at the normal school, as in the case of Mexico; or as a separate training phase, as in the case of Germany (see Chapter 2). Interestingly, the only exception to this pattern is in the use of technical language, especially for the Mexican future teachers, where the mean was lower than would be expected given the large means for stating the criteria—4.2, the largest (with Germany) among the six countries. Sampled U.S. future teachers also had a relatively high mean on their specification of criteria but they, like Mexico, also exhibited substantial variation. Such variation in the United States could reflect differences in program emphasis at the institutional level.

The above discussion is based on the notion that the breadth and depth of the students' declarative and procedural responses are indicative of a higher level of cognitive ability, and as such focuses not on the particular codes used but on the number thereof. To look further at the particular responses, we grouped the 23 substantive codes (16 of which represent examples per the text and are illustrated in Table 6.1) relevant to a planning-lesson activity into four basic perspectives on instruction (also listed in Table 6.1). We then examined how the future teachers used and applied these different sets of criteria—not to suggest that any one set is better than any other but simply to give a sense of the breadth of perspectives and country-specific profiles that were used and how they vary across the sampled future teachers from each of the six countries. If future teachers used any of the perspectives within a set, we coded them as using that type of criterion. This resulted in a dichotomous variable—using a category (1) versus not using that category (0). The estimated percentage of sampled future teachers is listed in Table 6.2.

The first set of criteria includes perspectives related to the goals and content of the lesson combined with the general approach or organization of the lesson; we label this as *lesson structure*. The second category focuses mostly on the nature of the *instructional interactions*. The third set of criteria is defined by

TABLE 6.2. Percentage of future teachers using the different perspectives on instruction in the lesson planning vignette.

Categories	Bulgaria	Germany	Mexico	South Korea	Taiwan	United States
Lesson Structure	10	53	38	50	22	53
Instructional Interactions	9	51	49	24	40	40
Instructional Materials	1	1	20	14	11	26
Motivational Issues	3	35	19	19	41	41

instructional materials and the *evaluation* of the student. The final set of criteria focuses on *motivational issues.*

Approximately half of the sampled German, South Korean, and U.S. future teachers used criteria related to the lesson structure—that is, addressing whether the lesson plan is organized and structured in a way that will accomplish the goal of the lesson focusing on area and volume.

Only about half again as many of the sampled Taiwanese future teachers (22%) used this type of criterion, with Mexico somewhere between (38%). Because future teachers can use multiple criteria, over half of the German future teachers also used instructional interaction perspectives, and approximately one third of the future teachers focused on motivation issues. This pattern reflects the strong emphasis lesson planning is given in the German Didaktik tradition (Tulodziecki, Herzig, & Blömeke, 2004). Since Bildung is not only a product but also a process, it matters how the instructional process is designed from the cognitive and the affective-motivational perspective with regard to the interaction of a teacher's goals, content requirements, and students' needs. Corresponding opportunities to learn play an important role in teacher education on a theoretical level at universities as well as on a practical level in the second, school-based phase of teacher education. The United States, like Germany, had sizeable proportions of its sampled future teachers (one third or more) using three of the four categories of perspectives.

In fact, across all six countries the only category not used very frequently dealt with the perspectives related to instructional materials/evaluation. Of course, this is also the narrowest category, hence some of the low use may be attributed to this. Bulgarian future teachers hardly used any of these criteria, while Taiwanese future teachers mainly focused on instructional organization and motivational issues. This reflects a strong emphasis in Taiwan that motivation is the key aspect of lesson planning. It is important to note that it is necessary to distinguish between the two East Asian countries in many respects. The achievement of future teachers in South Korea is very different from that of the Taiwanese, as is their response profile. This may reflect differences in opportunities to learn that are provided in the two countries (Chapter 2). In any case, it is helpful to challenge the tendency to treat East Asia as a uniform category, as is regularly done in the comparative literature.

SOCIAL CLASS AND THE ACHIEVEMENT GAP

The second vignette focuses on reasons for the social-class achievement gap and asks what future teachers would do in their own teaching to deal with the issue. The structure of the coding was the same as with the lesson plan, measuring both the declarative and procedural knowledge and the amount of technical language used. The degree of logical continuity between what they considered to be reasonable explanations for the achievement gap and how they would take such differences in socioeconomic status (SES) into account in their own teaching made up the third scale. The nature of the resulting scales parallel the scales used for the lesson plan vignette.

The coding scheme for the SES vignette also includes four perspectives: family characteristics, student characteristics, school characteristics, and teacher characteristics. The international team agreed on a comprehensive coding rubric for which two examples are given in Table 6.3, which document the range of codes. The first perspective represents preconditions of teaching that are mainly not under the control of teachers. In contrast, teacher characteristics are a function of the teachers' professional work. As with the lesson plan vignette, there was a code "others" to capture responses that did not fit into the coding scheme. Of the future teachers, 7.4% gave a response that had to be classified this way. This proportion can be regarded as suffi-

TABLE 6.3. Coding structure (breadth of perspectives) and examples for the explanation of (depth perspectives) as well as for the professional vocabulary of the lesson plan vignette.

Breadth of Perspectives	Depth of Perspectives	
	Declarative Knowledge	Professional Vocabulary
Family Characteristics	SES-Related Differences in Educational Aspiration Neighborhood Resources	Cultural Capital Role Models
Student Characteristics	SES-Related Differences in Motivation Time Spent on Homework	Self-Esteem Adaptation
School Characteristics	SES-Related Differences in Access to Technology Safety and Comfort	School Funding Tracking
Teacher Characteristics	Learning Expectations Teacher Quality	Pygmalion Effect Dealing with Heterogeneity

ciently low. Even if the differences between countries were significant ($\chi^2_{[5]}$ = 54.2, p < .0001), the range from 1.5 % in Germany to 16.8 % in South Korea still seems to be tolerable.

The means of the four scales for each of the countries are listed in Figure 6.3. What is quite surprising is that in discussing the reasons for such an achievement gap related to SES, there were no real differences among the countries. What is also notable is how many reasons were mentioned by the future teachers—only one or two on average. In terms of describing how they would deal with such an issue in their own classrooms, stark differences emerged. Here, rounding to the nearest whole number, the United States on average approached the issue using three out of the seven possible perspectives. All other countries used two perspectives or fewer. It might be a reasonable hypothesis to suggest that the reason for the higher mean in the United States is related to the unique history of this issue, especially as it intertwines with race in the United States. Germany comes the closest in their responses to the United States, especially when compared with the other countries, but it is most notable when compared to Taiwan and Bulgaria with means less than one. For Bulgarian future teachers the issue might be the same as described before—namely, the little amount of OTL related to general pedagogy in their typical teacher-preparation program. These differences among countries point to the possibility that teacher education matters especially in the area of general pedagogy as represented by these vignettes.

But quite surprisingly, differences among the countries change when considering the more technical aspects of the SES item. While U.S. and German future teachers suggested a broader approach in addressing SES in their own teaching, especially compared to Taiwanese future teachers, when it comes to the language used to describe that procedural (as well as declarative) knowledge it was the future teachers in Taiwan (and South Korea) who on average used the most professional terms. Mexico also presents an interesting scenario, since the country struggles with huge disparities in SES, as indicated in Chapters 1 and 2. However, the future teachers did relatively better speaking on the lesson plan vignette than they did on this one, and we know from Chapter 4 that, on average, there was a great deal of emphasis focusing on general pedagogy in their teacher preparation programs.

We now turn to an examination of the types of substantive arguments used by the sample of future teachers concerning the issue of the SES achievement gap. Four categories of response were used to characterize the perspectives related to their explanations of why the achievement gap occurs (see Table 6.3).

Table 6.4 includes the means, standard errors, and distributions. When it comes to explaining why such a gap exists, it is on this vignette that small

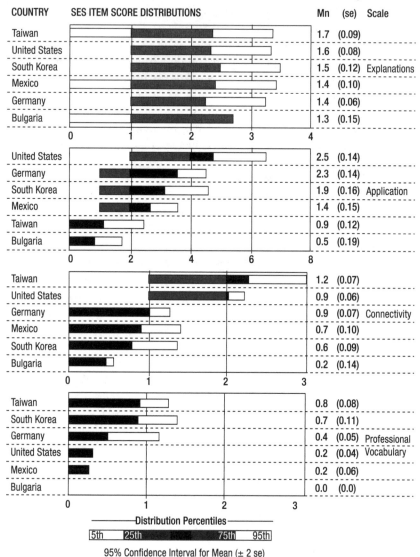

FIGURE 6.3. Country means for the four scales related to the SES vignette.

differences were revealed across the countries. Ignoring Bulgaria due to the low response rate, we focus on the other five countries. The future teachers in all five countries focused mostly on student characteristics as the explanation for the SES gap. In fact, in all but Mexico this type of response dominated— used by around 80% or more of the sampled future teachers. For Taiwan about one fourth of the sampled future teachers also used school funding as an expla-

TABLE 6.4. Percentage of future teachers in each country choosing different categories of explanation and accommodation for the SES vignette.

Categories	Bulgaria	Germany	Mexico	South Korea	Taiwan	United States
Explanations						
School Funding		3	10	7	23	10
Student Safety		1	3	4	11	4
Teacher Quality	18	9	3	1	3	14
Student Characteristics	2	85	58	78	93	85
Application						
Instructional Strategies	1	46	28	18	2	43
Curricular Adjustments		2	5	17	1	3
Motivational Strategies		22	1	4	9	16
Providing Extra Help	1	33	6	36	24	36
Involving Parents	3	16	6	1	14	21
Reducing School-Related Biases		4	1	31	8	20

nation. Virtually no one used teacher quality as a potential explanation for the gap. This is quite interesting given that this is the main feature under the control of teachers. It may indicate that teachers tend to move the responsibility away from themselves to other sources.

Turning to what these future teachers might choose to do in their own classrooms related to such differences in achievement across the different social classes, we first define the possible categories of accommodations suggested by the future teachers. Six categories were created (with examples of the professional vocabulary accepted by the international team in brackets):

- Instructional strategies (inclusive activities, group work)
- Curricular adjustments (cognitive demand, substantive focus)
- Motivational strategies (interest, confidence)
- Providing extra help (shadow education, tutoring)
- Involving parents (teacher-parent relationship, extracurricular activities)
- Reducing school-related biases (linguistic bias, SES–related bias)

The percentage of future teachers stating accommodations that fall into these six categories for each country are also found in Table 6.4. Approximately half of the sampled German and U.S. future teachers indicated they would respond to such an SES achievement gap through instructional strategies such as heterogeneous group work. This was also identified as an approach by around one fourth of the Mexican future teachers. In contrast, this approach was not used by hardly any of the Taiwanese future teachers (2%).

Curriculum adjustments were not considered by virtually any future teachers in all the countries except for South Korea, where approximately 20% stated such an approach. Providing extra help was also stated by a quarter or more of future teachers in the four countries other than Mexico (Bulgaria was not discussed due to small sample sizes with codable responses). South Korea, unlike the other four countries, had about 30% of its future teachers propose an approach of reducing school biases.

ASSESSING STUDENTS

The final vignette we used asked the future teachers to design up to four assessments during a unit on interpreting data. The plan includes when the assessments are to be given, what methods are to be used, and the reasons for using them. The same four parallel types of scales were used.

The first scale, focusing on declarative knowledge, was based on the reasons future teachers gave as to why they were doing these assessments. The second scale, on procedural knowledge, focused on the number of different assessment methods they proposed. Flow, or the measure of continuity, looked at the proposed assessment design to see if there was a logical connection between consecutive assessments. As was the case for the lesson plan and the SES vignette, this variable was scored from zero to two to indicate the strength of such connections. Finally, as with the other two vignettes, the fourth measure was a count of the number of appropriate technical terms used in describing their proposed assessment design.

Figure 6.4 presents the means for the four scales for each of the six countries. Looking at the number of reasons given, a clear pattern emerges. Rounding the values to the nearest whole number, the German future teachers gave on average five reasons, while the future teachers in the other five countries gave three. In this sense a pattern begins to emerge in which, at least at the level of declarative knowledge, German future teachers tend to exhibit a greater breadth of response.

For the assessment item we look more closely at the types of assessment methods used and when the various types were used in terms of the flow of the instruction. These results are presented in Table 6.5. The 20 or so methods available were coded into five groups:

1. Quiz-like activities
2. Homework or other in-class individual activities
3. In-class group projects or activities
4. Pre-tests or formative assessments
5. Written exams or post-tests

FIGURE 6.4. Country means for the four scales related to the student assessment vignette.

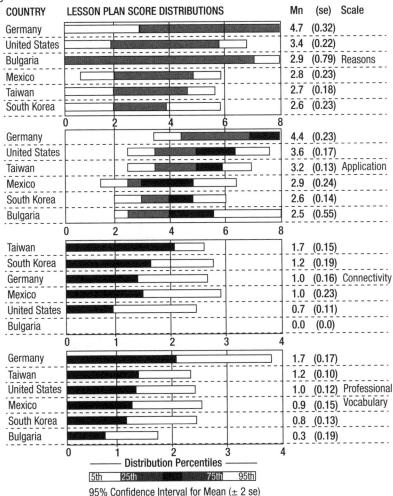

The values in the table represent the percentage of sampled future teachers in each country who chose each of the different methods at each of three time points. The three time points were defined in terms of the location of the assessment in the flow of the unit. We identified three time points: (1) the beginning of the unit, (2) during the unit, and (3) the end of the unit. We do this because different kinds of assessment techniques would likely be used at different points in the lesson. A pretest is a good illustration of why we divided the methods into different time points.

TABLE 6.5. Percentage of future teachers in each country choosing different
methods at three different points in the assessment vignette.

	Method	Bulgaria	Germany	Mexico	South Korea	Taiwan	United States	Total
Beginning of	Quiz		33	0	58	16	30	27
the Unit	Homework		25	32	24	54	25	31
	Projects		8	0	0	15	3	5
	Pre-tests		34	32	18	4	39	27
	Post-tests		0	35	0	12	4	10
	Total Percent		100	100	100	100	100	100
Middle of the	Quiz	76	24	4	24	25	25	26
Unit	Homework	18	28	54	28	43	37	38
	Projects	0	11	15	11	6	14	11
	Pre-tests	0	28	2	28	6	13	12
	Post-tests	7	10	25	10	20	9	13
	Total Percent	100	100	100	100	100	100	100
End of the	Quiz	25	23	1	23	18	35	25
Unit	Homework	25	16	31	16	41	24	30
	Projects	0	6	3	6	8	7	7
	Pre-tests	0	21	24	21	4	15	13
	Post-tests	50	34	41	34	29	19	26
	Total Percent	100	100	100	100	100	100	100

Over all countries at the beginning of the unit three types of assessments
were proposed by all but 15% of the sampled future teachers. These were quizzes, homework, and pre-tests. In Mexico, however, written exams were proposed instead of quizzes. It is also interesting to note that Taiwan and South
Korea, which share many practices, were different in one important way: 60%
of South Korean future teachers proposed quizzes and 24% proposed homework—the opposite of the Taiwanese future teachers.

In the middle of the unit not much difference occurred, but at the end of
the unit, where one might expect some differences across the countries or at
least across the types of assessments, essentially neither occurred. Bulgaria had
an interesting pattern of not proposing any testing at the beginning of the unit
but only during the unit and at the end, while for half of the teachers the proposed method was a written exam.

SUMMARY

In the previous sections we have reported the results for each of the three
vignettes separately. The question addressed in this section is what we have
learned across vignettes. This question can be phrased differently as: Do the
responses of the future teachers tell us anything in general about general pedagogy, or must we restrict ourselves to separate statements relative only to a particular type of pedagogical situation as we did in the field of mathematics with
distinguishing number, algebra, function, geometry, and data?

We do not believe that what we present here can answer this question definitively, as it is a complex substantive issue that intersects with complex psychometric issues. The three vignettes were each scored according to four constructs even though the particulars were different. These four were declarative knowledge, procedural knowledge, logical consistency, and the use of professional/technical language. Our examination of the data suggests that it is possible to combine the data for each of the four types across vignettes. More conceptual and psychometric work needs to be done and so we present these results only in a tentative way and as a useful way of summarizing a complex situation. Table 6.6 shows for each country and for each of the four questions the mean across the three vignettes. The unit for this analysis is the institution where both forms were given. What emerges is consistent in many ways with the findings of Chapter 4 with respect to OTL related to general pedagogy. German sampled future teachers scored the highest when it came to declarative knowledge, at least about these three pedagogical situations. Mexico and the United States also scored high, and Bulgaria the lowest.

For procedural knowledge the pattern is the same, indicating that for pedagogical knowledge both German and U.S. future teachers did well, at least relatively speaking. Mexican future teachers didn't do as well with procedural knowledge as one might expect given their higher performance on declarative knowledge.

Germany and the United States also did well on the logical consistency measure but here Taiwan was closer in performance than was the case with the two knowledge measures. Another observation from the data is the strong performance of the sampled Taiwanese future teachers in the area of the correct use of a professional/technical vocabulary. The same is true for South Korea. The differences here are most telling. Again, rounding to the nearest whole number, sampled Taiwanese future teachers had a score of 5, Germany and South Korea a score of 4, and Mexico and the United States a score of 3, with Bulgaria recording an average less than 1. Germany—which consistently had the highest mean on knowledge and logical consistency—dropped below both Taiwan and South Korea. We will return to these findings in Chapter 12.

TABLE 6.6. Country means and standard deviations for the four scales across the three vignettes.

Scales	Bulgaria Mean	SD	Germany Mean	SD	Mexico Mean	SD	South Korea Mean	SD	Taiwan Mean	SD	United States Mean	SD
1	5.9	1.6	10.3	0.8	8.9	2.1	6.5	0.8	7.5	1.6	9.3	2.6
2	5.0	1.3	10.5	0.9	8.1	1.4	7.3	0.8	7.7	0.7	9.7	2.0
3	0.6	0.9	3.3	0.5	2.7	1.0	1.7	0.2	2.9	1.2	3.0	1.0
4	0.2	0.1	3.5	0.4	2.7	0.8	4.1	1.2	5.1	1.1	2.6	0.8

What Do Future Teachers Believe About Teaching, Learning, and Mathematics?

By now we have learned about future teachers' opportunities to learn and the knowledge they had as they finished their programs. One could argue that there should be a direct correlation with their subsequent actions in the classroom. However, there is a reason Weinert (1999) divides competencies into cognitive abilities and the motivational, volitional, social disposition as well as the skills to apply those abilities. Teachers' professional convictions and their conception of values in terms of *beliefs* are crucial to their perception of classroom situations and their decision about what kind of knowledge to draw on and how to react (Leder, Pekhonen, & Törner, 2002; Leinhardt & Greeno, 1986). Beliefs connect knowledge and action. Therefore, if beliefs are operationalized specifically by both the content taught and the challenges presented by a classroom situation, then empirical evidence exists for a strong link between teacher beliefs and student achievement (Bromme, 2005).

For this reason, we carefully examined the professional beliefs of the future teacher sample, as well as their knowledge. Since beliefs can show different levels of proximity to behavior, we distinguished between *general professional beliefs* like epistemological beliefs about the nature of mathematics, as discussed by Hofer and Pintrich (2002), and *specific behavioral intentions* related to situations teachers would typically encounter (Ajzen, 1985). Whereas the first kinds of beliefs represent the future teachers' basic professional worldview, the latter kinds represent an indicator of their classroom performance.

In this chapter we present results about the two main dimensions of teachers' general professional beliefs (Calderhead, 1996; Cooney et al., 1998; Ernest, 1991a; Op't Eynde, De Corte, & Verschaffel, 2002; Thompson, 1992):

- epistemological beliefs about the nature of mathematics and about how to gain mathematical knowledge, as well as

FIGURE 7.1. Future teachers' beliefs measured in MT21.

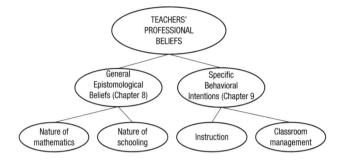

- epistemological beliefs about the nature of schooling, teaching, teacher education and professional development.

In the next chapter we report on the future teachers' behavioral intentions, including instructional behavior and classroom management (see Figure 7.1).

EPISTEMOLOGICAL BELIEFS ABOUT THE NATURE OF MATHEMATICS AND HOW TO GAIN MATHEMATICAL KNOWLEDGE

Epistemological beliefs refer to the *structure* and *formation* of knowledge (Buehl & Alexander, 2001; Hofer & Pintrich, 1997; Schommer-Aikins, 2002). The first perspective includes questions about how the nature of mathematics is perceived, for example, whether it is like an activity or more like a static and closed system. The second perspective includes questions about how mathematical knowledge develops: Is it predominantly based on natural talent or better apprehended through effort and support? Does it have to be transmitted or individually constructed, and what should be the main objective for its development?

The Nature of Mathematics

Beliefs about the nature of mathematics are one of the issues that have been more prominent in empirical research (Törner & Pehkonen, 1996). The majority of this research has focused on students; there is less empirical research on teacher beliefs. Grigutsch, Raatz, and Törner (1998) categorize epistemological beliefs about the nature of mathematics into four aspects:

1. Mathematics can be understood as a creative science that consists of discovery and problem solving. Examples for this would be statements like "Mathematics means creativity and new ideas," or, "If one engages in mathematical tasks, one can discover new things (e.g., connections, rules, concepts)."

2. Mathematics can be regarded as a useful science that can be applied to society and life. Examples for this would be statements like "Mathematics is useful for every profession," or "Many aspects of mathematics have practical relevance."

3. Mathematics could also be seen as a formal and logical science that has an axiomatic basis and develops by deduction. Examples for this perspective are statements like "Mathematical thought is characterized by abstraction and logic," or "Hallmarks of mathematics are clarity, precision, and unambiguousness."

4. Finally, mathematics could be identified as an algorithmic science that represents a collection of terms, formulas, and rules. Examples for this perspective are statements like "Mathematics is a collection of rules and procedures that prescribe how to solve a problem," or "Mathematics involves the remembering and application of definitions, formulas, mathematical facts, and procedures."

These four aspects describe two second-order dimensions of beliefs, namely, a dynamic perspective on mathematics represented by the creative and useful view, and a static perspective represented by the formal and algorithmic view.

In order to assess these beliefs, Grigutsch, Raatz, and Törner (1998) developed four scales. In a study with 310 German secondary mathematics teachers they found that teachers tended to show agreement with the useful and creative aspects of mathematics and a slight rejection of algorithmic aspects, whereas they were somewhat neutral to formal aspects. In a study with university mathematics instructors (Grigutsch & Törner, 1994), all aspects were supported, meaning that the dynamic and the static aspects coexist with each other. The scales have since been used in many studies. In MT21 a shortened version was used consisting of 20 items that had to be rated on a 6-point scale from 1 ("strongly disagree") to 6 ("strongly agree"). Following the prompt "To what extent do you agree or disagree with each of the following statements about mathematics?" the items included (in addition to others) the above-mentioned exemplary statements for each of the four scales. The reliability of the scales was high both across countries (at least $\alpha = .80$) and within most countries, where it was at least $\alpha = .75$. Only in South Korea did two of the scales drop below this level due to translation issues, but they were still at least at $\alpha = .70$.

Overall, future teachers at the end of teacher education in our six MT21 samples highly favored a dynamic perspective on mathematics (see Table 7.1). With both overall means around 5, the agreement favoring a view of mathematics as a useful and creative science was very strong. Agreement with a formal view was significantly lower and there was even less agreement with an algorithmic view. However, given a scale mean of 3.5 that indicated a neutral position, it has to be pointed out that the latter ratings still revealed agreement, albeit to a lesser degree.

The differences between the countries on each scale were statistically significant. Future teachers sampled in Mexico stood out as strong supporters of a view of mathematics as a creative and useful science, whereas Bulgarian future teachers were more doubtful about the first view and South Korean future teachers more doubtful about the latter view. Taiwan stood out as a strong supporter of a formalistic and algorithmic view, while German future teachers, whose mean was the smallest across all countries, indicated a slight disagreement with characterizing mathematics as an algorithmic science.

If one compares the two views characterized as dynamic, future teachers in Germany, South Korea, and Taiwan more strongly supported statements indicating the creative nature of mathematics than those indicating the useful nature. Whereas the ratings of the corresponding statements do not differ significantly in the United States and Mexico, Bulgarian teachers specifically support the usefulness of mathematics. With respect to the two static views, all countries except the United States acknowledged the formal nature of mathematics significantly more than the algorithmic nature.

Looking at the four standard deviations, South Korean future teachers showed a very homogenous response pattern, particularly with respect to a view on mathematics as a creative science, and future teachers in Taiwan and the United States showed fairly low variation as well. While we recognize the

TABLE 7.1. Country means and standard errors (se) for beliefs about the nature of mathematics.[1]

Country	Algorithmic		Usefulness		Creative		Formalism	
	Mean	*(se)*	*Mean*	*(se)*	*Mean*	*(se)*	*Mean*	*(se)*
South Korea	4.3	(0.1)	4.3	(0.1)	4.9	(0.1)	4.7	(0.1)
Taiwan	4.3	(0.0)	4.9	(0.0)	5.1	(0.0)	5.1	(0.0)
Bulgaria	4.2	(0.1)	4.9	(0.1)	4.6	(0.1)	4.8	(0.1)
Germany	3.3	(0.0)	4.7	(0.1)	5.1	(0.0)	4.3	(0.1)
United States	4.0	(0.1)	5.2	(0.1)	5.2	(0.0)	4.0	(0.1)
Mexico	3.5	(0.1)	5.5	(0.1)	5.4	(0.1)	4.1	(0.1)

homeogeneity in the two East Asian countries revealed in other studies, for example, on student achievement, the U.S. result is surprising given the usually high variation in U.S. data.

A median polish highlights the reality that Mexican future teachers in our sample had the most extreme beliefs about the nature of mathematics. They agreed particularly strongly with statements that indicated the creative and useful features of mathematics, while they showed significantly lower agreement than future teachers from the other countries when it came to statements indicating algorithmic and formal features. In contrast to such an antagonistic view on the nature of mathematics, South Korean future teachers showed the most balanced beliefs, as evidenced by the range of the means (see Figure 7.2 for a graphical representation). They characterized mathematics as creative and useful as well as formal and algorithmic.

As one would expect, strong positive correlations exist in all six MT21 countries between an algorithmic and a formal view of mathematics (see Figure 7.3). Correspondingly, strong positive correlations exist everywhere between the creative and useful views on mathematics, which represent the more dynamic beliefs.

There are no other clear generalizations that can be made across the six countries except that slight positive correlations dominate. This means that future teachers who agree with one generally tend to support the other scale as well. In this sense, their beliefs resemble those of mathematics experts as examined by Grigutsch and Törner (1994), which is perhaps related to having stud-

FIGURE 7.2. Future teachers' beliefs about the nature of mathematics (country means).

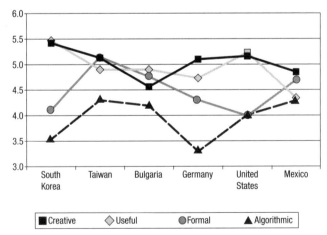

FIGURE 7.3. Correlations between future teachers' beliefs about the nature of mathematics (South Korea/Taiwan/Bulgaria/Germany/United States/Mexico).

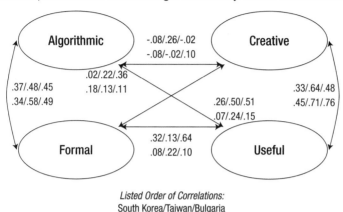

Listed Order of Correlations:
South Korea/Taiwan/Bulgaria
Germany/United States/Mexico

ied with such experts during their teacher preparation. This applies especially to future teachers in Taiwan.

Bulgarian future teachers are an interesting case since there are especially large correlations between useful, algorithmic, and formal statements. The more useful a future teacher regards mathematics, the more she believes in its algorithmic and formal nature. We assume that this pattern implies a very pronounced understanding of the complex relationship between the features of mathematics—namely, that mathematics can be very useful—but only if one masters the algorithms.

We have data from two countries about differences between license levels that lead to middle school teaching. In Germany, middle school teachers who trained as part of an elementary program showed an even stronger belief that mathematics is a useful science than future teachers who trained in a secondary program. Differences on the other three scales were less pronounced. In the United States future teachers who trained in an elementary or secondary program did not differ substantially. However, future teachers trained in a program specific for middle schools turned out to have stronger static views than the other groups.

The Formation of Mathematics Knowledge

Is mathematics learnable by most students? To what end should it be learned? And what would be the best way to teach it? These are the three basic questions behind our survey on future teachers' beliefs about the formation of mathematics knowledge. Early thinkers Bacon (1267/2000) and Kant (1786) discussed them because answers to these questions could reveal important insight into human nature and the purpose of education.

Those scales were only included on one of the two MT21 test forms. The resulting means are based on small sample sizes, especially in Bulgaria and South Korea, and caution is in order for any kind of conclusions. Since the test forms were randomly distributed to future teachers within each institution the results would be representative of the institution—but again, we remind the readers that we cannot assure their representativeness as a whole.

Is mathematics learnable by most? There are not many studies that try to capture beliefs about this question. A comparative study focusing on Chinese and U.S. teachers described different beliefs concerning the source of student success in mathematics: Chinese teachers viewed students' efforts as the reason for success in contrast to U.S. teachers, who believed in natural talent as the main determinant of student achievement (Stevenson et al., 1990). We captured this kind of belief with a scale that consisted of five items. Because of the high sensitivity of this issue they followed a prompt with which we tried to remove part of the social desirability one would expect in this kind of survey: "On a popular TV program several experts were invited to explain the puzzling phenomenon that student achievement in middle school mathematics varies widely. To what extent do you agree or disagree with each of the following statements that were made during the talk?" An example for the statements given, which were to be rated on a 6-point scale from 1 ("strongly disagree") to 6 ("strongly agree") would be "To be good at mathematics you need to have a kind of 'mathematical mind.'" The reliability of this scale was good across countries ($\alpha = .80$) and sufficient within most countries, although it drops below the critical benchmark of $\alpha = .70$ in Bulgaria.

Other studies point toward gender and ethnic differences in beliefs about the learning of mathematics. It seems as if teachers and parents regard girls by nature as less capable of learning mathematics compared to boys (Fennema, Carpenter, & Loef, 1990; Parsons, Adler, & Kaczala, 1982). This kind of belief was captured by a second scale, with two items covering each of the two categories mentioned; for example, "In general, boys tend to be naturally better at mathematics than girls." Again, the reliability of the scale is good across countries ($\alpha = .82$) and also within five of the six countries. In this case, Mexico has a relatively low reliability.

Inconsistent with support of this kind of statement would be the view that small children can already develop a basic understanding of mathematics that teachers must take into account. New content has to be connected to pre-existing mental concepts in order to be absorbed. While many mathematics teachers seem to be somewhat aware of this phenomenon, they still tend to underestimate the extent of prior understanding and treat children's minds as blank slates (Grassman, Mirwald, Klunter, & Veith, 1995; Hengartner & Röthlisberger, 1995; Wittmann, 2003)—with the undesirable effect that new ideas coexist with former mental concepts. An exemplary item in our two-item scale was "Children enter school with some important mathematical skills." The scale's reliability was very good, across countries and within four countries at least at α = .90.

Across countries, future teachers agreed with the notion of mental concepts of mathematics existing before children enter school (see Table 7.2). However, the differences between the six countries were highly significant. Mexican and German teachers sampled for MT21 showed the strongest support for this belief, whereas Bulgarian future teachers were the only group with more of a neutral position. Future teachers from the six MT21 countries slightly disagreed with statements that indicated natural talent as one of the main sources of student achievement in mathematics. The German and U.S. groups disagreed particularly strongly, whereas future teachers from the two Asian countries on average supported statements that indicated beliefs in natural ability. Across countries, future teachers even more strongly rejected the notion that mathematical abilities depended on biological categories like gender and ethnic background. Again, the differences between the six countries were highly significant. Strongest rejection in this area came from future teachers from Germany, whereas future teachers from Taiwan on average believed in categorical differences.

Median polish analyses revealed that Germany and Taiwan are also the two groups that deviated the most from the overall response patterns across the three scales, with the German students supporting particularly strong statements that

TABLE 7.2. Country means and standard errors (se) for beliefs about the formation of mathematics knowledge.

Country	Catagorical Differences		Pre-existing Concepts		Natural Ability	
	Mean	*(se)*	*Mean*	*(se)*	*Mean*	*(se)*
South Korea	2.6	(0.2)	3.8	(0.2)	3.9	(0.1)
Taiwan	3.9	(0.1)	3.9	(0.1)	3.8	(0.1)
Bulgaria	2.8	(0.2)	3.4	(0.2)	3.6	(0.1)
Germany	1.7	(0.1)	4.8	(0.1)	2.4	(0.1)
United States	2.3	(0.1)	4.3	(0.1)	2.4	(0.1)
Mexico	2.2	(0.1)	5.0	(0.1)	2.8	(0.1)

indicated children's understandings of mathematics even before they come to school and the Taiwanese students supporting particularly strong statements indicating differences in mathematics ability according to biological categories. The latter support is so strong that Taiwan is the only country with a non-antagonistic view on these ability concepts but a relatively homogenous support of all three approaches (see Figure 7.4). However, it has to be pointed out that the antagonism noticeable in the three Western countries—Germany, Mexico, and the United States—is less pronounced in Bulgaria and in South Korea as well because in these countries—unlike in Germany, Mexico, and the United States —natural ability still received some support. It was actually only the assumption of categorical differences that was rejected. One hypothesis is that these beliefs are influenced by the difficulty of the K–12 curriculum—that is, in those countries with the more difficult mathematics curriculum future teachers are more likely to believe in natural ability and categorical differences.

Taiwan is also the only country in which gender and ethnic differences received even more agreement than natural ability assumptions. In all the other countries, future teachers rejected the first belief but showed less willingness to reject the latter belief as well. It seems as if natural abilities were regarded as more tolerable if they were not related to categories. In general it is striking how much variation exists in all countries and on all scales. There is obvi-

FIGURE 7.4. Future teachers' beliefs about the formation of mathematical knowledge (country means).

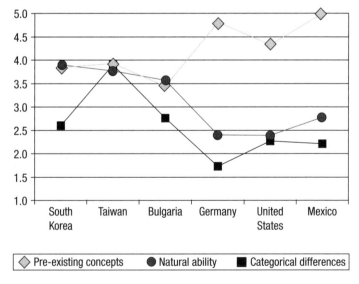

ously not much agreement about how mathematical knowledge is formed even within countries.

With respect to differences between future teachers trained in programs for different license levels, the most remarkable result repeats the aforementioned exceptional position of future teachers trained in a middle-school program. They agreed significantly more strongly with statements that indicated natural ability as the main source of achievement in mathematics. They agreed significantly less with statements that indicated children's mathematical understandings prior to schooling. In general, there is remarkably little variation between institutions with respect to beliefs about the formation of mathematical knowledge. In all countries except South Korea the between-institution variance was generally no more than 10%; in Bulgaria and Germany it was no more than 4%.

As expected, strong positive correlations exist between beliefs that indicate a biological predetermination of mathematics achievement (see Figure 7.5). The more future teachers from all six countries believe that mathematics is a natural ability one either does or does not have, the more they agree with categorical differences like gender or ethnic background as explanations of differences in mathematics achievement.

Relationships between these beliefs and beliefs about pre-existing concepts of mathematics differ across countries. Because the literature about pre-existing concepts stresses developmental aspects and the necessity of conceptual changes, we had expected that there would either be no systematic or even a negative relationship between beliefs about pre-existing concepts and beliefs about biological pre-determinations but, in any case, not a positive one. This

FIGURE 7.5. Correlations between future teachers' beliefs about mathematics learning (South Korea/Taiwan/Bulgaria/Germany/United States/Mexico).

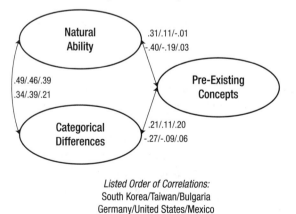

Listed Order of Correlations:
South Korea/Taiwan/Bulgaria
Germany/United States/Mexico

pattern shows up in Germany, the United States, and Mexico. The discussion in mathematics education in these countries can be characterized as highly influenced by Western traditions. In contrast, beliefs of future teachers, specifically in Taiwan but also in South Korea and partly in Bulgaria, are positively correlated with one another. Obviously, they do not regard these beliefs as incompatible. This likely reflects the thinking in Taiwan that rejects this Western literature as not applicable in countries with a more demanding curriculum, especially at the upper-secondary level.

To what end should mathematical knowledge be learned? Transmission and constructivism are fundamental paradigms in how human beings develop knowledge. With respect to teachers, another fundamental perspective has to be taken into account when we discuss the learning of mathematics—namely, their objectives for mathematics instruction. Objectives provide a higher-order structure for lesson planning and reflection. How much emphasis would teachers give to cognitive objectives, for example, compared to affective objectives? Six scales with altogether 28 items captured such beliefs in MT21. They cover cognitive, functional, and affective-motivational objectives for mathematics instruction as they are mentioned in standards from professional organizations as well as in those from states (KMK, 2004b; NCTM, 2000) and as they are discussed in educational psychology (Anderson et al., 2001) or didactics (Blum, Drüke-Noe, Hartung et al., 2006; Tulodziecki, Herzig, & Blömeke, 2004). The statements followed the prompt: "How much emphasis would you give to the following student objectives in teaching middle school mathematics?" They had to be rated on a 6-point Likert scale from 1 ("none at all") to 6 ("a great deal of emphasis"). Since these scales were part of only one of the two MT21 test forms, we again have to be very careful with generalizations. Our results should be regarded as first hypotheses only.

Cognitive objectives for mathematics instruction can be subdivided into lower-order objectives like the development of *mathematical skills* and *conceptual knowledge* and higher-order objectives like *reasoning* and the ability to *communicate* mathematical ideas:

- The development of mathematical skills is a basic precondition to successfully perform any kind of mathematical work (Heymann, 1996; Humenberger & Reichel, 1995). To dispose of a broad repertoire of algorithms reduces the cognitive load and frees mental capacity for higher-order tasks. It is therefore an important objective for mathematics instruction. The development of these kinds of skills was covered by seven items. Two examples were to "know mathematical algorithms" and to "learn to perform computations with speed and accuracy."

- The development of conceptual knowledge means to dispose of a mental representation of major mathematical concepts (Anderson et al., 2001; Mayer, 2003; Rittle-Johnson & Alibali, 1999), including how the concepts are related to one another. It is necessary to know the corresponding formal language and the symbolic representations in order to be able to connect the concepts to one another more than only superficially. Conceptual knowledge is a necessary precondition for understanding mathematical ideas and to be able to correctly apply mathematical skills. The conceptual-knowledge scale consisted of four items, of which to "understand mathematical concepts" and to "learn how mathematical ideas connect with one another" were two examples.
- Reasoning is a complex cognitive ability. It is always necessary if the algorithm that has to be used to solve a problem is unknown. MT21 covers two main mathematical tasks in which reasoning is highly involved: proofs and modeling. Proofs can be regarded as *the* mathematical activity. It is a formalized, step-wise procedure that is characterized by deduction from statements already proven. Mathematics educators have long been fighting for including proving in the school curriculum (Goldberg, 1992; Reiss, 2002) because it underpins an understanding of the logical structure of mathematics. Whereas proving in this regard refers to a within-mathematics activity, modeling refers to real-world problems that are solved with mathematical methods (Blum, Galbraith, Henn et al., 2007; Kaiser, 1995; Maaß, 2004). Modeling is a step-wise procedure as well, but of a different kind: The real-world problem has to be represented by a real-world model first before it can be translated into a mathematical model that can be worked on with mathematical methods. Then the mathematical solution has to be back-translated into a real-world solution. In MT21, six items covered reasoning as an objective for mathematics instruction. To "be able to prove mathematical statements" and to "be able to model real-world problems" were two examples of this scale.
- Finally, mathematical communication is an important objective for mathematics instruction. Students are supposed to learn to write essays, to talk about mathematics or to orally discuss different solutions of a mathematical problem (Hanna, 2000; Healy & Hoyles, 1998). This kind of ability is proven to lead to a better understanding of mathematical phenomena. Communication was captured by five items, of which to "be able to communicate about mathematics" and to "be able to engage in mathematics discourse" were examples.

The reliability of these cognitive scales is good across countries as well as within countries. Only one scale is below our benchmark of α = .70 in one country and this is the conceptual-knowledge scale in Germany. Functional objectives were captured with one scale. This kind of objective is narrowly focused on the mastery of mathematics classes and tests. So, there are no broader personal or societal accomplishments involved. Two exemplary items of this objective were to "be prepared for further study in mathematics" and to "be prepared for standardized tests." The scale's reliability is high everywhere.

Finally, affective-motivational objectives play an important role in discussions about mathematics instruction, not the least because of their long-term mediating effect on cognitive achievement. Only with sufficient interest is it possible for students to put long-term efforts into learning mathematics, even if there are setbacks (Krapp, 2001; Rheinberg, 2002). Interest and affection are usually closely related (Deci & Ryan, 1985). Correspondingly, high-achieving students like mathematics much better than low-achieving ones. In the MT21 survey, two exemplary items for affective-motivational objectives were to "enjoy dealing with mathematics" and to "have the feeling that mathematics is something he/she can do." Also, this scale's reliability is good across countries and within countries, with the possible exception of Mexico, where it is at α= .71.

It is amazing how evenly future teachers rated these objectives across countries. Given scale means of 3.5, cognitive objectives were as clearly emphasized overall as affective-motivational and functional ones (see Table 7.3). Affective-motivational objectives stood out, though, by being emphasized significantly more strongly than the other ones. It is also amazing how small the country variation was. The German students sampled for MT21 emphasized lower-order cognitive and especially functional objectives (this also applied to South Korea) less than students from other countries while Mexican students ex-

TABLE 7.3. Country means and standard errors (se) for objectives for mathematics instruction.

Country	Mathematical Skills		Reasoning		Communication		Functional Objectives		Conceptual Knowledge		Affective-Motivational	
	Mean	(se)	Mean	(se)	Mean	(se)	Mean	(se)	Mean	(se)	Mean	(se)
South Korea	4.5	(0.1)	4.4	(0.1)	4.4	(0.1)	3.9	(0.1)	4.7	(0.1)	5.4	(0.1)
Taiwan	4.6	(0.1)	4.7	(0.1)	4.4	(0.1)	4.8	(0.1)	5.0	(0.1)	5.4	(0.0)
Bulgaria	4.7	(0.1)	4.6	(0.1)	4.2	(0.2)	4.6	(0.1)	4.5	(0.1)	5.3	(0.1)
Germany	4.1	(0.1)	4.5	(0.1)	4.1	(0.1)	3.9	(0.1)	4.4	(0.1)	5.4	(0.1)
United States	4.4	(0.1)	4.8	(0.1)	4.6	(0.1)	4.6	(0.1)	4.8	(0.1)	5.5	(0.1)
Mexico	4.7	(0.1)	5.0	(0.1)	4.3	(0.1)	4.8	(0.1)	4.7	(0.1)	5.6	(0.1)

pressed somewhat more support of reasoning and Taiwanese students somewhat more support of conceptual knowledge—but overall, future teachers from all countries widely agreed on the importance of all objectives. Using Bonferroni adjusted statistical contrasts, the differences were not even statistically significant, which is—given the high number of cases—a strong indicator of cross-country homogeneity. Median polishes supported this interpretation. None of the countries stood out to an extent that would be remarkable.

Referring to the standard deviations, in all countries except Bulgaria, there was remarkably little variation on three of the four cognitive scales and on the affective-motivational scale. Obviously, within countries, future teachers agreed very much on the importance of these objectives. This applied also to future teachers in Germany and the United States coming from different programs. In neither of the two countries were substantial differences between these groups observed. Slightly more variation was noticed with respect to functional objectives as well as to communication abilities. In Germany and the United States, the latter were somewhat more strongly stressed by future teachers trained in a secondary program than by those trained in other programs. It could be that teachers relate these kinds of objectives to older students.

The correlations between beliefs about objectives for mathematics instruction were all positive (see Figure 7.6). This means that there is a general tendency across all countries either to value or to devalue more or less all objectives at the same time. However, there were differences in the extent to which this happens—and this between objectives on the one side and between countries on the other side. Across all countries, the relationship between support of mathematical skills as an objective and functional objectives was especially strong, which makes a lot of sense. The same applies to the two higher-order cognitive objectives reasoning and communication as well as to conceptual knowledge and communication. The latter demonstrates that conceptual knowledge—even if in general classified as a lower-order cognitive objective—from the perspective of future teachers represents a kind of bridge between lower- and higher-order skills with respect to student achievement.

Very low correlations were only observed for single countries, and this with respect to functional objectives. In Germany and Bulgaria, the latter were not systematically related to affective-motivational objectives, indicating a belief that test preparation alone is not regarded as sufficient to get children interested in mathematics. In South Korea and to an extent in Germany, functional objectives were not strongly related to conceptual knowledge and reasoning. These objectives are obviously regarded as not necessary to accomplish test preparation here.

Given all the indicators that point to homogenous response patterns, it is surprising that, with the exception of Bulgaria and the United States, variation

FIGURE 7.6. Correlations among future teachers' beliefs about objectives for mathematics instruction (South Korea/Taiwan/Bulgaria/Germany/United States/Mexico).

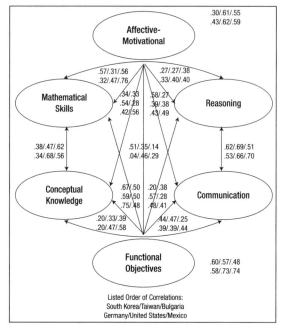

FIGURE 7.7. Institutional variation in the objectives for mathematics instruction of future teachers trained in elementary (left) and middle school programs (right).

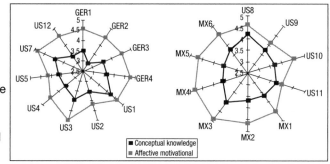

FIGURE 7.8. Institutional variation in the objectives for mathematics instruction of future teachers trained in secondary programs.

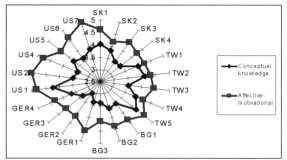

between institutions showed up in the other four countries (although in each country, only on one or two scales). To gain conceptual knowledge seems to depend most strongly on institutional characteristics. If one distinguishes not only between institutions but splits the programs in addition into license level, even more variation becomes apparent (see Figures 7.7 and 7.8).

EPISTEMOLOGICAL BELIEFS ABOUT
THE NATURE OF SCHOOLING AND TEACHING

A teacher's professional competencies are not only defined by the subject she is teaching but by the tasks that schools in our societies are expected to accomplish. In addition, the status of teachers in society, and the notion of whether teachers are born versus made also shape the structure of teacher education and can potentially influence what future teachers learn. Such epistemological beliefs about the nature of schooling, teachers, and professional development therefore represent another part of the MT21 beliefs survey. Our basic questions were: Which societal functions of schooling do future teachers value and which fundamental goals of schooling do they see as important? How do they perceive the teaching profession and what do they think about the teacher's role in the classroom? We assume that these kinds of beliefs are heavily shaped by cultural influences. Again, we have to point out that our results have to be regarded as hypotheses because the scales were only part of one of the two test forms, which means that the sample sizes are small.

The Nature of Schools

Functions of schooling. Why do we have institutions like schools? This is a basic theoretical question that can be answered from both an individual and a societal point of view (Fend, 1980; Parsons, 1959/1977). In modern societies, school has three main functions: integration, personalization, and selection.

- Every new generation has to get adjusted to core societal values and norms. Only if the majority of people accept core features of a society is its continuity secured. School contributes to integration into the society as a precondition of its reproduction by designing school life according to those core values and norms. The difference in power between groups of people, distributed according to a reasonable and convincing measure, is an example of this. Students have to accept that teachers, more knowledgeable and mature, are higher up in the hierarchy than they are. In the MT21 survey three statements that refer to integration as a function of schooling had to be rated on a 6-point

scale from 1 ("strongly disagree") to 6 ("strongly agree"). After initial
information about "The following statements relate to the nature and
purpose of schooling. Please indicate the extent to which you agree
or disagree with each," a prompt followed that said, "The main job of
schooling is to . . ." The integration scale consisted of three items, such
as "transmit the values of the national culture." Its reliability is high.

- Every new generation has to develop the individual's potential to be
  able to perform core societal tasks. Democracy needs politically mature
  citizens, just as the labor market needs well-trained employees. In this
  respect, to foster knowledge, skills, and competencies is as much a
  human right in a democratic society as it is a societal need. The school
  mainly contributes to personalization as a precondition of political and
  occupational reproduction by instruction but also by how the school
  life is designed. An example for the three-item personalization scale
  was to "support the personal development of each pupil/student." Also,
  this scale's reliability is good, across as well as within countries.
- Selection is the third important function of schooling. As already
  mentioned, there is a social divide in power but, in general, also in
  resources and jobs. In a democracy, their allocation must happen in
  a reasonable and convincing way. Whereas in the Middle Ages birth
  into an estate, such as being a member of the nobility, or peasantry
  determined the type of a person's societal role and participation,
  individual achievement has replaced birth in modern societies. Fend
  (1980, p. 29) described schooling, therefore, as the riddle or the screen
  between generations. Selection as a function of schooling was captured
  with a three-item scale that included, among others, the statement to
  "provide a fairer sorting of children than does occur elsewhere." The
  scale's reliability is very high.

The three functions are of equal importance for societies. However, we
have some indication from other studies that at least in some of the countries
teachers do not favor the third function (see, e.g., Fried, 2002). They perceive
selection somehow as contradictory to their pedagogical mandate to support
students' development.

Correspondingly, integration and personalization are the two functions of
schooling that were highly favored by future teachers across countries (see Table
7.4). With means around 5, their agreement is quite strong. In the case of integration this applied particularly to the Mexican sample, and with respect to
personalization it applied particularly to the German sample. In contrast to this
high agreement, future teachers overall took a more neutral view of selection
as a task of schools. However, the average across countries hides the fact that

TABLE 7.4. Country means and standard errors (se) for beliefs about the functions of schooling.

Country	Personalization		Integration		Selection	
	Mean	*(se)*	*Mean*	*(se)*	*Mean*	*(se)*
South Korea	4.7	(0.1)	4.6	(0.1)	4.5	(0.1)
Taiwan	5.0	(0.1)	5.0	(0.1)	4.5	(0.1)
Bulgaria	4.8	(0.2)	5.0	(0.2)	4.0	(0.2)
Germany	5.2	(0.1)	4.8	(0.1)	3.2	(0.1)
United States	5.0	(0.1)	4.6	(0.1)	3.1	(0.1)
Mexico	4.8	(0.1)	5.1	(0.1)	4.0	(0.1)

the two East Asian countries stood out by strongly supporting selection as a function of schooling and that the two Western countries—Germany and the United States—stood out on the other side—given a scale's mean of 3.5—by even slightly disagreeing with this function. Median polishes revealed that, in fact, these two countries showed the most extreme beliefs about the purpose of schooling while substantially more strongly endorsing personalization and less strongly endorsing selection. By contrast, the South Korean students homogeneously support all three functions of schooling.

The descriptives support these statements. South Korea is the only country in which there are no major differences between the means of the three scales, whereas the range of means is the largest in Germany and the United States. The latter are also the only countries where the full range of the scales had been used in the rating of selection as a function of schooling by future teachers. However, with the exception of Bulgaria, future teachers from all other countries responded fairly homogeneously to the two scales, which indicates the common belief that integration and personalization are functions of schooling.

The between-institution variation was at most 5%, and therefore very low in all countries for the two functions of integration and personalization. The low proportion of institutional variation applied to selection as a function of schooling in four countries as well. Only in South Korea and the United States was the variation slightly above 10%, which is still not very much. More variation showed up with respect to license levels. In Germany, future teachers trained in a secondary program agreed to a lower extent with integration but to a higher extent with selection as functions of schooling than future teachers trained in an elementary program. In the United States, future teachers trained in a middle-school program stood out. They also agreed more strongly with statements referring to selection as a function of schooling but they also supported integration more strongly than teachers coming from other programs.

All relationships between beliefs about the functions of schooling are positive (see Figure 7.9). This means that a tendency exists to equally support integration, personalization, and selection. However, a slight gap is visible with respect to selection and its correlation with the two other functions of schooling in Germany, Mexico, and also partly in the United States. The co-variation is much less pronounced in those countries than it is in South Korea, Taiwan, and Bulgaria.

Fundamental goals of schooling. The functions of schooling are probably closely connected to teachers' beliefs about fundamental goals of schooling. Should there be a strong focus on cognitive development which would be necessary for selection as a function of schooling? Should there also be a focus on personality development, which would be required in the case of personalization? Is there any need for teachers to go beyond instruction and do work on the design of school life as you would expect for integration purposes? The MT21 survey covered these questions with three short scales consisting of two items each. A prompt, "The main job of the teacher is to . . ." followed the introduction, "What do you understand to be the fundamental goal of teaching? Consider the following statements and indicate the degree to which you agree or disagree with each." The first scale brought up cognitive goals that had to be rated on a 6-point scale for which to "help the students grow cognitively" was an example. The second scale covered the issue of personality development with "to help the students grow socially" being an example. And the third scale

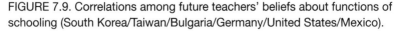

FIGURE 7.9. Correlations among future teachers' beliefs about functions of schooling (South Korea/Taiwan/Bulgaria/Germany/United States/Mexico).

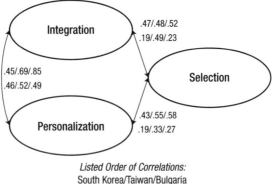

Listed Order of Correlations:
South Korea/Taiwan/Bulgaria
Germany/United States/Mexico

focused on institutional features like to "cooperate with parents." The reliability of all three scales was very high, which was across as well as within countries.

Cognitive development and the development of the student's personality receive a lot of agreement in all six MT21 samples (see Table 7.5). With the exception of the cognitive scale in Bulgaria, the countries' means are all around or even above 5.0, which means that they are at the high end of the 6-point scale. The high agreement is further demonstrated by the fact that only the future teachers sampled in Germany and Mexico use the whole range of the scale to rate the statements. It is especially surprising how homogenous future teachers agree on personality development as a fundamental goal of schooling where none of the means were below 5.0. With respect to cognitive development, the agreement of United States, Mexican, and German future teachers is the highest, whereas Bulgarian teachers are the only ones who agree on average significantly lower than at 5.0.

Compared to this high support of cognitive and personality goals, the agreement to the design of institutional features is lower but still positive in Bulgaria, Mexico, the United States, and especially in Taiwan. With a scale mean of 3.5, even a neutral view on the design of school life is shown by future teachers from South Korea and Germany. According to median polishes, the latter two countries are also the ones that show the most extreme beliefs: very high agreement with personality development and, in the case of Germany, cognitive development, but only low support of institutional features.

By contrast, future teachers from Taiwan attribute the same importance to all three goals of schooling. Future teachers from Bulgaria, the United States, and Mexico rate them nearly equally, even if the design of school life receives significantly less agreement in the latter two countries.

TABLE 7.5. Country means and standard errors (se) for the fundamental goals of schooling.

Country	Cognitive Development		Personality		School Life	
	Mean	*(se)*	*Mean*	*(se)*	*Mean*	*(se)*
South Korea	5.0	(0.1)	5.2	(0.1)	3.7	(0.1)
Taiwan	4.9	(0.1)	5.1	(0.1)	5.0	(0.1)
Bulgaria	4.7	(0.2)	5.0	(0.2)	4.5	(0.2)
Germany	5.3	(0.1)	5.3	(0.1)	3.8	(0.1)
United States	5.4	(0.1)	5.0	(0.1)	4.7	(0.1)
Mexico	5.4	(0.1)	5.2	(0.1)	4.6	(0.1)

Epistemological Beliefs About the Nature of Teaching

Besides beliefs about schooling, another epistemological aspect of professional competence is the nature of teaching. Related to teachers' objectives for instruction and to a transmission versus a constructivist perspective on teaching (see previous section) is how future teachers perceive the fundamental role of teachers in the classroom. Do they regard themselves as deliverers of true knowledge which has to be imparted to students, or do they regard themselves more as moderators of learning processes, which finally have to be managed by the students themselves?

Fundamental Role of Teachers in the Classroom

What is the fundamental role of teachers in the classroom? This final question in the section about future teachers' beliefs about mathematics, schooling, and teaching was captured by three statements that were to be rated on a 6-point scale from 1 ("not at all") to 6 ("to a major extent"). Corresponding to the above-mentioned basic distinction between a constructivist and a transmission view of teaching and learning, the teacher can be regarded as the only person in the classroom who has the correct knowledge of the content to be taught. In this view, it is the teachers' main role to "funnel" this knowledge into students' brains. That is, "A teacher has to impart knowledge to students."

If one looks at the average agreement of future teachers per country, it is possible to distinguish between three groups (see Figure 7.10). The samples from Germany and Mexico took a neutral view on the role of teachers as funneling knowledge into students. By contrast, future teachers from South Korea and Bulgaria show strong agreement with this view. The samples from Taiwan and the United States can be found between these extreme views. Within countries and license levels, there is a lot of variation in all countries. Even in

FIGURE 7.10. Country means and standard errors (se) for future teachers' beliefs about serving as knowledge deliverer (including the 95% confidence interval).

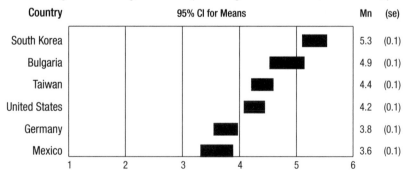

countries where future teachers usually show fairly homogenous beliefs, institutions exist that rate the statements about a teacher's role in the classroom either significantly higher or lower than other institutions.

SUMMARY AND CONCLUSIONS

If one looks across all beliefs scales, there are some basic tendencies that show up again and again. First, it is remarkable how *homogeneously* future teachers from South Korea and Taiwan view most of the issues, no matter whether they are subject related or generic. The within-country standard deviations of these two countries are much lower on almost all scales than the standard deviations for the other four MT21 countries. This indicates that some shared values about mathematics, teaching, and learning exist in South Korea and Taiwan, which probably reflects a relatively high level of social and cultural homogeneity in these two countries as compared with other countries (Hofstede, 2001; Triandis, 1995).

Second, given our expectation that we would find substantial cultural differences on virtually all scales, we were surprised that there are in fact several belief dimensions on which future teachers from all countries show essentially the same response patterns. This especially applies to those scales capturing beliefs about the nature of mathematics teaching and learning. Whereas we found substantial differences in future teachers' beliefs about the nature of mathematics as well as about the nature of schooling, our samples from the six countries pretty much agreed on core objectives for mathematics instruction and on ways by which students best learn the subject. This result points to a fairly globalized perspective on the teaching and learning of mathematics when it comes to fundamental issues (D'Ambrosio, 1995; Zaslavsky, 1996).

Third, as expected we found significant country differences in most of the cases and they pointed to a cultural split between East Asian countries on the one side and Western countries on the other side. However, in this case we also sometimes noted remarkably unexpected results, like substantial differences between South Korea and Taiwan. Whereas the future teachers in South Korea showed only a neutral view on the design of school life as a fundamental goal of teachers, the Taiwanese strongly supported this goal. This result reminded us that it is necessary to be careful with quick generalizations. With respect to the Western countries, the same caution is appropriate with respect to Bulgaria. Future teachers from this country were often bridging the divide between East Asian beliefs and Western beliefs. If the scales were related to content issues, more Bulgarian future teachers tended to show beliefs similar to future teachers from South Korea and Taiwan. This result probably indicates a traditionally strong position of mathematics even if the future teachers do not show the same outstanding performances as seen in earlier TIMSS studies.

CHAPTER 8

How Might We Expect Future Teachers to Teach?

In Chapters 5, 6, and 7 we have described results related to two major professional competencies specified in our conceptual framework—professional knowledge and professional beliefs. These do not necessarily characterize teacher performance in the classroom but are a part of the teacher competencies that are believed to contribute to quality classroom instruction. That these measures are not of teacher effectiveness is a limit of the MT21 study and we make no pretensions to the contrary. However, in order to simulate what instructional behavior these future teachers might engage in as they enter the classroom, we included a set of items in the future teacher questionnaire asking them hypothetically what they would do under different classroom scenarios. We fully recognize the limits of such an approach and do not paint it as more than it is, but feel that this approach might give some insight into how these future teachers envision their behavior as classroom instructors.

Whether these predispositions toward particular intended behaviors are realized or not, they are the images that future teachers carry with them as they leave their teacher preparation programs. As such, they likely tell us something about the type of teacher preparation they have received and the visions they carry in their heads of what teaching is like and what they think they should do in response to various situations. Variation in those images tells us something about the variability across future teachers, institutions and even, potentially, countries, which may help us then to understand differences in ideology or philosophy that guides teacher preparation. It must also be recognized here that these images could simply be ones that future teachers carry in their heads as a result of their own K–12 schooling experiences or more likely as some combination of both sets of experiences.

Our sampled future teachers have had to spend 4 to 6 years studying mathematics and pedagogy as well as observing, attending, and teaching in middle school classrooms. They also have had 12 to 13 years of experience in attending primary and secondary school themselves. As they leave all these experiences and the coursework behind, what do they believe mathematics instruction should look like? The questions we asked allow us to project what they might do with respect to key challenges as middle school mathematics teachers. These include two content-related aspects that are specific for mathematics instruction—calculator and computer usage, and problem solving in teaching mathematics to middle school students—as well as issues around instructional interaction. The issues around instructional interaction would include how they would see themselves responding to student errors in the mathematics they are doing, what approach they might take to help students who are having difficulties in mathematics, and more general issues of managing a classroom.

This chapter is divided into three major sets of intended behaviors related to being a teacher: classroom management, instructional organization, and instructional activities that are specifically related to mathematics. We take each and deal with its details, and in the last section look across these areas to see what general patterns might exist.

CLASSROOM MANAGEMENT

Any instructional activity depends on how a teacher manages to use the time she has at her disposal. The main objective is to avoid interruptions and disciplinary problems but to maximize students' time on task. Starting with Kounin (1970), research on classroom management has become a predominant research area (Anderson, Ryan, & Shapiro, 1989; Canter & Canter, 1976; Evertson & Weinstein, 2006). In this chapter, we use the term *classroom management* mainly in its narrow meaning of preventing and dealing with behavioral problems. Its instructional focus is discussed in the following paragraph, although we include one scale about motivational activities here as well in order to demonstrate the array of management strategies.

Specifically with respect to mathematics education, we know that classroom management and student achievement are closely related to each other (Einsiedler, 1997; Helmke, 2004; Wang, Haertel, & Walberg, 1993). Besides the cognitive level of mathematics problems given, the quality of classroom management is the most important predictor of achievement in mathematics if prior knowledge is controlled (Kunter, Dubberke, Baumert et al., 2006). Teachers are often mainly interested in learning how to *react* to disciplinary disturbances. However, research shows that a focus on preventing these kinds of interruptions by actively using certain strategies is a more promising way to maximize the time on task (Brophy & Good, 1986; Muijs & Reynolds, 2000). Only to react is neither effective nor in line with more complex learning activities like group work (Emmer & Stough, 2001). In several studies, this distinction between active and reactive classroom management strategies has proven to be reliable for distinguishing between teacher novices and teacher experts (Berliner, 1988; Livingston & Borko, 1989).

Active strategies include having the teacher and students develop and agree on rules for classroom behavior at the beginning of a school year. It is important that the teacher monitors these rules immediately and very carefully once they are established until they are routinely used by every student. Later on, she can be more relaxed and not follow up on every violation. Active strategies include practicing complex instructional activities as well. Specifically with respect to group work, students have to practice transferring between plenary work and group work, for example, while the teacher must smoothly transition among coincident instructional roles. Finally, important instructional strategies that are well suited to preventing behavioral problems include all kinds of motivational activities, starting with careful planning according to students' interests.

A great deal of evidence exists to support the importance of these strategies. Still, behavioral problems cannot be completely avoided. When they occur, it is important to react in a consistent and transparent manner: Students need to know why a teacher reacts the way she does. From the teacher's perspective, it is important to accept her responsibility to deal with these problems and not to postpone or externalize it.

We examine the future teachers' classroom management strategies by asking them what they would do in, or what they believed to be the best way to handle, different situations that teachers typically encounter in their classroom instruction. Again, we consider these as projections or simulations of what these future teachers will likely do when they become classroom teachers, recognizing there are limitations to such inferences.

Three situations were presented for future teachers' consideration. The first involves the future teacher imagining that she has been teaching for 2 months and one student has been consistently misbehaving in class, failing to turn work in, and scoring low on the assessments. The teacher writes a letter to the parents. The sampled future teachers were presented with a list of possible actions and asked to indicate if they would include or exclude each action from the letter to the parents. Indicators were formed for two types of issues that could be included in the letter. The first involved describing the problems—low grades and coming late to class—asking about outside school problems and finally proposing a meeting with parents and the student, together with a draft contract to use with the student. The second involved having the student tested for learning difficulties, moving him to a less demanding class, and suggesting the need for outside tutoring. In effect, these actions imply that the teacher is suggesting an approach that moves the problem away from herself to others as opposed to the first group of actions, which propose a joint solution wherein the teacher remains at the center of the solution. The means presented in Figure 8.1 indicate the extent to which teachers would, on average, include all of each specific action types in their letter. For example, a mean of 20% for proximal actions implies that, on average, future teachers would mention one of the possible five actions in their parent letter. Large country differences existed on the first scale.

In general, most sampled future teachers indicated that they would mention proximal actions more than referral actions, indicating they wanted to engage the parents in a solution. However, this was less the case for the German sampled future teachers than for the Taiwanese future teachers. Taiwanese sampled future teachers on average suggested using four of the five possible actions (81%) while the German future teachers indicated only about two actions (46%). Neither were German future teachers likely to use referral actions in the letter. Quite uniformly, except for Mexico, the vast majority of future teachers did not choose responses indicating they would externalize the problem by

FIGURE 8.1. Country means and standard errors (se) for future teachers' agreement with types of actions to include in a letter to parents about a child having difficulties in school with a 95% confidence interval (CI) for the means.

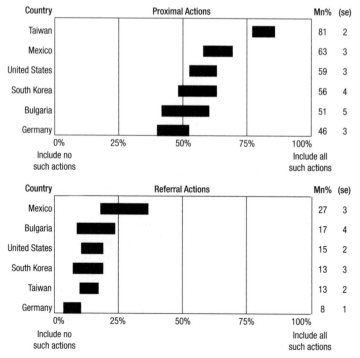

suggesting it needed to be addressed elsewhere through tutors or special classes. The low means may not be that the future teachers did not want to include the actions. It may also indicate that the actions are not even possible in some countries. For example, in Taiwan, all the students are assigned to a class at the beginning of their lower-secondary study and normally they are not allowed to switch classes until the end of the lower-secondary grades. In this case, an action such as "A suggestion that he be moved to a less demanding class section" is not possible in Taiwan. Only in Mexico was the mean for referral actions great enough to suggest most future teachers would specifically mention at least one of the three referral type actions. In the other countries there was still a noticeable minority who similarly suggested that the solution lay elsewhere. Virtually all of the variation in future teachers' responses was found at the individual future teacher level and not at the institutional level.

The second situation concerned the management of a middle school mathematics class. The future teachers were asked to imagine they are beginning to teach a new class and to what extent they would likely use a series of techniques both for the management of behavior and for the planning of instructions. Three scales were formed around different approaches, including: establishing rules, setting out consequences, and motivating them to behave by setting up instructional activities that capture their interest and involve them in different activities. The scales went from not at all (1) to most likely (6) in describing the extent to which they would likely use them in their class. Figure 8.2 provides the country means and standard errors for these scales.

Consider first management by establishing clear behavioral and disciplinary rules. We interpret these as follows: 1 and 2 (up to 3) indicate not likely to occur, 3 and 4 as somewhat of a 50–50 chance of occurring, and 5 and 6 (above 4) as a fairly likely activity for them to use in their class, at least as they see it upon leaving their teacher preparation programs. For class management by rules, the future teachers on average in all six countries indicated they would likely try this approach, although this was slightly less likely for the South Korean and Bulgarian future teachers. Management by motivation exhibited the same general results.

Management by consequences, where the students would be warned and rewarded only if they behaved appropriately, including the indication that students who were disturbing the class could be punished, produced extremely different results as well as greater cross-country variation. The German future teachers' mean was 2.3, indicating it would be quite unlikely that they, on average, would use this approach in their classroom. They were unique in their strong opposition to this approach among the six countries—significantly less likely to use this approach than those in any of our other countries. Similarly, but not as extremely, Bulgarian, Mexican, and U.S. sampled future teachers all had a neutral reaction on average, with means centering between three and four. South Korean future

FIGURE 8.2. Country means and standard errors for future teachers' agreement with aspects of classroom management with a 95% CI for the means.

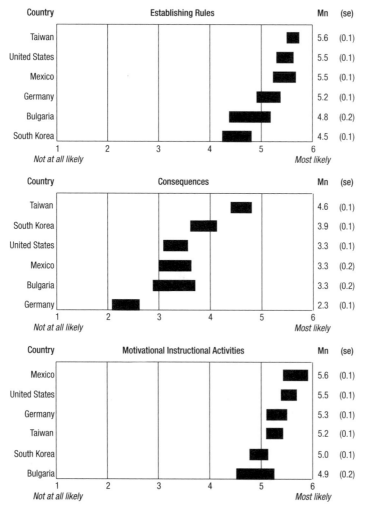

teachers had a mean of 3.9, indicating a more positive neutrality. The one country whose average indicated being positively inclined, although not strongly, to the use of such an approach was Taiwan, with a mean of 4.6.

Here again, in the area of classroom and instructional management there was a great deal of similarity across the six countries. Most favor assuming responsibility for a student having problems in their class as opposed to shifting the problem to someone else. Similarly, most believe the best way to manage a classroom is by rules and having a good and motivating learning environment and not by threatening punishment. There were some country differences, but more of degree rather than major categorical differences.

INSTRUCTIONAL ORGANIZATION

There is a large literature that suggests instructional organization is important to student learning. The focal point of schooling occurs as the content to be learned is introduced by the teacher to the students through the use of instructional materials and activities. How these are organized within the context of the classroom is most important. In fact, the time dimension associated with this encounter—the time spent focused on subject matter content—is an important resource (Schmidt et al., 2001). Elmore (1993) suggested that this is the most important resource that those in school leadership positions such as principals need to manage carefully to support student learning.

In this section, we explore how future teachers viewed several different aspects of instructional management when asked what they would use as they become teachers. We begin with a look at how they viewed two overarching philosophies and then move to a more detailed consideration. Again, we remind the reader that we do not believe this is necessarily how they actually will act when teaching, but we recognize this as the image they have of themselves regarding how they believe they would respond. It is an insight into their view of how they will act. This is a valuable potential outcome of teacher preparation, something that may imply their future actions; but even if it does not, at least it reveals the view they have of teaching as they enter the profession.

Four issues are explored in this section: which basic teaching methods the teachers are inclined to use, how they would structure a lesson, specific activities like group work, and the use of calculators and computers.

With respect to basic teaching methods, it is possible to distinguish between two approaches: one that includes more traditional activities and one that is close to constructivist thinking. In the first approach, the teacher steers and closely monitors most activities. Students do not work on larger projects, but take small steps. Drill and practice as well as relatively short but fast teacher-student interactions dominate the process. In the second approach, students often learn in groups by inquiring about complex phenomena according to self-developed strategies. Many different activities are applied (Fischer & Malle, 1985; Tulodziecki, Herzig, & Blömeke, 2004).

If students receive enough support—and this is an important precondition—students taught in the second, constructivist way are able to develop a deeper understanding of mathematics and achieve higher-order cognitions (Anderson, 2002; Smith et al., 2007; Tal, Krajcik, & Blumenfeld, 2006). If group work and other individual activities are included—an important precondition here—the first approach can be successful as well (Brophy & Good, 1986; Muijs & Reynolds, 2000).

The latter remark points to the importance of including group work into learning processes. Student interaction contributes to developing a shared understanding of a topic. Often, students are better able to explain a phenomenon to one another because their level of thinking matches. Reviews and meta analyses have summarized the evidence. It is possible to conclude that, across grades and subjects, group work has a positive effect on student achievement (Cobb, 1994; De Corte, Greer, & Verschaffel, 1996; Johnson, Johnson, & Stanne, 2000; Slavin, Hurley, & Chamberlain, 2003). In mathematics, classes with a lot of work in small groups show higher student achievement, specifically if it is substituted for traditional seat work (Helmke & Jäger, 2002; Slavin, 1996). Besides the advantages of social interaction, group work allows for dealing with heterogeneity in an intelligent way. Teachers have the chance to hand out problems according to the level of understanding and thereby win time to support students with difficulties (Dann, Diegritz, & Rosenbusch, 1999; Gutiérrez & Slavin, 1992; Schrader, 2001).

A last important but controversial aspect of teaching is the use of media; in mathematics education it is the use of calculators and computers that is discussed (Blömeke, 2003). Computers are supposed to help students gain a better understanding of complex mathematical phenomena by simulating them. In addition, students can learn individually, according to their own pace (Vosniadou, 1994). A wide range of calculation tools, drill-and-practice software, and simulation programs exists. In middle school, with respect to teaching quality, calculators that include graphs and dynamic geometry software are of major relevance. There is a lot of evidence that these kinds of media can support a better understanding of spatial relationships (Hartmann & Reiss, 2000; Souvignier, 1999). With respect to functions, students have the opportunity to explore their nature in a dynamic way before a more formal approach is introduced (Malle, 2000; vom Hofe, 2001). Studies show that problems associated with the traditional approach, such as a static idea of functions, can be avoided (Hischer, 2002; Mössner, 2000; Weigand & Weth, 2002).

First we examine the basic approach to instructional activities that future teachers feel to be appropriate in teaching middle school mathematics. The scale goes from "not at all" (coded 1) to "should receive a great deal of focus" (coded 6). With this type of scale we interpret 1 to 3 as not emphasizing the activity; 3 to 4 as being somewhat neutral about the activity and giving it little emphasis; over 4 as giving it emphasis; and 5 to 6 as suggesting such an activity should receive much emphasis and be a central part of instruction.

Twelve activities were included, ranging from having students work in small groups to reviewing homework. Two scales were formed. The first dimension can be thought of as the degree to which the emphasized activities chosen by the future teacher reflected a fairly standard or traditional approach to the teaching of middle school mathematics. It includes activities such as whole class instruction, seat work, reviewing homework in class, students working on problems at the board, and using assessments. The second scale is viewed as the more constructivist approach to instructional organization and includes activities such as small group work, having students do special projects, having discussions, and having students write about their thinking relative to mathematics. The country means are presented in Figure 8.3.

Virtually no differences existed across the countries on the use of traditional instructional activities. With one exception, the means all range across the values 4.4 to 4.8, indicating that on average these activities would receive a

FIGURE 8.3. Country means and standard errors for future teacher emphasis on two types of instructional organizations with a 95% CI for the means.

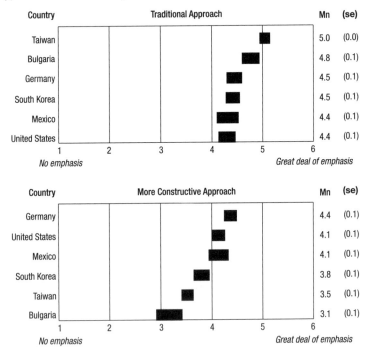

modest degree of emphasis. The only exceptions, although not large, were the means of 4.8 to 5.0 for the sampled future teachers in Bulgaria and Taiwan, indicating a greater degree of emphasis. Apparently there is somewhat of a universal agreement at the mean level across the countries indicating that traditional instructional activities are viewed positively and should receive at least some emphasis in their proposed future instruction.

The standard deviations are quite modest except in Mexico, Germany, and the United States, but even in those countries the variation is not at all large in magnitude. This implies (assuming a normal distribution) that 95% of the scale values will fall in the vicinity of 3.5 to 5.5, mostly consistent with giving some to a great deal of emphasis to these types of instructional activities. The point is, the results are suggestive not only of small differences across countries but across individual future teachers within countries as well. What little variation exists is virtually all at the individual future teacher level and not at the institution level (less than 5%).

The real variation occurs with the set of activities characterized as constructivist. The country means (also found in Figure 8.3) vary from 3.1 for Bulgaria, indicating little emphasis being given to these activities, up to 4.4 for Germany, which suggests allocating some emphasis to such activities. Rounding the mean values to whole numbers suggests a division among the countries, with Bulgaria and Taiwan at the low end in terms of emphasis and the other five suggestive of some emphasis. None of the country means suggested giving a great deal of emphasis to these types of activities. The variation within countries is small and, again, no substantial cross-institutional variation is present.

Figure 8.4 gives the country means for a select set of specific instructional activities (making up the above two scales), which indicated important cross-country differences. The future teachers' responses to these in terms of how much emphasis they thought to be appropriate in teaching middle school mathematics comes perhaps the closest to characterizing what they will likely do when they start teaching. For this reason we examine these individually to gain a better insight into those potential practices.

Using small groups in instruction was one such activity. We use the same interpretive frame employed throughout this chapter. Three countries' sampled future teachers (rounded to the nearest whole number) indicated giving a great deal of emphasis on average to this activity—Germany, Mexico, and the United States. All of the others indicated giving only some. Sampled future teachers in all countries except Mexico indicated on average that they would give much emphasis to whole-class instruction.

When it comes to intensely reviewing homework in class, sampled U.S. future teachers on average indicated the lowest degree of emphasis. Working

FIGURE 8.4. Country means and standard errors for future teacher emphasis on specific instructional activities with a 95% CI for the means.

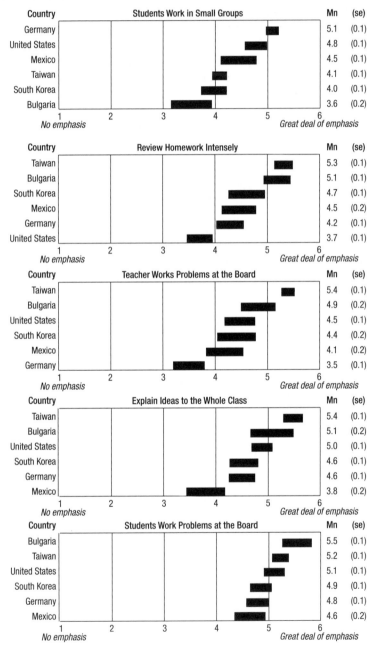

out mathematics problems on the board either by the teacher or by the students is an area where there were major differences among the countries. Major emphasis was suggested by the sampled future teachers in Bulgaria and Taiwan for having the teacher do this. In fact, the mean for Taiwan was 5.4 out of a possible 6.0. The other country means suggested a moderate degree of emphasis for this activity, except for Germany, whose sampled future teachers on average suggested very little emphasis for teachers working out problems on the board. For students working at the board, all six country means were in the range 4.6 to 5.5, indicating an activity that would be used quite frequently.

The second type of instructional issue we examined concerns the structure of a particular lesson for teaching a mathematics topic. Future teachers were asked to order different types of activities that they would include in their lesson, indicating what they feel would be the ideal sequence. Eleven activities were listed, although not all needed to be included—they could skip any that they would not include in their instruction. The activities were listed in this order: (1) practice the new content, (2) present a complex task (situated in the pupils' everyday life), (3) explore pupils' prior knowledge and conceptions, (4) assess pupils' achievement, (5) reflect on the learning process, (6) try to solve the task, (7) work on the new content, (8) present a simple task, (9) summarize, (10) overview the lesson goals and structure, and (11) discuss possible solutions. One summary of these data as presented in Figure 8.5 indicates the percentage of future teachers who included each of the 11 possible activities. The estimated percentage for each country is given in the figure.

Several important observations are possible. Almost all the Taiwanese future teachers (equal to or greater than 93%) included each of the 11 types of activities. Essentially there is a great deal of similarity across all countries in that typically more than 70% of all future teachers in each country included each of the 11 activities in their lesson plans (this does not imply that each future teacher included all of the 11 activities). Considering the cultural traditions surrounding education in these quite disparate nations, this is a remarkably large proportion that commonly included these activities in the structure of their proposed lessons. It suggests a common, cross-country sense of what the important components of instructional design should include. There are some country differences on some of the activities. For example, only 67% of South Korean sampled future teachers included presenting complex tasks, and only 63% of Bulgarian future teachers included an assessment of pupils. In contrast, 98% of future teachers in Germany and Taiwan included complex tasks and about 95% of future teachers in Mexico and Germany included pupil assessment. Bulgarian future teachers tended to use some of the activities less than was the case in the other countries.

FIGURE 8.5. Estimated percentage (standard error) with a 95% confidence interval for each lesson activity.

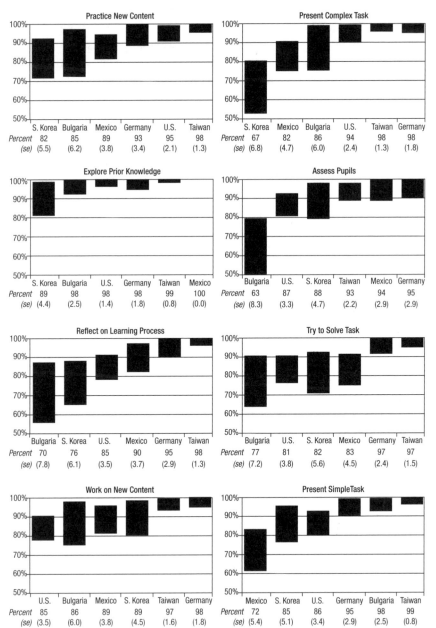

Practice New Content

	S. Korea	Bulgaria	Mexico	Germany	U.S.	Taiwan
Percent	82	85	89	93	95	98
(se)	(5.5)	(6.2)	(3.8)	(3.4)	(2.1)	(1.3)

Present Complex Task

	S. Korea	Mexico	Bulgaria	U.S.	Taiwan	Germany
Percent	67	82	86	94	98	98
(se)	(6.8)	(4.7)	(6.0)	(2.4)	(1.3)	(1.8)

Explore Prior Knowledge

	S. Korea	Bulgaria	U.S.	Germany	Taiwan	Mexico
Percent	89	98	98	98	99	100
(se)	(4.4)	(2.5)	(1.4)	(1.8)	(0.8)	(0.0)

Assess Pupils

	Bulgaria	U.S.	S. Korea	Taiwan	Mexico	Germany
Percent	63	87	88	93	94	95
(se)	(8.3)	(3.3)	(4.7)	(2.2)	(2.9)	(2.9)

Reflect on Learning Process

	Bulgaria	S. Korea	U.S.	Mexico	Germany	Taiwan
Percent	70	76	85	90	95	98
(se)	(7.8)	(6.1)	(3.5)	(3.7)	(2.9)	(1.3)

Try to Solve Task

	Bulgaria	U.S.	S. Korea	Mexico	Germany	Taiwan
Percent	77	81	82	83	97	97
(se)	(7.2)	(3.8)	(5.6)	(4.5)	(2.4)	(1.5)

Work on New Content

	U.S.	Bulgaria	Mexico	S. Korea	Taiwan	Germany
Percent	85	86	89	89	97	98
(se)	(3.5)	(6.0)	(3.8)	(4.5)	(1.6)	(1.8)

Present Simple Task

	Mexico	S. Korea	U.S.	Germany	Bulgaria	Taiwan
Percent	72	85	86	95	98	99
(se)	(5.4)	(5.1)	(3.4)	(2.9)	(2.5)	(0.8)

FIGURE 8.5. (*continued*)

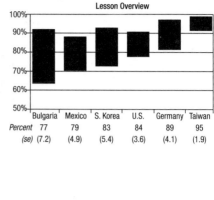

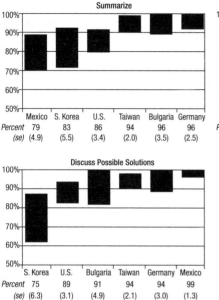

The next question, given the overall average of greater than 70% choosing each of the activities, is whether there is a similarity in the order in which they build these activities into their instructional design. The short answer is no, they do not order them in the same way—there was cross-country variation—but it is complicated and nuanced. Figure 8.6 shows the mean ranks over all the sampled future teachers in each country separately.

The differences across the countries are real and reflect different proposed lesson structures, but some of these differences can be overexaggerated. Given that there are 11 activities to be ranked, two activities that are ranked 7th and 10th in one country might be ranked 5th and 8th in another, suggesting differences; but the question would be, are they really significant—not statistically but in terms of reflecting a different lesson structure—or do they represent essentially the same lesson structure with some minor variations on the same theme? Both types of differences exist, as reflected in the means found in Figure 8.6. We focus on those we believe to be substantive in their implications.

First, several activities are, on average, clear regarding their placement in the overall lesson structure. "Prior knowledge" occurs early on in the lesson, as does the "lesson overview," the "consideration of a simple task," and "work on new content." Midway into the lesson structure, "solving the task" becomes a

FIGURE 8.6. Country means and standard errors for the rank order for each lesson activity with a 95% CI for the means.

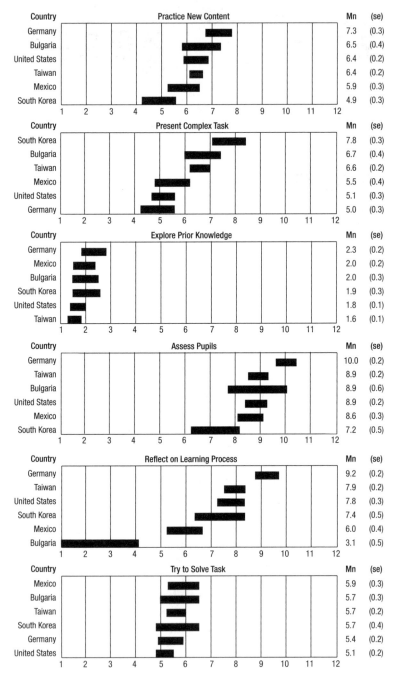

FIGURE 8.6. (*continued*)

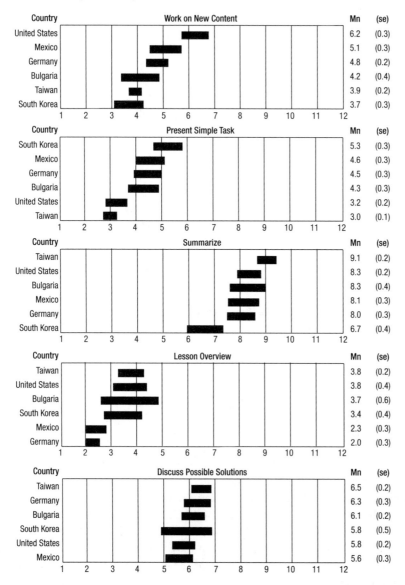

focal point, as does "discussion" and "practice." The lesson design ends with "re-flection," "summarization," and "assessment," except for Bulgaria, where future teachers tended to place "reflection" near the beginning.

What differs most distinctly across countries and hence is left out of the above summary is the inclusion of a complex task, such as a more complex

FIGURE 8.7. Country means and standard errors for reasons to use student group work in classroom instruction with a 95% CI for the means.

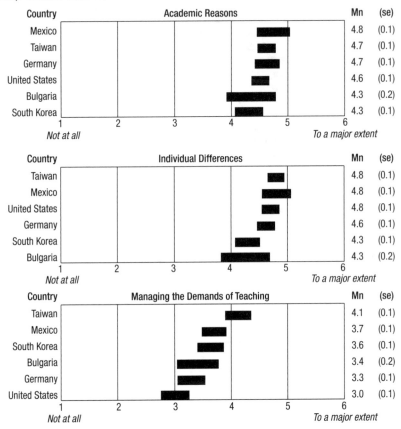

version of the simpler problem used at the outset of the lesson. Taiwanese and South Korean future teachers included the complex task toward the end of the lesson; in fact, in South Korea's case it had the highest average rank, implying it to be the last step. For both Taiwan and South Korea the complex task was three to four steps after the introduction of the simple task. However, in South Korea's case that step itself was more toward the middle of the lesson, after introducing the new content, rather than near the beginning of the lesson, as was the case with Taiwan.

By marked contrast, the typical U.S. model introduced the complex task essentially right after introducing the simple task, with only an overview of the lesson between the two. Practice occurred more toward the end of the lesson, while practice in both South Korea and Taiwan, on average, occurred earlier in the lesson and before the introduction of the complex task. German and Mexican future teachers were essentially the same as the sampled U.S. future teachers in their instructional design, while the Bulgarian future teachers were more similar to those in South Korea and Taiwan. Within each of the countries there was substantial variation on the individual rankings of each activity and virtually none of that variation implied cross-institutional variation. This implies that the country-level differences are shared by the institutions within the country.

The final instructional organizational issue concerns the use of group work. The future teachers were asked to what extent various beliefs served as reasons for why they would use student group work in their own teaching of mathematics. Ten beliefs were listed, including increasing students' independent learning, increasing student creativity, and good for dealing with classroom diversity, among others. The items were scored on a scale ranging from "not at all" (1) to "a major extent" (6). Scales were formed by three sets of reasons: academic, individual differences, and making teaching more manageable. The country means are presented in Figure 8.7. For the academic and individual differences scales, all the country means vary between 4.3 and 4.8, indicating that these types of reasons had strong emphasis in their proposed use of student work groups across all six countries.

The third scale, which highlighted reasons that made teaching more manageable, did show greater variation across countries. First of all, unlike the other two scales, which did have an impact on their decision to use student work groups, these types of reasons were in general less influential on the future teachers, ranging in value from 3.0 to 3.7 for five of the countries. For the sampled future teachers in Bulgaria, Germany, and the United States this reason had little, if any, influence, while in the other countries they had some limited influence. It was in Taiwan where this reason had the largest mean. Variation was small in all countries and for the three scales, but Bulgaria had slightly more variation, with the third scale having more variation than the other two. However, the differences were not large. In each country and for each scale, the percentage of the total variation that was attributable to cross-institutional variation was less than 10%. The only exceptions were on the individual differences scale in Mexico, where cross-institutional differences accounted for 20%.

Instructional organization, much like classroom management, found more similarity than differences, again reinforcing the general conclusion that across these six countries the future teachers' projections of what they will do as they become classroom teachers are remarkably similar. This is even true, as this section indicates, at the very focal point of education where student learning occurs—the lesson structure. The differences that do exist, however, appear to be relatively small. The variation among future teachers is not large and is mostly not attributable to institutional differences. The one more substantive difference that was notable related to where in the lesson structure simple and complex tasks are placed. The two Asian countries differ from the rest but especially from Mexico, Germany, and the United States.

INSTRUCTIONAL ACTIVITIES SPECIFICALLY AROUND MATHEMATICS

Here we look at future teachers' beliefs about the three issues related specifically to mathematics instruction. One issue that is somewhat contentious is the role that computers and calculators may have in middle school mathematics instruction. Figure 8.8 illustrates the country means and confidence intervals for future teachers in each country in terms of their agreement with the idea that it is important for middle grade students to learn to use calculators or computers in the mathematics class. From these data there is little agreement within or across countries on the issue, but the lack of agreement is especially noticeable across countries.

In general, sampled Taiwanese and South Korean future teachers view learning how to use such technology in the mathematics classes less positively. Around half or fewer don't strongly agree with the importance of students learning how to use the computer or calculator in class. This is especially the

FIGURE 8.8. Country means and standard errors for degree of future teachers' agreement with the importance of learning to use computers or calculators with a 95% CI for the means.

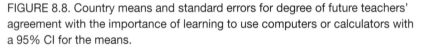

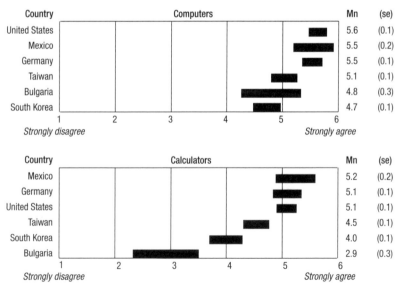

case for calculators, where only 28% of the Taiwanese future teachers and only 10% of the South Korean future teachers strongly believed that the mathematics classroom is where this should be learned. In the other countries, 60% or more felt strongly about the importance of learning the use of computers in the mathematics classes but less so about calculators. Particularly in Bulgaria, the sampled future teachers felt that the use of computers distracts students from learning the basic skills. Those in South Korea and Taiwan also expressed less enthusiasm for this practice. On the other hand, the U.S., German, and Mexican future teachers all felt strongly that students should learn to use computers and calculators in mathematics classes.

With respect to the importance of problem solving being included in mathematics instruction, the vast majority in all six countries strongly agreed. The one notable variation was that around one fourth of the Taiwanese future teachers felt that it was very important, but should be done at the higher grades because advanced mathematics was necessary to do it properly.

Data on the two other issues of how to handle student interactions around mathematics reveal greater similarity among countries than was the case with the above issues concerning mathematics itself. When asked what to do with students who are having difficulty, the approach the sampled future teachers in all countries said they would most likely take was to make students feel comfortable with mathematics and help them see that it can be fun. In fact, in all but Bulgaria, 60% or more of the sampled future teachers indicated that this would be their chosen approach.

Finally, we examine what future teachers said they would likely do when they encountered students responding incorrectly to questions in their mathematics classes. Each possible action on the part of the teacher was scored on a 6-point scale of strongly disagree (1) to strongly agree (6). The country means were all around 3 or 4 on the three scales we created, indicating a more neutral position, with 3 leaning to disagreeing with the stated approach and 4 leaning in the direction of agreeing with the approach. The first scale suggests that the teacher should ignore the error and move on. This was rejected by the sampled future teachers in all six countries with means of around 2. Furthermore, they almost all agreed (means of around 4) at least moderately that one approach would be for the teacher to ask the students themselves to evaluate and discuss the incorrect answers.

The little disagreement that existed was in the sampled future teachers' responses on how to handle student errors. On the last scale, where the proposed action centered on the teacher herself, the teacher would correct, highlight, or discuss the incorrect answers. The future teachers' ratings from all countries were between 3 and 4 on average, with 3 indicating a more negative (but not strongly) and 4 a more positive view of this approach. There were slight cross-country differences. Sampled future teachers in Bulgaria, South Korea, and Taiwan were more positive about this approach, while those in Germany, Mexico, and the United States were more negative, although the differences were not that large.

As these future teachers finished their teacher preparation, what these data suggest is that, with respect to the propensities they have as to how they would see themselves acting in the classroom under different circumstances or with respect to certain approaches, there are many commonalities among institutions and countries. They mostly believe in the importance of problem solving being in the curriculum and encouraging students who are having difficulty in mathematics by emphasizing that mathematics is fun, as well as using some combination of student and teacher assurances surrounding errors in student responses during class. Even so, there were some differences, although they were not large, in general. Where they do differ more is with respect to the role of calculators and computers in mathematics classes, the two Asian countries' future teachers together with the Bulgarians being much less inclined to believe this to be important compared to the German, Mexican, and U.S. future teachers.

A TYPOLOGY OF INSTRUCTIONAL ACTIVITIES

In the previous sections we have examined some five different types of instructional activities and management principles that the future teachers in our sample plan to utilize to varying degrees as they become classroom teachers, at least as they believe they will act. Do these different types of activities relate to each other in a way that there are different categories of teachers who employ a set of these in concert? Another way to ask this is, are there organizations, activities, and principles that work together to create an approach that is a combination of some of these different specific activities? We call these defined sets of activities a *typology of instructional activities*.

To explore this we examined the correlations among the five scales—including both instructional and classroom management activities that the future teachers might emphasize—and found the principle components of the covariance matrix. The principal components analysis identified two factors accounting for over 60% of the variance. The first factor characterizes variation on the most common pattern: a future teacher who is traditional in her instructional practices—who uses an approach to managing the classroom that emphasizes a combination of motivational activities, together with clearly established classroom rules—but who also, to a lesser extent, incorporates some of the student-centered approaches in her instruction and even warns students of possible consequences. The typical teacher with a high value on this dimension would suggest using whole-class instruction, reviewing homework regularly in class, and having students work at the blackboard, as well as organizing a classroom environment that maintains discipline by motivating students through different activities and their interests but also by establishing clear behavioral and disciplinary rules. We term this dimension the *eclectic approach scale*.

The second factor defines a contrast between a more student-focused approach to instructional and classroom management as contrasted with a more authoritative approach to both. The student approach includes future teachers who indicated they would have students work in small groups, write reports, and also write about their thinking in mathematics, as well as use an instructional organization approach toward motivating students as the way to manage the classroom. The authoritative approach includes the core of the traditional approach, but is now combined with a strong emphasis on maintaining discipline by warning students of consequences for disrupting the learning environment. This second dimension is termed the *management approach*, with positive values indicating a more authoritative approach, while the negative values indicate a more student-centered approach. This dimension splits the eclectic future teacher into two camps—those favoring the authoritative version versus those favoring the student-centered approach. Figure 8.9 shows the distribution of future teachers plotted against the two dimensions, with Figure 8.10 showing the same for the country means.

FIGURE 8.9. A plot of the institutional means in each country on the average degree of agreement with the eclectic and authoritative approaches.

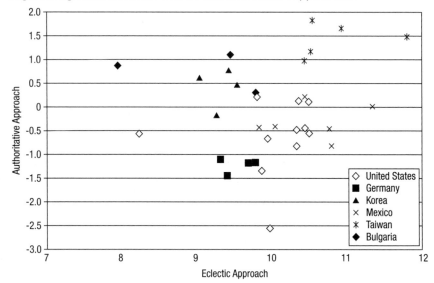

The two scales define the dimensions for both of the figures. The institutions plotted in Figure 8.9 range in values from around 8 to 12 on the degree of eclecticism scale and from -3 to +2 on the authoritative scale. What is interesting in this figure is the pattern of institutions by country. There were distinct clusterings of the institutions for South Korea, Taiwan, Bulgaria, Germany, and Mexico, indicating a communality of views on these two dimensions related to instructional design and classroom management. In other words, there is a country or cultural position on these issues in these five countries. The exception appears to be the United States, where there was substantially more variation among the institutions, with some more like South Korean or Bulgarian institutions and others more like German institutions. In general, most U.S. institutions are similar to Mexican institutions on these two dimensions.

Figure 8.10 shows the six country means. South Korean, Bulgarian, and Taiwanese future teachers are all, on average, more authoritative in their classroom and learning environment, especially those in Taiwan. Taiwanese future teachers, however, also are on average more eclectic and moderate in their authoritative approach by also building an environment through motivational activities. Mexico, Germany, and the United States are more student-centered in their approach, with German future teachers on average being the least eclectic and the most student-centered. We assume that these results most likely reflect recent discussions about teaching and learning.

FIGURE 8.10. A plot of the country means on the average degree of agreement with the eclectic and authoritative approaches.

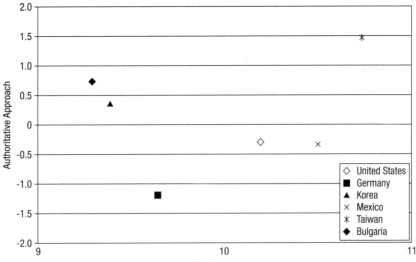

SUMMARY

One of the surprising findings of this chapter is that when we asked these future teachers to project themselves into the classroom and describe the types of activities in which they would engage or how they might organize their classroom from a management point of view, we found greater similarities than differences. It is as though the typical future teacher from each of the six countries would tend to act more similarly than differently on most of the areas of classroom and instructional management about which we asked. There were differences within the countries, but again, these were relatively small and what variation there was, was mostly about institutional or program difference within each country. There were also some cross-national differences, though mostly on the order of degree of agreement or extent of emphasis, not agree versus disagree or no emphasis versus extensive emphasis. Few differences were large, and those were noted in the chapter.

We began this chapter with caveats. The nature of the data allows us to speak about future teachers' perceptions of what they will do as teachers and about their beliefs regarding mathematics instruction, student learning, and the role of the teacher. We cannot claim to know how these future teachers will enact their practice in the classroom. Nevertheless, it is striking to note the relative convergence of images about what desirable mathematics classrooms look like—how classrooms are managed, what instructional activities are selected, and how lessons are structured.

This finding of apparent congruence in imagining the role of the mathematics teacher and the organization of mathematics instruction may well find support in larger cross-national analyses, such as that based on TIMSS work, which suggests shared notions about the role and work of the "universal math teacher" (Baker & LeTendre, 2005). It is important to consider how the shared views that TIMSS analyses offer describe perspectives of practicing teachers. In our data, we are able to explore how those intending to teach may already be learning to take on a set of views that reflects some larger shared claims in the profession of mathematics teaching. At the same time, we find that differences across countries—for example, in the value given to calculators and computers in mathematics classrooms, in the placement of complex tasks in the course of a lesson, or in the internalizing or externalizing of a student problem—are also important to note. Across countries we see impressive or surprising agreement without having uniformity. We also find within-country and program/institutional differences that are significant. This suggests, as research in other areas finds (Anderson-Levitt, 2002; LeTendre, Baker, Akiba et al., 2001; Ramirez, 2003), a kind of balance of some strong transnational, shared understandings with nevertheless distinct national or local instantiations.

CHAPTER 9

Using Cohort Comparisons to Explore How Future Teachers Change During Teacher Preparation: Difficulties, Findings, and Hypotheses

We set out in MT21 to explore whether teacher education matters—hence the title of this book. We knew the task to be complicated but were somewhat surprised about just how complex it was in an international context. The question we address in this and the next chapter is whether teacher education is related to future teacher knowledge and beliefs. As indicated in Chapter 3, little empirical research to date has addressed this issue.

Comparing institutions and nations on the professional knowledge of future teachers (Chapters 5 and 6), beliefs (Chapter 7), and instructional related intentions (Chapter 8) can be viewed as one way of examining the relationship of teacher preparation to such outcomes. The fact that some countries or institutions have a higher average performance on the knowledge scales or on the measured beliefs and dispositions than other countries or institutions can be viewed as one indication supporting the notion that teacher education matters. This would be especially true for differences among institutions within a country. This is further reinforced by the fact that these same institutions will likely vary in the opportunities they provide, as Chapter 4 illustrates—essentially, that variation in OTL reflects different definitions of teacher preparation. However, the looming question is whether the differences across institutions and countries in performance are mostly related to differences in the types of students who enter teacher preparation with different levels of knowledge or different views of mathematics and schooling, or whether those differences support the notion that teacher preparation through the opportunities provided is related to the development of professional competencies. This is the point of this and the next chapter.

Chapter 2 examined differences in the mathematics preparation of secondary students in the six countries. This was done by portraying the level of demand of the mathematics contained in the national standards for high school. There clearly were substantial differences in requirements for secondary students who intended to pursue college or university study among the six countries, implying likely country differences in the entry-level knowledge of future teachers. That point was again made in Chapter 11 by using international test results as a surrogate measure of country differences in the actual level of mathematics knowledge that is obtained by the typical secondary student. These were further adjusted to represent the entry-level mathematics knowledge of future teachers in each of the six countries. Substantial differences were again noted. Recognizing the implication of these country differences, that chapter also used the two cohorts to do a country-level analysis related to the question, "Does teacher education matter?" All of this supports the conjecture that the differences among countries for finishing future teachers could be attributable at least in part to differences in entry- level characteristics. This limits our ability to determine if the cross-national variation in performance is related to teacher preparation.

To have avoided this problem it would have been helpful to have longitudinal data on the future teachers. This would have meant measuring their knowledge and beliefs at the beginning of the preparation program and then tracking them through the next 4 to 6 years until they left the program to become teachers. With such data statistical adjustments would be possible, helping to disentangle the relationships. However, such data are difficult to obtain because of non-response over the years leading to data attrition and are costly both in terms of money and labor. This was beyond the resources of the MT21 project.

Even if longitudinal data were collected, the goal of studying the effect of teacher preparation would still be difficult. The selection processes that determine who is to become a future teacher are complicated and often it is almost impossible to determine at what point the preparation begins and hence when the initial data are to be collected. While the end point is definitive for future teachers, the beginning point is complicated by personal choice and program definition. For the institutions in our study the initial point began when the students were formally admitted to the program. In some cases this occurred as late as at the end of the third year of academic study at the university.

This then becomes the point at which the first measures can be collected. However, the difficulty is that what future teachers know and believe at that point may have already been influenced by coursework taken at the university before their formal admission into the program. To use these data together with the final measure taken when they are finished with their preparation program to define gain in knowledge or change in beliefs would surely underestimate the effect of teacher preparation. A further complication is that the program definitions of when they begin vary among institutions. Before this point only the students know if they are intending to enter teacher preparation and that, itself, can change over the first years of university study.

Our approach was to design a synthetic or cohort longitudinal study in which we measured the knowledge and beliefs of a sample of future teachers at the starting point defined by the program of the institution in which they were enrolled. This was Cohort I—representative of beginning future teachers. We used the measures obtained on this cohort as a comparison group for the finishing cohort (Cohort II) at that same institution. The validity of that difference as a measure of gain or change rests on the assumption that the two cohorts are essentially the same except for the additional time spent in teacher preparation. Another way of stating this assumption is that for each institution, Cohorts I and II are assumed to have come from the same population of entering future teachers. Unfortunately, we have no way of knowing whether the assumption is true except for the belief on the part of the country researchers that no definitive events occurred in their country over this time frame, which would have likely made the cohorts different in any major way. This, however, was not the case in Germany, where two of the institutions were affected by a structural change.[1]

Even without structural or other major changes, the composition of the cohorts can be different by factors other than chance, especially at the institutional level. One example results from cohort attrition created by beginning future teachers who drop out or flunk out of their teacher preparation programs. This caveat must be kept in mind as one examines the data in this chapter. The second caveat relates to the problem of defining the beginning point for teacher preparation, which affects our ability to estimate the relationship of teacher preparation to performance. This is especially true in those institutions in which the future teachers begin their formal preparation at a later point in their university studies. This is the same problem as it would have been even with longitudinal data.

The purpose of this chapter is to examine the results to see what we can learn in the vein of generating hypotheses and providing a foundation for the next chapter. We believe cohort differences provide one way to look at how future teachers might have changed. What it is not, however, is a set of results designed to establish the causal inference that teacher education matters or to characterize "real gains" defined at the individual level.

We provide these data recognizing what they are and what they are not. In the end what the results of this chapter do is provide quantitative comparisons between the two cohorts of future teachers distinguished by the point at which they are in their preparation programs. We believe evidence of substantial and consistent cohort differences would be supportive of the hypothesis suggesting that change could have occurred in the professional competencies of the future teachers as they finished their programs. It would be difficult to entertain the hypothesis that teacher education matters if the future teachers at the beginning of their teacher preparation already know the mathematics and pedagogy necessary to teach and have the beliefs that would be supportive of student learning, since little change would then be expected after their years in teacher preparation.

So in this chapter we look at the data to see if there are differences as we compare those at the beginning of teacher preparation (Cohort I) with those at the end (Cohort II) and use this as an indicator of potential average change in future teachers' competencies. The cohort differences can only be defined at the institutional level. To estimate the difference we subtracted the mean of each variable averaged over the Cohort I sample from the mean of the same variable averaged over Cohort II. What follows is a description of those findings.

WHAT TO LOOK FOR AND WHERE

The question arises as to the appropriate level—institution or country—when looking for cohort differences. Country comparisons are typically of more interest to readers than unnamed institutional comparisons. However, we decided to look at the data to determine where most of the variation on the dependent variables resided and to use that as the basis for making the choice. Looking at cohort change for the eight MT21 achievement tests the answer was clear: Most of the variation, if not all (in the case of geometry), was at the institutional level, not the country level, ranging from 98.4–100 %. Therefore, we focus on cohort differences at the institutional level in the next section, looking at the three broad areas of knowledge, beliefs, and instructional intentions. We conclude the chapter by briefly looking at the issue at the country level.

Before turning to the results it is important to understand the nature of the selection bias at the institutional level that is inherent in using the cohort difference as a statistical indicator of possible average change or, in the case of the achievement results, gain at the individual future teacher level. We do this here with respect to the eight achievement scales in mathematics and mathematics pedagogy. Chapter 5 characterized the distributions of the eight scales for those who completed their program, namely, teacher preparation *finishers*, both at the individual and the institutional level, which needs no further elaboration. Figure 9.1 shows the distributions for the eight knowledge scales for the students who are beginning their program (*beginners*). The distributions are defined over the 30 institutions in which such data were collected (four institutions did not collect Cohort I data). It is from this distribution and the one represented in Chapter 5 that the cohort comparisons are derived.

The variation in the institutional means for beginners across the 30 institutions indicates the presence of selection bias. This complicates the interpretation of the institutional differences described in the previous chapters as evidence that teacher education matters. These scores reflect what the future teachers knew about mathematics and mathematics pedagogy as they were admitted into their program. Because of the selection processes discussed previously, the knowledge acquired by the future teachers reflected in Figure 9.1 could have come from one or both of two sources—their own K–12 schooling and/or the university courses taken prior to officially beginning their teacher preparation program.

In a series of regression analyses we examined the source of this bias by modeling the five mathematics knowledge scales. The analyses were done at the institutional level. The variables included the average scale score of Cohort I, the average number of years they had been at the university before beginning their programs (a surrogate for the amount of coursework taken at the university), and the percentage of those beginners who had taken the most advanced mathematics course in their secondary program.

High school mathematics preparation was significantly related to each of the five mathematics knowledge scales. Time at the university was not. The mean effect for high school preparation in mathematics across the five mathematics knowledge scales was about one and a half, which means that the dif-

FIGURE 9.1. Institutional mean distributions for the eight knowledge scale scores for the beginning cohort future teachers.

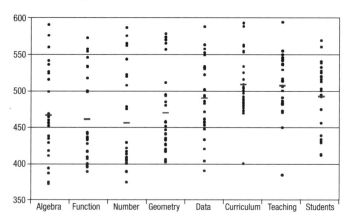

ference in scores between an institution that had none of its students entering teacher preparation having taken the most advanced high school mathematics course available and one in which all students had taken the most advanced high school mathematics course would be predicted to be nearly 150 points, or 1.5 standard deviations, which is a very substantial effect size for high school preparation.

What this clearly says is that there were differences among the 30 institutions with respect to the level of knowledge that future teachers brought with them into their teacher preparation programs. It would appear that a substantial portion of that was related to the mathematics they studied in high school and not so much to what they studied at the university before being admitted to their program—at least as conditioned on what knowledge they brought from their secondary education.

Table 9.1 shows that these differences in entry level knowledge vary not only among the institutions but also across countries. The U.S. sample of future middle school mathematics teachers had only 40% who had taken pre-calculus or calculus compared to over 90% of those in Taiwan who had taken the most advanced high school mathematics, including calculus topics.

The above discussion makes it clear that there is need to control for selection bias in the institutional comparisons as the students entering into teacher preparation programs do vary, on average, across institutions. This is likely related to selection criteria and entry requirements as well as official requirements for completing/graduating from secondary school. These analyses support the importance of estimating cohort differences as one way to address the inherent selection bias.

TABLE 9.1. Country means and standard errors (se) for percentage of Cohort I students having taken the most advanced high school mathematics course available and the number of years Cohort I students reported having been at the university before being admitted in their teacher preparation program.

	Percent with Highest High School Math		Years in Teacher Preparation Program	
	Mean	*(se)*	*Mean*	*(se)*
Bulgaria	49.0	(6.7)	2.0	(0.0)
Germany	63.0	(1.6)	2.6	(0.2)
Mexico	64.8	(6.5)	2.3	(0.3)
South Korea	83.8	(1.8)	1.0	(0.0)
Taiwan	93.8	(7.9)	2.9	(0.5)
United States	41.3	(4.9)	1.9	(0.2)

COHORT COMPARISONS AT THE INSTITUTIONAL LEVEL

Twenty-three of the 30 institutions had adequate sample sizes to be included in the institutional cohort comparisons. Positive values indicate that the mean of Cohort II was greater than the mean of Cohort I. This is the direction one would predict based on the assumption that the more time is spent in teacher preparation, the higher the score on the knowledge tests is. Such a direction in the mean differences would also be consistent with the notion that teacher education matters. Across the 23 institutions and the eight test areas, 71% of the cohort differences were positive. The remaining cohort differences were small negative values, none of which were statistically significant from zero, suggesting essentially no cohort differences. Of the positive differences, just under half of them were statistically significant but all of them point in the direction that is consistent with our hypothesis. Similar results were found for the general pedagogy test as well.

Figure 9.2 represents the institutional cohort mean differences for the professional competencies related to knowledge on the five mathematics scales as well as the three mathematics pedagogical scales. Each display shows the plot of the average score for the beginning cohort at each institution against the average score at the same institution for the cohort of students finishing their programs. The line drawn on the plots represents the points at which there is no difference—that is, the beginning and finishing cohorts have the same average performance. The extent to which the cohort difference for an institution deviates from the 45-degree line indicates the size of the cohort difference, with those institutions above the line being consistent with the hypothesis that, on average, future teachers gain in knowledge during teacher preparation. This was true in most of the institutions. The institutions below the line are ones in which there were no cohort differences as these values, although negative, were not statistically significant from zero. Geometry and Teaching were the two areas with the largest number of institutions showing essentially no difference between the two cohorts as most of the differences were small negative values that were not statistically significantly different from zero.

Consider Algebra first. All of the German, South Korean, and U.S. institutions had positive differences between the two cohorts, although for one South Korean institution the difference was not statistically significant from zero. However, Mexican and Taiwanese institutions had results that indicated no change between the beginning and finishing cohort, while the Bulgarian institutions varied.

The particulars associated with any one institution are not important, as this is not an evaluation study of these 23 teacher preparation institutions. They are meant to represent teacher preparation more generally. Looking at the other

FIGURE 9.2. Institutional cohort differences for the eight knowledge areas.

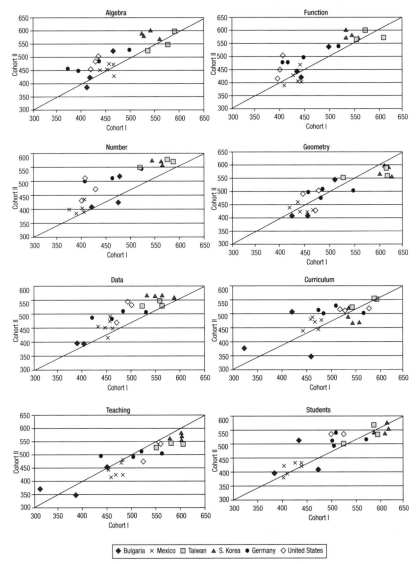

◆ Bulgaria × Mexico □ Taiwan ▲ S. Korea ● Germany ◇ United States

displays presents the same basic message: institutional variation is substantial in terms of the difference in performance between the two cohorts. The particulars change but the general pattern of cohort differences is much the same— some differences were very large and others were small or nonexistent. The two exceptions, as noted previously, were the geometry test and the pedagogical content knowledge test focusing on the instructional interactions related to the teaching of mathematics. In both cases there were no significant differences between the cohorts.

These cross-institutional cohort differences are at least mostly consistent with our hypothesis of a relationship between teacher preparation as defined at each institution and gain in professional competence in terms of knowledge. We documented in Chapter 4 large differences in terms of coursework or opportunity to learn more generally among the institutions. The question that remains is the extent to which the OTL differences in teacher preparation across institutions are related to these cohort differences in knowledge. This becomes the focus of the next chapter, where we build statistical models relating OTL to performance at the institutional level, including the beginning cohort means in the model. Those analyses will help us to understand better the implications of Figure 9.2.

Beliefs and Instructional Related Intentions

The same questions arise with respect to beliefs—the other type of professional competency that teacher preparation aims to influence. To what extent are the beliefs related to schooling and, in particular, to mathematics and mathematics education different between the two cohorts at the 23 sampled institutions? We took the differences between the two cohorts as we did for the knowledge scales. Because of the sheer number of belief scales (74) and the fact that we are using these results in an informal hypothesis-generating mode and not in a more formal hypothesis-testing mode (the substance of Chapter 10), we used a substantive criterion to determine whether the differences were sufficient both in number and magnitude to indicate the presence of a general pattern supporting our hypothesis of cohort change and, by implication, the likelihood of future teacher changes in beliefs related to their teacher preparation. In those cases where the change in belief exceeded a substantive criterion that defined a change in belief large enough to be meaningful given the scale range of five points—one-half a scale point—we recoded the scale as a one, and if the difference was not substantively significant it was coded as a zero.

There were 39 scales related to Chapter 7 (only 20 were discussed because of space limitations) and 35 such scales related to Chapter 8. We hypothesize that beliefs concerning instructional intentions would be the ones most influenced by teacher preparation while the more fundamental beliefs—about the role of schooling and teaching, the importance of mathematics, and views of what mathematics is as a formal discipline—would seem, a priori, the least likely to change during teacher preparation. On average across the 74 scales, substantively important cohort differences were noted in around 30% of the

23 institutions. There was, however, large variation across the 74 scales, with the percentage ranging from 0 to 96 with a standard deviation of around 20%. This pattern, together with the one noted for the knowledge scales, indicates a consistency which on the surface makes the hypothesis that teacher education matters seem reasonable and worthy of additional analyses and further study. To examine the specific nature of the cohort differences and to interpret it for each of the scales would make this chapter into a book itself. Our interest here is simply to demonstrate that for a large number of belief scales there were cohort differences. Almost all (20 out of 23) of the institutions recorded changes on more than 20 of the scales and an additional five institutions had changes on more than 50% of the 74 scales.

Looking at the other dimension—the beliefs themselves—some of the scales were more commonly ones on which change occurred across a larger number of institutions than was the case for the other scales. Over 35% of the scales indicated substantively significant differences between the two cohorts for at least a third or more of the institutions.

We first consider the 39 beliefs related to Chapter 7. All six of the scales from the item that asked future teachers to indicate how much emphasis they would give to various objectives in teaching middle school mathematics (see Chapter 7) demonstrated substantively significant cohort differences in more than half of the institutions. The number of institutions demonstrating this differed for each of the six scales and ranged from 52% to 78%. For all six of the scales there were institutions in which Cohort I indicated that they would give more emphasis to the objective than would Cohort II, and there were institutions in which the opposite was true. For the functional objective, focusing on future studies and exams, Cohort II suggested giving less emphasis as they did for the communication and reasoning objectives. Only two other scales demonstrated cohort differences for over 50% of the institutions. These scales were:

- the belief that the reason that student achievement in mathematics varies is because of differences between boys and girls and between different ethnic groups (52% of the institutions). Here the cohort of finishing future teachers was less likely to believe in such categorical differences than was the beginning cohort. This was true in 8 of the 12 institutions in which the cohort differences were significant; and
- the belief that mathematics is algorithmic in nature and involves a collection of terms, formulae, and rules (74% of the institutions). In the majority of those institutions (17 out of 23) Cohort II future teachers indicated less agreement with this belief than did Cohort I future teachers.

Given the nature of these beliefs and the large number of cohort differences, it seems reasonable that teacher preparation could have influenced such beliefs as they are related to a future teacher's conception of the *what* (the focus of mathematics instruction—algorithms, reasoning, motivation, etc.) and the *to whom* (whether all children can learn mathematics) of teaching. The two together define the essence of mathematics teaching.

Yet there were three belief scales on which significant cohort differences occurred in only two or fewer of the institutions. These scales were:

- the belief that mathematics is a formal body of knowledge defined by rigor and clarity of definitions (one institution);
- the belief about whether the purpose of schooling is to support the development of individuals (one institution); and
- a positive perspective on the teaching profession—that it is important for the country as well as something that offers personal satisfaction and status (one institution).

There were only two scales related to the instructional related intentions (Chapter 8) of the future teachers for which there were cohort differences in more than half of the institutions. This implies that one of our hypotheses was not borne out—there was no indication that these beliefs about their intentions to practice in a certain way in a simulated classroom situation are any more malleable than the more fundamental beliefs described previously. The variation is similar and the number of scales changed in a large percentage of institutions is very similar in pattern to the belief scales of Chapter 7.

There were two scales for which there were significant cohort differences in 57% and 96% of the institutions. The first scale stood out in that important substantive cohort differences occurred in nearly all of the institutions (in 22 out of 23 of them). The scale centered on the belief that using computers to solve mathematics problems distracts students from learning basic mathematics skills. The difference between the two cohorts was mixed—over 60% of the institutions reported that Cohort I indicated a stronger propensity than Cohort II to agree with this position. The other instructional related belief was that as future teachers they believed that teachers should avoid grouping students by ability. Here also there was a split, although in twice as many of the institutions, Cohort I more strongly agreed with this belief.

There were four scales in which only two or fewer of the institutions demonstrated substantive differences between the beginning and finishing cohorts. There was one item on which there were no significant cohort differences. That item asked what a new teacher should put in a letter to the parents for a child who was having behavioral as well as academic problems in class that were not going away. Specifically one scale indicated the degree to which they would externalize the problem, suggesting the need to refer the problem to a counselor, obtain further testing, and other such actions. The second scale indicated the degree to which they would take on the responsibility and indicate proximal solutions.

The other two scales were:

- the belief that students should learn how to use calculators and computers in the mathematics class (two institutions); and
- the degree of emphasis future teachers would place on the more traditional approach to teaching, including having students work at the board and whole class instruction as opposed to small-group instruction (two institutions).

COHORT COMPARISONS AT THE COUNTRY LEVEL

Mathematics and Mathematics Pedagogy Knowledge

Table 9.2 presents the mean level differences between Cohorts I and II for the eight mathematics and mathematics pedagogy knowledge scales together with their estimated standard errors and an indication of the significance level associated with testing if each of the cohort differences were significantly different from zero.

Over the six countries and for the eight scales the typical (median) cohort difference was about 15 score points or .15 of a standard deviation. However, the only country level–estimated cohort differences that were significantly different from zero were in the areas of Algebra (Germany, South Korea, and the United States), Function (Germany and South Korea), and Number (Germany). The gains for all three countries were especially large,

TABLE 9.2. Country means and standard errors (se) for differences between Cohorts I and II for the eight mathematics and mathematics pedagogy knowledge scales for each country.

	Algebra		Function		Number		Geometry		Data		Curriculum		Teaching		Students	
	Mean	*(se)*	*Mean*	*(se)*	*Mean*	*(se)*	*Mean*	*(se)*	*Mean*	*(se)*	*Mean*	*(se)*	*Mean*	*(se)*	*Mean*	*(se)*
Bulgaria	-	-	-	-	-	-	-	-	-	-	-	-	-	-	-	-
Germany	55.0	(11.0)	50.8	(8.9)	64.0	(16.3)	-	-	-	-	-	-	-	-	-	-
South Korea	48.4	(12.7)	40.8	(12.3)	-	-	-	-	-	-	-	-	-	-	-	-
Mexico	-	-	-	-	-	-	-	-	-	-	-	-	-	-	-	-
Taiwan	-	-	-	-	-	-	-	-	-	-	-	-	-	-	-	-
United States	51.1	(8.6)	-	-	-	-	-	-	-	-	-	-	-	-	-	-

Note. Only those means significantly greater than zero are displayed.

with values ranging from 41 for South Korea in functions to 64 for Germany in number, indicating effect sizes around .4 to .6 of a standard deviation.

One possible technical reason for the lack of significant gains for some of the countries in some of the test areas can be attributed to the nature of the distribution of the cohort differences across the institutions within a country. This was illustrated graphically in Figure 9.2, where some of the institutional cohort mean differences are negative (although not significantly so) or very small but positive, while others are positive and larger. One result associated with the nature of these institutional distributions was that when averaged to the country level, the mean cohort differences were small or essentially zero. This is consistent with variance components reported on earlier in this chapter that suggested that most of the variation is among institutions within countries.

Another reason could be related to the point made earlier concerning the definition of Cohort I, which has implications for the number of years' difference between the two cohorts. For those institutions with only 1 or 2 years between the two cohorts, the difference in the amount of coursework taken would also be smaller and hence the likelihood of smaller differences in performance would be greater. Taiwan is a good case in point, where the difference was typically 2 years compared to 3 for other countries. With less difference between the cohorts in university coursework and a high level of mathematics knowledge acquired during high school (see Chapter 11 and Figure 9.2), the cohort differences were typically small. The test scores for the beginning cohort were very high, supporting this contention—in fact, the mean performance of the beginners cohort of future teachers in Taiwan was higher in general than the mean performance of the finishers cohort of sampled teachers for all other countries except South Korea.

This implies that the level of mathematics knowledge necessary to perform well on the MT21 items was already present for the beginning cohort of future teachers in Taiwan. This does not imply that there were no differences in mathematics knowledge between the cohorts, only that this was the case in the more limited sense of knowledge necessary to perform well on the types of items used in this study. There is little reason to believe that the sampled future teachers had not acquired more knowledge of formal mathematics, especially at the more advanced level.

Teacher preparation is related to cohort gain for formal mathematics knowledge, at least in Germany, South Korea, and the United States, mostly in the areas of algebra, function, and number. Although not causal in nature because of the limits of the type of data, such large differences, especially in the case of Germany, give credible evidence of a likely teacher preparation effect. The one continuing caveat to that hypothesis is that the data are not longitudinal and the estimated gain is based on cohort longitudinal data. However, it seems reasonable not to expect major cohort differences other than that related to teacher preparation over such a short time frame, which is the necessary assumption being made. Its violation would introduce selection bias into the estimated gain. A more formal analysis of this relationship will be examined in Chapter 10.

One might have expected that there would be greater cohort differences for the three areas of mathematics pedagogy as this is not knowledge typically studied in high school or for that matter anywhere but in a teacher preparation program. However, this was not the case. There were, however, positive gains in Germany in two of the pedagogical areas—curriculum and student learning—that were marginally significant ($p < .10$ and $p < .13$). Bulgarian sampled future teachers also showed large gains in all three areas. The only other large gain was for the United States on the student scale. However, none of these were statistically significant from zero.

We need to point to the nature of our test and the scale we used as a possible explanation for the lack of significant differences. The variation among future teachers both within and across countries was very large, making it difficult to find statistical significance. Part of this variation reflects the state of knowledge but part of it also reflects measurement error. Mathematics pedagogy is a new field of research and its definition is still unclear, as discussed in Chapter 5. There clearly is the need for more work to develop a test that reflects OTL in mathematics pedagogy in a better way. One of the main challenges in this context is to capture its nature in a way that is valid across countries with their cultural differences.

The other area of professional competence was general pedagogy. Looking at the total score for the lesson plan item described in Chapter 6 as an example, we found only one statistically significant cohort difference—Germany. However, all countries showed cohort differences in which Cohort II outperformed Cohort I, although not statistically significant.

Professional Beliefs

Over the 39 belief scales focusing on fundamental beliefs (Chapter 7) the general results suggest limited cohort differences at the country level. German sampled future teachers changed their beliefs on 12 of the scales where the change was statistically significant. For the other countries, statistically significant cohort differences occurred on three scales for South Korean future teachers and on only one or two scales for the remaining three countries with the exception of the United States.

However, if one were to include marginally significant results ($.05 > p > .1$), an additional 21 such changes occurred: five in Bulgaria, five in Germany, two in South Korea, one in Mexico, three in Taiwan, and five in the United States. On no belief scale were all of the countries' future teachers on average different between the two cohorts.

Only two belief scales demonstrated a significant cohort difference (p < .10) in more than two countries, and these two scales had a significant difference in only three countries. The first of these measured the degree to which they believed that mathematics was a creative endeavor. Sampled future teachers in the final year of preparation from Germany, South Korea, and the United States. were more positive toward this belief than were the beginning cohort future teachers. The second concerned the future teachers' beliefs about mathematical abilities being dependent on biological categories such as gender or ethnic background or on natural ability. Again, changes in this belief were significant in Germany, South Korea, Bulgaria, and Mexico. The differences indicated that those finishing their teacher preparation expressed less support for the idea that ability and such categorical differences play a part in students' mathematics ability. The one exception was the finishing cohort in Bulgaria which on average indicated more support for the idea that differences in student ability were related to gender or other categorical differences than did the beginning cohort.

Behavioral Related Intentions

In this section we examine country change on those beliefs that come the closest to characterizing what the likely classroom and instructional practices of these future teachers are likely to be. It is also the area as indicated previously that we hypothesize should show the most change as these are beliefs more about what one does in practice and not on more deeply held beliefs about fundamental notions of mathematics and schooling.

Our hypothesis was not borne out. Germany once again had the most statistically significant cohort differences—a total of 12 with 8 of them significant at the .05 level. Other countries had only three or four statistically significant changes except Bulgaria, which had only one marginally statistically significant difference. Three of the items and their scales are worth discussing because the average estimated cohort difference is substantial and in several countries the average differences are statistically significant.

The first of these are the scales characterizing how the future teacher believes a middle school teacher should respond to student errors in class. The two scales with significant change are: (1) asking other students to become involved; and (2) whether the teacher should directly address the error. In Mexico, the difference between the finishing cohort and the beginning cohort on average was a more positive view toward having other students become involved in discussing the answers or providing the correct answer (p < .029). The same pattern was marginally significant in both Germany and Taiwan. The finishing cohort in both the United States (p < .003) and Mexico endorsed less strongly the idea that teachers should directly address student errors in their class than the beginning cohort, although this difference was only marginally significant in Mexico (p < .067). The U.S. finishing cohort was different in one respect in that they were less enthusiastic about having other students become involved than was the beginning cohort.

The final set of items concerned the future teachers' beliefs about how a teacher should handle various types of student diversity in the classroom. A single item stated that ability grouping should be avoided and another item stated that teachers should assign more complex problems to the more able students which is, in effect, a form of tracking. The sampled German future teachers at the end of their preparation ended up more positive about ability tracking by providing the more able students with more complex problems going beyond the examples done in class than those at the beginning of the program (p < .055). Mexican future teachers were also more likely to use this approach (p < .076). This practice was also endorsed more strongly by the final cohort in the United States (p < .001). The negatively stated item that ability grouping should be avoided was embraced less by the final cohort in Germany than the beginning cohort (p < .007). However, the final cohort in South Korea more strongly expressed that ability groups should be avoided than did the beginning cohort (p < .001).

SUMMARY

What this chapter indicates is that future teachers in the cohort finishing their program had greater knowledge of mathematics, especially related to algebra and functions, than did those in the beginning cohort at most (71%) but not all of the 23 institutions included in the analyses. Our hypothesis is that the difference likely reflects at least in part the input of the teacher preparation program associated with that institution. We also found such differences between the cohorts in the beliefs they held and for the instructionally related intentions related to classroom instruction and management, at least in responding to simulated situations.

All of this lends support to our hypothesis that teacher preparation is related to the cohort changes we observed in this chapter—namely, that teacher education matters. These hypotheses are just that—conjectures—since such causal inferences are beyond the limits of these data. The formal models examining the relationship of teacher preparation to cohort differences in teacher competencies both of knowledge and beliefs are summarized in the next chapter using the measures of OTL described in Chapter 4 as the defining elements of teacher preparation.

CHAPTER 10

The Role of Opportunity to Learn in Teacher Preparation

The previous chapter explored country and program differences to uncover evidence of what relationships teacher preparation may have had on the professional competencies of future teachers. In this chapter we take a more formal statistical modeling approach by relating the most salient feature of teacher preparation—OTL—to different sets of competencies: knowledge and beliefs. For each of these areas we examine the effects of OTL on a conceptually coherent group of measures. In each analysis we are looking for the relationship that exposure to OTL in teacher education has with respect to the specific measures discussed. Finally, we draw some conclusions that are more appropriately considered to be hypotheses about how teacher education makes a difference.

RESEARCH RELATED TO TEACHER PREPARATION

Undoubtedly teacher preparation institutions structure the learning opportunities they offer (their OTLs) concordant with a specific perspective and philosophy on how best to prepare competent, highly qualified teachers within their contextual constraints. As we begin to look for the difference that participation in such a program may make, that is, the effect of teacher preparation, the importance of an overarching theoretical model plays an important role. The conceptual framework presented in Chapter 3 provides an outline of the theoretical constructs and relationships hypothesized as we approached this work. Previous research provided fertile ground for identifying possibly fruitful lines of inquiry, yet no single theory-driven definition of the outcomes of interest—professional competencies in areas of mathematics; mathematics knowledge specific to the teaching of mathematics; general pedagogical knowledge; and the practices, dispositions, and beliefs associated with good teaching—were readily evidenced. This was not a uniquely identified challenge but was repeatedly noted as a systemic issue confronting teacher education research in the over 800-page volume *Studying Teacher Education*, published by AERA (Blömeke et al., 2008; Clift & Brady, 2005; Floden & Meniketti, 2005; Grossman, 2005; Wilson & Youngs, 2005; Zeichner, 2005; Zeichner & Conklin, 2005). Thus, the major contribution of this chapter is to examine the effect of specific teacher preparation learning experiences to some important competencies that may be viewed as teacher preparation outcomes.

MODELING THE RELATIONSHIP
BETWEEN OTL AND TEACHER COMPETENCIES

Recognizing the hierarchical nature of the survey data collected from future teachers—that is, future teachers clustered within teacher preparation institutions—the appropriate model to use in exploring how future teachers' opportunities to learn are related to what they know, believe, or how they might teach is a two-stage nested regression model, sometimes referred to as a Multi-Level model. In such models, the outcome variable of interest is defined at the individual (stage 1) level while the independent variables or predictors may be defined at either the individual or institutional (stage 2) level or both. Variables defined and employed at the individual level of the analysis highlight the effects of individual differences or choices. Variables defined and included at the institutional level reflect differences between institutions in characteristics, policies, and/or practices.

In this chapter, specific OTL variables were included in the regression analyses as predictors at two levels, both at the individual level and at the mean level for each of the participating institutions. Including OTL at both levels enables us to explore both the effects of personal choice—to the extent that such is possible, as some students electing to take certain types of courses—and the effects of institution policies, as some require all students to take certain types of courses while other institutions do not. In addition, a pseudo pre-test was created and used in the regressions. This pre-test was formed using the data collected from the beginning cohort of future teachers. The beginning cohort scores served as the pre-test for the finishing cohort at the same institution. Thus, these cohort longitudinal measures were only available at the institutional level.

As noted in the previous chapters, *when* students became a part of the teacher preparation program varied across the institutions—in some cases during the 1st year of post-secondary education, and in other cases the 2nd or even 3rd year of teacher preparation. Given this situation, a variable was included in these analyses to represent the number of years between the beginning and finishing cohort. Finally, the regressions also included country contrasts for the U.S. versus Bulgaria, Germany, Mexico, South Korea, and Taiwan.

The rationale for which specific independent variables were included in an analysis was based on the principle of including all of those OTL variables which by conceptual analyses would likely cover content topics that would be related to the particular competency being modeled. We erred on the side of inclusiveness but did not include OTL variables that were similarly defined. Care was taken to distinguish between individual and institutional effects. The goal of this chapter is not, however, to differentiate between individual and institutional effects, as both of these are legitimate evidence of teacher preparation effects, but simply to use an appropriate statistical model to discern whether teacher preparation does indeed matter.

RELATIONSHIP OF OTL TO FUTURE TEACHER COMPETENCIES—KNOWLEDGE

Knowledge of Mathematics

Few would argue that coursework in formal mathematics is not necessary for the preparation of quality middle school teachers, but which courses and how many are subtler issues for which there is less empirical evidence. As a result, the OTL variables included in the models presented in this section include seven of the variables related to opportunities to learn formal mathematics (excluding the history of mathematics), and OTL related to coverage toward gaining a deeper understanding of the school topics related to each particular dependent variable. Also included was the number of courses taken in mathematics pedagogy. Subsets of these variables were included in five separate models, one for each of the mathematics knowledge areas—number, geometry, algebra, function, and data.

The short answer to the question posed for this section is yes, OTL is related to one of the desired future middle school teacher competencies—their knowledge of formal mathematics as it relates to and provides the theoretical foundation for the type of mathematics found in middle and high school curricula around the world and hence the type of mathematics knowledge they will need to teach. For all five knowledge areas, opportunities to study calculus and advanced mathematics were found to be statistically significantly related to the knowledge scores at the individual and/or the institutional level (see Table 10.1). Advanced mathematics, which included topics from multivariate calculus, analysis, differential equations, topology, and differential geometry, was related to all five knowledge scales at the individual future teacher level.

TABLE 10.1. Multi-level analysis results relating mathematics content knowledge to OTL.

	Algebra			Function			Number			Geometry			Data		
	Est	(se)	p<	Est	(se)	p<	Est	(se)	p<	Est	(se)	p<	Est	(se)	p<
Intercept	367.9	(39.2)	0.0000	391.6	(50.2)	0.0000	365.2	(37.6)	0.0000	386.5	(42.4)	0.0000	385.4	(26.1)	0.0000
Future Teacher Level															
Mathematics Pedagogy	-2.6	(9.1)	0.7744				-6.1	(8.5)	0.4732	-1.9	(9.5)	0.8402	3.7	(8.5)	0.6626
Linear Algebra	24.9	(8.9)	0.0055	24.3	(8.0)	0.0026							5.6	(6.6)	0.3908
Number Theory	-10.4	(6.9)	0.1303												
Geometry	-3.1	(8.9)	0.7281							-4.3	(9.2)	0.6398			
Probability & Stat										-6.6	(8.9)	0.4560			
Adv Math	25.6	(12.3)	0.0379	43.5	(11.0)	0.0001	50.0	(11.3)	0.0000	35.4	(12.8)	0.0058	33.5	(11.2)	0.0028
Abstract Algebra	30.6	(9.1)	0.0007	18.7	(7.9)	0.0177	17.0	(9.2)	0.0664	22.4	(10.5)	0.0325	19.3	(9.1)	0.0332
Basic Calculus	28.8	(10.1)	0.0043	22.4	(9.2)	0.0149									
Working With / Understanding															
Number Topics							0.4	(1.7)	0.8116						
Geometry Topics										-1.0	(1.9)	0.5772			
Function Topics				1.4	(1.6)	0.3769									
Institution Level															
Mathematics Pedagogy	29.5	(35.6)	0.4157	-72.2	(46.9)	0.1372	26.5	(38.3)	0.4962	21.0	(43.9)	0.6378			
Linear Algebra	-50.1	(43.6)	0.2635												
Number Theory	23.3	(25.8)	0.3763												
Geometry	97.6	(40.7)	0.0259							110.7	(42.8)	0.0170			
Probability & Stat				-102.5	(62.5)	0.1144	-60.9	(65.6)	0.3620	-28.0	(63.4)	0.6632			
Adv Math	-117.8	(60.6)	0.0653	166.0	(39.3)	0.0003	102.7	(38.3)	0.0131	-114.0	(68.8)	0.1121			
Abstract Algebra	89.0	(41.0)	0.0414	79.5	(34.6)	0.0308				67.2	(41.0)	0.1149			
Basic Calculus	55.8	(34.2)	0.1172												
Working With / Understanding															
Number Topics							5.0	(11.1)	0.6536						
Geometry Topics										3.2	(12.7)	0.8017			
Function Topics				0.1	(12.1)	0.9923									
Country Contrast vs United States															
Bulgaria	9.5	(21.6)	0.6641	79.0	(23.1)	0.0023	14.6	(22.7)	0.5267	17.7	(23.9)	0.4680			
Germany	60.7	(15.4)	0.0007	87.2	(14.4)	0.0000	68.4	(16.3)	0.0003	47.5	(23.0)	0.0505			
Mexico	-9.4	(20.8)	0.6576	-13.3	(18.4)	0.4776	-43.3	(23.6)	0.0792	-26.7	(30.4)	0.3888			
South Korea	123.5	(28.5)	0.0003	127.9	(29.3)	0.0002	124.2	(30.7)	0.0005	133.7	(32.7)	0.0005			
Taiwan	113.6	(23.3)	0.0001	130.4	(21.2)	0.0000	114.1	(22.5)	0.0000	131.5	(25.0)	0.0000			

Note. In this, and in all Chapter 10 tables reporting multi-level results, blank spaces indicate that the independent variable in the corresponding row was not included in the model for the dependent variable defining the corresponding column. None of the negative coefficients are statistically significantly different from zero.

Algebra knowledge was not only related to OTL in calculus and advanced mathematics but also OTL related to the study of linear and abstract algebra. The estimated effects at the individual future teacher level were sizeable in magnitude across all four variables—about one third of a standard deviation, which is a relatively strong relationship given that we are talking about just one topic or course.

The pattern of relationships was similar for the Function test as well, which measures knowledge of the second major aspect of middle and high school algebra. Since many of the topics included in the definition of advanced mathematics are related to analysis, the large estimated effect size[1] is understandable. For the abstract algebra course there also was a statistically significant relationship at the institutional level, both for the Function test (p <. 001) and for the Algebra test (p <. 041).[2] This indicates that the differences in OTL across institutions are related to differences in achievement, even after controlling for these relationships at the individual future teacher level.

The presence of such aggregate effects implies that for some of these dependent variables there is variation in course-taking at the institutional level (within countries) that additionally contributes to achievement. Exactly what the genesis of this is, however, is not entirely clear. Most likely these differences are related to some combination of cross-institutional distinctions in course requirements, course offerings, informal expectations among students to take more courses even though not required, and the mathematics backgrounds of students entering the program, resulting in more advanced course-taking. Whichever of these factors triggers the observed institutional variation—which may very well not be the same at every institution—the estimated institutional effect size, when combined with the individual effect size, indicates a strong relationship between OTL and performance on both the Algebra and the Function tests.

For the geometry area there was a significant institutional relationship for course-taking in geometry (p < .017) but not at the individual future teacher level. Nevertheless, basic calculus and advanced mathematics were significantly related to achievement. Evidently most of the achievement-related variation in geometry course-taking is at the institutional level, which likely stems from differential course requirements or course offerings by the institutions.

For the Number and Data tests, basic calculus and advanced mathematics were, again, significantly related to achievement, with basic calculus also having a significant effect at the institutional level. Perhaps somewhat strangely, there also was a significant institutional effect relating geometry to gain on the Data test. We assume that this effect is partly triggered by the nature of our Data test. The items require knowledge of iconic representations, which is often gained in geometry classes.

The two categories of OTL included in these models that did not have a significant relationship to any of the five dependent variables characterizing mathematics knowledge were advanced mathematics for school topics and formal mathematics pedagogy. This can probably be attributed to the somewhat lower reliability of these scales and a floor effect due to the low proportion of future teachers who had studied these topics. Still, it also indicates that formal mathematics might be better learned in formal mathematics classes.

Sampled U.S. future teachers were statistically significantly outperformed by Taiwanese and South Korean future teachers in all of the knowledge areas for the unadjusted means (see Chapter 5) and for the adjusted contrasts of the means—controlling for differences in opportunity (where the estimated contrasts defined with respect to the United States are given in Table 10.1). They were also outperformed by the German future teachers in all areas except data, and by Bulgarian future teachers in functions. After also adjusting for prior knowledge (using test data from the beginning teachers as a surrogate pre-test at the institutional level), the magnitude of all of these estimated mean contrasts with the United States were reduced, even eliminating some of the significant differences for both South Korea and Taiwan on the Data test and the Geometry test. Although not significant, the mean difference on the Function test between both South Korean and Taiwanese future teachers, when contrasted with future teachers in the United States, was reduced by half after adjusting for the surrogate pre-test and OTL.

Such a reduction in the magnitude of the estimated country contrasts likely implies that country differences reflect not only differences in program definitions as reflected in OTL but also differences in the preparation in formal mathematics that future teachers have had at the secondary level in combination with differences in the mathematics ability of students who enter teaching. Country admissions and recruitment procedures could also impact the latter. As a result, country differences are not only a reflection of differences in teacher preparation but, at least to some extent, encompass the divergences that begin with a future teacher's grade 1 school enrollment. From TIMSS we know that there are large differences in the coherence and rigor of the K–12 curriculum in Taiwan and South Korea compared to that of the United States and the other countries (Schmidt et al., 2001; see also Chapter 2).

Knowledge of Mathematics Pedagogy

Pedagogical content knowledge includes understanding mathematics but also encompasses what needs to be understood in order to teach lower-secondary students school mathematics topics. Three areas were identified by the literature: knowledge related to the K–12 curriculum, including what it covers and what the mathematical reasons are as to why certain topics precede others (curriculum); knowledge about the nature of instructional interactions surrounding the teaching of mathematics, such as knowing how to ask questions that help students develop a deeper understanding of mathematics (teaching); and knowledge about student learning, including what types of errors they make and the misconceptions they may have (student).

For each of the three variables a model was specified that included OTL variables from the broad categories of formal mathematics, school mathematics, mathematics pedagogy, practical mathematics pedagogy, the practical aspect of general pedagogy, and classroom-related experiences. Different OTL variables were included for each of the different dependent variables. All of the items used to measure pedagogical content knowledge included mathematics and as such, at least theoretically, both mathematics and pedagogical knowledge would be necessary to successfully respond to the MT21 items. As a result, OTL measures included course-taking in formal mathematics, school mathematics, and mathematics pedagogy. The analyses for the three mathematics pedagogical knowledge scales include the institutional level cohort-defined pre-test.

For *curriculum pedagogical knowledge*, the OTL variables in the model included formal mathematics coursework in number theory; the history of school mathematics; advanced school mathematics; and two measures of classroom-related experiences—the number of different types of opportunities to gain practical experience and the number of weeks of practice (student) teaching. OTL in number theory was included because the organization of the school curriculum is strongly related to number.

The pre-test and time variable as well as coursework in number and the OTL defined by the study of advanced school mathematics were not statistically significantly related to curriculum knowledge (see Table 10.2—the number of years between the cohorts was eliminated from the final model). In fact, only the history of school mathematics at the institutional level was significantly related to performance (p < .024). Put simply, knowledge of the K–12 curriculum was not well predicted from these OTL variables. However, the significance of the history of school mathematics is important to note as its relationship to knowledge of the mathematics curriculum likely derives from an understanding of how mathematics itself evolved and how this is related to the way mathematics topics are structured and sequenced in the K–12 curriculum. Its significance at the institutional level most likely derives from the fact that this is a course that is not even offered at all institutions, and which certainly is not required if it is offered. It most likely reflects differences in program emphases. Our inclusion of coursework in number theory was somewhat borne out by the positive coefficient for number theory at the institutional level; however, it was not statistically significant (p < .11).

TABLE 10.2. Multi-level analysis results relating OTL to mathematics pedagogy knowledge.

	Curriculum			Teaching			Students		
	Est	*(se)*	*p<*	*Est*	*(se)*	*p<*	*Est*	*(se)*	*p<*
Intercept	616.3	(127.5)	0.0001	343.1	(164.3)	0.0555	265.0	(102.3)	0.0236
Future Teacher									
General Pedagogy							-25.8	(17.6)	0.1432
Instructional Planning and Classroom Management				-18.7	(9.2)	0.0417			
Mathematics Pedagogy				17.3	(12.3)	0.1621	18.0	(13.3)	0.1765
History of School Mathematics	-0.8	(8.5)	0.9264						
Number Theory	-5.1	(8.4)	0.5450						
Abstract Algebra				17.7	(10.4)	0.0892			
Instructional Interaction Around Mathematics				4.1	(5.4)	0.4524			
Methods of Teaching Algorithms, Non-Routine Problems, and Proofs				-8.7	(4.2)	0.0390			
Teaching Mathematics in the Lower Secondary Level				0.9	(4.2)	0.8337			
Understanding How Students Learn Mathematics							-4.8	(3.0)	0.1065
Working with and Understanding Lower Secondary Math Topics	-0.6	(2.6)	0.81				3.0	(2.7)	0.2659
Number of Opportunities to Gain Practical Experiences	2.3	(1.6)	0.15	3.0	(1.6)	0.05	2.9	(1.6)	0.0694
Amount of Time to Gain Practical Experiences (in Weeks)	0.1	(0.2)	0.72	0.6	(0.2)	0.02	0.5	(0.2)	0.0342
Methods of Solving School Mathematics Problems							3.6	(8.0)	0.6488
School Mathematics Topics							-7.7	(9.9)	0.4399
Opportunity to Gain Practical Experiences—TP							0.2	(3.7)	0.9474
Opportunity to Gain Practical Experiences—OTL							-18.3	(7.3)	0.0124
Institution									
Beginning Cohort Performance	-0.3	(0.2)	0.2422	0.3	(0.3)	0.2840			
General Pedagogy							80.4	(108.2)	0.4715
Instructional Planning and Classroom Management				-95.8	(61.9)	0.1441			
Mathematics Pedagogy				31.2	(47.8)	0.5248	207.0	(78.0)	0.0210
History of School Mathematics	121.8	(49.2)	0.0235						
Number Theory	75.0	(44.6)	0.1100						
Abstract Algebra				83.5	(44.1)	0.0793			
Instructional Interaction Around Mathematics				95.9	(39.0)	0.0277			
Methods of Teaching Algorithms, Non-Routine Problems, and Proofs				-62.3	(32.9)	0.08			
Teaching Mathematics in the Lower Secondary Level				-59.6	(31.6)	0.08			
Understanding How Students Learn Mathematics							-57.6	(23.2)	0.0287
Working with and Understanding Lower Secondary Math Topics	-19.5	(20.0)	0.34				56.9	(20.5)	0.0166
Number of Opportunities to Gain Practical Experiences	2.8	(11.1)	0.80	17.9	(10.2)	0.10	-4.4	(13.9)	0.7555
Amount of Time to Gain Practical Experiences (in Weeks)	1.0	(2.3)	0.67	-0.7	(1.8)	0.70	-2.7	(2.4)	0.2695
Methods of Solving School Mathematics Problems							-99.9	(54.9)	0.0938
School Mathematics Topics							90.3	(73.4)	0.2421
Opportunity to Gain Practical Experiences—TP							55.7	(28.9)	0.0782
Opportunity to Gain Practical Experiences—OTL							-123.1	(57.7)	0.0541
Number of Years Between Beginning and Finishing Cohorts							32.1	(15.0)	0.0534
Contrast vs United States									
Bulgaria	-99.1	(41.5)	0.0283	-50.0	(41.0)	0.2424	-105.3	(56.3)	0.0863
Germany	-2.5	(22.5)	0.9127	-26.5	(26.9)	0.3417	-61.0	(51.8)	0.2622
Mexico	-122.8	(39.2)	0.0058	-60.3	(29.9)	0.0636	-247.4	(78.4)	0.0083
South Korea	-29.0	(26.7)	0.2917	58.3	(36.2)	0.1290	-37.8	(51.8)	0.4795
Taiwan	27.4	(26.5)	0.3142	23.9	(28.3)	0.4124	3.3	(40.7)	0.9371

Pedagogical content knowledge related to the teaching of mathematics was modeled with course-taking in general mathematics pedagogy, abstract algebra, and instructional planning and classroom management. Also included were future teachers' judgments about the extent of OTL related to: instructional interactions around mathematics; methods of teaching, algorithms, nonroutine problems and proofs; and teaching mathematics at the lower-secondary level. Classroom-related experiences were also included. The surrogate pre-test was again not significant. Three variables were significantly and positively related to performance in this area. They were the extent of opportunity related to instructional interactions around mathematics ($p < .03$), the number of different types of practical experiences gained during their programs ($p < .05$), and the number of weeks in which they were involved in having major responsibility for teaching mathematics in the schools ($p < .02$). This result nicely reflects the importance of practical experiences in teacher education. There is a growing body of research studies that points out that teachers are only able to make sense of their declarative knowledge—which is undoubtedly a necessary precondition for this process—when they get the chance to practice it (Blömeke, 2002). Teaching is a procedural activity. Therefore, teachers need to restructure and connect many different areas of knowledge in order to perform well (Berliner, 2001). The result also reflects the skill-related nature of our Mathematics Pedagogy test. Items in this part are focused on specific classroom situations that a teacher has to organize.

Interestingly, the extent of opportunity in the practical aspects of instructional interactions around mathematics was significantly related to residual gain at the institutional level. The extent of OTL in this area is most likely gained in coursework in mathematics pedagogy. The availability of such an emphasis in those courses varies across institutions within the six countries, likely reflecting philosophical diversity regarding the extent to which inclusion of such practical issues is appropriate in teacher training. In terms of its relationship to residual gain, it is essentially an institutional issue.

There is also a marginally significant effect for abstract algebra at both the institutional level ($p < .08$) and at the individual future teacher level ($p < .09$). It could be hypothesized that this is picking up the effect of formal mathematics as it defines the mathematics content of many of these mathematics pedagogy items that focus on algebra. Two other significant relationships indicate a negative relationship of OTL to gain—methods of teaching algorithms, nonroutine problems, and proofs ($p < .04$), and instructional planning and classroom management ($p < .04$)—which is difficult to understand. One hypothesis is that the future teachers and institutions where more of these types of OTLs are present and taken, are at the institutions which on average perform at lower levels.

The third pedagogical content knowledge scale was student learning, which focused on knowledge related to how students think about and learn mathematics. Included in the model were OTL variables characterizing coursework in both general and mathematics pedagogy, advanced school mathematics, understanding how students learn mathematics, methods of solving school mathematics problems, and also classroom-related experiences. The surrogate pre-test was not statistically significant.[3]

Future teachers, who spent more time (measured as the number of weeks) with the full responsibility for teaching mathematics classes for more than 1 day a week, scored higher on the Student Learning Knowledge test ($p < .03$). In addition, a marginally significant ($p < .07$) relationship was noted for the number of different types of K–12 practice experiences. These relationships were at the future teacher level. The remaining significant relationships were defined at the institutional level. They confirm our interpretation of the results with respect to the teaching scale. The larger the average number of formal courses taken or topics covered in the courses taken in general mathematics pedagogy by the future teachers at an institution, the larger the mean performance ($p < .02$). There was also a positive relationship at the individual future teacher level, but it was not significant. Recall that one of the courses included in this category was the psychology of student learning, which presumably would address many issues that would be directly related to performance on this test.

The other significant institutional effect was the study of lower-secondary school topics ($p < .02$). This course (or courses) focuses on studying the mathematics that provides the theoretical background of the mathematics found in the school curriculum. One anomalous result was a similar effect for the average extent of OTL related to the practical topic of understanding how students learn mathematics. What is difficult to understand is that this relationship is negative, implying that institutions that have on average a higher extent of coverage on the part of future teachers also have lower academic achievement in this area ($p < .03$). Rather than supporting the sort of counterintuitive conclusion that such courses would actually decrease knowledge in this area, it seems far more likely that it is reflecting the zero-sum nature of any teacher preparation program. That is, time in teacher education is finite and increasing emphasis in one area must ultimately come at the expense of emphasis in another. Therefore, it might well be that those institutions that provide the most emphasis on understanding how students learn provide very little emphasis on some other of the very critical areas pertinent to developing competencies in this area.

After accounting for differences in OTL, several significant differences in pedagogical performance among countries still exist. However, sampled Taiwanese, South Korean, and German future teachers do not differ significantly from the U.S. future teachers on any of the three test areas. They did in some areas on the unadjusted means reported in Chapter 5. For example, Taiwan outperformed the United States in all three areas and South Korea did on two of them.

Knowledge of General Pedagogy

In the real world of classroom instruction, teachers must use their knowledge of mathematics together with their knowledge of both mathematics pedagogy and general pedagogy to develop lesson plans and then to implement the plans. The design of a lesson plan with regard to how a particular topic will be taught is a fundamental skill for quality teaching. It not only demands knowledge of the particular mathematics defining the lesson but also strategies for teaching the particulars related to the topic as well as knowledge of how one constructs a lesson plan and, even more fundamentally, how a lesson should flow—for example, how you begin, and where and how practice enters the sequence.

The general pedagogy measure asked future teachers to critique a lesson plan for teaching surface area and volume. The fitted model includes OTL variables related to formal or theoretical general pedagogy; the formal study of geometry, as this is the mathematics area of the lesson; the extent of opportunity related to different types of classroom experiences; and studying the practical aspects of mathematics pedagogy related to teaching mathematics at the middle school level. Also included in the model was the number of weeks of student teaching.

The surrogate pre-test measure was not significant (see Table 10.3). The practical aspects of mathematics pedagogy related to the teaching of mathematics were marginally related to residual gain at the individual future teacher level ($p < .08$). OTL defined by the number of different classroom-related experiences was also significant. This was significant at the individual level ($p < .00001$). There was also one marginally significant effect at the institutional level related to the coursework in geometry ($p < .09$). After adjusting for differences in OTL, only Germany was marginally significantly different from the United States.

These results lead to an interesting conclusion. Obviously, general pedagogical knowledge as defined by the lesson plan item requires different types of classroom experiences, such as observing instruction and practicing teaching, before one is able to apply the pedagogical knowledge acquired during teacher education, as in coursework related to the teaching of mathematics at the lower-secondary level, to classroom situations. In this sense, practical experiences in classrooms can be regarded as an important learning opportunity during teacher education and, in this case, the more varied the type of experience the larger the residual gain in performance on the lesson-planning item. Also, a marginally statistically significant relationship was found for opportunity to learn related to coursework in geometry ($p < .09$). The fact that the knowledge of geometry is

TABLE 10.3. Multi-level analysis results relating OTL to general pedagogical knowledge.

Source	General Pedagogy		
	Est	(se)	p<
Intercept	1.3	(0.2)	0.7997
Future Teacher Level			
General Pedagogy	0.9	(1.0)	0.3712
Geometry	0.4	(0.6)	0.5307
Teaching Mathematics in the Lower Secondary Level	0.3	(0.2)	0.0751
Number of Opportunities to Gain Practical Experiences	0.4	(0.1)	0.0000
Amount of Time to Gain Practical Experiences (in Weeks)	0.0	(0.0)	0.4263
Institution Level			
General Pedagogy	3.1	(4.9)	0.5437
Geometry	5.4	(3.0)	0.0882
Teaching Mathematics in the Lower Secondary Level	0.3	(1.1)	0.7862
Number of Opportunities to Gain Practical Experiences	0.7	(0.7)	0.3443
Amount of Time to Gain Practical Experiences (in Weeks)	-0.1	(0.2)	0.6998
Country Contrast vs United States			
Bulgaria	-3.9	(2.6)	0.1600
Germany	4.1	(2.2)	0.0732
Mexico	2.4	(1.6)	0.1537
South Korea	-2.1	(1.5)	0.1744
Taiwan	0.8	(1.5)	0.5973

marginally significant at the institutional level is likely related to the fact that the content of the lesson plan is related to geometry and, as was indicated earlier, there was substantial variation in OTL in this area among the institutions, especially in Taiwan and Bulgaria (see Chapter 3).

RELATIONSHIP OF OTL TO FUTURE TEACHER COMPETENCE—BELIEFS

An Overview

In Chapters 7 and 8 we looked at a range of beliefs about professionally related topics. In these chapters we distinguished between two groups of beliefs:

those that represented a general perspective on the profession and those that were more closely related to specific instructional approaches in the classroom. General profession beliefs such as the nature of mathematics, the role of a teacher, and characteristics of students and student learning were the focus of Chapter 7. In Chapter 8 we explored another set of beliefs that were more closely associated with specific aspects of classroom teaching, such as how a teacher should handle errors expressed by students, the rationale and appropriate use or non-use of student work groups, and many practical aspects of establishing and maintaining classroom decorum that supports and encourages student learning in the classroom. We looked at this set of beliefs about practical aspects of teaching and learning in classrooms for possible insight into how these future teachers might conduct themselves once they have a classroom and students of their own.

The goal of teacher education is not only to provide the requisite subject matter knowledge, which in our case is mathematics, and the knowledge of the teaching and learning process; but also to equip individuals with a professional perspective and an array of professional practices that will inform and shape the teacher's classroom practices. Although all teacher education programs provide specific learning opportunities that are intended to foster the development of a professional perspective and influence attendant beliefs, it is not always clear which specific experiences are most germane to this process. In the previous section we explored the specific OTL experiences that were related to our measures of future teachers' knowledge of mathematics, mathematics pedagogy, and general pedagogy. In this section we take on the task of identifying the specific learning opportunities that are related to various professionally related beliefs.

Our discussion in Chapters 7 and 8 included many such beliefs. Here we highlight a select few and, using the same analytical approach used in the previous section, explore which learning opportunities are most closely associated with them. The rationale for the selection of the few discussed in this section is twofold. First is simply the practical consideration of needing to focus on smaller sets of beliefs than all those detailed in Chapters 7 and 8. Given this, the specific ones discussed below were selected because we felt these were the ones that are most likely—given the state of research—connected to classroom performance, and which we hypothesized would most likely be the ones that OTL would have affected.

From Chapter 7 we selected eight belief scales to explore their relationship to OTL. Two of these relate to the nature of mathematics: the idea that mathematics is a useful and applicable tool in most any profession or situation and the idea that mathematics is algorithmic, entailing the use of many definitions, rules, procedures, routines, and strategies. Two more scales have to do with how much emphasis certain types of student objectives should be given in teaching lower-secondary/middle grades mathematics. The two we discuss here are the objective to develop students' mathematical reasoning and problem solving and the objective to have students acquire the mathematical algorithms, rules, and skills and the facility to accurately make use of them. Three scales address the role of schooling in society and the role of the teacher. One addressed the role of schooling in appropriately sorting students. Another has to do with the idea that a teacher is a provider of knowledge to students, and the last is the idea that a fundamental goal of teachers is to foster community cooperation. The final belief scale has to do with the idea that certain individuals have innate mathematical abilities while others do not.

A more extensive selection of classroom practice-related beliefs from Chapter 8 was selected for discussion here. These include three ideas about how to organize and manage a classroom, selecting among instructional practice emphases, how a teacher should handle errors expressed by students, and the rationale and appropriate use of student work groups.

A Summary of the OTL Relationships

A teacher preparation program for those who will teach mathematics generally includes learning experiences that have four different emphases: mathematics, mathematics pedagogy, general pedagogy, and practical experiences. The models in the previous section concerning the development of mathematics and mathematics pedagogy knowledge focused on the OTL effects associated with courses or learning experiences devoted to mathematics or mathematics pedagogy (education), as there seems to be little theoretical or practical rationale for the contribution of general pedagogy topics to such knowledge. For example, there seems to be little reason to expect that a course focusing on general classroom management principles would increase one's knowledge of algebra or the role of proof in the 8th-grade mathematics curriculum. However, in exploring the relationships between various OTL experiences and various professionally related beliefs, we need to consider the possible effects of all four types of experiences. Initial analyses led to the elimination of some of these possible OTL experiences from those reported here.

Across the 7 general professional beliefs and 11 classroom practices described above there were a total of 30 specific statistically significant OTL effects: 8 significant OTL effects among the 7 beliefs and 22 significant OTL effects among the 11 classroom practices. There were an additional 7 OTL effects that were marginally significant—that is, effects with $.05 < p < .1$.

In addition to these OTL effects, there were 28 country effects. This means that after controlling for the effect of OTL on the various beliefs or classroom practices, the adjusted means were different for future teachers in one or more of the other five countries compared to U.S. future teachers. The number of such effects underscores the importance of including country in analyzing the relationship of OTL to these beliefs, and reinforces the results discussed in previous chapters about differences in the way future teachers think about these beliefs from one country to the next. Most of the effects uncovered in the analyses were at the individual level.

The most frequent OTL variable to demonstrate a relationship with any of the beliefs was the total number of courses or topics future teachers indicated having in the area of general pedagogy. This included topics such as the history, philosophy, or sociology of education; educational psychology; general methods of teaching; classroom management; and principles and theory of instruction. Most of the relationships were positive, indicating that the more courses and/or topics in this area that the future teacher encountered, the more strongly the future teacher endorsed a specific belief or classroom practice. All but one of the significant relationships were with those beliefs relating to specific classroom practices. We will go into details below, but as a first summary we want to point out that in contrast to a lot of skepticism in the literature, beliefs may be influenced during teacher education, and this mainly through pedagogy classes and mainly with respect to specific classroom behavior. However, the picture is very nuanced, as the reader will discover. A second OTL variable—methods of teaching algorithm, nonroutine problems and proofs—demonstrated almost as many significant relationships with various beliefs. Most were with four general professional beliefs while the other two were with two classroom-practice areas. More specific OTL effects are explained in the following sections.

General Professional Beliefs

Table 10.4 presents the results for three areas of professional beliefs: epistemological beliefs about the nature of mathematics, the importance of various objectives in teaching students mathematics, and how one thinks about categorical differences and mathematics ability. One might expect that as one studies mathematics one's perspective on the nature of mathematics as a discipline and its applicability and usefulness in the world would be affected. However, to the contrary, epistemological beliefs are by nature deeply rooted in a student's personality (Hofer & Pintrich, 2002) and most likely changed only by a whole set of experiences rather than by the study of one topic. The results of the OTL regressions on these two beliefs, presented in Table 10.4, demonstrate an intriguing relationship between studying mathematics and these two epistemological perspectives on the discipline.

TABLE 10.4. Multi-level analysis results relating OTL to general professional beliefs.

Source	Algorithmic			Usefulness			Math Skills			Math Reasoning			Category Differences		
	Est	(se)	p<	Est	(se)	p<	Est	(se)	p<	Est	(se)	p<	Est	(se)	p<
Intercept	4.11	(0.71)	0.000	4.61	(0.45)	0.000	3.33	(0.39)	0.000	4.02	(0.26)	0.000	2.23	(0.58)	0.001
Future Teacher															
Number of Courses Taken in Mathematics	-0.01	(0.01)	0.520	0.00	(0.01)	0.830	0.01	(0.01)	0.353	0.01	(0.01)	0.517	0.00	(0.01)	0.830
Mathematics Pedagogy	-0.13	(0.11)	0.236	0.08	(0.11)	0.463	-0.04	(0.10)	0.677	0.03	(0.09)	0.785	-0.01	(0.13)	0.463
History of School Mathematics	0.03	(0.07)	0.632	0.09	(0.07)	0.204	-0.09	(0.06)	0.131	0.02	(0.06)	0.718			
School Mathematics Topics	0.07	(0.08)	0.414	0.07	(0.08)	0.365	0.12	(0.06)	0.045	0.06	(0.06)	0.263			
Teaching Including Classroom Management													0.04	(0.03)	0.153
Instructional Interaction Around Mathematics	0.05	(0.05)	0.330	0.08	(0.05)	0.114	0.03	(0.07)	0.649	0.16	(0.07)	0.016			
Methods of Teaching Algorithms, Non-Routine Problems, and Proofs	0.07	(0.04)	0.074	-0.01	(0.04)	0.887	0.03	(0.03)	0.314	-0.02	(0.02)	0.320			
Teaching Mathematics in the Lower Secondary Level	-0.06	(0.04)	0.097	0.05	(0.04)	0.229	0.09	(0.03)	0.002	0.09	(0.03)	0.001			
Working with and Understanding Lower Secondary Math Topics	0.06	(0.02)	0.008	0.02	(0.02)	0.392	0.00	(0.03)	0.987	0.00	(0.03)	0.998			
Institution															
Number of Courses Taken in Mathematics	-0.09	(0.05)	0.126	0.05	(0.04)	0.202	0.01	(0.03)	0.643	0.00	(0.02)	0.872	0.02	(0.05)	0.607
Mathematics Pedagogy	0.36	(0.73)	0.622	-0.32	(0.45)	0.489	-0.37	(0.45)	0.416	-0.72	(0.29)	0.024	-0.06	(0.54)	0.915
History of School Mathematics	-0.05	(0.59)	0.935	0.42	(0.38)	0.284	0.01	(0.33)	0.986	0.40	(0.24)	0.110			
School Mathematics Topics	-0.22	(0.66)	0.742	-0.21	(0.43)	0.626	0.21	(0.25)	0.412	0.20	(0.15)	0.204			
Teaching Including Classroom Management													-0.01	(0.16)	0.973
Instructional Interaction Around Mathematics	-0.41	(0.51)	0.427	0.54	(0.34)	0.129	-0.18	(0.40)	0.656	-0.31	(0.27)	0.263			
Methods of Teaching Algorithms, Non-Routine Problems, and Proofs	0.22	(0.42)	0.608	-0.25	(0.27)	0.374	0.04	(0.21)	0.859	0.14	(0.15)	0.358			
Teaching Mathematics in the Lower Secondary Level	0.21	(0.42)	0.615	-0.23	(0.29)	0.427	-0.02	(0.20)	0.908	-0.10	(0.14)	0.496			
Working with and Understanding Lower Secondary Math Topics	0.21	(0.21)	0.338	0.00	(0.14)	0.971	0.02	(0.18)	0.903	-0.04	(0.12)	0.746			
Country Contrast vs United States															
Bulgaria	0.51	(0.34)	0.151	-0.36	(0.22)	0.127	0.20	(0.19)	0.298	-0.28	(0.13)	0.049	0.22	(0.25)	0.378
Germany	-0.70	(0.30)	0.029	-0.39	(0.18)	0.049	-0.28	(0.16)	0.087	-0.35	(0.10)	0.003	-0.20	(0.25)	0.429
Mexico	-0.76	(0.41)	0.081	0.27	(0.27)	0.338	0.40	(0.28)	0.158	0.17	(0.19)	0.381	-0.19	(0.28)	0.493
South Korea	0.28	(0.37)	0.448	-0.74	(0.24)	0.006	0.14	(0.22)	0.527	-0.11	(0.16)	0.493	0.29	(0.28)	0.321
Taiwan	0.46	(0.29)	0.124	-0.56	(0.19)	0.008	0.09	(0.18)	0.631	-0.08	(0.12)	0.531	1.30	(0.26)	0.000

The algorithmic scale, which defined mathematics as entailing the use of many definitions, rules, procedures, routines, and strategies was significantly related at the individual future teachers' level to their exposure to developing a deep understanding of various middle school mathematics topics. Neither the number of formal mathematics courses taken nor the extent of their exposure to mathematics education courses and/or topics demonstrated a significant relationship. Two other OTL experiences, for example, methods of teaching algorithms, nonroutine problems, and proofs; and specific methods for teaching middle school mathematics, demonstrated marginally significant relationships ($p < .1$).

This suggests that, at least for those who are preparing to teach, endorsing an algorithmic perspective on mathematics is more closely related to the study of school mathematics and various aspects of teaching mathematics in schools than it is to coursework in formal mathematics. Inasmuch as this epistemological perspective encompasses the focus of much classroom interaction and instruction, this seems quite reasonable at first glance. However, the picture that emerged is a bit more nuanced than this. The OTL experiences related to more general methods of teaching mathematics, as opposed to the more specific methods of teaching algorithms, proofs, and so on, demonstrated a marginally significant negative relationship, suggesting that these types of experiences may not emphasize this perspective. Therefore, we assume that this relationship cannot be discussed without taking the absolute level of endorsement into account.

In Chapter 7 we reported that the means for the algorithmic scale were lowest in Germany, followed by Mexico and then the United States. The regressions reveal that, having controlled for OTL on this belief, the algorithmic belief is significantly less among the future teachers in our German sample than among those in the United States and marginally significantly less among the Mexican sampled future teachers. In contrast, none of the OTL experiences demonstrated a significant relationship with the usefulness epistemological perspective on mathematics. Perhaps this is the case because those who are interested in teaching mathematics have already adopted this perspective. Recall from Chapter 7 that this was one of the most strongly endorsed epistemological perspectives of the four in virtually all of our six countries.

Another set of beliefs discussed in Chapter 7 dealt with the extent to which future teachers thought different objectives should be emphasized in teaching mathematics. One of the surprises that emerged in that discussion was the general lack of country-level differences across the different objectives. Given the substantial OTL differences noted in previous chapters, how do these OTL differences relate to various teaching objectives? OTL regressions were analyzed with two teaching objectives scales: one that emphasized the development and practice of mathematics skills, such as algorithms, rules, computational skill, and speed; and another that emphasized mathematical reasoning, such as proofs and modeling real-world situations.

Neither of these demonstrated a significant relationship with either mathematics or mathematics education formal coursework or with formal coursework related to school mathematics topics. Both did, however, demonstrate a significant relationship at the individual future teacher level with the extent to which they had the opportunity to learn general methods for teaching mathematics at the lower-secondary level (see Table 10.4). In both instances, the more experience future teachers had with learning such methods, the more emphasis they indicated for these two types of learning objectives. This effect is most likely due to the fact that it is mainly in these kinds of classes that meta-questions of teaching and learning are discussed—namely, not only how to teach mathematics, but also to what extent to teach mathematics in school. This interpretation is supported by the results that the more specific OTL experiences related to teaching proofs and nonroutine problems—the essence of mathematical reasoning—didn't display a significant relationship with the mathematical reasoning objectives. The nature of these specific topics probably implies that future teachers learn how to do that without substantial learning time spent on reflecting why.

In this respect, again, broader OTL experiences related to instructional interactions around mathematics—for example, probing students' prior understandings, misconceptions, analyzing student responses, and so on—did demonstrate a significant relationship to the emphasis afforded mathematical reasoning objectives. Obviously learning about how students think and reason mathematically, learning how to analyze student responses and how to develop questions to stimulate students' mathematical reasoning (all a part of this OTL scale) brings into focus the importance of emphasizing mathematical reasoning objectives more saliently than focusing on actual methods of doing proofs or constructing real-world models. In contrast to the lack of significant country differences reported in Chapter 7, once OTL experiences are statistically controlled, the mean emphasis for mathematical reasoning is lower for the future teachers from both Bulgaria and Germany than for those from the United States ($p < .05$ and $p < .01$, respectively). In addition, the emphasis afforded mathematical skills objectives among the German future teachers is marginally significantly lower than for the U.S. future teachers ($p < .1$).

Who is capable of learning mathematics? It would be very significant to see that beliefs about who can learn mathematics is affected by OTL experiences. In Chapter 7 we learned that future teachers from Germany, Mexico, and the United States expressed the least support for the belief that mathematical ability is determined by ethnic or gender identity, although this scale (category differences) did not demonstrate strong support in any country but Taiwan. Curiously, it appears from our analyses that no OTL experience is significantly related to this particular belief (see Table 10.4). It would seem that one's perspective on this belief—the capacity to learn mathematics being associated with one's gender or ethnic identity—is not subject to the type of OTL experiences measured by MT21. It might also be that, similar to one's perspective about the usefulness of mathematics, this is a belief that those who decide to become future mathematics teachers have already settled in their own thinking, so little is subject to their OTL experiences in teacher preparation. After controlling for all the non-significant OTL effects on this belief, it comes as no surprise that those future teachers in Taiwan demonstrated a significantly greater endorsement of this belief than did U.S. future teachers.

The last set of general professional beliefs from Chapter 7 that we consider here relate to the fundamental purpose or goal of three aspects of education: the goals of a teacher (beyond the support of cognitive and personal development of students—participation in the design of school life), the role of the teacher in the classroom (teachers as knowledge providers), and the purpose of schooling itself (selection). The results of the OTL relational analyses are presented in Table 10.5.

Among this group of general professional beliefs only the amount of formal general education coursework demonstrated a significant relationship. This seems reasonable in considering school life (community development) as one of the fundamental goals of a teacher since it is not obvious from one's own school experience as a student but has to be learned, yet it then seems odd to encounter the lack of any such relationship with the other two beliefs in Table 10.5. Instead, once again the topic of teaching algorithms, nonroutine problems, and proofs showed a strong significant relationship to one of the scales, and this is the role of a teacher as a knowledge provider. Given the conceptual overlap of the OTL and the belief scale, this result makes perfect sense. The significant country contrasts that we observed simply reflect the mean differences reported in Chapter 7.

Beliefs Related to Classroom Practices

The last group of beliefs that is considered here comes from those centering around actual classroom practices that were reported in Chapter 8. Near the beginning of Chapter 8 we discussed what future teachers reported they would likely do when students make errors in the classroom. Three scales represented different approaches to this situation: One was simply to ignore the error and move on; another was to ask other students the same question or to have other

TABLE 10.5. Multi-level analysis results relating OTL to professional beliefs about schools and teaching.

Source	School Life			Knowledge Provider			Selection		
	Est	(se)	p<	Est	(se)	p<	Est	(se)	p<
Intercept	4.44	(0.25)	0.000	2.92	(0.55)	0.000	2.87	(0.36)	0.000
Future Teacher									
General Pedagogy	0.39	(0.18)	0.030	0.05	(0.17)	0.760	0.26	(0.20)	0.201
Instructional Planning and Classroom Management	0.12	(0.12)	0.323				-0.16	(0.13)	0.222
Mathematics Pedagogy				-0.03	(0.16)	0.839			
Instructional Interaction Around Mathematics				-0.08	(0.05)	0.129			
Methods of Teaching Algorithms, Non-Routine Problems, and Proofs				0.20	(0.04)	0.000			
Opportunity to Gain Practical Experiences—TP				-0.07	(0.04)	0.108			
Amount of Time to Gain Practical Experiences (in weeks)				0.00	(0.00)	0.105			
Institution									
General Pedagogy	-0.10	(0.65)	0.884	-0.11	(0.63)	0.858	1.56	(0.94)	0.108
Instructional Planning and Classroom Management	0.48	(0.52)	0.37				-0.67	(0.74)	0.373
Mathematics Pedagogy				0.21	(0.56)	0.709			
Instructional Interaction Around Mathematics				-0.07	(0.36)	0.848			
Methods of Teaching Algorithms, Non-Routine Problems, and Proofs				0.17	(0.35)	0.635			
Opportunity to Gain Practical Experiences—TP				0.04	(0.33)	0.904			
Amount of Time to Gain Practical Experiences (in weeks)				-0.01	(0.02)	0.469			
Country Contrast vs United States									
Bulgaria	-0.29	(0.21)	0.181	0.43	(0.31)	0.190	0.96	(0.31)	0.005
Germany	-0.48	(0.16)	0.006	-0.04	(0.31)	0.907	0.21	(0.25)	0.390
Mexico	-0.04	(0.17)	0.805	-0.56	(0.24)	0.030	0.60	(0.24)	0.018
South Korea	-0.80	(0.25)	0.004	0.82	(0.27)	0.006	0.88	(0.36)	0.021
Taiwan	0.23	(0.13)	0.074	-0.02	(0.23)	0.928	1.14	(0.19)	0.000

students evaluate what had been said; the last approach was to have the teacher address the error in some direct manner. What types of coursework or learning opportunities might be associated with these various approaches? Table 10.6 displays the results from the OTL analyses with these beliefs.

As may be seen from the table, there is no single OTL experience that is significantly associated with all three of these approaches. For individual future teachers, three experiences were significantly and negatively related to

TABLE 10.6. Multi-level analysis results relating OTL to beliefs related to classroom practices.

Source	Ignore			Ask Other Students			Teacher Addresses		
	Est	*(se)*	*p<*	*Est*	*(se)*	*p<*	*Est*	*(se)*	*p<*
Intercept	2.51	(0.63)	0.001	3.86	(0.50)	0.000	3.99	(0.59)	0.000
Future Teacher									
Number of Courses Taken in Mathematics	-0.03	(0.01)	0.025	0.00	(0.01)	0.822	0.00	(0.01)	0.904
General Pedagogy	-0.05	(0.23)	0.837	0.53	(0.26)	0.044	0.15	(0.20)	0.462
Instructional Planning and Classroom Management	0.10	(0.13)	0.435	-0.12	(0.15)	0.412	-0.05	(0.12)	0.645
Mathematics Pedagogy	0.16	(0.15)	0.276	-0.03	(0.16)	0.839	-0.11	(0.13)	0.374
Methods of Solving School Mathematics Problems	0.13	(0.09)	0.143	-0.12	(0.10)	0.238	0.05	(0.08)	0.521
School Mathematics Topics	-0.22	(0.11)	0.036	-0.06	(0.12)	0.621	0.08	(0.09)	0.384
Instructional Interaction Around Mathematics	-0.14	(0.05)	0.005	0.10	(0.06)	0.064	-0.03	(0.04)	0.522
Understanding How Students Learn Mathematics	0.00	(0.03)	0.951	-0.02	(0.04)	0.649	0.01	(0.03)	0.846
Opportunity to Gain Practical Experiences	0.14	(0.05)	0.004	-0.03	(0.05)	0.582	0.03	(0.04)	0.463
Number of Opportunities to Gain Practical Experiences	-0.01	(0.02)	0.646	0.00	(0.02)	0.964	0.04	(0.01)	0.008
Institution									
Number of Courses Taken in Mathematics	-0.06	(0.05)	0.226	-0.03	(0.04)	0.536	0.00	(0.05)	0.942
General Pedagogy	-1.22	(1.30)	0.359	-0.32	(1.08)	0.769	-1.02	(1.21)	0.411
Instructional Planning and Classroom Management	0.73	(1.02)	0.484	-0.15	(0.88)	0.866	0.87	(0.95)	0.371
Mathematics Pedagogy	-0.16	(0.78)	0.835	-0.86	(0.63)	0.188	0.41	(0.73)	0.577
Methods of Solving School Mathematics Problems	0.35	(0.42)	0.427	0.36	(0.33)	0.289	-0.23	(0.40)	0.576
School Mathematics Topics	-0.23	(0.73)	0.756	0.07	(0.60)	0.905	-0.16	(0.68)	0.819
Instructional Interaction Around Mathematics	-0.01	(0.32)	0.964	0.48	(0.28)	0.106	-0.43	(0.29)	0.160
Understanding How Students Learn Mathematics	0.05	(0.24)	0.838	-0.23	(0.20)	0.276	0.05	(0.22)	0.816
Opportunity to Gain Practical Experiences	0.18	(0.29)	0.533	-0.33	(0.24)	0.189	0.34	(0.26)	0.218
Number of Opportunities to Gain Practical Experiences	-0.14	(0.11)	0.209	0.29	(0.09)	0.006	-0.20	(0.10)	0.062
Country Contrast vs United States									
Bulgaria	0.67	(0.40)	0.116	0.44	(0.33)	0.201	0.79	(0.38)	0.050
Germany	0.38	(0.32)	0.254	0.42	(0.25)	0.105	0.09	(0.30)	0.764
Mexico	0.17	(0.49)	0.736	0.31	(0.41)	0.461	0.71	(0.46)	0.139
South Korea	0.80	(0.58)	0.187	0.55	(0.48)	0.269	0.89	(0.54)	0.118
Taiwan	0.54	(0.31)	0.105	0.53	(0.26)	0.056	0.99	(0.29)	0.003

ignoring student errors: the amount of formal coursework in mathematics, the formal study of school mathematics topics, and the opportunity to learn about instructional interactions around mathematics, that is, how students think. In fact, ignoring student errors is one of the approaches that is typical for a lay approach, whereas in teacher education a strong focus is on trying to capture the misconception behind an error and how to deal with it. Dealing with student errors can be regarded as one of the fundamental professional competencies of teachers. This result demonstrates how OTL in mathematics and mathematics pedagogy work together in this case. In contrast, practical opportunities such as preparing mathematics lessons, trying out new approaches to teaching, and planning lessons with fellow students or teachers were positively associated with ignoring student error. One might be tempted to see this as an illustration of the tension between the theory one learns in formal coursework and the realities of classroom practice, but this is not necessary. More likely, the overwhelming reality of classroom experience with its rapid and multidimensional nature challenges teachers, especially at the beginning of their careers (Berliner, 2001). They do not have the skills and routines to deal with heterogeneous challenges (Neuweg, 1999)—without denying the necessity.

The opportunity to learn about instructional interactions around mathematics was the OTL experience at the individual future teacher level that was significantly related to more than one approach to responding to student error. This was negatively related to the "ignore" approach but was positively related to asking other students in an attempt to respond to the student error. The amount of coursework relating to formal general pedagogy topics was also positively related to this approach. Asking other students to weigh in on ideas expressed in a class is one of the general principles of leading or facilitating a class discussion, a common theme in many general education courses as such discussions may occur in virtually any type of classroom.

We also encountered one of the few institutional-level OTL relationships in this area. Those institutions that provided more practical classroom experiences for future teachers demonstrated a positive relationship with asking other students in response to a student error. As we have pointed out before, complex skills like this one require a lot of practical experience before teachers feel safe to apply them. The positive relationship of practical experiences at the institutional level, probably an indicator of required and supervised activities, may be evidence for the need of more mentoring, support, and supervision of beginning teachers (Blömeke & Paine, 2009). Intriguingly, this same OTL experience at the institutional level is negatively related to students' endorsement of the idea that the teacher should somehow respond to student errors. Even more curious is the positive relationship at the individual future teacher level between the amount of practical classroom experiences and the idea that the teacher should respond to errors. These results support a similar interpretation. During institutionally required and supervised practical experiences, educators may try to implement the "involve students" approach with their future teachers when dealing with errors instead of letting them respond to errors themselves. However, it may be that this requirement is too demanding and that future teachers prefer to correct mistakes.

In Chapter 8 no country differences were observed in future teachers' endorsement of the idea that other students be involved in responding to a student error. Once OTL differences are controlled, however, we note a significant contrast between those in the United States and Taiwan, with future teachers in Taiwan more strongly endorsing this approach. After controlling for OTL experiences, future teachers in Taiwan and Bulgaria demonstrated a greater endorsement of the idea that the teacher should address student errors than did those in the United States. In Chapter 7 the means for the United States and Bulgaria did not appear to be different. Again, the differences that emerge here after controlling for OTL experiences illustrate the importance of considering the role of OTL.

Table 10.7 details the results of the OTL regressions for three of the classroom management scales appearing in Figure 8.2. Here the practical oppor-

TABLE 10.7. Multi-level analysis results relating OTL to classroom management beliefs.

Source	Warn of Consequences			Motivational Instructional Activities			Establishing Rules		
	Est	(se)	p<	Est	(se)	p<	Est	(se)	p<
Intercept	1.92	(0.52)	0.001	4.32	(0.31)	0.000	4.64	(0.22)	0.000
Future Teacher									
General Pedagogy	-0.47	(0.23)	0.039	0.22	(0.14)	0.122	0.23	(0.16)	0.150
Instructional Planning and Classroom Management	0.21	(0.14)	0.136	-0.07	(0.09)	0.447	-0.09	(0.10)	0.392
Opportunity to Gain Practical Experiences	0.08	(0.03)	0.022	0.09	(0.02)	0.000	0.04	(0.02)	0.098
Institution									
General Pedagogy	0.87	(1.00)	0.391	0.89	(0.60)	0.151	-0.49	(0.45)	0.278
Instructional Planning and Classroom Management	0.17	(0.89)	0.850	-0.23	(0.53)	0.672	0.38	(0.41)	0.358
Opportunity to Gain Practical Experiences	-0.08	(0.20)	0.690	-0.10	(0.12)	0.416	-0.09	(0.08)	0.315
Country Contrast vs United States									
Bulgaria	0.41	(0.38)	0.297	-0.24	(0.23)	0.308	-0.41	(0.17)	0.022
Germany	-0.84	(0.28)	0.007	-0.24	(0.17)	0.167	-0.49	(0.12)	0.000
Mexico	0.20	(0.34)	0.569	0.17	(0.20)	0.423	0.14	(0.15)	0.365
South Korea	0.55	(0.41)	0.186	-0.42	(0.24)	0.096	-0.76	(0.18)	0.000
Taiwan	1.31	(0.25)	0.000	-0.11	(0.15)	0.473	0.08	(0.10)	0.424

tunities such as preparing mathematics lessons, trying out new approaches to teaching, and planning lessons with fellow students or teachers demonstrated a positive relationship with all three approaches to creating a classroom learning environment: Warn students of consequences for classroom disturbances/ inappropriate behaviors, adjust instruction in an attempt to motivate students more, and establish rules for students' classroom behavior that are clearly communicated to students.

The belief that students should be warned of the consequences of disturbing the classroom has a negative relationship at the individual future teacher level to the amount of formal coursework in the area of general pedagogy. To a layperson such a result sounds counter-intuitive, but in fact research on classroom management has found strong evidence that following such a reactive and short-term strategy fails in the long run. Here, motivational instructional strategies and clear rules have proven to be much more successful. The significant country contrasts with the United States found in Table 10.7 are all consistent with the country differences discussed in Chapter 8.

Table 10.8 has the results of the OTL analyses on two different approaches to lower-secondary mathematics classroom instruction. These are the same two approaches presented in Figure 8.3 and discussed in Chapter 8. As can be seen in Table 10.8, one OTL experience—the opportunity to learn specific methods for teaching algorithms, how to solve nonroutine problems, and proofs—is positively related to the traditional approach but negatively related to the more constructivist approach. This means that within each institution, students who reported having more opportunities to learn about the methods for teaching these specific mathematics topics expressed less emphasis for constructivist approaches such as having students work in small groups, write reports, or do special projects, and greater emphasis on more traditional instructional activities such as the teacher explaining ideas to the whole class, intensely reviewing homework, or having students work out mathematical problems at the board.

One general pedagogy formal course exhibited a negative relationship with the traditional approach—instructional planning and classroom management. Many traditional instructional practices such as lecture or whole-class presentations have been criticized, and teachers have been encouraged to employ more student-centered practices. This might explain this relationship here, as a general course—that is, a non-mathematics specific course—might well de-emphasize traditional approaches and promote other instructional activities. Research has documented the important role that subject matter has in determining classroom instructional activities (Stodolsky & Grossman, 1995). Methods of teaching algorithms and nonroutine problems and proofs have a significant positive relationship to belief in the traditional approach and a significant negative relationship to belief in the more constructive approach. Since this type of opportunity relates to teaching advanced mathematical methods, these positive and negative relationships might imply that future teachers were told in such courses to use the more traditional approach in the teaching of such methods. After controlling for OTL experiences at both the individual future teacher and the institution level, all the country contrasts are consistent with the differences in country means, as reported in Chapter 8.

TABLE 10.8. Multi-level analysis results relating OTL to approaches to teaching mathematics.

Source	Traditional Approach			More Constructivist Approach		
	Est	*(se)*	*p<*	*Est*	*(se)*	*p<*
Intercept	3.09	(0.36)	0.000	2.77	(0.39)	0.000
Future Teacher						
General Pedagogy	0.24	(0.15)	0.113	0.04	(0.15)	0.783
Instructional Planning and Classroom Management	-0.15	(0.09)	0.096	-0.04	(0.09)	0.648
Mathematics Pedagogy	0.03	(0.09)	0.712	-0.01	(0.09)	0.900
Teaching Including Classroom Management	0.00	(0.03)	0.942	0.01	(0.03)	0.842
Instructional Interaction Around Mathematics	0.05	(0.05)	0.302	0.09	(0.05)	0.056
Methods of Teaching Algorithms, Non-Routine Problems and Proofs	0.08	(0.03)	0.011	-0.07	(0.03)	0.022
Teaching Mathematics in the Lower Secondary Level	-0.05	(0.03)	0.146	0.04	(0.03)	0.193
Opportunity to Gain Practical Experiences—TP	0.02	(0.03)	0.630	-0.01	(0.03)	0.740
Number of Opportunities to Gain Practical Experiences	0.01	(0.01)	0.428	0.01	(0.01)	0.587
Institution						
General Pedagogy	-0.27	(0.62)	0.665	0.09	(0.68)	0.900
Instructional Planning and Classroom Management	0.40	(0.57)	0.490	0.37	(0.62)	0.557
Mathematics Pedagogy	-0.08	(0.39)	0.832	-0.49	(0.42)	0.262
Teaching Including Classroom Management	0.03	(0.19)	0.885	0.16	(0.21)	0.464
Instructional Interaction Around Mathematics	-0.20	(0.30)	0.517	0.02	(0.33)	0.959
Methods of Teaching Algorithms, Non-Routine Problems and Proofs	-0.01	(0.23)	0.956	-0.13	(0.25)	0.596
Teaching Mathematics in the Lower Secondary Level	-0.02	(0.25)	0.945	0.08	(0.27)	0.762
Opportunity to Gain Practical Experiences—TP	0.32	(0.23)	0.175	-0.04	(0.24)	0.865
Number of Opportunities to Gain Practical Experiences	-0.07	(0.07)	0.326	-0.02	(0.07)	0.771
Country Contrast vs United States						
Bulgaria	0.40	(0.21)	0.071	-0.63	(0.23)	0.012
Germany	0.49	(0.19)	0.022	0.62	(0.21)	0.009
Mexico	0.09	(0.21)	0.671	0.18	(0.23)	0.438
South Korea	0.33	(0.31)	0.313	0.18	(0.34)	0.600
Taiwan	0.67	(0.15)	0.000	-0.38	(0.16)	0.027

The last group of instructional practice beliefs to be considered is those dealing with the use of student work groups, which was first reported in Figure 8.7 in Chapter 8. These beliefs address three reasons why teachers might make use of student work groups as a part of their instruction. One was to further academic goals such as increasing students' independent learning, or to encourage them to develop their own solution strategies. Another reason suggested that student work groups could help the teacher address individual differences by providing a more social climate or integrating students with special needs. A final reason teachers might use student work groups is that this was simply a practical solution as materials were available for such groups or because they lessen a teacher's workload.

Results of the OTL analyses for these three ideas about the use of student work groups appear in Table 10.9. Not too surprisingly, the amount of formal general pedagogy coursework is positively related to all three. This means that within each institution, those future teachers who covered more of these topics indicated a stronger support for each of the three different rationales for using student work groups. This does not support the idea that any of these reasons were explicitly discussed in any course. What is perhaps more likely is that as students were increasingly exposed to the idea of student work groups as an effective instructional strategy, any rationale for their use became more acceptable. Within each institution, those future teachers who reported having had the formal instructional planning and classroom management course

TABLE 10.9. Multi-level analysis results relating OTL to use of student work groups.

Source	Academic Reasons			Individual Differences			Managing Teaching		
	Est	(se)	p<	Est	(se)	p<	Est	(se)	p<
Intercept	3.42	(0.24)	0.000	3.36	(0.25)	0.000	2.39	(0.26)	0.000
Future Teacher									
General Pedagogy	0.44	(0.16)	0.008	0.39	(0.16)	0.018	0.43	(0.20)	0.029
Instructional Planning and Classroom Management	-0.21	(0.10)	0.046	-0.11	(0.10)	0.307	-0.16	(0.13)	0.207
Institution									
General Pedagogy	-0.57	(0.62)	0.369	-0.70	(0.66)	0.302	-2.08	(0.68)	0.005
Instructional Planning and Classroom Management	0.81	(0.50)	0.117	1.18	(0.53)	0.035	1.22	(0.55)	0.036
Country Contrast vs United States									
Bulgaria	-0.17	(0.20)	0.405	-0.37	(0.22)	0.096	0.10	(0.22)	0.648
Germany	0.11	(0.16)	0.474	-0.03	(0.17)	0.873	0.24	(0.17)	0.179
Mexico	0.41	(0.16)	0.017	0.38	(0.17)	0.034	0.94	(0.18)	0.000
South Korea	-0.18	(0.24)	0.456	-0.15	(0.25)	0.571	1.01	(0.26)	0.001
Taiwan	-0.03	(0.12)	0.826	0.14	(0.13)	0.316	0.94	(0.13)	0.000

less strongly endorsed academic reasons for using student work groups. After controlling for OTL experiences at the individual future teacher level and the institutional level, the country contrasts were mostly consistent with the mean differences reported in Chapter 8.

SUMMARY

In general, opportunity to learn from each of the major domains of teacher education was related to the development of teacher knowledge in these 34 institutions. What is also related to mathematics pedagogical knowledge in the areas of teaching and the student as well as general pedagogical knowledge related to lesson planning is the variety of classroom-related experiences and the number of weeks of classroom teaching. This clearly indicates the salience of school-related experience. Also, many of the relationships of OTL to these pedagogical test areas are defined by the extent of opportunity related to practical learnings and not just the more theoretical aspects of pedagogy. The results suggest that teacher education, as defined by the learning opportunities provided, likely has an impact on the professional knowledge of future teachers as they leave their teacher preparation program.

One of the surprises in looking for OTL relationships to the set of beliefs in this chapter is that the amount of formal coursework in mathematics pedagogy—in contrast to the formal coursework in general pedagogy, which was quite often significantly associated with beliefs as outcomes of teacher education—did not demonstrate a significant relationship with any of these: not with the general professional beliefs nor with any of the beliefs more directly related to actual classroom practices. What did demonstrate a number of significant relationships with these beliefs, however, was a range of scales indicating the extent to which future teachers had been exposed to a range of very specific types of learning experiences, for example, specific methods for teaching proofs or algorithms, exploring how students think about mathematics (including misconceptions), general principles of teaching mathematics (as opposed to simply general teaching methods), and gaining a deep understanding of various lower-secondary school mathematics topics. Does this pattern of OTL relationships with these beliefs suggest that formal coursework in mathematics pedagogy is not important? On the contrary: What these analyses point to is the precise sort of experiences likely encountered within these courses that do demonstrate significant relationships with the beliefs. In this respect, the analyses begin to point to the types of experiences that teacher preparation programs may want to emphasize in such courses to influence the sort of beliefs included in this chapter.

Clearly, opportunities to learn designed by institutions and experienced by future teachers are related to teacher competencies as they finish their teacher preparation programs. This is true both of knowledge, beliefs, and predispositions of how to respond in the classroom as a new teacher. Several areas of OTL are broadly related to many competencies, others to a more limited set. Perhaps the best summary of this chapter is Table 10.10, which shows the pattern of statistically significant relationships for each OTL variable across all the various competencies—both beliefs and knowledge. The table is self-explanatory.

Opportunity to learn appears to be as important in developing the professional knowledge of future teachers as it is in developing the knowledge of middle school students. The sampled U.S. institutions fall behind in the type and amount of mathematics content covered compared to the sampled Taiwanese and South Korean institutions. This pattern is also true in terms of mathematics pedagogy. However, for the theoretical aspects of pedagogy, U.S. institutions cover a greater portion of such topics relative to mathematics courses than is true in these two countries. Just as important, the belief that the preparation of future teachers might be done without any preparation in practical pedagogy seems unwise and should certainly be reconsidered, especially as the data indicate the presence of varied classroom-related experiences in other sampled institutions. The real question, then, is not whether such experiences are necessary, but rather what is the nature and the extent of the learning opportunities in each of the areas that should be available for future teachers. It is quite revealing but far from conclusive that the countries whose middle-grade students continually perform well on the international benchmark tests have the teachers who have been trained with extensive educational opportunities in mathematics as well as in the practical aspects of teaching mathematics to their students.

TABLE 10.10. Summary of the statistically significant relationships of OTL to professional competencies.

	Algebra	Function	Numbers	Geometry	Data	Curriculum	Teaching	Student	General Pedagogy	Algorithmic	Usefulness	Math Skills	Math Reasoning	Category Differences	School Life	Knowledge Provider	Selection	Ignore	Ask Other Students	Teacher Addresses	Warn of Consequences	Motivational Instructional Activities	Establishing Rules	Traditional Approach	More Constructivist Approach	Academic Reasons	Individual Differences	Managing Teaching
Abstract Algebra	FT/IN	FT/IN																										
Adv Math	FT	FT	FT	FT	FT																					FT	FT	FT/IN
Basic Calculus	FT	FT/IN	IN	FT	FT/IN																					FT	IN	IN
Geometry	IN	—	—	IN	FT/IN																							
Linear Algebra	FT	FT																										
Number of Courses Taken in Mathematics				—										—						—				—	—			
Probability & Stat				—														FT	—			—						
History of School Mathematics						IN																						
Mathematics Pedagogy		—	—	—			—	IN	—		—	—	IN	—				—	—	—		—		—	—			
Methods of Solving School Mathematics Problems				—			—	—			—	FT	—	—				—	—	—		—		—	—			
School Mathematics Topics		—					—	—		—	—	—		—				—	—	FT	FT	—		—	—	FT	FT	FT/IN
Working with / Understanding Lower Sec. Function Topics		—		—																								
Working with / Understanding Lower Sec. Geometry Topics																												
Working with / Understanding Lower Sec. Number Topics			—																									
Working with / Understanding Lower Sec. Math Topics				—		—	—	IN		FT	—	—	—					—				—		—	—			
General Pedagogy						—	—	—	—	FT					FT	FT	—	FT	FT	—	FT	—	—	—	—			
Instructional Planning and Classroom Management						—	FT	FT	—	—					—	—		—	—	—	—	—	—	—	—			
Amount of Time to Gain Practical Experiences (in Weeks)						—	FT	—	FT																			
Number of Opportunities to Gain Practical Experiences						—	—	—										—	IN	FT	—	FT	—		—			
Number Theory	—				IN																							
Opportunity to Gain Practical Experiences																		FT	—	—	FT	FT	—	—				
Opportunity to Gain Practical Experiences—OTL							FT																					
Opportunity to Gain Practical Experiences—TP							—	—										FT	—	—		—		—	—			
Instructional Interaction Around Mathematics							IN	IN		—			FT												—			
Methods of Teaching Algorithms, Non-Routine Problems, and Proofs							FT			—		—	—			FT		FT						FT	FT			
Teaching Including Classroom Management										—		—	—					—						—	—			
Teaching Mathematics in the Lower Secondary Level							—		FT	—		FT	FT					—		—		—		—	—			
Understanding How Students Learn Mathematics								IN																				

Note. Statistically significant relationships are indicated in the table by the letters FT (future teacher) or IN (institution), defining the level at which the relationship exists. Potential relationships that are not significant are indicated by —. Blank spaces indicate that the implied relationship was not modeled.

CHAPTER 11

The Cost of Teacher Preparation

This chapter explores two issues related to teacher preparation using both MT21 data and other country level data. The first concerns the role of teacher salaries in influencing who chooses to enter the field of lower-secondary mathematics teaching. The second, using standard economic models, estimates the cost associated with teacher preparation.

Previous chapters have shown that substantial differences exist in the preparation of future middle school teachers of mathematics among the six countries studied. At one end of the spectrum, future teachers in Taiwan and South Korea are extensively prepared in mathematics. At the other end of the spectrum, Mexico and the United States provide less course-taking in higher levels of mathematics and focus their course experiences for future teachers more on pedagogy.

From an economic perspective, teachers are a key input for the production of students' mathematics achievement in schools. In middle schools, much more than half the costs of schooling are associated with teacher compensation. Furthermore, there is increasing evidence that the greater teachers' teaching skills, the more students learn (Boyd, Grossman, Hammerness et al., 2008; Boyd, Lankford, Loeb et al., 2008; Carnoy, Brodziak, Loyalka et al., 2006; Clotfelter, Ladd, & Vigdor, 2007; Hill, Rowen, & Ball, 2005). For many years, economists resisted the idea that improving the quality of education would require more resources (see, e.g., Hanushek, 1994), but the new evidence on the relation of teachers' knowledge and teaching skills to student outcomes is changing this view.

Increasing teachers' mathematics skills inevitably does require resources. These resources might be invested directly in the mathematics, mathematics pedagogical, and general pedagogical preparation of future teachers in teacher education programs (Darling-Hammond & Youngs, 2002); in improving K–12 mathematics preparation of the whole population of (ultimately) secondary school graduates (Schmidt, Tatto, Bankov et al., 2008),[1] some of whom may then become middle school teachers; or in paying higher salaries to teachers so that high school graduates who are better at mathematics are attracted into the teaching profession.

In this chapter, we attempt to understand how and how much the six countries in our sample invest in teachers' mathematics skills—that is, (a) whether future teachers' knowledge at the end of their teacher education is largely the result of the knowledge they bring to the program from secondary schooling or the result of what they may have learned in their teacher education program, and (b) how much teacher education costs per student.

Future teachers in Taiwan and South Korea scored highest in all mathematical content areas at the end of their teacher education, and future teachers in Mexico and the United States (along with Bulgaria) scored the lowest. Future teachers in Germany were somewhere in the middle in their content knowledge.

However, future teachers in the United States (and Germany) know more about general pedagogy than do future teachers in Taiwan and South Korea. Those in Mexico, despite the reported focus on pedagogy in their training, scored lower than the U.S. future teachers in their knowledge of general pedagogy, but generally higher than the two Asian countries. Bulgarian future teachers scored quite low in general pedagogical knowledge.

According to the three resource-investment possibilities described above, economists would have several plausible explanations for these differences.

- Taiwan and South Korea could be investing many more resources in the education of each future teacher, particularly in mathematics content knowledge, once they enter teacher education and hence are able to provide a higher level of mathematics training than the other four countries. However, Taiwan and South Korea could invest very little in pedagogical training compared to other countries, such as the United States.

- Taiwanese and South Korean secondary school graduates may already have a higher *average* level of mathematics preparation, making it relatively cheaper to provide a high level of mathematics content preparation to future teachers who want to teach mathematics. In effect, future teachers in Taiwan and South Korea may be starting ahead, mathematically, of future teachers in the other four countries when they enter their teacher education programs. For the same or smaller investment of resources per future teachers' education, Taiwan and South Korea could therefore prepare future mathematics teachers to a higher level of mathematics content knowledge than in the other four countries. They may also start out with future teachers who have a lower general pedagogical knowledge, and for the same investment per student as in other countries, end up with teachers who have relatively lower levels of pedagogical knowledge.

- Taiwan and South Korea may pay teacher salaries that are relatively higher compared to competing mathematics-oriented professions, so even if secondary school graduates were not better prepared in mathematics, on average, than in the other four countries, Taiwan and South Korea could be recruiting future teachers into teacher education programs who were among the better mathematics students at the completion of secondary school. This would produce the same result as in the previous case: Future teachers in Taiwan and South Korea would be entering their teacher education with already higher levels of mathematics knowledge than future teachers in the other four countries.

This chapter explores all three of these possibilities. Naturally, with only six countries in the sample, it will be difficult to draw hard and fast conclusions about the economics of how countries produce better-prepared mathematics middle school teachers and our data contain many caveats, but as in the other chapters, we may be able to observe suggestive patterns.

COUNTRY SPENDING ON TEACHER PREPARATION

Some countries spend relatively more to produce mathematics teachers than others. As part of the collaborative project, participants collected cost data from the teacher education programs surveyed. Participants in the MT21 project were asked to estimate the costs per student of training mathematics teachers and to compare them with the costs per student of training bachelor's or equivalent national degree students in the sciences (physics, chemistry, life sciences). They were asked to gather data in several institutions in each country, if possible.

One of the complexities in such a comparison is that in some countries— namely, Taiwan (5 years), Germany (6 years) and in some U.S. states (5 years)— obtaining a teaching degree requires more time than gaining a degree in science. The estimated costs by country are shown in Table 11.1.

- The costs per student for Bulgaria are national and based on the allowances given each university per student according to the department in which they are enrolled. Secondary mathematics teachers are trained in the mathematics department (this is the higher figure), and primary teachers are trained in education departments (this is the lower figure). Middle school teachers are mainly drawn from the secondary school teacher pool, so the higher figure is

Table 11.1. Costs of middle school mathematics teacher and science profession university education, 4-year bachelor's degree, by country.[2]

Country	Secondary School Mathematics Teacher Training Cost		Science Profession Training Cost	
	(2006 Dollars)	*(2006 PPP dollars)*	*(2006 Dollars)*	*(2006 PPP dollars)*
Bulgaria	7,300–10,800	18,300–27,100	10,800	27,100
Taiwan	14,000–17,600	24,400–30,700	8,400–10,900	14,600–19,000
Germany	68,300–72,700	62,800–66,800	40,000	36,800
South Korea	16,400–31,300	20,600–39,300	40,000–43,300	50,100–54,300
Mexico	18,900	28,600	18,500–27,000	28,000–40,800
United States	40,000–60,000	40,000–60,000	40,000–60,000	40,000–60,000

Note. Costs estimated by MT21 participating institutions. PPP: To adjust for exchange rates, we re-estimated costs for all countries based on purchasing power parity dollars. Reported instructional costs for South Korea are $9,840– $18,800 for secondary school teachers and $24,000– $26,000 for scientists. The corresponding PPP dollar amounts are $12,300–$23,600 for teachers and $30,100– $32,600 for scientists. The reported South Korean costs are multiplied by 1.67 to account for non-instructional spending. The reported Taiwan estimates are multiplied by 1.2 to include administrative overhead. Lower German estimate is for secondary school teachers and the higher estimate is for middle school teachers.

more relevant. Mathematics teachers are trained in two subjects—mathematics and one other.

- Per-student costs for Germany were only estimated for one university, and this may be a high-cost example. Germany's teacher training costs may be generally high for three reasons: First and most important, future teachers are required to take a second level of courses after they get their formal university degree, and Germany is the only country that requires such added training. This additional phase, where the teachers do student teaching and continue taking courses, is expensive because teachers are paid a stipend in addition to the costs of their schooling. One-half of this stipend is pay for teaching regular classes, so that should not be counted as a cost of training since it releases regularly employed teachers to do other work. The second reason is that mathematics teachers have to minor in other subjects (primary school teachers) or major in a second subject (middle and secondary school teachers), in addition to taking courses at all three levels in primary or general education. At the end of the 4.5 years of the first phase of studies, German future middle and secondary teachers have the equivalent of two master's degrees. To make these first-phase costs for future middle and secondary school teachers somewhat more comparable to costs in other countries, we deducted 22.2% of the first-phase costs—this is the equivalent of a full year of study, the extra time it takes to get a second major. These instructional costs net out spending on research but include administrative overhead related to instruction. The first-phase costs in Germany are approximately equivalent to the higher end estimates of teacher education costs in South Korea and Taiwan. The third reason is that the exchange rate of the euro to the dollar is relatively high. In 2004, the year for which German costs were estimated, the rate was 1.2 U.S. dollars for 1 euro. To adjust for exchange rate issues, we reestimated costs for all countries based on purchasing power parity (PPP) dollars.

- The Mexican teacher training costs were also only estimated for the principal teacher training university and, as in the case of Germany, the Mexican costs for this particular university appear to be high-end estimates. To verify this upward bias, we would need to have estimates for other education programs, but these are difficult to obtain. Nevertheless, we were able to estimate Mexican costs for science profession training in many different universities across the country.

- Estimates of mathematics teacher training in South Korea and Taiwan were made for three different universities in each country. The original South Korean estimates we received were only for instructional costs (salaries of professors and staff plus materials at the departmental level). We assumed that instructional costs were 60% of total costs of training a student—this is an educated guess—so South Korean costs per student may be either underestimated or overestimated. The Taiwan estimates for mathematics teacher education took into account the cost per student of a bachelor's degree plus the cost of completing the required education credits for a teaching certificate plus the costs of completing a teaching internship (this is estimated as the salary costs of professors supervising intern teachers). The cost estimates include salary costs (instructional costs) plus the maintenance costs of facilities. Other administrative overhead is not included, so we added in 20% administrative overhead to make the figures more comparable with the other countries.

- The U.S. costs were based on estimated spending per student in 14 of the California state universities in 2005–2006 plus nine other public universities chosen at random in eight other states for the same year. None of these universities were represented in the U.S. MT21 sample of future teachers. Costs per student in U.S. universities may be overestimated because in many cases, department costs are averaged over bachelor's degree and master's degree students. The latter requires more resources. All cost estimates assume that it takes 4 years to get a degree, even though in certain states, such as California, teachers are required to get a bachelor's degree in a subject first and then a teaching certificate, which requires up to an extra year of courses. Costs per Full Time Equivalency (FTE) education student in California state universities vary from $8,000/year to $33,000/year, with 11 of the 14 universities' costs in the $8,000–$14,000 range. The three high-cost outliers have relatively low numbers of education students. The mean for the 14 California universities is $12,500. The cost per FTE education student in the 9 other U.S. universities varies from $5,000 to $22,000 per year, with 7 of the universities in the $10,000–$17,000 range. The mean cost per FTE education student in the 9 universities is $12,600. Engineering costs per student are similar in the California State University system and in the 9 universities outside California—$13,600 per year. Our upper-end figure for the United States assumes a 5-year degree.

The results suggest that costs of teacher training were generally not much different than training costs for science majors in three of the countries but were higher in Taiwan, Germany, and some U.S. states (such as California) where, in addition to getting a bachelor's degree, future teachers must take extra training to get a teaching degree; and in South Korea, where the costs of teacher education appear to be considerably lower than those for getting a science degree. The costs of teacher education are higher in Germany because, as noted, future teachers must study additional years while working as an apprentice teacher (paid a stipend and given practical training under supervision).

To compare the costs of mathematics teachers' and scientists' education across countries, it is more useful to measure the costs in purchasing power parity (PPP) dollars, which weight currencies by the cost of a typical basket of consumer goods in each country. The benchmark is still the U.S. dollar, so the baskets of goods are weighted relative to the costs in the United States. For example, in Bulgaria in 2006, a dollar would buy 2.5 times as much as in the United States at prevailing exchange rates; in Germany, about 0.92 as much; in South Korea, about 1.25 times as much; in Mexico, about 1.5 times as much; and in Taiwan, about 1.75 times as much.

The lower part of the table reports the PPP dollar comparisons of teachers' and scientists' education costs. Germany spent much more per student than the other five countries on teacher education; and Bulgaria, Taiwan, Mexico, and South Korea spent approximately the same per student on their teacher training. The United States spent more than those four countries but less than Germany. The upper estimate for South Korea, representing one of the three universities sampled, is approximately the same as the lower-end estimate in the United States.

Bulgaria and Mexico's and, to some extent, the United States's spending on teacher education are consistent with a lower provision of mathematics content training plus mathematics pedagogical training for middle school teachers. Germany seems to spend more for the amount of mathematics knowledge it imparts to its teachers, but this is an artifact of the large amount that Germany spends on practical training for future teachers after university. Taiwan and South Korea appear to spend less than seems required to provide the high level of mathematics knowledge its future teachers have at the end of their teacher education. The United States may spend too much relative to the amount of mathematics it teaches its future teachers, but the up side is that, according to what we have seen, future teachers in the United States did well on general pedagogical knowledge, which appears to be the emphasis of U.S. teacher education.

Another way to look at this pattern is that there are relatively small differences in the cost of educating scientists in the six countries. The United States tends to spend at the higher end, along with South Korea. Mexico and Germany spend less, and Bulgaria somewhat less than those two. Taiwan spends much less. The higher cost of educating mathematics teachers in Germany and the lower costs in South Korea appear to be related to how those countries allocate public monies to teacher education rather than how much they are spending on higher education. Germany in particular requires a relatively long apprenticeship period for its teachers, which doubles its cost per student and makes it much more expensive to train a teacher than a scientist.[3] Taiwan, in contrast, seems to be allocating relatively low public monies to higher education generally.

Thus, from the cost-of-education view, there is some evidence that Germany spends more on teacher education and delivers less in the mathematics knowledge that teachers take away from their teacher preparation than either Taiwan or South Korea—assuming the level of mathematics knowledge of those entering university teacher preparation as discussed in the next section. German future teachers, however, may gain significantly more pedagogical knowledge and perhaps more practical skills. Bulgaria and Mexico spend less and also deliver a lot less. The United States spends somewhere in the middle of the range and delivers poorly on some elements (mathematics content) and well on others (pedagogy).

One of the problems with this analysis, however, is that it only looks at the end point of future teacher outcomes. It may well be that in countries such as Taiwan and South Korea future teachers enter with relatively high mathematics knowledge and gain relatively little; or the opposite may be true, that South Korea and Taiwan are very efficient producers of teacher education. It is therefore important to analyze spending on teacher education relative to some sense of the gain in knowledge occurring in the teacher education process.

THE HIGH SCHOOL ADVANTAGE

South Korea and Taiwan likely have an advantage in teaching future teachers advanced mathematics because the average mathematics knowledge of high school graduates in the two countries is already high when they enter teacher education. One indicator of how much mathematics knowledge high school graduates have in each country is the TIMSS or PISA results for that country. TIMSS tests 8th graders and PISA, 15-year-olds (Table 11.2).

According to the 1995 TIMSS (also applied in Mexico but never released), 8th-grade students in Bulgaria and South Korea were better prepared in mathematics than those in Germany and the United States, but only by 0.3 standard deviations. By 1999, these scores had changed somewhat, with Bulgarian students doing worse and South Koreans doing better. Taiwan students scored the same as South Koreans. Assuming that the future teachers surveyed in our six-country study were in 8th-grade in 1997–1998, the 1995–1999 test scores probably approximate the *relative levels* of the beginning average ability across countries of high school graduates as they entered teacher education, assuming that relative ability levels of high school graduates are similar to those of 8th graders in these six countries. This also assumes that all countries are able to attract average secondary school graduates into teaching.

Taking the 2000 PISA scores as another approximation of the levels of mathematics content knowledge of our cohort of future teachers suggests that

TABLE 11.2. TIMSS and PISA mathematics scores by country and year of test, 1995–2006.

	TIMSS 1995	TIMSS 1999	TIMSS 2003	TIMSS 2007	PISA 2000	PISA 2003	PISA 2006
Bulgaria	527	511	476	464			413
Taiwan		585	585	598			549
Germany	509				490	500	504
South Korea	581	587	589	599	547	552	547
Mexico					387	382	406
United States	492	502	504	508	493	472	474

Note. Data obtained from Beaton et al., 1997(TIMSS 1995); Mullis et al., 2000 (TIMSS 1999); Mullis et al., 2004 (TIMSS 2003); OECD, 2001 (PISA 2000); 2004 (PISA 2003); 2007 (PISA 2006).

in South Korea (and almost certainly in Taiwan), future teachers entered teacher education with about 0.5 standard deviation of mathematics knowledge more than future teachers in the United States and Germany, and considerably more than a standard deviation higher mathematics content knowledge than future teachers in Bulgaria and Mexico.

These test score results suggest that—focusing only on teachers' mathematics knowledge as an end goal—the lower spending per future teacher on mathematics teacher preparation in PPP dollars in South Korea and Taiwan may be justified because of the high mathematics knowledge of South Korean and Taiwanese high school students. However, lower spending per future teacher on mathematics teacher preparation is certainly not justified in Mexico or Bulgaria (taking the most recent scores in Bulgaria) if these two countries want to produce well-prepared mathematics teachers. The German and U.S. cases are more difficult to interpret. The United States spends more per future teacher on mathematics teacher preparation than all but Germany, but is the amount sufficient to overcome the relatively low average mathematics knowledge of U.S. secondary students who form the pool of future teacher candidates? Germany's spending per future teacher on mathematics teacher preparation is high, but much of the money goes for practical training and the second major. If mathematics content knowledge is important in effective teaching, should Germany shift its resources to improve the mathematics knowledge of the secondary school graduates who are studying to become teachers?

However, we need to be careful in using TIMSS and PISA scores as a proxy for the relative mathematics knowledge of those who go on to post-secondary education. Not all 8th graders or 15-year-olds (those who were tested in the TIMSS and PISA tests) enter a university, and not all those who enter a university enter teacher education programs. We do not have data on the TIMSS or PISA scores of university entrants or teacher education students, but we do know the proportion of the age group enrolled in higher education in each of six countries under study. These figures vary in the years 1999–2006 from only about 20% in Mexico to about 85% in South Korea (see Table 11.3).

We need to make three assumptions to approximate the mean scores of those who entered teacher education in 2003 or 2006. The first is that all those in the TIMSS or PISA age group were in school and therefore eligible to take the PISA—thus, the PISA or TIMSS score is representative of the test scores in that age group. For all the countries in the MT21 sample except Mexico, this is a fair assumption. For Mexico, the figure for net enrollment in the 9th and 10th grades is closer to 60–65 %. We assume that this 65% is the upper 65% of the achievement distribution were all 100% of those eligible, agewise, to take the test. This is probably not an unreasonable assumption.

The second assumption is that if, say, 43% of the age cohort attends higher education as in Bulgaria in 2005, that 43% is in the upper 43% of the PISA test score distribution. This means that the mean PISA score for this group of students would be the 78th percentile [100 − (43 ÷ 2)]. For the United States, the PISA score of entering post-secondary students would be [100 − (78 ÷ 2)]. There are two issues with this assumption: (1) the figures for the proportion of the age group attending post-secondary education are approximate and probably considerably overestimate the proportion going to 4-year university, more in some countries than others (for example, in the United States, probably less than 40% of the age cohort attends a university); (2) the assumption rests on the proposition that there is a very high correlation between educational attainment and mathematics score, and we know from empirical studies (e.g., Bowles, Gintis, & Osborne, 2001) that parents' income and other family characteristics are as good or better predictors of educational attainment than academic achievement, even though the two are correlated. The first of these issues biases our estimates downward and the second upward. It is probable that the downward bias is greater, but we do not have sufficient data to support that claim.

The third assumption is that those in teacher education have mean mathematics scores equal to the average PISA scores of those who enter higher education as a whole. For Mexico, since about 22% of the age cohort attends higher education and the PISA score is already for a group of 8th graders that is in the upper 65% of the age group achievement range, those attending higher education are assumed to be in the upper 33% of the test-score distribution. The mean for that group is the 83rd percentile of the PISA score [100 − (33 ÷ 2)]. So, if young Mexicans entering teacher preparation institutions have similar mathematics achievement as average university entrants, they would have PISA mathematics scores approximately equal to the 83rd percentile of PISA takers. Unfortunately, this assumption may not be as accurate in some countries as it is in others. In particular, because of much higher relative monetary rewards to teaching in Taiwan and South Korea, those entering teacher preparation may come from a much higher average mathematics ability pool than in the other four countries. Similarly, much lower relative payoffs to teaching in the United States may have the opposite effect, drawing future teachers from a lower-than-average university entrant ability pool. We will discuss these possible biases in the next section on teacher recruitment.

The results of adjusting for the fraction of the age cohort entering post-secondary education are shown in Table 11.3. We want to stress that these are only approximations of how those entering teacher preparation institutions might score on the PISA, but they can serve as a starting point to suggest the relative mathematics knowledge of secondary students who go on to attend higher education. Once we adjust the scores for the gross enrollment rate in

TABLE 11.3. PISA test scores adjusted for average percent of age cohort enrolled in higher education, 2000–2005.

Country	% Age Group Enrolled in 9th & 10th Grades (PISA Test)	% Age Group Enrolled in Higher, Est. Average, 2000–2005	Distributional Point Used for PISA Score Estimate	Estimated 2003 PISA Score for Entrants	Estimated 2006 PISA Score for Entrants
Bulgaria	95+	43	78th percentile	515	496
Taiwan	95+	70	65th percentile	606	594
Germany	95+	46	77th percentile	565	582
South Korea	95+	81	60th percentile	570	573
Mexico	65	22	83rd percentile	472	490
United States	95+	78	61st percentile	528	502

Note. Sources: Percent enrolled for all but Taiwan: World Bank (2005). *World Development Indicators* for gross enrollment in higher education, and for Taiwan, personal correspondence from Taiwan participants in this study. Test scores: OECD, 2004, Annex B1, Table 2.1c; OECD, 2007, Table 6.2c. For those countries that did not take the PISA in 2003 (Bulgaria, Taiwan), we estimated average PISA mathematics scores on the basis of a regression of PISA on TIMSS scores for those countries that took both in 2003 (459 for Bulgaria and 568 for Taiwan).

higher education, we see that the students who are enrolled in higher education in three of the countries—Taiwan, Germany, and South Korea—average high mathematics scores, with Taiwan at the very top, Germany second, and South Korea third (remember, these are adjusted for the fact that a very high fraction of the South Korean age group attends post-secondary education and a much lower fraction of the age group in Germany attends post-secondary), and the three other countries—Bulgaria, Mexico, and the United States—average much lower scores. The difference is that PISA mathematics scores are falling in Bulgaria and the United States but seem to be rising in Mexico. In any case, there is hypothetically 0.5 to 1.0 standard deviations higher estimated mathematics performance among higher education students in Taiwan, South Korea, and Germany than in Bulgaria, Mexico, and the United States.

When we link these test scores to the spending on teacher education, the results begin to be generally more consistent with what we might expect. One set of lower-spending countries—Bulgaria and Mexico—bring in a pool of higher education students with relatively low mathematics knowledge to their teacher education programs from secondary schools, even though in Mexico this is a fairly elite fraction of the age group. This combination of relatively lower mathematics knowledge brought from secondary schools with the relatively lower spending per future teacher surely helps explain why future teachers in Bulgaria and Mexico score lower on the mathematics content knowledge tests applied to the sample of future teachers covered in this study. Taiwan and South Korea also spend relatively fewer resources on teacher education but they bring relatively high mathematics knowledge students into teacher education programs and end up with final-year future teachers who have relatively high mathematics content knowledge. The United States brings high school students into teacher education with relatively low mathematics knowledge, and spends a moderate to high amount to train them and produce teacher education graduates with relatively low mathematics content knowledge but relatively high pedagogical knowledge.

German students who attend higher education appear to bring relatively high PISA scores to their institutions of higher education. Although German teacher education is expensive, much of the expense is in the 2 years of practical training required of future teachers after their academic preparation (as noted, equivalent academic preparation costs in Germany are about the same as in South Korea). At the end of the process, German future teachers in this sample did much better on the mathematics content knowledge portion of the evaluation than those in the United States but not as well as Taiwanese and South Korean future teachers. This could be consistent with the similar first-phase training costs in Germany, South Korea, and Taiwan if our assumptions about who enters teaching from the pool of university entrants have accurately captured the German PISA scores of those who enter teacher preparation, but underestimated the scores of those who are recruited into teaching in South Korea and Taiwan.

THE RECRUITMENT OF
HIGH MATHEMATICS ABILITY STUDENTS INTO TEACHING

Until now we have assumed that in terms of mathematics content knowledge learned in secondary school, the future teachers attending the teacher education institutions surveyed in each country are more or less representative of average higher education students. Yet this is not necessarily the case. Those who are studying to be teachers may have much lower or higher mathematical ability than students choosing other professions, and this may be influenced by how much teachers are paid to teach mathematics relative to salaries in competing professions.

We posit that the earnings over a lifetime associated with various professional-level occupations have a significant influence on occupational choice. This is not the only factor influencing choice. Individuals choose occupations because they are drawn to the type of work associated with the occupation, and certainly because they have the abilities that it requires. Often, these abilities are affirmed or even discovered in school, with teachers and other adult role models often influencing choices made by adolescents. In addition, cultural factors such as gender stereotyping push (or even force, through discrimination) individuals to enter certain types of work and not others. Opportunities for work also vary among countries, so occupational choice is not equal everywhere in the world even for university graduates.

We have no way of comparing the preference for teaching as a profession among the six countries, but we can compare the salaries of teachers with other professions and how they are changing over time. These estimates of teachers' relative salaries give some indication of how economically attractive teaching may be to prospective future teachers in the six countries and whether this attractiveness has increased or decreased in the past 10 years.

The relative salaries of teachers are usually thought of only in terms of how much governments are willing to pay to attract quality teachers. There is no doubt that some societies are more disposed than others to reward teachers. However, teachers' relative salaries are also a function of how much the private and public sectors have to pay for competing skills. In the case of mathematics teachers, the competing professions are mathematics-oriented and include scientists, engineers, social scientists, and accountants. In societies where there is a greater supply of mathematics skills relative to demand, the relative salaries of mathematics middle school teachers may be high because the salaries of mathematics-oriented professionals are moderated by the availability of individuals who are good at mathematics.

The more widely mathematical skills are available in the labor force, the smaller the difference in wages might be between workers in jobs requiring such skills and those in other professions, such as teaching, where the emphasis is on other skills. Thus, if all high school graduates have relatively high mathematics skills, the premium for jobs requiring such skills would not be as great as it would in economies where mathematics skills are more rare. Yet mathematics skills do vary greatly in national student populations. If teachers are not picked (and paid) mainly for their mathematics skills, they are likely to have lower mathematics skills than engineers, scientists, accountants, and workers in other mathematics-intensive professions. So even in countries where the average high school graduate is relatively (to other countries) well-trained in mathematics, it is possible that it would be difficult to recruit individuals with adequate mathematics knowledge to become teachers if teachers are paid much less than those in mathematics-intensive professions.

Countries such as the United States may find it expensive to match the better mathematics teacher preparation in other countries in part because of the relatively high salaries of university-educated engineers, mathematicians, and scientists compared to university-educated mathematics teachers and mathematics teacher-trainers. These high salaries are the result of a relatively small pool of high-level mathematics skills and a very high demand in industry for workers with high mathematics skills. Nevertheless, if a country ends up paying teacher salaries that are significantly lower than those in competing professions, it is likely that young people entering teaching will have less than average (for university students) mathematics content knowledge acquired in high school. A number of studies in the United States, for example, have estimated that the majority of students studying to be teachers come from the lower part of the Scholastic Aptitude Test (SAT) score distribution (e.g., Murnane, Singer, Willett et al., 1991).

The evidence on the relationship between relative salaries of teachers and the quality of teaching is not easy to find. In the United States, the subject has been one of considerable controversy. One recent study has estimated the relative pay of teachers in the United States (Allegretto, Corcoran, & Mishel, 2004). In summarizing the literature on the relationship between teacher quality and relative wages, it concludes:

> Existing evidence on the relationship between teacher pay and teacher quality is divided. In the short run, pay increases do not appear to have noticeable effects on the quality of candidates entering the teaching profession. Over the long run, however, trends in relative teacher pay seem to coincide with trends in teacher quality. (Allegretto, Corcoran, & Mishel, 2004, p. 6)

We construct age-earnings curves for men and women in mathematics-intensive occupations and in teaching by level of their education (first university degree, master's degree). These can show how mathematics teachers fare compared to their competing professionals in each of the countries we studied. It is important to separate the analysis by gender (see Corcoran, Evans, & Schwab, 2002), because the labor markets for men and women in most countries differ and salary structures are often also different. In all six of the MT21 countries, we were able to estimate age-earnings profiles for 2 different years, one in the 1990s and the other in 2000 or later. This allowed us to observe possible changes in relative earnings in recent years and whether the trends are confirmed at different points in time.[4]

The results in Table 11.4 suggest that other than in the United States, female secondary school teachers are well paid relative to female scientists in the six MT21 countries (we assume that middle school teachers are considered secondary school teachers). However, except for Taiwan and South Korea, male teachers get considerably lower salaries than male scientists. Female teachers' salaries are declining relative to female scientists' salaries in all but the United States, probably because wage discrimination against women in scientific occupations is gradually declining. In Germany, it appears that the decline is part of a more general decrease in teachers' salaries relative to salaries in science professions. This may be the result of incorporating former German Democratic Republic teachers into the teaching force because federal states could not employ these teachers as civil servants but only under part-time contracts. Yet this may also have been part of a more general policy of public spending cuts that resulted from the high cost of reunification. With the private sector doing well economically in the 1990s, the relative salaries of teachers fell.

In terms of male salaries, the two countries in the study where future teachers are the best trained in mathematics—Taiwan and South Korea—are also the best paid relative to scientists. The countries with future teachers scoring lowest on the mathematics content knowledge test—Bulgaria, Mexico, and the United States—also have the lowest relative male salaries for teachers. Although female teachers are relatively well paid in Bulgaria and Mexico compared to female scientists, it is evident that this is largely so because female scientists are so poorly paid relative to male scientists. Further, by the early 2000s, female teachers' relative salaries seemed to have fallen considerably in Bulgaria, so recruiting bright secondary graduates into teaching probably began to be more difficult. This may also be the case in Germany, where teachers' relative salaries fell steadily in the 1990s.

The salary data suggest that Taiwan and South Korea should be able to attract those secondary school graduates going to university with perhaps higher than average mathematics ability and, as we have seen (Table 11.3), average ability there is high by world standards. Bulgaria and the United States are likely to be attracting graduating secondary school students who have below-average mathematics skills into teaching. Since university students' average mathematics skills are not high there (Table 11.4), it is likely that those who enter teacher education programs in Bulgaria and the United States are not well prepared in mathematics compared to those in Taiwan or South Korea, even though they may be specializing in mathematics teaching. One mitigating circumstance in Bulgaria is that unemployment rates were relatively high in the 1990s and early 2000s, so that the teaching profession may still have been attractive because it provided relatively secure employment.

It appears that Mexico is probably recruiting women into teaching with the average mathematics skills of university students. The main issue is that those mathematics skills are much lower than the mathematics knowledge of university students in Taiwan, South Korea, or Germany. This is true even if only about one fourth of the Mexican university age cohort attends post-secondary education. We should also point out that Mexican women scored about 10 points lower than men on the PISA 2003 and PISA 2006 mathematics test. This is not

TABLE 11.4. Secondary teacher/scientist earnings ratios by gender, male/female scientist earnings ratio, GDP/capita, and GINI coefficients, by country, early 2000s.

Country	Male Teacher/Scientist Salary Ratio	Female Teacher/Scientist Salary Ratio	Male/Female Scientist Ratio	GDP/Cap (2000 PPP $)
Bulgaria				
1995	0.58	1.11		6,229
2001	0.55	0.81	1.9	
Taiwan				
1997	1.01	1.08	1.03	25,000
2004	1.04	0.98		
Germany				
1990	1.19	1.1	1.14	26,075
1995	1.1	1.04		
2000	0.79	0.85		
South Korea				
1996	0.96	1.02	0.97	15,202
2004	0.99	0.91		
Mexico				
1996	0.74	1.11		
2004	0.78	1.07	1.58	8,920
United States				
1995	0.63	0.71	1.21	34,134
2000	0.64	0.74		

Note. Source: Salary ratios: Carnoy et al., 2006. The salary ratio is the average ratio of the age categories: 25–29, 30–34, and 35–44 years old, and are for teachers and scientists with a university bachelor's degree. GDP per capita: World Bank (2005).

a huge difference, but it means that if Mexico is counting on filling its middle school teaching ranks with women, the mathematics skills of those students studying to become teachers would be somewhat lower, on average, than the average shown in Table 11.4.

German students studying to be mathematics teachers may be coming from a pool of less than average mathematics ability university students if relative salaries are an indicator of the attractiveness of the teaching profession. If some middle school teachers are trained in elementary education programs, as is common in the United States as well as in Germany, these teachers are paid less and may come from a pool of university entrants with much lower mathematics knowledge. However, on average, the mathematics test scores of German students entering university are probably high. This suggests that those students entering teacher education may not be as able mathematically as those in Taiwan or South Korea, but German future teachers are probably still very strong in mathematics, in international terms. According to the data collected in this study, German future teachers come out of their preparation with higher mathematics content knowledge than future teachers in all countries but South Korea and Taiwan. If we just consider German first-phase training, which is in the same range as the high end of South Korean and Taiwan costs per student, this could be seen as a logical result. However, the second phase of teacher preparation in Germany adds a significant amount to the total costs. Such practical training may be important to teaching mathematics in terms of pedagogical knowledge and instructional routines and therefore produce other benefits, but apparently not additional mathematics knowledge.

AN APPROXIMATION OF
COST-EFFECTIVENESS OF TEACHER EDUCATION

We can use the MT21 data (see Chapter 5, Figures 5.6 and 5.10) to estimate a form of "value-added" of teacher education in the six countries. The "beginning cohort" mathematics content knowledge scores and the "final year" scores in each country represent a measure of gain in learning for future teachers during their training (see Chapters 3 and 9 for definitions, assumptions, and caveats). The main problem with this estimated value-added is that in each country the number of years between the year of study of the beginning cohort and the ending cohort varies. Another problem is that the two cohorts represent different groups of future teachers, so that in some countries there may be major differences between the two cohorts and very little difference in others.

With these caveats in mind, using the data in Figures 5.6 and 5.10, we estimated the finishing cohort test score values for the five mathematics content knowledge areas and the three pedagogical content knowledge areas across the six countries (see Table 11.5). The analyses were controlled for the corresponding beginning cohort test score values and country. The country coefficients represent how scores on each test area in that country compare to the United States.[5] This is summarized in the following equation:

$$ETS_{ij} = \alpha + \beta\, BTS_{ij} + \Sigma\gamma_j\, C_j + \varepsilon$$

Where ETS_{ij} = End test score on sub-area i in country j;
BTS_{ij} = Beginning test score on sub-area i in country j;
C_j = country dummy variables;
and, ε = the error term.

TABLE 11.5. Parameter estimates for predicting the finishing cohort knowledge scores controlled for country and the knowledge scores of the beginning cohort.

Variable	Finishing Cohort Mathematics Content Knowledge (MCK)	Finishing Cohort Mathematics Pedagogical Content Knowledge (PCK)	Finishing Cohort MCK plus PCK
MCK Beginning Cohort	0.546***		
PCK Beginning Cohort		0.83***	
MCK + PCK Beginning Cohort			0.772***
Bulgaria	0.55	16.83	3.86
Germany	40.80***	4.09	27.44***
South Korea	59.80***	-15.80	15.25
Mexico	-18.66**	4.23	-9.99
Taiwan	37.50**	2.95	5.53
Intercept	214.54***	83.26	114.3***
Adjusted R2	0.96	0.92	0.87
N	30	18	48

Notes. Source—MT21 Surveys, Cohort I future teacher test scores and Cohort II future teacher test scores. Country coefficients shown in table are relative to U.S. future teacher test scores.

statistically significant at the .05 level of significance; * statistically significant at the .01 level of significance.

These results suggest that future teachers in three countries (Taiwan, Germany, and South Korea) made significantly higher gains in mathematical content knowledge during their teacher education training than did future teachers in the United States. Future teachers in Bulgaria made about the same gains as those in the United States, and future teachers in Mexico made significantly lower gains than those in the other five countries. It should be noted that German future teachers had more years of training than future teachers in the other countries between the point in their studies that the beginning cohort was tested and when the finishing cohort was tested.

The second regressions suggested that there were no statistically significant differences among countries in the gains in pedagogical knowledge between the beginning future teacher cohort and the finishing future teacher cohort, although South Korean future teachers tended to gain less and Bulgarian future teachers more. The third regression ran all eight of the test scores for each country's future teachers. Overall, German future teachers showed a positive overall gain compared to U.S. future teachers (and, implicitly, other countries' future teachers).

Since it could be argued that the United States puts more emphasis on pedagogy in its teacher education, the fact that it made the same gains as other countries in pedagogical knowledge and its final-year future teachers scored relatively high on the three elements of pedagogical knowledge, the United States could be considered to have a reasonably cost-effective teacher education program. However, if effectiveness is measured in terms of added mathematics knowledge, this is not the case. On the other hand, since South Korea and Taiwan spend relatively little on their teacher education and their future teachers' gains in mathematics knowledge are relatively high, with similar gains in pedagogical knowledge compared to U.S. future teachers, it could be argued that the cost-effectiveness of teacher education in those two countries is much higher than in the United States. At the other end of the spectrum, Mexico and Bulgaria do not spend much on their teacher education, but they do not get much for their expenditures, either.

The analysis in this section also confirms that Germany is difficult to gauge in terms of cost-effectiveness. Spending on teacher education is higher than in the United States, but German future teachers have higher gains in mathematics knowledge than U.S. future teachers and end up at comparable levels with U.S. future teachers in pedagogical knowledge. So the Germans spend more than the Americans but seem to get more, at least in terms of the test score gains of future teachers on these tests.

SUMMARY

Table 11.6 summarizes our economic analyses of teacher education in these six countries.

- Bulgaria, Mexico, and the United States recruit students into teacher education who have relatively low mathematics scores and, in the case of Mexico and the United States, relatively high pedagogical knowledge scores. These three countries spend low (Bulgaria) to moderate (Mexico) to moderately high (U.S.) amounts of PPP dollars per student to educate future teachers, have relatively low value-added in both mathematics and general pedagogical knowledge between the cohort beginning and the cohort finishing teacher education, and produce future teachers with relatively low levels of mathematics content knowledge and low (Bulgaria), moderate (Mexico), and relatively high (U.S.) levels of pedagogical knowledge. These results are consistent with Mexico's and the United States' emphasis on pedagogical training. But the results also suggest that future teachers in the three countries are rather poorly trained in mathematics, at least compared to the others in the sample. They start with relatively

TABLE 11.6. Summary of economic analyses of mathematics middle school teacher education in six countries.

Country	Mathematics Ability Recruitment Pool (TIMSS/PISA Scores of Potential College Students)	Teacher Pay as Predictor of Recruitment into Mathematics Education	Spending per Student to Produce a Mathematics Teacher Education Graduate	"Value-Added" of Math Content Knowledge and Pedagogical Knowledge During Teacher Education	Overall Impact on New Teachers' Mathematics Teaching Capacity
Bulgaria	Began high in 1990s, declined to middle levels by 2003, and continued to decline somewhat.	Male teachers paid much less than male scientists; female teachers were at parity with female scientists, now paid less.	Spending per student is relatively low in PPP dollars despite double subject requirement.	Value-added in math content relatively low and pedagogical knowledge similar to student teachers in other countries.	Math teacher education probably recruiting low-middle math scoring students, spends little on training, producing relatively low value-added and low result.
Taiwan	Has consistently been very high, among the highest in the world.	Male and female teachers are paid similar salaries (perhaps higher) as scientists.	Spending in mathematics education is relatively low despite high teacher certification requirements.	Value-added in math content relatively high and value-added in pedagogical knowledge similar to student teachers in other countries.	Math teacher education recruits high scoring students, spends relatively little on their training, producing relatively high math content knowledge in new teachers, but not as high pedagogical knowledge.
Germany	University students have high mathematics scores.	Male and female teachers had very high salaries relative to scientists in the early 1990s, but teachers' relative salaries have declined sharply by 2000.	Spending in mathematics education is relatively high because of high teacher certification requirements and double subject requirement.	Value-added in math content relatively high and value-added in pedagogical knowledge similar to student teachers in other countries.	Math teacher education probably recruits lower scoring students from a high average scoring pool, spends relatively more on their training, and produces two-subject teachers with middle level math knowledge and relatively higher pedagogical knowledge— reasonably cost effective.
South Korea	Has consistently been very high, among the highest in the world.	Male and female teachers are paid salaries similar to those of scientists.	Costs of teacher education are relatively low compared to other countries and to South Korean scientists' education.	Value-added in math content relatively high and value-added in pedagogical knowledge lower than for student teachers in other countries.	Math teacher education recruits high scoring students, spends relatively little on their training, but produces relatively high math knowledge but low pedagogical knowledge in new teachers.
Mexico	University students probably at low-middle OECD level math scores, also increasing somewhat.	Male teachers paid less than male scientists, but female teachers more than female scientists.	Costs of teacher education are relatively low.	Value-added in math content relatively much lower and value-added in pedagogical knowledge similar to student teachers in other countries.	Math teacher education recruits average/ lower scoring (female) students from middle level pool, spends relatively little to train them, resulting in relatively low math knowledge and moderately high pedagogical knowledge in new teachers.
United States	Has consistently been at middle levels, but is gradually declining.	Both male and female teachers paid much less than scientists.	Costs of teacher education vary among institutions, but most are middle range compared to other countries' costs.	Value-added in math content relatively low and value-added in pedagogical knowledge similar to student teachers in other countries.	Math teacher education recruits lower scoring students from middle level pool, spends moderately on their training, resulting in relatively low math knowledge but relatively high pedagogical knowledge in new teachers.

lower levels of mathematics preparation and get little value-added in mathematics knowledge during their teacher education.

- Taiwan and South Korea recruit students with very high levels of mathematics content knowledge into teacher education, spend only a moderate amount per student to educate them, achieve relatively high value-added in the mathematics content knowledge element of teacher education, and produce future teachers with high levels of mathematics content knowledge. Yet, at the same time, these two countries have average value-added in this part of teacher education and produce future teachers with relatively lower levels of pedagogical knowledge. These results make sense considering that the initial level of mathematics knowledge—probably very high—among those who are studying to become teachers may allow Taiwanese and South Korean teacher-training programs to spend relatively little on teacher education and still produce future teachers with high mathematics knowledge. Yet, possibly as a result of the relatively lower levels of spending on teacher education and somewhat less emphasis on general pedagogy, they produce future teachers with relatively lower levels of pedagogical knowledge.

- In Germany, the mathematics knowledge of the future teachers at the beginning of their training might be expected to be lower than it is, given our estimated PISA mathematics scores for German university students. One possible explanation for the lower than expected beginning scores is that our PISA estimates are biased upward. A second possible reason is that in the 2000s, teacher salaries relative to salaries in competing mathematics-oriented professions may have fallen low enough to attract to teacher preparation programs only those German students with much lower than average levels of mathematics ability. Yet it is also the case that German future teachers scored relatively high on the pedagogical knowledge test and that the overall value-added on the combined mathematical content and pedagogical knowledge tests was higher than in other countries. If we focus only on the costs of the first phase of teacher preparation in Germany, this suggests that teacher education spending in Germany is reasonably cost-effective.

Thus, at one end of the spectrum, Taiwan and South Korea can recruit young people into mathematics teacher education from a very well mathematically prepared pool of secondary school graduates by paying teachers relatively high salaries compared to competing mathematics-oriented professionals. However, the government spends only moderate amounts per student on teachers' education. The reported outcomes suggest that this still results in very well-prepared future teachers when it comes to mathematics content knowledge but less so for general pedagogical knowledge.

At the other end of the spectrum, three countries (Bulgaria, Mexico, and the United States) have a recruiting pool of only middle-scoring (in mathematics) secondary school graduates. Bulgaria's teachers' salaries have been falling steadily in relative terms since the 1990s, so it is likely that those entering teacher education have relatively lower mathematics skills than in the past. Bulgaria then spends relatively little to train them. Mexico has a similar, middle-level recruitment pool for mathematics teacher education and pays relatively high salaries to female teachers (female students average lower mathematics scores than males), so should be able to recruit average mathematics-level female students into teaching. However, Mexico spends only moderate amounts on teacher education. The end result: Future middle school teachers in Bulgaria and Mexico have relatively low mathematics content knowledge and, in the Bulgarian case, also very low general pedagogical knowledge.

The United States is a particularly interesting case since the average level of mathematics knowledge in the recruitment pool for teacher education (secondary school graduates attending 4-year colleges/universities) is almost certainly only middle level (about the OECD average). Since teacher salaries are relatively low compared to scientists for both men and women, it also likely that a career in teaching attracts considerably more secondary school students from the lower half of the mathematics knowledge distribution (see, e.g., Henke, Chen, Geis et al., 2000, for the likelihood of entering the teaching profession based on a quartile of college entrance test scores). Furthermore, most U.S. teachers are trained in moderate-cost teacher education programs. This is less the result of lower costs in teacher education than the fact that most U.S. future teachers are educated in public colleges where costs are relatively modest, about $10,000–$12,000 per student per year, including student services and administrative overhead. In the California state college/university system, for example, teacher education only provides certification or master's degree courses and has costs per student that are similar to engineering programs in the same institutions. It appears from Chapter 4 that, based on the number of hours of instruction, a higher proportion of the resources spent on teacher education in the United States is allocated to pedagogical training and a lower proportion on mathematics than in most of the other countries. This may help explain why future teachers in the U.S. sample of this study scored relatively low on mathematics content knowledge but high on the pedagogical elements of the test.

Putting more resources into U.S. middle school mathematics teachers' education could significantly raise future teachers' mathematics skills but may not be sufficient to equal those in countries where mathematics skills are substantially higher or produce sufficient numbers of more highly skilled middle school mathematics teachers, for two reasons. Average mathematics knowledge among U.S. college students is much lower than in Taiwan, South Korea, or Germany, and because of the relatively low salaries and prestige of teaching in the United States, the college students enrolled in teacher education are likely to average much lower mathematics skills than the large number of students in science, engineering, and economics/business. A combination of recruitment incentives and better mathematics training would be needed to simultaneously draw secondary school and college students with higher mathematics ability into teaching and to increase significantly the mathematics knowledge of U.S. future teachers.

A potential problem for the future is that U.S. students' average PISA scores in mathematics seem to be declining over time. There is contrary evidence from the 8th-grade mathematics scores on the National Assessment of Educational Progress (NAEP), which have climbed 0.6 standard deviations between 1990 and 2009. If the PISA scores correctly capture reality, improving future teachers' mathematics knowledge outcomes may require policy makers to take measures that both increase the recruitment of secondary graduates with higher mathematics achievement into teaching and increase the mathematics training required for middle school mathematics teachers. If the NAEP scores correctly reflect reality, the level of mathematics knowledge of those entering U.S. teacher preparation programs could very well rise in the future, providing an opportunity to raise the standard of mathematics training of middle school teachers with only moderate levels of additional spending.

CHAPTER 12

Concluding Thoughts
and Some Hypotheses

Preparing highly qualified teachers is undoubtedly the central goal of teacher education in every country and in every institution entrusted with this mission. Accordingly, each teacher preparation institution organizes a set of courses and experiences that are designed to equip future teachers with a set of competencies that they can take with them into the classroom. The desired cognitive competencies necessary for a mathematics teacher to be successful in the classroom are generally agreed upon in the literature and encompass three types of competencies: (1) mathematics knowledge, (2) pedagogical knowledge related to the teaching and learning of mathematics, and (3) general pedagogical knowledge related to instructional practices and schooling more generally.

In addition, the literature points to the importance of professional beliefs as another set of competencies as they are viewed as the bridge between the knowledge competencies and the actual practice of classroom teaching. These beliefs include general epistemological beliefs about the nature of mathematics and the nature of schooling, as well as specific behavioral intentions about instruction and classroom management.

Within state or national guidelines, different institutions design different sets of course offerings and practical experiences reflecting different philosophies and ideologies of how best to accomplish the goal of developing these professional competencies in future teachers. These then become the de facto definitions of teacher preparation. For that reason we examined the course offerings and practical experiences at each of the 34 institutions included in this study. We did this by asking the institutions for their formal requirements and the future teachers for an accounting of what courses/topics they had covered during teacher education and whether they had had the opportunity to gain experience through a number of very specific classroom-related activities. The set of questions we posed addressed four areas: formal mathematics,

mathematics pedagogy, general pedagogy, and practical school-related experiences. Collectively, we have examined and discussed this set of courses and experiences as representing the future teachers' opportunities to learn (OTL) as provided by their formal program of teacher preparation.

We also differentiated OTL related to the formal or the more theoretical aspects of pedagogy courses, such as the history of school mathematics; the psychology of mathematics learning; the philosophy, history, and sociology of education; education psychology; and instructional theory from the more practical aspects of pedagogy, gained not only through coursework but also through the practice aspects of teacher preparation like classroom visits, teaching practice lessons, and student teaching.

The MT21 data clearly indicated that OTL in these areas varies appreciably across the 34 institutions studied, with the institutional patterns further clustering by country which, at least in practice, represents different visions of teacher preparation. In addition, we have documented that these differences in OTL are related to differences in performance with respect to our measures of the major cognitive and belief competencies of concern in teacher education. These relationships occur both at the individual future teacher level and at the institutional level. In effect, what we have found is evidence to suggest that the variations in course-taking across future teachers and institutions is related to variations in future teacher knowledge and beliefs. The unmistakable conclusion is that teacher education does, indeed, matter.

In none of the 34 institutions were any of the four areas of OTL not addressed in some way. What did vary was the total amount of time spent on course requirements (as measured in total clock hours), the amount of coursework in each of these areas, and the number of different types of school-related experiences. Consider first the formal requirements for these 34 institutions. We found that, on average, the total amount of course-taking as indicated by the number of clock hours of course requirements over all of teacher preparation varied substantially across the countries. For example, Taiwanese institutions on average required over 550 more clock hours over the four years than did U.S. institutions. It is essential to point out that some of these differences, if not the majority of them, stem from different governmental policies that regulate teacher preparation, but this insight only serves to underline the important differences we documented.

Taiwanese sampled institutions on average required that over half (56%) of the clock hours be allocated to the study of mathematics. The secondary preparation programs in the United States required on average 30% while the elementary programs required only 20%. Germany was very similar to the United States but future teachers there are required to attain a second full major. Mexico required no formal mathematics. The only mathematics instruction Mexican sample future teachers had was in their mathematics pedagogy courses. A basic calculus sequence and a linear algebra course were taken by virtually all of the sampled Taiwanese future teachers. This was also true for sampled South Korean future teachers for whom mathematics instruction represented 43% of their total course-taking load. But of all the countries in MT21, Bulgaria required the largest proportion of mathematics course-taking—almost 60%.

Sampled future teachers in the two Asian countries also took more advanced coursework such as analysis, differential equations, and abstract algebra than did those in any of the other countries, including Bulgaria and the United States. There were clear differences in OTL related to formal mathematics. The statistical analyses suggested significant and large relationships of such OTL to performance on the MT21 mathematics knowledge test at both the individual future teacher level and at the institutional level.

For mathematics knowledge the opportunities that are related to higher levels of performance at the future teacher level include coursework primarily in linear algebra and calculus, but also abstract algebra and advanced mathematics including analysis, topology, and differential geometry. Coursework in the more formal aspects of mathematics pedagogy, as well as in advanced school mathematics, was not related to such performance. This suggests the hypothesis that mathematics content knowledge related to the topics typically taught worldwide in middle school is best developed in formal mathematics courses. Some specific additional relationships were found for algebra and geometry involving OTL in the corresponding area—that is, abstract and linear algebra and axiomatic, analytical and non-Euclidean geometry, respectively.

The country-level patterns that emerged on our measures of mathematics knowledge were consistent with the OTL provided by the various programs/institutions. On the algebra test the Taiwanese and South Korean future teachers outperformed the German and U.S. future teachers by one to one and one-half standard deviations—a very large difference. Mexico and Bulgaria were similar to Germany and the United States. On the functions test future teachers from the United States and Mexico were outperformed even more while Bulgaria and Germany performed slightly better.

The patterns for mathematics pedagogy were somewhat different. Other than the Mexican future teachers and the German future teachers in an elementary preparation program, the differences in the amount of coursework required did not vary as much as was the case for mathematics. Mexico and the elementary preparation program in Germany required that around one fourth of the total clock hours of preparation be focused on mathematics pedagogy. In contrast, the other countries and programs required only around 3% to 11%. Formal analyses relating the variation in OTL to the variation in test scores of mathematics pedagogical knowledge were significant, although the estimated relationships were not as strong as they were for the mathematics test.

With respect to the performance of future teachers on our measures of mathematics pedagogical knowledge, however, no general patterns emerged. Curriculum knowledge seemed primarily related to coursework on the history of school mathematics. Perhaps such knowledge of history contributes to an understanding of how and why the curriculum is organized as it is. For pedagogical knowledge related to the teaching of mathematics, OTL on instructional interactions related to mathematics was significant—as would be expected—but so was the amount of practical experience gained in schools. It seems as if not only coursework but working in a school environment increases knowledge, as has been claimed in the literature on teacher induction.

For knowledge of student learning, the major significant effect was formal coursework in mathematics pedagogy and coursework related to understanding school mathematics at the middle school level. All of these relationships were defined at the institutional level, implying differences in philosophy as to what constitutes important pedagogical knowledge and what types of experiences and coursework leads to that development. Apparently different institutions have different views on this and they are related to what future teachers learn during their teacher preparation. In addition, variation among future teachers in terms of the practical experience of actually teaching mathematics to middle school students was related to how well students learn mathematics. This was not the case with mathematics knowledge; country patterns in mathematics pedagogy knowledge were not entirely consistent with the OTL country patterns.

To make these patterns simpler to look at, we combined the three separate pedagogical tests—curriculum, teaching, and students—into one score. We also used both the conditional (i.e., mathematics pedagogy knowledge conditioned on mathematics knowledge) and unconditional (i.e., straight performance on the mathematics pedagogy items) mathematics pedagogy scores as reported on in Table 5.6. This means we averaged six scores for each country. By including both versions of the mathematics pedagogy scores, we treat them equally in terms of informing us about mathematics pedagogy knowledge.

We found the patterns for South Korea, Taiwan, the United States, and the secondary program in Germany to be consistent. All three required somewhat the same relative amount of clock hours in mathematics pedagogy and their total scores were somewhat similar—510, 518, 520, and 513. Bulgaria was very similar in their relative allocation of time to mathematics pedagogy but their total score was substantially lower—440.

Inconsistently, the Mexican and the elementary program in Germany allocated almost a quarter of their preparation time to mathematics pedagogy yet scored only at or below the other countries. The explanation in both cases is likely related to their relatively low coverage of mathematics, which is related to such pedagogy as discussed in Chapter 5.

Examining the patterns with respect to performance on the general pedagogy measures is yet another story. In contrast to mathematics pedagogy, very large differences in the relative amount of clock hours allocated to general pedagogy were evident across the six countries. Bulgaria and Mexico served as the polar opposites, with sampled Bulgarian institutions requiring only about 5% contrasted with Mexican institutions, which on average required 75% (including practical experiences). Also on the high side were Germany (including the coursework obtained during the second phase) and the United States, with about 25–30% for each of its two programs—elementary and secondary preparation of future middle school teachers. The two Asian countries allocated around 10% to general pedagogy coursework—although, keep in mind that 10% of the total clock hours in Taiwanese institutions could be more than what was allocated in another country.

At the institutional level there was also large variation in OTL, and that variation was related to variation in the test scores associated with the lesson plan item (the only one administered to the entire sample). For performance on the general pedagogy assessment, opportunities to engage in classroom-related experiences such as teaching and observing mathematics lessons was the dominant influence; but OTL related to geometry, which was the substantive nature of the mathematics content of the lesson plan item, and OTL related to the teaching of mathematics at the middle school level were also marginally significant.

To explore these relationships a bit further, we did an analysis of the test results somewhat like that for mathematics pedagogy, where we averaged over the four scores for the lesson plan items discussed in Chapter 6 to obtain a total score. German, U.S., Taiwanese, and Mexican future teachers scored the highest (in that order) on the total general pedagogy measure. By comparison, Mexico, the United States, and Germany (in that order) allocated the most clock hours relative to the total to the study of general pedagogy, which is consistent, in general, although not in specific order to the pattern for the test results.

Taiwan seems not to fit the pattern as its institutions allocated on average only 7% to the study of general pedagogy as compared to the 25% to 75% for the other top three performers in general pedagogy. However, the 7% is not a big difference from the 25% in terms of the absolute number of clock hours because of Taiwan's larger number of required hours overall. It is also the case that developing lesson plans is a part of mathematics pedagogy courses which is not included in the 7%. In addition, it is important to keep in mind that the Taiwanese future teachers were sampled during their 1-year practicum (which was not included in the total number of clock hours) with many school-based experiences while the formal coursework took place during the first 4 years at the university. It is likely that the practical experiences support the acquisition of pedagogical knowledge.

As a final analysis we combined the mathematics pedagogy and general pedagogy scores and found that sampled U.S. future teachers would be ranked first among the six countries, with German future teachers second. This is quite consistent with the fact that these two countries allocated a large percentage of their preparation hours to pedagogy-related coursework.

Mexico allocated the most amount of time to pedagogy, both absolutely and relatively. Yet their total pedagogy score placed them only in a tie for fourth place with South Korea. There are probably very different reasons for the low test results of the two countries. It is reasonable to assume that in the case of the South Korean sample, the outcome is a function of their OTL. South Korea is the country with the second lowest amount of pedagogy coursework. In Mexico, however, the result is probably more a function of the low entrance characteristics of the future teachers (see Chapter 11).

Using the total mathematics score and the total pedagogy score, an interesting pattern emerges. Taiwanese future teachers performed in the top tier[1] in mathematics and in the middle tier in pedagogy, while Germany was in the middle tier in terms of mathematics but in the top tier in pedagogy. The United States was distinct. The mathematics knowledge level of sampled future middle school mathematics teachers placed them in the lowest tier, but they were in the top tier in pedagogical knowledge. However, separating the mathematics pedagogical knowledge into its two components shows the effect of the low mathematics performance. For general pedagogy they remain in the top tier, but for mathematics pedagogy they drop to the low end of the second tier when mathematics knowledge is not conditioned out of the mathematics pedagogy score; when it was conditioned out, they remained in the top tier (with the highest score).

Perhaps related to this pattern of performance for the United States is the observation that the variation in OTL (as reported by the future teachers) across the sampled U.S. institutions is the largest of any of the six countries in the area of formal mathematics course-taking and also in the area of formal mathematics pedagogy course-taking. The latter includes courses such as the psychology of student learning, history of school mathematics, and methods of teaching mathematics. Yet the United States was the least variable in terms of the coverage of the general pedagogy topics. In fact, there was no institutional variation for general pedagogy. As Chapter 10 indicated, these measures of OTL were related to the knowledge measures, and greater variation in the relevant OTL—especially variation created by institutions at the lower end of the distribution—had the effect of lowering the average scores for the United States in mathematics and mathematics pedagogy. This was not the case for general pedagogy.

For the professional beliefs, significant relationships were also found with the OTL variables both in terms of formal courses and in terms of practical knowledge often gained through practical experiences with K–12 schools. In general, what we have shown is that opportunity to learn from each of the major domains of teacher education was related to the development of teacher knowledge, professional beliefs, and instructionally related behavioral intentions in these 34 institutions from the six countries participating in MT21.

What is also related to both types of pedagogical knowledge as well as to the professional beliefs of future teachers is the variety of classroom-related experiences and the number of weeks of classroom teaching. This clearly indicates the salience of school-related experience. Also, many of the relationships of OTL to these pedagogical test areas and beliefs were defined by the extent of opportunity related to the practical knowledge of how one actively functions in the classroom in terms of instruction (e.g., asking questions that stimulate deeper thought) and classroom management, and not just the more theoretical aspects of pedagogy. The results suggest that teacher education as defined by the learning opportunities provided is related to the professional knowledge of future teachers as they leave their teacher preparation programs.

The data were especially clear about the importance of formal mathematics coursework as shown by the MT21 data. This was not as clear for pedagogical course-taking. But we have to be careful with the implications concerning the relationships or lack of relationships of OTL in the areas of mathematics pedagogy and general pedagogy. Mathematics pedagogy knowledge is operationalized relatively closely to mathematics knowledge in MT21 and, even in its most pedagogical aspects, mathematics pedagogy is limited to short descriptions of students' difficulties or errors. However, teaching is a very complex activity addressing large groups of students over a very long time period (e.g., a whole school year) and in addition consisting of multiple tasks at the same time. OTL in mathematics pedagogy as well as in general pedagogy is to a large extent focused on these three features, which we could not measure in MT21 because it is hard to measure them in a paper-and-pencil format.

The lesson plan item is the only one that requires at least some long-term procedural knowledge. So, conclusions about the relationship of OTL to mathematics pedagogy or general pedagogy knowledge have to be regarded with caution. There could also be a slight gap between what is measured as OTL in MT21 in these areas and what is done in teacher education. This gap is probably greater than with regard to mathematics because mathematics is a relatively standardized set of content in comparison to the less well defined areas of mathematics pedagogy and general pedagogy.

Opportunity to learn appears to be as important in developing the professional knowledge of future teachers as it is in developing the knowledge of middle school students. The sampled U.S. institutions were behind in the type and amount of mathematics content covered compared to the Taiwanese and South Korean sampled institutions. The same was true for the typical student in 8th grade, as evidenced by TIMSS results. This pattern is also true in terms of mathematics pedagogy. However, for the theoretical aspects of pedagogy, U.S. institutions covered a greater portion of such topics relative to mathematics courses than was true in these two countries. Clearly just as important, the belief that the preparation of future teachers might be done without any preparation in practical pedagogy seems unwise and should certainly be reconsidered, especially as the analyses indicated the relationship of classroom-related experiences to professional competencies. Again, the Taiwanese future teachers indicated more extensive opportunities to acquire such practical pedagogical knowledge.

The real question, then, is not whether such experiences are necessary but rather what is the nature and the extent of the learning opportunities in each of the areas that should be available for future teachers. It is quite revealing but far from conclusive that the countries whose middle-grade students continually perform well on the international benchmark tests have the teachers who have been trained with extensive educational opportunities in mathematics and mathematics pedagogy as well as in the practical aspects of teaching mathematics to their students.

Several observations are worth noting with respect to professional beliefs—both the beliefs about the nature of mathematics and schooling as well as beliefs about instructional- and management-related behavioral intentions. In general, it was quite surprising to the research team to learn how much commonality there was in terms of such beliefs and dispositions. To be specific, there was substantial homogeneity of beliefs across all six countries with respect to beliefs about the nature of mathematics teaching and learning.

These included agreement on the core objectives of mathematics instruction and on the ways students learn. This suggests there may well exist an emerging global perspective in these areas.

There also were many similarities related to what future teachers believed about how they would act in various simulated instructional situations and in classroom management. This, too, represents a convergence about instructional activities in mathematics. However, there were differences as well. There were big differences in beliefs about the nature of mathematics and the nature and purposes of schooling. These seemed to reflect cultural views, although they could also be related to differences in the difficulty of the K–12 curricula, especially with respect to beliefs about the nature of mathematics. There was some evidence of the possibility of an east-versus-west divide on some of these scales, with Bulgaria somewhat in the middle bridging the two cultures. This was especially true for content-related issues, where Bulgarian future teachers were more like those in Taiwan and South Korea. However, an alternative explanation might be related to the differences among the countries in the difficulty of the mathematics studied, especially if mathematical knowledge is related to beliefs about mathematics.

Differences were also apparent among future teachers on what type of instructional approach they intended to follow. The sample divided along two dimensions, the first characterizing the degree to which the future teaches proposed teaching in more traditional ways (including homework, using the blackboard, giving tests, etc.) versus preference for more constructivist ways (e.g., small groups, writing journals, group projects). The other dimension characterized the future teachers' position about how to manage the classroom. One end of the scale was an authoritative position where consequences related to behavior were the most important way of maintaining order. The other end of the scale referred to approaches that would work to help the students be more motivated and in that way stay focused and not have behavioral problems.

Taiwanese future teachers, on average, were more authoritative and proposed following the traditional approach. They were the highest of all six countries on both of these dimensions. The other pole was defined by the German sampled future teachers who were the absolute opposite—lowest on the traditional approach and the most reliant on motivational strategies to manage the classroom. Sampled U.S. future teachers were slightly more traditional on average and slightly more inclined to use motivational techniques for classroom management.

Another major difference involved the proposed lesson structure. There were some universals as to when certain types of activities would occur but there were also some distinct differences, the main ones centering on where and what kind of examples should be used. South Korean and Taiwanese future teachers included both simple and complex examples in their lessons, usually including these in the beginning or middle of the lesson. By contrast, sampled U.S. future teachers tended mostly to use simple examples and to include them at the very end of the lesson.

After cataloguing all the results and noting similarities and differences, where does all of this lead us? As to research, we have developed methodologies that worked well in a first and hopefully groundbreaking cross-country study but still need to be further developed. These include developing a better definition of mathematics pedagogical knowledge and better ways to assess it. Also, we have developed a vignette approach to measuring general pedagogical knowledge in an international context. We have learned what does not work well—such as scaling over different types of vignettes—but we need to develop better ways to scale such measures. We have developed ways to measure opportunities to learn in teacher education. Overall, they reflect reasonably well the nature of OTL in mathematics, mathematics pedagogy, general pedagogy, and practical experiences in our six countries. However, as always in international comparisons, we have to be somewhat cautious with respect to the cross-country validity of self-reported data.

From a policy perspective, it is tempting to move beyond the data and to make sweeping recommendations. We refrain from doing that as our samples are small and non-random, but what we can do is generate some hunches or hypotheses. We do this recognizing the limitations and caution the reader to note these limitations.

There are three approaches to teacher education that emerge from the data. These are exemplified by Taiwan, Germany, and the United States. In Taiwan (and South Korea) the students who enter teacher preparation are well prepared mathematically. In other words, these institutions can recruit from the high end of the mathematics achievement distribution. For Taiwan this was illustrated by the high scores for the beginning cohort for the country as a whole. This recruitment is facilitated by teaching jobs that provide high salaries relative to other professions and high social status. Their focus in preparation requires a high level of formal mathematics and the program is provided at moderate cost. As a result, the output in terms of teacher competence is high in mathematics and more moderate in pedagogy.

By contrast, Germany at a first glance does not seem to achieve an end product in terms of future teachers with a high degree of mathematics knowledge commensurate with the students who enter teacher preparation with a relatively high initial knowledge and given the high costs associated with a program that spans over 6 or more years. This conclusion must be moderated by three facts. First, the German future middle school teachers have to be prepared in two distinct subject matters. In this respect, the costs of one German teacher actually have to be compared with the costs of some fraction higher than one reasonably well-trained teacher in other countries. The picture that emerges then changes. At the cost of high achievement in mathematics knowledge, Germany having greater flexibility in its teaching force is able to avoid out-of-field teaching—a problem that is present in many countries. It is hard to determine how much that fraction is.

Second, there are two types of preparation programs in which future middle school teachers can be prepared with different selection criteria and with different program requirements, especially in mathematics. Given the extensive preparation in pedagogy, especially at the second institution, it is not surprising that the output in terms of pedagogical knowledge is extremely strong.

Third, including teacher salaries as an indicator of how attractive the teaching profession is in comparison to other professions in which mathematics is important, Taiwan and South Korea probably attract students with higher entrance knowledge into teacher education. So, even if the mathematics knowledge of beginning students is high in an international context, it is lower than it is in high-achieving Asian countries.

Finally, the United States represents yet a third approach. Recruitment by the institutions secure future teachers whose level of mathematics knowledge is average by international standards and in many cases come from the lower half of the achievement distribution. Costs are moderate and the programs (those prepared in elementary, middle school only, and secondary programs) focus heavily on general pedagogy but little on formal mathematics, with the exception of those prepared as secondary teachers, as was the case for the German institutions. The output is consistent—a low level of mathematics knowledge and a strong level of pedagogical knowledge.

From the U.S. and German perspectives one of the key policy questions centers around whether to maintain the different types of preparation programs for middle school mathematics teachers. In both countries there are differences between the programs both in terms of OTL and in terms of the knowledge level attained. In both countries those who are prepared in the secondary program have higher levels of mathematics knowledge.

Whether it is a good idea to prepare these teachers in elementary preparation programs becomes an issue of equity. Lower-secondary teachers, even those prepared in elementary programs, have to teach up to grade 10. These grades are highly important with respect to future opportunities for the students, for example whether they can go to a vocational high school or pass the Abitur and maybe even attend the university. It seems hard to defend a system where some of the middle school students have better trained teachers than others.

For the United States it is also a similar question of what types of preparation programs should be made available but also of examining the relative allocation of time within those programs to various areas of study. The United States is unique in that around one third of the total clock hours in teacher preparation are focused on general liberal arts requirements. That leaves a smaller part for the preparation specific to becoming a teacher. Within that part available for teacher preparation, a major question becomes the amount of mathematics to be required relative to the amount of pedagogy and what is the best balance.

The average amount of mathematics is lower than it is in other countries (with the exception of Mexico) and this becomes critical to teacher preparation, especially when one considers two other factors: (1) the low level of the U.S. K–12 curriculum (see Chapter 2) from which future teachers obtain their initial knowledge of mathematics; and (2) many if not most of the future teachers, especially those entering elementary or middle school preparation programs, come from the lower half of the mathematics ability distribution. This implies that another policy issue for the United States is whether recruitment can be changed to interest more high school students with more knowledge in mathematics to enter teacher preparation. With generally low relative salaries, this is more difficult.

Mexico and Bulgaria have more specific policy conundrums. For Mexico it is the absence of formal mathematics coursework in the preparation program— unique among the six countries with almost a total focus on pedagogical training. Bulgaria, in contrast, mostly ignores pedagogical training but has a strong focus on mathematics.

In the end, what the field of teacher preparation and those of us who conducted this study really want to know is the answer to the ultimate question of how middle school students achieve in mathematics as a result of the different approaches to teacher preparation. We have examined the competencies viewed as essential for quality teaching and found them related to teacher preparation, but in the end it is how those are used to engage effective student learning in the classroom.

In other words, the question is whether any of this makes any difference for student learning. We conclude this book not knowing the answer to that question but with two pictures worthy of further thought, shown in Figure 12.1 on the following page.

FIGURE 12.1. Future teacher mean level mathematics knowledge of functions (upper) and mathematics pedagogical knowledge about student learning (lower) plotted against the mean level performance of 8th graders (on an international test—TIMSS/PISA—adjusted for GDP and the rigor of the K–8 curriculum) for the six countries.

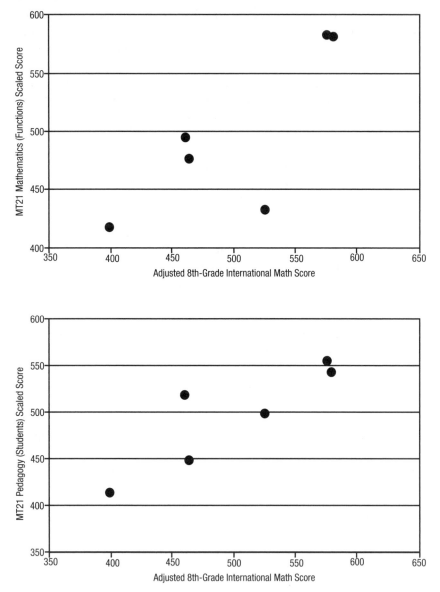

Notes

Chapter 1

1. We refer to teachers and future teachers throughout the book as if they were females. This is, of course, not the case and is done for convenience of exposition. In this study the majority of future teachers were females.
2. The discipline officer maintains order when teachers are not present and is a member of the class's executive board, all of whom were elected by the class.

Chapter 2

1. This format of the examination was used during the time of the MT21 study. Now the format is changed and it varies across institutions.
2. The MT21 sample fell under the pre-2004 regulations, which required a full year on-site practicum.
3. Some important background about the data in Figure 2.8:

   - It is not expected that any country's intended curriculum exactly match the TAC composite. The composite is the result of a statistical analysis representing what is commonly covered across the top-achieving countries.
   - As previously mentioned, Germany's recently established national standards specify the curriculum only for grades 4 and 8. To present comparable results for Germany we analyzed the standards used in one of the federal states, which are a good representation of the standards for Germany as a whole.
   - The intended curriculum of South Korea, one of the top-achieving countries identified in the TIMSS, is closely aligned with the TAC profile.
   - The United States does not have a set of national standards. The intended curriculum that is depicted for grades 1 through 8 in Figure 2.8 was derived from the standards for grades 1 through 8 for all 50 states. If 26 or more states intended to cover a particular topic at a particular grade, then it was considered to be intended for coverage in the United States.

4. Documents were analyzed as part of a curricular study that was completed in Fall 2003.

Chapter 3

1. In Taiwan, 1 year was required before 2004, a half-year has been required since 2009, while either 1 or a half-year was required between 2004 and 2009.

Chapter 4

1. This focus on the specific content of learning opportunities is not intended to invalidate other approaches to various attendant features of content exposure which some have included in their discussions of OTL but, rather, identifies the focus of our discussions. We use the definitions of OTL developed in the work of Carroll (1962, 1963) and the IEA studies (Schmidt, 1993; Schmidt & Burstein 1993; Schmidt, Wolfe, & Kifer, 1993; and Schmidt & Kifer, 1989). See Schmidt and Maier (2009) for a history of the concept as well as a discussion of how this has been broadened to include many other pedagogical and contextual elements in the work of others.

2. An institutional questionnaire was filled out by each of the 34 institutions. Three did not respond with enough detail to be included in the descriptions developed here. Institutions were asked to provide data in clock hours but, except for Bulgaria, institutions typically listed semester hours. All semester hours were converted into clock hours by multiplying the semester hours by the number of weeks in one semester that each institution reported.

   • Semester hours in Germany last 45 minutes, in contrast to most of the other countries, where one semester hour equals 50–60 minutes. To make the German semester hours more consistent with the rest of the countries, the 45-minute semester hours were converted into 50-minute semester hours. Total clock hours were then calculated by multiplying the semester hours by 15 (one German semester = 15 weeks). However, according to our informant, even those calculations are not completely equivalent to the U.S. semester hours because in the United States, students' schoolwork finishes with the semester, but in Germany, students continue working on essays and exam preparation after the end of the semester. Another point where Germany differs from most other countries is the provision of teacher training in two consecutive phases, where Phase I is a theory-based teacher preparation that occurs at a university setting and Phase II is primarily a practical training with more courses in general pedagogy and subject matter pedagogy. Phase II takes place outside of the university, upon students' completion of Phase I.

   • The amount of hours for Mexico is disproportionately high when compared to the other countries. It has been calculated from the National Studies' Plan, which sets the curriculum for all normal schools in Mexico. The plan lists the number of hours per week for each course that future teachers take in a given semester. This number was multiplied by 16 to reflect the length of one semester as reported by our informant, although according to the Studies' Plan, there may be as many as 18 weeks in a semester, so the total number of hours is likely even higher. Our informant also suggested that the mathematics courses listed in the Studies' Plan are in fact courses in mathematics pedagogy rather than mathematics. These amount to 56 semester hours (896 clock hours). Finally, the Mexican Studies' Plan indicates that a significant portion of time in teacher preparation (30% of time, 68 credits) is devoted to practical experiences. Due to the difficulty of estimating the time involved, these are not included in the other countries' calculations, which may explain why Mexico's total clock hours is so large.

- Taiwan—information was provided in semester hours; 1 semester hour (50–60 minutes) = 18 contact hours; total instructional time = semester hours × 18.
- South Korea—information was provided in semester hours; 1 semester hour (50 minutes) = 15 contact hours per semester; total instructional time = semester hours × 15.
- United States—individual institutional questionnaires sometimes reflected several different programs. The tables summarize information for elementary and secondary programs only. Information about middle school–specific programs or majors was included in the elementary program summaries.

3. We use the term *semester unit* in place of semester hour so as to avoid the confusion of semester hours with clock hours. See endnote 2 for the details.

4. This was confirmed with the Mexican Ministry of Education.

5. The list of topics was derived internationally so as to accommodate all topics/ courses covered in any of the six countries. There is no expectation that all of these would be taken by an individual future teacher or that all of them would be necessarily offered in each of the 34 institutions or each of the six countries.

6. The greatest difficulty in interpreting these topics as courses occurs in Germany, where the term *course* as typically understood in the United States is not applicable. There, the basic unit is a *lecture*, especially on the undergraduate level (*grundstudium*) and especially in mathematics and general pedagogy. A lecture has typically a much larger audience than a course in the United States—more than 100 and up to 300 or 400 students are not uncommon—and meets only once a week. Due to the low number of courses or lectures respectively, their content usually covers a broad range of topics. So, many of the topics listed could be covered in only one lecture.

7. To make these nonrandom samples as representative as possible in each of the six countries, MT21 weighted the results. We did this by obtaining estimates from previous years of the number of teachers prepared at each of the sampled institutions. Using those measures of size, we generated a set of weights to provide estimates from the sampled institutions that were more consistent with the output of each institution.

8. The standard errors were calculated recognizing the low intra-class correlations. This is true throughout the book. They likely slightly underestimate the sampling error.

9. We used maximum likelihood procedures to estimate the variance components treating the institutions within countries as random.

10. The total variance was estimated using maximum likelihood estimates derived from a variance decomposition. This addresses the question of whether the total variance is the result of institutional differences in terms of what is required or in terms of what individual students opt to take among various alternatives where there are no formal requirements associated with the taking of particular courses.

The percent of variance attributable to the two levels was estimated based on this estimate of the total variance. The standard errors being more easily understood and reflective of the total variance were included in the tables.

11. A median polish was used to analyze the mean percentages in Table 4.3.

12. The median polish indicated many interaction effects.

13. Interaction effects revealed through the median polish analysis.

14. A similar approach was done for formal mathematics course-taking but without success, as there were many different patterns taken by few future teachers.

15. For general pedagogy, many of the topics listed in the questionnaire are covered in one or more courses. We felt this was more the case in this area than in mathematics or mathematics pedagogy. We use the term *topics* more heavily in this section to remind the reader of this possibility. However, in some cases—in certain countries—these are courses.

16. Given the wording—*full responsibility*—and its varied meanings in the different countries—sizeable numbers of students in some of the countries did not answer the question. We believe that their lack of response reflects this ambiguity in their minds as to what constitutes full responsibility. What we had intended is what typically is referred to as student teaching in the United States.

17. The sampling of future teachers in German second-phase institutions could not distinguish between those at the beginning of their studies from those near the end; hence, the estimate is probably too low in terms of characterizing the total for future teachers at the end of their preparation.

18. These scales were developed through a combination of conceptual and empirical analyses. Items were grouped conceptually and then subjected to a covariance structure analysis. Some adjustments were made to the conceptually defined scales. The number of separate items in each of the scales varied: classroom management and professional practice (3); instructional interaction around mathematics (7); methods of teaching algorithms, proofs, and nonroutine problems (4); teaching mathematics in middle school (2); understanding how students learn (1); deep understanding of middle school math topics (5); planning, preparing, and practicing mathematics lessons (4). Across all six countries, reliability ranged from .90 (for both the methods of teaching algorithms, proofs, and nonroutine problems and the planning, preparing, and practicing of mathematics lessons scales) to .95 (deep understanding of middle school math topics). Reliability within each country for these ranged from .79 for the planning, preparing, and practicing of mathematics lessons scale in Bulgaria to .96 for the deep understanding of middle school math topics scale in both Germany and Taiwan.

19. To do this we ignored our a priori classifications of the items into the seven scales and subjected the 29 items as a whole to a median polish analysis.

20. The ratios are not as large as they were in terms of required clock hours. The differences are most likely related to variation in course credit for different courses.

Chapter 5

1. Both Mathematics Content Knowledge (MCK) and Mathematics Pedagogy Knowledge (MPK) items were used to assess future teachers' mathematics

knowledge. MCK items focused on five content areas: algebra, data, functions, geometry, and number; and MPK items were related to three areas: curriculum, teaching, and students. The items were allocated to two forms that were randomly assigned to students. Most of the items had multiple parts and each part was scored dichotomously. The distribution of score points is shown in the following table.

Distribution of Score Points by Contents and Type Combination

	Algebra	Data	Function	Geometry	Number	Total
Score Points for Mathematics Knowledge Only	10	3	7	7	7	34
Score Points for Mathematics Pedagogy Knowledge	4	9	12	10	23	58
Total	14	12	19	17	30	92

It was assumed that to answer all of these items correctly, knowledge of the specific mathematics content areas would be required. In addition, for MPK items, specific pedagogy knowledge embedded in the items would also be required. In other words, all items should be involved to obtaining MCK scores for each content area, whereas only items with embedded pedagogy knowledge should be used to obtain MPK scores for each of the three sub-areas. We used a two-stage approach.

First, to preserve the domain validity of the items, the One-Parameter Item Response Theory (Rasch) model was used to estimate the person score underlying the future teachers' responses to a specific set of items according to the content by type combination. Since no person responded to both forms, the estimates were done separately for each form and then equated to form a single scale for that set of items. (Note: Equivalent groups were assumed. If the combination had a sufficient number of common items, the estimation procedure yielded comparable estimates for each form. If there was an insufficient number of common items, separate estimates were obtained for each form and equipercentile equating was used to obtain a single scale for the combination.)

A total of 18 sets of scores were estimated. These were for the 10 cells in the above table plus 5 overall content scores (across both types of items) and 3 separate scores for the 3 MPK areas not shown in the table, with 15, 20, and 23 items, respectively, for Curriculum, Teaching, and Students. These scores were referred to as domain or strand scores. Note that the 3 MPK scales were reflective of both mathematics content and mathematics pedagogy knowledge of the future teachers. They were the unconditional MPK scores used for the analyses presented in the book.

The second stage was to construct the MCK scores from the domain scores. Since all 18 domain scores were assumed to be reflective of content knowledge and pedagogy knowledge, a latent covariance structure model was used to extract the MCK scores. The model assumed the five inter-correlated latent MCK scales to be uncorrelated with the three intercorrelated MPK scales. The results produced five estimated MCK and three MPK factor scores. Note that structurally, the three MPK scores were defined without the influence of mathematics knowledge or conditional—independent of mathematics—content knowledge.

Essentially, these estimated factor scores were composites of the domain or strand scores. The estimated reliability of the individual scales and the average correlations with the different types of items are shown in the table below.

Math Content Knowledge

	Algebra	Function	Number	Geometry	Data
Estimated Reliability	.81	.79	.81	.85	.82
Average Score by Item Correlation					
Mathematics Content Items	.51	.44	.57	.54	.66
Mathematics Pedagogy Items	.11	.14	.13	.14	.13

Note. For MCK scores, the average correlations were with items for the specific mathematics content area.

Math Pedagogy Knowledge Scores

	With Math Knowledge			Uncorrelated with Math		
	Curriculum	Teaching	Students	Curriculum	Teaching	Students
Estimated Reliability	.66	.78	.83	.62	.65	.88
Average Scores by Item Correlation						
Mathematics Content Items	.16	.19	.21	-.17	-.19	.04
Mathematics Pedagogy Items	.25	.32	.38	.16	.13	.31

Note: For MPK scores, the average correlations were with items for all the mathematics content areas.

2. The estimated variance components were derived through maximum likelihood procedures as implemented in statistical anaylis software (SAS).
3. We simply estimated the mean of the conditional distribution conditioning on the total mathematics content knowledge scale which was the average of the five content knowledge scale scores.

Chapter 7

1. Throughout this chapter with only a couple of exceptions the tables are ordered by region, Asia (South Korea and Taiwan); Europe (Bulgaria and Germany); and America (United States and Mexico). This is based on our hypothesis that beliefs are more culturally influenced and that one such cultural influence might be regional. Organizing the tables in this way facilitates examining this hypothesis.

Chapter 9

1. Cohort II was trained either as lower-secondary teachers or as lower- and upper-secondary teachers, whereas Cohort I was trained either as primary and lower-secondary teachers or as lower- and upper-secondary teachers. In addition, the sampled institutions represented different proportions of the four regions/institutions in Cohorts I and II.

Chapter 10

1. We use the term *effect size* with reference to standard analysis of variance terminology. No assumption is made on our part that these estimated effects are indicative of a causal relationship. We use effect size to indicate in standard deviation terms the size of the estimated relationship.

2. For this area of teacher competence we did not include the surrogate pre-test as much of the mathematics was taken in the first 2 years, and given the problems of identifying future teachers at the beginning of their progress it seemed inappropriate. In fact, we did run these analyses, including the surrogate pre-test, and found no appreciable difference from the results reported for South Korea.
3. The variable was dropped from the final model.

Chapter 11

1. In the United States, mathematics scores on the National Assessment of Educational Progress test have risen steadily for 4th and 8th graders since the early 1990s, so that by 2009, they were about one standard deviation higher than in 1990 for 4th graders, and about 0.6 standard deviations higher for 8th graders. There has been no solid explanation for these gains. Neither have the gains been carried over into the 12th-grade NAEP results.
2. Notes: (1) German costs of teacher preparation are divided into two parts. The first phase is the traditional classroom-based training, with estimated instructional costs (including administrative overhead) of $42,900–$48,500 (2006 dollars) for the 4.5 years training of secondary and middle school teachers. Considering that middle and secondary school teacher degrees require two majors plus general pedagogy courses and the second major takes an extra year of instruction, we reduced these instructional costs by 22.2% (1/4.5 years) to make them comparable with the other country training. The second and more expensive phase of teacher training is the 2-year practical classroom training, during which student teachers receive a stipend. The total cost of the second phase is a high $60,000 (2006 dollars) for both middle and secondary school teachers. However, one half of this practical training cost is student teacher stipend, and about one half of the time the student teachers teach, they are replacing regular teachers, so we deduct the cost of that time from training costs. The other half of the second phase cost is for supervisors, and one third of the supervisory cost is for second subject (not mathematics) supervision. So we reduce supervisory cost by one third. The total per-student cost of the practical training is therefore $35,000. The costs shown in the table equal the sum of the costs of the two phases; (2) Costs per student for the United States were estimated for education schools and engineering departments by using department budgets and FTE enrollment to estimate direct instructional costs per student, and adding administrative plus other noninstructional costs for the university as a whole divided by the total number of FTE students enrolled in the university.
3. It is also worth mentioning that the German diploma graduation rate in university subjects such as science or mathematics is considerably lower than the graduation rate for those in teacher education, making the cost of a science graduate as high or higher than that of a teacher education graduate.
4. A major issue in estimating the earnings in different occupations, particularly when making a comparison with teaching, is whether to use yearly earnings (salary) or earnings per hour (wages). Full-time teachers in most countries have duties that require the normal 35–40 hours per week associated with full-time

work. But also in most countries, teachers teach only 10 months per year. Taking into account this vacation period, their hourly earnings usually compare more favorably with hourly earnings in other professions than do their salaries. Many economists consider hourly earnings a better measure of compensation because they measure the cost of the trade-off between working an hour and consuming leisure time. Economists would argue that hourly wages are a better predictor of whether an individual would choose one type of work over another. Teaching offers the possibility of working fewer than 12 months and a somewhat shorter work day at school and this is particularly favorable in most societies for women, who even in postindustrial economies still have primary responsibility for child-rearing. Nevertheless, for those who are concerned with absolute earnings, and in economies where it is difficult to get vacation jobs, annual earnings are probably a better comparison between teacher earnings and those in competing occupations. In addition, as pointed out by Allegretto, Corcoran, and Mishel (2004), there are often inconsistencies in measurement of the number of hours that teachers and other professionals work per week and how many weeks they work per year, leading to inaccurate estimates of wages per hour.

5. The regression estimates are shown in Table 11.5.

Chapter 12

1. The six countries were divided into three tiers based on the relevant scores with two countries in the top tier, three in the middle tier, and one in the lowest tier for total pedagogy and two in each tier for mathematics.

References

Abell Foundation (2001a). Teacher certification reconsidered: Stumbling for quality. Baltimore, MD: Abell. Retrieved September 30, 2003, from www.abell.org/pubsitems/ed_cert_1101.pdf/.

Abell Foundation (2001b). *Teacher certification reconsidered: Stumbling for quality—appendix. Review of research teacher certification and effective teaching.* Baltimore, MD: Abell. Retrieved September 30, 2003, from www.abell.org/pubsitems/ed_cert_appendix_1101.pdf.

Adey, P., Csapo, B., Demetriou, A., Hautamäki, J., & Shayer, M. (2007). Can we be intelligent about intelligence? Why education needs the concept of plastic general ability. *Educational Research Review, 2,* 75–97.

Aebli, H. (1983). *Zwölf grundformen des lehrens: Eine allgemeine didaktik auf psychologischer grundlage* [Twelve basic forms of instruction: General didactics on a psychological basis]. Stuttgart, Germany: Klett.

Ajzen, I. (1985). From intention to action: A theory of planned behavior. In J. Kuhl & J. Beckman (Eds.), *Action-control: From cognition to behavior* (pp. 11–39). Heidelberg, Germany: Springer.

Akiba, M., LeTendre, G. & Scribner, J. P. (2007). Teacher quality, opportunity gap, and national achievement in 46 countries around the world. *Educational Researcher, 36*(7), 369–387. Princeton, NJ: Educational Testing Service.

Allegretto, S. A., Corcoran, S. P., & Mishel, L. (2004). *How does teacher pay compare? Methodological challenges and answers.* Washington, DC: Economic Policy Institute.

Anderson, L. W., Krathwohl, D. R., Airasian, P. W., Cruikshank, K. A., Mayer, R. E., & Pintrich, P. R. (Eds.). (2001). *A taxonomy for learning, teaching and assessing: A revision of Bloom's Taxonomy of Educational Objectives.* New York: Longman.

Anderson, L. W., Ryan, D. W., & Shapiro, B. (Eds.). (1989). *The IEA classroom environment study.* New York: Pergamon Press.

Anderson, M. (1992). *Intelligence and development: A cognitive theory.* London: Blackwell.

Anderson, R. D. (2002). Reforming science teaching: What research says about inquiry. *Journal of Science Teacher Education, 13*(1), 1–12.

Anderson-Levitt, K. M. (2002, April). Teaching culture as national and transnational: A response to teachers' work. *Educational Researcher, 31*(3), 19–21.

Ausubel, D. P. (1968). *Educational psychology: A cognitive view.* New York: Holt, Rinehardt, & Winston.

Baartman, L. K. J., Bastiaens, T. J., Kirschner, P. A., & Van Der Vleuten, C. P. M. (2007). Evaluating assessment quality in competence-based education: A qualitative comparison of two frameworks. *Educational Research Review, 2*(2), 114–129.

Bacon, R. (2000). *The opus majus of Roger Bacon.* Bristol, United Kingdom: Thömmes. (Original work published 1267).

Baker, D., & LeTendre, G. K. (2005). *National differences, global similarities: World culture and the future of schooling.* Palo Alto, CA: Stanford University Press.

Ball, D. L., Hill, H. C., & Bass, H. (2002). *Developing measures of mathematics knowledge for teaching*. Ann Arbor: University of Michigan Press.

Ball, D. L., Hill, H. C., & Bass, H. (2005). Knowing mathematics for teaching: Who knows mathematics well enough to teach third grade, and how can we decide? *American Educator*, 14–22.

Baumert, J., & Kunter, M. (2006). Stichwort: Professionelle kompetenz von lehrkräften [Keyword: Professional competencies of teachers]. *Zeitschrift für Erziehungswissenschaft [Journal of education science]*, 9, 469–520.

Beaton, A. E., Mullis, I. V. S., Martin, M. O., Gonzalez, E. J., Kelly, D. L., & Smith, T. A. (1997). *The mathematics achievement in the middle school years: TIMSS 1995*. Chestnut Hill, MA: TIMSS International Study Center, Boston College.

Bellenberg, G., & Thierack, A. (2003). *Die ausbildung von lehrerinnen und lehrern in Deutschland: Aktueller stand und reformbestrebungen [Teacher education in Germany: Status quo and reform tendencies]*. Opladen, Germany: Leske and Budrich.

Berliner, D. C. (1988). Implication of studies of expertise in pedagogy for teacher education and evaluation. In Educational Testing Service (Ed.), *New directions for teacher assessment: Proceedings of the 1988 ETS Invitational Conference* (pp. 39–67). Princeton, NJ: Educational Testing Service.

Berliner, D. C. (2001). Learning about and learning from expert teachers. *International Journal of Educational Research*, 35, 463–482.

Berliner, D. C. (2004). Describing the behavior and documenting the accomplishments of expert teachers. *Bulletin of Science Technology & Society*, 24(3), 200–212.

Birenbaum, M. (2003). New insights into learning and teaching and their implications for assessment. In M. Seegers, F. J. R. C. Dochy, & E. Cascallar (Eds.), *Optimizing new modes of assessment: In search of qualities and standards* (pp. 13–36). Dordrecht, Netherlands: Kluwer.

Bishop, A. J. (1991). *Mathematical enculturation: A cultural perspective on mathematics education*. Dordrecht, Netherlands: Kluwer.

Blömeke, S. (2001). B. A.- und M. A.-abschlüsse in der lehrerausbildung—Chancen und problem [B.A. and M.A. degrees in teacher education—Benefits and problems]. In N. Seibert (Ed.), *Probleme der lehrerbildung: Analysen, positionen, lösungsversuche [Problems of teacher education: Analyses, positions, and solutions]* (pp. 163–183). Bad Heilbrunn/Obb, Germany: Klinkhardt.

Blömeke, S. (2002). *Universität und lehrerausbildung [University and teacher education]*. Bad Heilbrunn, Germany: Klinkhardt.

Blömeke, S. (2003). Lehren und lernen mit neuen medien: Forschungsstand und forschungsperspektiven [Teaching and learning with new media: State of research and research perspectives]. *Unterrichtswissenschaft [Instruction Research]*, 31, 57–82.

Blömeke, S. (2004). Empirische befunde zur wirksamkeit der lehrerbildung [Empirical findings about the effectiveness of teacher education]. In S. Blömeke, P. Reinhold, G. Tulodziecki, & J. Wildt (Eds.), *Handbuch lehrerbildung [Handbook of teacher education]* (pp. 59–91). Bad Heilbrunn/Braunschweig, Germany: Klinkhardt/Westermann.

Blömeke, S. (2005). *Lehrerausbildung—lehrerhandeln—schülerleistungen: Perspektiven nationaler und internationaler empirischer bildungsforschung [Teacher education—teacher performance—student achievement: Perspectives of national and international empirical research in education]*. Public Lecture on December 10, 2003, at Humboldt University. Berlin, Germany: Humboldt-Universität.

Blömeke, S., Felbrich, A., & Müller, C. (2008). Theoretischer rahmen und untersuchungsdesign [Theoretical framework and study design]. In S. Blömeke, G. Kaiser, & R. Lehmann (Eds.), *Professionelle kompetenz angehender lehrerinnen und Lehrer: Wissen, überzeugungen und lerngelegenheiten Deutscher mathematik-studierender und -referendare—erste ergebnisse zur wirksamkeit der lehrerausbildung [Professional competencies of future teachers: Knowledge, beliefs, and opportunities to learn for German mathematics teachers—First results about the effectiveness of teacher education]* (pp. 15–48). Münster, Germany: Waxmann.

Blömeke, S., Felbrich, A., Müller, C., Kaiser, G., & Lehmann, R. (2008). Effectiveness of teacher education: State of research, measurement issues, and consequences for future studies. *ZDM— The International Journal on Mathematics Education, 40*(5), 719–734.

Blömeke, S., Herzig, G., & Tulodziecki, G. (2007). *Gestaltung von schule: Eine einführung in schultheorie und schulentwicklung [The formation of schools: An introduction to school theory and school development]*. Bad Heilbrunn/Obb, Germany: Klinkhardt.

Blömeke, S., & Kaiser, G. (2010). Mathematics teacher education and gender effects. In H. Forgasz, K.-H. Lee, J. Rossi Becker, & O. Bjorg Steinsthorsdottir (Eds.), *International perspectives on gender and mathematics education*. Charlotte, NC: Information Age Publishing.

Blömeke, S., Kaiser, G., & Lehmann, R. (Eds.). (2008). *Professionelle kompetenz angehender lehrerinnen und Lehrer: Wissen, überzeugungen und lerngelegenheiten Deutscher mathematik-studierender und-referendare—erste ergebnisse zur wirksamkeit der lehrerausbildung [Professional competencies of future teachers: Knowledge, beliefs, and opportunities to learn for German mathematics teachers—First results about the effectiveness of teacher education]*. Münster, Germany: Waxmann.

Blömeke, S., & Paine, L. (2008). Getting the fish out of the water: Considering benefits and problems of doing research on teacher education at an international level. *Teaching and Teacher Education, 24*(8), 2027–2037.

Blömeke, S., & Paine, L. (2009). Berufseinstiegs-programme für lehrkräfte im internationalen vergleich [Occupation entrance programs for instructors in the international comparison]. *Journal Für Lehrerinnen- und Lehrerbildung [Journal for Teaching and Teacher Education], 9*(3), 18–25.

Blömeke, S., Paine, L., Houang, R. T., Hsieh, F.-J., Schmidt, W. H., Tatto, M. T., Bankov, K., Cedillo, T., Cogan, L., Han, S.-I., Santillan, M., Schwille, J. (2008). Future teachers' competence to plan a lesson: Conceptual and methodological challenges in the assessment of pedagogical knowledge and first results of a six-country study on the efficiency of teacher education. *ZDM—The International Journal on Mathematics Education, 40*(5), 749–762.

Blum, W., Drüke-Noe, C., Hartung, R., & Köller, O. (Eds.). (2006). *Bildungsstandards mathematik: Konkret. Sekundarstufe I: Aufgabenbeispiele, unterrichtsanregungen, fortbildungsideen [Standards for school mathematics: Specifics. Lower secondary school: Sample problems, suggestions for instruction, and ideas for in-service training]*. Berlin, Germany: Cornelsen Scriptor.

Blum, W., Galbraith, P. L., Henn, H.-W., & Niss, M. (Eds.). (2007). *Modeling and applications in mathematics education. The 14th ICMI Study*. Berlin, Germany: Springer.

Blum, W., Neubrand, M., Ehmke, T., Senkbeil, M., Jordan, A., Ulfig, F., & Carstensen, C. H. (2004). Mathematische Kompetenz [Mathematical literacy]. In M. Prenzel, J. Baumert, W. Blum, R. Lehmann, D. Leutner, M. Neubrand et al. (Eds.), *PISA 2003: Der bildungsstand der jugendlichen in Deutschland—Ergebnisse des zweiten internationalen vergleichs [PISA 2003: Student achievement in Germany—Results of the second international comparison]* (pp. 47–92). Münster, Germany: Waxmann.

Blumer, H. (1969). *Symbolic interactionism: Perspective and method*. Englewood Cliffs, NJ: Prentice-Hall.

Bodensohn, R., Schneider, C., & Jäger, R. S. (2007). *Studierende drängen in das lehramt! Haben wir anlass zu kompetenzbeobachtung und studierendenauswahl? Studie über studienanfänger an der Universität Koblenz-Landau in Landau [Students push into teacher education! Do we have a need to monitor their competencies or to select them? A study about beginning university students at the University of Koblenz Landau in Landau]*. Landau, Germany: Zentrum für Lehrerbildung.

Bowles, S., Gintis, H., & Osborne, M. (2001). The determinants of earnings: A behavioral approach. *Journal of Economic Literature, 39*(4), 1137–1176.

Boyd, D., Grossman, P., Hammerness, K., Lankford, R. H., Loeb, S., McDonald, M., Reininger, M., Ronfeldt, M., & Wyckoff, J., (2008). Surveying the landscape of teacher education in New York City: Constrained variation and the challenge of innovation. *Education Evaluation and Policy Analysis, 30*, 319–343.

Boyd, D., Lankford, H., Loeb, S., Rockoff, J., & Wyckoff, J. (2008). The narrowing gap in New York City teacher qualifications and its implications for student achievement in high-poverty schools. *Journal of Policy Analysis and Management, 27*(4), 793–818.

Broadfoot, P. (1996). *Education, assessment and society. A sociological analysis.* Buckingham, England: Open University Press.

Broadfoot, P., & Osborn, M. (1991). French lessons: Comparative perspectives on what it means to be a teacher. *Oxford Studies in Comparative Education, 1,* 69–88.

Bromme, R. (1994). Beyond subject mattter: A psychological topology of teachers' professional knowledge. In R. Biehler, R. W. Scholz, R. Sträßer, & B. Winkelmann (Eds.), *Mathematics didactics as a scientific discipline: The state of the art* (pp. 77–88). Dordrecht, Netherlands: Kluwer.

Bromme, R. (1997). Kompetenzen, funktionen, und unterrichtliches handeln des lehrers [Competencies, responsibilities, and instructional performance of teachers]. In F. E. Weinert (Ed.), *Psychologie des unterrichts und der schule [Psychology of instruction and schooling]* (pp. 177–212). Göttingen, Germany: Hogrefe.

Bromme, R. (2005). Thinking and knowing about knowledge: A plea for and critical remarks on psychological research programs on epistemological beliefs. In M. H. G. Hoffmann, J. Lenhard, & F. Seeger (Eds.), *Activity and sign—grounding mathematics education.* New York: Springer.

Brophy, J. (1999). *Teaching.* Brussels: International Academy of Education.

Brophy, J. E., & Good, T. L. (1986). Teacher behavior and student achievement. In M. C. Wittrock (Ed.), *Handbook of research on teaching* (3rd ed., pp. 328–375). London: Macmillan.

Brown, D. F., & Rose, T. D. (1995). Self-reported classroom impact of teachers' theories about learning and obstacles to implementation. *Action in Teacher Education, 17*(1), 20–29.

Brühwiler, C. (2001). Die bedeutung von motivation in der lehrerinnen- und lehrerausbildung [The relevance of motivation in teacher education]. In F. Oser & J. Oelkers (Eds.), *Die wirksamkeit der lehrerbildungssysteme: Von der allrounderbildung zur ausbildung professioneller standards, Nationales Forschungsprogramm 33 [The effectiveness of teacher education systems: From the all-around education to the education of professional standards, National Research Program 33]* (pp. 343–397). Chur/Zürich, Switzerland: Rüegger.

Buckley, D. M. (1982). Teacher language complexity and pupil task involvement. *Research in Science Education, 12*(1), 50–54.

Buehl, M. M., & Alexander, P. (2001). Beliefs about academic knowledge. *Educational Psychology Review, 13,* 382–418.

Byrne, B. M. (2003). Testing for equivalent self-concept measurement across culture. In K. A. Bollen & S. J. Long (Eds.), *Testing structural equation models* (pp. 136–162). Newbury Park, CA: Sage.

Calderhead, J. (1996). Teachers' beliefs and knowledge. In D. C. Berliner & R. Calfee (Eds.), *Handbook of Educational Psychology* (pp. 709–725). New York: Macmillan.

Canter, L., & Canter, M. (1976). *Assertive discipline: A take-charge approach for today's educator.* Santa Monica, CA: Lee Canter & Associates.

Capps, L. R., & Pickreign, J. (1993, September). Language connections in mathematics: A critical part of mathematics instruction. *Arithmetic Teacher, 41*(1), 8–12.

Carnoy, M., Brodziak, I., Loyalka, P., Reininger, M., & Luschei, T. (2006). *How much would it cost to attract individuals with more math knowledge into middle school (lower secondary) teaching: A seven-country comparison.* Palo Alto, CA: School of Education, Stanford University.

Carroll, J. B. (1962). The prediction of success in intensive foreign language training. In R. Glaser (Ed.), *Training research and education* (pp. 87–136). Pittsburgh, PA: University of Pittsburgh Press.

Carroll, J. B. (1963). A model of school learning. *Teachers College Record, 64*(8), 723–733.

Clarke, D. (2003). International comparative research in mathematics education. In A. J. Bishop, M. A. Clements, C. Keitel, J. Kilpatrick, & F. K. S. Leung (Eds.), *Second international handbook of mathematics education* (pp. 143–184). Dordrecht, Netherlands: Kluwer.

Clift, R. T., & Brady, P. (2005). Research on methods courses and field experiences. In M. Cochran-Smith & K. M. Zeichner (Eds.), *Studying teacher education: The report of the AERA Panel on Research and Teacher Education*. Mahwah, NJ: Lawrence Erlbaum.

Clotfelter, C., Ladd, H., & Vigdor, J. (2007). *How and why do teachers matter for student achievement?* Cambridge, MA: National Bureau of Economic Research, Working Paper 12828.

Cobb, P. (1994). Where is the mind? Constructivist and sociocultural perspectives on mathematical development. *Educational Researcher, 23*, 13–20.

Cochran-Smith, M., & Zeichner, K. M. (Eds.). (2005). Studying teacher education: The report of the AERA Panel on Research and Teacher Education. Mahwah, NJ: Lawrence Erlbaum.

Cooney, T. J., Barry, E. S., & Bridget, A. (1998). Conceptualizing belief structures of preservice secondary mathematics teachers. *Journal for Research in Mathematics Education, 29*(3), 306–333.

Corcoran, S., Evans, W. N., & Schwab, R .S. (2002). *Changing labor market opportunities for women and the quality of teachers, 1957–1992.* National Bureau of Economic Research, Working Paper 9180. Available at www.nber.org/papers/w9180.

Czerwenka, K., & Nölle, K. (2000). Probleme des erwerbs professioneller kompetenz im kontext universitärer lehrerausbildung [Problems of the acquisition of professional competencies in the context of university teacher education]. In O. Jaumann-Graumann & W. Köhnlein (Eds.). *Lehrerprofessionalität—lehrerprofessionalisierung [Teacher professionalism—teacher professionalization]* (pp. 67–77). Bad Heilbrunn, Germany: Klinkhardt.

D'Ambrosio, U. (1995). Multiculturalism and mathematics education. *International Journal on Mathematics, Science, Technology Education, 26*(3), 337–346.

Dahrendorf, R. (1965). *Bildung ist bürgerrecht: Plädoyer für eine aktive bildungspolitik. [Education is a civil right: Plea for an active educational policy].* Hamburg, Germany: Nannen.

Dann, H.-D., Diegritz, T., & Rosenbusch, H. S. (1999). *Gruppenunterricht im schulalltag: Realität und chancen [Group work in the everyday classroom: Reality and chances].* Erlangen, Germany: Universitätsbibliothek.

Dann, H.-D., Müller-Fohrbrodt, G., & Cloetta, B. (1981). Sozialisation junger lehrer im beruf: "Praxisschock" drei jahre spatter [Socialization of young teachers into the profession: "Practice shock" 3 years later]. *Zeitschrift für Entwicklungspsychologie und Pädagogische Psychologie [Journal of Developmental Psychology and Educational Psychology], 13*, 251–262.

Darling-Hammond, L., & Youngs, P. (2002). Defining "highly qualified teachers": What does "scientifically-based research" actually tell us? *Educational Researcher, 31*(9), 13–25.

Deci, E. L., & Ryan, R. (1985). *Intrinsic motivation and self-determination in human behavior.* New York: Plenum.

De Corte, E., Greer, B., & Verschaffel, L. (1996). Mathematics teaching and learning. In D.C. Berliner & R.C. Calfee (Eds.), *Handbook of educational psychology* (pp. 491–549). New York: Simon & Schuster Macmillan.

Dierick, S., & Dochy, F. J. R. C. (2001). New lines in edumetrics: New forms of assessment lead to new assessment criteria. *Studies in Educational Evaluation, 27*, 307–329.

Dochy, F., Gijbels, D., & Segers, M. (2006). Learning and the emerging new assessment culture. In L. Verschaffel, F. Dochy, M. Boekaerts, & S. Vosniadou (Eds.), *Instructional psychology: Past, present and future trends* (pp. 191–206). Oxford, United Kingdom: Elsevier.

Dupriez, V., Dumay, X., & Vause, A. (2008). How do school systems manage pupils' heterogeneity? *Comparative Education Review, 52*(2), 245–273.

Eberle, T. & Pollak, G. (2006). Studien- und berufswahlmotivation von Passauer lehramtsstudierenden [Motivation of student teachers in Passau regarding program and occupational choices]. In N. Seibert (Ed.), *Paradigma. Beiträge aus forschung und lehre aus dem Zentrum für Lehrerbildung und Fachdidaktik [Paradigm: Contributions from research and teaching at the Center of Teacher Education and Subject Didactics]* (pp. 19–37). Passau: Zentrum für Lehrerbildung und Fachdidaktik. Retrieved November 21, 2007, from www.uni-passau.de/fileadmin/dokumente/einrichtungen/zlf/paradigm/2006_10.pdf/.

Educational Testing Service (ETS). (2005). *The praxis series: Principles of learning and teaching: grades 5–9 (0523)*. Princeton, NJ: Author.

Einsiedler, W. (1997). Unterrichtsqualität und leistungsentwicklung: Literaturüberblick [Instructional quality and achievement development: Literature survey]. In F. E. Weinert & A. Helmke (Eds.), *Entwicklung im grundschulalter [Development at the primary school age]* (pp. 225–240). Weinheim, Germany: Beltz Psychologie Verlags Union.

Elmore, R. (1993). School decentralisation: Who gains? Who loses? In J. Hannaway & M. Carnoy (Eds.), *Decentralization and school improvement: Can we fulfill the promise?*(pp. 33–54). San Francisco, CA: Jossey-Bass.

Emmer, E. T., & Stough, L. M. (2001). Classroom management: A critical part of educational psychology, with implications for teacher education. *Educational Psychologist, 36,* 103–112.

Eraut, M. (1994). *Developing professional knowledge and competence*. London: Falmer Press.

Ernest, P. (1991a). Mathematics teacher education and quality. *Assessment and Evaluation in Higher Education, 16*(1), 56–65.

Ernest, P. (1991b). *The philosophy of mathematics education*. London: Falmer Press.

Evertson, C. M., & Weinstein, C. S. (Eds.). (2006). *Handbook of classroom management: Research, practice, and contemporary issues*. Mahwah, NJ: Erlbaum.

Eye, A. V. (1999). Kognitive komplexität: Messung und validität [Cognitive complexity: Assessment and validity]. *Zeitschrift für Differentielle und Diagnostische Psychologie [Journal of Differential and Diagnostic Psychology], 2,* 81–96.

Fend, H. (1980). *Theorie der Schule [Theory of schooling]*. München, Germany: Urban and Schwarzenberg.

Fennema, E., Carpenter, T. P., & Loef, M. (1990). *Teacher belief scale: Cognitively guided instruction project*. Madison: University of Wisconsin Press.

Fennema, E., Peterson, P., Carpenter, T., & Lubinski, C. (1990). Teachers' attributions and beliefs about girls, boys, and mathematics. *Educational Studies in Mathematics, 21,* 55–69.

Fischer, R., & Malle, G. (1985). *Mensch und mathematik [Humans and mathematics]*. Mannheim, Germany: BI Wissenschaftsverlag.

Floden, R., & Meniketti, M. (2005). Research on the effects of coursework in the arts and sciences and in the foundations of education. In M. Cochran-Smith & K. M. Zeichner (Eds.), *Studying teacher education: The report of the AERA Panel on Research and Teacher Education*. Mahwah, NJ: Lawrence Erlbaum.

Fraser, B. J., Walberg, H. J., Welch, W. W., & Hattie, J. A. (1987). Syntheses of educational productivity research. *International Journal of Educational Research, 11,* 145–252.

Freudenthal, H. (1983). *Didactical phenomenology of mathematical structures.* Dordrecht, Netherlands: D. Reidel.

Fried, L. (2002). *Pädagogisches professionswissen und schulentwicklung: Eine systemtheoretische einführung in die grundkategorien der schultheorie [Professional knowledge of teachers and school development: A system-theoretical introduction to the basic categories of school theory]*. Weinheim, Germany: Juventa.

Goetz, T., Pekrun, R., Zirngibl, A., Jullien, S., Kleine, M., vom Hofe, R., et al. (2004). Leistung und emotionales erleben im fach mathematik [Achievement and emotional experiences in mathematics]. *Zeitschrift für Entwicklungspsychologie und Pädagogische Psychologie [Journal of Developmental Psychology and Educational Psychology], 18*(3/4), 201–212.

Goldberg, E. (1992). Beweisen im mathematikunterricht der sekundarstufe 1: Ergebnisse— schwierigkeiten—möglichkeiten [Proofs in lower-secondary mathematics: Results—difficulties—chances]. *Mathematikunterricht [Mathematics instruction], 38*(6), 33–46.

Goldhaber, D. D., & Brewer, D. J. (2000). Does teacher certification matter? High school teacher certification status and student achievement. *Educational Evaluation and Policy Analysis, 22*(2), 129–145.

Grassmann, M., Mirwald, E., Klunter, M., & Veith, U. (1995). Arithmetische kompetenzen von schulanfängern [Arithmetic competencies of school beginners]. *Sachunterricht und Mathematik in der Primarstufe [Social Sciences and Mathematics in Primary School], 23*, 302–321.

Grigutsch, S., Raatz, U., & Törner, G. (1998). Einstellungen gegenüber mathematik bei mathematiklehrern [Epistemological beliefs of mathematics teachers about mathematics]. *Journal für Mathematik-Didaktik [Journal for Mathematics Didactics], 19*, 3–45.

Grigutsch, S., & Törner, G. (1994). Mathematische weltbilder bei sudienanfängern: Eine erhebung [Mathematical world views of beginning university students: A survey]. *Journal für Mathematikdidaktik [Journal for Mathematics Didactics], 15*, 211–251.

Grossman, P. L. (1990). *The making of a teacher: Teacher knowledge and teacher education.* New York: Teachers College Press.

Grossman, P. (2005). Research on pedagogical approaches in teacher education. In M. Cochran-Smith & K. M. Zeichner (Eds.), *Studying teacher education: The report of the AERA Panel on Research and Teacher Education.* Mahwah, NJ: Lawrence Erlbaum.

Gutiérrez, R., & Slavin, R. E. (1992). Achievement effects of the nongraded elementary school: A best evidence synthesis. *Review of Educational Research, 62*, 333–376.

Ham, S.-H., Kim, R.-Y., & Tanner, P. (2008). *Taking beliefs and knowledge seriously: The problems of language and scaling in alternative methods for comparative research on teacher knowledge.* Paper presented at the Comparative & International Education Society (CIES) Conference in 2008 in New York.

Hambleton, R. K. (2002). Adapting achievement tests into multiple languages for international assessment. In A. C. Porter & A. Gamoran (Eds.), *Methodological advances in cross-national surveys of educational achievement* (pp. 58–79). Board on International Board Comparative Studies in Education, Center for Education, Division of Behavioral and Social Sciences and Education. Washington, DC: National Academy Press.

Hanna, G. (2000). Proof, explanation and exploration: An overview. *Educational Studies in Mathematics, 44*, 5–23.

Hanushek, E. (1997, Summer). Assessing the effects of school resources on student performance: An update. *Educational Evaluation and Policy Analysis, 19*(2), 141–164.

Hanushek, E. (2009). The economic value of education and cognitive skills. In G. Sykes, B. Schneider, & D. N. Plank (Eds.), *Handbook of education policy research.* (pp. 39–56). New York: Routledge.

Hanushek, E. A. (1994). *Making schools work: Improving performance and controlling costs.* Washington, DC: Brookings Institution.

Hanushek, E. A., & Wößmann, L. (2006). Does educational tracking affect performance and inequality? Differences-in-differences evidence across countries. *Economic Journal, 116*(510), 63–73.

Hartmann, J., & Reiss, K. (2000). Auswirkungen der Bearbeitung räumlich-geometrischer Aufgaben auf das Raumvorstellungsvermögen [Effects of working on spatial-geometrical tasks on the spacial visualization capacity]. In D. Leutner & R. Brünken (Eds.), *Neue medien in unterricht, aus und weiterbildung: Aktuelle ergebnisse empirischer pädagogischer forschung [New media in instruction, pre- and inservice training: New results of empirical educational research]* (pp. 85–93). Münster, Germany: Waxmann.

Healy, L., & Hoyles, C. (1998). *Justifying and proving in school mathematics* (Technical report on the nationwide survey). London: Institute of Education, University of London.

Heine, S., Lehmann, D. R., Peng, K., & Greenholtz, J. (2002). What's wrong with cross-cultural comparisons of subjective Likert scales? The reference group effect. *Journal of Personality and Social Psychology, 82*(6), 903–918.

Hengartner, E., & Röthlisberger, H. (1995). Rechenfähigkeit von Schulanfängern [Numeracy skills of school beginners]. In H. Brügelmann, H. Balhorn, & I. Füssenich (Eds.), *Am rande der schrift: Zwischen sprachenvielfalt und analphabetismus [At the edge of the writing: Between language variety and illiteracy]* (pp. 66–86). Lengwil, Switzerland: Libelle.

Helmke, A. (2004). *Unterrichtsqualität: Erfassen, bewerten, verbessern* [Instructional quality: Measuring, evaluating, improving] (3rd Ed.). Seelze, Germany: Kallmeyersche Publishing House.

Helmke, A., & Jäger, R. S. (Eds.). (2002). *Das projekt MARKUS:Mathematik-gesamterhebung Rheinland-Pfalz: Kompetenzen, unterrichtsmerkmale, schulkontext. [The MARKUS project: Mathematics survey Rhineland-Palatinate: Competencies, instructional characteristics, and school context.]* Landau:Verlag Empirische Pädagogik.

Henke, R. R., Chen, X., Geis, S, & Knepper, P. (2000). *Progress through the teacher pipeline: 1992– 1993 college graduates and elementary and secondary teaching as of 1997.* Washington, DC: National Center for Education Statistics.

Herzog,W., Müller, H.-P., Brunner,A., & Herzog, S. (2004, March). Studien- und berufswahlmotive aus berufsbiographischer sicht: Erste ergebnisse einer studie zu karriereverläufen von primarlehrpersonen [Motives of program and occupational choices from a biographical point-of-view: First results of a study on career processes of primary teachers]. In B. Weinmann-Lutz, *Lehrern werden—und bleiben studien zur (selbst-)rekrutierung und zum verbleib im beruf [Becoming a teacher—and remaining it. Studies on (self-)recruitment into the occupation].* Working group conducted at the Bildung über die Lebenszeit [Education over the Lifetime] International Congress Conference at the University of Zurich, Switzerland.

Heymann, H.W. (1996). *Allgemeinbildung und mathematik [General education and mathematics].* Weinheim, Germany: Beltz.

Hill, H. C., & Ball, D. L. (2004). Learning mathematics for teaching: Results from California's mathematics professional development institutes. *Journal for Research in Mathematics Education, 35*(5), 330–351.

Hill, H. C., Ball, D. L., Sleep, L., & Lewis, J. M. (2007). Assessing teachers' mathematical knowledge: What knowledge matters and what evidence counts? In F. Lester (Ed.), *Handbook for Research on Mathematics Education* (2nd ed.) (pp. 111–155). Charlotte, NC: Information Age Publishing.

Hill, H., Rowen, B., & Ball, D. L. (2005). Effects of teachers' mathematical knowledge for teaching on student achievement. *American Educational Research Journal, 42*(2), 371–406.

Hill, H., Schilling, S. G., & Ball, D. L. (2004). Developing measures of teachers' mathematics knowledge for teaching. *The Elementary School Journal, 105,* 11–30.

Hischer, H. (2002). *Mathematikunterricht und neue medien [Mathematics instruction and new media].* Hildesheim, Germany: Franzbecker.

Hofer, B. K., & Pintrich, P. R. (1997).The development of epistemological theories: Beliefs about knowledge and knowing and their relation to learning. *Review of Educational Research, 67,* 88–140.

Hofer, B. K., & Pintrich, P. R. (2002). *Personal epistemology: The psychology of beliefs about knowledge and knowing.* Mahwah, NJ: Lawrence Erlbaum.

Hofstede, G. (2001). *Culture's consequences: Comparing values, behaviors, institutions, and organizations across nations* (2nd ed.).Thousand Oaks, CA: Sage Publications.

Hopmann, S., & Riquarts, K. (1995). Didaktik und/oder curriculum: Grundprobleme einer international vergleichenden didaktik [Didactics and/or curriculum: Fundamental problems of an comparative didactics]. In S. Hopmann & K. Riquarts (Eds.), *Didaktik und/oder curriculum [Didactics and/or curriculum]* (pp. 9–34).Weinheim, Germany: Beltz.

HRK—Hochschulrektorenkonferenz (Ed.). (2007). *Von Bologna nach Quedlinburg: Die reform des lehramtsstudiums in Deutschland. [From Bologna to Quedlinburg: The reform of teacher education in Germany].* Bonn, Germany: BMBF.

Humenberger, J., & Reichel, H.-C. (1995). *Fundamentale ideen der angewandten mathematik und ihre umsetzung im unterricht [Fundamental ideas of applied mathematics and their application in instruction].* Mannheim, Germany: BI Verlag.

Jäger, R. S., & Milbach, B. (1994). Studierende im lehramt als praktikanten—eine empirische evaluation des blockpraktikums [Future teachers as trainees: An evaluation of the practicum]. *Empirische Pädagogik [Empirical Pegagogy], 8*(2), 199–234.

Johnson, D., Johnson, R., & Stanne, M. (2000). *Cooperative learning methods: A meta-analysis.* Retrieved September 24, 2009, from www.clcrc.com/pages/cl-methods.html.

Jonsson, A., & Svingby, G. (2007). The use of scoring rubrics: Reliability, validity and educational consequences. *Educational Research Review, 2*(2), 130–144.

(KMK) Sekretariat der Ständigen Konferenz der Kultusminister der Länder in der Bundesrepublik Deutschland [Secretariat of the Standing Conference of the Ministers of Education and Cultural Affairs of the States in the Federal Republic of Germany]. (Ed.). (2003). *Bildungsstandards im fach mathematik für den mittleren schulabschluss [Standards of school mathematics for graduation at the end of lower-secondary school].* Bonn, Germany: Author.

(KMK) Sekretariat der Ständigen Konferenz der Kultusminister der Länder in der Bundesrepublik Deutschland [Secretariat of the Standing Conference of the Ministers of Education and Cultural Affairs of the States in the Federal Republic of Germany]. (2004a). *Bildungsstandards im fach mathematik für den mittleren schulabschluss (jahrgangsstufe 10)[Standards of school mathematics for graduation at the end of lower-secondary school (grade 10)].* München, Germany: Wolters Kluwer.

(KMK) Sekretariat der Ständigen Konferenz der Kultusminister der Länder in der Bundesrepublik Deutschland [Secretariat of the Standing Conference of the Ministers of Education and Cultural Affairs of the States in the Federal Republic of Germany]. (2004b). *Standards für die lehrerbildung: Bildungswissenschaften [Standards for teacher education: Education sciences].* Resolution of the conference of Ministers for the Arts and Culture on October 16, 2004. Bonn, Germany: Author.

(KMK) Sekretariat der Ständigen Konferenz der Kultusminister der Länder in der Bundesrepublik Deutschland [Secretariat of the Standing Conference of the Ministers of Education and Cultural Affairs of the States in the Federal Republic of Germany]. (Ed.). (2005). *Eckpunkte für die gegenseitige anerkennung von Bachelor- und Masterabschlüssen in studiengängen, mit denen die bildungsvoraussetzungen für ein lehramt vermittelt warden [Cornerstones for the mutual acknowledgement of Bachelor and Masters degrees in programs where the prerequisites for the teaching profession are obtained].* Resolution of the conference of Ministers for the Arts and Culture on June 02, 2005. Bonn, Germany: Author.

Kaiser, G. (1995). Realitätsbezüge im mathematikunterricht: Ein überblick über die aktuelle und historische diskussion [Real-world connections in mathematics instruction: An overview of the current and historical discussion]. In G. Graumann, T. Jahnke, G. Kaiser, & J. Meyer (Eds.), *Materialien für einen realitätsbezogenen mathematikunterricht [Materials for mathematics instruction with real-world connections]* (Vol. 2, pp. 66–84). Hildesheim, Germany: Franzbecker.

Kane, R. G., Sandretto, S., & Heath, C. (2002). Telling half the story: A critical review of the research into tertiary teachers' beliefs. *Review of Educational Research, 72*(2), 177–228.

Kang, N.-H. & Hong, M., (2008). Achieving excellence in teacher workforce and equity in learning opportunities in South Korea. *Educational Researcher, 37*(3), 200–207.

Kant, I. (1786). *Metaphysische anfangsgründe der naturwissenschaft [Metaphysical rudiments of the natural science].* Riga, Latvia: Johann Friedrich Hartknoch.

Keeves, J. P. (1992). Longitudinal research methods. In J.P. Keeves (Ed.), *The IEA technical handbook* (pp. 15–38). Hague, The Netherlands: International Association for the Evaluation of Educational Achievement.

Klieme, E., Schümer, G., & Knoll, S. (2001). Mathematikunterricht in der sekundarstufe I. "aufgabenkultur" und unterichtsgestaltang [Mathematics instruction in lower-secondary school: "A culture of working on problems" and instructional organization]. In Bundesministerium für Bildung und Forschung [Federal Ministry for Education and Research] (Ed.). *TIMSS—Impulse für Schule und Unterricht [TIMSS—Impulses for school and instruction]* (pp. 43-57). Bonn, Germany: BMBF.

Kline, S. L., Pelias, R. J., & Delia, J. G. (1991). The predictive validity of cognitive complexity measures on social perspective-taking and counseling communication. *International Journal of Personal Construct Psychology, 4*, 347–357.

Köller, O., & Klieme, E. (2000). Geschlechtsdifferenzen in den mathematisch-naturwissenschaftlichen leistungen [Gender differences in mathematics and science achievement]. In J. Baumert, W. Bos, & R. H. Lehmann (Eds.), *Dritte internationale mathematik- und naturwissenschaftsstudie: Mathematische und naturwissenschaftliche bildung am ende der schullaufbahn (Vol. II: Mathematische und physikalische kompetenzen am ende der schullaufbahn [Third international mathematics and natural science study: Mathematical and scientific literacy at the end of schooling (Vol. II: Mathematical and physical literacy at the end of schooling)]* (pp. 373–404). Opladen, Germany: Leske & Budrich.

Kotzschmar, J. (2004). *Hochschulseminare im vergleich: Chancen und ergebnisse unterschiedlicher lehrformen in der wissenschaftlichen ausbildung von lehrkräften [University seminars compared: Chances and results of different kinds of teaching in the academic phase of teacher education].* Frankfurt am Main, Germany: Peter Lang.

Kounin, J. S. (1970). *Discipline and group management in classrooms.* New York: Holt, Rinehart & Winston.

Kozol, J. (2006). *The shame of the nation: The restoration of apartheid in schooling in America.* New York: Random House.

Krapp, A. (2001). Interesse [Interest]. In D. H. Rost (Ed.), *Handwörterbuch pädagogische psychologie [Concise dictionary of educational psychology]* (2nd ed., pp. 286–294). Weinheim, Germany: Psychologie Verlags Union.

Krauss, S., Kunter, M., Brunner, M., Baumert, J., Blum, W., Neubrand, M. et al. (2004). CO-ACTIV. Professionswissen von lehrkräften, kognitiv aktivierender mathematikunterricht und die entwicklung von mathematischer kompetenz [COACTIV. Professional competence of teachers, cognitively activating instruction, and the development of students' mathematical literacy]. In J. Doll & M. Prenzel (Eds.), *Bildungsqualität von schule: Lehrerprofessionalisierung, unterrichtsentwicklung und schülerförderung als strategien der qualitätsverbesserung [Education quality of schooling: Teacher professionalism, instruction development and student support as strategies of quality improvement]* (pp. 31–53). Münster, Germany: Waxmann.

Krauthausen, G., & Scherer, P. (2007). *Einführung in die mathematikdidaktik [Introduction to the mathematics education].* München, Germany: Elsevier.

Kunter, M., Dubberke, T., Baumert, J., Blum, W., Brunner, M., & Jordan, A. (2006). Mathematikunterricht in den PISA-klassen: Rahmenbedingungen, formen und lehr-lernprozesse [Mathematics instruction in PISA classes: Context conditions, forms, and learning processes]. In M. Prenzel, J. Baumert, W. Blum, R. Lehmann, D. Leutner, M. Neubrand et al. (Eds.), *PISA 2003. Untersuchungen zur Kompetenzentwicklung im Verlaufe eines Schuljahres [PISA 2003. Studies on the development of competencies over one school year]* (pp. 161–194). Münster, Germany: Waxmann.

Lampert, M. (2001). *Teaching problems and the problems of teaching.* New Haven, CT: Yale University Press.

Leder, G. C. Pekhonen, E., & Törner, G. (Eds.). (2002). *Beliefs: A hidden variable in mathematics education?* Dordrecht, Netherlands: Kluwer.

Leinhardt, G., & Greeno, J. (1986). The cognitive skill of teaching. *Journal of Educational Psychology, 78,* 75–95.

LeTendre, G., Baker, D. P., Akiba, M., Goesling, B., & Wiseman, A. (2001). Teachers' work: Institutional isomorphism and cultural variation in the U.S., Germany, and Japan. *Educational Researcher, 30*(6), 3–15.

LeTendre, G. K., Hofer, B. K., & Shimizu, H. (2003). What is tracking? Cultural expectations in the United States, Germany, and Japan. *American Educational Research Journal, 40*(1), 43–89.

Little, T. D. (1997). Mean and covariance structures (MACS) analyses of cross-cultural data: Practical and theoretical issues. *Multivariate Behavioral Research, 32*(1), 53–76.

Livingston, C., & Borko, H. (1989). Cognition and improvisation: Differences in mathematics instruction by expert and novice teachers. *American Educational Research Journal, 26,* 473–498.

Ma, L. (1999). *Knowing and teaching elementary mathematics.* Mahwah, NJ: Lawrence Erlbaum.

Maaß, K. (2004). *Mathematisches modellieren im unterricht[Mathematical modeling in instruction]*. Hildesheim, Germany: Franzbecker.

Malle, G. (2000). Funktionen untersuchen—ein durchgängiges thema [Examining functions—a constant topic.]. *Mathematik Lehren [Teaching Mathematics] 103*, 4–7.

Mayer, R. E. (2003). *Learning and instruction*. Upper Saddle River, NJ: Prentice Hall.

Mayr, J. (2003). *Lehrern werden? Abschlussbericht zum projekt evaluierung des beratungsmaterials "lehrer/ in werden?" [Become a teacher? The final report on the project evaluation of the consulting material "become a teacher?"]*. Linz, Austria: Pädagogische Akademie der Diözese [Educational Academy of the Diocese].

McDonald, J. P. (1992). *Teaching: Making sense of an uncertain craft*. New York: Teachers College Press.

Möller, J., & Köller, O. (2004). Die genese akademischer selbstkonzepte: Effekte dimensionaler und sozialer vergleiche [The genesis of academic self concepts: Effects of dimensional and social comparisons]. *Psychologische Rundschau [Psychological Review], 55*, 19–27.

Monk, D. H., & King, J. A. (1994). Multilevel teacher resource effects on pupil performance in secondary mathematics and science: The case of teacher subject-matter preparation. In R. Ehrenberg (Ed.), *Choices and consequences: Contemporary policy issues in education* (pp. 29–58). Ithaca, NY: ILR Press.

Mössner, A. (2000). Funktionen dynamisch untersuchen [Dynamically examining functions]. *Mathematik Lehren [Mathematics Teaching], 103*, 22–50.

Muijs, D., & Reynolds, D. (2000). School effectiveness and teacher effectiveness in mathematics: Some preliminary findings from the evaluation of the mathematics enhancement programme (primary). *School Effectiveness and School Improvement, 11*, 273–303.

Mullis, I. V. S., Martin, M. O., Gonzalez, E. J., & Chrostowski, S. J. (2004). *TIMSS international mathematics report. TIMSS 2003*. Chestnut Hill, MA: TIMSS & PIRLS International Study Center, Boston College.

Mullis, I. V. S., Martin, M. O., Gonzalez, E. J., Gregory, K. D., Garden, R. A., O'Connor, K. M., Chrostowski, S. J., & Smith, T. A. (2000). *TIMSS international mathematics report. TIMSS 1999*. Chestnut Hill, MA: TIMSS International Study Center, Boston College.

Mullis, I. V. S., Martin, M. O., Smith, T. A., Garden, R. A., Gregory, K. D., Gonzalez, E. J., et al. (2003). *TIMSS assessment frameworks and specifications 2003* (2nd ed). Chestnut Hill, MA: TIMSS International Study Center, Boston College.

Murnane, R., Singer, J. D., Willett, J. B., Kemple, J. J., & Olsen, R. J. (1991). *Who will teach*. Cambridge, MA: Harvard University Press.

(NBPTS) National Board for Professional Teaching Standards. (2003). *What teachers should know and be able to do*. Retrieved June 28, 2005, from www.nbpts.org/pdf/coreprops.pdf.

(NCTM) National Council of Teachers of Mathematics. (1991). *Professional standards for teaching mathematics*. Reston, VA: Author.

(NCTM) National Council of Teachers of Mathematics (2000). *Principles and standards for school mathematics*. Reston, VA: Author.

National Council on Teacher Quality. (2010). *Evaluating the fundamentals of teacher training programs in Texas* (p. 148). Washington, DC: Author.

National Research Council. (2003). *Understanding others, educating ourselves: Getting more from international comparative studies in education*. (C. Chabbott, & E. J. Elliott (Eds.). Washington, DC: National Academy Press.

National Research Council. (2010). *Preparing teachers: Building evidence for sound policy*. Committee on the Study of Teacher Preparation Programs in the United States, Division of Behavioral and Social Sciences and Education (p. 232). Washington, DC: National Academy Press.

Nespor, J. (1987). The role of beliefs in the practice of teaching. *Journal of Curriculum Studies, 19*(4), 317–328.

Neuweg, G. H. (1999). *Könnerschaft und implizites wissen: Zur lehr-lerntheoretischen bedeutung der erkenntnis- und wissenstheorie Michael Polanyis [Skill and tacit knowledge: On the importance of Michael Polanyi's theory of cognition and epistemology for the learning theories]*. Münster, Germany: Waxmann.

Niggli, A. (2004). Welche Komponenten reflexiver beruflicher Entwicklung interessieren angehende Lehrerinnen und Lehrer? Faktorenstruktur eines Fragebogens und erste empirische Ergebnisse [Which components of reflective professional development are of interest to future teachers? Factorial structure of a questionnaire and first empirical results]. *Schweizerische Zeitschrift für Bildungswissenschaften [Swiss Journal of Educational Sciences], 26*(2), 343–362.

OECD (Organization for Economic Cooperation and Development). (2001). *Knowledge and skills for life*. Paris: OECD, PISA.

OECD. (2004). *Learning for tomorrow's world*. Paris: OECD, PISA.

OECD. (2007). *Science competencies for tomorrow's world*. Paris: OECD. PISA.

OECD. (2008a). *Education at a glance 2008: A briefing note for Mexico*. Paris: OECD. PISA.

OECD. (2008b). *Education at a glance 2008: A briefing note for Korea*. Paris: OECD. PISA.

OECD. (2010). *Programme for International Student Assessment*. Retrieved on July 12, 2010, from www.pisa.oecd.org.

Op't Eynde, P., DeCorte, E., & Verschaffel, L. (2002). Framing students' mathematics-related beliefs: A quest for conceptual clarity and a comprehensive categorization. In G. C. Leder, E. Pehkonen, & G. Törner (Eds.), Beliefs: *A hidden variable in mathematics education?* (pp. 13–37). Dordrecht, Netherlands: Kluwer.

Oser, F. (1997a). Standards in der lehrerbildung. Teil 1: Berufliche kompetenzen, die hohen qualitäsmerkmalen entsprechen [Standards of teacher education. Part 1: Professional competencies which correspond to high quality characteristics]. *Beiträge zur Lehrerbildung [Contributions to Teacher Education], 1997*(1), 26–37.

Oser, F. (1997b). Standards in der lehrerbildung. Teil 2: Wie werden standards in der schweizerischen lehrerbildung erworben? Erste empirische ergebnisse [Standards of teacher education. Part 2: How are standards in Swiss teacher education acquired? First empirical results]. *Beiträge zur Lehrerbildung [Contributions to Teacher Education], 1997*(2), 210–228.

Oser, F., & Oelkers, J. (Eds.). (2001). *Die Wirksamkeit der Lehrerbildungssysteme. Von der Allrounderbildung zur Ausbildung professioneller Standards. Nationales Forschungsprogramm 33 [The effectiveness of the teacher education system. From the All-around education to the education of professional standards. National research program 33]*. Chur & Zürich, Switzerland: Rüegger.

PACT Consortium (2005). *Performance assessment for California teachers*. Retrieved November 17, 2008, from www.pacttpa.org.

Pajares, F. (1992). Teachers' beliefs and educational research: Cleaning up a messy construct. *Review of Educational Research, 62*, 307–332.

Parsons, T. (1977). Die schulklasse als soziales system: Einige ihrer funktionen in der Amerikanischen gesellschaft [The school class as a social system: Some of its functions in American society]. In T. Parsons, *Sozialstruktur und persönlichkeit [Social structure and personality]* (2nd ed., pp. 161–193). Frankfurt, Germany: Fachbuchhandlung für Psychologie. (Original work published in 1959)

Parsons, J. E., Adler, T. F., & Kaczala, C. M. (1982). Socialization of achievement attitudes and beliefs: Parental influences. *Child Development, 53*, 310–321.

Peterson, P. L., Fennema, E., Carpenter, T. P., & Loef, M. (1989). Teachers' pedagogical content beliefs in mathematics. *Cognition and Instruction, 6*(1), 1–40.

Picht, G. (1964). *Die Deutsche bildungskatastrophe. Analyse und dokumentation [The German education disaster. Analysis and documentation]*. Olten, Switzerland: Walter.

Postlethwaite, N. T. (1967). *School organization and student achievement: A study based on achievement in mathematics in twelve countries*. Stockholm, Sweden: Almqvist & Wiksell.

Prenzel, M., Baumert, J., Blum, W., Lehmann, R., Leutner, D., Neubrand, M., Pekrun, R., Rolff, H. G., Rost, J., & Schiefele, U. (2004). (Eds.). *PISA 2003. Der bildungsstand der jugendlichen in Deutschland—ergebnisse des zweiten internationalen vergleichs [PISA 2003. Student achievement in Germany—results of the second international comparison]*. Münster, Germany: Waxmann.

Putnam, R. T., & Borko, H. (2000). What do new views of knowledge and thinking have to say about research on teacher learning? *Educational Researcher, 29*, 4–15.

Ramirez, F. O. (2003). Toward a cultural anthropology of the world. In K. M. Anderson-Levitt. (Ed.), *Local meanings, global schooling: Anthropology and world culture theory*. New York: Palgrave Macmillan.

Reiss, K. (2002). Beweisen, begründen und argumentieren. Wege zu einem diskursiven mathematikunterricht [Proving, reasoning and debating. Strategies for discursive mathematics instruction]. In W. Peschek (Ed.). *Beiträge zum Mathematikunterricht [Contributions to mathematics instruction], 2002* (pp. 39–46). Hildesheim, Germany: Franzbecker.

Rheinberg, F. (2002). *Motivation* (4th ed.). Stuttgart: Kohlhammer.

Richardson, V. (1996). The role of attitudes and beliefs in learning to teach. In J. Sikula (Ed.), *The handbook of research in teacher education* (2nd ed., pp. 102–119). New York: Macmillan.

Richardson, V., & Placier, P. (2001). Teacher change. In *Handbook of research on teaching* (4th ed., pp. 905–947). Washington, DC: American Educational Research Association.

Rittle-Johnson, B., & Alibali, M. W. (1999, March). Conceptual and procedural knowledge of mathematics: Does one lead to the other? *Journal of Educational Psychology. 91*(1), 175–189.

Robitaille, D. F., McKnight, C. C., Schmidt, W. H., Britton, E., Raizen, S., & Nicol, C. (1993). *TIMSS monograph No 1: Curriculum framework for mathematics and science.* Vancouver, Canada: Pacific Educational Press.

Sabers, D. S., Cushing, K. S., & Berliner, D. C. (1991). Differences among teachers in a task characterized by simultaneity, multidimensionality, and immediacy. *American Educational Research Journal, 28*(1), 63–88.

Scheerens, J., & Bosker, R. J. (1997). *The foundations of educational effectiveness*. Oxford, England: Pergamon.

Schmidt, W. H. (1993). The distribution of instructional time to mathematical content: One aspect of opportunity to learn. In L. Burstein (Ed.), *The IEA Study of Mathematics III: Student growth and classroom processes* (pp. 129–145). Tarrytown, NY: Pergamon Press.

Schmidt, W. H., & Burstein, L. (1993). Concomitants of growth in mathematics achievement during the population A school year. In L. Burstein (Ed.), *The IEA study of mathematics III: Student growth and classroom processes* (pp. 309–327). Tarrytown, NY: Pergamon Press.

Schmidt, W.H., & Houang, R.T. (2007). Lack of focus in the mathematics curriculum. In T. Loveless (Ed.), *Lessons learned: What international assessments tell us about math achievement*. Washington, DC: Brookings Institution Press.

Schmidt, W. H., Jorde, D., Cogan, L. S., Barrier, E., Gonzalo, I., Moser, U., et al. (1996). *Characterizing pedagogical flow: An investigation of mathematics and science teaching in six countries*. New York: Springer.

Schmidt, W. H., & Kifer, E. (1989). Exploring relationships across population A systems: A search for patterns. In F. D. Robitaille & R. A. Gardens (Eds.), *The IEA study of Mathematics II: Contexts and outcomes of school mathematics* (pp. 209–231). Tarrytown, NY: Pergamon Press.

Schmidt, W. H., & Maier, A. (2009). Opportunity to learn. In G. Sykes, B. L. Schneider, & D. N. Plank (Eds.), *Handbook on Education Policy Research* (pp. 541–549). New York: Routledge.

Schmidt, W. H., McKnight, C., Cogan, L. S., Jakwerth, P. M., & Houang, R. T. (1999). *Facing the consequences: Using TIMSS for a closer look at U.S. mathematics and science education*. Dordrecht, Boston, and London: Kluwer.

Schmidt, W. H., McKnight, C. C., Houang, R. T., Wang, H., Wiley, D., Cogan, L. S., et al. (2001). *Why schools matter: A cross-national comparison of curriculum and learning*. San Francisco, CA: Jossey-Bass.

Schmidt, W. H., McKnight, C. C. & Raizen, S. A. (1996). *Splintered vision: An investigation of U.S. science and mathematics education: Executive summary*. East Lansing: U.S. National Research Center for the Third International Mathematics and Science Study, Michigan State University.

Schmidt, W. H., Tatto, M. M., Bankov, K., Blömeke, S. Cedillo, T., Cogan, L., Han, S. I., Houang, R., Hsieh, F. J., Paine, L., Santillan, M., & Schwille, J. (2008). *The preparation gap: Teacher education for middle school mathematics in six countries.* East Lansing: Center for Research in Mathematics and Science Education, Michigan State University.

Schmidt, W. H., Wang, H. A., & McKnight, C. C. (2005). Curriculum coherence: An examination of U.S. mathematics and science content standards from an international perspective. *Journal of Curriculum Studies, 37*(5), 525–559.

Schmidt, W. H., Wolfe, R. G., & Kifer, E. (1993). The identification and description of student growth in mathematics achievement. In L. Burstein (Ed.), *The IEA study of Mathematics III: Student growth and classroom processes* (pp. 59–100). Tarrytown, NY: Pergamon Press.

Schommer-Aikins, M. (2002). An evolving theoretical framework for an epistemological belief system. In B. Hofer & P. Pintrich (Eds.), *Personal epistemology: The psychology of beliefs about knowledge and knowing.* Mahwah, NJ: Lawrence Erlbaum.

Schrader, F.-W. (2001). Diagnostische kompetenz von eltern und lehrern [Diagnostic competencies of parents and teachers]. In D. H. Rost (Ed.), *Handwörterbuch pädagogische psychologie [Concise dictionary of educational psychology]* (2nd ed., pp. 68–71). Weinheim, Germany: Psychologie Verlags Union.

Schulz, W. (2009). Questionnaire construct validation in the International Civic and Citizenship Education Study (pp. 113–135). In *IERI monograph series: Issues and methodologies in large-scale assessment* (Vol. 2). Hamburg, Germany and Princeton, NJ: IEA-ETS Research Institute.

Schutz, A. (1967). *The phenomenology of the social world* (G. Walsh & F. Lehnert, Trans.). Evanston, IL: Northwestern University Press.

Seidel, T., & Shavelson, R. J. (2007). Teaching effectiveness research in the past decade: The role of theory and research design in disentangling meta-analysis results. *Review of Educational Research, 77*(4), 454–499.

Shavelson, R. J., Gao, X., & Baxter, G. (1996). On the content validity of performance assessments: Centrality of domain specification. In M. Birenbaum & F. J. R. C. Dochy (Eds.), *Alternatives in assessment of achievements, learning processes and prior knowledge* (pp. 131–141). Boston: Kluwer.

Short, R. J., & Short, P. M. (1989). Teacher beliefs, perceptions of behavior problems and intervention preferences. *Journal of Social Studies Research, 13*(2), 28–33.

Shulman, L. S. (1985). Paradigms and research programs in the study of teaching: A contemporary perspective. In M. C. Wittrock (Ed.), *Handbook of research on teaching.* (3rd ed, pp. 3–36). New York: Macmillan.

Shulman, L. (1986). Those who understand: Knowledge growth in teaching. *Educational Researcher, 15* (2), 4–14 [AERA Presidential Address].

Shulman, L. S. (1987). Knowledge and teaching: Foundations of the new reform. *Harvard Educational Research, 57*, 1–22.

Slavin, R. E. (1994). Quality, appropriateness, incentive, and time: A model of instructional effectiveness. *International Journal of Educational Research, 21*, S141–S157.

Slavin, R. E. (1996). *Education for all.* Lisse, Netherlands: Swets & Zeitlinger.

Slavin, R. E., Hurley, E. A., & Chamberlain, A. M. (2003). Cooperative learning and achievement: Theory and research. In W. M. Reynolds & G. E. Miller (Eds.), *Handbook of psychology: Educational psychology* (Vol. 7, pp. 177–198). New York: Wiley.

Smith, T. M., Desimone, L. M., Zeidner, T. L., Dunn, A. C., Bhatt, M., & Rumyantseva, N. L. (2007). Inquiry-oriented instruction in science: Who teaches that way? *Educational Evaluation and Policy Analysis 29*(3), 169–199.

Sorensen, C. W. (1994). Success and education in South Korea. *Comparative Education Review, 38*(1), 10–35.

Souvignier, E. (1999). Die verbesserung räumlicher fähigkeiten durch computerunterstützte fördermaßnahmen. Zwei evaluationsstudien [Improvement of spatial abilities by computer-aided supporting measures. Two evaluation studies]. *Zeitschrift für Pädagogische Psychologie [Journal of Educational Psychology], 13*, 4–16.

Spearman, C. (1927). *The abilities of man.* New York: Macmillan.

Spencer, L., & Spencer, S. (1993). *Competence at work: Models for superior performance.* New York: Wiley.

Stark, R., & Mandl, H. (2000). *Das theorie-praxis-problem in der pädagogisch-psychologischen forschung— ein unüberwindbares transferproblem? (Forschungsbericht Nr. 118) [The theory–practice problem in educational-psychological research—An insurmountable transfer problem? (Research report No. 118)].* München, Germany: LMU, Lehrstuhl für Empirische Pädagogik und Pädagogische Psychologie [Chair for empirical pedagogy and educational psychology].

Staub, F. C., & Stern, E. (2002). The nature of teachers' pedagogical content belief matters for students' achievement gains: Quasi-experimental evidence from elementary mathematics. *Journal of Educational Psychology, 94,* 344–355.

Stevenson, H. W., Lee, H. Y., Chen, C., Lummis, M., Stigler, J. W., Liu, F., et al. (1990). Mathematics achievement of children in China and the United States. *Child Development, 61,* 1053–1066.

Stevenson H. W., Lee, S.-Y., Chen, C., Stigler, J. W., Hsu, C.-C., Kitamura, S., & Hatano, G. (1990). A study of American, Chinese, and Japanese children [Monograph]. *Monographs of the Society for Research in Child Development, 55*(1/2), i–119.

Stodolsky, S. S., & Grossman, P. L. (1995). The impact of subject matter on curricular activity: An analysis of five academic subjects. *American Educational Research Journal, 32*(2), 227–249.

Stuhlmann, K. (2005). Entwicklung der lern- und leistungsmotivation im übergang von der adoleszenz ins frühe erwachsenenalter [Development of learning and achievement motivation in the transition of the adolescent to the early adult age]. *Zeitschrift für Sozialisation und Erziehung [Magazine for Socialization and Education], 25*(1), 67–81.

Suter, L. E. (2000). Is student achievement immutable? Evidence from international studies on schooling and student achievement. *Review of Educational Research, 70,* 529–545.

Taconis, R., Van der Plas, P., & Van der Sanden, J. (2004). The development of professional competencies by educational assistants in school-based teacher education. *European Journal of Teacher Education, 27,* 215–240.

Tal, T., Krajcik, J. S., & Blumenfeld, P. (2006). Urban school teachers enacting project-based science. *Journal of Research in Science Teaching, 43*(7), 722–745.

Thompson, A. G. (1992). Teachers' beliefs and conceptions: A synthesis of research. In D. A. Grouws (Ed.), *Handbook of research on mathematics teaching and learning* (pp. 127–146). New York: Macmillan.

TIMSS & PIRLS International Study Center. Retrieved July 12, 2009, from http://timss.bc.edu/.

Törner, G., & Pehkonen, E. (1996). On the structure of mathematical belief systems. *Zentralblatt der Didaktik der Mathematik. [Central Sheet of the Didactics of Mathematics], 4,* 109–112.

Triandis, H. C. (1995). *Individualism and collectivism.* Boulder, CO and Oxford, England: Westview Press.

Tulodziecki, G., Herzig, B., & Blömeke, S. (2004). *Gestaltung von unterricht: Eine einführung in die didaktik [Organization of instruction: An introduction to the didactics].* Bad Heilbrunn, Germany & Braunschweig, Germany: Klinkhardt & Westermann.

Ulich, K. (2000). Traumberuf lehrer/in? Berufsmotive und die (un)sicherheit der berufsentscheidung [Is being a teacher the occupation of a dream? Motives for occupation choices of future teachers and the (in)security of the decision]. *Die Deutsche Schule [The German School], 92,* 41-53.

Urhahne, D. (2006). Ich will biologielehrer(-in) werden! Berufswahlmotive von lehramtsstudierenden der biologie [I want to become a biology teacher! Motives for occupation choices of future biology teachers]. *Zeitschrift für Didaktik der Naturwissenschaften [Magazine for Didactics of the Natural Sciences], 12,* 127–157.

Valverde, G. A., & Schmidt, W. H. (2000). Greater expectations: Learning from other nations in the quest for "world-class standards" in U.S. school mathematics and science. *Journal of Curriculum Studies, 32*(5), 651–687.

van de Vijver, F. J. R., & Tanzer, N. K. (1997). Bias and equivalence in cross-cultural assessment: An overview. *European Review of Applied Psychology, 47,* 263–279.

Vollrath, H.-J. (2001). *Grundlagen des mathematikunterrichts in der sekundarstufe [Foundations of mathematics instruction in the secondary school].* Heidelberg, Germany: Spektrum Akademischer Verlag.

vom Hofe, R. (2001). Funktionen erkunden—mit dem Computer [Exploring functions—with the computer]. *Mathematik Lehren [Mathematics Teaching], 105*, 54–58.

Vosniadou, S. (1994). From cognitive theory to educational technology. In S. Vosniadou, E. De Corte, & H. Mandl (Eds.), *Technology-based learning environments: Psychological and educational foundations* (pp. 11–18). Berlin: Springer.

Wang, M. C., Haertel, G. D., & Walberg, H. J. (1993). Toward a knowledge base for school learning. *Review of Educational Research, 63*, 249–294.

Weigand, H.-G., & Weth, T. (2002). *Computer im mathematikunterricht: Neue wege zu alten zielen [Computer in mathematics instruction: New ways to old goals]*. Heidelberg, Germany: Spektrum.

Weinert, F. E. (1999). *Konzepte der kompetenz. Gutachten zum OECD-projekt "definition and selection of competencies: Theoretical and conceptual foundations (DeSeCo)" [Concepts of competence. Expertise on the OECD project "definition and selection of competencies: Theoretical and conceptual foundations (DeSeCo)"]*. Neuchatel, Switzerland: Bundesamt für Statistik.

Weinert, F. E. (2001). Concept of competence: A conceptual clarification. In D. S. Rychen & L. H. Salganik (Eds.), *Defining and selecting key competencies* (pp. 45–66). Göttingen, Germany: Hogrefe.

Westbury, I. D. (1995): Didactic and curriculum theory. Are they the two sides of the same coin? In S. Hopmann & K. Riquarts (Eds.), *Didactic and/or curriculum* (pp. 233–263). Kiel, Germany: IPN 1995.

Wiggan, G. (2007). Race, school achievement, and educational inequality: Toward a student-based inquiry perspectives. *Review of Educational Research, 77*, 310–333.

Wiley, D. E., & Wolfe, R. G. (1992). Major survey design issues for the IEA Third International Mathematics and Science Study. *Prospectus, 22*, pp. 207–304.

Wilson, S. M., Floden, R. E. & Ferrini-Mundy, J. (2001). *Teacher preparation research. Current knowledge, gaps, and recommendations*. Washington DC: Center for the Study of Teaching and Policy. Retrieved September 30, 2003, from http://depts.washington.edu/ctpmail/PDFs/Teacher-Prep-WFFM-02-2001.pdf.

Wilson, S., & Youngs, P. (2005). Research on accountability processes in teacher education. In M. Cochran-Smith & K. M. Zeichner (Eds.), *Studying teacher education: The report of the AERA Panel on Research and Teacher Education*. Mahwah, NJ: Lawrence Erlbaum.

Wittmann, E. C. (2003). Was ist mathematik und welche pädagogische bedeutung hat das wohlverstandene fach für den mathematikunterricht auch in der grundschule [What is mathematics and what educational relevance does the well-understood subject have for mathematics instruction in the primary school]? In M. Baum & H. Wielpütz (Eds.), *Mathematik in der grundschule: Ein arbeitsbuch [Mathematics in the primary school: A work book]*. Seelze, Germany: Kallmeyer.

World Bank (2005). *World development indicators*. Washington, DC: Author.

Wu, C. J. (2009). *Education in Taiwan 2009* (p. 10). Taipei: MOE.

Zaslavsky, C. (1996). *The multicultural math classroom: Bringing in the world*. Portsmouth, NH: Heinemann.

Zaslavsky, O., & Leikin, R. (2004). Professional development of mathematics teacher educators: Growth through practice. *Journal of Mathematics Teacher Education, 7*, 5–23.

Zeichner, K. M. (2005). A research agenda for teacher education. In M. Cochran-Smith & K. M. Zeichner (Eds.), *Studying teacher education: The Report of the AERA Panel on Research and Teacher Education*. Mahwah, NJ: Lawrence Erlbaum.

Zeichner, K. M., & Conklin, H. G. (2005). Teacher education programs. In M. Cochran-Smith & K. M. Zeichner (Eds.), *Studying teacher education: The Report of the AERA Panel on Research and Teacher Education*. Mahwah, NJ: Lawrence Erlbaum.

About the Authors

Kiril Bankov (Bulgaria) is a professor of mathematics and mathematics education at the Faculty of Mathematics and Informatics, University of Sofia, Bulgaria. He teaches future mathematics teachers and is closely involved in their preparation for entering the field of mathematics and mathematics pedagogy. Kiril Bankov worked as a mathematics coordinator at the International Study Center for the TEDS-M IEA study (2007–2009). He was also the National Research Coordinator (NRC) of TIMSS 1995, TIMSS 1999, and TIMSS 2003 in Bulgaria. Now he is a member of the international mathematics item review committee for TIMSS. Kiril Bankov has served as an educational assessment consultant in several World Bank projects. His research interests include educational measurement and evaluation (with a focus on student mathematics achievement) and mathematics teacher education and development.

Sigrid Blömeke, born in 1965, has been a Full Professor of Instructional Research at Humboldt University of Berlin in Germany since 2002. Prior to her appointment at Humboldt, she was an Associate Professor of Teaching and Learning with ICT at the University of Hamburg. From 2007 through 2009, she was a Visiting Scholar at Michigan State University in the United States. Dr. Blömeke received her teacher education degree, "Erstes Staatsexamen für die Sekundarstufe II," in social sciences and history in 1991; her PhD (Dr. phil.) in education in 1999; and her "Habilitation" in education in 2001. Her areas of research include the modeling and measurement of teacher competencies, international comparisons, and research on the effectiveness of ICT in instruction. She is the German head of IEA's "Teacher education and development study: Learning to teach mathematics (TEDS-M)" and the head of the recently released German federal funding initiative, "Modeling and measurement of competencies in higher education."

Martin Carnoy is the Vida Jacks Professor of Education at Stanford University School of Education. Prior to coming to Stanford, he was a Research

Associate in Economics, Foreign Policy Division, at the Brookings Institution. He is also a consultant to the World Bank, Inter-American Development Bank, Asian Development Bank, UNESCO, IEA, OECD, UNICEF, International Labour Office. Dr. Carnoy is a labor economist with a special interest in the relation between the economy and the educational system. To this end, he studies the U.S. labor market and the roles of race, ethnicity, and gender in the labor market; the U.S. educational system; and educational systems in many other countries. He uses comparative analysis to understand how education influences productivity and economic growth; how and why educational systems change over time; and why some countries educational systems are marked by better student performance than others'. He has studied extensively the impact of vouchers and charter schools on educational quality and has recently focused his research on differences in teacher preparation and teacher salaries across countries, as well as larger issues of the impact of economic inequality on educational quality. Dr. Carnoy received his BA in Electrical Engineering from the California Institute of Technology, and his MA and PhD in Economics from the University of Chicago.

Tenoch Cedillo was born in Mexico City. He received his PhD in 1996 from the Department of Mathematics, Statistics and Computing at the Institute of Education, University of London. Since 1979, he has been a Senior Lecturer in the Department of Mathematics at the National Pedagogical University in Mexico City. Dr. Cedillo was Academic Secretary of the National Pedagogical University from 2001 to 2007. Since 2000, he was awarded as National Researcher by the National Council of Science and Technology. Since 2007, he has served as Policy Director of the General Direction for Teachers Education of the Mexican Ministry of Education.

Leland S. Cogan is a Senior Researcher in both the Institute for Research on Mathematics and Science Education at Michigan State University and the U.S. Research Center for the Teacher Education Study in Mathematics (U.S. TEDS-M). He earned undergraduate degrees in microbiology and psychology and a PhD in educational psychology from Michigan State University. He has taught courses in educational psychology and educational research methods. He coordinated data collection and analyses for the Survey of Mathematics and Science Opportunities (SMSO), a multinational project that researched and developed the instruments used in the Third International Mathematics and Science Study (TIMSS). He has co-authored technical reports, articles, and books, including *Characterizing Pedagogical Flow, Facing the Consequences, Why Schools Matter* and *The Preparation Gap: Teacher Education for Middle School Mathematics in Six Countries*. His research interests include evaluation of mathematics and science curricula, mathematics and science classroom instruction, and the preparation of mathematics and science teachers

Shin-Il Han is associate professor in the department of education at the Sung-kyunkwan University, Seoul, Korea. Previously, he was senior researcher at the Korean Council for University Education. In 1992, he received his BA in Theology from Methodist Theological University in Korea; in 1995, he received his M.A. in Educational Measurement and Statistics from the University of Iowa; in 1999, he received his PhD in Higher Education from the University of Iowa. Recently, he has focused his research and writing on university teaching and learning and university administration, Korean educational policy, and the general education programs of Korean universities.

Richard T. Houang is Director of Research for the Institute for Research on Mathematics and Science Education and for the PROM/SE project (Promoting Rigorous Outcomes in Mathematics and Science Education). He also holds faculty appointments in measurement and quantitative methods. His research interests concern issues of academic content in K–12 schooling and the effects of curriculum on academic achievement. He is interested in the different aspects of modeling such relationships. Dr. Houang received his PhD from the University of California at Santa Barbara. He joined the faculty at Michigan State University in 1979 and has taught courses in quantitative methods, multivariate statistics, measurement and psychometrics. His research interests include latent trait models, imputation, and the measurement of curriculum. He was the Associate Director for the U.S. National Research Center for TIMSS (Third International Mathematics and Science Study). Dr. Houang has also published in numerous journals, including the *American Education Research Journal*, *Educational Studies in Mathematics*, and *Perceptual and Motor Skills,* and he has presented numerous papers at conferences.

Feng-Jui Hsieh is an associate professor in the Department of Mathematics at the National Taiwan Normal University, where she instructs on the teaching of mathematics. She received her PhD from Purdue University. Dr. Hsieh has researched mathematics learning, mathematics teaching, teacher education, and pre- and inservice teacher professional development. She has served as chairwoman of Taiwan's first evaluation committee of the junior high school mathematics textbook, as a member of the first evaluation committee of the elementary school mathematics textbook, and as a member of the committee to develop the first national curriculum standards for private textbook publishers at the senior high school level. She has received grants from Taiwan's National Science Council and Ministry of Education. Hsieh serves as Taiwan's representative on two international studies administered by the International Association of the Evaluation of Educational Achievement and the National Science Foundation. She also has served as a member of the Common Core State Standards Initiative Validation Committee.

Lynn Paine is a professor of teacher education, and an adjunct professor of sociology and women's studies. Her work focuses on comparative and international education and the sociology of education, with an emphasis on the relationship between educational policy and practice, the links between education and social change, and issues of inequality and diversity. Much of her work has involved the comparative study of teachers, teaching, and teacher education and is supported by research in China, the United States and England.

Marcela Santillan was born in Mexico City. She is a Mathematician at the National Autonomous University of Mexico and carried out postgraduate studies on Mathematics at Rutgers, The State University of New Jersey. Her research on mathematics education was done in the Department of Mathematics, Computing and Statistics at the Institute of Education, University of London. She has been a Senior Lecturer in the Department of Mathematics of the National Pedagogical University since 1980. She was Rector of the National Pedagogical University between 2001–2006. Since 2007, Marcela Santillan has been the General Director of Teacher Education in the Mexican Ministry of Education.

William H. Schmidt received his undergraduate degree in mathematics from Concordia College in River Forrest, IL and his PhD from the University of Chicago in psychometrics and applied statistics. He carries the title of University Distinguished Professor at Michigan State University and is currently co-director of the Education Policy Center, co-director of the U.S.–China Center for Research, and co-director of the NSF PROM/SE project. He holds faculty appointments in the Departments of Educational Psychology and Statistics at MSU. Previously he served as National Research Coordinator and Executive Director of the U.S. National Center, which oversaw participation of the United States in the IEA-sponsored Third International Mathematics and Science Study (TIMSS). He has published in numerous journals including the *Journal of the American Statistical Association, Journal of Educational Statistics,* and the *Journal of Educational Measurement.* He has co-authored seven books including *Why Schools Matter.* His current writing and research concerns issues of academic content in K–12 schooling, assessment theory, and the effects of curriculum on academic achievement. He is also concerned with educational policy related to mathematics, science, and testing in general. He was awarded the Honorary Doctorate Degree at Concordia University in 1997, received the 1998 Willard Jacobson Lectureship from The New York Academy of Sciences, and is a member of the National Academy of Education.

John Schwille is professor and assistant dean for international studies in education at Michigan State University. In 2013 he will celebrate a 50-year career in international research in education, which he started as a doctoral student in 1963. Since 1972, after initial research on France and French education, one of his primary interests has been in cross-national studies of educational achievement, primarily in civic education and mathematics. Currently, he is co-director of the seventeen-nation TEDS-M teacher education in mathematics study, the first international assessment of student learning in higher education based on national samples. He has also worked extensively on international development in education, primarily in Africa, with major projects first in Burundi, then Guinea, and now Tanzania. At the same time, he has been a college administrator at MSU for over 25 years and is responsible for developing an international dimension in research, teaching, and outreach throughout the college.

Maria Teresa Tatto is an associate professor at the College of Education in Michigan State University, where she has taught since 1987. Her research is characterized by the use of an international-comparative framework to study educational reform and educational policy and their impact on schooling—particularly the role of teachers, teaching, and learning—within varied organizational, economic, political, and social contexts. Tatto's other research interests include the influence of early childhood education on improved knowledge levels for the rural poor, the role of values education on citizenship formation, and the development of effective policies to support the education of children of migrant workers in the United States. Tatto's work combines the use of quantitative and qualitative approaches and methods and provides a unique perspective on the study of these complex issues. She has taught in Mexico, France, and the United States, and has served as a consultant to the World Bank for the governments of Mexico, Colombia, Peru, and the Dominican Republic. She is currently the Principal Investigator for the IEA Teacher Education Study in Mathematics (TEDS-M) and president of the Comparative and International Education Society (CIES).

Index

323

More praise for *Exchange Traded Funds and E-mini Stock Index Futures*

"Dave Lerman has written a comprehensive book that thoroughly describes the important role of ETFs and Stock Index Futures in overall portfolio management. A must-read for sophisticated and active investors on a difficult subject matter that Dave has made easy to understand. Investors should now realize the value and power that these tools can play in the enhancement of their portfolios."

—Jack Blackburn,
Senior Business Relationship Manager,
Lind-Waldock & Co.

"Lerman is one of the most detailed-intensive market researchers I know. This book demonstrates his uncanny ability to understand the true guts of the markets."

—Mark D. Cook, professional trader,
Cook Investments

Wiley Trading

EXCHANGE TRADED FUNDS AND E-MINI STOCK INDEX FUTURES

DAVID LERMAN

John Wiley & Sons
New York • Chichester • Weinheim • Brisbane • Singapore • Toronto

To my extraordinary wife, Jeane

To my parents, Louis and Corrine Lerman, who have taught me about
encouragement, determination, and hard work

This book is printed on acid-free paper. ♾

Copyright © 2001 by David Lerman. All rights reserved.

Published by John Wiley & Sons, Inc.
Published simultaneously in Canada.

This publication is designed to provide accurate and authoritative
information in regard to the subject matter covered. It is sold with the
understanding that the publisher is not engaged in rendering professional
services. If professional advice or other expert assistance is required, the
services of a competent professional person should be sought.

Library of Congress Cataloging-in-Publication Data

Lerman, David.
    Exchange traded funds and e-mini stock index futures / by David Lerman.
      p. cm—(Wiley trading)
    Includes bibliographical references and index.
    ISBN 0-471-44298-4 (cloth : alk. paper)
    1. Exchange traded funds. 2. Stock index futures. I. Title. II. Series.

  HG6043.L47 2001
  332.63′228—dc21

                        2001035979

Printed in the United States of America.

10 9 8 7 6 5 4 3 2 1

CONTENTS

PREFACE

Incredulously, on May 5, 1997, I found myself standing in line at 6:00 A.M. with hundreds of other folks. On this beautiful spring morning, we were waiting to file into the Aksarben Coliseum just outside Omaha, Nebraska. The doors would not open for another hour, and the meeting would not start until 9:30. When the meeting began, the place was packed with about 9,000 attendees. A typical corporate annual meeting attracts a few hundred, perhaps a thousand, investors. But this was no typical annual meeting. It was the "capitalists' Woodstock": the annual meeting of Warren Buffett's Berkshire Hathaway. And the venue was a hockey rink! When the greatest investor in the history of civilization entered the building, a thunderous applause broke out.

Warren took his customary place next to Berkshire Hathaway's vice chairman, Charlie Munger, and the formalities of the annual meeting took the usual ten minutes. Meeting over. At this point the real reason for the gathering began: the Q&A session. You see, the question-and-answer portion of the Berkshire Hathaway annual meeting is when investors—many of them richly rewarded for holding their shares—get to ask the ultimate investing expert any question imaginable. And Warren aims to please, since the Q&A sessions usually run four to six hours. A dozen or so microphones were placed around the coliseum, and the faithful lined up for the greatest teaching thrill of their investment lives. This year, one of the first questions came from a middle-aged woman who wanted Buffett's opinion regarding high investment fees relative to performance in the mutual fund arena. Buffett prefaced his reply by saying, "The typical investment manager, even some of the good ones, have little chance of beating the S&P 500 over the long run." Jaws dropped, and heads turned. Many in attendance that day were in fact money managers. Berkshire also held a boat-load of Salomon common stock, one of the world's premier investment banks that also managed billions in assets. Here was the world's greatest stock picker, a man with a thirty-five-year track record that had smashed the S&P 500 to bits—and he was talking about the great

advantages of indexing. The irony exploded across Aksarben. Class was
in session.

As Buffett was amassing one of the great track records of all time,
John Bogle was quietly amassing an extraordinary track record of a different kind, a thousand miles away in Valley Forge, Pennsylvania. The
Vanguard Group's flagship fund, the Vanguard Index Trust, which
tracks the S&P 500 Composite Index, was slowly, but inexorably fulfilling the Oracle of Omaha's prediction. Over the past quarter of a century, the S&P 500 Index, and thus the Vanguard Index Trust, had
handily beat most active managers (i.e., stock pickers). The fund com-
menced operations 25 years earlier with $11 million in assets. By the
end of 1999, the fund had surpassed $100 billion in assets and shortly
after had became the largest mutual fund in the United States.

Buffett was right: the majority of investment managers fail to outperform their benchmark over the long run. That is likely to continue.
To be sure, there will be periods when they will prevail. But the past 30
years has shown them to be on the losing end of a very tough comparison. Today more than $2.5 trillion are indexed (passively managed)
worldwide—about $1.4 trillion in the United States.

At a recent seminar that I gave to hundreds of attendees, someone
asked if I thought that indexing had "lost some of its momentum."
When I responded that the evidence pointed to the contrary, the ques-
tioner replied, "How do you figure?" I rattled off the following in rapid-
fire succession:

- There is nearly $70 billion invested in exchange traded funds
  (ETFs), up from zero eight years ago!
- The S&P 500 Depositary Receipts (also known as SPDRs or Spiders) trade 7 million shares a day and usually are at the top of
  the American Stock Exchange's list of most active issues.
- The QQQ, an ETF that tracks the Nasdaq-100 index, traded over
  2.5 million shares on its first day less than two years ago. It usually is the most active issue on the American Stock Exchange
  (and now trades 20 times that amount).
- Average daily volume in the Chicago Mercantile Exchange's new
  E-Mini S&P 500 Index futures contract has grown over, 1000
  percent (from under 10,000 a day to over 100,000 per day) in the
  past three years.
- The Chicago Mercantile Exchange's new E-Mini Nasdaq-100
  Index futures contract traded 2,400 contracts at its inception in

June 1999. Average daily volume now exceeds 80,000 contracts—
a 33-fold increase in less than 18 months! (The mini S&P and
mini Nasdaq now trade over 100,000 contracts per day.)

• In the past few months, Barclays Global Investors has successfully launched dozens of new ETFs, called iShares, to help investors create index strategies. These funds duplicate a host of
well-known indexes such as the Russell 2000, S&P/Barra Growth
and Value Indexes, and dozens more.

In short, these new index products have far exceeded the most optimistic expectations and indicate that, at least for now, the momentum
for index investing is on the increase. I asked the gentleman if he was
clear on the momentum issue. He replied, "Crystal!"

As the indexing revolution continues, these new stock index products such as ETFs and CME's E-mini stock index futures are starting
to grab the attention of investors large and small. Unfortunately, these
products are so new and encompass so many different indexes that
some investors, especially novices, are having difficulty keeping up
with the changing landscape. The aim of this book is to provide a comprehensive view of these new stock index products—how they work,
how traders can use them, and how long-term investors can use them.
I will also go into:

• How individuals can use these products to mimic some of the indexing strategies of the largest institutional investors and obtain
excellent returns.

• Asset allocation and related strategies, such as the core-satellite
approach, which allow combining indexing strategies using ETFs,
with the seemingly hereditary desire to pick stocks (after all,
there is a little Warren Buffett in all of us!).

• Trading, hedging, and spreading strategies using the popular E-
mini stock index futures at Chicago Mercantile Exchange.

Although this book is aimed at the beginning- to intermediate-level
investor, I believe it offers investors, advisers, and traders of all experience levels several benefits. I hope to challenge you, even quiz you, so
that when you are finished, you'll be able to make informed decisions
regarding short-term and long-term strategies using these new stock
index products.

Class is in session!

ACKNOWLEDGMENTS

Many thanks to the individuals and institutions below that played a part in the writing of this book.

First to Jim McNulty, the CEO of Chicago Mercantile Exchange Inc. for giving permission to move forward on the project. Rick Redding, Brett Vietmeier, and Gail Moss (also at CME) played important roles.

Thanks also to Nicholas Lopardo and Gus Fleites at State Street Global Advisors for reading parts of the manuscript and making important suggestions.

At the AMEX, Mike Babel and Diane Fezza provided helpful information along the way.

Jay Baker from Spear, Leeds & Kellogg also explained some of the critical details of market making and the creation/redemption process. Tim Jarvis from JP Morgan/Chase and Tom Centrone from the Bank of New York also filled in crucial details on these products. Rick Rosenthal of Sydan and Jon Peabody of Rock Island Securities provided great input in terms of the Chicago Stock Exchange's role in Exchange Traded funds.

And finally, thanks to those folks at John Wiley and Sons. Pam van Giessen and Claudio Campuzano for orchestrating this whole project, the copyeditors and typesetters who took the manuscript with all its flaws and created the finished project.

Part I

FROM RANDOM WALK TO A TRILLION-DOLLAR PHENOMENON

"Yeah, but can he beat the S & P 500?"

Credit: Hank Blaustein

1

FROM RANDOM WALK TO A TRILLION-DOLLAR PHENOMENON: WHY INDEXING WORKS SO WELL

In 1973, Burton Malkiel published the first of seven editions of *A Random Walk Down Wall Street*. The book, which I urge all investors to read, describes how investors are better off buying and holding a passive index fund rather than trying to buy and sell individual securities or actively managed mutual funds. *Random walk*, a term coined by academicians, states that the short-term fluctuations in the stock market cannot be predicted and argues that analysts' reports, newsletter touts, and chart formations are useless in gauging long-term market trends. In fact, random walkers are convinced that a monkey throwing a dart at the stock pages of a newspaper could choose a portfolio of stocks as well as most of the Harvard M.B.A. types on The Street.

Malkiel goes on to describe a virtual "wrestlemania" between the academic world and Wall Street. In the academic corner, we have modern portfolio theory (MPT), the capital asset pricing model (CAPM), and a stable of Nobel laureates. In Wall Street's corner, there are the fundamental analysts, the technical analysts. and some very highly paid investment managers. Over the past 30 or so years, observers have witnessed these forces beating each other over the head with an endless stream of beta coefficients, alphas, earning upgrades and downgrades, reiterated buy recommendations, and outside-day inside-day false breakouts!

Malkiel goes so far as to say, "Financial forecasting appears to be a science that makes astrology look respectable."[1] This unflattering statement reminds me of a popular analyst who recently recommended purchase of Yahoo! common stock while at the same time setting a price target well above its then current price. Not only did Yahoo! fail to hit that target, but it proceeded to lose over 60 percent of its value in the next four months! Another analyst recently downgraded a dot-com stock—*after* it lost 95 percent of its value. To be sure, there are some great money managers, traders, and analysts, and some academic studies have made great contributions to the investing world. But the fact remains that the S&P 500 index has beaten most of the stock-picking profession. And for those who claim that active management stacks up more favorably against a broader benchmark, such as the Wilshire 5000, I urge them to examine the evidence in Exhibit 1.1 and Exhibit 1.2.

What further conclusions can we draw?

- Markets are, for the most part, efficient (inefficiencies can usually be arbitraged away, and inadequate liquidity or profit potential makes them unexploitable).
- The average manager still cannot beat the appropriate benchmarks, and thus is not likely to add value in the long run.

Exhibit 1.1   The Case for Indexing: Percentage of Mutual Funds Outperformed by the S&P 500, 1972–2000

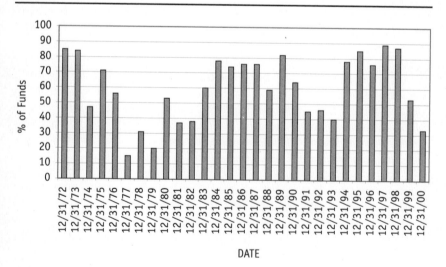

Note: The funds referred to are general equity mutual funds.
Source: CME Marketing/Standard & Poor's/The Vanguard Group.

- Some active managers can obtain returns above the benchmarks, but investors must possess tremendous skills and resources to identify them. Warren Buffett, Bill Miller (manager of the Legg Mason Value Trust), Ralph Wanger (manager of the Acorn Funds), and a handful of other great managers can and do beat their benchmarks on a consistent basis.

Some win, some lose, but on average, they're average.[2]

Barton Waring, Barclays Global Investors

About the same time as the publication of Malkiel's book and a few years after the random walkers began to insult active managers, the seeds of the indexing revolution were planted. Bill Fouse and John Mc-Quown, both working at Wells Fargo Bank, were the first to implement indexing. The first indexed portfolio was constructed in 1971 by Fouse and McQuown for the pension fund of a large corporation and was actually based on the New York Stock Exchange (NYSE) Composite index. The NYSE Composite is basically every issue traded on the

Exhibit 1.2 Percentage of Mutual Funds Outperformed by the Wilshire 5000 Index, 1972–1999

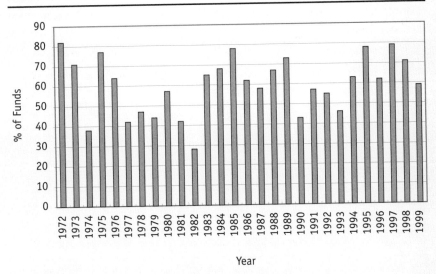

Note: The funds referred to are general equity mutual funds.
Source: CME, Standard & Poor's, The Vanguard Group.

NYSE; hence, the number of stocks is enormous. Outright purchase of every stock proved cumbersome and it is easy to imagine the custodial headaches that ensued. Remember, too, that there was no SuperDot system (for electronic order routing to the NYSE specialist), and automation was a far cry from the technology we now take for granted. Wells later abandoned indexing using the NYSE Composite and in 1973 began to index based on the S&P 500 Composite. The first clients were Wells's own pension fund and the pension plan of Illinois Bell.

Wells had some company in the early 1970s. Batterymarch Financial Management and American National Bank both indexed client money in 1974, and adherents to efficient market theory recognized the beginning of a new investment vehicle. In December 1975, John Bogle, who had just started the Vanguard Group, introduced the first indexed mutual fund. Its name: *First Index Investment Trust*. The fund began operations with $11 million in assets. No one could have predicted what was to unfold for indexed investments over the next quarter of a century, but one thing can be said for certain: Investors are noticing now and opening their wallets . . . big time.

How can you explain the numbers in Exhibit 1.3? How has this "if you can't beat 'em, join em" philosophy of investing gathered so much

Exhibit 1.3   Growth of Indexing of U.S. Tax-Exempt Institutional Assets, Year End 1977–June 30, 2000

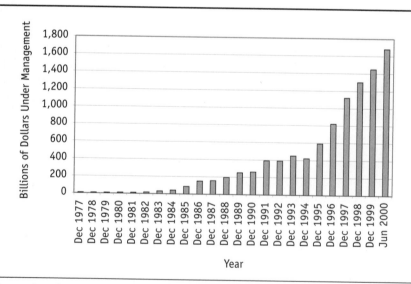

Source: Data from Pension and Investments Annual Survey.

momentum in so little time? The answer is simple: It works. After all is said and done, indexed investors have more money left in their pockets over time than if they had invested the same money in a typical actively managed mutual fund. We have established unequivocally that the S&P 500 composite outperforms most mutual fund managers over time. However, we must gain an understanding of why this occurs and then examine some of the other reasons that indexing has become a trillion-dollar phenomenon.

Why is the S&P 500 such a formidable competitor? There are basically six reasons that this benchmark has trumped the competition:

1. Investment management fees
2. Transaction costs and portfolio turnover
3. Taxes
4. Cash drag
5. Mid-cap and small-cap holding bias
6. Additional costs

INVESTMENT MANAGEMENT FEES

The average annual expense ratio for a typical equity mutual fund is about 1.40 percent per year (or 140 basis points). You can find the fund's annual expense ratio in its prospectus, but if you wish to avoid being lulled to sleep reading a prospectus, I urge you to visit Morningstar's Web site (www.morningstar.com) to find a whole range of data on just about any mutual fund, including annual expense ratios (although a little due diligence might not hurt—a fund's prospectus is full of facts, and you may learn something about your investments!). The annual expense ratio expresses the percentage of assets *deducted* each fiscal year for fund expenses including management fees, administrative fees, operating costs, 12b-1 fees, and all total costs incurred by the fund. Brokerage costs and transaction fees, as well as all sales loads, front- or back-ended, *are not included* in the annual expense ratio. Since bull markets idolize active stock pickers (in bear markets, they are tarred and feathered), some of the gods of investing make appearances at retail money shows, where they fill ritzy hotel ballrooms with thousands of people clamoring to get stock "picks." But these portfolio managers do not come cheap. Many have salaries and bonuses in the high six-figures. Some earn even more. Peter Lynch, the legendary manager at Fidelity, easily earned his salary by blowing past his benchmark for over 15 years. Most, however, are not as fortunate. These costs are one part of the total annual expenses paid out of a fund's assets. All the mailings, the annual reports, the ability to call a fund representative at 2:00 A.M. and Web access cost money. You have to determine if these costs are worth the returns.

Now, 140 basis points might not sound like a lot, but over time, it is a considerable cost. The average index fund is at least 100 basis points cheaper, and the average exchange traded fund (ETF) is cheaper still. What is a 1.0 percent cost advantage worth? If you start with $10,000 and obtain a return of 10 percent, after 25 years you will have $108,340. The same $10,000 with a return of 11 percent will have grown to $135,854. The difference is about $27,500—a major sum here, enough for a fully loaded Ford Explorer, a down payment on a typical house in the United States (excluding Silicon Valley), or a trip around the world for two with first-class Airfare and five-star hotel accommodations. ETFs and index funds in general, however, have a tremendous advantage in that annual expense ratios are a fraction of those of a typical fund. There are no star managers here (although Vanguard's Gus Sauter, who runs most of Vanguard's index funds, including the largest mutual fund in the United States, does receive a great deal of press and adeptly finds a way to *beat* his benchmarks sometimes. More on Sauter later.). No gigantic research staff trying to find the next Cisco or Microsoft. No Cray Y-MP supercomputers looking for strange market anomalies to try to exploit. No bloated costs. Simple. Advantage: Passive guys win this one.

TRANSACTION COSTS AND PORTFOLIO TURNOVER

It used to be that if you bought 100 shares of a stock, you would pay about $90 at a full-service firm. Then the discounters arrived and brought commissions to the $25 to $50 range. Then the deep discounters, and later, in the 1990s, the on-line brokers came on board charging $5 to $10 for the same 100 shares. Institutions such as pension fund managers and mutual funds managers obviously pay far less in brokerage commissions since they buy huge numbers of shares—usually in blocks of 10,000 to 100,000 shares and up. Nevertheless, despite extremely low commissions, these costs add up. The estimated transaction costs to a fund are between 0.5 percent and 1.0 percent per annum. In a recent presentation to the Investment Analysts Society, John Bogle said the transaction costs represent about 0.7 percent of a fund's assets, or 70 basis points.[3] Hence, when transaction costs are added to the aforementioned expenses, you have a whopping 200 to 210 basis point drag on a portfolio every year. Unfortunately, there are even

Exhibit 1.4 Turnover Rates and Expense Ratios, Selected Funds

	Turnover Rate		Expense Ratio	
Fund	1988	1998	1988	1998
Evergreen Income and Growth	81%	133%	1.01%	1.25%
Invesco Blue Chip Growth	116	153	.81	1.04
Templeton Growth	11	48	.69	1.08
Fidelity Magellan	101	34	1.14	.61
Vanguard 500 Index	10	6	.22	.18

Source: Morningstar Mutual Fund 500, 2000 Edition.

more costs to the investor. Some managers buy stocks and hold them for quite some time. Buffett's favorite holding period is "forever." Many of his holdings have been in Berkshire's portfolio for at least a decade. Washington Post Co. has been in the portfolio since 1974. His turnover rate is extremely low. In light of this, one would think that funds would have a powerful incentive to lower turnover and thus transaction fees. Surprisingly, though, part of the industry seems to be doing the opposite. In the mid 1970s, turnover for most funds was at the 30 percent level. A quarter-century later, turnover for a general equity mutual fund now stands at 108 percent. As Exhibit 1.4 shows, while some funds have held the line or even reduced their turnover and expense ratios, others have gone in the opposite direction.

True, some commissions will be incurred. It's part of the business, and there's nothing wrong with that. But when managers become so short term oriented that they turn over their entire portfolio in a little more than a year, the costs start to become burdensome. The old adage, "You can never go broke taking a profit," rings true. But continue adding cost after cost, and soon the take by various financial intermediaries becomes too large to overcome, even for the above-average stock picker. And one of the biggest costs has yet to be brought to the discussion. It comes in a three-letter acronym that seizes every American investor: the IRS.

*The investment success of investors in the aggregate is
defined—not only over the long-term but every single day—
by the extent to which market returns are consumed by
financial intermediaries.*

John Bogle, speaking to the Investment
Analysts Society of Chicago[4]

TAXES

Some of us have had the pleasure of filling out form 1040—Schedule D for Capital Gains and Losses. It is a simple form if you buy or sell a couple of stocks throughout the year. My Schedule D used to take about an hour of work. Then I decided to invest in (and later sell) some mutual funds. For the 1999 filing year, it took almost three hours just for the Schedule D portion. I can think of better things to do than figure the average cost basis of my mutual fund shares (although many funds actually calculate your tax basis for you). Worse, you then have to pay taxes on any income, as well as realized gains the fund had during the year. This can be a substantial drag on returns, and the IRS is one financial intermediary that will sooner or later get its cut. The one bright side to paying taxes is that you have made money! But to give more than your fair share is un-American. The only sport more popular than our national pastime is tax avoidance (Notice I said tax *avoidance*, which is legal, as opposed to tax *evasion*, which is illegal.) Sadly, this is one sport that many mutual funds and investment managers fail to participate in. If fact, there is little or no discussion of the tax issues surrounding mutual fund investment. Large ads in the financial press tout a particular fund as the number one performer during a particular period. I have yet to see an ad proudly displaying after-tax returns. Most discussions in prospectuses center around the general statement that the shareholder will pay taxes on all income distributions and capital gains distributions.

How big is the IRS's cut? The Chicago presentation at which Jack Bogle spoke provided a wealth of knowledge, and I took copious notes. According to the Bogle Financial Markets Center, the impact of taxes on an actively managed portfolio is roughly 160 basis points. I couldn't believe it. I have been in this industry for awhile, but like many other investors, I never paid close attention. Since I had heard some estimates that were somewhat lower and some that were 100 basis points higher, I decided to find out for myself where in that range things really fall. I paged through the 2000 edition of the Morningstar 500 booklet and chose a few of the larger, more well-known funds. Exhibit 1.5 illustrates the results of this informal experiment.

The 172 basis points was in the same ballpark as Bogle's figure. Then I pulled out my tax records for the last couple of years and computed the amounts with my personal holdings in the Mutual Qualified fund and the Acorn International fund. Averaging my tax burden over the past two years for Mutual Qualified and one year for the Acorn International, I came up with 1.78 percentage points, or 178 basis points.

Exhibit 1.5 Pretax vs. After-Tax Returns, Selected Funds

Fund	10-Year Annualized Return	10-Year Annualized Return, Tax Adjusted	Tax Impact in Basis Points
T. Rowe Price Blue Chip Growth	28.28	27.82	46
AIM Constellation	21.16	20.33	83
Vanguard 500	18.07	16.97	110
Gabelli Asset	16.31	14.36	195
Fidelity Growth Company	23.63	21.39	224
Janus Fund	20.58	18.11	247
Mutual Qualified	14.25	11.25	300
Average			172 or 1.72%

Note: All data are for ten years ending December 31, 1999, except T. Rowe Price, which is five years, ending December 31, 1999.
Source: Morningstar Mutual Fund 500, 2000 Edition.

(Morningstar's computation reflects the maximum capital gains rate of 39.6 percent. Many Americans do not fall into that tax bracket. Too, many Americans do not hold funds 10 years either.)

The tax implications alone are enormous. Every time a fund manager sells a stock, he or she incurs transaction costs. Every time a fund manager sells a stock, he or she creates a taxable event (unless it is sold at a loss). Every time a fund manager creates a taxable event, the IRS wants to be part of that event. Let's summarize:

Annual expenses	140 basis points
Transaction costs	70 basis points
Taxes	170 basis points
Subtotal (there is more to come)	*380 basis points*

CASH DRAG

Most equity investment managers are paid to invest in equities, but even the most aggressive among them are rarely 100 percent in stocks. They always hold some cash reserves for picking up stocks in the future or to meet redemptions should an investor cash out shares. A very small subset of funds is 100 percent invested (index funds among them).

Others are 90 percent or more invested in stocks. Some less. The remaining allocation, which can range from 1 percent to 30 percent depending on the fund, may be in bonds, and some may be in cash—Treasury bills (T-bills), repurchase agreements, and other money market instruments. Cash is a great thing to have on hand in a bear market. However, for most of the past eighteen years, investors have had an amazing run. Any investor holding even small amounts of cash suffered from cash drag—the drag on a portfolio's performance in a rising market due to holding excessive cash. Cash returns have been in the 4–7 percent range for most of the past few years. Imagine holding 10 percent of your assets in cash earning single-digit returns while the S&P 500 was up over 20 percent each year from 1995 to 1999. That is cash drag, and almost every investor, small and large, experiences it. It is also very hard to determine the overall impact since cash levels change so much. It also depends on market returns. Suffice it to say that the impact is between 20 basis points and over 200 basis points. If cash balances are at 10 percent or greater, then it is entirely possible, given the returns of the past few years, that the drag could reach 200 basis points. Given long-run returns of 11 percent to 13 percent in the equity markets and cash levels between 5 percent and 10 percent, the cash drag should be approximately 40 to 50 basis points.

MID-CAP AND SMALL-CAP BIAS

Another reason that investment managers have a hard time beating their benchmark is their style of investing. Many general equity mutual funds have a healthy dose of middle-capitalization and small-capitalization (midsize and small-size stocks) issues. The S&P 500 is primarily a large-capitalization index. Therefore, if mid- and small-size stocks lag the overall market, the manager will lag too. When the active camp claims victory over the S&P 500, it is usually in an environment when midsize and small-cap stocks have substantial rallies.

ADDITIONAL COSTS

In addition to the layers of costs already painfully detailed, there are costs associated with upfront sales charges levied by some mutual funds. Sales charges, or *loads* as they are called, vary from 1.00 percent to 8.75 percent. Some fixed-income funds even charge a 6.75 percent (or greater) load. Usually, funds sold by brokers are of the load variety, and it is from that sales charge that they are paid their commission. Sometimes the load is paid upfront, and sometimes loads are back-ended, meaning you pay the load when you sell the fund. The annual expense ratio of a fund *does not include loads of any kind!* So if you use brokers and purchase funds with front- or back-end loads, this is another layer of cost. The longer you hold a loaded fund, however, the lower the per-annum cost of the sales charge.

In addition, the tax costs reflect only federal taxes, not state or local taxes. In some states with certain types of investors, this would add yet more costs. And one other item can hurt the performance of a fund: Poor stock picking! There are some managers on the street who just do not possess stock picking acumen.

Given that the mid-cap bias is hard to measure and that not all funds have sales charges, we will eliminate these costs from our final tally of various fund costs:

Annual expenses	140 basis points
Transaction costs	70 basis points
Taxes	170 basis points
Cash drag	40 basis points

Total costs   ***420 basis points, or 4.2 percentage points***

Now we will go one step further and put this in dollar terms. But first we have to set the ground rules and make some assumptions in terms of time, rate of return, and so on.

Over the past 75 or so years, the returns of the U.S. stock market as measured by the S&P 500 have averaged about 11.3 percent. This is a very representative period; it includes several major wars, one depression, one severe and dozens of minor recessions, a few S&L and banking crises, Watergate, Monica-gate, and Chad-gate. Stock market returns over the past 50 years have averaged about 13.3 percent (and this time frame includes the fabulous fifties, the best decade for stocks in the past 70 years—even better than the nineties) and the past 40 years about 12.0 percent. Over the past 20 years, the market has returned on average just shy of 18 percent. But the past 20 years have been extraordinarily kind to investors, and to assume the next 20 years will be just as generous is a real stretch.

So in my illustration, I use 11.3 percent returns for the market and a 40-year time horizon—about the same length of time many of us will be accumulating money (ages 25 to 65). Lets further assume that before expenses, the average fund outperforms the market by 100 basis points, or 1.00 percentage point per year (a very generous assumption). John Bogle has some data demonstrating that equity funds outperformed the Wilshire 5000 over the past 15-year period by 50 basis points.[5] However, the study did not account for "survivorship bias," which would certainly have eradicated that 50 basis points and a lot more. When you look at the group that beat the market by 50 basis points, you are looking only at funds that were around or survived the whole 15-year period. Many funds that existed at the start of the study (but did not make it to the end) do not appear in the data. They may have merged or been liquidated, but no matter where they went, the funds that failed to deliver adequate returns are gone. Had they been included, they would certainly have lowered the returns of the group as a whole.

In a similar study, Burton Malkiel found that from 1982 to 1991, the survivors experienced annual returns of 17.1 percent.[6] But all funds—survivors and those that did not make it to the end—provided returns of only 15.7 percent, a 1.4 percent bias. A similar study with a 15-year period ending in 1991 showed a survivorship bias of over 4.2 percent.[7] So to award mutual funds a 100 basis point advantage is truly an act of kindness.

In addition, I will not include cash drag costs, loads, and mid- and small-cap bias since they are harder to gauge. I include only expenses, transaction fees, and taxes.

We'll start with $10,000 and compound it at 11.3 percent (return of S&P 500 or the market). Then we will compound at 12.3 percent (for the fund—again, before expenses). Exhibit 1.6 shows how much costs matter—how much the intermediaries and the IRS take as their cut. Clearly, in Exhibit 1.6, the indexer has almost a quarter of a million more dollars at the end of the period, adjusting for costs, and that's after spotting the active manager 100 basis points.

Now you can understand why Buffett has held some of his stocks for decades. Less turnover means fewer "taxable events." Less turnover means fewer transaction fees. Now you can also see why the active investment management community has such a hard time beating the S&P 500. Those little boxes that appear at the lower right-hand corner of your CNBC telecast continuously display updated levels of the major indexes, including the S&P 500. That number does not have to pay taxes, does not have expenses, does not have brokerage commissions, does not charge a load, and could not care less about midsize stocks, upgrades, downgrades, or anything else. Yes, an index fund designed to

Exhibit 1.6   Impact of Costs on Investment Returns

Index Fund

$10,000

@ 11.3%	for 40 years, no expenses or taxes	becomes $724,100
@ 11.1%	[11.3 – .20% expenses = 11.10%][a]	becomes $673,800
@ 10.25%	[11.1 – .85% taxes = 10.25%][a]	***becomes $495,600***

Average Fund

$10,000

@ 12.3%	for 40 years, no expenses or taxes	becomes $1,035,600
@ 10.2%	[12.3% – 2.1% expenses = 10.2%]	becomes $ 486,700
@ 8.5%	[10.2% – 1.7% taxes = 8.5%]	***becomes $ 261,300***

---

[a]The typical index fund is about twice as tax efficient as its passive counterpart. The Vanguard 500 has an annual expense ratio of .18 percent and virtually no turnover costs. The average fund has 1.4 percent annual management fee plus .7 percent in turnover costs, for a total expense of 2.1 percent.

mimic the S&P 500 would incur costs. However, the costs would be substantially lower than the average investment manager. Costs matter. They matter so much that a couple of trillion dollars (up from virtually nothing 20 years ago) has been sucked into indexing like a huge vacuum. But the story gets better, as we will see in Parts II and III. Exchange traded funds and E-mini stock index futures can be even cheaper than index funds.

2

THE PLAYERS

While ETFs and E-mini stock index futures owe their birth to a few individuals, it was really a panoply of institutions that made them the success they are now. To the institutionally inclined, they are household names. To the retail investor, they may be only vaguely familiar. So that you can really appreciate and gain a full understanding of these great products, you should know something about the players behind them.

INSTITUTIONAL MANAGERS OF ETFs

The three institutions highlighted here are the managers of most of the ETFs listed so far in the United States.

Barclays Global Investors

Perhaps the largest institutional money manager in the world, and certainly the largest indexer on the planet, Barclays Global Investors (BGI) had $833 billion under management as of June 2000. Headquartered in San Francisco, BGI is the world's largest provider of structured investment strategies such as indexing, tactical asset allocation, and quantitative active strategies. While BGI is known for being involved primarily in passive indexing strategies, it derives nearly 40 percent of its revenues from active money management. This giant money manager has evolved over the years, as have many other financial corporations in the United States, through a series of brilliant mergers. The current form of BGI is an amalgam of Wells Fargo Investment Management (which in the early 1970s pioneered the first indexing strategies using the NYSE composite index, and later the S&P 500), Nikko Securities, and BZW Investment Management (the investment management arm of Barclays Bank PLC). In 1990, Wells Fargo Investment advisers merged with Nikko Securities to form Wells Fargo Nikko Investment Advisors (WFNIA). Then in 1996, Barclays Bank PLC bought WFNIA and merged it with its own investment management division, BZW Investment Management. The combined entity was named Barclays Global Investors. Continuing a quarter-century of innovation in quantitative investment management, BGI launched its WEBS ETF (World Equity Benchmark Securities) in 1996. It launched iUnits or Canadian ETFs in 1999 and then continued with a huge rollout of its iShares ETF products in the United States in mid-2000. Patricia Dunn is BGI's CEO. Interestingly, Dunn started out as a temporary secretary at Wells Fargo Investment advisers in 1976 and worked her way to the top spot at BGI. *Fortune* named her to the number 11 spot in its top 50 female executives. Lee Kranefuss is BGI's managing director in charge of the iShares product.

State Street Global Advisors

State Street Global Advisors (SSgA), the sixth largest money manager in the world and the first (and world's largest) manager of ETFs, is the investment management arm of State Street Corporation located in Boston. As of June 2000, SSgA had $720 billion in assets under management and was named the number 2 indexer in *Pension and Investments'* annual update on indexing.[1] In addition, SSgA is the dominant player in the custody services business and has over $7 trillion (yes trillion with a capital "T") in custodial assets. If you own a mutual fund, chances are that that fund does business with SSgA or its parent. Considered the leader in the ETF market, in 1993 SSgA partnered with the American Stock Exchange and launched the first ETF—the Standard & Poor's 500 Depositary Receipts or SPDR, now the largest ETF, with assets of nearly $24 billion. As of late 2000, SSgA had over a 50 percent market share in the ETF market (in terms of assets) and is manager of the S&P Select Sector SPDRS. SSgA launched streetTRACKS ETFs in 2000 based on Dow Jones, Morgan Stanley, Fortune, and Wilshire indexes. Of the 78 ETFs launched in the United States as of November

29, 2000, 19 are managed by SSgA. Nick Lopardo is SSgA's CEO. Gus
Fleites, a principal of SSGA, is in charge of, among other responsibilities, SSgA's exchange-traded products.

Bank of New York

The Bank of New York (BNY) is the oldest U.S. bank in existence
today. In 1784, Alexander Hamilton, then a prominent New York attorney, helped forge the new business in an era when banking was in
its infancy. (Hamilton went on to become the first secretary of the
treasury under George Washington.) Over the next 216 years, the BNY
left its fingerprints on government, Wall Street, and the business world
at large. The first loan obtained by the new U.S. government was
arranged with BNY. When the NYSE was formed in 1792, the first corporate stock to be traded was BNY. It is now a major player in trust
management, custodial services, fund administration and accounting,
transfer agent services, and passive investment management. It manages the hugely successful Nasdaq-100 Index Shares (the QQQ) ETF
and the S&P MidCap 400 (mid-cap SPDRs, or spiders; ticker symbol:
MDY) ETF. The QQQ and the MDY are the second and third largest
ETFs in terms of asset size. BNY also manages the popular Merrill Lynch
HOLDRS (Holding Company Depositary Receipts). In fact, it is the
world's largest depositary for American and global depositary receipts,
allowing non-U.S. companies to offer dollar-denominated securities to
investors in the United States and Europe. BNY accounts for approximately two-thirds of all public-sponsored depositary receipt programs.
Tom Centrone, a vice president at BNY, is responsible for the passive
investment management of the QQQ and S&P MidCap 400 ETFs. He
also headed the group that helped launch the Nasdaq-100 ETF.

THE EXCHANGES AND MARKET MAKERS

ETFs owe their success to more than the trust managers. The exchanges that provide the forum for trading and the market makers and
specialists who provide liquidity have also made vital contributions to
these great instruments.

American Stock Exchange

For much of its history, the American Stock Exchange (AMEX) traded
mostly stocks. During the 1970s and 1980s, the AMEX gained more

prominence as many of the companies listed on the exchange were involved in energy. As energy prices spiked in the late 1970s, volume too rose significantly. But as the energy boom of the late 1970s turned to bust, volume declined and remained unremarkable for many years. Then the AMEX got into the derivatives business and started trading options on stocks and stock indexes. The exchange thrived, and volume soared, as did seat prices. Then an interesting octogenarian named Nathan Most had a brilliant idea to blend certain aspects of mutual funds and the trading liquidity of stocks into one instrument. Although it took a while for the idea to catch on with the regulators and lawyers, as well as the AMEX development team (the entire new-products team consisted of Most and coworker Steve Bloom), in 1993 the AMEX launched the first ETF: the Standard & Poor's 500 Depositary Receipts, or SPDRs. As this new market began to attract interest, traders combined the SPDR abbreviation with the AMEX exchange ticker symbol SPY. As a result, the instrument was affectionately referred to as SPYDERS, or SPIDERS. The fund now had all the ingredients for a raging success: easy to remember, simple in design, the name recognition of the underlying S&P 500, gobs of liquidity. The rest is history. The AMEX now has a virtual lock on the ETF market. In the late 1990s, the AMEX's upward momentum was so strong that Nasdaq, which itself had just overtaken the NYSE in volume, decided to merge with the AMEX.

Chicago Mercantile Exchange Inc.

Until 1972, Chicago Mercantile Exchange Inc. (CME) traded traditional commodity futures on livestock such as pork bellies and live cattle. Then, in 1972, under the direction of Leo Melamed and guidance from the Nobel laureate economist Milton Friedman, the CME launched futures contracts based not on livestock or grains but on currencies. With the first financial futures contracts, a new era was born. In the early 1980s, the CME introduced interest rate and stock index futures products as well. The Eurodollar futures contract went on to become the most extraordinary futures contract in the history of finance, trading 500,000 to 700,000 contracts per day (each with a $1 million notional value). The Eurodollar contract helped establish CME as a global powerhouse in risk management. In April 1982, CME launched S&P 500 stock index futures. Within a few years, average daily dollar volume in S&P 500 futures had overtaken that of the NYSE. The S&P 500 had reached critical mass.

But by 1997, after 15 years of rising markets, the notional value of the S&P 500 futures contract had reached an unprecedented $400,000.

Most futures contracts have notional values that are far less. A mere 1 percent move in the contract was equal to $4,000—far greater than the usual one-day move in beans, cattle, or crude futures. More important, the upfront performance bond margin (a deposit that futures traders must place when trading futures, see Part III) was becoming too large for the average trader, and some switched to competing products. Of several possible solutions suggested by CME's board of governors, one was to launch a smaller, more investor-friendly-size contract. It would be similar to its bigger brother in all respects except two: It would be one-fifth the size or "mini-size," and it would trade exclusively on CME's GLOBEX$_2$ electronic trading system. Hence, the E-mini S&P 500 was launched in September 1997. The E-mini S&P 500 futures contract far exceeded even the most optimistic projections. Within two years, average daily dollar volume exceeded the S&P 500 SPDRs at the AMEX, and within three years volume had exploded 1,000 percent from its launch. The mini went on to become one of CME's largest volume futures contracts, second only to Eurodollar futures. Lightning struck twice when CME launched a mini version of its successful Nasdaq-100 futures contract (for many of the same reasons) in June 1999. Astoundingly, the E-mini Nasdaq 100 grew faster than the E-mini S&P 500, and within one year of trading, it had pulled ahead of the QQQ at the AMEX in terms of average daily dollar volume. Clearly, CME's equity index complex was firing on all cylinders.

Spear, Leeds & Kellogg

One comment heard universally from large institutions and retail investors is the depth of the market in many ETFs. Where deep, liquid markets do exist, some of the credit goes to the specialist firms on the AMEX floor and other regional exchanges.

Spear, Leeds & Kellogg (SLK) is the largest specialist firm on the floors of both the NYSE and AMEX. As a specialist, it is responsible for making markets in each of its assigned companies. Markets are to be fair, orderly, and efficient. In addition, SLK tries to make these markets as deep and liquid as possible. Recently bought by Goldman Sachs, SLK has about $2 billion in capital and over 2,000 employees. It is the specialist for many of the AMEX's exchange-traded funds, including the SPY, S&P Select Sector SPDRs, and DIAMONDS, to name just a few. SLK routinely quotes deep markets (100,000 shares and up) at very narrow bid-offer spreads. Only in the most volatile of markets will these spreads widen. And when something this liquid widens, it usually means that spreads all across the financial spectrum are similarly expanding.

Part of the reason for the deep liquid markets in ETFs is the ability of specialists to hedge their market-making activities in other markets such as S&P 500 futures. In fact, SLK has direct lines to all major trading floors, including CME's S&P 500 futures pit. If, as part of its market-making activity, SLK suddenly finds itself long a few hundred thousand SPY and thinks the exposure might cause losses should the market fall (even temporarily) before it can unload the position, the firm could mitigate this risk with an appropriate position in S&P 500 futures or another vehicle such as S&P 500 options. Thus, although some view ETFs and futures as "competitive" instruments, they can actually complement each other.

Susquehanna Partners

Susquehanna Partners (SP) is a powerhouse of another sort on the street. Unlike Goldman Sachs, Morgan Stanley, JP Morgan, and the other investment banks on Wall Street that trade and engage in underwriting and a host of other activities, SP pretty much sticks to trading—and in a huge way. Underwriting initial public offerings and bonds is not SP's specialty; trading in securities, options, and futures is. SP, with some of the best personnel in the business, accounts for 2 percent of NYSE volume and 10 percent of the volume cleared through the Options Clearing Corporation (the clearinghouse that clears equity options and options on cash indexes). It also is one of the largest index arbitrageurs in the marketplace. It has specialist privileges in 400 to 500 equity options and is a force in over-the-counter currency options market as well. With all this trading acumen, it comes as no surprise that SP was chosen to be the specialist in many ETFs, including the QQQ, the S&P Midcap 400 (MDY), and several of Merrill Lynch's HOLDR trusts such as the Biotech HOLDRS (BBH), Internet HOLDRS (HHH), and the B2B Internet HOLDRS (BHH), to name a few. These markets too possess good liquidity and depth of market, depending on market conditions. SP is also very active in overseas markets and trades in the financial markets of 20 countries.

Hull Group, L.L.C.

The Hull Group is a quantitatively oriented, technology-driven market maker in equities and equity derivatives that is also involved in transaction services.* Founded by Blair Hull in 1985, Hull built the proprietary trading firm into a worldwide market player. Like Susquehanna and other major market makers, Hull takes the "other side" of just about any exchange-based trade. Superb financial engineering and electronic systems have helped it create an edge that allows it to be one of the major players worldwide and thus was assigned to be the specialist for many ETFs, particularly the BGI iShares. Hull is the market maker in the iShares S&P 500, iShares S&P MidCap 400, the iShares Russell 1000 Index and Russell 1000 Value index, and many others. (It is interesting to note that Goldman Sachs purchased SLK in 2000. Shortly before the SLK purchase, Goldman Sachs acquired Hull Trading Group. Hence, two of the major players in ETFs are now owned by Goldman Sachs.)

Other Important Firms

Spear Leeds, Susquehanna Partners, and Hull Trading are the specialists for the majority of the ETFs listed on the AMEX. Other important firms too have contributed to the success of the 100 or so ETF products launched as of March 2001. They are listed here with a sampling of some of the ETFs that they make markets in. In addition, the Chicago Stock Exchange (CSX) trades a significant amount of ETF volume. Some of the CSX's specialists are also listed along with a sampling of some of the ETFs they make markets in.

Wolverine Trading/AMEX

Broadband HOLDRS
Dow Jones U.S. LargeCap Growth streetTRACKS
Dow Jones U.S. SmallCap Value streetTRACKS
Morgan Stanley Internet streetTRACKS

KV Execution Services L.L.C./AMEX

Fortune e50 Index
Pharmaceutical HOLDRS

---

*I remember receiving a call from someone representing Hull Trading many years ago in response to sending a resumé. The gentleman asked if I had expertise in stochastics and multivariate analysis. I said no. He asked if I could program in C and in Pascal languages. Starting to feel totally unqualified by this time, I said no. He asked if I had experience in statistical arbitrage. I said no. Did I get an interview? No! But watching Hull's meteoric rise in the trading markets was not too much of a surprise after learning that it tends to look for those who are adept with technology and mathematics.

Select Sector SPDR Consumer Staples
Morgan Stanley High-Tech 35 Index streetTRACKS
Select Sector SPDR Basic Industries
Dow Jones U.S. LargeCap Value streetTRACKS
Dow Jones U.S. SmallCap Growth streetTRACKS
Dow Jones Global Titans streetTracks
Market 2000 HOLDRS

AIM Securities/AMEX

MSCI iShares Australia
MSCI iShares Austria
MSCI iShares Canada
MSCI iShares Italy
MSCI iShares Malaysia

AGS/STR/OTA/AMEX

Telecommunication HOLDRS
Software HOLDRS
Select Sector SPDR Utilities
Select Sector SPDR Industrial

Rock Island/CSX

Financial Sector SPDR
Energy Sector SPDR
Technology Sector SPDR
Biotech HOLDRS

Sydan/CSX

SPDRs
Pharmaceutical HOLDRS
Wireless HOLDRS
Morgan Stanley Internet streetTRACKS

Dempsey/CSX

Nasdaq 100 Index Shares
Russell 2000 Value
Russell 2000 Growth

In Part II detailed information tables show each ETF, along with a comprehensive display of data, rankings, and information.

MAJOR PLAYERS IN INDEXING OVERALL

ETFs and mini stock index futures are only two (albeit important) aspects of the trillion-dollar indexing phenomenon. Several other very large participants, although not currently involved in the ETF or futures side of indexing, play a dominant role that cannot be ignored. Some have been mentioned already. Exhibit 2.1 gives a picture of how big some of the players are.

We also cover some of the major equity derivatives players—those that are active in index arbitrage and program trading—in the section on index arbitrage.

Exhibit 2.1   Leading Passive and Enhanced Index Managers, June 30, 2000

Company	Total U.S. Institutional Tax-Exempt Assets (billions of dollars)
Barclays Global Investors	$525.6
State Street Global Advisors	337.5
TIAA-CREF	110.7
Vanguard Group	92.7
Deutsche Asset Management	92.4
Mellon Capital	74.6
Northern Trust Quantitative	59.9
J.P. Morgan	48.1
Fidelity	46.1
Dimensional Fund	24.8
Alliance Capital	24.7
Prudential Insurance	20.7
PIMCO (Pacific Investment Management)	20.5
Lincoln Capital	20.2
Merrill Lynch Asset Management	19.1
World Asset Management	16.8

Source: Data from Pension and Investments, September 4, 2000.

3

THE INDEXES

As of March 1, 2001, there were approximately 100 ETFs and HOL-DRS. Many cover key industry benchmarks such as the Standard & Poor's Indexes, Russell Indexes, and Dow Jones Products. Others are less well known, cover narrow-based sectors, or are so new that they do not yet have much operating history. Given time and the right market conditions, the volume and asset bases of these products will grow substantially. In this chapter, I give some details of the major indexes that are either key benchmarks or have ETFs tied to them that have attracted a large number of assets or trading volume. For example, the SPY, which tracks the Standard & Poor's 500 Composite Index, is the largest of the ETFs, with assets of nearly $25 billion. Its average daily volume is about 7 million shares. The S&P 500 is also a key benchmark and has the most money indexed to it, so it will obviously get more attention than other less established indexes.

STANDARD & POOR'S

Standard & Poor's is the financial services segment of the McGraw-Hill Companies, which have provided independent and objective financial information, analysis, and research for nearly 140 years. It is also recognized as a leading provider of equity indexes. Investors around the globe use S&P indexes for investment performance measurement and as the basis for a wide range of financial instruments, such as index funds, futures, options, and, of course, ETFs. Its flagship index, the S&P 500 Composite, is one of the most popular indexes in all of finance and one of the key benchmarks for money manager performance. Over 400 companies around the globe have licenses with Standard & Poor's for their index products. The influence and name recognition of the S&P 500 is unparalleled in finance.

S&P 500 Index

Key Statistics on the S&P 500, March 2, 2001

Mean market value	$ 21.0 billion
Median market value	$ 8.3 billion
Largest company market value	$441.0 billion
Smallest company market value	$773.0 million[1]

The original S&P index was a weekly index of 233 U.S. stocks, first published in 1923 (see the timeline at the back of the book). By 1941 the index had grown to 416 issues. And by 1957 it had grown to 500 issues and evolved into what we now know as the S&P 500 Composite.

The S&P 500 Index is a capitalization-weighted index that tracks the performance of 500 large-capitalization issues. The total value of all the companies in the index as of this writing is about $11 trillion and represents about 75 percent of the total capitalization of the entire U.S. stock market (usually measured by the Wilshire 5000 Index, which contains over 6,000 stocks). The correlation between the S&P 500 and the gigantic Wilshire 5000 index is quite high: nearly .97, despite having substantially fewer stocks. The investment returns between the two indexes have also been similar over the 29 or so years that both indexes have been available. Furthermore, of the $1.4 trillion indexed in the United States, about $ 0.9 to $ 1.1 trillion is indexed to the S&P 500. Each year, thousands of money managers have the single-minded goal of outperforming the S&P 500. Few accomplish this goal. Although the S&P 500 is not perfect, it provides an excellent measure of the stock market.

Over the years, S&P 500's complexion has changed. Thirty years ago, it was a tribute to industrial America (then the "new economy"— and now the "old economy"). IBM, AT&T, GM, and Kodak graced the top spots in the index. GE was number nine. By the late 1970s, six of the top 10 issues were oil companies. In 2000, only one oil company was in the top 10 (ExxonMobil), and four of the top spots were taken by the high-tech companies Cisco, Intel, Microsoft, and EMC (see Exhibit 3.1).

Exhibit 3.1 The Ten Largest Stocks in the S&P 500: A Three-Decade Snapshot

1969	1979	1989	2000
1. IBM	IBM	Exxon	General Electric
2. AT&T	AT&T	General Electric	Cisco
3. General Motors	Exxon	IBM	ExxonMobil
4. Eastman Kodak	General Motors	AT&T	Microsoft
5. Exxon	Amoco	Philip Morris	Pfizer
6. Sears	Mobil Oil	Merck	Citigroup
7. Texaco	General Electric	Bristol Myers Squibb	Wal-Mart
8. Xerox	Standard Oil	Du Pont	AIG
9. General Electric	Chevron	Amoco	Intel
10. Gulf Oil	Atlantic Richfield	Bell South	EMC Corp

In early 2000, technology composed about one-third of the capitalization of the index. The downdraft in technology issues during 2000–2001 reduced that concentration to the 20 percent level.

Calculating this popular index is relatively easy; maintaining it is another task entirely. It is a capitalization-weighted index. This means you take the number of shares of a stock, say General Electric, and multiply by the stock price. (Put another way, capitalization is how much in dollars it would take to buy every share of General Electric.) GE has 9.9 billion shares outstanding and trades at about $43 per share. Multiplying the two yields a capitalization (also known as *market cap* or *market value*) of $425 billion as of March 2001. Cisco Systems has nearly 7.1 billion shares outstanding and trades for $22 per share, giving it a market cap of $156 billion. S&P adds up the market caps of these and the other 498 names in the index and comes up with a number of about $11.0 trillion. That number is then divided by the divisor (approximately 8,900) to give the S&P 500 composite value: about 1,235 as of March 2001. The divisor changes in response to changes in the index. To ensure continuity, S&P adjusts the divisor every time one stock is substituted into the index in the case of merger activity.

The stocks in the S&P 500 Index are determined by a combination of general guidelines and a nine-member committee headed up by David Blitzer, the vice president and chief economist at S&P and chairman of the Standard & Poor's index committee. When any stock is considered for adding to the index, Blitzer's committee makes the final decision. In 1999, there were 30 changes in the index, and in 1998 there were nearly 50.

General Guidelines for Adding Stocks to the S&P Indexes

- *Market value:* S&P indexes are market value weighted.[2]
- *Industry group classification:* Companies selected for the S&P indexes represent a broad range of industry segments within the U.S. economy.
- *Capitalization:* Ownership of a company's outstanding common shares is carefully analyzed in order to screen out closely held companies.
- *Trading activity:* The trading volume of a company's stock is analyzed on a daily, monthly, and annual basis to ensure ample liquidity and efficient share pricing.
- *Fundamental analysis:* The financial and operating conditions of a company are rigorously analyzed. The goal is to add companies to the indexes that are relatively stable and keep turnover low.
- *Emerging industries:* Companies in emerging industries and new industry groups (industry groups currently not represented in the indexes) are candidates as long as they meet the general guidelines for adding stocks.

General Guidelines for Removing Stocks from the S&P Indexes

- *Merger, acquisition, or leveraged buyout:* A company is removed from the indexes as close as possible to the actual transaction date.[3]
- *Bankruptcy:* A company is removed from the indexes immediately after Chapter 11 filing or as soon as an alternative recapitalization plan that changes the company's debt-to-equity mix is approved by shareholders
- *Restructuring:* Each company's restructuring plan is analyzed in depth. The restructured company as well as any spin-offs are reviewed for index inclusion or exclusion.
- *Lack of representation:* The company no longer meets current criteria for inclusion or is no longer representative of its industry group.

S&P MidCap 400 Index

Key Statistics on the MidCap 400 Index, March 2, 2001

Total market value	$816.0 billion
Mean market value	$ 2.2 billion
Median market value	$ 2.0 billion
Largest company market value	$ 10.3 billion
Smallest company market value	$102.0 million

The MidCap 400 measures the performance of the midsize company segment of the U.S. market. It consists of 400 domestic stocks chosen for market size, liquidity, and industry group representation. It is also capitalization weighted (market value weighted) and was the first benchmark targeted to mid-tier companies. The MidCap 400 index is used by 95 percent of U.S. managers and pension plan sponsors. About $25 billion is indexed to the S&P MidCap 400.

S&P SmallCap 600 Index

Key Statistics on the S&P Small Cap 600 Index, February 2, 2001

Total market value	$ 340.0 billion
Mean market value	$ 566.0 million
Median market value	$ 474.0 million
Largest company market value	$ 3.0 billion
Smallest company market value	$ 28.0 million

The S&P SmallCap 600 Index consists of 600 domestic stocks chosen for market size and liquidity. Liquidity measures are bid-offer spreads, share turnover, and share ownership. Like the MidCap 400 and the 500, the SmallCap 600 is capitalization weighted. The small-cap sector in the United States has captured the interest of institutional and retail investors over the past several years.

Subindexes

Each of the indexes described has subindexes based on the two primary styles of investing: growth and value. For example, the S&P 500 has a growth subindex named the S&P 500/Barra Growth Index and a value subindex called the S&P 500/Barra Value Index. Barra is a well-known quantitative group that provides innovative models, software, consulting, and money management services to its clients. In May 1992,

Standard & Poor's and Barra jointly released the S&P 500/Barra Growth and S&P 500/Barra Value indexes designed to track two of the predominant styles of investing in the U.S. equity market: growth and value investing. The subindexes are constructed by dividing the stocks in the S&P 500 according to each company's book-to-price ratio. The value index contains S&P 500 Index companies that have higher book-to-price ratios and vice versa for the growth index. ETFs are available on all three of the primary indexes, as well as the S&P/Barra subindexes.

NASDAQ

Key Statistics on the Nasdaq 100 Index, March 2, 2001

Total market value:	$ 2.0 trillion
Median market value:	$ 20.1 billion
Largest company market value	$306.0 billion
Smallest company market value	$ 2.7 billion

In the mid-1960s, the Securities and Exchange Commission (SEC) released a study that characterized the over-the-counter (OTC) securities market as fragmented and obscure. The regulator then put the National Association of Securities Dealers (NASD) in charge of fixing the problem with a mandate to automate the system. By 1968, construction began on an automated OTC securities system then known as the National Association of Securities Dealers Automated Quotation system (NASDAQ). Interestingly, that same year Gordon Moore and Robert Noyce founded a corporation by the name of Integrated Electronics, which went on to become Intel Corporation, one of the greatest of many success stories that came out of the Nasdaq stock market. Even more intriguing was that a few months after Intel was born, computer scientists at the Advanced Research Project Agency (ARPA) and Bolt, Beranek, and Newman invented and implemented a way for computers to be networked, creating the precursor to today's Internet. On February 8, 1971, Nasdaq's system began its first official day of trading.

Less than 30 years later, in 1994, Nasdaq passed the NYSE in annual share volume. The Nasdaq Composite Index now contains over 4,800 companies representing a market capitalization of over $3 trillion. The Nasdaq stock market now regularly trades over 1 billion shares per day and is home to dozens of corporate giants in technology, biotechnology, telecommunications, and other sectors. Frequently, you'll hear the media referring to the Nasdaq market as being up or down on any given day. And that little box in the corner of your TV when you are watching CNBC or some other financial program usually quotes the Nasdaq Composite Index. However, there is another Nasdaq index. Called the Nasdaq-100, it is composed of the top 100 nonfinancial companies in the Nasdaq stock market. Hence, there is some confusion. At CME we are constantly getting calls concerning the futures contract and the cash Nasdaq composite—and therein lies the problem. The composite and the 100 are two different indexes! The QQQ is based on the Nasdaq-100 index, *not the composite*. The regular-sized and E-mini Nasdaq-100 futures are based (obviously) on the Nasdaq-100 Index, *not the composite index*. The NDX options contract at the CBOE is based on the Nasdaq-100, as is the MNX (mini-NDX option). In fact all derivatives and trading vehicles are based on the Nasdaq-100.

The Nasdaq-100 is a modified capitalization-weighted index. The calculations for a modified cap-weighted index are a bit deep, so we'll stick to the basics here. Modified cap weighting involves adjustments to the capitalizations of the various components of the Nasdaq-100 index. For example, at the end of 1999, Microsoft had an actual market cap of just over $600 billion—about 5.9 billion shares outstanding at $101 per share. Yet Mister Softee's (the street's nickname for Microsoft derived from its ticker symbol, MSFT) capitalization in the Nasdaq-100 calculation turns out to be $389 billion as of December 31, 1999. How did MSFT lose $211 billion of market cap? A little modification. Nasdaq adjusts the market capitalization of the members of the 100 so that no one individual issue would grow too large relative to the rest of the index. Still, Microsoft is a large percentage of the index, as are Cisco, Intel, Oracle, and some others. Without these modifications to their market values, they would in all probability account for too large a proportion of the index.

RUSSELL INDEXES

Key Statistics on Russell Indexes, March 2, 2001

	Russell 3000	Russell 1000	Russell 2000
Total market value	$13.0 trillion	$11.9 trillion	$1.1 trillion
Mean market value	$4.6 billion	$12.6 billion	$552.0 million
Largest company market value	$441.0 billion	$441.0 billion	$4.1 billion
Smallest company market value	$3.0 million	$9.0 million	$3.0 million

Frank Russell Company, one of the world's leading investment consultants, is also involved in performance measurement, analysis, and investment management. A few statistics underscore the role that Russell plays in indexing:

- Over $100 billion is invested in funds using Russell indexes as a model.
- Investment Management Assets exceed $50 billion worldwide.
- Frank Russell's consulting arm serves 200 major clients in 25 countries, with $1 trillion in assets.
- Several Russell indexes have become benchmarks for specific areas of investment management. For example, the Russell 2000 Index is a well-known benchmark for the small capitalization sector.

In 1984, Frank Russell launched the first members of its family of U.S. equity indexes. Leading off was the Russell 3000 Index. Russell wanted to create an index that represented the entire U.S. equity market available to investors, so the index included 3,000 issues and adjusted for certain factors such as cross-holdings and the number of shares in private hands (which would not be available to investors in the marketplace float). These 3,000 companies represented about 98 percent of the investable U.S. equity universe. (It would take the addition of thousands more very small companies to include the other 2 percent—companies so small that the typical fund manager would have a rough time trying to deal in.) Russell further split the index, by capitalization, into several additional indexes. The Russell 1000 Index is composed of the largest 1,000 stocks (top third) in the Russell 3000 Index. The top 1,000 covers about 92 percent of the value of the entire 3,000-stock index. The Russell 2000 Index is the smallest 2000 companies in the Russell 3000 index and represents 8 percent of the capitalization of the index. Thus, all Russell indexes are subsets of the Russell 3000.

Recall that the S&P 500 is a pure capitalization-weighted index, and the Nasdaq-100 is a modified capitalization-weighted index. The Russell indexes are also capitalization weighted, but some adjustments have been made, and investors should be aware of them. The purpose of these adjustments is to exclude from market calculations the capitalization that is not available for purchase by investors. Member companies are ranked by their available market capitalization, which is calculated by multiplying the price by available shares. Available shares are shares that are available for trading. Unavailable shares would fall under the category of employee stock ownership plans (ESOPs). If an ESOP owns a certain amount of the capitalization, then Russell adjusts for this in the calculation of the stocks capitalization. Cross-ownership of shares in a company (in the index) by another company (in the index) would also represent unavailable shares and would require adjustment by Russell.

In addition, unlike the Standard & Poor's indexes, which makes additions and deletions in an ongoing or as-needed fashion, Russell indexes are reconstituted annually to reflect changes in the market. When a stock leaves the index for whatever reason—bankruptcy, merger activity, or something else—it is not replaced. Hence, the Russell 2000, for example, may actually have fewer than 2,000 issues at any point in between annual reconstitution. Reconstitution (also called *rebalancing*) occurs on May 31 each year and becomes effective one month later.

Russell, like Standard & Poor's, has also developed style indexes based on the growth and value disciplines of investing. Russell uses price-to-book ratios and long-term-growth estimates in determining which issues fall into the growth or value camp. Hence, the Russell 3000, 2000, and 1000 have growth and value indexes. ETFs exist on all of these indexes. In addition, although CME does not have an E-mini Russell 2000 futures (as of yet), it does have a regular-size futures contract based on the Russell 2000 Index.

DOW JONES

Key Statistics on the Dow Jones Industrial Average, March 2, 2001

Total market cap	$ 3.76 trillion
Average market cap	$122.0 billion
Largest market cap	$527.0 billion
Lowest market cap	$ 11.0 billion

From a business point of view, the *Wall Street Journal* is probably one of the most perfect business franchises—one that could not be duplicated even if a competitor had billions of dollars to work with. It offers a product that people gladly pay 75 cents for every day. It is also a demographic dream, distributed in every major city and every major financial center in the world. Generally its readers have incredible buying capability; the average net worth of its readers is nearly in the seven figures. These demographics, along with vast readership (it usually ranks among the top three newspapers in terms of readership, along with the *New York Times* and *USA Today*), allow it to receive top dollar for advertising space.

This perfect business was started by Charles Henry Dow and Edward Jones, and Dow Jones remains the publisher of the *Journal* to this day. The first edition of the *Wall Street Journal* appeared in July 1889. Dow and Jones, along with Charles M. Bergstresser, were previously employed by the Kiernan News Agency, but they all left Kiernan to start Dow Jones & Company in November 1882. Bergstresser's name was left out because it was too long despite the fact that he actually bankrolled the new firm. The *Journal* evolved out of a publication that Dow created called the *Customer's Afternoon Letter*, a daily two-page financial news bulletin that also covered an average of 11 stocks (nine of them were railroad issues). On May 26, 1896, the Dow Jones Industrial Average (DJIA), comprising 12 smokestack companies, made its debut. The DJIA grew to encompass 30 large industrial companies and became a popular business barometer. Of the 12 original companies, only one (General Electric) remains in the DJIA.

More than 104 years later, the DJIA is one of the world's best-known stock measures and consists of 30 of the largest and most liquid blue-chip stocks in the United States. The average is maintained by the editors of the *Wall Street Journal*. Although they have made several changes over the past 10 years, there were long periods when there were no changes at all. Recently, Microsoft and Intel were added to the average, and though some experts questioned the validity of Microsoft's being an "industrial" enterprise, they nevertheless welcomed the technological update to the well-known average.

The DJIA, unlike the S&P 500 (and many other indexes), is a price-weighted average. The highest price issues hold the most influence over the average. A stock split would, in effect, decrease a stock's influence. A 1 percent move in a $90 stock like IBM would have a greater impact than a 1 percent move in a $40 stock like Wal-Mart. On the other hand, if GE, for example, advanced one point and General Motors declined one point, there would be no affect on the DJIA. However, in a price-weighted index such as the S&P 500 or Russell 1000, that same scenario would cause an increase in the index because GE's market-cap is so much larger than General Motors.

Prices of the 30 issues in the DJIA are simply added up and divided by a divisor. (Adjustments in the divisor over the years have reduced it so much that it went below 1.00 a few years ago, effectively transforming the divisor into a multiplier!) Indeed, with the Dow divisor now standing at .17, each one-point move in a Dow component creates a more than five-point move in the index. Such exaggerations in price movements have caught the eye of the investing public and the media. It is also one of the reasons (though a small one) that so little money is indexed to the DJIA relative to other indexes. Having only 30 components is another factor that the Street seems to dislike.

The ETF based on the DJIA, the DIAMONDS Trust, is one of the more successful ETFs. Excellent name recognition and great market making by Spear Leeds & Kellogg has engendered an ETF that trades over 900,000 shares per day and has $2 billion in assets. ETFs exist on many other Dow indexes, including the Dow Jones Total Market Index, the Dow Jones Global Titans Index, and various style and sector indexes (all covered in Part II).

WILSHIRE ASSOCIATES

Wilshire Associates Incorporated is an independent advisory company that provides investment products, consulting, and tools to investment managers, fund sponsors, and individuals. Wilshire serves over 400 organizations in over 20 countries representing over $2 trillion in assets.

Wilshire's flagship index is the Wilshire 5000 Total Market Index. It represents the broadest index for the United States equity market, measuring the performance of all U.S. headquartered equity securities with readily available price data. When it was originally created (1974), the index contained nearly 5000 stocks. But it has grown to over 6500 issues reflecting the growth in the number of companies in the United States as a whole.

In 1983, Wilshire introduced the Wilshire 4500 Index by removing the 500 stocks in the S&P 500 creating an index primarily of mid- and small-sized stocks. While no ETF exists for either of these indexes as of mid 2001, on May 31, 2001, the AMEX launched an ETF based on the Vanguard Group's Total Market Index mutual fund. This fund does track the Wilshire 5000. On its first day of trading, the ETF traded over 2 million shares—a great start by any standard.

MSCI INDEXES

These indexes were founded in 1969 by Capital International S.A. as the first international performance benchmarks. Benchmarking had made great inroads in the United States, and as investment overseas increased dramatically, the need for metrics on foreign markets became evident. Capital International's indexes facilitated the comparison of many world markets. In 1986, Morgan Stanley, the investment banking powerhouse, acquired the rights to these indexes. The result was Morgan Stanley Capital International (MSCI). MSCI's database contains nearly 25,000 securities covering 50 countries. It calculates nearly 3,000 indexes daily and services a client base of over 1,200 worldwide.

One of the advantages of MSCI and its foreign indexes is consistency. Although many foreign stock exchanges calculate their own indexes, comparing them to one another is difficult because of differences in representation of local markets, mathematical differences in formulas, adjustments, and reference and base dates. MSCI applies the same rigorous criteria and calculation methodology across many of its indexes, including emerging stock market indexes. Moreover, it tries to create indexes noted for depth and breadth of coverage in a particular country. Each MSCI country index attempts to have at least 60 percent of the capitalization of a country's stock market reflected in the calculation. All single-country indexes are capitalization weighted.

In 1996 the AMEX launched ETFs based on 17 MSCI country indexes. These products were affectionately known as WEBS—the acronym for World Equity Benchmark Securities. BGI was the manager of the WEBS products, and when it launched its iShares ETFs, the WEBS name was changed to iShares MSCI Index Fund Shares. The 23 iShares MSCI Index funds now listed on AMEX offer investors large and small vehicles for investing overseas.

Exhibit 3.2 summarizes and compares the indexes discussed in this chapter.

Exhibit 3.2 A Comparison of U.S. Equity Indexes

Index	S&P 500	S&P Mid Cap 400	S&P Small Cap 600	Russell 1000	Russell 2000	Russell 3000	Dow Jones Industrial Average	Nasdaq 100	Wilshire 5000
Total market capitalization[a]	$10.9 trillion	$815 billion	$339 billion	$11.9 trillion	$1.0 trillion	$13.0 trillion	$3.6 trillion	$2.0 trillion	$13.2 trillion
Percentage of total U.S. market	77%	7%	2%	92%	8%	98%	18%	19%	100%
Market representation	Large cap	Mid-cap	Small cap	Large cap	Small cap	Overall market	Large cap	Tech, telecom	Overall market
Approximate number of members	500	400	600	1,000	2,000	3,000	30	100	More than 6,000
Weighting in calculation of index	Cap weighted	Cap weighted	Cap weighted	Cap weighted with float adjustment	Cap weighted with float adjustment	Cap weighted with float adjustment	Price weighted	Modified cap weighted	Cap weighted
Additions or selections of members	Committee/ guidelines	Committee/ guidelines	Committee/ guidelines	Annual reconstitution	Annual reconstitution	Annual reconstitution	By committee	Annual rebalance	As needed
Growth and value-style indexes	Yes	Yes	Yes	Yes	Yes	Yes	Yes	No	Yes
ETF on underlying	Yes	Yes	Yes	Yes	Yes	Yes	Yes	Yes	No
Futures on underlying	Yes— CME	Yes— CME	No	Yes— NYBOT	Yes— CME	No	Yes— CBOT	Yes— CME	No

[a]As of March 2, 2001.
Source: CME Index Products Marketing.

Part II

EXCHANGE TRADED FUNDS

"No way! I'm a day-trading major, too!"

4

ETFs: BEGINNINGS, ADVANTAGES, ATTRIBUTES

When Nathan Most was growing up in Los Angeles during the depression, he used to hike the trails all over the southern California mountains. "Southern California wasn't like it is now. It was wide open. We'd go out into the desert and we could see the Milky Way."[1] Seventy years later, Nate Most has not lost his zeal for exploring. In fact, this 86 year old could teach the financial engineers a few things. I originally thought of putting his story in Chapter 2 on the players but soon realized that his persona puts him at a level much higher.

In the late 1980s, the AMEX was struggling. The NYSE and the Nasdaq stock market were snapping up all the new listings. New listings to exchanges are like new products to a corporation. A blockbuster stock with heavy trading volume could contribute enormously to revenues. True, many Nasdaq issues did migrate to the Big Board (the NYSE). But many companies on the cutting edge of technology, biotechnology, and telecommunications chose to list or remain on Nasdaq. The Nasdaq would go on to bill itself as the "market for the next 100 years," and the NYSE was arguably the most prestigious securities exchange in the world. Intel and Apple (and eventually Microsoft) and the rest of the techno-leaders were carrying Nasdaq to record volume. The Nasdaq's holy trinity of Microsoft, Cisco, and Intel would at one time hold three of the top four spots in the S&P 500 and the top three issues in the Nasdaq-100 Index. The great bull market also lifted the NYSE record activity as well as seat prices. But the AMEX's volume was lackluster—around 20 million shares per day, according to Most. Most and colleague Steven Bloom were in charge of new product development in derivatives and were tired of seeing the equity side struggle to get new listings. Most thought that there had to be a better way. He had a background in commodities and was thus familiar with the idea of warehouse receipts (In commodities, you hear stories of people being fearful of getting 5,000 bushels of soybeans dumped in their driveway. In theory, if you did fail to sell your contracts before final settlement, the beans would delivered to a grain silo–storage warehouse facility, and you would have a piece of paper—a warehouse receipt—showing ownership of those 5,000 bushels of soybeans, thus sparing you discomfort.) Most and Bloom also knew about mutual funds and wondered if the two could be blended into a hybrid security—a warehouse receipt for shares of stock.

Most's idea grew after the crash of 1987. As expected, there were plenty of naysayers. The attorneys initially told him that the SEC would never approve this type of instrument. Most, who was in his mid-seventies at the time, finally convinced AMEX senior management to give it a try. The AMEX chose wisely and with Most and Bloom's guidance forged ahead. After years of legal wrangling and obtaining exemptions from the 1940 Securities and Exchange Act, things started moving. The AMEX enlisted Kathleen Moriarty, an attorney, who was enormously helpful in getting the product through the regulatory maze. The final push came from the head of the SEC, Richard Breeden, who reportedly liked the product. Most told me in an e-mail that he never thought it would be as successful as it turned out to be. No one told him ETFs would not work, just that approval from regulators would never come.

Most worked with State Street Bank to do the fund management and wanted a product that would compete with the hugely successful Vanguard Index products and the 20 basis point annual management fee. SSgA was the only one that came close at the time. Hence, the first ETF, the Standard & Poor's Depositary Receipt, is really a warehouse receipt for a basket of stocks (stocks in the S&P 500) in a fund! Nate was not just a player but the inventor of ETFs. There was no real rocket science here, no massively paralleled supercomputers crunching and optimizing, no huge research and development staff. There was merely a desire to see an idea through despite the obstacles and a willingness to do whatever it takes.

In late January 1993, against all regulatory odds, the AMEX launched the S&P 500 Depositary Receipts. Spiders were born, and the AMEX was on its way again. Volume on the first day was spectacular.

Average daily volume for the first full month of operation was over 300,000 shares per day. Within a few years, volume regularly hit 1 million shares a day, and the SPY ticker symbol was atop the AMEX most-active list constantly.

Most is still hard at work in the ETF field and at age 86 shows no signs of slowing down. In fact, after many years at the AMEX, he is now the president of the iShares Trust, which is responsible for nearly 60 ETFs managed by Barclays Global Investors. Bloom continues to preach the ETF gospel, now as a principal at Capmark, a consulting firm. Bloom also assisted the Nasdaq in launching the Nasdaq-100 Index Shares and with *Fortune* magazine in its indexes. He continues to work with ETFs on a worldwide basis.

In the year 2000 alone, over 60 ETFs were introduced. AMEX trades around 80 ETFs, and they are springing up all over the globe, as well as on other U.S. exchanges. In 1993, the SPDR trust had less than $2 billion in assets. The assets of all ETFs in the United States are now over $70 billion. And as the financial press and mutual fund rating outfits such as Morningstar broaden their coverage beyond traditional mutual funds and cover ETFs, interest is certain to snowball.

ETFs are available on nearly every major broad market, style, and sector indexes in the United States. Investors large and small have a large number of choices. BGI, SSgA, and other major players have put together an assortment that would make the finest index aficionado feel like a kid in a candy store.

Here are the reasons that ETFs (and E-mini stock index futures) have captured so many assets in so little time:

- Easy to understand
- Intraday trading access
- ETF strategies can be enjoyed by institutions as well as individuals
- Attractive and universally accepted indexes and sectors
- Low cost
- Liquidity
- No short-selling restrictions
- Trade on regulated exchanges
- Tax advantages

In the chapters that follow, we discuss these attributes in considerable detail. Then we discuss how ETFs are produced, move on to applications and strategies, and profile the major ETFs—those with a huge asset base or a large average daily trading volume or that are an important benchmark or sector. Many of the examples are drawn from the most active and popular ETFs. Exhibits list all the important items an investor or trader needs to know about each ETF, including tickers, volume, bid-offer spreads, and fees. We then discuss additional products such as Merrill Lynch's HOLDRS products and international investing with ETFs. Later in this book, we put together some sample portfolios for investors of all risk-reward profiles. After all, that is one of the biggest questions novice investors ask: How do I put together a portfolio without a lot of knowledge of the investing process?

EASY TO UNDERSTAND

ETFs trade just like stocks. You can buy most of them in any increment you want (HOLDRS have a 100-share minimum), and they can be traded out of any brokerage account or margin account, including online brokerage firms. They are elegant in their simplicity. They combine the attributes of mutual funds and individual equities. They are two-dimensional; the only thing the investor cares about is up and down, as opposed to the options trader, who has to think in four dimensions (up, down, time, and volatility). Instead of trying to choose from the 10,000 mutual funds currently available, some of which have confusing multiple classes (e.g., Class A, B, or C shares), ETFs narrow the field considerably and therefore simplify investors' decisions immensely.

The popular S&P 500 Spiders (SPY) demonstrate the simplicity of these products. The SPY mimics the S&P 500, which is currently trading at around 1,300. At the same time, the SPY is trading at 130, one-tenth the size. Spiders are designed as securities with a market value approximating one-tenth the value of the underlying index. A word of caution here: Not all ETFs are priced at one-tenth the value of their respective indexes. The QQQ, for example, which tracks the Nasdaq-100 Index, is currently at 50, while the underlying index is at 2000. Hence, the QQQ has a market value of one-fortieth of the underlying index (a two-for-one split in early 2000 effectively changed the value from one-twentieth to one-fortieth). As an illustration, if the S&P 500 were to advance 10 percent from 1300 to 1430, the SPY would similarly advance about 10 percent, to 143. The investor would receive virtually the same rate of return as the index and the same rate of return as if he had bought a standard index mutual fund that mimics the S&P 500, minus a few costs.

INTRADAY TRADING ACCESS

Several years ago, I decided to invest some money in a popular mutual fund. I wrote out the check on a Sunday evening and mailed it Monday morning. By the time the check arrived at the mutual fund and I received my shares, it was Friday. It was just my luck that the momentum players were in the market in full force, and the broad market had advanced dramatically over the week. By Friday, the S&P 500 was about 5 percent higher than it had been five days earlier.

One of the most powerful advantages of ETFs is the ability to buy or sell them throughout the day, much as you would a typical stock. There is no waiting for the 4:00 EST close of the NYSE to determine what you'll pay for your shares, no waiting for the mail, no waiting for the back office processing (as efficient as it is), no restrictions on switching in or out of your fund. Make a phone call to your stock broker or a point-and-click through your on-line broker, and you're invested in the broad market or sector of your choice. True, constant turnover in the form of day trading or actively trading ETFs can defeat the purpose of indexing, whose prime goal is to reduce costs. Nevertheless, the flexibility and the freedom to adjust positions, especially for registered investment advisers or institutional investors, is compelling.

APPEAL TO A BROAD RANGE OF INVESTORS

Whether you are the manager of a billion-dollar pension fund or a smaller retail investor armed with only $2,500 in capital (but a strong opinion on the market), there is an ETF and a strategy for you.

Let's say you manage a pension fund, and part of your fund is indexed to the Russell 2000. You think that an overheated market will cool over the near term, and you want to tilt (i.e., weigh your portfolio toward a certain style) your portfolio more toward the value end of the Russell 2000, since value stocks tend to outperform their growth brethren in down markets. The manager could accomplish this by purchasing an ETF, specifically the iShares Russell 2000 Value shares. If an individual thought that the Internet economy was poised for an advance, she could purchase the Fortune e-50 streetTRACKS, which is an ETF comprising 50 leading Internet economy stocks, including Internet hardware, software, telecom, and e-commerce. Clearly, ETFs fill the needs of a variety of investors.

UNIVERSALLY ACCEPTED INDEXES (BENCHMARKS)

Add up the major index provider's product lines, and you have literally thousands of indexes. While many of these function as benchmarks for investors the world over, only a small subset of broad market indexes, style indexes, and sector indexes garners most of the attention. Indeed, of the trillions of dollars indexed in the United States and abroad, much of the indexed money finds its way into a very small number (compared to the total playing field) of benchmarks that are characterized by high visibility and recognition in the investment realm. ETFs cover each of these highly visible and important benchmarks.

LOW COST

Some of the advantages of ETFs are real standouts. Cost is one of them. Despite rising asset bases and the concomitant economies of scale, many mutual funds have shown rising, not falling, expenses over their operating history. On the other hand, the bargain basement costs of most ETFs would impress even the most ardent cheapskate. Exhibits 4.1 and 4.2 illustrate the incredibly low-cost structure of ETFs.

Zeroing in on the broad-based indexes, the evidence is overwhelmingly in favor of ETFs when considering costs. The typical broad-based mutual fund is approximately 10 times more expensive than its ETF counterpart. If you take away any lesson from this book it is this: *Costs matter!* Saving 50 to 100 basis points per year over the course of an investing lifetime can mean a substantial amount of money.

LIQUIDITY

One characteristic evident in most of the U.S. financial markets is liquidity. In the U.S stock market, it is easy to transact blocks of 10,000, 50,000, or even 100,000 shares of stock for many of the issues in the S&P 500 and the Nasdaq-100. Most institutional firms like Bear Stearns, Goldman, Morgan, and Merrill Lynch have block trading desks that regularly transact 100,000 shares or more. In short, buying or selling 500,000 shares of GE or Microsoft is not a difficult task. On the other hand, transacting that many shares of a typical mid-cap or small-cap issue might take some finessing.

When discussing ETFs, eventually the question comes up: Given their relatively short history, isn't liquidity a concern? Two of the major

Exhibit 4.1 Annual Expenses of Various Funds and ETFs

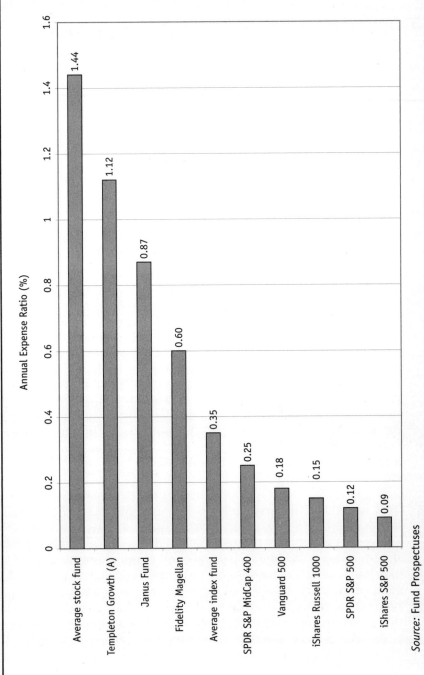

Annual Expense Ratio (%)

Average stock fund	1.44
Templeton Growth (A)	1.12
Janus Fund	0.87
Fidelity Magellan	0.60
Average index fund	0.35
SPDR S&P MidCap 400	0.25
Vanguard 500	0.18
iShares Russell 1000	0.15
SPDR S&P 500	0.12
iShares S&P 500	0.09

Source: Fund Prospectuses

Exhibit 4.2 General Cost Comparisons: Mutual Funds and ETFs

| | Annual Expense Ratios (in basis points) | |
	Exchange Traded Funds	Mutual Fund
Broad-based	9–20	144
International	50–99	194
Sector	20–60	166
Style	18–25	133–154

Source: Morningstar Mutual Fund 500, 2000 ed. (Chicago, 2000), p. 36.

determinants of liquidity are bid-offer spreads and the size (or depth) of those spreads. If you had access to quotes and you brought up the market for General Electric, your screen would tell you that the market was 42.20 × 42.30, 500 × 500—meaning that the highest bid for GE is currently 42.20 and the lowest offer is 42.30. The size of the bid and offer is 500 × 500. In other words, there are 50,000 shares (500 is shorthand for 50,000—you must add two zeros) bid at 42.20 and 50,000 shares offered at 42.30. In reality, GE's size would probably say 999 × 999 (i.e., the market is deeper than 100,000 on both the bid and the offer sides). Compare this to the quote I once saw on Dairy Queen, which traded as a public company before Berkshire Hathaway bought the company recently: INDQA: 34 × 35½, 2 × 2. This was a bid-offer spread of 1½ points—large enough to drive a Lincoln Navigator through—and a depth of only 200 shares! Many of the large-cap stocks in the S&P 500 have bid-offer spreads of one-quarter point or less. The most liquid issues (e.g., GE, IBM, Wal-Mart) have bid-offer spreads of 12 cents or less. The size is usually five to six figures, meaning that you can transact 50,000 to 100,000 shares at the bid or offer.

I remember the first time I pulled up a quote on SPY. I was astounded: SPY 92 × 92⅛ (decimalization had not arrived yet), 999 × 999. This meant that Spiders were more liquid than virtually all individual stocks in terms of bid-offer spreads *and* depth. I was amazed. I also didn't believe it. So I made a few calls, and each contact confirmed the depth of the market. One individual, who was very familiar with Spear Leeds & Kellogg, the specialist in SPY on the floor of the AMEX, added that you could probably do 500,000 SPY at the bid or offer or very close to it! Spiders were less than five years old at the time, and their liquidity rivaled the top tier large-cap stocks like GE, IBM, and Wal-Mart! Exhibit 4.3 shows some detailed comparisons of bid-offer spreads and size for various ETFs and a few stocks for comparison.

Exhibit 4.3 Bid-Offer Spreads in Selected ETFs and E-Mini Stock Index Futures

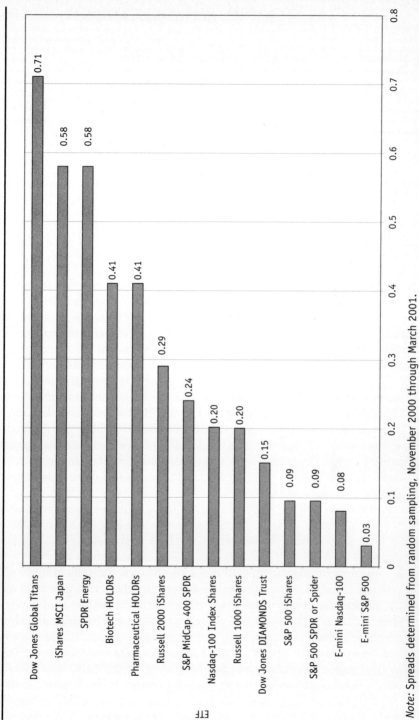

Note: Spreads determined from random sampling, November 2000 through March 2001.

Exhibit 4.4 SPY Bid-Offer Spread
Distribution, January 1993–December 1999

Range between Bid and Offer	% of Total
1/64–1/16	0.83
5/64–1/8	10.41
9/64–3/16	67.15
13/64–1/4	20.99
17/64–5/16	0.36
21/64–3/8	0.14
Greater than 3/8	0.12

Clearly, not all ETFs share the same depth of liquidity as the S&P 500 Spiders; however, the specialists in many of these ETFs have done an excellent job in providing liquidity and depth to the market. As a general rule, the more money following an index, the tighter the bid-offer spread and depth. It is also the bid-offer spreads of the underlying stocks in the index that are of critical importance in determining liquidity. Market conditions play an important role too; extremely volatile markets nearly always produce wider bid-offer spreads. Hence, markets are not always tight, even in the most liquid securities. Exhibit 4.4 illustrates a frequency distribution of the SPY bid-offer spread. It shows that 99 percent of the time, the bid-offer spread was one-quarter point or less. This includes some of the more volatile markets in history, including the severe sell-offs in 1997 and 1998 during the Russian and Asian financial crises.

NO UPTICK RULE ON ETF SHORT SALES

It's no surprise that narrow, deep markets attract a large number of investors. However, two prerequisites for critical mass (aside from quality market makers) in the marketplace are the presence of a pool of speculators and the existence of large institutional hedgers. If either is missing, bid-offer spreads will be a large chasm. True, speculators who can't wait for the opening bell love to go short securities as much as they go long. Institutions (and retail traders too) also need the ability to short securities or futures without obstacles. With stocks, there is the well-known short-sale uptick rule: you need an uptick in a stock's price to initiate a short sale. Like stock index futures, ETFs do not require an uptick to initiate a short sale. Thus, all traders can quickly and efficiently go short as easily as they go long. An investor with holdings in technology, health care, or utilities could short ETFs as a hedge against his holdings. If a large institution was prohibited from using futures (unfortunately, some are, despite the manifold benefits they offer), the investor could short ETFs to protect against an adverse move in his portfolio.

TRADE ON REGULATED EXCHANGES

Nearly all existing ETFs in the United States trade on the AMEX. However, other exchanges, eager to share in a hot product, are beginning to list ETFs. In the fall of 2000, the Chicago Board Options Exchange (CBOE) listed an ETF on the well-known OEX index (the S&P 100). In December 2000, the NYSE listed an ETF on the S&P Global 100, which comprises some of the largest capitalization issues across the globe. In addition to the low costs and excellent liquidity, investors, especially smaller retail accounts, are attracted to exchange traded instruments because of what I call the credibility element. U.S. security and commodity exchanges have several layers of regulatory protection. Anything that trades on the AMEX, NYSE, or CBOE is subject to the scrutiny of the SEC. In addition, these exchanges have in-house surveillance and compliance and audit departments to help ensure the integrity of the markets. In short, the average investor has considerable trust in the U.S. markets.

On the other hand, large, sophisticated institutional investors are active on exchanges but also in off-exchange, OTC, and interbank markets. These are markets where regulation sometimes is nonexistent. But given the resources, deep pockets, and contacts of the average institutional investor, wading in the currents outside regulated exchanges is commonplace.

TAX ADVANTAGES

Indexing is one way to help mitigate the burden of taxes on investment returns. ETFs beat the average mutual fund in tax efficiency, and because of their unique structure, they are more tax efficient than even the typical indexed mutual fund. In a declining market, for example, a traditional open-ended mutual fund manager may sell securities to raise cash to meet redemptions. Selling usually results in that proverbial "taxable event": a capital gain for the fund and tax regulations of investment companies (mutual funds) that force funds to pass

Exhibit 4.5　Capital Gains Distributions: SPY and Selected Mutual Funds

	SPDR	Vanguard Index 500	Fidelity Magellan	Washington Mutual Investors	Investment Company of America	Mutual Shares
1993	0.03	0.03	6.50	0.39	0.75	1.26
1994	0.00	0.20	2.64	0.41	0.60	0.91
1995	0.01	0.13	4.69	1.09	0.91	2.56
1996	0.12	0.25	12.85	1.20	1.03	1.74
1997	0.00	0.59	5.21	1.66	2.60	1.58
1998	0.00	0.42	5.15	2.60	2.94	1.29
1999	0.00	1.00	11.39	3.11	3.04	1.58
2000	0.00	0.00	4.69	2.5	2.08	2.51
Cumulative, 1993–2000	0.16	2.62	48.43	12.96	13.95	13.43
% pretax return (5 years)	99.0	95.7	83.8	83.6	85.5	76.5

Notes: Capital gains distributions are in dollars.
Magellan's net asset value has averaged around 100 over the past five years. Its distributions are thus not as high as they appear here.
Source: Morningstar and SPDR prospectus.

all capital gains on to investors. Most ETFs, though, have tax advantages because of a redemption-in-kind or payment-in-kind mechanism. Qualified participants (specialists, institutional investors) are able to redeem ETF shares for shares in the underlying stocks. No cash changes hands, as in the case with mutual funds. This creation and redemption process (discussed in Chapter 5) does not result in a taxable event for the ETF (it may cause a taxable event for the creator or redeemer, but not for the ETF itself). Although in-kind mechanisms abate taxes, they do not eliminate them altogether. If the ETF has to sell positions as a result of a change in the underlying index, the resulting capital gains or losses will be passed down to investors (see Exhibit 4.5). Taxes also apply to capital gains and losses when ETF positions are offset. So a trader who bought the SPY at 120 and sold it six months later will pay tax on the appropriate capital gain (short term). All dividends and interest realized by the ETF will also be passed down to the investor. Nevertheless, given that ETFs track a particular index, portfolio turnover is dramatically lower within ETF structures than the average mutual fund.

CONCLUSION

ETFs are attractive for a variety of reasons, but the real drivers to their popularity are a combination of very low costs, excellent liquidity, and their important role in helping investors battle against burdensome taxes. Because ETFs blend the attributes of indexing and the key advantages outlined in this chapter, it is not hard to see why they have amassed $70 billion in assets so quickly. Exhibits 4.6 and 4.7 summarize the comparisons between ETFs and traditional mutual funds.

Exhibit 4.6   Comparing Attributes: ETFs and Mutual Funds

	Exchange Traded Funds	Mutual Funds
Intraday trading	Investors can trade ETFs throughout the trading day. As with stocks, they can use market, limit, stop, and applicable order types.	Mutual funds are purchased at net asset value only at 4:00 P.M. EST.
Fees	Annual expense fees are very low, ranging from .09 to .99 percent.	Annual expenses usually range from .12 to 2.5 percent.
Commissions	Like stocks, a commission will be charged to ETF investors when buying or selling.	No commissions are charged to buy funds, but many funds charge sales loads.
Tax advantages	Structure and low turnover result in lower taxes in general.	While index mutual funds experience low turnover, actively managed funds have dramatically higher turnover.
Short selling	Short selling is allowed; no uptick is required.	In general, short selling is not allowed with mutual funds.
Redemption	In-kind redemption results in ETFs' being exchanged for an underlying portfolio of securities—not usually a taxable event.	When funds sell holdings, the taxable event is created, and gains or losses must be reported.
Margin trading	ETFs, like stocks, can be margined.	Margin is generally not allowed for the typical user.

Exhibit 4.7 Contrasting ETF and Mutual Fund Investing

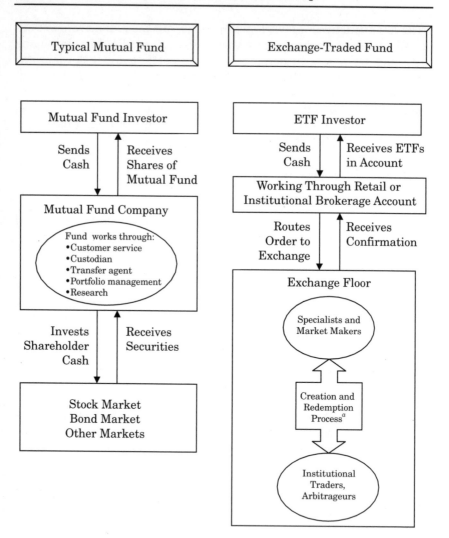

[a]Usually requires a minimum of 50,000 shares.

5

DETAILS: ETF STRUCTURES AND THE CREATION-REDEMPTION PROCESS

Exhibits 4.6 and 4.7 illustrated the many differences between traditional mutual funds and ETFs, but there are also important structural differences among ETFs. As easy to understand and trade as these products are, ETFs can be like fancy sportscars: fun to drive, but you might not want to tinker with what's under the hood. Of the 100 or so ETFs currently available, three primary structures prevail:

- Exchange traded unit investment trusts
- Exchange traded open-end mutual funds (or managed investment companies)
- Exchange traded grantor trusts

The SPY, MidCap SPDRs, QQQs, and DIAMONDS are actually *unit investment trusts* (UIT) that trade on the AMEX trading floor. They fall under the Investment Company Act of 1940 (40-Act) and thus have a few SEC exemptions. The holdings of UIT ETFs must completely replicate the holdings of the underlying index; there can be no optimizing. (Some index funds do not buy all the issues in an underlying index but instead *optimize* a portfolio to behave as closely to the index as possible without owning 100 percent of the components. For example, many total stock market index funds mimic the Wilshire 5000 Index, but none that I am aware of buys each of the more than 6,000 stocks in the index. Researchers find an optimal subset of the 6,000 issues using statistical sampling methods and can get virtually all the returns with fewer than half the stocks.) Lending of the ETF's portfolio of securities is also not allowed under a UIT structure; dividends paid by the underlying stocks cannot be reinvested and are usually paid to fund holders on a regular basis.

BGI's iShares and the Select Sector SPDRs are structured as *open-end indexed mutual funds* (or managed investment companies). This type of fund too falls under the guise of the 40-Act. Open-end companies generally are free from some of the restrictions that UITs have. They do not have to replicate the underlying basket or index completely. They can reinvest dividends when they are paid out. In truth, most of the iShares funds do replicate their underlying indexes. However, the iShares MSCI products are actually optimized baskets of international indexes. They do not buy every issue in the index. Open-end companies also can lend out their securities (which is done at a fee) and thus collect extra cash flow. They also have more freedom to deal in other types of securities or financial instruments such as derivatives.

The third type of ETF structure is the *grantor trust*. The holding company depositary receipts (HOLDR) products developed by Merrill Lynch that trade on the AMEX floor fall under this category. HOLDRS give an investor ownership in a basket of stocks of 20 companies. Each HOLDR started with a basket of 20 companies, but because of merger and restructuring in some of the component stocks, some HOLDRS now hold fewer than 20 companies. Odd lotters need not apply; investors are required to buy no fewer than 100 shares. Given that the Biotechnology HOLDR trades at 130, the $13,000 minimum price is a bit steep for smaller investors. HOLDRS are not regulated investment companies like the two previous types of ETFs. HOLDR owners receive all dividends on their shares and annual reports, and they have voting rights. They can also redeem HOLDRS for a small charge, creating a position in each of the 20 or so stocks in the instrument. However, HOLDRS are fully invested in the underlying securities; there is no investment optimization here as in open-end ETFs. HOLDRS are also prohibited from lending securities. Exhibit 5.1 summarizes the three main ETF models.

THE CREATION AND REDEMPTION PROCESS

The creation and redemption of ETFs basically involves exchanging ETF "shares" (there are no certificates issued for ETFs; everything is a book entry) for a portfolio of stocks or exchanging a portfolio of stocks

Exhibit 5.1 ETF Structures

ETF Characteristic	Exchange Traded Unit Investment Trust	Open-End Investment Company	Grantor Trust
ETF product example	SPY, MDY, QQQ	iShares, Select Sector SPDRs	HOLDRS
Registered investment company under Investment Company Act of 1940	Yes	Yes	No
Voting rights regarding portfolio	Trustee	Adviser	Investor
Securities lending	No	Yes	No
Derivatives are allowed	No*	Yes	No
Optimize or completely replicate underlying index	Must fully replicate	Can optimize underlying	Must fully replicate
Dividends and income	Cannot reinvest dividends	Can reinvest dividends	Dividends distributed to investor
Investor ability to lend shares for short selling	Yes	Yes	Yes
Tax treatment and distributions	Enjoys in-kind status but distributes gains and dividends	Enjoys in-kind status but distributes gains and dividends	Treated the same as owning securities
Creation units and redemption	Yes—50,000 share minimum	Yes—50,000 share minimum	Yes—100 share minimum

*Not specifically disallowed, but many UITs not set up for use.

for shares. To be involved in the creation and redemption process, the minimum number of ETF "shares" is usually 50,000. At the current price of the Spiders, that represents $6.5 million—chump change for a pension fund, but a major investment for most of us. So unless your net worth is considerable, you will get to enjoy trading or investing in ETFs, but you will not be able to exchange your Spiders for the underlying S&P 500 stocks and vice versa. The story that follows will demonstrate why the requirement is 50,000 shares.

Beyond a 50-mile radius of the Chicago Mercantile Exchange, many people confuse the major exchanges. People call CME (a futures exchange) to obtain stock quotes, to find out why S&P added or deleted a certain stock (we have no control over these issues), and to find out about ETFs even though they trade 800 miles away in New York on the AMEX. In trying to be a good citizen, I'll talk to anyone. A person who owned 100 shares of the S&P 500 Depositary Receipts—SPY—called and inquired as to how he could convert his 100 Spiders into the stocks in the S&P 500. I held back a chuckle and explained that his 100 Spiders were worth $13,000, and it would be mighty difficult to spread $13,000 among the 500 members of the index in their exact proportion. Even if it could be done, he would have hundreds of stocks in fractional amounts (1.2 shares of McDonalds, 0.59 share of Bausch & Lomb, 0.45 shares of Campbell Soup, and so on). It would be a back-office nightmare, and the costs and fees would take his $13,000 down considerably. The caller understood and finally admitted, "I guess when I don't like the market anymore I could just sell the things." I replied, "That's the beauty of ETFs. No need for the headaches that come with owning 500 individual stocks. Let the big players who have the computers and processing resources to do that sort of thing."

For the minute details of creation units and redemption units, I urge you to read the SPDR prospectus offered by the AMEX. Although it is written by legal experts and is loaded with jargon, it has some intriguing facts. Moreover, a knowledge of the process is beneficial. For those who want to do a little homework, I will outline the salient points with schematic diagrams and provide a creation example.

Because the vast majority of ETF traders and investors buy and sell in the secondary market on the floor of the AMEX, they do not realize that these instruments need a mechanism or process to be created and redeemed. ETFs are created by institutions and other large investors in block-size *creation units* of 50,000 (and multiples of 50,000). Creating 50,000 SPDRs, for example, requires that the creator deposit into the trust a portfolio of stocks that replicates or very closely approximates the composition of an underlying index—in the SPDR case, the stocks of the Standard & Poor's 500 Index. Only authorized participants (APs) can create or redeem. Obviously, a large institution can qualify to become an AP or work through a firm that is an AP.

Redemptions in blocks of 50,000 can also be transacted. The AP deposits the 50,000 SPDRs into the trust, and the investor receives a portfolio of stocks that replicates the S&P 500. Creators and redeemers also pay creation and redemption fees and are responsible for accrued dividends, interest payments, and custodial and transfer fees for the underlying portfolio. Exhibits 5.2 and 5.3 illustrate the basic steps in the creation and redemption process.

Exhibit 5.2   Creation Unit Process

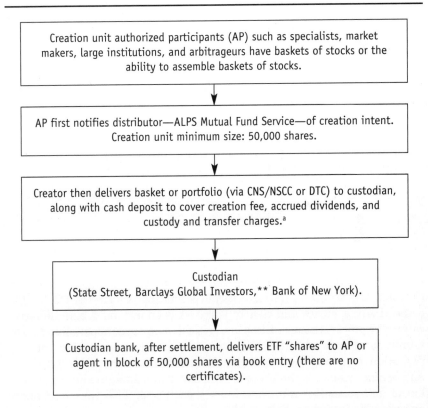

Creation unit authorized participants (AP) such as specialists, market makers, large institutions, and arbitrageurs have baskets of stocks or the ability to assemble baskets of stocks.

AP first notifies distributor—ALPS Mutual Fund Service—of creation intent. Creation unit minimum size: 50,000 shares.

Creator then delivers basket or portfolio (via CNS/NSCC or DTC) to custodian, along with cash deposit to cover creation fee, accrued dividends, and custody and transfer charges.[a]

Custodian
(State Street, Barclays Global Investors,** Bank of New York).

Custodian bank, after settlement, delivers ETF "shares" to AP or agent in block of 50,000 shares via book entry (there are no certificates).

[a]CNS/NSCC is the Continuous Net Settlement System of the National Securities Clearing Corporation. DTC is the Depository Trust Company. These two entities merged recently to form DTCC: Depository Trust and Clearing Corporation. DTCC acts as a clearing and depository agent for securities, including the portfolio of stocks delivered as part of the creation process.
**Custodial services for BGI's iShares is Investors Bank and Trust.

Exhibit 5.3   Redemption Process

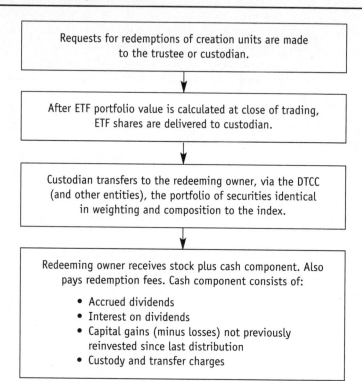

Several other parties are involved in the process including ALPs Mutual Funds Distributor, SEI Investments, the Depository Trust Company (DTC), and the National Securities Clearing Corporation (NSCC). The DTC and the CNS recently merged to form the DTCC. Because the paperwork and clearing process is enormous despite massive computer power, these entities are critical. They are responsible for the administration and back office procedures for the creation and redemption process. They also clear and settle trades, hold securities, and basically ensure the process goes smoothly. Imagine buying a basket of 500 securities and then having each one, with the exact share amounts, delivered to the custodian with near-perfect reliability. Imagine the record keeping involved with hundreds of stock certificates and hundreds of dividend payments four times per year. As investors, we buy and sell ETFs with the greatest of ease. However, behind the scenes, brokers, dealers, banks, trust companies, clearing corporations, and other institutions constantly work together and maintain a relationship with the DTCC.

ETF "shares" are not issued like traditional stock certificates but rather are held in book-entry form. The DTCC or a nominee is the record owner of all ETF shares. Investors holding shares are beneficial owners who are on DTCC records (or its participants), so the DTCC acts as a depository for shares. The beneficial owners of these shares are not entitled to physical delivery of certificates, nor can they have ETF shares registered in their names.

A CREATION PROCESS EXAMPLE

Now we turn to an example of how the creation process would look using the Nasdaq-100 Index shares, the QQQ. Exhibits 5.2 and 5.3 were general illustrations. In this QQQ example, we add more detail.

The Entities in the Process

First, I'll review the many entities involved in the QQQ creation process and their responsibilities.

Index Licensor: Nasdaq.   The index licensor is responsible for the construction and calculation of the Nasdaq-100 index, the underlying index for the QQQs. The licensor is also responsible for all additions to and deletions from the Nasdaq-100 and rebalancing of the index. Each day Nasdaq calculates and distributes the index weightings to other players in the ETF arena.

Fund Adviser/Manager: Bank of New York.   BNY is responsible for portfolio management and ensuring that it replicates the Nasdaq-100 index as much as possible. It also publishes the portfolio composition file (PCF) to the marketplace. This is a critical file that tells "creators" exactly what stocks and how many shares of each component will have to be delivered to the custodian. (See Exhibit 5.4.)

Distributor.   For most ETFs, including the QQQs, the distributor is ALPS Mutual Fund Services or SEI Investments. All creation orders are processed and approved by the distributor before any portfolio deposits are made to the custodian. Any creation order instructions can be rejected by ALPS if they are not submitted in proper form. ALPS

Exhibit 5.4 Nasdaq-100 Portfolio Composition File Illustration

	Company	Ticker	Price	Weighting in Index (%)	Dollar amount per Creation Unit	Number of Shares to Be Deposited with Custodian
1	Microsoft	MSFT	57	8.25	$197,175	3,459
2	Intel	INTC	30.5	5.61	134,079	4,396
3	Cisco	CSCO	23.25	4.66	111,374	4,790
4	Qualcomm	QCOM	62.75	4.03	96,317	1,535
5	Oracle	ORCL	17.25	3.11	74,329	4,309
6	JDS Uniphase	JDSU	28.5	2.84	67,876	2,382
7	Amgen	AMGN	72.875	2.67	63,813	876
8	Sun Microsystems	SUNW	21.125	2.38	56,882	2,693
9	Veritas Software	VRTS	59	2.05	48,995	830
10	Ciena	CIEN	69.625	1.93	46,127	663
100	Inktomi	INKT	9.375	0.087	$ 2,079	222

Net assets per share: $47.80
Minimum shares: 50,000
Market value of creation unit: $47.80 × 50,000 = $2.39 million
The portfolio composition file is at the heart of the creation process. The NSCC takes the PCF file and creation and redemption instructions sent by the custodian and bursts, or explodes, the file into securities transactions in each of the underlying Nasdaq-100 index components. The NSCC then provides transaction details to the authorized participant and the custodian. Settlement of bursted trades occurs in a normal three-day time frame via the NSCC's continuous net settlement system (CNS).

then sends creation or redemption instructions to the index receipt agent (the trustee).

Authorized Participant. The AP is usually a broker-dealer, professional trading house, institutional firm, or specialist. For QQQs, the specialist is Susquehanna Partners on the AMEX floor. (For orders executed on the Chicago Stock Exchange, the specialist is Dempsey).

Index Receipt Agent or Custodian. In the case of QQQs, the Bank of New York is the manager and the custodian (also known as the index receipt agent and trustee). It is responsible for the trade settlement for the ETF and the underlying basket. It also facilitates the creation unit–redemption unit process through the clearing process by sending the creation and redemption instruction file (from the distributor) to NSCC. Bank of New York also maintains and hold the assets: the Nasdaq-100 Index and all its components.

Clearing: National Securities Clearing Corporation (NSCC). NSCC has been renamed the DTCC after its merger with the Depository Trust. As an illustration, let's say the QQQ specialist wants to create more QQQs. Somehow, the 100 issues or names that make up the Nasdaq-100 need to get to the trustee in a reliable fashion. The NSCC clears and settles all the trades for the portfolio baskets, as well as the ETFs. The NSCC also receives the PCF from the trustee and disseminates the list of component stocks on this file. It accepts the creation and redemption instructions from the trustee in a process called *bursting*, it transacts the trades for each of the 100 stocks in the Nasdaq-100 Index in the exact share amount according to the PCF file and the number of creation units desired. The clearing and settlement are accomplished through the continuous net settlement system of the NSCC, which provides all the trade details to both parties: the AP and the trustee.

Transfer Agent and Depository: Depository Trust Company. BNY functions as the transfer agent for QQQs. These entities hold certificates in book entry form, perform record keeping, and provide fund distribution services.

An Analogy for How It Works

Obviously, there is a huge division of labor in the ETF creation process. But it is amazingly efficient and with 100 ETFs with $80 billion in assets, the process is remarkably smooth. Perhaps using the Internet as an analogy, this process is more easily understood. Many of us have downloaded files or data off the Internet. Think of the PCF as a file of securities or a list of stocks. Your browser connects you to the Internet, and a complex maze of switches and routers gets you to the destination or Internet address. With ETFs, the file (PCF) gets routed through intermediaries (ALPS, NSCC, and DTC) that direct the list of securities to the correct destination: the trustee.

Reduced to its most simplistic form, QQQ creation merely involves depositing a massive portfolio of securities into the hands of the trustee. A look at this portfolio will drive home just what is involved in QQQ creation.

The Illustration

Exhibit 5.4 shows an abridged illustration of the top components in the Nasdaq-100 portfolio composition file; it recreates the Nasdaq-100 basket exactly. On this particular day, Microsoft was the largest stock in the Nasdaq-100 and accounted for 8.25 percent of the index. Intel was the second largest and had a weighting in the index of 5.6 percent. Cisco was next with 4.66, and so on down the line with the other 97 components. The minimum creation unit size is 50,000 shares of QQQ. With the net asset value in early March 2001 of about $47.80, the dollar value of a creation unit would be approximately $2.39 million.

Assume for a moment you are an authorized participant and must deliver this $2.39 million basket of 100 names to the custodian. How many Microsoft shares must you deliver? How much Intel and all the other components must the creator deposit? The calculations in the PCF are basic math. If Microsoft is 8.25 percent of the index, then 8.25 percent of the $2.39 million, or about $197,175, must be put into Microsoft. Since Microsoft was trading at $57 per share on this same day, that would amount to 3,459 shares to be deposited. Intel would be 5.6 percent of the $2.39 million, or $134,080. At $30 per share, this would amount to 4,396 shares. The entire PCF file is duplicated in a similar manner, and the NSCC makes sure that each share of all 100 members clears and settles for custodian and authorized participant. Any accrued dividends, cash settlement amounts, and the fee for creation are also settled by the NSCC.

ETFs and Tracking Error

Closed-end mutual funds have achieved some success over the past few decades. These funds have a fixed number of shares (open-end funds can constantly issue new shares and grow larger and larger). One of the great conveniences was that they traded like listed stocks on the NYSE or AMEX, much as ETFs do now. One of the less desirable characteristics of closed-end funds was that they could trade at a premium or discount to their net asset value (NAV). In the mid-1990s, when emerging markets were white hot, I remember the Templeton Emerging Markets closed-end fund trading at 20 percent premium to the NAV of the stocks in its portfolio. At the time, Mark Mobius was running the fund, and he was considered one of the greats when it came to investing in far-away places like Thailand, Africa, India, and Russia. Mobius reportedly logged over 200,000 miles per year in his quest for potential investments in the last frontiers of investing. The phenomenal returns from some of these markets, along with the appeal of a great manager, apparently gave investors a perfect excuse to check their brains at the door (myself included). Investors, for reasons unbeknown to me, thought that it was worth paying 15 to 20 percent more than the underlying portfolio was worth; in effect, people were paying $1.20 for $1.00—not the sort of behavior that will land you on the Forbes 400 list. Similarly, some closed-end funds traded at severe discounts to their NAV. Exacerbating the situation was the fact that large traders and arbitrageurs had no in-kind redemption mechanism as they do with ETFs. For example, you could not easily buy "cheap" shares of closed-end funds trading at a significant discount to NAV and sell a basket of the more expensive underlying portfolio. This process is sometimes referred to as *arbitrage*—the process of simultaneously buying and selling similar or identical instruments to take advantage of price discrepancies. Buying gold in New York for $300 per ounce and immediately selling it in London for $301 per ounce is an example of arbitrage. It is usually a risk-free or nearly risk-free strategy and practiced by many major financial institutions worldwide. The activities of arbitrageurs, while profitable, also help generate liquidity in markets and, more important, help to keep prices in line. Because of regulations and the way closed-end funds were structured and managed, arbitrageurs had no mechanism by which they could take advantage of these price discrepancies as they could in other markets. The result is that large discounts and premiums to NAV persisted.

When ETFs began making their mark on Wall Street, discussion ensued as to whether they would exhibit the same characteristic. Two primary questions emerged: Would large discounts and premiums to NAVs occur, and would the price returns of ETFs mirror the returns on the underlying index? It turns out that while ETFs did trade at premiums and discounts to their NAVs, the discrepancies or "tracking error" (as the quantitative types on Wall Street referred to them) were very small. Traders and arbitrageurs were quite active in ETFs because of the ability to do in-kind creation and redemption of portfolios. This in-kind mechanism is one of the traits that helps set ETFs apart from closed-end funds. When tracking error does rear its head, arbitrageurs and institutions take advantage of these price discrepancies and thus help bring prices back in line, or close to it.

Still, as small as the tracking error is, any amount is enough to show up on the radar of a billion-dollar institution. Let's examine some real numbers to get a handle on tracking error:

1999 total return on S&P 500 Index	21.04 percent
1999 total return on SPY	20.39 percent
1999 total return on NAV	20.84 percent
1999 tracking error—ETF to index	−.65 percent
1999 tracking error—NAV to index	−.20 percent

If you had $100 million (a small amount for an institution) invested in the ETF instead of the underlying stocks in the S&P 500 itself, you would have underperformed the index by 65 basis points. That is $650,000. Interestingly, in 1998, the SPY actually *outperformed* the underlying index by 8 basis points. On a day-to-day basis, too, one can see that while ETFs track their NAVs and underlying indexes closely, tracking error does exist. In some of the less liquid ETFs, the tracking error is a bit larger. The last trade in a less liquid ETF may be much higher or lower than the current bid/offer spread and create the impression of even greater tracking error than those witnessed with the SPDR or QQQ. Investors with substantial sums of capital on the line need to keep a close eye on tracking error.

What are the reasons for tracking error?

- *Fees and Expenses.*   Fees and expenses take a significant toll on the total return of a mutual fund. Although ETFs have some of the lowest annual expense ratios in the business, these fees cause some underperformance relative to their indexes over time. Higher fees usually lead to greater underperformance.

- *Portfolio replication.*   Some ETFs are required to replicate their underlying index completely. Others, using computers and financial engineering, can closely approximate, or optimize, a portfolio to look very much like the actual index. Say you have an ETF that mimics the S&P 500. The ETF may own only 450 of the stocks in the index. The optimized basket of 450 issues may track the underlying S&P 500 very closely—sometimes maybe perfectly. But because it is missing some of the components, it will display tracking error from time to time.

• *Dividend reinvestment.*   We have discussed the dividend reinvestment policies of the various ETF structures. UIT structures cannot reinvest dividends. They hold the payment in cash equivalents and distribute them to investors quarterly. The lack of daily reinvestment means that the return of the ETF will not perfectly match the total return of the underlying index. The extra cash is a drag in up markets, but serves as a small cushion in down markets. ETFs structured as open-ended investment companies, on the other hand, can reinvest dividends daily. Overall, the effect is very small due in part to the fact that the 18-year-old bull market in stocks has caused dividend yields to drop to historically low levels—about 1.3 percent in the case of the S&P 500 and virtually zero in the case of the Nasdaq-100.

• *Changes in the underlying index.*   Over the past few years, there have been dozens of changes in the S&P 500. Every year without fail, the Russell indexes undergo their annual reconstitution, with hundreds of changes in their components. Although it is a positive thing for market barometers to be updated to reflect the times, it plays havoc with those managing index funds. Witness what occurred when Yahoo! and JDS Uniphase were added to the S&P 500. As investors saw the stocks rocket after the announcement of the addition of these two tech favorites to the index, behind-the-scenes fund managers were busy rebalancing billion-dollar portfolios, buying Yahoo! and Uniphase and selling hundreds of other issues to make sure that they duplicated the S&P 500 as closely as possible. The market impact and transaction costs alone take a toll on index funds. The impact is likely to be similar with ETFs. Timing issues also can cause tracking error in ETFs depending on when the new component stock is added to the index versus when it is added to the ETF underlying portfolio.

• *Nonsynchronous closing of ETFs with underlying.*   Trading on the NYSE closes at 4:00 P.M. Eastern Standard Time (EST). Thus, the majority of the stocks in the S&P 500 stop trading at 4:00 P.M. However, some ETFs on the AMEX floor continue to trade for another 15 minutes. That additional 15 minutes can be a very lackluster trading period, but trading occasionally erupts during that window of time. Many earnings announcements are made after the NYSE closing, and when they exceed (or fail to meet) expectations, all hell can break loose while certain instruments continue to trade.

Imagine for a second that you are a registered investment adviser. You have clients, some of them indexed to the S&P 500 using ETFs. It is month end or quarter end. At 4:00 P.M., the S&P 500 closes at 1300. The SPY and the IVV (iShares S&P 500 ETF) are both trading very close to 130 (one-tenth the value of the S&P 500). At 4:01, a very important component in the index announces that it will not meet Wall Street's expectations. The ETFs have 14 more minutes to trade and might very well sell off, as happened several times in 2000 when a company made such announcements. The ETFs may close at 129.00 at 4:15 P.M. EST. Someone indexed via ETFs will have a one full point tracking error due to that 15-minute window of additional trading. When stocks open for trading the next morning, the index will play catch-up (all other things being equal, it would then trade at 1290). But—and this is a very important *but*—quarterly statements for the ETF holder will be based on the 4:15 close. The benchmark S&P 500 will use the 4:00 closing value. One point on a $130 issue is .77 percent, and 77 basis points of tracking error that is artificially created because of this nonsynchronous close of the two instruments.

A similar problem occurs with stock index futures. When some large institutional investors that use futures as part of synthetic indexing strategies noticed how the nonsynchronous close of futures and the cash caused tracking errors in their portfolios, CME came up with a novel way of addressing the issue. To reduce or eliminate this tracking error, CME settles all domestic stock index futures to a *fair-value settlement* at the end of each month. Hence, no matter what futures do in the 15-minute window, they are settled according to their fair value. Instead of calculating the fair value itself, CME surveys or polls some of the largest institutions in the field and takes an average of the sample. The results of the fair value survey are then disseminated shortly after the 3:15 Chicago close.

A TRADING EXAMPLE

This trading example shows how institutional traders and market makers work in concert with supply and demand and how they interact with the creation and redemption process to provide a liquid trading environment for ETFs. It also demonstrates why ETFs show remarkably low tracking errors.

Let's assume that the Spiders (SPY) are trading at about 130.00. The market, as quoted by Spear, Leeds & Kellogg, the specialist in SPY, is 130 bid, 130.13 offered. The size is 999×999. This is an excellent spread and very good depth of market. Let's also assume that the NAV is 130.00.

A broker acting on behalf of a large institutional trader places an order to buy 100,000 shares of SPY "at the market" (the best available price—130.13). Again, we assume that Spear Leeds is on both sides of the bid and offer and decides to sell the broker the 100,000 SPY and is now short 100,000 SPY at 130.13. This is a common occurrence and part of the duties of the specialist, who is responsible for making two-sided markets and ensuring a fair and orderly market. This market was fair and orderly, and SLK discharged its duties by making a two-sided market. The institution is happy since it gets its SPY without moving the bid-offer and gets its shares all at one price in a very quick execution. However, SLK is now short 100,000 shares of SPY (remember that all specialists go long and short stocks as part of their role as market makers). It can hope that the market declines in the next few minutes or hours and that it can cover the short at a profit. It does run the risk that the market will rocket upward—not a comforting situation when short 100,000 SPY. I can assure you that SLK (as well as other specialists) did not become one of the top market makers on the NYSE based on hope. What would likely transpire is one of the following:

- SLK can hedge using S&P 500 futures and buy enough futures contracts to hedge or ensure against an adverse price move (upward in this instance) until it trades out of the 100,000 SPY position.
- It can hedge by buying the underlying portfolio at an NAV of 130. It would have to buy a $13 million portfolio to hedge 100,000 SPY. After buying the stocks in the S&P 500, it could deposit them using the creation unit process to the custodian. Then the custodian would issue ETF "shares" (remember, in book entry form) for 100,000 SPY.

Here is a summary of the second choice:

1. SLK was originally short 100,000 SPY at 130.13 for a credit of $13,013,000.
2. SLK was long 100,000 SPY at 130.00 via the creation unit process for a debit of $ 13,000,000.
3. The net profit from the trade and hedge is $13,000, minus expenses.

CONCLUSION

You can now begin to comprehend why tracking errors with some ETFs remain relatively low. If discrepancies become too large, arbitrage traders or institutions take advantage of these discrepancies in a nearly identical fashion to the example in this chapter. The act of "doing" arbitrage trades usually brings prices back in line.

6

GENERAL STRATEGIES USING ETFs

ETFs offer institutional and individual investors a wide range of strategies. Many are simple to implement for even novice investors. Others take a bit more understanding of the markets. Their intraday trading feature and the ability to sell ETFs short allow investors to implement strategies that are impossible with regular mutual funds. In this chapter, I briefly explore the following strategies:

- ETFs as core index holdings
- Active trading
- Hedging
- Cash equitization and cash management
- Sector Bets
- Filling benchmark or style gaps
- Gaining exposure to international markets
- Tax strategies

Later in this book, we will go over some of these in more detail.

ETFs AS CORE INDEX HOLDINGS

Given their low-cost, user-friendly nature, ETFs make great building blocks for core investment holdings. For many individual investors (institutions too use them to build indexed portfolios), they offer a simple way to gain market exposure in broad-based indexes, international indexes, and various market sectors.

ACTIVE TRADING

I recently did a seminar for a large brokerage firm, and one of the account executives confessed to me that he had a client who made 30 trades a day in the Nasdaq-100 Index shares (QQQ). Short of being a full-time professional trader, 30 is quite a lot of trades. I have already noted that turnaround on the SPY is less than a month, and for the QQQ it is less than a week. Clearly, speculators love ETFs. One look at the volume statistics confirms this. While they are a great tool for active traders (although I am convinced futures would probably be better for the active trader—see Part 3), frequent transactions will eliminate most, if not all, of the advantages that ETFs bring to the table. Several trades per day or more mean higher transaction costs and lots of taxable events. Of course, if you are one of those with a nose for short-term market movements, more power to you. But remember, there are also proprietary trading desks at institutional firms like Goldman, Morgan, Merrill, Deutsche Bank, and so on that successfully trade for a living. There are also some active individual traders who make six-figure incomes trading in and out of stocks and ETFs. Beware, though; this is extremely difficult to accomplish. So do your homework before you quit your day job and think for a moment about that famous Clint Eastwood line in *Dirty Harry*: "Do you feel lucky?"

HEDGING

Another strategy practiced by investors (mostly institutional) is hedging. For the uninitiated, *hedging* is simply insuring against an adverse price move. For a billion-dollar portfolio manager or an investor with $100,000 in a 401(k) plan, a bear market would be such an adverse move.

The great bull market of the past 18 years has nevertheless witnessed some gut-wrenching declines, especially the mother of all corrections in October 1987. The fall of 1997 and 1998 also displayed some fireworks on the downside. Those accustomed to initiating hedging strategies will find ETFs very simple to use. If you have a negative view on the market (short term or long term), you can sell short ETFs. Should the market decline, the profits on the "short leg" would offset the losses on the portfolio. Of course, should the market advance, you will not participate in the rally; your "short hedge" will lose money, and those losses will offset the gains made by your portfolio. More on this later on.

CASH EQUITIZATION

Hugely popular with larger investors but very useful for individual investors too, cash equitization is a strategy that helps investors mitigate what is known as *cash drag*. While some fund managers prefer to have cash in the portfolio, especially asset allocation and balanced funds, others loathe too much cash; cash is not what they are paid to hold. But in the good old days, the checks would roll in the door, with some well-known funds taking in tens of millions of dollars or more each business day. With all that cash coming in, investing money in a timely fashion became a problem. If a fund held even small amounts of cash while the market was marching upward, it would underperform.

ETFs allow an investor to gain quick exposure to many popular indexes or sectors, thereby mitigating the drag caused by holding cash and other money market equivalents. For actively managed portfolios, ETFs could be employed until the manager decides which issues to add to the portfolio. In truth, this strategy is usually done with futures. But some indexes, such as the Russell 3000 Growth Index, have an ETF but not a futures contracts. In these cases, the ETF could prove a valuable strategic tool.

SECTOR BETS

Peter Lynch, the legendary fund manager of the Fidelity Magellan Fund, at one point owned over a thousand stocks (the average mutual fund owns far less). Often he could not satiate his appetite for a sector with just one or two stocks. For example, one savings and loan stock was not enough. When he became smitten with a sector, he bought as many of the issues in that sector as he could. And since he was at the helm of what was then the largest mutual fund in the world, he had no problem owning 20 or so savings and loan stocks. Even well-heeled investors would be hard pressed to try this tactic, and for the small investor it is impossible. This is not the case with ETFs. There are dozens of sector ETFs and HOLDRS instruments. Not sure which biotech wonder will provide the cure for cancer? Buy a whole biotech basket with

Biotech HOLDRS. You then own 20 of them, and if one company gets the thumbs down from the Food and Drug Administration because its new drug killed everyone in clinical trials, you have the benefit of diversity. Can't decide among Pfizer, Merck, and Bristol-Myers Squibb? Buy them all and a few others via Pharmaceutical HOLDRS.

Institutional investors can use ETFs to increase exposure to a specific segment of the market. Say, a small to midsize pension fund has 3.5 percent of assets in utility issues but desires a 5 percent weighting in this sector. There are three choices to help increase exposure: DJ US Utilities iShares, Utilities Sector SPDRs, and Utilities HOLDRS.

FILLING BENCHMARK OR STYLE GAPS

ETFs can be skillfully used to adjust style or benchmark gaps. Let's say a particular manager has a portfolio mix of large-cap growth and value stocks. She notes the wide gap in valuation between growth and value and thinks that value will outperform in the next few quarters or years. She could tilt her style toward the value end of the spectrum using an ETF such as the S&P 500/Barra Value Index, the Russell 1000 Value Index, or the Dow Jones US Large Cap Value streetTRACKS.

GAINING EXPOSURE TO INTERNATIONAL MARKETS

There are debates on the merit of investing overseas. Some in the field think that international investing provides added diversity and the opportunity to profit from opportunities abroad that have already been exploited in the more mature U.S. markets. Others disagree; they do not believe that overseas markets achieve diversification. The evidence they give is that the severe declines over the past 18 years in the U.S. markets have been accompanied by equally severe drops in international markets. Diversification means that when part of your portfolio zigs, the other part zags. When the U.S. markets fell precipitously in 1998 as a result of the long-term capital management fiasco and the Asian and Russian crises, overseas markets also dropped severely. Where was the diversification? cried the critics of overseas investing. Warren Buffett added more fuel to the fire when he commented that he did not necessarily need to look overseas for opportunities. There are plenty of international companies in the United States on the NYSE. For example, Berkshire owns 200 million shares of Coca Cola which does business in nearly 200 countries. Other critics say that the dual risks involved in overseas investing of market risk and currency risk make the investment process even more difficult. Proponents, however, have offered up the *efficient frontier* concept, which shows that adding an international component can help returns while lowering risk.

No matter who you believe, investors have voted with their bank accounts. Hundreds of billions of U.S. dollars in international stocks reside in the portfolios of Americans. For the individual investor, ETFs offer a way to gain broad exposure across many overseas markets as well as individual countries through MSCI iShares series.

Jim Rogers, the famed hedge fund manager who has spent most of the past five years traveling around the world on a motorcycle (his experiences were chronicled in the excellent book *Investment Biker*), was fond of going long and short entire countries. Several years ago, he was quite bullish on Austria and bearish on certain other countries. With the MSCI iShares, it would be possible to "short countries" while going long other countries. Beware, though: Only seasoned investors with a knowledge of world markets should attempt this strategy. In addition, investors must acknowledge that investing in the correct country is only half the problem. They must get the currency correct too. If, for example, you invested in the MSCI iShares Japan and the underlying stocks did well but the yen currency dropped sharply in world currency trading, your gains would be trimmed by foreign exchange losses—not the kind of news an investor wants to hear. Overall, the international ETFs add yet another weapon to the investors' arsenal.

TAX STRATEGIES

As I write this section, the year 2001 is three months old, and many sectors have taken a drubbing—technology and telecommunications especially. The Nasdaq-100 is 62 percent off its highs and the dot-com "space" is, well, empty space, with many issues off 95 percent or more. Tax selling appears to be in full force as investors position themselves to offset any gains with some losses to reduce their tax burden for the 2000 filing year.

ETFs can be useful in tax planning strategies and help investors sidestep the IRS wash sale rules, which disallow losses if substantially identical securities were bought within 30 days of the sale. I had a conversation with a woman who had good realized gains in Johnson & Johnson and Enron but had some fairly significant losses in MCI/Worldcom, AT&T, and Global Crossing. I suggested she consult her accountant or tax attorney for verification but that I was almost certain she could sell her telecoms at a loss, which would help offset some of her gains. She objected on the grounds that she liked the telecom sector and strongly believed that the troubles with her three stocks were temporary, adding that she did not want to risk being out of the sector during the 30-day wash sale window. I responded by saying that if she sold her losers now, she probably would not have to wait 30 days if she bought an ETF that covered that sector since the fund holdings are substantially different from her holdings. Hence, she could offset some gains with losses and still retain exposure in the sector. She paused, then pulled out a day-timer the size of a Buick and jotted a few notes to call her accountant and check out telecom ETFs with her broker.

These strategies and many more are available to ETF investors. Later chapters further this discussion with more examples and some case studies.

7

ETF HIGHLIGHTS

This chapter takes a detailed look at 26 popular ETFs—those with either a huge asset base or large average daily volume relative to other ETFs. I also highlight a few that have smaller asset bases and daily turnover because of some other unique characteristics. These details are presented in ETF highlight (or summary) pages. Each major ETF has its own full-page summary and description, along with pertinent information for investors.

As of early 2001, over 100 ETFs were available, nearly all of them trading on the AMEX. One ETF trades on the NYSE and one on the Chicago Board Options Exchange. This number is certain to expand dramatically in the United States and overseas as well. In fact, Deutsche Bank, one of the largest index players in the world, recently launched ETFs in Europe. Vanguard, Pro-Funds, and Nuveen have all announced plans to introduce ETFs on some of their existing products or new ones.

The information presented here is comprehensive and would take substantial time and resources for the average investor to procure. These 26 ETFs represent the lion's share of volume and assets under management. The top four—the QQQ, S&P 500 Spiders, MidCap Spiders, and the Dow Jones DIAMONDS—represent over 75 percent of the ETF asset base as of early 2001. All major categories are covered, including broad-based and style indexes, sector ETFs and HOLDRS, international ETFs and single-country ETFs.

GUIDE TO ETF HIGHLIGHT PAGES

The categories, terms, and information on the ETF highlight pages are outlined in this section and follow their order of appearance on the page. Anyone who has studied the Value Line Investment Survey or Morningstar will have no trouble following the highlight pages and can skip this guide. If you are a newcomer to ETFs or the investment scene, welcome. This guide references Exhibit 7.1, the S&P 500 Depositary Receipt.

- *Assets in trust*—the total assets held by the trust as of March 16, 2001 (HOLDRS assets are as of February 28, 2001). This number is subject to change. By publication date, the assets could be dramatically higher—or lower. Only a half dozen or so ETFs have assets above $1 billion. Larger asset bases usually are accompanied by higher daily trading volume. SPY is the largest as of March 2001, with over $23 billion in assets.
- *Average daily volume*—the average daily turnover for all of 2000, as well as a figure for most of first quarter 2001. SPY traded over 10 million shares per day as of March 21, 2001. If the ETF was recently launched and did not trade for the entire year, then the reference date is noted (such as December 2000 or February 2001). BGI launched dozens of new ETFs in 2000 starting in May and continuing with additional new products throughout the year.
- *Size of ETF share*—Some ETFs trade at approximately one-tenth the value of their underlying indexes, some at one-fifth the value. The QQQ trades at one-fortieth the value of the Nasdaq-100 Index. Hence, if the Nasdaq-100 trades at 2000, the QQQ will be priced at about 50.00 per share. The SPY trades at one-tenth the underlying S&P 500. If the S&P 500 index is at 1200.00, then SPY will be priced around 120.00.
- *Annual expense fee*—the amount the trust charges in fees per year (in percent). For ETFs, all expense fees are below 1.00 percent. Most are below .60 percent, and some are below .25 percent. At .12 percent, SPY is one of the lowest of all the ETFs (the

iShares S&P 500 has the lowest expenses: .09 percent). Shop around. Compare these fees to some of the traditional mutual funds you may own or other investments. *Caveat:* This fee does not take into account the commission you will have to pay a broker to buy and sell shares of ETFs.

- *Ticker, NAV ticker*—The ticker symbol (SPY) is what you need to get quotes from your broker or to place orders. In addition, many on-line services require a ticker symbol in order to provide you with charts or quotes. The NAV ticker symbol (SXN) allows you to get the intraday NAV of the underlying trust on certain quote systems. This figure should be very close to the actual price of the ETF (see the tracking error section in Chapter 5). These symbols are good on a Bloomberg terminal but might not be the correct symbols for other quote systems. Contact your quote vendor for details.
- *Trading hours*—the normal hours of trading. Many ETFs trade after the 4:00 P.M. EST close of the markets, and there could be significant price movement during this 15-minute window. Twenty-four hour trading is available in stock index futures but not with ETFs.
- *Bid-offer spread*—the bid-offer spread, in basis points, that is, the difference between the highest available bid and the lowest available offer. With SPY, the spread is usually a tight 10 to 15 cents. That spread on a $120 stock would come out to be .10 to .12 percent, or 10 to 12 basis points for SPY. This spread was obtained by random sampling of markets at various times between November 2000 and March 2001.
- *Price*—the closing AMEX prices as of March 21, 2001. Remember that tracking error will exist between the ETF as it trades on the AMEX floor and the basket of underlying securities. Institutional trading, arbitrage, and excellent market making by the specialists usually keep the tracking error low.
- *Dividends*—ETFs may or may not pay a dividend. Most are in the March, June, September, and December quarterly cycle. Others pay dividends or distributions semiannually.
- *Began trading*—A handful of ETFs were around pre-1998; most have been launched in the past two years, and some have very short operating histories. Do not be surprised if you cannot find any data on one-year or three-year returns or trading histories.

SPY is the oldest. The Select Sector SPDRS, MDY, DIA, and iShares MSCI have been around longer than most other ETFs.

- *Structure*—There are three types of ETF structures: (1) unit investment trusts (UITs), (2) open-ended mutual fund or managed investment company, and (3) grantor trust. (See Figure 5.1 for a review.)
- *Manager*—the entity that manages the assets of the trust. State Street Global Advisors, Barclays Global Investors, and Bank of New York handle these duties for nearly all ETFs.
- *Specialist*—the primary market maker on the floor of the AMEX (or NYSE, CBOE) that is responsible for making a fair and orderly market. The market makers do a very good job overall in making markets. The success these instruments enjoy is due in part to the liquidity provided by market makers. Note that a significant amount of ETF volume trades at the Chicago Stock Exchange.
- *Top members*—the top 10 components of the underlying index and their percentage weights in that index. Given that some underlying indexes are composed of 2,000 or more issues, I cannot list them all. Also, the top 10 members are constantly in flux. Cisco was number one weighting in the S&P 500 for a day and has since fallen down the top-10 rankings dramatically. For HOLDRS, I have listed all the stocks in the ETF since the number is usually 20 or fewer (although the Market 2000+ HOLDR has 50 members).
- *ETF summary*—pertinent insight into the ETF or its underlying index as of the writing of this book.

BROAD-BASED INDEX AND STYLE ETFs

The broad-based index and style ETFs in Exhibits 7.1 through 7.10 do not require advanced knowledge of the investment process; they are designed to simplify the investment landscape. If you want exposure to a particular part of the market—say, small-cap value—you could merely purchase the iShares Russell 2000 Value ETF or the S&P SmallCap/ Barra 600 Value ETF. If you are bullish, you enter an order to go long. If you are bearish, sell what you already own, or sell short to take advantage of a downward move. (Chapter 10 presents case studies on how to establish more complex positions, and Chapter 11 is dedicated to the subject of assembling portfolios of various ETFs as part of an investment program.)

Exhibit 7.1 ETF Highlights—Standard & Poor's 500 Depositary Receipts (SPY)

Assets in trust (March 16, 2001)	$23.2 billion
Average daily volume (2000)	7,669,444 shares
Average daily volume (2001)*	10,318,675 shares
Size of ETF share	1/10th S&P 500 Index
Annual expense fee	.12%
Ticker	SPY
NAV ticker	SXV
Trading hours	9:30 A.M.–4:15 P.M. (EST)
Bid-offer spread	9 basis points
Price March 21, 2001	114.26
Dividends	Quarterly; March cycle
Began trading	January 1993
Structure	UIT
Manager	State Street Global Advisors
AMEX specialist	Spear, Leeds & Kellogg

*YTD March 21, 2001.

Top Members and Weightings in Underlying Index as of March 20, 2001

General Electric	3.9%	Wal-Mart	2.1%
Microsoft	2.7%	AIG	1.8%
ExxonMobil	2.7%	AOL Time Warner	1.6%
Pfizer Inc.	2.3%	Merck	1.6%
Citigroup	2.2%	IBM	1.5%

Summary

The S&P 500 covers about 78 percent of the market capitalization of the U.S. market. It is the key benchmark in this country for mutual funds and pension funds alike. In terms of assets, SPY is the largest of the ETFs. As far as liquidity, Spear, Leeds and other market makers can accommodate just about any order. SPY trades nearly 10 million per day, so it is an investor's and trader's dream. How important is this benchmark? Over $1 trillion is indexed to the S&P 500. For 12 basis points a year, anyone can own the entire S&P 500. (And for those who find that budget really tight, BGI's S&P 500 iShares accomplishes the same goal for 9 basis points annually.)

Exhibit 7.2   ETF Highlights—Nasdaq-100 Index Tracking Stock (QQQ)

Assets in trust (March 16, 2001)	$20.54 billion
Average daily volume (2000)	27,673,809 shares
Average daily volume (2001)*	63,487,000 shares
Size of ETF share	1/40th Nasdaq-100 Index
Annual expense fee	.18%
Ticker	QQQ
NAV ticker	QXV
Trading hours	9:30 A.M.–4:15 P.M. (EST)
Bid-offer spread	20 basis points
Price (March 21, 2001)	41.30
Dividends	NA
Began trading	March 1999
Structure	UIT
Manager	Bank of New York
AMEX specialist	Susquehanna Partners

*YTD March 21, 2001.

Top Members and Weightings in Underlying Index as of March 20, 2001

Microsoft	8.9%	Amgen	2.7%
Intel	5.4%	JDS Uniphase	2.7%
Qualcomm	4.5%	Sun Microsystems	2.3%
Cisco	4.5%	Dell Computer	2.1%
Oracle	3.1%	VoiceStream Wireless	2.0%

Summary

"Would've should've could've," says the AMEX ad for the Nasdaq-100 ETF. All those stocks you wanted a piece of 5 and 10 years ago are now wrapped in a nice package. In less than two years, the QQQ, sometimes referred to as "Cubes," has risen to the top of the charts in volume. This Nasdaq-100 ETF averages around 40 million shares per day. In asset size, it is the number two ETF, and despite the recent slide in the Nasdaq-100 Index, assets are poised to overtake the SPY in the not-too-distant future. Spreads are tight and widen only during violent moves.

Exhibit 7.3 ETF Highlights—Standard & Poor's MidCap 400 SPDR (MDY)

Assets in trust (March 16, 2001)	$3.68 billion
Average daily volume (2000)	842,857 shares
Average daily volume (2001)*	1,125,265 shares
Size of ETF share	1/5 S&P MidCap 400 Index
Annual expense fee	.25%
Ticker	MDY
NAV ticker	MXV
Trading hours	9:30 A.M.–4:15 P.M. (EST)
Bid-offer spread	24 basis points
Price (March 16, 2001)	83.65
Dividends	Quarterly (March, June, September, December)
Began trading	May 1995
Structure	UIT
Manager	Bank of New York
AMEX specialist	Susquehanna Partners

*YTD, March 21, 2001.

Top Members and Weightings in Underlying Index as of December 29, 2000

Millennium Pharmaceutical	1.49%	Genzyme	.96%
Waters Corp	1.19%	DST Systems	.95%
Concord EFS Inc	1.11%	Univision	.94%
Idec Pharmaceutical	1.07%	Rational Software	.84%
Cintas	.99%	Cadence Design	.73%

Summary

In 2000, the S&P 500, the Dow, and the Nasdaq all had negative returns. With the vicious decline in technology and the market overall that year, there were few places to hide. The only major broad-based index showing a gain in 2000 was the S&P MidCap 400, which in fact outperformed its bigger brother, the S&P 500, by 23 full percentage points. MidCap SPDRs were a great way for investors to take advantage of this huge move in midsize companies. They are also a good vehicle for extending asset allocation beyond large stocks.

Exhibit 7.4   ETF Highlights—The Dow Jones DIAMONDS Trust (DIA)

Assets in trust (March 16, 2001)	$2.24 billion
Average daily volume (2000)	1,394,000 shares
Average daily volume (2001)*	2,190,129 shares
Size of ETF share	1/100 Dow Jones Industrials
Annual expense fee	.18%
Ticker	DIA
NAV ticker	DXV
Trading hours	9:30 A.M.–4:15 P.M. (EST)
Bid-offer spread	15 basis points
Price (March 21, 2001)	96.21
Dividends	Monthly
Began trading	January 1998
Structure	UIT
Manager	State Street Global Advisors
AMEX Specialist	Spear, Leeds & Kellogg

*YTD, March 21, 2001.

Top Members and Weightings in Underlying Index as of December 29, 2000

JP Morgan	9.14%	ExxonMobil	4.89%
IBM	6.33%	Merck	4.01%
Hewlett-Packard	5.71%	United Technologies	3.93%
Johnson & Johnson	5.13%	General Motors	3.68%
Minnesota Mining	5.03%	Procter & Gamble	3.67%

Summary

The Dow Jones Industrial Average is the only major large-cap index covered in this book that is price weighted. It also has the fewest components. These two traits probably explain why less institutional money is indexed to the Dow 30, compared with the S&P and Russell indexes. Nevertheless, investors and traders alike are attracted to the DIAMONDS, which are among the top five most active ETFs on the AMEX in share volume and in terms of asset size. Name recognition and the venerable 104-year-old history are a plus. DIA trades over 1 million shares per day.

Exhibit 7.5   ETF Highlights—iShares Russell 1000 Index Fund (IWB)

Assets in trust (March 16, 2001)	$206 million
Average daily volume (2000)	22,423 shares
Average daily volume (2001)*	50,842 shares
Size of ETF share	1/10 Russell 1000 Index
Annual expense fee	.15%
Ticker	IWB
NAV ticker	NJB
Trading hours	9:30 A.M.–4:15 P.M. (EST)
Bid-offer spread	20 basis points
Price (March 21, 2001)	60.00
Dividends	Quarterly (March, June, September, December)
Began trading	May 2000
Structure	Open-end mutual fund
Manager	Barclays Global Investors
AMEX specialist	Hull Trading

*YTD, March 21, 2001.

Top Members and Weightings in Underlying Index as of December 31, 2000

General Electric	4.0%	Merck	1.8%
ExxonMobil	2.5%	Intel	1.7%
Pfizer	2.4%	AIG	1.7%
Cisco	2.3%	Microsoft	1.4%
Citigroup	2.2%	SBC Communications	1.4%

Summary

Over $14 billion is indexed to the Russell 1000. The total market capitalization represents about 90 percent of the U.S. equity market. Although it has nearly twice the number of issues as the S&P 500 (remember, Russell does not immediately add new issues but waits until the annual rebalancing, so you may have fewer than 1,000 issues), its correlation to the S&P is 99.4 percent. Still, some investors like the broader coverage of the Russell 1000. With only 6 months of trading history, the ETF has attracted a significant amount of assets and trades with very good liquidity.

Figure 7.6 ETF Highlights—iShares Russell 2000 Index Fund (IWM)

Assets in trust (March 16, 2001)	$629.2 million
Average daily volume (2000)	115,563 shares
Average daily volume (2001)*	364,765 shares
Size of ETF share	1/5 Russell 2000 Index
Annual expense fee	.20%
Ticker	IWM
NAV ticker	NJM
Trading hours	9:30 A.M.–4:15 P.M. (EST)
Bid-offer spread	29 basis points
Price (March 21, 2001)	88.00
Dividends	Quarterly (March, June, September, December)
Began trading	May 2000
Structure	Open-end mutual fund
Manager	Barclays Global Investors
AMEX specialist	Susquehanna Partners

*YTD, March 21, 2001.

Top Members and Weightings in Underlying Index as of December 31, 2000

Caremark Rx Inc.	0.4%	Amerisource Health	0.3%
Laboratory Corporation	0.4%	Enzon	0.3%
Invitrogen	0.3%	Investors Financial	0.3%
Health Net	0.3%	Astoria Financial	0.3%
Manugistics	0.3%	Gallagher AJ & Co.	0.3%

Summary

While the Russell 1000 and 3000 indexes are well known in institutional circles, the Russell 2000 also enjoys wide popularity among individual investors. Designed to be a benchmark for small-capitalization stocks, over $20 billion is indexed to the Russell 2000. As such, its correlation to the S&P 500 is only about 76 percent. Despite the excellent relative performance of the S&P 500, there have been many periods when small-size issues excelled. When those times return, this ETF should shine. Although the Russell 2000 showed a decline for the year 2000, it outperformed the S&P 500.

Exhibit 7.7   ETF Highlights—iShares Russell 3000 Index Fund (IWV)

Assets in trust (March 16, 2001)	$385.2 million
Average daily volume (2000)	48,548 shares
Average daily volume (2001)*	74,229 shares
Size of ETF share	1/10 Russell 3000 Index
Annual expense fee	.20%
Ticker	IWV
NAV ticker	NMV
Trading hours	9:30 A.M.–4:15 P.M. (EST)
Bid-offer spread	26 basis points
Price (March 21, 2001)	62.50
Dividends	Quarterly (March, June, September, December)
Began trading	May 2000
Structure	Open-end mutual fund
Manager	Barclays Global Investors
AMEX specialist	Hull Trading

*First quarter 2001.

Top Members and Weightings in Underlying Index as of December 31, 2000

General Electric	3.8%	Merck	1.7%
ExxonMobil	2.4%	Intel	1.6%
Pfizer	2.3%	AIG	1.4%
Cisco	2.1%	Microsoft	1.4%
Citigroup	2.0%	SBC Communications	1.3%

Summary

Not content with 500 or 1,000 stocks? The Russell 3000 is the broadest of the broad market indexes that has an ETF (as of January 2001, there is no ETF on the Wilshire 5000 Index). The underlying index contains just over 2,900 stocks (the ETF is optimized and contains about 2,760 issues). Owning this ETF will give you exposure to about 98 percent of the total capitalization of the stock market in the United States. So for 20 basis points, the ETF provides you with the vehicle to own virtually the entire universe of stocks in the United States. You'll have plenty of company too: $52 billion is indexed to the Russell 3000.

Exhibit 7.8   ETF Highlights—iShares S&P 500/Barra Growth Index Fund (IVW)

Assets in trust (March 16, 2001)	$125.9 million
Average daily volume (2000)	48,548 shares
Average daily volume (2001)*	57,055 shares
Size of ETF share	1/10 underlying index
Annual expense fee	.18%
Ticker	IVW
NAV ticker	NJG
Trading hours	9:30 A.M.–4:15 P.M. (EST)
Bid-offer spread	18 basis points
Price (March 21, 2001)	55.390
Dividends	Quarterly (March, June, September, December)
Began trading	May 2000
Structure	Open-end mutual fund
Manager	Barclays Global Investors
AMEX specialist	Hull Trading

*YTD, March 21, 2001

Top Members and Weightings in Underlying Index as of December 31, 2000

General Electric	8.3%	AIG	4.0%
Pfizer	5.1%	Merck	3.8%
Cisco Systems	4.8%	Intel	3.5%
Wal-Mart	3.3%	Oracle	2.8%
Microsoft	4.0%	Coca Cola	2.6%

Summary

Until recently, investors had few options when it came to style investing or quantitative investment management. With BGI's iShares and State Street's streetTRACKS, the choices are numerous. Using basic quantitative methods (primarily price-to-book value), Standard & Poor's and Barra separated the growth stocks from the value stocks in the S&P 500 Index. This ETF replicates the growth stocks. Think of it as the S&P 500 with only the Microsofts, Pfizers, and Intels. Slower-growing value issues were put into the S&P 500/Barra Value index, which also has an ETF. From 1995 through 1999, Barra Growth had beaten Barra Value and the S&P 500. In 2000, though, Value trounced both indexes.

Exhibit 7.9   ETF Highlights—iShares S&P 500/Barra Value Index Fund (IVE)

Assets in trust (March 16, 2001)	$374.1 million
Average daily volume (2000)	46,268 shares
Average daily volume (2001)*	79,871 shares
Size of ETF share	1/10 underlying index
Annual expense fee	.18%
Ticker	IVE
NAV ticker	NME
Trading hours	9:30 A.M.–4:15 P.M. (EST)
Bid-offer spread	20 basis points
Price (March 21, 2001)	59.00
Dividends	Quarterly (March, June, September, December)
Began trading	May 2000
Structure	Open-end mutual fund
Manager	Barclays Global Investors
AMEX specialist	Hull Trading

*YTD, March 21, 2001.

Top Members and Weightings in Underlying Index as of December 31, 2000

ExxonMobil	5.1%	Nortel Networks	1.7%
Citigroup	4.3%	Philip Morris	1.6%
SBC Communications	2.7%	Tyco International	1.6%
Verizon Communications	2.3%	Wells Fargo	1.6%
Royal Dutch Petroleum	2.2%	Morgan Stanley	1.5%

Summary

The returns in growth stocks for the latter half of the 1990s were outrageously high. The result was that many investors took their eyes off the rest of the investment landscape. In fact, value investors took a lot of heat in the latter part of the 1990s. Even Warren Buffett, who compounds money better than anyone else, took heat. Only when growth headed south in 1999 did investors once again take notice of value. Some proponents of value investing claim that value wins in the long run. This ETF represents the value side of the growth-value debate. It takes out the high fliers and leaves in issues like GE, ExxonMobil, and Citigroup. The Barra/Value ETF has about 390 companies in it. The other 110 of the S&P 500 are in the growth index. In addition, the value index is significantly less volatile than is its growth counterpart.

Exhibit 7.10   ETF Highlights—Other Broadbased and Style ETFs

ETF	Ticker	Expenses	Assets (millions)
Barclays Global Investors iShares			
S&P 500 iShares	IVV	.09%	$2,460
S&P MidCap 400 iShares	IJH	.20	165
S&P MidCap/Barra Growth iShares	IJK	.25	137
S&P MidCap/Barra Value iShares	IJJ	.25	77
S&P SmallCap iShares	IJR	.20	199
S&P Small Cap/Barra Growth iShares	IJT	.25	26
S&P Small Cap/Barra Value iShares	IJS	.25	60
Russell 1000 Growth iShares	IWF	.20	153
Russell 1000 Value iShares	IWD	.20	166
Russell 2000 Growth iShares	IWO	.25	115
Russell 2000 Value iShares	IWN	.25	245
Russell 3000 Growth iShares	IWZ	.25	20
Russell 3000 Value iShares	IWW	.25	32
DJ US Total Market iShares	IYY	.20	61
State Street Global Advisors streetTRACKS			
FORTUNE 500 streetTRACKS	FFF	.20	49
DJ US LargeCap Growth streetTRACKS	ELG	.20	22
DJ US LargeCap Value streetTRACKS	ELV	.20	37
DJ US SmallCap Growth streetTRACKS	DSG	.25	13
DJ US SmallCap Value streetTRACKS	DSV	.25	23
HOLDRS			
Market 2000+ HOLDRS	MKH	NA	$316

Note: Asset figures for Market 2000 HOLDRS are from February 28, 2001; all others are from March 16, 2001.

SECTOR ETFs

The sector ETFs include HOLDRS, Select Sector Spiders, and other sector ETFs that allow investors to fine-tune their holdings more aggressively. Starting with Exhibit 7.12, are highlight pages for six of Merrill Lynch's HOLDRS products, a few of the Select Sector Spiders, and a streetTRACKS ETF.

I previously mentioned HOLDRS as part of a discussion on various ETF structures. We need to return to these unique ETFs because they have an interesting history and a few quirks that investors should be aware of. Recent changes by Merrill Lynch have also mitigated some of the problems caused by these quirks.

In July 1998, the Brazilian telecommunications company Telebras split off and sold most of its operating divisions. The result was a mish-mash of a dozen companies (in ADR form) created from the parent company and dubbed "baby bras."[1]

Many retail investors were mystified as to which of the ADRs to keep and which to discard. They understood Telebras but did not understand its progeny. Merrill thought perhaps investors would benefit from a vehicle that allowed all the pieces to be put back together. It repackaged the 12 baby bras ADRs into a structured product called Telebras Holding Companies depositary receipts (Telebras HOLDRS), with the ticker symbol TBH. It was an instant success. Assets were just under $5 billion initially, and average daily volume quickly topped 1 million shares. Investors had their Telebras, and Merrill had a hit.

In September 1999, Merrill came back for more by launching Internet HOLDRS (ticker HHH). The timing was exquisite; investors could not get enough of the Net, and many lacked the resources to put together a diversified portfolio of very expensive Internet stocks, and at the time there were only a handful of mutual funds dedicated to this sector. Exhibit 7.11 shows the original and current issues in the Internet HOLDRS ETF. Notice first the share amounts. With HOLDRS, investors actually own shares in each component—in some cases, a single share. Each 100 HOLDRS, the minimum amount for purchase, give the buyer beneficial ownership in each stock. If a stock splits, the number of shares of that component will increase in the HOLDR. Investors receive annual reports from each member in the ETF (warn the mail delivery person), have voting rights (watch for proxy statements), and receive dividends. In addition, if a stock drops out, it will not be replaced. That is why some HOLDRS do not have 20 issues. The HHH has 17 because several members were merged with or acquired by other companies (some of the acquiring companies were themselves HOLDR components).

Exhibit 7.11   Internet HOLDRS Portfolio

Company Name	Original Share Amounts	Current Share Amounts
America Online Inc.	21	42
Yahoo! Inc.	13	26
Amazon.com Inc.	9	18
EBay Inc.	6	12
At Home Corp.	17	17
Priceline.com	7	7
CMGI Inc.	5	10
Inktomi Corp.	3	6
Real Networks	4	8
Exodus Communications	4	16
E*Trade	12	12
DoubleClick	2	4
Ameritrade Holdings	8	9
Lycos	4	0[a]
CNET	4	4
PSI Net	3	6
Network Associates	7	7
EarthLink Network	2	6.23[b]
Mindspring Enterprises	3	0[c]
Go2Net, Inc.	1	0[d]
Total number of companies	20	17

[a]Acquired by Terra Networks and distributed.
[b]As a result of the Mindspring merger.
[c]Acquired by EarthLink.
[d]Acquired by Infospace and distributed.

Hence, for your investment, you get a basket of 17 Internet companies. You can also create and redeem HOLDRS in a similar fashion to the way you would create or redeem the SPY. So if you absolutely must take possession of those 6.23 shares of EarthLink, you pay the trustee (Bank of New York) a fee of $10.00, and you'll receive your shares in EarthLink and the other 16 members of the Internet HOLDRS. The ETF highlight pages show the components and the percentage weighting of each component rather than the share amounts.

The Merrill HOLDRS products were a huge success. Early on, though, there were some growing pains. First, there was very little detailed information on the products. If you were well wired or had a Bloomberg terminal, you could dig up the details. But a retail investor who would not think of shelling out $1,500 each month for a Bloomberg terminal had to rely on a broker, make lots of phone calls, or search the Web, which had little information itself on the products. Then Merrill realized how popular HOLDRS had become and finally put up a Web site dedicated to HOLDR products only: www.holdrs.com. The first problem was solved. The second problem was a lot tougher.

In February 2000, Merrill launched the Internet Architecture HOLDRS (ticker symbol IAH) product. One of its components was Hewlett-Packard Corporation. A few months later, HP spun off a division called Agilent Technologies. Investors who owned the IAHs suddenly found themselves with about 2.7 shares of Agilent. Indeed, one investor called CME thinking perhaps we would know about this. (Remember that many people do not differentiate the exchanges, and this caller thought HOLDRS traded at the CME.) He was lucky. I knew because I had read something in the press around the time of his call. I told the caller that he actually owned HP as a result of buying the IAH. He was entitled to HP dividends, annual reports, proxy statements, and, of course, spin-offs! He had fewer than three shares of Agilent. I said, "It gets worse." He wanted to know how 2.7 shares of a spin-off could get worse. I said those three letters—IRS—and also mentioned a commission would be involved should he decide to sell his 2.7 shares. The commission would probably eat away most of the value of the shares. And for tax purposes, he would have to calculate a cost basis for those shares received as part of the HP spin-off. Part of the HOLDRS structure was that this kind of transaction must be distributed to the owner of the HOLDR.

Merrill realized the problems that small distributions were causing and certainly did not want to see the product suffer as a result of corporate distributions and IRS rulings. In November 2000, it announced that it would not distribute shares and fractions but would keep them in the trust as long as the merging or acquiring companies were in the same sector. Merrill also went the extra mile and put a cost-basis calculator on the HOLDRS Web site to assist investors with taxation issues pertinent to HOLDRS distributions. The second problem was thereby solved.

There are now 17 HOLDRS products (as of mid 2001). The most recent is the Retail HOLDRS. Look for more because investors have voted with their accounts. They like the flexibility that comes with being able to invest in one particular sector of the market. Exhibits 7.12 through 7.17 illustrate some of the more active HOLDR products. Later in Chapter 7, more details on the remaining products will be listed in spreadsheet form.

Exhibit 7.12   ETF Highlights—Biotech HOLDRS (BBH)

Assets in trust (February 28, 2001)	$1.42 billion
Average daily volume (2000)	886,000 shares
Average daily volume (2001)*	1,069,171 shares
Annual expense fee†	$8.00 per 100 shares
Minimum purchase	100 shares
Ticker	BBH
NAV ticker	IBH
Trading hours	9:30 A.M.–4:00 P.M. (EST)
Bid-offer spread	41 basis points
Price (March 21, 2001)	107.45
Options	Yes; AMEX/CBOE
Began trading	November 1999
Structure	Grantor trust
Manager	Bank of New York
AMEX specialist	Susquehanna Partners

*YTD, March 21, 2001.

† The custody fee for HOLDRS is $2.00 per quarter per round lot, to be deducted from any cash dividend or other cash distribution. The trustee will waive any portion of the custody fee that exceeds the total cash dividend or distributions received.

Members as of December 31, 2000

Genentech	21.1%	Human Genome Science	3.3%
Amgen	17.3%	Sepracor Inc.	2.8%
Immunex	10.0%	Gilead Sciences	1.9%
Applera Corporation	9.9%	Affymetrix Inc.	1.7%
Biogen	4.6%	Biochem Pharmaceutical	1.7%
Idec Pharmaceutical	4.5%	Icos Corp.	1.2%
Millennium Pharmaceutical	4.4%	Enzon	1.1%
Medimmune Inc.	4.2%	Applera	.9%
Chiron	4.2%	QLT Inc.	.8%
Genzyme	3.7%	Alkermes Inc.	.7%

Summary

The second of Merrill Lynch's very popular HOLDRS products, Biotech HOLDRS is the largest in terms of assets and the most heavily traded. Conservative investors might want to stay away from the BBH, however; it went from 100 to 240, and back to 120—all within a year! You get a nice portfolio of leading-edge biotech companies with these ETFs, but remember that six issues make up two-thirds of the portfolio. If you believe that biotech represents the next mother lode in investing, step right up. Bring lots of money, though; as you must buy 100 shares, and at the recent price, that means $10,700.

Exhibit 7.13   ETF Highlights—Internet HOLDRS (HHH)

Assets in trust (February 28, 2001)	$212 million
Average daily volume (2000)	892,000 shares
Average daily volume (2001)*	330,000 shares
Minimum purchase	100 shares
Annual expense fee†	$8.00 per 100 shares
Ticker	HHH
NAV ticker	HHI
Trading hours	9:30 A.M.–4:00 P.M. (EST)
Bid-offer spread	50–70 basis points
Price (March 21, 2001)	31.60
Options	Yes; AMEX/CBOE
Began trading	September 1999
Structure	Grantor trust
Manager	Bank of New York
AMEX specialist	Susquehanna Partners

*YTD, March 21, 2001.

†The custody fee for HOLDRS is $2.00 per quarter per round lot to be deducted from any cash dividend or other cash distribution. The trustee will waive any portion of the custody fee that exceeds the total cash dividend or distributions received.

17 Members as of December 31, 2000

America Online	37.5%	CNET Networks	1.6%
Yahoo!	20.0%	Ameritrade Holdings	1.6%
eBay Inc.	10.2%	CMGI Inc.	1.4%
Exodus Communication	8.2%	Double Click	1.1%
Amazon.Com Inc.	7.2%	EarthLink	.8%
Inktomi Corp.	2.8%	Network Associates	.8%
At Home Corp.	2.4%	Priceline.com	.2%
E*Trade Group	2.3%	Psinet Inc.	.1%
Real Networks	1.8%		

Summary

Internet HOLDRS (HHH) were the first Merrill HOLDRS product since the Telebras HOLDRS. Notice that, there are only 17 issues, although originally this HOLDR started with 20 stocks. When a stock disappears for whatever reason (e.g., merger), it is not replaced under the grantor trust structure. In this fund, Lycos, Mindspring, and Go2Net were on the original list. This ETF is not for the faint of heart, as the Internet space can provide plenty of ups and downs. Notice too that America Online and Yahoo! comprise more than half the index.

Exhibit 7.14   ETF Highlights—Semiconductor HOLDRS (SMH)

Assets in trust (February 28, 2001)	$422 million
Average daily volume (2000)	557,228 shares
Average daily volume (2001)*	1,446,695 shares
Minimum purchase	100 shares
Annual expense fee†	$8.00 per 100 shares
Ticker	SMH
NAV ticker	XSH
Trading hours	9:30 A.M.–4:00 P.M. (EST)
Bid-offer spread	47 basis points
Price (March 21, 2001)	44.01
Options	Yes; AMEX/CBOE
Began trading	May 2000
Structure	Grantor trust
Manager	Bank of New York
AMEX specialist	Susquehanna Partners

*YTD, March 21, 2001.

†The custody fee for HOLDRS is $2.00 per quarter per round lot to be deducted from any cash dividend or other cash distribution. The trustee will waive any portion of the custody fee that exceeds the total cash dividend or distributions received.

20 Members as of December 31, 2000

Texas Instruments	21.3%	Altera Corp.	3.2%
Intel Corp.	18.4%	Teradyne	2.3%
Applied Materials	10.1%	KLA-Tencor	2.1%
Micron Technology	6.5%	Atmel Corp.	1.9%
Analog Devices	6.3%	LSI Logic	1.7%
Maxim Integrated	4.9%	Novellus Systems	1.4%
Linear Technology	4.7%	National Semiconductor	1.2%
Xilinx Inc.	4.7%	Advance Micro Devices	1.1%
Broadcom Corp.	3.4%	Amkor Technology	0.6%
Vitesse Seminconductor	3.4%	Sandisk Corp.	0.6%

Summary

These companies are the major players in the development, manufacturing and marketing of chips for the high-tech industry. Even new-generation gallium chips (manufactured by Vitesse Semi) are represented in the Semiconductor HOLDRS. SMH is one of the more active HOLDRS products.

Exhibit 7.15 ETF Highlights—Pharmaceutical HOLDRS (PPH)

Assets in trust (February 28, 2001)	$554 million
Average daily volume (2000)	156,896 shares
Average daily volume (2001)*	312,005 shares
Minimum purchase	100 shares
Annual expense fee†	$8.00 per 100 shares
Ticker	PPH
NAV ticker	IPH
Trading hours	9:30 A.M.–4:00 P.M. (EST)
Bid or offer spread	41 basis points
Price (March 21, 2001)	89.20
Options	Yes; AMEX/CBOE
Began trading	February 2000
Structure	Grantor trust
Manager	Bank of New York
AMEX specialist	KV Execution

*YTD, March 21, 2001.

†The custody fee for HOLDRS is $2.00 per quarter per round lot to be deducted from any cash dividend or other cash distribution. The trustee will waive any portion of the custody fee that exceeds the total cash dividend or distributions received.

17 Members as of December 31, 2000

Pfizer	23.4%	Biovail Corp.	1.4%
Merck & Co.	18.0%	Forest Lab.	1.2%
Johnson & Johnson	12.0%	Andrx Corp.	1.0%
Bristol-Myers Squibb	11.6%	Allergan	0.8%
Eli Lilly & Co.	8.2%	IVAX Corp.	0.5%
Schering Plough	6.9%	Watson Pharmaceutical	0.4%
American Home Products	6.7%	ICN Pharmaceutical	0.3%
Abbott Laboratories	5.9%	Mylan Laboratories	0.2%
King Pharmaceuticals	1.4%		

Summary

Although technology offered the best returns at the end of the 1990s, the next best sector was health care, including drugs. Well-above-average return on equities, combined with a solid demographic play (aging of America), make these HOLDRS interesting for those who want aggressive growth with a little less risk than the biotech industry. This ETF offers a nice blend of the bluest of blue chip drug makers, along with representation in the generic drug segment, over-the-counter medicines, hospital supplies, and related areas.

Exhibit 7.16 ETF Highlights—Telecom HOLDRS (TTH)

Assets in trust (February 28, 2001)	$365 million
Average daily volume (2000)	128,017 shares
Average daily volume (2001)*	94,909 shares
Minimum purchase	100 shares
Annual expense fee†	$8.00 per 100 shares
Ticker	TTH
NAV ticker	ITH
Trading hours	9:30 A.M.–4:00 P.M. (EST)
Bid-offer spread	47 basis points
Price (March 21, 2001)	49.35
Options	Yes; AMEX/CBOE
Began trading	February 2000
Structure	Grantor trust
Manager	Bank of New York
AMEX specialist	AGS/STR/OTA

*YTD, March 21, 2001.

†The custody fee for HOLDRS is $2.00 per quarter per round lot to be
deducted from any cash dividend or other cash distribution. The trustee will
waive any portion of the custody fee that exceeds the total cash dividend or
distributions received.

18 Members as of December 31, 2000

SBC Communications	24.1%	Sprint Corp. (PCS group)	2.3%
Verizon Communications	20.4%	Sprint Corp. (FON group)	2.3%
Bell South	11.5%	Level 3 Communication	1.8%
Qwest Communications	9.9%	Telephone and Data System	1.7%
AT&T	8.1%	Global Crossing	1.6%
WorldCom	5.7%	Broadwing Inc.	0.9%
Nextel Communications	2.8%	McLeod USA	0.8%
BCE Inc.	2.7%	Century Telephone Inc.	0.7%
Alltel Corp.	2.3%	NTL Inc.	0.6%

Summary

Telecom HOLDRS are a mixture of Ma Bell; a few baby bells; wireless, local,
and long distance companies; and fiber-optic infrastructure operations. The
sector, represented by TTH, also has cooled somewhat from above-average
performances in years past. Clearly, AT&T and WorldCom, which have
suffered severe declines, have exerted a huge negative drag on this ETF.

Exhibit 7.17 ETF Highlights—Broadband HOLDRS (BDH)

Assets in trust (February 28, 2001)	$216 million
Average daily volume	206,989 shares
Average daily volume*	361,847 shares
Minimum purchase	100 shares
Annual expense fee†	$8.00 per 100 shares
Ticker	BDH
NAV ticker	XDH
Trading hours	9:30 A.M.–4:00 P.M. (EST)
Bid-offer spread	50–60 basis points
Price (March 21, 2001)	27.06
Options	Yes; AMEX/CBOE
Began trading	April 2000
Structure	Grantor trust
Manager	Bank of New York
AMEX specialist	Wolverine

*YTD, March 21, 2001.

†The custody fee for HOLDRS is $2.00 per quarter per round lot to be deducted from any cash dividend or other cash distribution. The trustee will waive any portion of the custody fee that exceeds the total cash dividend or distributions received.

20 Members as of December 31, 2000

Nortel Networks	19.6%	Applied Micro Circuits	3.3%
Qualcomm	14.4%	SDL Inc.	3.3%
Corning Inc.	10.4%	Sycamore Networks	2.4%
Lucent Technology	8.6%	PMC-Sierra Inc.	1.7%
Motorola	8.0%	Scientific Atlanta	1.4%
JDS Uniphase	7.3%	RF Micro Devices	1.2%
Tellabs Inc.	4.9%	Conexant Systems	0.7%
Comverse Technology	4.7%	Next Level Communications	0.3%
Broadcom Corp.	3.7%	Terayon Corp.	0.2%
Ciena Corp.	3.7%	Copper Mountain	0.1%

Summary

This ETF consists of companies that develop, manufacture, and market products and services that facilitate the transmission of data, video- and voice more quickly than over traditional phone lines. These companies are on the cutting edge of technology and make things such as pump lasers, fiber-optic cable, filters, and switches.

For equity investors, sector ETFs offer the potential for dramatically higher returns (along with some extra risk). We witnessed this with Internet mutual funds in 1998 and 1999 when many of these sector funds rewarded risk-taking investors with triple-digit gains. Rather than laboring over which stock to pick, a sector ETF offers investors an entire basket within a sector. A couple of stories illustrate the benefits of sector investing.

In the fall of 1990 during an investment management class that I taught at a local college, we were discussing some of the events in the market. They were exciting days. The markets were still recovering from the junk bond debacles of the late 1980s as well as the crash of 1987. By August 1990, the Dow had fallen over 20 percent. War in the Persian Gulf was a real threat, and nonperforming loans and real estate problems were creating havoc with the nation's banking system. Citigroup had fallen from $36 per share to under $10. Chase Manhattan fell from $44 to $14 (these prices were before numerous splits over the years). Brokerage firms and other financial stocks were lower too, and investors were fearful. One student made a comment that every investor knows but seldom acts on. During a discussion period, she explained that this was the time to buy: "Isn't it, 'Buy low, sell high' that we always hear about? Banks are not going to disappear, and they are giving the best and biggest banks away in a 75 percent off sale. Didn't Warren Buffett scoop up shares in American Express during times of trouble, and look what happened to him!" I told her that if she was that convinced, she should take advantage of the sale and buy a few bank and financial stocks. She said she had only a few thousand dollars that she could invest and that would not buy much. I told her to try sector funds. If this discussion came up today, I would be able to point her to four sector ETFs that could capitalize on such a hunch.

An investor I knew who worked in the pharmaceutical field asked me to review her portfolio. It had some diversification but was lagging in several major sectors. Despite her vast knowledge of the drug and medical industry, she had no investments in that sector, which had compounded money at rates between 20 and 25 percent for most of the previous 15 years. In the January 8, 2001, edition of *Barron's*,[2] a table reports the top (and bottom) funds over a 15-year time period. Guess which sector was number one? Health care/drugs. In fact, funds that invested in that sector captured three of the top five slots. I told her to buy what she was familiar with. She said she would like too but had no time to analyze stocks, so I told her about sector investing. With ETFs, filling a hole in a portfolio can be done with a single call to your broker.

I like to tell both sides of a story. I discuss risks with investors and students far more than returns, so it is only fair to point out that in the same *Barron's* table, the biggest laggards over the past 15 years have also been concentrated in certain sectors: precious metals and natural resources. All have been victims of a deflationary environment and have caused the destruction of vast amounts of investor capital. You'd have been better off putting the money in your pillow! And there lies the heart of the sector debate: If you are in the right sector, you have home-run potential; get it wrong, and it might cost you. Either way, sector ETFs allow investors a tactical method of enhancing a portfolio. (See Exhibits 7.18 through 7.23.)

INTERNATIONAL INVESTING

There are so many wonderful opportunities outside the borders of the United States that on the surface it would be foolish to ignore them. But investors must be careful. A look at Japan around 1990 serves as a sobering illustration.

In late 1989, the Nikkei 225 stock average, one of Japan's primary market barometers, stood at just under 40,000. It had had a persistent rise for most of the previous decade and had recently entered a near-parabolic phase upward. Analysts called for the Nikkei to continue to rise to 50,000 or 60,000 in coming years. During the 1970s and 1980s, Japan had taken a major chunk of business from the big three automakers in the United States. Frustrated Americans were losing lots of economic battles to Japan. U.S. auto and consumer electronics manufacturers found that they faced a difficult, perhaps impossible, task of competing with the Japanese. Japanese real estate also was in a major bubble phase. A small house cost millions. Japanese lenders had to invent intergenerational mortgages because there would be no way to pay off the gargantuan mortgages in 30 years.

Then one day they rang the bell (that's Street jargon for, "Its time to *sell!*"). In Japan the bell rang when someone published *The Japan That Can Say No.*[3] A few months later, in January 1990, the bell rang loudly. Several major Wall Street firms issued Nikkei put warrants— a type of long-term put option. Buying such warrants is a bearish strategy. Selling, writing, or issuing them was a bullish kind of move. Although the firms all knew how to hedge their exposures, the fact that so many issued the warrants at almost the same time was incredible—so incredible that I bought a few at 10 and sold them at 15 a few days later. I thought I was a genius. Then I proceeded to watch them go to 50 before they expired.

The point is that Japan unraveled. Those who had ventured into Japan watched the huge profits they had reaped quickly melt away.

Exhibit 7.18   ETF Highlights—Financial Select Sector SPDR Fund (XLF)

Assets in trust (March 16, 2001)	$701 million
Average daily volume (2000)	523,013 shares
Average daily volume (2001)*	698,571 shares
Size of ETF share	1/10th underlying index
Annual expense fee	.28%
Ticker	XLF
NAV ticker	FXV
Trading Hours	9:30 A.M.–4:00 P.M. (EST)
Bid-offer spread	42 basis points
Price (March 21, 2001)	24.92
Dividends	Quarterly; March cycle
Options	Yes; AMEX
Began trading	December 1998
Structure	Open-end mutual fund
Manager	State Street Global Advisors
AMEX specialist	Spear, Leeds & Kellogg

*YTD, March 21, 2001.

Top Members and Weightings in Underlying Index as of September 30, 2000

Citigroup	12.3%	Wells Fargo	3.8%
AIG	11.2%	FNMA	3.6%
Morgan Stanley DW	5.2%	Chase Manhattan	3.1%
Bank of America	4.3%	Merrill Lynch	2.7%
American Express	4.1%	Charles Schwab Corp.	2.5%

Number of stocks in ETF: 74

Summary

Financial SPDRs contain a wide variety of financial services companies, including money center and regional banks, investment bank and brokerage firms, and insurance companies. This sector displayed very good relative returns in 2000, and many investors consider it as a play on the boomer generation. The common wisdom is that banks, brokers, and insurance companies will be prime beneficiaries as boomers save for their retirement and finance the education of their children. Despite good long-term performance by many members of this sector, financials are interest rate sensitive and suffer downdrafts during periods of rising interest rates.

Exhibit 7.19 ETF Highlights—Energy Select Sector SPDR Fund (XLE)

Assets in trust (March 16, 2001)	$232 million
Average daily volume (2000)	346,825 shares
Average daily volume (2001)*	258,876 shares
Size of ETF share	1/10th underlying index
Annual expense fee	.28%
Ticker	XLE
NAV ticker	EXV
Trading hours	9:30 A.M.–4:00 P.M. (EST)
Bid-offer spread	58 basis points
Price (December 26, 2000)	31.44
Dividends	Quarterly; March cycle
Options	Yes; AMEX
Began trading	December 1998
Structure	Open-end mutual fund
Manager	State Street Global Advisors
AMEX specialist	Susquehanna Partners

*YTD, March 21, 2001.

Top Members and Weightings in Underlying Index as of December 31, 2000

ExxonMobil	21.9%	Chevron Corp.	4.4%
Royal Dutch Petroleum	15.2%	Coastal Corp.	2.9%
Enron	7.8%	Conoco	2.7%
Texaco Inc.	4.6%	Anadarko Petroleum	2.7%
Schlumberger	4.6%	El Paso Energy	2.6%

Number of stocks in ETF: 30

Summary

The long gas lines and the Arab oil embargo of the 1970s seemed a distant memory until the U.S. and world economic engines started to consume energy at a rate that far outstripped supply in the late 1990s. Throw in the very cold winter of 2000–2001, energy shortages in the western United States, and high gas pump prices, and the term *energy crisis* begins to resurface. The energy sector ETF invests in the major oil and gas companies, suppliers, and pipeline companies, as well as exploration and research companies. Many components are "old economy" companies that form the foundation of numerous portfolios, large and small.

Exhibit 7.20 ETF Highlights—Technology Select Sector SPDR Fund (XLK)

Assets in trust	$922 million
Average daily volume (2000)	671,825 shares
Average daily volume (2001)*	883,505 shares
Size of ETF share	1/10th underlying index
Annual expense fee	.28%
Ticker	XLK
NAV ticker	KXV
Trading hours	9:30 A.M.–4:00 P.M. (EST)
Bid-offer spread	39 basis points
Price (March 21, 2001)	25.25
Dividends	Quarterly; March cycle
Options	Yes; AMEX
Began trading	December 1998
Structure	Open-end mutual fund
Manager	State Street Global Advisors
AMEX specialist	Susquehanna Partners

*YTD, March 21, 2001.

Top Members and Weightings in Underlying Index as of September 30, 2000

Cisco	9.5%	IBM	4.8%
Microsoft	7.7%	Sun Microsystems	4.5%
Intel	6.7%	Nortel Networks	4.4%
Oracle	5.4%	America Online	3.0%
EMC	5.3%	AT&T	2.7%

Number of stocks in ETF: 90

Summary

Technology Spiders had a very successful launch in December 1998. Four months later, however, when the Nasdaq-100 Index shares made its debut, many thought the XLK would suffer in volume. Both, though, have survived and thrived, and both are in the top ten in assets under management and daily turnover out of the 100 or so existing ETFs. Despite similar price performance, the S&P Technology Sector Index (the underlying index) is composed not only of Nasdaq issues like Intel, Microsoft, and Cisco, but also has many NYSE-listed tech issues. The share price, too, is more affordable for the retail investor (about half the QQQ price).

Exhibit 7.21 ETF Highlights—Fortune e-50 streetTRACKS (FEF)

Assets in trust (March 16, 2001)	$14 million
Average daily volume (2000)	15,886 shares
Average daily volume (2001)*	1,738 shares
Size of ETF share	1/10th Fortune e-50 Index
Annual expense fee	.20%
Ticker	FEF
NAV ticker	FEY
Trading hours	9:30 A.M.–4:15 P.M. (EST)
Bid-offer spread	75–100 basis points
Price (March 21, 2001)	36.00
Dividends	NA
Options/futures	No/yes (CME)
Began trading	October 2000
Structure	Open-end mutual fund
Manager	State Street Global Advisors
AMEX specialist	KV Execution

*YTD, March 21, 2001.

Top Members and Weightings in Underlying Index as of September 30, 2000

Oracle	9.1%	JDS Uniphase	4.4%
Microsoft	9.0%	Juniper Networks	4.3%
Cisco	8.3%	Sun Microsystems	3.3%
America Online	7.5%	Qwest Communications	3.0%
Intel	6.5%	EMC Corp.	3.0%

Number of stocks in ETF: 50

Summary

Launched in October 2000, the uniquely constructed Fortune e-50 index is designed to track 50 companies selected from the following subsectors: e-companies, Internet communications, Internet hardware, and Internet software and services. Moreover, it is a modified-capitalization-weighted index, and thus the weighting of any company is adjusted depending on what percentage of the company's revenue is derived from the Internet. For example, Worldcom, a component of the e-50, is usually regarded as a long-distance telecom company. However, Worldcom is also one of the largest Internet service providers in the United States, and thus Worldcom's capitalization is modified to reflect that 15 percent of its revenues come from the Internet.

Exhibit 7.22   ETF Highlights—Consumer Staples Select Sector SPDR (XLP)

Assets in trust (March 16, 2001)	$198 million
Average daily volume (2000)	177,381 shares
Average daily volume (2001)*	114,981 shares
Size of ETF share	1/10th underlying index
Annual expense fee	.28%
Ticker	XLP
NAV ticker	PXV
Trading hours	9:30 A.M.–4:00 P.M. (EST)
Bid-offer spread	80 basis points
Price (March 21, 2001)	23.51
Dividends	Quarterly
Options	Yes, AMEX
Began trading	December 1998
Structure	Open-end mutual fund
Manager	State Street Global Advisors
Specialist/market maker	KV Execution

*YTD, March 21, 2001.

Top Members and Weightings in Underlying Index as of September 30, 2000

Pfizer Inc.	12.6%	Eli Lilly and Comp.	4.2%
Merck	7.6%	Procter and Gamble	4.0%
Coca Cola	6.2%	Pharmacia Corp.	3.5%
Johnson & Johnson	5.9%	American Home Products	3.4%
Bristol-Myers Squibb	5.2%	Amgen Inc.	3.3%

Number of stocks in ETF: 68

Summary

Food and medicine, like energy, are obvious necessities. This ETF invests in a broad range of such consumer staples as food, beverages, and retail—a sector that tends to hold up well during economic weakness.

Exhibit 7.23 ETF Highlights—Other Sector ETFs and HOLDRS

ETF	Ticker	Expenses	Assets (millions)
Select Sector SPDRs (State Street)			
Basic Industries Select Sector SPDR	XLB	.28%	$73
Cyclical/Transport Select Sector SPDR	XLY	.28	95
Consumer Services Select Sector SPDR	XLV	.28	82
Industrial Select Sector SPDR	XLI	.28	38
Utilities Select Sector SPDR	XLU	.28	56
iShares (Barclays Global Investors)			
DJ US Basic Materials iShares	IYM	.60	9
DJ US Chemicals iShares	IYD	.60	16
DJ US Consumer Cyclical iShares	IYC	.60	25
DJ US Consumer Non-Cyclical iShares	IYK	.60	14
DJ US Energy iShares	IYE	.60	42
DJ US Financial iShares	IYF	.60	57
DJ US Financial Services iShares	IYG	.60	26
DJ US Healthcare iShares	IYH	.60	71
DJ US Industrial iShares	IYJ	.60	22
DJ US Internet iShares	IYV	.60	13
DJ US Technology iShares	IYW	.60	82
DJ US Telecom iShares	IYZ	.60	55
DJ US Utilities iShares	IDU	.60	28
streetTRACKS (State Street)			
MS Internet streetTRACKS	MII	.50	5
MS High Tech 35 streetTRACKS	MTK	.50	58
Merrill Lynch HOLDRS (Bank of New York)			
Internet Architecture HOLDRS	IAH	NA	247
Internet Infrastructure HOLDRS	IIH	NA	209
B2B Internet HOLDRS	BHH	NA	370
Software HOLDRS	SWH	NA	11
Utilities HOLDRS	UTH	NA	66
Regional Bank HOLDRS	RKH	NA	86
Oil Service HOLDRS	OIH	NA	131
Wireless HOLDRS	WMH	NA	97

Note: Assets as of March 16, 2001; HOLDRS assets as of February 28, 2001.

Over the next five years, the Nikkei would decline by more than half. Eleven years later, the Nikkei continues in a downward spiral. There is no doubt that Japan will recover, and the Nikkei 225 will rise again, but the recovery may take a while. Remember that after peaking at 380 in 1929, the Dow Jones Industrials did not return to that level for over a decade. Diversification outside U.S. borders carries real risk.

Despite Japan's current woes and despite the meltdown of the Russian stock index, the Hang Seng index (Hong Kong), the SET index (Thailand), and dozens of other major indexes, U.S. investors had nearly $600 billion in international funds as the new century began. Pension funds too allocate a percentage of their assets to overseas markets. It is not unusual to find 5 percent, 10 percent, or more allocated to international markets. Let's look at the returns of U.S and international stocks during certain periods over the last 16 years. Exhibit 7.24 shows the returns on the S&P 500 Index and the MSCI EAFE Index (EAFE stands for Europe, Australasia and Far East). MSCI's EAFE Index is one of the more prominent barometers of international markets.

The EAFE Index "won" the return race seven years, while the S&P 500 won eight times. Interestingly, the EAFE Index was on fire from 1985 through 1989, then struggled for much of the next seven years. The S&P 500 had a tremendous run from 1995 through 1999 and well-above-average returns for many of the other years shown. The crux of the matter is a long-term outlook. The numbers in Exhibit 7.24 represent 15 years of investment performance. Those planning to invest internationally with ETFs or other vehicles need to keep this kind of perspective and understand three kinds of risk:

- *Currency risk.* Although the Mexican stock market has had remarkable rates of returns during part of the last 25 years, the peso underwent severe devaluations. This not only paralyzes economies; it is a killer of stock markets. When your fund owns foreign equities, it sells dollars to buy the currencies of the markets it is interested in. If a fund manager or ETF invests in German equities, those stocks will be bought with euro currency. A manager who wants Japanese stocks has to buy them with yen. If the euro or yen declines, anyone holding stocks priced in those currencies will be holding a stock in a declining currency and will suffer a loss on the currency portion of the investment. The actual up-and-down movements of the stock are something entirely separate. You could make 10 percent in a foreign stock and still face 10 percent currency losses, for a net gain of zero.
- *Political risk.* During the Asian economic crises, some governments, notably Malaysia, enacted capital controls and restric-

Exhibit 7.24 Returns on the Wilshire 5000 Index and the MSCI EAFE Index

Year	S&P 500 Index Returns (%)	MSCI EAFE Returns (%)
1985	32.6	56.7
1986	16.0	69.9
1987	5.2	24.6
1988	16.6	28.3
1989	31.7	10.5
1990	−3.1	−23.5
1991	30.5	12.1
1992	7.6	−12.2
1993	10.1	32.6
1994	1.3	7.8
1995	37.6	11.2
1996	23.0	6.1
1997	33.4	1.8
1998	28.6	20.0
1999	21.0	27.0
2000	−10.0	—

Source: CME Index Products.

tions. Foreign investors had a rough time during the crises. (See the ETF highlight on Malaysia in Exhibit 7.30.) Unstable capital flows, political instability, and civil wars have all been painfully played out in many emerging markets. Although risk is present in all markets, it is not likely we will see civil war in the United States anytime soon.

- *Liquidity risk.* In the United States we are blessed with extraordinarily liquid markets. Small investors and $20 billion institutions have few problems getting orders filled in large-cap stocks and the U.S. Treasury markets. True, London, Tokyo, and Hong Kong are world financial market dealing centers that also have tremendous liquidity. But many other regions, especially in emerging markets like India, Eastern Europe, and Africa, have far lower trading volumes, and their clearing and settlement systems are not nearly as efficient as in the United States, Western Europe, or other major financial centers.

All of these forces pose risks to investors. Only investors who can assess the risks should consider making any kind of investment, especially one halfway across the planet. Do your homework! (See Exhibits 7.25 through 7.31.)

Exhibit 7.25 ETF Highlights—iShares Standard & Poor's Europe 350 Fund (IEV)

Assets in trust (March 16, 2001)	$139 million
Average daily volume (2000)	47,148 shares
Average daily volume (2001)*	37,635 shares
Annual expense fee	.60%
Ticker	IEV
NAV ticker	NLG
Trading hours	9:30 A.M.–4:15 P.M. (EST)
Bid-offer spread	54 basis points
Price (March 21, 2001)	65.00
Dividends	NA
Options	No
Began trading	July 2000
Structure	Open-end mutual fund
Manager	Barclays Global Investors
AMEX specialist	Susquehanna Partners

*YTD, March 21, 2001.

Top Members and Weightings in Underlying Index as of December 31, 2000

Vodafone ADR	4.0%	Novartis	2.4%
Nokia	3.6%	Royal Dutch Petroleum	2.3%
BP Amoco	3.3%	Total SA (b)	2.0%
Glaxo Smith Kline	3.2%	AstraZeneca	1.7%
HSBC Holdings	2.4%	Nestle	1.6%

Number of stocks in ETF: 326

Summary

For those wishing to venture outside the United States, this ETF invests across a broad spectrum of large-cap European equities. Financial, consumer, technology, and energy issues make up 75 percent of the index. The iShares S&P Europe ETF holds 326 issues (optimized portfolio of the actual 350) mostly from the following countries: Austria, Denmark, Finland, France, Germany, Ireland, Italy, the Netherlands, Norway, Portugal, Spain, Sweden, Switzerland, and the United Kingdom

Exhibit 7.26   ETF Highlights—streetTRACKS Dow Jones Global Titans Index (DGT)

Assets in trust (March 16, 2001)	$27 million
Average daily volume (2000)	3,109 shares
Average daily volume (2001)*	1,487 shares
Annual expense fee	.50%
Ticker	DGT
NAV ticker	UGTNV
Trading hours	9:30 A.M.–4:00 P.M. (EST)
Bid-offer spread	71 basis points
Price (March 21, 2001)	76.75
Distributions	2 per year
Options	No
Began trading	September 2000
Structure	Open-end mutual fund
Manager	State Street Global Advisors
AMEX specialist	KV Execution

*YTD, March 21, 2001.

Top Members and Weightings in Underlying Index as of September 30, 2000

General Electric	9.0%	Citigroup	3.8%
Cisco Systems	6.1%	Vodafone Grp. PLC	3.6%
ExxonMobil	4.9%	BP Amoco PLC	3.2%
Intel Corp.	4.2%	IBM	3.1%
Microsoft	4.0%	AIG	3.0%

Number of stocks in ETF: 50

Summary

The Dow Jones Global Titans Index seeks to provide an effective representation of the world's largest global companies. Each year, Dow Jones chooses from a universe of the world's largest stocks. It ranks companies based on market capitalization, assets, book value, sales and revenue, and profits. Convention says that international funds invest exclusively outside the United States, whereas global funds invest overseas and within the United States. This ETF is heavily weighted with U.S. multinational corporations, as the "Global Titans" name would imply: United States, 64.7 percent; United Kingdom, 11.1 percent; Switzerland, 6.8 percent; Finland, 3.6 percent; Netherlands, 3.4 percent; Germany, 3.4 percent; Japan, 3.2 percent; and France, 3.3 percent.

Exhibit 7.27   ETF Highlights—iShares MSCI Japan Index Fund (EWJ)

Assets in trust (March 16, 2001)	$531 million
Average daily volume (2000)	445,238 shares
Average daily volume (2001)*	693,876 shares
Annual expense fee	.84%
National currency†	Japanese yen
Ticker	EWJ
NAV ticker	INJ
Trading hours	9:30 A.M.–4:00 P.M. (EST)
Bid-offer spread	58 basis points
Price (March 21, 2001)	11.00
Distributions	2 per year
Options	No
Began trading	March 1996
Structure	Open-end mutual fund
Manager	Barclays Global Investors
AMEX specialist	AIM Securities

*YTD, March 21, 2001.

†All iShares MSCI country funds are bought and sold in U.S. dollars.

Top Members and Weightings in Underlying Index as of September 30, 2000

Toyota Motor Corp.	6.2%	Matshushita Elec. Indus.	2.3%
Nippon Telephone & Tel.	5.2%	Mizuho Holding	2.1%
Sony Corp.	3.6%	Nomura Securities	1.9%
Bk of Tokyo-Mitsubishi	2.6%	Sumitomo Bank	1.8%
Takeda Chemical	2.5%	Fujitsu	1.8%

Number of stocks in ETF: 206

Summary

Formerly called WEBs, iShares MSCI Japan Index fund is a straightforward play on Japan's largest and most established public companies. The MSCI Japan Index accounts for about 60 percent of the market capitalization of all publicly traded equities in Japan. These ETFs provide U.S. investors with tools to invest easily in foreign markets at reduced costs. Remember, though, that investing overseas entails risk other than the local market going up or down. A decline of the Japanese yen against the U.S. dollar would adversely affect the U.S.-based investors. In addition, the ETF may or may not track the performance of the Nikkei 225, one of Japan's most popular stock market benchmarks.

Exhibit 7.28 ETF Highlights—iShares MSCI Germany Index Fund (EWG)

Assets in trust (March 16, 2001)	$145 million
Average daily volume (2000)	79,000 shares
Average daily volume (2001)*	69,636 shares
Annual expense fee	.84%
National currency†	Euro
Ticker	EWG
NAV ticker	WDG
Trading hours	9:30 A.M.–4:00 P.M. (EST)
Bid-offer spread	71 basis points
Price (March 21, 2001)	16.35
Distributions	2 per year
Options	No
Began trading	March 1996
Structure	Open-end mutual fund
Manager	Barclays Global Investors
AMEX specialist	AIM Securities

*YTD, March 21, 2001.

†All iShares MSCI country indexes are bought and sold in dollars.

Top Members and Weightings in Underlying Index as of December 31, 2000

Allianz	13.4%	Bayer	4.6%
Deutsche Telekom	12.1%	Deutsche Bank	4.4%
Siemens	11.4%	Dresdner Bank	4.4%
E.ON AG	5.4%	SAP AG	4.2%
Muenchener Rueckver	5.4%	DaimlerChrysler	3.7%

Number of stocks in ETF: 48

Summary

This ETF holds 48 of the components of the MSCI Germany index. These 48 stocks represent nearly three-quarters of the total capitalization of all publicly traded stocks in this market. This single-country ETF has good liquidity, particularly in view of the complexion and added risks of foreign markets. Weakness in German equities and the euro caused this ETF to slide in 2000. However, the German and UK markets exhibit relatively low volatility when compared with other MSCI country indexes.

Exhibit 7.29 ETF Highlights—iShares MSCI United Kingdom Fund (EWU)

Assets in trust (March 16, 2001)	$165 million
Average daily volume (2000)	71,603 shares
Average daily volume (2001)*	63,518 shares
Annual expense fee	.84%
National currency†	British pound sterling
Ticker	EWU
NAV ticker	INU
Trading hours	9:30 A.M.–4:00 P.M. (EST)
Bid-offer spread	67 basis points
Price (March 21, 2001)	15.40
Distributions	2 per year
Options	No
Began trading	March 1996
Structure	Open-end mutual fund
Manager	Barclays Global Investors
AMEX specialist	Spear, Leeds & Kellogg

*YTD, March 21, 2001.

†All iShares MSCI country indexes are bought and sold in dollars.

Top Members and Weightings in Underlying Index as of December 31, 2000

Vodofone Airtouch	10.0%	Royal Bank of Scotland	3.6%
Glaxo Smith Kline	8.0%	Lloyds TSB Group	3.4%
BP Amoco	6.3%	British Telecom.	3.2%
HSBC Holdings	4.8%	Barclays	2.7%
AstraZeneca	4.6%	Diageo	2.1%

Number of stocks in ETF: 103

Summary

The MSCI UK Index holds about 120 securities, most of them listed on the London Stock Exchange. The ETF invests in 103 of these issues—about two-thirds of the total UK market capitalization. After the United States and Japan, the United Kingdom's market cap is the third largest in the world. In 2000–2001, most world markets slid, and the UK indexes were no exception. Investors should note, however, that the UK market has the lowest volatility of all the MSCI country indexes that have ETFs (10.9 percent, compared to 57 percent for Brazil and 41 percent for South Korea).

Exhibit 7.30 ETF Highlights—iShares MSCI Malaysia Index Fund (EWM)

Assets in trust (March 16, 2001)	$88 million
Average daily volume (2000)	98,019 shares
Average daily volume (2001)*	28,882 shares
Annual expense fee	.84%
National currency†	Malaysian ringgit
Ticker	EWM
NAV ticker	INM
Trading hours	9:30 A.M.–4:00 P.M. (EST)
Bid-offer spread	100+ basis points
Price (March 21, 2001)	4.90
Distributions	2 per year
Options	No
Began trading	March 1996
Structure	Open-end mutual fund
Manager	Barclays Global Investors
AMEX specialist	AIM Securities

*YTD, March 21, 2001.

†All iShares MSCI country indexes are bought and sold in dollars.

Top Members and Weightings in Underlying Index as of December 31, 2000

Telkom Malaysia	15.0%	British Amer. Tobacco	4.4%
Tenaga Nasional	14.4%	Commerce Asst. Holding	4.0%
Malayan Banking	13.2%	YTL	3.1%
Malaysia Inter. Ship.	4.7%	Resorts World	3.0%
Sime Darby	4.6%	Public Bank (FGN)	2.7%

Number of stocks in ETF: 61

Summary

The 61 stocks that the iShares MSCI Malaysian Index Fund holds represent about 60 percent of the total market capitalization of this market. Most trade on the Kuala Lumpur Stock Exchange. This ETF is for those who can withstand risk and then some. Not only has the Malaysian market exhibited extreme volatility, but the government also imposed stringent capital controls as a result of the general economic deterioration in Asia in September 1998, and the creation and redemption process for ETFs was completely disrupted. Without this process, trading in the ETF occurred at levels materially different from the underlying NAV. The moral of the story: Be extremely careful! Emerging markets can be very profitable, but there can be enormous risk attached to those returns.

Exhibit 7.31   ETF Highlights—Other International and Country (ETFs)

ETF	Ticker	Expenses	Assets (in millions)
iShares MSCI Australia	EWA	.84%	$ 45
iShares MSCI Austria	EWO	.84	11
iShares MSCI Belgium	EWK	.84	10
iShares MSCI Brazil	EWZ	.99	16
iShares MSCI Canada	EWC	.84	18
iShares MSCI France	EWQ	.84	69
iShares MSCI Hong Kong	EWH	.84	63
iShares MSCI Italy	EWI	.84	37
iShares MSCI Mexico	EWW	.84	34
iShares MSCI Netherlands	EWN	.84	32
iShares MSCI Singapore	EWS	.84	58
iShares MSCI South Korea	EWY	.99	17
iShares MSCI Spain	EWP	.84	30
iShares MSCI Sweden	EWD	.84	12
iShares MSCI Switzerland	EWL	.84	37
iShares MSCI Taiwan	EWT	.99	104
Broad-based global indexes			
iShares S&P/TSE 60 Index Fund	IKC	.50	9
iShares S&P Global 100	IOO	.20	97
iShares EMU	EZU	.84	48
European 2001 HOLDRS	EKH	NA	71

Note: Assets as of March 16, 2001. HOLDRS assets as of February 28, 2001

TOP ETF FUNDS

The top ETFs ranked by their average daily volume in the year 2000 are listed in Exhibit 7.32. The top ETFs ranked by assets under management are listed in Exhibit 7.33. Exhibit 7.34 ranks the top ETFs by market share. Exhibit 7.35 lists a brief statistical summary of every ETF available in early 2001 and Exhibit 7.36 shows the growth of ETF assets since 1993. ETFs not covered with a separate full-page highlight receive some treatment here.

Exhibit 7.32 Top ETFs Ranked by Year 2000 Average Daily Volume

Rank	ETF Name	Ticker	Average Daily Volume (shares)
1	Nasdaq-100 Index Shares	QQQ	27,673,809
2	S&P Depositary Receipts ("Spiders")	SPY	7,669,444
3	Dow Jones Industrial DIAMONDS	DIA	1,394,444
4	Internet HOLDRS	HHH	892,063
5	Biotechnology HOLDRS	BBH	886,111
6	S&P MidCap 400 Depositary Receipts	MDY	842,857
7	Technology Select Sector SPDRs	XLK	671,825
8	Semiconductor HOLDRS	SMH	557,228
9	Financial Select Sector SPDRs	XLF	523,015
10	Internet Infrastructure HOLDRS	IIH	491,813
11	Business to Business Internet HOLDRS	BHH	483,333
12	iShares MSCI Japan Index	EWJ	445,238
13	Energy Select Sector SPDRs	XLE	346,825
14	iShares S&P 500	IVV	212,820
15	Broadband HOLDRS	BDH	206,989
16	Consumer Staples Select Sector SPDRs	XLP	177,381
17	Pharmaceutical HOLDRS	PPH	156,896
18	Cyclical/Transportation Select Sector SPDR	XLY	140,079
19	Telecom HOLDRS	TTH	128,017
20	Utilities Select Sector SPDRs	XLU	115,873
21	Russell 2000 iShares	IWM	115,563
22	iShares MSCI Malaysia Index	EWM	98,619
23	iShares MSCI Germany Index	EWG	83,527
24	iShares MSCI United Kingdom Index	EWU	71,603
25	Russell 3000 iShares	IWV	48,548

Source: AMEX, CME Index Product Marketing.

Exhibit 7.33   Top ETFs Ranked by Assets Under Management

Rank	ETF Name	Ticker	Assets Under Management March 16, 2001
1	S&P 500 SPDR	SPY	$23,177,760,240
2	Nasdaq-100 Index Tracking Stock	QQQ	20,542,054,000
3	S&P 400 MidCap SPDR	MDY	3,682,750,500
4	iShares S&P 500	IVV	2,460,374,000
5	DJIA DIAMONDs	DIA	2,241,566,310
6	Biotech HOLDRS	BBH	1,423,794,715
7	Select Sector SPDR—Technology	XLK	921,836,000
8	Select Sector SPDR—Financial	XLF	700,891,410
9	iShares Russell 2000	IWM	629,200,000
10	Pharmaceutical HOLDRS	PPH	554,048,321
11	iShares MSCI-Japan	EWJ	531,267,730
12	Semiconductor HOLDRS	SMH	422,027,955
13	iShares Russell 3000	IWV	385,154,000
14	iShares S&P 500/BARRA Value	IVE	374,078,500
15	Telecommunications HOLDRS	TTH	365,565,960
16	Market 2000+ HOLDRS	MKH	315,581,369
17	iShares Russell 2000 Value	IWN	245,551,500
18	Select Sector SPDR—Energy	XLE	232,730,000
19	Broadband HOLDRS	BDH	216,218,970
20	Internet HOLDRS	HHH	212,619,120
21	iShares Russell 1000	IWB	206,108,000
22	iShares S&P SmallCap 600	IJR	199,420,000
23	Select Sector SPDR—Consumer Staples	XLP	198,932,000
24	Internet Architecture HOLDRS	IAH	175,241,750
25	iShares Russell 1000 Value	IWD	166,290,000

Source: AMEX, CME Index Products Marketing.

Exhibit 7.34 Top ETFs Ranked by Market Share

ETF	Ticker	Market Share (%)
S&P 500 SPDR	SPY	37.44
Nasdaq-100 Index Tracking Stock	QQQ	31.06
S&P 400 MidCap SPDR	MDY	5.38
DJIA DIAMONDS	DIA	3.84
iShares S&P 500	IVV	3.53
Biotech HOLDRS	BBH	1.84
Select sector SPDR-Technology	XLK	1.56
iShare Russell 2000	IWM	1.17
Select Sector SPDR-Financial	XLF	1.02
iShares MSCI-Japan	EWJ	0.80
Semiconductor HOLDRS	SMH	0.77
iShares Russell 3000	IWV	0.71
Pharmaceutical HOLDRS	PPH	0.69
iShares S&P 500/BARRA Value	IVE	0.54
Telecommunication HOLDRS	TTH	0.49
iShares Russell 2000 Value	IWN	0.44
iShares S&P SmallCap 600	IJR	0.44
iShares Russell 1000 Growth	IWF	0.43
Select Sector SPDR-Energy	XLE	0.37
iShares Russell 1000 Value	IWD	0.35

Source: AMEX/CME Index Product Marketing

Market share is expressed as a percent of total EFT assets. As of June 1, 2001 total ETF assets, including HOLDRS was about $77 billion. While the list of ETF offerings continues to grow most of the assets and activity is concentrated in 20 or so products. As of June 1, 2001, 103 ETFs exist in the United States. The top ETFs account for 81% of assets. The top 10 ETFs account for nearly 90% of assets and the top 20 account for 93% of total ETF assets.

Exhibit 7.35 All ETFs by Category/Type

ETF Name	Ticker	Manager	Launch Date	Index Type	ETF Volume: Avg. Daily Vol. Jan–Mar 2001	Expense Ratio (%)
S&P 500 SPDR or Spider	SPY	SSGA	Jan. 1993	Large cap	10,318,675	0.12
S&P 500 iShares	IVV	BGI	May 2000	Large cap	228,995	0.09
S&P 500/Barra Growth iShares	IVW	BGI	May 2000	Large cap/growth	57,055	0.18
S&P 500/Barra Value iShares	IVE	BGI	May 2000	Large cap/value	79,871	0.18
S&P 100 iShares	OEF	BGI	Oct. 2000	Large cap	3,878	0.20
S&P MidCap 400 SPDR	MDY	BNY	May 1995	Mid cap	1,125,265	0.25
S&P MidCap 400 iShares	IJH	BGI	May 2000	Mid cap	81,052	0.20
S&P MidCap/Barra Growth iShares	IJK	BGI	Jul. 2000	Mid cap/growth	38,625	0.25
S&P MidCap/Barra Value iShares	IJJ	BGI	Jul. 2000	Mid cap/value	19,440	0.25
S&P Small Cap iShares	IJR	BGI	May 2000	Small cap	78,751	0.20
S&P Small Cap/Barra Growth iShares	IJT	BGI	Jul. 2000	Small cap/growth	8,158	0.25
S&P Small Cap/Barra Value iShares	IJS	BGI	Jul. 2000	Small	33,031	0.25
Russell 1000 iShares	IWB	BGI	May 2000	Large cap	50,842	0.15
Russell 1000 Growth iShares	IWF	BGI	May 2000	Large cap/growth	48,454	0.20
Russell 1000 Value iShares	IWD	BGI	May 2000	Large cap/value	90,375	0.20
Russell 2000 iShares	IWM	BGI	May 2000	Small cap	364,765	0.20
Russell 2000 Growth iShares	IWO	BGI	Jul. 2000	Small cap/growth	91,744	0.25
Russell 2000 Value iShares	IWN	BGI	Jul. 2000	Small cap/value	61,409	0.25
Russell 3000 iShares	IWV	BGI	May 2000	Broad market	74,229	0.20
Russell 3000 Growth iShares	IWZ	BGI	Jul. 2000	Broad market/growth	5,725	0.25
Russell 3000 Value iShares	IWW	BGI	Jul. 2000	Broad market/value	4,435	0.25

ETF Name	Ticker	Manager	Launch Date	Index Type	ETF Volume: Avg. Daily Vol. Jan-Mar 2001	Expense Ratio (%)
Nasdaq-100 Index Shares	QQQ	BNY	Mar. 1999	Large cap/tech	63,487,000	0.18
Dow Jones Industrial Diamonds Trust	DIA	SSGA	Jan. 1998	Large cap	2,190,129	0.18
DJ US Total Market iShares	IYY	BGI	Jun. 2000	Broad market	25,253	0.20
DJ US Large Cap Growth streetTRACKS	ELG	SSGA	Sep. 2000	Large cap/growth	1,422	0.20
DJ US Large Cap Value streetTRACKS	ELV	SSGA	Sep. 2000	Large cap/value	2,856	0.20
DJ US SmallCap Growth streetTRACKS	DSG	SSGA	Sep. 2000	Small cap/growth	865	0.25
DJ US SmallCap Value streetTRACKS	DSV	SSGA	Sep. 2000	Small cap/value	775	0.25
FORTUNE 500 streetTRACKS	FFF	SSGA	Oct. 2000	Large cap	7,529	0.20
SPDR Basic Industries	XLB	SSGA	Dec. 1998	Sector	90,018	0.28
DJ US Basic Materials iShares	IYM	BGI	Jun. 2000	Sector	4,740	0.60
DJ US Chemicals iShares	IYD	BGI	Jun. 2000	Sector	7,525	0.60
SPDR Cyclical/Transportation	XLY	SSGA	Dec. 1998	Sector	338,560	0.28
DJ US Consumer Cyclical iShares	IYC	BGI	Jun. 2000	Sector	9,404	0.60
SPDR Consumer Staples	XLP	SSGA	Dec. 1998	Sector	114,980	0.28
DJ US Consumer Non Cyclical iShares	IYK	BGI	Jun. 2000	Sector	10,235	0.60
SPDR Consumer Services	XLV	SSGA	Dec. 1998	Sector	41,332	0.28
SPDR Energy	XLE	SSGA	Dec. 1998	Sector	258,876	0.28
DJ US Energy iShares	IYE	BGI	Jun. 2000	Sector	26,395	0.60
SPDR Financial	XLF	SSGA	Dec. 1998	Sector	698,571	0.28

Exhibit 7.35 (*continued*)

ETF Name	Ticker	Manager	Launch Date	Index Type	ETF Volume: Avg. Daily Vol. Jan-Mar 2001	Expense Ratio (%)
DJ US Financial iShares	IYF	BGI	May 2000	Sector	26,435	0.60
DJ US Financial Services iShares	IYG	BGI	Jun. 2000	Sector	8,500	0.60
DJ US Healthcare iShares	IYH	BGI	Jun. 2000	Sector	26,285	0.60
SPDR Industrial	XLI	SSGA	Dec. 1998	Sector	48,116	0.28
DJ US Industrial iShares	IYJ	BGI	Jun. 2000	Sector	3,031	0.60
DJ US Internet iShares	IYV	BGI	May 2000	Sector	30,705	0.60
MS Internet streetTRACKS	MII	SSGA	Sep. 2000	Sector	4,998	0.50
FORTUNE e-50 streetTRACKS	FEF	SSGA	Oct. 2000	Sector	1,738	0.20
DJ US Real Estate iShares	IYR	BGI	Jun. 2000	Sector	17,747	0.60
SPDR Technology	XLK	SSGA	Dec. 1998	Sector	883,505	0.28
DJ US Technology iShares	IYW	BGI	May 2000	Sector	50,296	0.60
MS High Tech 35 streetTRACKS	MTK	SSGA	Sep. 2000	Sector	110,933	0.50
DJ US Telecom iShares	IYZ	BGI	May 2000	Sector	20,595	0.60
SPDR Utilities	XLU	SSGA	Dec. 1998	Sector	41,602	0.28
DJ US Utilities iShares	IDU	BGI	Jun. 2000	Sector	26,802	0.60
Biotech HOLDRS	BBH	BNY	Nov. 1999	Biotech/health	1,069,171	$8/yr
B2B Internet HOLDRS	BHH	BNY	Feb. 2000	Internet	496,660	$8/yr
Pharmaceutical HOLDRS	PPH	BNY	Feb. 2000	Drugs/health	312,005	$8/yr
Internet HOLDRS	HHH	BNY	Sep. 1999	Internet	330,424	$8/yr
Telecom HOLDRS	TTH	BNY	Feb. 2000	Telecommunications	94,909	$8/yr

ETF Name	Ticker	Manager	Launch Date	Index Type	ETF Volume: Avg. Daily Vol. Jan–Mar 2001	Expense Ratio (%)
Market 2000+ HOLDRS	MKH	BNY	Aug. 2000	Broad market	29,415	$8/yr
Broadband HOLDRS	BDH	BNY	Apr. 2000	Telecommunications	361,847	$8/yr
Internet Infrastructure HOLDRS	IIH	BNY	Feb. 2000	Internet	220,858	$8/yr
Internet Architecture HOLDRS	IAH	BNY	Feb. 2000	Internet	104,567	$8/yr
Semiconductor HOLDRS	SMH	BNY	May 2000	Technology	1,446,695	$8/yr
Regional Bank HOLDRS	RKH	BNY	Jun. 2000	Financial	59,425	$8/yr
Utilities HOLDRS	UTH	BNY	Jun. 2000	Utilities	77,378	$8/yr
Software HOLDRS	SWH	BNY	Sep. 2000	Technology	72,449	$8/yr
Wireless HOLDRS	WMH	BNY	Nov. 2000	Telecommunications	26,338	$8/yr
Oil Service HOLDRS	OIH	BNY	Jan. 2001	Energy services	140,317	$8/yr
European 2001 HOLDRS	EKH	BNY	Jan. 2001	International	12,565	$8/yr
iShares MSCI Australia	EWA	BGI	Mar. 1996	Country/International	15,326	0.84
iShares MSCI Austria	EWO	BGI	Mar. 1996	Country/International	7,694	0.84
iShares MSCI Belgium	EWK	BGI	Mar. 1996	Country/International	5,672	0.84
iShares MSCI Brazil	EWZ	BGI	Jul. 2000	Country/International	38,747	0.99
iShares MSCI Canada	EWC	BGI	Mar. 1996	Country/International	20,062	0.84
iShares MSCI EMU	EZU	BGI	Jul. 2000	Country/International	19,949	0.84
iShares MSCI France	EWQ	BGI	Mar. 1996	Country/International	37,736	0.84
iShares MSCI Germany	EWG	BGI	Mar. 1996	Country/International	69,636	0.84
iShares MSCI Hong Kong	EWH	BGI	Mar. 1996	Country/International	55,409	0.84
iShares MSCI Italy	EWI	BGI	Mar. 1996	Country/International	19,635	0.84

Exhibit 7.35 *(continued)*

ETF Name	Ticker	Manager	Launch Date	Index Type	ETF Volume: Avg. Daily Vol. Jan–Mar 2001	Expense Ratio (%)
iShares MSCI Japan	EWJ	BGI	Mar. 1996	Country/International	693,876	0.84
iShares MSCI Malaysia	EWM	BGI	Mar. 1996	Country/International	28,882	0.84
iShares MSCI Mexico	EWW	BGI	Mar. 1996	Country/International	51,189	0.84
iShares MSCI Netherlands	EWN	BGI	Mar. 1996	Country/International	9,185	0.84
iShares MSCI Singapore	EWS	BGI	Mar. 1996	Country/International	32,571	0.84
iShares MSCI South Korea	EWY	BGI	May 2000	Country/International	34,972	0.99
iShares MSCI Spain	EWP	BGI	Mar. 1996	Country/International	21,300	0.84
iShares MSCI Sweden	EWD	BGI	Mar. 1996	Country/International	22,369	0.84
iShares MSCI Switzerland	EWL	BGI	Mar. 1996	Country/International	17,058	0.84
iShares MSCI Taiwan	EWT	BGI	Jun. 2000	Country/International	34,972	0.99
iShares MSCI UK	EWU	BGI	Mar. 1996	Country/International	63,518	0.84
iShares S&P Europe 350 Index Fund	IEV	BGI	Jul. 2000	Country/International	37,635	0.60
iShares Canada TSE 60	IKC	BGI	Jun. 2000	Country/International	5,822	0.50
DJ Global Titans streetTRACKS	DGT	SSGA	Sep. 2000	Country/International	1,487	0.50
S&P Global 100 iShares	IOO	BGI	Dec. 2000	Country/International	3,632	0.40

Exhibit 7.36 Worldwide Growth of ETF Assets

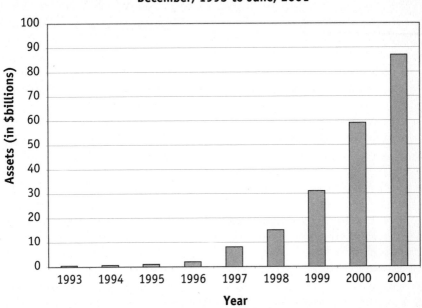

December, 1993 to June, 2001

2001 assets as of June 1, 2001

Source: State Street Global Advisors

REVIEW QUIZ (PARTS I AND II)

Since quiz shows are all the rage on TV, we will review the material thus far. With some of the questions that follow, more than one answer might be correct. All answers can be found within the first seven chapters. (The answer key is at the back of the book.)

1. Which of the following individuals have had a prominent role in the history of indexing?
   a. John Bogle
   b. Burton Malkiel
   c. John McQuown
   d. Bill Fouse

2. Index assets in the United States represent approximately:
   a. $1.4 trillion.
   b. $1.4 billion.
   c. $140 billion.
   d. $140 trillion.

3. List four reasons that most money managers underperform the S&P 500.
   a.
   b.
   c.
   d.

4. Which of the following is *not* a capitalization-weighted index?
   a. S&P 500
   b. Nasdaq-100
   c. Dow Jones Industrials
   d. Russell 1000

5. Exchange traded funds were "invented" by:
   a. Al Gore.
   b. Peter Lynch.
   c. Warren Buffett.
   d. Nate Most and Steve Bloom.

6. Most ETFs trade on:
   a. AMEX.
   b. CME.
   c. NYSE.
   d. CBOE.

7. Which of the following pairs is mismatched?
   a. S&P 500/large caps
   b. Russell 1000/small caps
   c. Russell 2000/small caps

8. Creation and redemption of ETFs usually involves:
   a. 50,000 shares or more.
   b. trustee.
   c. DTCC.
   d. All of the above

9. Which of the following are specialists most directly involved in?
   a. Maintaining a fair and orderly market
   b. Clearing of trades
   c. Distribution and marketing of ETFs

10. The largest ETF in terms of volume is:
    a. MidCap Spiders.
    b. S&P 500 Spiders.
    c. Nasdaq-100 Index Shares.
    d. Biotech HOLDRS.

11. Owning which of the following ETF would likely result in receiving an annual report through the mail from each component company?
    a. S&P 500 iShares
    b. S&P 500 Spiders
    c. Telecom HOLDRS
    d. Dow Jones Global Titan

12. Tracking error can be defined as the:
    a. difference between the ETF price and the net asset value of the underlying stocks.
    b. difference between the ETF dividend rate and the bid-offer spread.
    c. difference between ETF trading hours in the United States versus Japan.
    d. None of the above.

13. S&P 500 Spiders are priced at
    a. one-tenth the underlying index.
    b. one-fifth the underlying index.
    c. one-fortieth the underlying index.
    d. one-half the underlying index.

14. iShares MSCI country ETFs have two risks above and beyond the market risk of the stocks in the fund. These risks are:
    a.
    b.

15. The three primary ETF structures are?
    a. UITs, revocable trusts, irrevocable trusts
    b. GIFT trusts, Grantor Trusts and revocable trusts
    c. Closed end funds, open end funds and UITs
    d. UITs, open ended mutual funds and Grantor trusts

16. The approximate number of ETFs as of early to mid-2001 is?
    a. 50
    b. 1000
    c. 100
    d. 500

17. Which of the following would probably exhibit the highest volatility?
    a. iShares MSCI Brazil
    b. iShares MSCI United Kingdom
    c. iShares MSCI Germany
    d. iShares MSCI Switzerland

18. The minimum number of shares required to buy HOLDRS is?
    a. 1
    b. 10
    c. 1000
    d. none of the above

19. In its simplest form, creation of ETFs involves:
    a. buying 50,000 ETFs
    b. registering 50,000 ETFs with the SEC
    c. depositing the underlying stocks with the custodian in exchange for ETF "shares"
    d. selling 50,000 ETFs

20. ETFs trade on which of the following exchanges:
    a. AMEX
    b. Chicago Stock Exchange
    c. NYSE
    d. CBOE
    e. All of the above

21. Which of the following Indexes is rebalanced annually:
    a. Russell 3000
    b. Russell 2000
    c. Russell 1000
    d. All of the above

22. Which of the following ETFs is not a sector fund?
    a. Nasdaq Biotechnology iShares
    b. Telecom HOLDRS
    c. Pharmaceutical HOLDRS
    d. iShares MSCI EMU fund

23. Which of the following ETFs was launched first?
    a. S&P 500 iShares
    b. S&P 500 SPDRs
    c. iShares MSCI funds
    d. DIAMONDS

24. iShares MSCI country funds are traded in dollar terms
    a. True
    b. False

25. In May of 2001, the Vanguard group launched its first ETF (VIPERS). The ETF was based on:
    a. The Wilshire 4500 Index
    b. The Vanguard Total Stock Market Index Fund
    c. The Russell 3000 Index
    d. The Vanguard Index 500 fund
    e. None of the above.

Part III

THE FASTEST-GROWING INDEX PRODUCTS: E-MINI S&P 500 AND E-MINI NASDAQ-100 FUTURES—APPLICATIONS AND CASE STUDIES

"Gee, Regis, only a million?"

Credit: *Grant's Interest Rate Observer*. Reprinted with permission.

8

E-MINI STOCK INDEX FUTURES: THE HISTORY AND BASIC NOMENCLATURE

June 5, 1997, was a very interesting day for many of us in CME's Marketing Division. Susan O'Toole, who headed up Retail Marketing Programs, a few other colleagues, and I were huddled in Susan's office for a teleconference call. On that day, Dow Jones was going to announce which U.S. derivatives exchanges would be awarded product licenses— that is, who would get the rights to trade various derivative products based on the DJIA. Several exchanges were in the running to be granted licenses for Dow Jones futures, options on futures, and options on the cash Dow Jones itself. The CME and its cross-town rival, the CBOT, were jockeying for the futures licensing rights. Other exchanges were vying for ETF and cash options licensing rights.

Fourteen years earlier, the CBOT had attempted to launch a Dow futures contract (actually a Dow lookalike). After all, the Kansas City Board of Trade (KCBOT) had the Value Line Stock Index contract, and the CME had the S&P 500 futures contract. However, a strange turn of events had transpired. Dow Jones sued the CBOT, contending that it had violated all sorts of trademarks and that it would in no way allow futures contracts to be associated with its venerable index. The whole thing ended up in court, and the CBOT lost the case. It eventually introduced a futures contract based on the Major Market Index, which consisted of 20 blue chip stocks—many of them in the Dow 30. It had some good success initially but eventually failed. (It then traded at the CME, where it also failed.)

The CBOT was the oldest and at the time largest futures exchange in the U.S., and it was out of the stock index futures game completely. So when Dow Jones decided to license its indexes, the CBOT saw it as an excellent opportunity to get back into stock index futures. As the 1990s progressed, the CME had increased its market share in stock index futures to around 96 percent. It had the flagship product in the S&P 500 futures (launched in 1982) along with the S&P MidCap 400, Russell 2000, and Nasdaq-100 futures. It would have been a great addition to CME's stellar line-up in stock index futures—a virtual stock index dream team. The pressure was on; some at CME thought it would be a major debacle if the CME failed in its attempt to "get the Dow contract." Others questioned whether the CME would have to pay too high a price. Dozens of people in several departments at the CME worked long hours on the Dow Jones' Request for Proposal. Hence, when the moment of truth came, our hearts were pounding. Finally, Peter Kann, chairman and CEO of Dow Jones, announced that the CBOT would get the rights to trade futures and options on futures on the DJIA. The CBOE would get the rights to trade options on the cash Dow Jones Industrials, and AMEX would trade an ETF that was later named the DIAMONDs trust. It took awhile, but we all exhaled, spent a few moments commiserating, and then realized we did not have time to ponder the agony of defeat. It was time to do battle. CME's chairman, Jack Sandner, former chairman Leo Melamed, the CME board of governors, and the Equity Index Committee lost no time in deciding to roll out a competing product. Actually, it killed two birds with one stone. The S&P 500 was becoming so large that smaller retail traders could no longer afford the upfront performance bond (margin). If it continued to grow, smaller traders would migrate to competing stock index futures at other exchanges, or they would trade the Dow as soon as it became available. At over $400,000 notional amount, the average daily dollar moves were far greater than any other financial futures contract. CME leaders had discussed trading a more investor-friendly version of the S&P 500 for quite some time. A miniature version of the big S&P seemed like a very good idea. Some of the powers that be at the CME insisted on another condition: This miniature version of the S&P 500 would trade exclusively on the GLOBEX$_2$ electronic trading system, and it would trade virtually 24 hours a day. The concept of an all-electronic miniature Standard & Poor's 500 futures contract—E-Mini S&P 500, for short—was born. We knew that the CBOT would probably launch around October, perhaps sooner. The CME, with all its infrastructure (nearly a thousand GLOBEX terminals all over the world) and stock index expertise in place, was able to launch the E-Mini in September, a full month before the CBOT's Dow Futures.

With the launch of every futures contract at any exchange are inevitable naysayers, but the response to the E-Mini S&P 500 was overwhelmingly positive right from the start. Of course, a few predicted that it would die shortly after launch and that the name recognition of the Dow would prevail. We made friendly wagers with the naysayers. The stakes were that the loser would buy dinner at any New York restaurant. Susan O'Toole and I scheduled and then performed 16 product launch seminars starting in July. The instant I stepped in front of 340 people at the Beverly Regent Wilshire in Los Angeles, I knew the E-mini would be gigantic. There was a buzz in the air like no other seminar we had done (and we had done over a thousand). The seminar lasted two hours, and I remained another two hours answering questions about the E-mini. In San Francisco, Seattle, Atlanta, and Vancouver, we had crowds two to three times larger than average. In Washington, D.C., and New York City, we had standing room only.

On that September day, we were in Denver, and this time we would know the first-day volume just before the seminar began. The news was much better than I could have imagined. On its first day, the E-mini traded 7,494 contracts, a huge number for day 1 (the big S&P traded just under 4,000 on its inaugural day). For most of the first month, volume was between 7,000 and 11,000 contracts per day. When the Dow launched a month later, volume hit 20,000 contracts on two occasions. Then it settled down to about the same level as the E-Mini S&P 500. They traded neck and neck for about nine months at about 10,000 to 12,000 per day. After a year or so, the E-Mini S&P started to pull away from the pack, and it never looked back. Soon it was doing 20,000 contracts per day. After only two years, the mini was averaging 40,000 per day, while the Dow was still trading a successful 20,000 per day.

Any exchange in the world would love to have a contract that was trading these numbers after a mere two years of history, but the E-mini was just getting started. At 40,000 per day, it exceeded our wildest expectations. In 1999 and 2000, electronic trading steamrolled through the financial community. The ECNs, the E*Trades, and Ameritrades were opening millions of accounts. Charles Schwab had 7 million accounts, and 82 percent of those trades were executed on-line. Growth was parabolic, as was the behavior of stock prices during those years. Add to this mix the fact that many CME members were clamoring for GLOBEX terminals to trade this raging success. Average daily volume on the E-Mini S&P reached 75,000 contracts before long. On many days, it exceeded 100,000 contracts per day, and on March 13, it traded a whopping 180,000 contracts. It is now the second most actively traded contract at the CME and one of the great success stories of the past 10 years. The dinner in New York was wonderful, and I enjoyed it and the thrill of victory immensely.

Interestingly, the Nasdaq-100 futures were also gaining in volume. And with the Nasdaq-100 passing century marks with chilling regularity, this contract too started to get rather large. By 1999, senior management at CME began contemplating, an E-Mini Nasdaq-100 futures. Sequels in the movie industry are rarely as good as their predecessor, but what do you think would happen if you combined the excitement and the volatility of the Nasdaq-100 with the ability to trade nearly 24 hours on an electronic platform? Let's examine the record.

When Alan Greenspan decided to cut interest rates by 50 basis points in early January 2001 during the middle of the trading session, the market rocketed upward. The Nasdaq-100 was up 399 points and the E-Mini Nasdaq futures traded 115,000 contracts—not bad, especially when you consider that it had not reached its second birthday and that day 1 volume was 2,400 contracts. Exhibits 8.1 and 8.2 show that that investors have voted: They love the E-mini stock index futures.

Exhibit 8.1   E-Mini S&P 500 Average Daily Volume by Month, September 1997–February 28, 2001

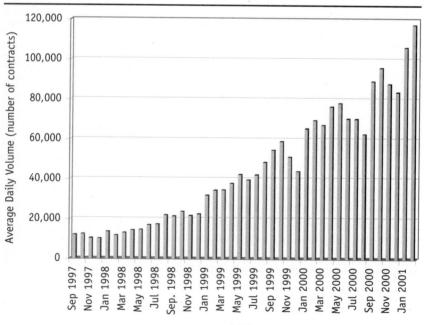

DATE

Exhibit 8.2   E-Mini Nasdaq-100 Average Daily Volume by Month, July 1999–February 28, 2001

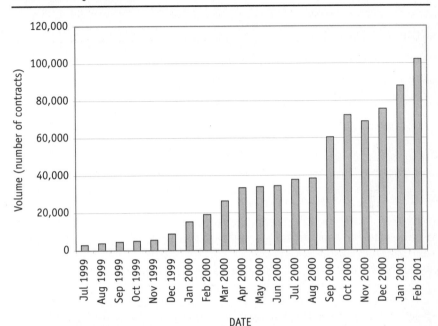

DATE

Source: CME Index Products Marketing.

As successful as the SPY and QQQ had become, their futures cousins—the E-Mini S&P 500 and E-Mini Nasdaq-100—quickly began to dominate in terms of average daily dollar volume. The QQQs were averaging an unbelievable 60 million shares per day, or about $3 billion in dollar volume, in early 2001. Volume in the E-Mini Nasdaq-100 futures averaged about 100,000 contracts per day, but each contract is worth about $40,000 (as of early 2001), giving it an average daily dollar volume of about $4 billion. The E-Mini S&P 500 futures average daily dollar value is about $6.0 billion versus $1 billion for the SPY. Comparisons such as these lead investors to believe that the instruments are competitive products. However, a growing number of industry professionals believe that the products are complementary. This makes perfect sense when you dig deeper into the arbitrage and spreading relationships between ETFs and futures. I already noted that the specialists will lay off market-making risk in the futures. The more ETF business that gets transacted (especially in ETFs that have futures or options contracts), the more activity there will be in futures, as has been the obvious case with the E-Mini S&P and E-Mini Nasdaq.

In Parts I and II, I documented the fundamentals of ETFs and their role in the world of indexing, and we will return to these popular products. Now, we will examine the fundamentals of E-mini stock index futures and discuss how they have made a substantial contribution to indexing and how traders have found them to be an indispensable tool. But first I provide a brief primer on futures. (Readers with a knowledge of futures can skip the rest of this chapter and go to Chapter 9, which covers the details of the E-Mini S&P 500 and E-Mini Nasdaq-100 products.

I begin by building a case for trading E-mini stock index futures and then describe some of the barriers to these instruments, which at times are subject to controversy. Along the way, we cover the required nomenclature and then build on that knowledge with easy-to-follow illustrations. Then we address risk, mark-to-market and settlement issues, setting up accounts, and margin comparisons between stocks and index futures. A little homework or study will be required. Readers with absolutely no investing experience in stocks, bonds, mutual funds, or any other aspect of finance will find this section a challenge, but not an insurmountable one. For those with some investing experience, especially in indexing or for those who have bought stocks or mutual funds, assimilation should be relatively easy.

Reading this chapter will be worth your time. Even if you never trade a stock index futures contract in your life, a knowledge of these instruments may make you a better investor and trader. The futures markets often provide excellent indicators of market direction on a short- or intermediate-term basis. At the very least, you will understand a little better how markets work and how they are interrelated. If professionals keep an eye on stock index futures, it might be a good idea for readers to do so too.

THE CASE FOR TRADING INDEX FUTURES

Investors should consider index futures for a number of reasons.

Excellent Profit Potential

There are few other investments that offer the potential for large returns that index futures do. While stocks have enjoyed excellent gains in the past 18 years, other investments have offered less-than-spectacular gains. Index futures, and futures in general, offer return potential that is several times larger than equities, albeit at greater risk. One might argue that the amazing gains posted by Internet stocks from

1997 through early 2000 are arguably as good as, if not better than, index futures. Just consider the initial public offering of VA Linux, a technology company that soared from 30 to 340 in its first few hours of trading. On its first day as a public company, VA Linux provided investors nearly a 700 percent gain—decades of investment returns—in a mere six hours of trading! No doubt that those returns would give index futures a run for the money. However, the gains of that era have long faded, and this sort of "bubble behavior" occurs rarely (less than a year later, VA Linux common stock rests at 12.00 per share). High return potential is nearly always present in index futures and does not require any kind of new paradigm.

Cost Advantages and Affordability

The transaction costs in index futures are significantly cheaper than with stocks. And as cheap as ETFs are as investments, futures—the E-mini stock index futures in particular—are even less expensive. Consider the costs of assembling a portfolio of stocks, let alone a basket of 500 of them. In just about any comparison, the index futures will win hands down.

Capital Requirement and Leverage

The capital requirement to purchase 500 SPY would be $58,000. To purchase 500 SPY on margin would cost an investor $29,000. In addition, that investor would have to borrow the other $29,000 from the broker and pay an interest rate. One E-Mini S&P 500 futures contract is worth about $58,000 at this writing. The capital requirement would be around $4,313, and there would be no borrowing requirement as with stocks. Although this kind of leverage is not for all investors, those who understand the concept of leverage can realize the advantages of this powerful tool in their trading plan. Any homeowner can grasp the concept of leverage; you can buy a $200,000 house for a much smaller down payment—say, 10 percent, or $20,000. Index futures work in a similar fashion. Those who wish to mitigate some of the leverage could put up more than the minimum capital requirement.

Unique Trading Opportunities

Spreading and arbitrage are two of the primary strategies available to futures traders. While arbitrage can be accomplished only by those with access to enormous amounts of capital (institutions, professional traders, specialists), spreading is one strategy that nearly all index futures

traders can take advantage of. Spreading involves the simultaneous buying and selling of futures contracts to take advantage of price disparity.
For example, if you thought large-cap stocks were going to outperform
mid-cap stocks, there are strategies you can apply to futures that will
allow you to profit from this opinion. This same strategy using individuals stocks would require very deep pockets and a high degree of sophistication. (I provide a case study on this strategy later in Chapter 10.) While
there is risk of loss in spreading, arbitrage, properly executed, is a risk-
free strategy.

Tax Advantages

ETFs offer tax efficiencies of their own, but so do index futures. Futures
contracts in general are taxed at different rates from plain old stocks,
bonds, and mutual funds. An investor in the 39.6 percent tax bracket
would pay this rate on gains on stocks held less than 1 year. An index
futures trader would likely pay much less in taxes on a gain on a futures position held less than 1 year. This is because under IRS rules,
futures contracts (or Section 1256 contracts) are treated by the 60/40
rule. Some of the gain, 60 percent, is taxed at more favorable rates, and
some, 40 percent, is taxed at ordinary income rates.

Unparalleled Excitement

An analogy best describes trading futures and all the excitement that
goes with it. Go to your nearest BMW dealer and test-drive the sporti-
est model available. Then go test-drive a Lambourghini. In fact, some
psychographic studies (studies that determine psychological profiles, or
how people think, versus demographic studies, which show age, income,
and other tangible statistics) on traders show that they are attracted to
things that move. They love action. Instead of hiking, they climb Mt.
Everest. Instead of a picnic, they go bungee jumping or hang-gliding.
They drive not Ford Mavericks but fast cars. It is unlikely you will find
a gardening enthusiast among them. Index futures no doubt are fast
paced and exciting and will get your heart racing. As the exchange dis-
claimers say, "Futures trading isn't for everyone." Time for a gut check.

BARRIERS TO TRADING FUTURES

Given all the advantages, you might think everyone would trade futures. However, there are some barriers, and a brief list might prove

valuable at this point. First, the distribution channel for futures is much smaller than for stocks. There are probably 600,000 stock brokers. There are probably only about 40,000 to 60,000 commodity brokers in the United States. Hence, a veritable army is out there selling traditional investments. Second, there is a general lack of knowledge about futures. Many Americans have at least some of their investments tied to the stock and bond markets. The explosion in IRA and 401(k) accounts and other retirement vehicles has at least forced the typical U.S. worker to come to grips with the most rudimentary investment concepts, but very few Americans have any exposure to the futures markets. Many do not know that these financial instruments have become some of the most successful products available.

Another barrier is the competition provided by stock market returns. An investor-trader making 22 points a day in Juniper Networks is hardly going to consider alternative investment products. Who is going to trade wheat futures when Qualcomm goes up 1,000 percent in 13 months? The returns in the U.S. markets have been just too compelling recently. However, as is always the case, things will cool down (they already have), and investors will concentrate on other types of investments. Futures will be one of those areas.

There is also the perception (real or otherwise) that futures trading is a difficult, risky undertaking. The belief is that only full-time professionals profit consistently; less serious participants lose more often than not. After one of CME's E-Mini S&P launch seminars, a participant came up to me and commented that he would like to trade futures but that they seemed "too risky" for him. We talked more, and it turned out that he had sold a very profitable business for several million dollars. Much of it was bankrolled in U.S. T-bills and tax-free muni bonds. But he had his "cool" money pot—money that he could afford to lose. I asked him what type of investing he did with this account. Given his comment about futures, I expected it to be filled with rock-solid blue chips and utility stocks. He confessed that he had few thousand shares of iVillage.com, a smattering of Microstrategy Inc., and an amount more than he cared to discuss of Red Hat common stock. I was flabbergasted! Here was an individual leery of the risks of index futures, and his principal holdings in one account were down at the time an average of 50 to 75 percent! (In the remaining months of 2000, all of these issues continued the death spiral that cut their value by over 90 percent.) I asked him how he could be afraid of the risks in futures when some of his investment vehicles were far riskier. It is nearly impossible for the S&P 500 to drop 75 to 90 percent of its value in less than a year, and if it did decline that much, we all would have a very big problem on our hands. Returns on our investment would be the least of our concerns. On a pure movement basis looking at standard deviations, dot-com stocks and Internet stocks in general are far more volatile than index futures—or many other types of futures, for that matter. After wrestling with the risk issue for nearly an hour, he finally realized that index futures were not as risky as his "cool money" investments. He rightfully concluded that some of the risk he had been hearing about lay in the leverage aspect of futures, which could be controlled with a greater down payment (performance bond margin) and better risk management.

I furthered his education by saying a wise index futures trader learns to cut losses and would never ride a position down as far as he did with his risky stocks. I added that his brokerage firm's risk control department would also monitor all positions and would not let losses mount by too much on a position without requesting additional margin. Putting down $5,000 to control a basket of stocks worth $65,000 is the leverage part of the equation that many people cannot come to terms with. Losing $1,000 on a $65,000 investment and losing the same $1,000 on a $5,000 investment is still $1,000. Psychologically, a gain or loss of $1,000 on a $5,000 investment is 20 percent of capital—but it is only 1.5 percent of a $65,000 investment. One of the advantages of trading index futures is that you are forced to exercise good risk and money management habits. You are forced to be disciplined. In fact, if you examined the habits of successful investors throughout history I think you'll find two important traits surface: They all have discipline (remember all the heat Warren Buffett took over not investing in technology? Who is laughing now?), and they all have good money management and risk management skills. Not too many skilled traders or investors I know will ride a stock like iVillage.com from 120 to 2. The gentleman thanked me, and we parted ways.

Potential investors often quote the phrase that 90 percent of futures traders lose some of their capital. I heard one gentleman make this statement at a conference once. I challenged him and the other 200 attendees by offering a $100 bill to the first person (and only one) who could provide me with an audited (by a large accounting firm) study showing unequivocally that 90 percent of futures traders lose money. Ten years later and thousands of subsequent challenges, I still retain my $100.

Learning and successfully trading index futures is not easy. On the other hand, it does not require a Ph.D. in stochastic calculus. Investing in any way requires effort and study, but this holds true in any facet of life. You must be willing to do what it takes to achieve any success.

THE LANGUAGE OF INDEX FUTURES

Before one can become comfortable in any discipline of investing, a little homework is required. Before one can learn the great benefit of futures, he/she must learn the language.

Futures Exchanges Price Discovery and Risk Transfer

Futures markets have played a role in the U.S. economy dating back to the mid-1800s. They were originally used by agricultural producers and consumers to transfer the price risk of commodities (crops, livestock, and so on) that were harvested each year. Futures markets today encompass financial instruments such as currencies, interest rates, and, of course, stock indexes. The risk transfer mechanism of futures markets is quite unique. Say you were a cattle farmer. As the owner of live cattle (live only for a little longer, as they will eventually make it to your local meat market or restaurant), your concern is to get the best price possible for your cattle. Higher prices are a good thing; lower prices will erode your profits and may lead to losses. However, if you are a fast food chain and buy huge amounts of beef each year, lower prices are more desirable for you; higher prices would force you to pay more for beef and charge more for hamburgers. An adverse price move for the cattle rancher is lower prices and for the user such as the fast food chain, it is higher prices.

A futures exchange like CME is where these two parties can get together (through brokers) and transfer their respective risks. The user, concerned about higher prices, could buy or lock in cattle (beef) prices now through the futures market if prices were attractive. The question at this point is, If the user is buying, who will sell? Go back to the producer or cattle rancher. His concern is lower prices in the future. If he could sell his livestock now, for "future" delivery, presumably at satisfactory prices, you would have a seller. This adverse price move dilemma faces thousands of cattle ranchers throughout the world, as well as thousands of users. The exchange provides the vehicle (live cattle futures) and the infrastructure (the exchange) whereby the many parties wishing to transfer the risk of adverse price moves can connect with each other. The process of ensuring against an adverse price move is called *hedging*. In our example, the rancher and the user would be hedging against adverse price moves. Hedgers are a very large part of the futures markets.

Futures markets are also a vehicle that provide a way of collecting all the bids and all the offers and bringing them together in a central location. The prices at which these trades are executed determine the best current market price. This is often referred to as *price discovery*. The result is that about 17,000 live cattle futures contacts trade hands every day on the floor of the exchange. Each trade represents someone assuming the risk of higher or lower cattle prices. Users and producers are two of the main ingredients in a liquid futures contract. Speculators are also a vital part of the equation. They commit their capital and make two-side markets (bids and offers) in exchange for a chance to profit. The three, working in concert, have long been the backbone of the price discovery mechanism, as well as the liquid futures markets that are evident today.

Futures Contracts Defined

A *futures contract* is an obligation to buy or sell a specific quantity of a commodity at a certain price by a specific delivery date. A futures contract month, also called the *delivery month*, identifies the month and year in which the futures contract ceases to exist and when the obligation of the contract must be fulfilled. If the futures contract is not offset (sold off if someone previously bought or bought back if previously sold short) before the delivery date, it will be settled by exchange of the physical commodity, or settlement will occur in cash, as is the case with many futures contracts, including E-mini stock index futures. If you own a November soybean futures contract, for example, and do not offset (sell it) the contract before the November delivery date, you will, in effect, be obligated to take physical delivery of 5,000 bushels of soybeans. However, the E-Mini S&P futures contract is cash settled. No delivery of stocks or certificates occurs. You will get the difference, in cash, credited or debited to your account depending on the price you bought the contract at and the final settlement price of the contract. Physical delivery and cash settlement are the two primary means of settling futures contracts in the United States. (Each soybean futures contract, traded at the CBOT calls for delivery of 5,000 bushels of beans. In practice, the beans will probably be stored in a warehouse or grain elevator, and you might receive a call from the elevator supervisor wanting to know what you want to do with your beans. The vast majority of all futures contracts are offset before the delivery date. The only participants that would take actual delivery of the beans or cattle would be large users and producers, such as a food company or processor that needs the commodity.)

GETTING STARTED TRADING INDEX FUTURES

Before we get into the details of opening accounts, the mechanics of margin, and the daily settlement system used in futures, there are a few important questions investors must address:

- Are you willing and prepared to deal with the risks of trading futures? Do you understand the concept of leverage?
- Do you satisfy the financial requirements for trading futures? (These requirements are set by each brokerage firm and can differ substantially from broker to broker.) With $1,000, you could buy a few shares of just about any ETF, but that sum is not even near the minimum to open a futures account at many futures brokers. Some require $5,000 to $10,000. A few require much more, depending on what and how much you will trade. The exchange minimum margin for the E-Mini Nasdaq-100 is currently $6,750 (and subject to change).
- Is your personality well suited for the fast pace gains and losses? I once told someone who wanted to get into commodities trading to reconsider. He was the type who went crazy upon losing a $50 wager on the Super Bowl. I told him that if he couldn't handle $50 losses, he would have trouble dealing with a loss 10 or 20 times that amount. But if you have experienced large losses at one time or another and still slept like a rock, then maybe you are wired up for futures trading.

Opening an Account

Many investors call the CME and inquire as to whether they can trade futures from the same account that they trade stocks. No. Futures trading can only be executed out of a futures account opened through a licensed or registered futures broker. (This too is one of the barriers preventing more widespread trading of futures.) You need a different type of account altogether, as well as a different kind of broker. Some brokers are dual licensed: they have a stock broker license and a futures broker registration. But even if your broker is dual licensed, you still have to open a futures account to transact E-mini stock index futures. This is because of the regulations surrounding futures trading compared with stock trading. Stock brokerage accounts are regulated by the SEC; futures accounts are regulated by a separate entity, the Commodity Futures Trading Commission (CFTC).

Selecting a futures broker may require some effort. Ask friends, or attend some conferences specializing in investing. Perhaps your stockbroker has individuals on staff who are registered to execute futures trades. You can also go to the Web sites of the exchanges themselves and check out the clearing members of the exchange. The CME has 70 or 80 clearing members, many of which will open retail customer accounts for trading E-mini stock index futures, assuming you meet the financial suitability requirements of that firm. You may have to speak with several brokers before you feel comfortable with the relationship. You must be able to trust your broker and that he or she will provide the level of service that you require. Over the years, surveys have revealed that the some of the critical issues that cause customers to close their accounts is a lack of trust or bad service. Pay particular attention to these issues when talking with prospective brokers. Discount brokers are also available with futures for those wanting execution only.

Assuming you have done the necessary due diligence, have the prerequisite trading capital and the personality to trade index futures (not too mention a knowledge of the basic mechanics of trading, which is coming up), and have selected a futures broker who can provide you with trust and service, then you can go forward and open an account. To do this you must fill out and sign a variety of documents, including account applications, risk disclosure documents, and performance bond agreements that prove that you are aware of the risks and the nature of leverage in futures trading. These documents and the broker will also disclose how much capital will be required to open a trading account, as well as performance bond margin issues, maintenance margin issues, commissions, and other details. *Make sure you completely understand these details before ever executing any trade in futures.* I receive hundreds of phone calls each month at the exchange. Many callers ask intelligent, stimulating, and sometimes humorous questions before they start trading. Others, however, do not do their homework. They ask questions *after* they put on a trade that should have been addressed *before* they put the trade on. This category of calls can result in vast disappointment, as well as serious loss of capital. Do your homework, and ask lots of questions. Call me at the CME if you have to, but do not go into this venture unprepared!

The Exchange Clearing House

The Clearing House is the entity through which all futures (and options) transactions are settled. It is responsible for ensuring the transfer of funds and guaranteeing the financial performance of each contract. All E-mini stock index futures trades are cleared through the CME Clearing House. All other CME products, including the E-Mini Nasdaq-100 futures, are cleared through the Clearing House as well. On any given day, $1 billion in performance bond margins is transferred across the CME's Clearing House books. On days with extreme market moves, an amount four to five times that is transferred. The primary manner in which the Clearing House ensures the performance of all parties to futures contracts is by the performance bond margin system and the variation margin settlement system (sometimes referred to as *mark-to-market Settlement*).

Performance Bond Margins

At the time you open your account, you will be required to make a deposit of cash or securities (usually in the form of T-bills), or both. This deposit opens your account and serves to meet the minimum performance bond requirements of trading futures. For E-mini stock index futures, the CME establishes minimum initial and maintenance performance bond requirements. Your broker's requirements may be higher, but they cannot be lower than CME minimums. And although you deposit the funds with your broker, the CME Clearing House ultimately is the holder of those margin deposits once a trade is initiated. This is one of the many financial safeguards in place that protect the system from risk and ensure a smooth flow of funds between buyers and sellers and their brokerage firms. The Clearing House transfers funds to accounts through your clearing member firm. Hence, gains will be credited to your account and losses debited from your account by the Clearing House through your firm. Think of the Clearing House as a giant back office system set up to monitor all positions, risk, and money transfers and to hold billions in collateral by performance bond deposits. The CME's Clearing House is one of its greatest assets and has served CME customers very well. Exhibit 8.3 outlines how a trade is done and how the clearing firm where you hold your account interacts with you and the exchange Clearing House.

As of March 28, 2001, the CME minimum initial performance bond margin for the E-mini S&P 500 futures was $4,313. This is the minimum margin deposit that the CME will accept (although a particular broker may request more) before you can trade. Margin levels can and do change, depending mostly on the volatility of the markets. So if we entered a period of extreme volatility, look for performance bond margins to increase. The performance bond margin of the E-Mini Nasdaq-100 was about $ 6,750 on March 28, 2001, and the Mini Nasdaq-100

Exhibit 8.3 How a Trade Is Done

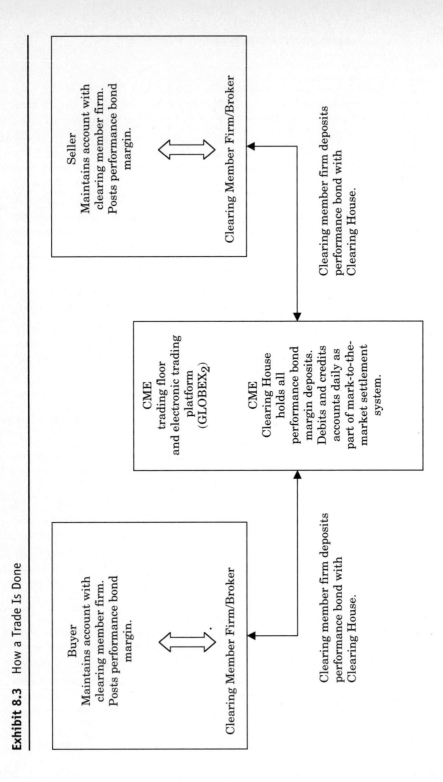

has a smaller contract value. Why? Remember that the more volatile an instrument is, the more margin is required. What is more volatile: the S&P 500 Index or the Nasdaq-100 Index? If you guessed the Nasdaq-100, you are correct. The volatility of all those tech stocks has made the Nasdaq-100 cash index, and thus the E-Mini Nasdaq-100 futures, which track the underlying index, more volatile. Indeed, the Nasdaq-100 is more than twice as volatile as the S&P 500; hence, you have to provide a larger performance bond margin deposit. A quick glance at Exhibit 8.4 below shows how much more volatile and will give you an understanding of why the Clearing House requires a greater performance bond deposit for the E-Mini Nasdaq 100 compared with the E-Mini S&P 500. The daily ranges of some other actively traded futures are included in the exhibit for comparison.

Similarly, if your account or position falls to the maintenance margin requirement, the firm will reach out and touch you: You will receive a *margin call*—a phone call requesting that you deposit additional funds into your account. For the E-Mini S&P futures, the maintenance margin requirement is $3,450, a difference of $863 from the initial margin requirement. Hence, if your position goes against you (by $863), then you will receive a call to deposit enough cash to bring your account or position back up to the initial margin level, and you have to act quickly. You either have to keep adequate amounts of cash in your account to cover such contingencies, or you will have to wire the money. Often the firm requires the cash in a matter of hours. If it does not arrive and the market continues to be volatile and the associated risk has the potential to cause the investor or the firm to suffer large losses, then the firm has the right to liquidate the position, whether or not you

Exhibit 8.4 Average Daily Dollar Range and Volatility of Various Futures Contracts (Jan.-Sep. 2000 time frame)

Futures	Average Daily Dollar Range	Historical Volatility
S&P 500	$ 6,990	22.04%
E-Mini S&P 500	1,432	22.04
Nasdaq-100	17,627	53.99
E-Mini Nasdaq-100	3,573	53.99
T-bonds	869	8.84
Crude Oil	1,064	42.33
Live Cattle	210	13.38
Corn	202	23.15

think the market will bail you out. This is very similar to margin buying in stock brokerage accounts. If you do not meet a margin call on time, the firm has the right (read your disclosure documents) to offset the position.

Variation Margin and the Mark-to-Market Settlement System

At the end of each trading day and each trading day that your position remains open, the contract value is *marked-to-the-market*; that is, your account is debited or credited based on that day's trading session. If you have gains, your account will be credited; if you have losses, your account will be debited. This is sometimes referred to as *variation margin*. Again, all variation margin passes from customer, to clearing member firm (broker), to Clearing House. Thus, if you profited by $500 during the day's trading, the Clearing House will credit your firm, and your firm will credit your account. The next chapter provides an illustration that features the mark-to-the-market process.

CONCLUSION

By now, you have probably surmised that the margin process with equities is vastly different than with futures, though both serve to protect customer, broker, and the system as a whole. Exhibit 8.5 summarizes the differences between futures trading and stock trading.

Futures performance bond requirements, maintenance requirements, and the mark-to-the-market process are all part of the financial safeguard system in place to protect the entire industry. This system gives futures trading rock-solid credit standing because losses are not allowed to accumulate. The Clearing House looks at every account and every firm on each trading day to ensure that adequate financial requirements are met. If extremely volatile conditions arise, the Clearing House can examine these accounts several times per day if it feels necessary to guarantee performance. It is these stringent measures that establish the financial integrity of the CME Clearing House, which gives billion-dollar pension funds as well as retail investors the confidence to transact business in the futures markets at the CME. Often potential futures traders ask if there is an SIPC type of organization in futures trading. (The Securities Investors Protection Corporation, SIPC, insures investors' accounts in case a firm were to run into financial difficulties.) I tell them not exactly, but our clearing members are some of the most solid, prestigious firms in the world—firms like Gold-

Exhibit 8.5 Futures and Stock Trading: A Comparison

	Futures	Stocks
Type of broker	Series 3 Registered	Series 7 Registered
Minimum to open account	Usually $5,000 to $10,000	$2,000 for margin account, sometimes less to open cash account
Paperwork	Account application Risk disclosure documentation Performance bond agreements Financial and suitability documents	Account application Other documents for margin trading and options trading
Settlement	Mark-to-the-market daily by Clearing House	T + 3 (trades settle three days later)
Margin	Initial performance bond deposit subject to exchange minimums	50% per current Regulation T of Federal Reserve Bank of New York
Short selling	Yes, no uptick required	Yes; uptick required
On-line trading available	Yes	Yes
Regulation	CFTC	SEC
Insurance or financial safeguards	Clearing House Financial Safeguards	SIPC or Security Investors Protection Corporation
Commission style	Round turn—commission covers the cost of both buying and selling	One way. Commission paid on buy and sell side of trade

man Sachs, Morgan Stanley, JP Morgan Chase, Merrill Lynch, and Salomon Smith Barney. Also, the CME Clearing House manages $25 billion in collateral deposits, administers more than $1 billion in letters of credit, and moves an average $1 billion per day in settlement payments. On January 3, 2001, when Alan Greenspan, chair of the Fed, lowered rates in mid-trading session, the Clearing House moved a record $6.4 billion in settlement payments through the banking system. Also remember the following:

- There has never been a failure by a clearing member to pay settlement variation to the Clearing House.
- There has never been a failure by a clearing member to meet a performance bond call.
- There has never been a failure by a clearing member to meet its delivery obligations.
- Most important, there has never been a failure of a clearing member resulting in a loss of customer funds.

9

E-MINI STOCK INDEX FUTURES: CONTRACT HIGHLIGHTS, TRADING FUNDAMENTALS, BASIS, AND FAIR VALUE

Once you have mastered futures basics, such as performance bond margins, the mark-to-market settlement process, and account specifics, it is time to learn how a futures contract ticks. Hundreds of futures contracts trade on federally regulated futures exchanges in the United States, and each of these exchanges trades contracts that are somewhat unique to it. For example, CME's most active contracts are Eurodollar futures and stock index futures, including the E-minis. The CBOT's flagship products are the U.S. Treasury bond and note contracts and corn and soybean futures. The New York Mercantile Exchange's (NYMEX) most active products are crude oil, heating oil, and natural gas. Each of these products has specific contract specifications: the details describing the size of the contract, delivery (also known as settlement) dates, minimum price fluctuations (referred to as "ticks"), and settlement procedures. These contract specs or highlights are determined by the exchanges themselves and formulated during the research and development process before they are submitted to the CFTC for review and approval. Often exchanges gather information from the futures industry (or product-related industry users or potential users) to help design the contract for the greatest possible chance of success. Futures contracts, like all other products launched in the business world, do not always succeed. Many products in every type of business fail within a few years or less, and futures contracts are no different. Later in this chapter I discuss a few of the reasons that some contracts are more successful than others.

The E-Mini S&P 500 futures contract is a scaled-down version of its bigger brother, the S&P 500 Index futures contract. The Mini S&P is a smaller, more investor-friendly size, and it trades exclusively on an electronic trading system (named GLOBEX$_2$); in contrast, the larger contract is pit-traded during the day (8:30 A.M. to 3:15 P.M. central time) and traded on GLOBEX when the pits are closed. The Mini S&P 500 is valued at roughly $58,000 (as of March 21, 2001), one-fifth the size of the regular or big S&P 500, valued at $287,500.*

CONTRACT SPECIFICATIONS

Exhibits 9.1 and 9.2 show the contract specifications for the E-Mini S&P 500 futures and E-Mini Nasdaq-100 contracts, respectively. Take a close look at them because we will use this information, along with the concepts covered in the previous chapter, to illustrate the mechanics of trading the contract.

Ticker Symbol

The ticker symbol, listed first, functions much like the ticker symbols with stocks and ETFs. You use the symbols to obtain quotes from the appropriate quote vendors. Although many Web sites offer free quotes on stocks—some are delayed, some are real-time quotes—getting quotes for the E-mini contracts takes a little more effort. If you do not have the appropriate software and exchange hookup, then you can go to CME's Web site (www.cme.com) and obtain real-time quotes by going through a sign-up procedure. Although real-time quotes were offered for free at the introduction of the mini contracts, it is likely a small fee will be charged going forward. Since stocks and ETFs do not have quarterly settlements as futures do, the symbol ES is combined with another symbol or code that identifies the expiration month. The code for March is *H*, for June it is *M*, for September it is *U*, and for December it is *Z*. So "ESZ" would mean the E-Mini S&P 500, December delivery. NQH is the symbol for the March E-Mini Nasdaq-100 futures. (A note

---

*The values of the S&P 500 and other indexes in this book sometimes differ from example to example or chapter to chapter. This is not meant to confuse the reader, but to show how fluctuations in the indexes cause the contract sizes to change constantly. In late 2000 and January 2001, the S&P 500 was trading above 1300. By March, it had dropped significantly to 1160. I could have written each example with the same price and contract values but that would hardly be realistic given that the market constantly fluctuates. Besides, it is this constant changing that provides the opportunity to profit!

Exhibit 9.1   E-Mini S&P 500: Contract Specifications and Highlights

Ticker symbol	ES
Contract size	$50 × E-Mini S&P futures price
Minimum price fluctuation	.25 index point = $12.50 per contract
Trading hours (GLOBEX system)	Virtually 24 hours. No trading between 3:15 P.M. and 3:45 P.M. Trading begins again on Sundays at 5:30 P.M.
Contract months	March, June, September, December
Last day of trading	Trading can occur up to 8:30 A.M. central standard time on the third Friday of the contract month
Quarterly futures settlement	Cash settled to the special opening quotation on Friday morning of the S&P 500 cash index

Exhibit 9.2   E-Mini Nasdaq-100: Contract Specifications and Highlights

Ticker symbol	NQ
Contract size	$20 × E-Mini Nasdaq-100 futures price
Minimum price fluctuation	.50 index point or $10 per contract
Trading hours	Virtually 24 hours. No trading between 3:15 P.M. and 3:45 P.M. Trading begins again on Sundays at 5:30 P.M.)
Contract months	March, June, September, December
Last day of trading	Trading can occur up to 8:30 A.M. central standard time on the third Friday of the contract month
Quarterly futures settlement	Cash settled to the special opening quotation on Friday morning of the Nasdaq-100 index

of caution here: Some quote systems have unique codes or symbols, so consult with your vendor for the appropriate symbols.)

Contract Size

The contract size is sometimes referred to as the contract multiplier. The Mini S&P 500 traded at 1150.00 as of March 2001. To get the contract size, multiply $50 times 1150.00, which equals $57,500. Thus, each Mini S&P 500 futures contract has a contract size or value of $57,500—a lot larger than one share of the SPY or QQQ! (It takes about 500 SPY to equal the dollar value of one Mini S&P contract or 800 QQQs to equal the value of one mini Nasdaq-100 contract.) Another way of looking at it is that with each 1 point the futures moves, the value changes by $50. If the futures rise by 10 points, the value of the contract increases by $500. Therefore, if you bought one contract of the E-Mini S&P 500 at 1,150 and sold it a week later for 1,160, you would profit by $500 (10 points × $50 per point). With the E-Mini Nasdaq-100, the contract size is $20 multiplied by the Mini Nasdaq-100 futures contract price. It recently changed hands at 2,000. The contract value would be $20 × 2,000 = $40,000.

Minimum Price Fluctuation

When you watch a quote screen or perhaps CNBC, you will notice the minimum increment that the cash S&P 500 index can change is .01 points. The cash index can go from 1200.07 to 1200.08 but not from 1200.07 to 1200.071. Futures contracts have different minimum increments or minimum tick values. For the Mini S&P 500, the minimum tick is .25 index point. Since each full index point is worth $50.00, a quarter of that equals $12.50. Thus, the minimum price change you will see in the Mini S&P is .25 point, and that represents a dollar amount of $12.50. The contract might move 1.00 point at a time or .50 point at a time, but never less than .25 point. The following cash and futures price sequences (from January 2001) illustrate the point:

Cash S&P 500	Mini S&P 500 Futures
1299.75	1299.50
1299.77	1299.75
1299.78	1300.00
1299.91	1299.75
1299.98	1300.00
1300.00	1300.25
1300.01	1300.00
1300.04	1300.25
1300.03	1300.50
1300.09	1300.25
1300.11	1300.00
1300.10	1300.25
.01 pt minimum increment	.25 pt minimum increment

With the Mini Nasdaq-100 futures, the minimum price change or tick value is .50 point. Similar to the cash S&P 500, the underlying cash Nasdaq-100 index can move in .01 point increments. Given that a full point is worth $20 in the futures, then .50 point would equal $10. In reality, the S&P 500 or Nasdaq-100 cash indexes rarely move the minimum increment. When the market is volatile, as it has been in recent years, jumps are usually much higher than the .01 point level. It is not uncommon for the Nasdaq-100 cash index to experience price jumps of 1.00 point or more. So if you look at a quote screen and see the cash Nasdaq-100 at 2000.22 and the price 15 seconds later reads 2001.50 (1.28 points higher), do not be alarmed. The S&P 500 cash index also often jumps in increments greater than the .01 point minimum.

Trading Hours

Trading hours are virtually 24 hours. In recent years, investors have cheered the expansion of trading hours. Many firms have expanded their trading hours past the 4:00 P.M. NYSE close. Nevertheless, stocks do not trade on a 24-hour basis yet. The interbank foreign exchange markets have been trading 24 hours for decades, and stock index futures at the CME have been trading around the clock since the 1992 inception of electronic trading on the exchange's GLOBEX trading system. To some who are less familiar with futures, around the-clock access to index futures seems like overkill. However, many events occur outside the normal trading day, such as government economic announcements or corporate earnings announcements, and having access to the market during these situations is an advantage that traders like. Too, events overseas sometimes cause a flurry of overnight activity. With 24-hour availability, traders can initiate, close out, or adjust positions in response to action in overseas markets.

Contract Months and Last Day of Trading

Both E-Mini S&P 500 and E-Mini Nasdaq-100 contracts have the same four expiration months: March (H), June (M), September (U), and December (Z). On the last day of trading, generally the third Friday of the contract month, trading ends at 8:30 A.M. Most contracts are offset, or "rolled," to the next quarterly expiration, many days before the last trading day. Very few traders hold contracts until the final settlement, and those who do are usually professional traders with complex positions on their books. The CME's Web site has calendars that indicate the last trading day for all of its products. For those without Web access, the exchange can provide literature that provides these important details.

Quarterly Futures Settlement

All stock index futures, including the mini-index products, are cash settled based on a special opening quotation (SOQ) of the relevant underlying index. The SOQ for the S&P 500 index is based on the opening price of each component stock in the index on expiration Friday. The NYSE or AMEX opening price is used for stocks listed on the NYSE or AMEX, respectively. The first transaction price is used for Nasdaq component stocks in the S&P 500. The Mini Nasdaq-100 futures, however, settle to an SOQ computed from a five-minute volume-weighted average of each component stock's opening prices (VWOP). The SOQ calculations for the Mini S&P and Mini Nasdaq are usually available by 10:00 or 11:00 A.M. central time. The concept of SOQ is relevant only if you are holding a mini-index futures contract (or options position) until the last trading day. This is a practice that the majority of traders avoid.

Example

Now that you know some basic terms and specifications, let's work through an example that will highlight many of the concepts. Exhibits 9.3 to 9.6 illustrate step by step how a typical trade using the E-Mini S&P 500 futures might look. It demonstrates how profits and losses accrue and how the Clearing House collects and pays margins, and it provides a comprehensive look at the trading process. As with ETFs, there are transaction costs to trade futures. But unlike stocks and ETFs, where a commission is charged on both the buy and sell sides, futures commissions are *round turns*, meaning you pay once to get in and out of the trade. In this particular example, an investor with a bullish opinion on the market goes "long" on E-mini S&P 500 futures at 1,300.00. Several days later the trade becomes profitable and the investors decides to offset (sell) the position at 1,315.00. The example shows how several entities are involved in clearing the trade and cash flows. Clearly, a lot of intermediate steps are involved between initiating the position and closing it out.

Exhibit 9.3   Trading the E-Mini S&P 500: An Example, End of Day 1

Date	January 16, 2001
Investor's outlook	Bullish
Strategy	Buy one March E-Mini S&P 500 futures (or long 1 ESH)
Initial performance bond margin	$5,000 (CME minimum margin is $4,313, but for this example we will use $5,000)
Initial position and price	Long 1 ESH @ 1300.00
Price at end of day 1	1300
Profit or loss on position, in points, from previous day	0
Profit or loss on position, in dollars, from previous day	0
Mark-to-market settlement or variation margin	0
Current value of position	$5,000 ($5000 + day 1 variation margin of 0)
Comments	Trader goes long one ESH (E-Mini S&P 500 futures) at 1300.00. At end of first day, ESH closes or settles at 1300.00. Trader thus has neither profit nor loss on position. No variation margin credit or debit on day 1.

Exhibit 9.4   Trading the E-Mini S&P 500: An Example, End of Day 2

Date	January 17, 2001
Investor's outlook	Still bullish
Strategy	Still long
Initial performance bond margin	$5,000 (CME minimum margin is $4,313 but for this example we will use $5,000)
Initial position and price	Long 1 ESH @ 1300.00
Price at end of day 2	1305
Profit or loss on position, in points, from previous day	5-point gain (1305 − 1300 = 5 points)
Profit or loss on position, in dollars, from previous day (day 1)	$250 profit (5 points × $50 per point = $250)
Mark-to-market settlement or variation margin	$250 variation margin credited to account
Current value of account	$5,250 ($5000 + day 1 variation of $250)
Comments	At end of day 2, trader's position is up 5 points, or $250. Clearing House credits variation margin of $250 to the account via broker. (Performance bond margin subject to change.)

Exhibit 9.5   Trading the E-Mini S&P 500: An Example, End of Day 3

Date	January 18, 2001
Investor's outlook	Still bullish
Strategy	Still long
Initial performance bond margin	$5,000 (CME minimum margin is $4,313, but for this example we will use $5,000)
Initial position and price	Long 1 ESH @ 1300.00
Price at end of day 3	1299
Profit or loss on position, in points, from previous day	6-point loss (1299 − 1305 = −6 points)
Profit or loss on position, in dollars, from previous day (day 2)	$300 loss (6 point loss × $50 per point)
Mark-to-market settlement or variation margin	$300 variation margin loss debited to account
Current value of account	$4,950
Comments	On day 2 the trader made $250. But on day 3, he lost $300, resulting in an overall loss of $50 since initiating the trade. At Clearing House level, profit and loss is equal to sum of variation margin settlements for each day: 0 + $250 − $300 = −$50.

Exhibit 9.6   Trading the E-Mini S&P 500: An Example, End of Day 4, Trade Closed Out

Date	January 19, 2001
Investor's outlook	No longer bullish
Strategy	Sell or offset position at end of day 4
Initial performance bond margin	$5,000 (CME minimum margin is $4,313, but for this example we will use $5,000)
Initial position and price	Long 1 ESH @ 1300.00
Price at end of day 4	1315
Profit or loss on position, in points, from previous day	16-point gain (1315 − 1299 = 16 points)
Profit or loss on position, in dollars, from previous day (day 3)	$800 gain (16 point gain × $50 per point)
Mark-to-market settlement or variation margin	$800 variation margin gain credited to account
Current value of account	$5,750
Comments	Market rallies 16 points as trader exits or sells position at 1315. Day 4 variation margin is $800. Sum of all variation margins: 0 + $250 − $300 + $800 = $750 or final ESH price minus initial × $50 per point, which equals 1315 − 1300 = 15 points × $50 or $750.

SOURCES OF INFORMATION AND PRICES ON
MINI STOCK INDEX FUTURES

Intraday and closing price quotes are accessible to just about anyone with a PC and a modem, but there are many other sources for information on prices:

- Brokers
- Information services and quote vendors, such as Reuters, Dow Jones Markets, Bloomberg, and CQG
- Major daily and weekly newspapers
- CME's Web site, www.cme.com, or www.bloomberg.com
- Private advisory services
- Financial programs on radio and TV

In the past few years, the prices of quote vendor services have come down dramatically. It was not uncommon, 10 to 15 years ago, for a trader to spend $1,000 or more per month for quote and other services such as charting and analysis packages. For a fraction of that amount, serious traders now have access to information that was previously available only to professionals and institutions.

Those with no PC or Internet access depend largely on their broker or the financial media. Your broker will be able to provide you with any information related to trading. The *Wall Street Journal* and *Investors Business Daily*, as well as CNBC and CNN, carry price information on the major futures contracts traded in the United States, including the E-mini stock index products. A caveat here: The intraday movements of the Mini S&P and Mini Nasdaq-100 can sometimes be quite large, and relying on the daily newspapers for updated prices can be risky. By the time you get tomorrow's prices, you may already have experienced some losses. If the losses are great enough, your broker will not wait until the next day either to give you a maintenance margin call.

Exhibit 9.7 illustrates how information is formatted in some of the major financial and daily newspapers. It is similar to stock information, with the addition of expiration months.

Most major daily newspapers carry the opening price, the intraday high and low prices from the previous day, and the close or settlement price and net change from the previous trading session. There are also volume figures and open interest statistics as well. The E-Mini S&P 500 and E-Mini Nasdaq-100 trade very actively and have a solid open interest. Open interest is one gauge of liquidity. Contracts with low open interest have not attracted an adequate critical mass of traders and hedgers and thus display poorer relative liquidity. Average daily

Exhibit 9.7   E-Mini S&P 500 and E-Mini Nasdaq-100 Prices in the Financial Press

E-Mini S&P 500 Index futures $50 × index

	Open	High	Low	Settle	Change	Lifetime High	Lifetime Low	Open Interest
Sep	1301.75	1321.50	1299.00	1315.00	8.00	1450.00	1267.00	47,365
Dec	1321.50	1340.75	1320.00	1335.00	8.00	1399.00	1285.50	1,250

Estimated volume: 123,400 contracts
Volume Friday: 115,452 contracts   Open Interest: 48,615

E-Mini Nasdaq-100 Index futures $20 × index

	Open	High	Low	Settle	Change	Lifetime High	Lifetime Low	Open Interest
Sep	2301.50	2321.50	2120.00	2120.00	−98.00	4100.00	2100.00	33,212
Dec	2350.50	2371.50	2170.00	2170.00	−95.00	4150.00	2150.00	522

Estimated volume: 95,000 contracts
Volume Friday: 91,004 contracts   Open Interest: 33,734

Note: Open interest is the total number of contracts outstanding that have not been offset. It is often an indicator of how much activity or interest there is in a futures contract.

volume is another indicator of liquidity. A trader wants to trade in liquid markets, with easy entry and exit. Contracts with low open interest and volume of fewer than a few hundred contracts should probably be traded only by more experienced traders. Exhibit 9.8 compares the major equity index futures in the United States.

LIQUIDITY

What are the forces that create liquidity? Why do some contracts trade 80,000 contracts a day and have a five- or six-figure open interest, while others trade much less? Successful futures contracts, including S&P futures, generally share five attributes:

- Large underlying cash market
- A large pool of speculators (either in open outcry or electronic platform)
- A large pool of hedgers
- The presence of arbitrageurs (with a product easy to arbitrage)
- The presence of spreaders

Exhibit 9.8 A Comparison of Various U.S. Equity Index Futures Contracts

Futures Contract	Exchange	Multiplier	Index Value	Contract Size	Average Daily Volume (in contracts)	Open Interest
E-Mini S&P 500	CME	$ 50	1200	$ 60,000	117,413	79,854
E-Mini Nasdaq-100	CME	20	1800	36,000	102,200	82,705
S&P 500	CME	250	1200	300,000	85,831	514,179
Nasdaq-100	CME	100	1800	180,000	21,918	53,631
Dow Jones Industrials	CBOT	10	10200	102,000	13,134	22,580
Russell 2000	CME	500	460	230,000	1,998	19,022
S&P 400 MidCap	CME	500	460	230,000	1,047	16,054
NYSE Composite Index	NYBOT	500	605	302,500	298	2,592
Russell 1000	NYBOT	500	621	310,500	229	8,199
Mini Value Line Index	KCBOT	100	1142	114,200	62	0
Value Line Index	KCBOT	500	1142	571,000	61	303
FORTUNE e-50	CME	20	350	7,000	28	123
ISDEX	KCBOT	100	225	22,500	2	64

Note: Volume and open interest data for CME products are as of February 28, 2001. All others are as of January 30, 2001.

If we did a quick attribute check on Eurodollar futures, U.S. Treasury note futures, crude oil futures, and the S&P 500 futures (Mini S&P included), we would see a very large underlying cash market in each. The amount of Eurodollar paper and U.S. government securities outstanding is in the tens of trillions of dollars. We are all aware of how large the energy market is, since it is a vital necessity. The S&P 500 Index has a total market value of $11.5 trillion. Each of the preceding contracts is traded either in a large trading pit or on electronic trading systems that reach every corner of the world. This means plenty of speculators committing capital and making markets. Many mutual fund companies and pension funds, large and small, use S&P futures directly or indirectly to hedge their portfolios or synthetically replicate an indexing strategy. Arbitrage, a major contributor to liquidity, as well as to keeping prices in line, is quite common in the Eurodollar, foreign exchange, U.S. government securities, and S&P 500 futures areas. Take away one or perhaps two of these attributes, and liquidity will suffer. If none of these attributes is present, it is extremely unlikely that the product would have enough sponsorship or participation to survive. You need a confluence of participants executing dozens of strategies—from simple long strategies to complex cash futures arbitrage—in order to attain critical mass.

CASH AND FUTURES

Before we try to absorb some of these strategies, we have to tackle one more subject: the relationship between a stock index futures contract such as the E-Mini S&P 500 and its underlying cash index. No other subject generates as many inquiries to the index products department at CME as does the relationship between cash and futures. Will understanding this relationship make you a better trader? Maybe. Will ignoring it have negative consequences? In my opinion, it might help you achieve a bit more precision in your trading, especially if you have little or no experience in stock index futures. According to many of the tales I've heard, many poor trades can be traced to a lack of knowledge of the cash-futures relationship or basis.

If you look at a quote screen or the financial press, you'll notice that the E-Mini S&P 500 futures (and its big brother) track the underlying cash S&P 500 Index quite closely. Indeed, the correlation between them is extremely high (above 98 percent). As this discussion unfolds, you will see why they track so well. You will probably also notice that the E-Mini S&P 500 futures trade at a premium over the cash index.

(The big S&P 500 also trades at a premium over cash. And although the Mini S&P 500 and the big S&P 500 trade on two different platforms—electronic and open outcry, respectively—the prices of the two futures contracts trade extremely close to each other throughout the day.) For example on January 18, 2001, I took a sampling of Mini S&P 500 futures quotes (and the larger S&P 500 futures contract) and at the exact same time jotted down the underlying cash index. The results are shown in Exhibit 9.9.

During most of the trading session, the futures traded between 9 and 11 points higher than the cash index—a 9–11 point premium. The difference between the futures contract price and the cash prices is often referred to as *basis* or *cash-futures basis*. Typically, but not always, both large and Mini S&Ps trade at a premium to their underlying cash index. Over time, the premium can and does change, and

Exhibit 9.9 Sampling of Mini S&P 500 Futures and Cash Index Quotes

Time	E-Mini S&P 500 Futures[a]	Standard S&P 500 Futures[a]	Cash S&P 500 Index	Premium E-Mini over Cash Index
10:00 A.M.	1345.75	1345.80	1336.19	9.56
10:15	1348.00	1348.00	1338.13	9.87
10:30	1347.75	1348.00	1337.32	10.43
10:45	1347.75	1347.70	1338.30	9.45
11:15	1348.75	1348.70	1339.04	9.71
11:30	1353.50	1353.50	1343.23	10.27
11:45	1354.75	1354.80	1344.23	10.52
12:03 P.M.	1357.25	1357.50	1346.04	11.21
12:17	1359.50	1359.50	1349.10	10.40
12:30	1359.75	1359.70	1348.34	11.41
12:45	1358.25	1358.00	1347.15	11.10
1:00	1360.00	1360.00	1349.26	10.74
1:15	1363.00	1363.00	1352.07	10.93
1:30	1358.75	1358.80	1348.84	9.91
2:45	1360.50	1360.50	1349.06	11.44
3:00	1357.50	1357.50	1347.97	9.53

Note: Cash closes at 3:00 P.M. CST; futures remain open until 3:15 P.M.

[a]March 2001 futures contracts, 57 days until March expiration.

under certain circumstances, it disappears altogether. The futures could, in effect, trade at a discount to the cash index. Why do S&P futures exhibit this pattern? Several factors are responsible for the basis in stock index futures markets, and they usually have to do with *cost of carry*. In other words, interest rates, the dividend yield on the underlying index, and the number of days to the final settlement of the quarterly futures all contribute to the basis phenomenon. Let us break it down a little at a time.

Assume for a moment that I gave you $65,000 (the contract value of the E-mini on January 18, 2001) on the condition that you index the money to the S&P 500 index. You have two choices: (1) take all the money and buy each of the stocks in their exact percentage in the index or (2) buy an E-Mini S&P 500 futures contract. Let's examine the ramifications of each choice.

If you spent the entire sum buying each issue (assuming you could buy all 500 with such a small sum of money), you would own all 500 stocks and also be entitled to the dividend stream of these stocks. But you would also lose any interest previously earned on that money, and you might actually pay interest to finance a purchase of stocks, as pros on the Street often do. After all, you "spent" the cash on stocks that would otherwise have earned interest at money market rates. The dividend yield on the S&P 500 index is about 1.3 percent at this writing. The interest costs would have been around 6.0 percent. That is a difference of 4.7 percentage points.

For the second choice, you buy an E-Mini S&P 500 futures contract instead. Remember your basics from this and the prior chapter: The E-mini has a value of around $65,000 (as of January 2001), but you do not have to put down the full amount. You can meet the performance bond margin requirement with only $4,688. The remaining $60,312 can be left to earn interest. Both choices essentially replicate a basket of the S&P 500 index stocks. With choice 1, you own the stocks directly, and with choice 2, you "own" them via a futures contract that trades virtually identically with the underlying index (see Exhibit 9.9). If you chose the futures, you get to take the bulk of the money you would otherwise have spent on stocks and earn money market rates on it. However, the futures contract pays no dividends!

In summary:

Choice 1

- Spends $65,000 buying all stocks in the index
- Gets dividends (+1.3 percent); pays interest (–6.0 percent)
- Overall cash flow difference: –4.7%

Choice 2

- Buys E-Mini S&P 500 futures contract
- Forfeits dividend (–1.3 percent); gains interest (+6.0 percent)
- Overall cash flow difference: + 4.7 percent

Choice 1 clearly costs the investor 4.7 percent in return, while choice 2 provides a cash flow swing of +4.7 percent. This cost disadvantage of carrying the stocks is what causes the cash S&P 500 to trade under the futures price. This cost of carry is critical with all futures contracts and is the primary reason we observe a cash-futures basis.

The discussion does not end here, since the passage of time has a large effect on the cost of carry. The closer we get to the futures contract's expiration date, the less the cost of carry becomes. A 4.7 percent cost of carry over a 57-day period will obviously be greater than the same 4.7 percent over a 10-day period. As a result, the premium will shrink as the quarterly futures expiration nears. With 57 days to expiration, dividends at 1.3 percent, and interest rates at about 6.0 percent, the premium of futures over cash should be about 9.8 points. For most of the day on January 18, we traded slightly above and below that value. As the expiration date nears, there will no longer be any dividends, and there will no longer be an interest cost because the E-Mini S&P 500 futures and regular S&P 500 futures will no longer exist after final settlement. At this point, the premium will equal zero, and cash will equal futures. This phenomenon, where the premium shrinks as expiration approaches, is a critical point in stock index futures and is known as convergence. Exhibit 9.10 illustrates how the cost of carry eventually goes to zero as we approach expiration and the cash-futures basis dissolves. If we had done the observations on December 31, 2000, instead of January 18, 2001, the numbers would have looked different because the cash and futures markets were at a different level and we had 75 days until the March S&P 500 expiration and over two weeks of additional carry costs. Hence, the premium would have been approximately 13 points.

At this point, a curious investor might ask, how were we able to tell on January 18 that the premium should have been about 9.8 points, as stated a few sentences ago? The answer is that the relationship between dividends, interest rates, days to expiration, and so on is brought together mathematically in a formula known as theoretical fair value:

$$\text{Futures theoretical fair value} = \text{Cash} (1 + [r - d][x/365])$$

Exhibit 9.10   Convergence of June S&P 500 Futures with Cash S&P 500 Index

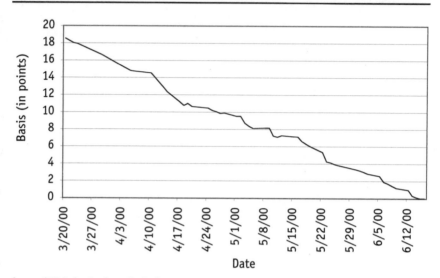

Source: CME Index Products Marketing.

where:
    cash = underlying cash S&P 500 Index
    r   = financing costs
    x   = number of days until expiration of S&P futures
    d   = annualized dividend yield of S&P 500

The futures fair value formula will allow you to calculate a theoretical value for the E-Mini S&P 500 or the regular S&P 500 futures contract using the cash index, interest rates, dividends, and time to expiration.

We'll work through an example using the actual values available on January 18, 2001, at 10:00 A.M. Chicago Time:

Cash S&P 500	= 1336.19
Interest rate/financing costs	= 6.0 percent
Number of days until expirations	= 57 days
Dividends to yield	= 1.3 percent
Futures theoretical fair value	= 1336.19 (1 + [.06 − .013] [57/365])
	= 1345.99

Theoretical premium   = Fair value – actual value of
                                               cash index
                                             = 1345.99 – 1336.19
                                             = 9.80 points

Actual premium   = Actual futures – actual value
   (E-Mini over cash)   of cash index
                                             = 1345.75 – 1336.19
                                             = 9.56 points

If you calculate a theoretical value for the futures and you know the cash index at any given point, then you subtract the two and get a theoretical premium. However, you will soon notice that the theoretical premium level and the actual premium level throughout the trading session are often different. In our example earlier, we said the theoretical premium should be about 9.8. In reality, it trades above and below that point throughout the day. This is a normal occurrence, since supply and demand fluctuate throughout each trading day depending on conditions, order flow, news events, and so on. The premium starts to capture a great deal of attention when the actual premium diverges from the theoretical premium by a wide amount. For example, if premium is calculated to be 9.8 points, it is perfectly normal to trade between 0 and 1.5 to 2.0 points above or below the premium. However, if the actual premium level rose substantially above the theoretical premium or dropped significantly below the theoretical premium, things would begin to happen. At this point, some savvy professional traders would begin to ply their skills in a trading strategy called *index arbitrage*—one of the many strategies that fall under the heading of program trading. These skilled professionals are called *arbitrageurs*, and they remain a mystery to the average investor despite the widespread attention that program trading and index arbitrage receive in the press. The topic of index arbitrage is a bit complicated but is nevertheless a subject that a stock index futures trader should be very familiar with.

At this point in the stock index class I teach, I usually ask my students the following question: Can you think of three scenarios where the cash-futures basis or premium would actually equal zero? Many can provide one obvious answer: at expiration, cash will equal futures. We just covered that topic. The other two answers usually elude students. What causes the E-Mini S&P 500 futures to trade above the cash index? Look at the relative level of interest costs versus dividend yields. Interest rates are almost always higher than dividend yields.

What would happen if interest rates were the same level as dividend yields? Play with the fair value equation:

Futures theoretical fair value = cash $(1 + [r - d] \, x/365])$

where
   r = interest costs (like other formula)
   cash = underlying S&P cash (like other formula)
   x = number of days to expiration
   d = projected dividend yield

We will use January 18 values again but instead put in 3 percent (.03) for interest rates as well as 3 percent (.03) for dividend yields.

$$\text{Futures fair value} = 1336.19 \, (1 + [.03 - .03] \, [57/365])$$
$$= 1336.19 \, (1 + [0] \, 57/365])$$
$$= 1336.19 \, (1 + [0])$$
$$= 1336.19 = \text{cash or Futures} = \text{Cash}$$

You would see that if dividends and interest rates were equal, that whole side in between the parentheses becomes 1 and the futures fair value equals the cash index.

By this time, a student or someone in a seminar usually calls out, "So what?" They complain that we are dealing with pie-in-the-sky theoretical trivia—to which I respond, "Really?" Go look up the yield on interest rates and the dividend yield on stocks in November 1993. You will see something very interesting: Yields on the S&P 500 cash index were in the 2.9 percent area. Yields on 3-month LIBOR (London Interbank Offered Rate), a common measure of financing costs, were about 2.9 percent. Futures traded at very low to almost nonexistent premiums to cash, and some investors were confused. But for most of the history of the big S&P 500 futures, as well as the E-Mini S&P 500 contract, interest rates have been higher than dividend yields. However, many years ago, dividend yields were the same as or higher than interest rates. While this scenario is not likely to arise soon, it is possible, and you should be aware of the implications of fair value and premium levels to stock index futures. In addition, outside the United States, the relative levels of interest rates and dividend yieldsl can be very different.

The third scenario that would produce zero basis is extreme bearish sentiment. It is a little more common than the previous example, which has happened for only one short time in the past 18 years. The best example regarding extreme bearish sentiment was during the Persian

Gulf War. Before Operation Desert Shield became Desert Storm, there were many attempts to resolve the situation peacefully. In one final attempt to avoid war, U.S Secretary of State James Baker and Iraqi Foreign Minister Tariq Aziz had a meeting. At the news conference that followed, Baker uttered those unforgettable words: "Regrettably—we could not come to terms with the Iraqi government." Traders all over the world did not need to hear anything beyond the "regrettably" part. Within 20 seconds, the S&P futures (no minis at that time) were obliterated by 13 full points, a huge move back then. In a few more moments, they were down about 20 points or $10,000 per contract (the S&P multiplier back in 1990 was $500). It took the cash S&P and Dow Jones about 15 to 20 minutes to catch up. Stock index futures are usually more responsive than the underlying cash index. This is because it takes longer for buying and selling pressure to manifest itself in stocks because there are so many that trade on the NYSE, AMEX, and Nasdaq. Even with electronic order routing, large-scale buying and selling—the kind observed on this memorable day—does take a few minutes or longer. Large-scale buying or selling in stock index futures contracts is much easier (one contract, one exchange versus several hundred stocks on multiple exchanges) and therefore much more responsive.

The point is that after the Baker-Aziz news conference, the futures went from a normal premium situation to no premium, and for a few brief minutes they even traded at a discount to cash. The sentiment, even if it was for only a short time, was so extremely bearish that the premium dissolved in an instant. The market was on shaky grounds already, banks were weak, recession was in the air, and this was the last thing the stock market needed to hear. For the contrarians or those with ice in their veins, it was a good buying opportunity. After weeks of bombing sorties, the ground war began, and it was over in a flash. That was the bottom. The market never looked back and mounted one of the greatest advances in history over the next decade. In fact, the 1990s was the second best decade in history. Extreme bearish sentiment can last only so long.

One last point regarding basis and we will move on. The cash S&P closes at 4:00 P.M. eastern standard time. The S&P futures (mini and regular) keep trading until 4:15 EST. Many news announcements come out right after the 4:00 close. Stocks cannot react because they are closed for the day, but the futures can and have some significant moves during that 15-minute window. As a result, the basis or premium can be artificially distorted on some days. An example will make this easier to grasp. We start with these statistics:

Time	Cash	Futures	Premium
4:00	1300.00 closed	1310.00	10.00

Then Company X announces lower-than-expected earnings at 4:05 P.M., causing a sell-off in futures, which are still open for 10 more minutes. Most NYSE stocks cannot react because they are closed; some Nasdaq issues get hit in after-hours sessions. We end up like this:

Time	Cash	Futures	Premium
4:05	1300.00 closed	1308.00	8.00
4:10	1300.00 closed	1306.00	6.00
4:15	1300.00 closed	1305.00 now closed	5.00

But like all other artificial moves, the marketplace corrects the situation the next morning, and the normal cash futures basis is established either by the cash opening 5.00 points lower, while the futures are unchanged (they already made their move prior day). Or the market shrugs off the news overnight, and the futures will gain back the 5 points of lost basis while the cash market treads water. Either way, a 5-point premium probably will not last long in an environment where the normal premium is 10. Arbitrage activity or ordinary supply and demand always work to reestablish equilibrium.

10

SHORT-TERM STRATEGIES USING E-MINI STOCK INDEX FUTURES AND ETFs

Now that you are armed with several chapters of basic information, it is time to see what futures and ETFs are capable of in terms of applications and strategies. In Chapter 6, we discussed in broad terms the many strategies available using ETFs. Chapter 9 gave a brief example using E-Mini S&P 500 futures. In this chapter, we look at several strategies and applications that will begin to give you a fuller understanding of the capabilities of ETFs and E-mini stock index futures.

As a review and to create a transition into the strategy section, let's first compare some of the major characteristics of ETFs and E-mini stock index futures. Exhibit 10.1 highlights some of the comparisons between Spiders and the Mini S&P 500 futures. Exhibit 10.2 illustrates the same comparison for the QQQ and E-Mini Nasdaq-100 futures products.

We will cover nine strategies in detail. Some involve stock index futures; others focus on ETF applications. You can implement some applications with both futures and ETFs. We start out with the topic of hedging using the E-Mini S&P 500 futures, then cover anticipatory hedging, and move on to spread trading. *Spreading* is a technique that allows a trader to profit from disparate price movements in the stock market. For example, a capitalization spread would allow a trader to profit from mid-cap stocks outperforming large-cap stocks. The last remaining strategies will educate you on the many opportunities available using futures and ETFs.

Exhibit 10.1   Comparing S&P 500 and E-Mini S&P 500 Futures with Spiders

	S&P 500 Futures	E-Mini S&P 500 Futures	SPDRs
Where traded	CME	CME	AMEX
Type of instrument	Futures contract	Futures contract	ETF/unit investment trust
Ticker symbol	SP	ES	SPY
Underlying index	S&P 500	S&P 500	S&P 500
Multiplier	$250 × index	$50 × index	1/10th of the S&P 500 cash index
Dollar value (with futures @1,160.00)	$290,000	$58,000	$116 per share
Average daily volume ($)	$30 billion	$7 billion	$1 billion
Trading platform	Pit and electronic via GLOBEX	Electronic only via GLOBEX	AMEX floor specialist (Spear Leeds and Kellogg)
Minimum capital required[a]	Margin: 7.4% ($21,563)	Margin: 7.4% ($4,313)	50% Reg T Margin
Transaction costs: bid-offer	2–7 basis points	4–8 basis points	9–13 basis points
Transaction costs: management fee	None	None	12 basis points per annum
24-hour trading	Yes	Yes	No
Options	Yes	Yes	No

[a]As of June 21, 2001. Subject to change.
Source: CME Index Products Marketing.

HEDGING INVESTMENT PORTFOLIOS USING E-MINI STOCK INDEX FUTURES

Over the past 18 years, the U.S. stock market has enjoyed one of the greatest run-ups in history. As measured by the benchmark S&P 500 Index, the annualized compounded return on the market was around 17 percent. Investors small and large have become more market literate as the number of mutual funds exceeds 9,000 and the number of 401(k) accounts in the United States nears 30 million. In fact, for many, the 401(k) account represents one of their largest assets, if not the

Exhibit 10.2 Comparing Nasdaq-100 and E-Mini Nasdaq-100 Futures with the QQQ

	Nasdaq-100 Futures	E-Mini Nasdaq-100 Futures	Nasdaq-100 Tracking Stock QQQ
Where traded	CME	CME	AMEX
Type of instrument	Futures contract	Futures contract	ETF/unit investment trust
Ticker	ND	NQ	QQQ
Underlying index	Nasdaq-100 Index	Nasdaq-100 Index	Nasdaq-100 Index
Multiplier	$100	$20	1/40th Nasdaq-100 Index
Dollar value (futures @ 1,800.00)	$180,000	$36,000	45
Average daily volume	$5.0–7.0 billion	$4–5 billion	$2.5–3.0 billion
Trading platform	Pit and electronic via GLOBEX	Electronic— GLOBEX only	AMEX specialist (Susquehanna Partners)
Minimum capital requirement[a]	$33,750 or 19% of value	$6,750 or 19% of value	50% Reg. T Margin
Transaction costs: bid-offer	17–38 basis points	8–16 basis points	16+ basis points
Transaction costs: management fees	None	None	18 basis points per annum
24-hour trading	Yes	Yes	No
Options	Yes	No	Yes

[a]As of June 21, 2001. Subject to change.
Source: CME Index Products Marketing.

largest. Trillions of dollars also reside in taxable mutual funds and with private money managers.

But as we all know, stock values do not only move upward. Stocks slid nearly 20 percent in just a few months in 1998's third quarter, causing jitters among investors in the U.S. markets. In addition, investors experienced declines during the 2000 calendar year as the S&P 500 showed a double-digit loss, and the Nasdaq-100 was also down substantially. Many wondered how bad it could get and if there was a way to protect their portfolios from significant losses.

In fact, there are ways to protect a portfolio of stocks using a variety of futures strategies. This section focuses on one in particular: using stock index futures to hedge equity portfolios. I also illustrate how investors can use stock index futures to gain market exposure—the so-called *anticipatory hedge*. Before we outline the strategies, there are a few items to consider:

- *Size of portfolio.* CME's flagship S&P 500 contract had a notional value (or contract size) of around $335,000 as of January 2001. The E-Mini S&P 500, which trades very close to its larger brother, has a value about one-fifth the size, or $67,000. Hence, investors with IRAs or 401(k) accounts or portfolios less than $67,000 in size would not be able to use these products effectively. For example, consider an investor who has $25,000 in an index fund that replicates the S&P 500 composite. If the investor wanted to hedge using the CME's Mini S&P 500, he would be hedging a $25,000 portfolio with an instrument valued at $67,000; he would be "overhedged" by $42,500 (you could say his hedge would be out of balance).
- *Construction of the portfolio.* To benefit from using the various CME stock index products, the investor's portfolio must have a significant component of U.S. equities. Many investors, especially more conservative ones, have sizable stakes in bonds, money market funds, convertible securities, and so on. CME stock index futures are not designed to hedge fixed-income instruments, but to hedge equity portfolios that correlate highly with a particular index such as the S&P 500, S&P MidCap 400, Nasdaq-100, and Russell 2000.
- *Correlation of equity portfolios to CME stock index products.* Assume that you have a large enough portfolio and that it is composed mainly of U.S. equities. The next step is to determine how closely the portfolio tracks the underlying indexes on which CME stock index futures are based. For example, the S&P 500 comprises mostly larger-capitalization stocks such as General Electric, Cisco, Microsoft, and ExxonMobil (and 496 other issues). If you owned shares in an S&P 500 Index fund or even a fund or portfolio that had a lot of large-capitalization stocks, the correlation of the fund should be high, and the S&P 500 or Mini S&P 500 futures contract might be a good vehicle to hedge against a declining market. On the other hand, if your portfolio were to in-

clude smaller-capitalization stocks or even midsize stocks, the
correlation of these stocks to the S&P 500 would be lower, and a
futures contract based on the S&P 500 may not be suitable for
your hedging purposes. A more appropriate hedge might be constructed using Russell 2000 futures or S&P MidCap 400 futures.
Of course, you would first have to determine how well your portfolio tracks these indexes.

- *Tax considerations.* The taxation of futures is different from other
investments and depends on the taxpayer's status and strategy.
Is the taxpayer a trader? Investor? Dealer? Hedger? Any gains or
losses arising from these transactions usually are subject to both
the mark-to-market and the 60/40 rule at the end of the tax year.
Generally this type of transaction is reported on the appropriate
IRS form (Form 6781—Gains/Losses from Section 1256 Contracts
and Straddles) and transferred to the Schedule D filing. A tax adviser can determine which rules apply. While tax treatment of an
overall hedging strategy may be complicated, the protection offered by such a strategy merits consideration.

PROTECTING YOUR PORTFOLIO

Exhibit 10.3 displays several mutual funds along with investment returns and other information during a period in 2000, a year of generally
declining stock prices. Why did I pick these funds? When the market
heads south, certain mutual fund investors that have a modicum of
knowledge of hedging begin to call CME. During a couple of nasty
weeks in the market, I received numerous inquiries about hedging mutual fund holdings and other portfolios using the E-minis. The exhibit
shows the fund holdings they were interested in hedging as the identi-
fier. Here I briefly recount some of the discussions, though I have no
idea if these investors ever acted after these conversations took place.

Along with fund name and amount invested, the exhibit lists price
data for an eight-week period, including the percent return. I have also
included the performance of the underlying cash indexes and their
corresponding futures contracts since those would be the instruments
used to hedge the funds. The table also includes some data on *R-
squared values.* R-squared ranges from 0 to 100 and reflects the percentage of a fund's movements that are explained by movements in its
benchmark index. (R-squared is *not* a predictor of relative performance
or profitability.) An R-squared of 100 means that all movements of a
fund are completely explained by movements in the index. Thus, index

Exhibit 10.3 Using E-Mini Stock Index Futures to Hedge Portfolios

Investor/Fund	Amount Invested	Price, Mar. 24, 2000	Price, May 24, 2000	Percentage Return	R-Squared
Vanguard Index 500	$400,000	140.74	127.54	−9.38	100
Janus Fund	110,000	50.34	40.65	−19.25	72
T. Rowe Price Blue Chip	52,000	39.75	35.56	−10.54	95
Mutual Qualified	900,000	17.14	17.64	2.90	67
S&P 500 Cash	NA	1527.46	1399.05	−8.41	NA
June S&P 500 Futures	NA	1555.40	1401.70	−9.88	NA

Note: On 3/24/01, S&P 500 futures continued trading until 3:15, running up considerably after the cash markets were closed. Their "fair value" was approximately 1545.00. At this level, the percentage decline from March 24 to May 24 would have more closely matched the cash decline. In fact, it would have been 9.4 percent.

funds that invest only in S&P 500 stocks will have an R-squared very close to 100 since they invest in the index itself. A low R-squared means that very few of the fund's movements are explained by movements in its benchmark index. Put another way, funds with lower R-squared values move to the beat of a different drummer and will not mimic the moves of the S&P as well over the long run. In very general terms, high R-squared values mean a portfolio has a good correlation with its benchmark, the S&P 500.

The first investor had a $400,000 balance in the Vanguard 500 Index fund. I told him he had an adequate balance and that his correlation to the S&P 500 is perfect. It should be; the fund perfectly replicates the index. That fund was down about 9.4 percent. The S&P 500 futures (and the Mini S&P 500) were down about 9.88 percent. Basically the fund was a very good candidate for hedging—if he chose to do so. He had a large enough portfolio and a good correlation with the futures, so it would have been a good hedge.

The second investor had $110,000 in the Janus Fund. The amount invested was not adequate for the regular S&P 500 futures but could be hedged using two Mini S&P futures. However, two minis would have a value of $140,000. He would be hedging a $110,000 investment with a "$140,000 insurance policy"; he would be overhedged. This is not a bad situation in a bear market, but it is a bit risky should stocks move upward. I also told him that the fund was a bit concentrated and had a large tilt toward technology. This explains why it declined twice as much as the index did. Hence, if this investor hedged using the E-Mini S&P 500, he would have made some profits on the hedge but not enough to cover the severe decline the portfolio experienced. In summary, the tracking error and concentrated nature of the portfolio could be a problem.

The next caller had $52,000 in the T Rowe Price Blue Chip fund. Again, this fund correlated well with the overall market, with a high R-squared. S&P futures would have been useful as a hedge in this case too. But, unfortunately, this investor had too small a portfolio. Even one Mini S&P 500 contract is too large for the amount of assets to be hedged. The person then asked if these new "Spider stocks" might be useful. I replied yes and sent her to the AMEX.

The last caller had almost a million dollars in the Mutual Qualified Fund, which I know well. Although the investor did have a large enough asset base, some items made this fund a less attractive candidate for hedging with S&P futures. The Mutual Qualified Fund is loaded with stocks that many other fund managers would never touch. Michael Price, who ran it for most of its operating history (before he sold his fund company to Franklin Templeton), had an interesting collection of investments. The portfolio had a huge value tilt, including many bankruptcy candidates, companies reorganizing out of bankruptcy, junk debt, and a whole collection of investments that much of the Street avoided. Too bad for them; this and other Mutual Series portfolios had amassed a superb track record (except for during the dotcom mania, where many value investors were left in the dust by technology). Indeed, as 2000 unfolded and much of the technology space became toxic waste, Mutual Qualified did what it usually does in adverse markets: it went up. If this investor had hedged, he would have made money on the hedge as the market slid and would have profited on the investment being hedged since the fund was up 2.9 percent during this time frame. It is nearly impossible to profit on both sides of a hedge! All things considered, the low correlation means that S&P 500 futures would not provide a good, reliable hedge in this case. (During the 1973–1974 bear market, when the S&P was down nearly 50 percent, Price's flagship fund, now run by the great team he left behind, was down less than 2 percent, an amazing but little-known accomplishment in the investing world.) This investor must closely consider the size of the portfolio to be hedged, the construction, and the correlation to the futures contract. If an investor had investments primarily in small-cap issues, then the Russell 2000 futures might be more appropriate than the S&P 500 in this case.

THE STRATEGIES

We now provide details on how such hedges might be constructed. Remember that hedging is insuring against an adverse price move. An adverse price move to a fund holder is a down market. Thus, hedges of this sort are also called *short hedges*, since the investor would have to sell short a futures contract to protect against an adverse price move. If the market did slide, the hope is that the profits on the short hedge would offset the losses on the portfolio of stocks.

Strategy 1: Hedging a Portfolio with Stock Index Futures

Suppose you own a mutual fund or portfolio of stocks that is highly correlated with the S&P 500 composite index (R-squared = 98). The current value of the portfolio is $140,000:

Time frame:	Early November
Outlook:	Short-term bearish; looking for a decline of at least 10 to 15 percent.
Strategy:	Sell two E-Mini S&P 500 futures contracts to hedge portfolio. Each E-Mini S&P futures is worth $70,750 (1415 × $50 per point = $70,750); thus, two contracts would be required to hedge a $140,000 portfolio.
Current S&P 500 index (cash):	1,400.00 points
Current E-Mini S&P 500 futures (December futures):	1,415.00 points. Futures contracts usually trade at a premium to the cash index due to cost-of-carry factors. As expiration of the futures contract nears, this premium will converge toward zero.

Four weeks later, the S&P 500 declines 15 percent to 1190.00, your portfolio declines 15.5 percent, and December future declines 15.5 percent to 1195.00.

To determine the effectiveness of a hedging program, the hedger must calculate the profit/loss on each leg—i.e., the hedging instrument and the portfolio being hedged.

Profit/Loss Picture

Value of portfolio early November	$140,000
Value of portfolio early December	$118,300
Profit/loss on portfolio	–$21,700

Value of E-Mini S&P 500 in early November	$70,750 (1415 × 50 = $70,750)
Value of E-Mini S&P 500 in early December	$59,750 (1195 × 50 = $59,750)

Gain on short hedge	+$11,000
× 2 ($140,000 portfolio required two futures)	+$22,000

Hedged Portfolio

Loss on portfolio	–$21,700
Gain from futures hedge	+$22,000
Overall profit/loss	+$ 300

Unhedged Portfolio

Loss on portfolio	–$21,700
Gain from futures hedge	NA
Overall profit/loss	–$21,700

In this hypothetical example, the hedge using E-mini stock index futures fully protected the portfolio against a decline. The decline in your portfolio was offset by gains in the two E-Mini S&P futures contracts. You preserved the value of your portfolio despite a significant decline in the market of 15 percent! On the other hand, if the market had advanced, the portfolio's gains would have been offset by losses on the two E-Mini S&P 500 futures contracts. If this were to occur, you would have had to consider removing your hedge by buying back the short futures contracts so you could participate in any further upside action.

Strategy 2: The Anticipatory Hedge: Using Stock Index futures to Gain Market Exposure

You are expecting a large cash infusion from selling your business. You plan to invest the cash proceeds (about $150,000) in the market, primarily in high-tech stocks, at the close of the deal in four to five months. Your problem now is that you are very bullish near-term, especially on technology stocks, but you lack sufficient cash to construct a portfolio immediately. Your strategy is to execute a long hedge by buying three E-Mini Nasdaq-100 futures contracts (three contracts are worth approximately $150,000 in January 2001). The strategy has these advantages: It is easy to execute, less costly, and more efficient than buying a basket of stocks, and the initial cash outlay or performance bond would be much less than $150,000 (in fact, it would be less than 15 percent of that amount—about $7,000 per contract × 3, or $21,000).

If the market rose before you received the $150,000 in proceeds, the futures would also tend to rise, allowing you to participate in the advance. Four to five months later, you could purchase the stocks. The higher price that you would pay would be offset by the profits in the futures contracts. If the prices of stocks (and therefore the Nasdaq-100) declined, your futures contracts would lose money. However, the cost to purchase your portfolio would also be reduced. This *anticipatory long hedge*, as it is sometimes called, allows you to enter the market immediately at a fraction of the cost.

Over the past 15 years, CME's stock index futures product line has seen tremendous growth. Much of the success in these products stems from their advantages to large institutions such as banks, pension funds, and mutual funds. Used properly, these products provide superb risk management and trading opportunities. Their usefulness, however, is not limited to billion-dollar institutions. Suitable individual investors with adequate risk capital and the appropriate type of portfolios can successfully employ these vehicles too.

Strategy 3: Spreads Using Stock Index Futures

We all read about certain market professionals who turn a profit year in and year out. George Soros, Michael Steinhardt, and dozens of others have racked up annualized returns of 20 to 30 percent for 20 to 30 years. It seems that there are some money managers, individuals, or proprietary trading houses that mint money. What is it that separates professional traders such as these from the rest of the pack?

First, they use all available resources and tools. They invest and trade more than just stocks and bonds. They trade options, futures, and other derivatives when the opportunity presents itself. Second, they are willing to play down markets; they are willing to sell short when they feel that a particular stock, sector, or asset class within the financial markets will head south. How many investors out there have tried to profit from a down market? Not many. And although the primary trend of the market has been up for much of the past 18 years, there have been some excellent seasons in which short selling would have been lucrative. The third item that sets these investors apart is their ability to recognize and take advantages of disparities in the markets. One of the many ways to play some of these disparities is with spreads in stock index futures. Spreading is a distant cousin to arbitrage, the simultaneous purchase and sale of similar or identical instruments to take advantage of small, short-lived price discrepancies. It is largely a risk-free venture. Spreading with futures is similar to arbitrage, but the price discrepancies usually last for days, weeks, months, or longer instead of being available for mere moments. Spreads also have some risk, but they have advantages too:

- In general, spreads carry lower risk than outright long or short positions.
- With spreads, you can divorce yourself from the prevailing thinking in that you do not have to predict the direction of the market. You only have to identify the disparity.
- Spreads allow you to profit in up or down markets.
- Spreading with futures usually results in lower performance bond margins.
- For most investors, it is cheaper than buying and selling a basket of stocks.

Let's look at how a typical spread would work using the E-Mini S&P 500 futures and the S&P MidCap 400 futures (contract specifications for the MidCap 400 index are provided in Exhibit 10.4). To see why we are choosing these two index futures, let us examine the returns for various indexes for the calendar year 2000:

S&P 500	−10.14%
DJIA	−6.18%
Nasdaq-100	−36.84%
Russell 2000	−4.20%
S&P MidCap 400	+16.21%

Exhibit 10.4   S&P MidCap 400 Index Futures Contract Specifications

Ticker symbol	MD
Contract size	$500 × S&P MidCap 400 Index futures
Minimum price fluctuation	.05 index point = $25 per contract
Trading hours	8:30 A.M.–3:15 P.M. (regular trading hours or pit-traded hours)
	3:45 P.M.–8:15 A.M. (Globex trading hours)
Contract months	March, June, September, December (H, M, U, Z)
Last day of trading	The Thursday prior to the third Friday of the contract month
Quarterly futures settlement	Settled in cash on final day of trading to the special opening quotation (SOQ) on Friday morning of the S&P MidCap 400 Index

Most major indexes were down, especially the tech-heavy Nasdaq-100. The Russell 2000, composed primarily of small stocks, was also down, but by not nearly as much as the Nasdaq-100 and the S&P 500. The MidCap 400, the benchmark for midsize companies, left the rest of the market in the dust, not only showing a gain for 2000, but outperforming the S&P 500 by 26 percentage points. In addition to manifesting themselves in the stock markets, these disparities also show up in currency markets, agricultural markets, and the fixed-income market (in particular, along the yield curve in U.S. Treasuries).

By spring 2000, technology issues were undergoing a significant correction. The large-cap S&P 500 was also correcting, but to a much smaller degree. But the MidCap 400 was showing gains on the year. One April day, I received a phone call from a good trader/friend I'll refer to as the Gnome of Zurich (*Gnome of Zurich* was a term coined by an English politician decades ago to describe currency and gold traders in Switzerland. They had a reputation at the time of being very clever speculators. You can read a hilarious account of the Gnomes of Zurich in Adam Smith's *The Money Game*).[1] The Gnome who called me liked to trade Mini S&Ps and Mini Nasdaq-100 futures and also loved to trade spreads. He had noticed over the course of a few weeks that the midsize stocks were holding their ground during the sell-off that engulfed other sectors of the market. He also reminded me that the S&P 500 had five superlative years of performance—five straight years with returns greater than 20 percent. This is unequaled in financial history.

The Gnome figured that it was time for small stocks and midsize stocks to have their day. Admittedly, over the past few years, many folks have prematurely predicted the arrival of the small- and mid-cap renaissance. The Gnome is not your average trader, and he was one of those who watched those Super Bowl dot-com ads and proclaimed that the bell was clanging loudly and was giddy over the possibilities of a top in tech. He also knew that the technology sector at that time composed over 30 percent of the S&P 500 and figured that if it was heading south, it would create a huge drag on the performance of the S&P 500 Index. He stated in no uncertain terms, "The time is ripe. Time to go long mid-caps and short large caps." Let's see how his trade worked out, since I was privy to some of the details. Here is the information for April 28, 2000:

> Long 3 September S&P MidCap
>   futures (MDU is ticker symbol)   @   488.25
> Short 10 September E-Mini
>   S&P 500 futures (ESU is ticker symbol)   @ 1481.50
>
> Dollar value of long 3 MDU = $732,375
> Dollar value of short 10 ESU = $740,750

The reason for the 3-to-10 ratio is to establish a dollar-neutral position. The Gnome wanted to be long a certain dollar amount of mid-cap futures and short the same (or nearly the same) dollar amount of large-cap futures for the strategy to be effective. In this example, he was long a $732,000 basket of mid-cap issues and short a $740,000 basket of large-cap issues. He could also have done the trade in a 3-to-2 ratio by going long three MidCap futures and short two regular-sized S&P 500 contracts. Normally, the performance bond margin for a 10 short Mini S&P 500 alone would be about $47,000 ($4,688 × 10). The margins for the MidCap futures would also add to the bill. However, the performance bond margin for this spread trade is substantially lower. Why? Because spreads tend to reduce risk. You are simultaneously long one section of the market and short another in virtually equal amounts. Because there is generally less risk than the outright long or short position, the firms and the Clearing House reduce the margins. To duplicate this strategy with stocks would take an incredible amount of capital.

Let us see how things progressed.

By the end of May, the overall market had drifted lower, led by Nasdaq stocks. The S&P 500 was also lower. But the S&P MidCap 400 index was only slightly lower:

MDU = 484.80 (mid-caps down .71 percent)
ESU = 1443.75 (large-caps down 2.54 percent)

P/L long MDU = 484.80 − 488.25 × $500 × 3   = −$ 5,175
P/L short ESU = 1443.75 − 1481.50 × $50 × 10 = +$18,875
P/L spread   = +$13,700

Note in these figures that the S&P MidCap 400 futures have a $500 multiplier, the Mini S&P 500 a $50 multiplier, and the regular S&P 500 a $250 multiplier. (See the contract specifications.)

One of the great advantages to spread trading is that spreads can work in up and down markets. The Street is filled with bright financial types who are paid handsome sums to predict Fed Chairman Greenspan's next move or to predict where GNP will be in the fourth quarter of 2004. The trader of a spread can divorce himself from prevailing wisdom—he doesn't care what Greenspan does, doesn't care if GNP rises a little, doesn't care if the employment cost index jumps a point or two. He/she only cares about the spread between the large- and small-caps. During this time only one thing matters and that is that mid-sized stocks go up more than large-caps do or that mid-cap stocks go down less than large-caps do. In this case, by May 31, 2000, the S&P MidCap 400 futures were down .71 percent. The Gnome lost over $5,000 on that part of the spread (each part of a spread is called a *leg*). But the large-caps measured by the Mini S&P 500 futures declined an even greater amount—2.54 percent—and that leg of the spread showed a profit of $18,875. Overall, the profit on the spread was $13,700 at this point.

By the end of June, large-caps rallied a bit and caused the spread to give up some of its gains:

MDU = 488.30 (mid-caps up .01 percent from inception of trade)
ESU = 1468.00 (large-caps down .91 percent from inception of trade)

P/L long MDU = 488.30 − 488.25 × $500 × 3   = + $75
P/L short ESU = 1468.00 − 1481.50 × $50 × 10 = + 6,750
P/L spread   = +$6,825

But as summer progressed and the market regained some of its footing, midsize issues began to hit their stride. Here are the figures for July 19, 2000:

MDU = 511.25 (mid-caps up 4.7 percent since inception of trade)
ESU =1498.00 (large-caps up 1.1 percent since inception of trade)

$$\text{P/L long MDU} = 511.25 - 488.25 \times \$500 \times 3 \qquad = +\$34,500$$
$$\text{P/L short ESU} = 1498.00 - 1481.50 \times \$50 \times 10 \quad = \underline{-\$\ 8,250}$$
$$\text{P/L spread} \qquad\qquad\qquad\qquad\qquad\qquad\quad = +\$26,250$$

The S&P MidCap 400 Index widened the gap over the S&P 500 Index and for the remainder of the 2000 never looked back. In summary, the spread worked very nicely. It worked in a rising market and a falling market, without having to predict which way the market was going. The risk in this kind of trade would only be if you surmised wrong, and mid-cap stocks underperformed large-caps.

This type of strategy would be particularly useful to someone wishing to capitalize on the well-known *January effect*: the seasonal tendency for small and midsize stocks to outperform large-cap stocks during the beginning of the year. Although it does not happen every year, it is something traders keep their eye on. As late December approaches (sometimes the effect arrives as early as November), stocks that have depreciated significantly, usually small- and mid-cap stocks (large stocks tend to hold up better in major slides), fall victim to even greater seasonal selling pressure due to selling for tax purposes. Investors bail out of major losers, take the loss for tax purposes, and sometimes repurchase these or other issues in January so as not to run afoul of the IRS 30-day wash-sale rule. When the new year begins, the tax selling abates, and sometimes there is buying pressure during January. New-year contributions to IRA and 401(k) accounts and mutual fund quarter-end and year-end window dressing also contribute to this seasonal tendency. The overall result is that small-cap and mid-cap stocks tend to outperform large-cap issues in January. Sometimes the effect carries further into the new year. Like Pavlov's dogs, the press is replete with its lists of stocks to buy for that proverbial January bounce. There are two problems with this, though.

First, how much of the investing public has enough capital to put together a diversified package of small- or mid-cap stocks? Second, what if the overall market, including small- and mid-cap stocks, heads south in an important way? Many investors are well short of the capital required to assemble a large enough portfolio of these types of stocks, and if the market does decline, the outright owner of stocks loses money. Hence, the benefits of trading a spread are clear. Spreads can work in a down market and cost much less (in terms of capital required and commissions) than buying even 5 or 10 small- and mid-cap stocks, and the investor gets the movement of 400 midsize companies in the case of the S&P MidCap 400. An investor who thought that small stocks were going to outperform their larger brethren could then go long Russell 2000 futures and short the S&P 500 futures or the Mini S&P futures in the appropriate ratio.

In a similar vein, investors could also spread style indexes with both futures and ETFs. For example, each year from 1995 through 1999, the S&P 500/Barra Growth Index outperformed the S&P 500/Barra Value Index:

Year	Growth Index	Value Index
1995	38.13%	36.99%
1996	23.97	22.00
1997	36.52	29.98
1998	42.16	14.69
1999	28.25	12.73
2000	−22.07	5.99

An investor who caught even a small part of that multiyear trend would have profited and could have traded the spread from both sides. As the new paradigm finally wore out its welcome in April 2000, the old economy came thundering back, and the S&P 500/Barra Value Index trounced its growth counterpart by 28 full percentage points. Both the Growth and Value futures trade at CME. There are also iShares ETFs on both. The investor has literally dozens of spreading strategies available. Exhibit 10.5 shows some of the possibilities. They all can be played from both sides too. When properly implemented, these strategies can unlock a multitude of opportunities that were previously available to only a few professionals and institutions.

Strategy 4: Using ETFs to Implement Sector Shifts

The myriad of sector ETFs and HOLDRS products have made the shift into and out of various sectors much easier for both individual investors and institutional giants. Many of the major firms on Wall Street perform lengthy and detailed analysis. They analyze reams of fundamental, technical, and economic data and rate various sectors as more attractive or less attractive. They then recommend to clients appropriate overweighting in attractive sectors and underweighting in unattractive sectors. Before we get into the strategy, we'll examine the breakdown of the major sectors and their weights in the S&P 500 benchmark as of December 31, 2000, shown in Exhibit 10.6.

Assume a high-net-worth portfolio of $25 million invested according to the weight-in-portfolio column in Figure 10.6, $4.5 million, or 18 percent, is invested in the technology sector. This investor's firm, whose

Exhibit 10.5 Spread Matrix

Outlook	Spread Choices	Instruments Available
Large-cap outperforms mid-cap	Long S&P 500, short S&P MidCap 400	Futures (CME), SPDRs, iShares (AMEX)
Large-cap outperforms small-caps	Long S&P 500, short Russell 2000	Futures (CME), iShares (AMEX)
Large-cap outperforms small-caps	Long S&P 500, short S&P SmallCap	SPDRs/iShares (AMEX)
Large-cap outperforms small-caps	Long Dow DIAMONDs, short Russell 2000 or S&P SmallCap	DIAMONDs, iShares (AMEX)"
Large-cap outperforms small-caps	Long Russell 1000, short Russell 2000	Futures (CME, NYBOT), iShares/(AMEX)
Large-cap outperforms small-caps	Long Russell 1000, short S&P SmallCap	iShares (AMEX)
Large-cap growth outperforms large-cap value	Long S&P 500/Barra Growth, short S&P 500/Barra Value	Futures (CME) and iShares (AMEX)
Large-cap growth outperforms large-cap value	Long Russell 1000 Growth, short Russell 1000 Value	iShares (AMEX)
Large-cap growth outperforms large-cap value	Long DJ US LargeCap Growth, short DJ US LargeCap Value	streetTRACKS (AMEX)
Mid-cap growth outperforms mid-cap value	Long S&P/Barra Midcap Growth, short S&P/Barra Midcap Value	iShares (AMEX)
Small-cap growth outperforms small-cap value	Long S&P SmallCap/Barra Growth, short S&P SmallCap/Barra Value	iShares (AMEX)
Small-cap growth outperforms small-cap value	Long Russell 2000 Growth, short Russell 2000 Value	iShares (AMEX)
Small-cap growth outperforms small-cap value	Long DJ US SmallCap Growth, short DJ US SmallCap Value	streetTRACKS (AMEX)
Total market growth outperforms total market value)	Long Russell 3000 Growth, short Russell 3000 Value	iShares (AMEX)

Exhibit 10.6 Sector Weighting Shifts

Sector	Index Weighting (%)	Weight in Portfolio (%)	"Firm" Recommends (%)	
Technology	20.0	18.0	22	(overweighting)
Finance	16.9	15.0	20	(overweighting)
Health care	14.0	14.0	14	(normal weighting)
Consumer services	11.8	11.8	11.8	(normal weighting)
Capital goods	8.9	8.9	8.9	(normal weighting)
Consumer nondurables	7.4	7.4	7.4	(normal weighting)
Energy	6.7	6.5	6.5	(small underweighting)
Other	14.3	18.4		

research she follows closely and respects, recommends a 22 percent weighting in technology, or $5.5 million exposure. The investor decides to raise her tech exposure by $1.0 million by going long the Technology Select Sector SPDR. At $37.00 per share, she would need to buy just over 27,000 shares. (She could buy the DJ US Technology iShares or the MS High Tech 35 streetTRACKS as alternatives.) There are two reasons for choosing ETFs as opposed to just picking the stocks: cost and time. Execution in the ETF is a simple one-transaction deal. It is not necessary to research several possible companies as candidates since the sector Spider covers the entire spectrum in technology. The costs of one transaction are very low, and the liquidity is excellent. Using the Financial Select Sector SPDRs, the investor could also raise her financial sector threshold to the desired level just as easily.

Underweighting a sector or eliminating it altogether are also possible using the ETFs. For example, suppose an investor wants to own the S&P 500 ex-utilities. I had a conversation with the head of a small endowment fund that was largely indexed to the S&P 500. He expressed his dislike for utilities and wished he could own the S&P without the utilities exposure. I thought this was a strange wish; endowments are typically on the conservative side, and utility investing is in keeping with that degree of risk. I explained that he could remove the utilities in one clean sweep by selling Utility SPDRs. I asked the size of his endowment, and he said small—about $50 million. I knew that utilities as a sector composed about 2.0 percent of the S&P

500 and the Utilities Select Sector SPDR traded around $25 per share. I pulled out my calculator and tapped a few numbers: .02 × $50 million/$25 = 40,000. I told him he could have his wish by selling 40,000 Utility Select Sector SPDRs. He thanked me for the information and said farewell. I hoped he did not excise his utility exposure since one of the best-performing sectors that year was utilities.

Until the advent of ETFs, this kind of flexibility required very deep pockets and institutional connections. Now, anyone armed with enough money to open a brokerage account can benefit.

Strategy 5: Using ETFs to Gain Country or Regional Exposure

I took a call in 1998 around the time of the Asian and Russian crises. The Dow and S&P were getting hammered; they were down about 20 percent. Some of the Asian markets were decimated. Hong Kong's Hang Seng went from 15,000 to below 10,000. The Malaysian market melted down, and Singapore also suffered severe losses (as did Thailand, Korea, and Taiwan). Nevertheless, an investor just returned from the region was impressed with the progress there since her last trip many years ago. She knew things were cheap and thought that in 5 to 10 years, these countries would be back in vogue. She had about $10,000 to invest. I said futures were out of the question since the only futures we trade in the region was the Nikkei 225 and the margin was quite a bit higher than $10,000. We did not have futures on the Singapore Straits Times index or on any Malaysian or Korean index. We did have a Dow Jones Taiwan Index, but it just could not develop enough activity, and the time zone difference was a problem (although it is not with the Nikkei for some reason). I could not help her but suggested she call her broker and buy 100 shares each of every WEBS product in the region. (WEBS stands for World Equity Benchmark Shares—since renamed iShares MSCI.) The Singapore WEBS traded below $7.00 per share, and Malaysian WEBS were going for about $3.50 per share. It was a 30 to 50 percent off sale in the Pacific Rim! And she would have enough left over to pick up some Latin American bargains too. She seemed delighted.

The region did recover, although some economies are still in the doldrums. The WEBS did appreciate some in the next year or so. And if sector and style investing are not enough, with the iShares MSCI and other regional and international ETFs, obtaining fast, easy exposure to just about any point on the globe is within your grasp.

Strategy 6: Using Futures or ETFs to Relieve a Hostage Crisis

From 1998 through the early part of 2000, many Silicon Valley employees hit the mother lode in investing. Lush stock options and holdings in corporations whose stocks had soared in a few months created new millionaires. But many of these newly rich were held hostage to their holdings or stock options. Many had lock-ups of six months or more and also did not want to face the tax liability. After all, the gains were immense. Why would anyone want to share up to 39.6 percent of their wealth with Uncle Sam? In retrospect, this thinking proved foolish; many investors now look back and would gladly have paid their taxes rather than be left holding shares that have declined substantially.

One person in this situation had thousands of shares of a high-tech firm and could not get out for a while. This person was scared that his net worth was going to be wiped away before his eyes. Could he do something in Nasdaq futures? Yes, he could. But he might want to check with his company and his brokerage firm for any restrictions. He would need capital to come up with the performance bond margin, and he would need several E-Mini Nasdaq-100 futures to cover the entire amount should he wish to go that route (as an alternative, he could hedge part of his holdings). Remember that he had lots of stock but not lots of cash, and there would be risks. He could sell short E-Mini or regular Nasdaq-100 futures. If technology overall got wrecked (which it eventually did) he would have some kind of hedge, some insurance, should his company be dragged through the mud too. But the risk would be if the Nasdaq-100 held up or continued to rally and his company slumped in the market. Then his hedge would lose, and his stock would lose value. One additional risk would be if both stock and the Nasdaq-100 soared. He would lose on the hedge, which would offset the gain on his rising stock holdings—unless the stock rose much more than the Nasdaq-100 index, in which case his profits in the stock would more than offset losses in the index hedge. ETFs could have worked too, but they would have required a lot more capital given the margin rules on selling ETFs short. I wish I knew the outcome.

Some of these situations are quite intriguing. Imagine being worth mid six-figures or even seven-figures and not being able to touch the stock. Then imagine the stock starts heading south. This individual's plight was shared with thousands of other corporate workers in the tech industry. Too few people are aware of the strategies made possible through futures, ETFs, and other types of derivatives.

Strategy 7: Perils of an Index Fund Manager: Using Stock Index Futures for Cash Equitization

If you take a close look at the Morningstar performance data on the Vanguard 500 Index Fund, you'll begin to notice something intriguing. At several intervals, the fund has beaten the index. For instance, the three years ending January 26, 2001, saw the fund up 13.80 percent on an annualized basis—4 basis points better than the S&P 500 itself. Any normal investor would expect the fund at best to match the performance of the index minus any fees and expenses. Thus, the best the investor would hope for would be the index minus 18 basis points. With Vanguard's performance, the investor no doubt is left wondering how the manager pulls off this feat. There are probably two reasons. First, the Vanguard Group is dedicated to bringing costs down like few other firms are. Second the manager, Gus Sauter, skillfully uses futures contracts sometimes to buy the S&P 500 on the cheap. If the index were at 1300.00 and you could, through skillful trading, buy it at 1299.00, you would pick up a bit of performance edge. Do this often enough, and the savings would add up to a few basis points of performance advantage. A few basis points might add only a few cents on small accounts, but on mid- and larger-size accounts over 5 or 10 years, the cheapskate factor will make a significant difference.

How would a manager accomplish this? By using futures when they provide a price advantage. The theoretical fair value of stock index futures comes into play in this strategy. Let's look at some prices. Assume that a manager has $1 million to invest:

S&P 500 futures (E-Mini and regular) at:	1311.00
Cash S&P 500 Index trading at:	1300.00
Actual basis	11.00
Days to expiration	90 days
Interest rate or financing costs	6.0 percent
Dividend yield on index	1.3 percent

The theoretical fair value of futures should be equal to:

$$\text{cash } (1 + [r - d] [x/365])$$
$$1300.00 (1 + [.06 - .013] [90/365])$$
$$1315.10$$

Here is the theoretical basis:

Theoretical fair value minus actual cash S&P
1315.10 − 1300.00
15.10 points

Now, further assume you are an index fund manager, and your back office informs you that $1 million in new money needs to be invested. As an index fund, that cash must be invested immediately. If the market was up 3 percent the next day and he held cash instead of the stocks in the S&P 500, then he would experience a cash drag and underperform the index.

If you were an index fund portfolio manager and saw the data above, what would you do? Would you invest the $1 million in the actual stocks in the index—that is, buy the cash instrument (very easy to do with a computer)—or would you buy the futures? The fair value of the S&P 500 is 1315.10. But due to short-term supply and demand conditions, the futures are 4.10 points cheaper than they are supposed to be given interest rates, dividends, and time to expiration. Anytime a skilled index fund manager could buy the futures 4.10 points cheaper, he would seize the opportunity. For large and midsize funds, it is likely the manager would use the regular-size S&P 500 futures (with value about $335,000). For smaller accounts, the E-Mini S&P 500 might be used.

This relationship between the relative prices of cash and futures plays out daily. For traders and arbitrageurs, the fair value is quite important in establishing buy and sell points. Similarly, it is important for fund managers to earn every basis point of performance possible. Skillfully exploiting anomalies in cash and futures is one tool that will help managers accomplish this goal.

This technique is called *cash equitization* because it allows the manager to invest in equities ("equitize") by purchasing futures contracts. Instead of spending the $1 million on stocks, he is doing so synthetically by futures. Buying three S&P 500 futures contacts with a value of $335,000 each is the same as buying a $1 million basket of stocks in the S&P 500 index. (In reality, the three futures give $1 million in exposure, but the performance bond margin requirement for the three contracts would be about $70,000.) The exposure is identical, but with the futures at a discount from fair value, the S&P 500 index is cheaper in price. Later, as the cash and futures basis returns to normal, the portfolio manager could then choose to invest cash while selling or offsetting the futures contracts as time passes. The manager could also hold the futures until expiration. If, on the other hand, the futures were priced at 1318.10—3.00 points more expensive than they are supposed to be—the manager would avoid the futures and buy the cash basket instead.

Strategy 8: "The Perfect Storm"—
A Case Study in Oversold Markets

In late March 2001, the market was suffering a devastating storm, with damages in the hundreds of billions of dollars. On March 22, 2001, we had three perfect ingredients coming together. A bad month for the market was getting worse as the Dow sliced through 10,000, then 9900, 9800, 9700, and on down. Tech was taking even more punishment. The S&P futures were down over 40 points. The Dow was down about 330 points.

The phone rang. It was the Gnome of Zurich, imitating the meteorologist in the movie *The Perfect Storm*: "First, you have huge selling. Every major index and sector is heading south. The monthly relative strength index [RSI] is 16! [A monthly reading below 20 is extremely oversold and extremely rare.] Second, you have the S&P 500 collapsing, well beyond the lower boundary on the Bollinger Band chart—indicative of massive selling. Just a few moments ago, the third ingredient came into play. CBOE's volatility index [sometimes a market barometer of fear] is 40.65 percent [average is about half that level]. Waves of panic selling are crashing down on the market. This kind of selling climax will produce a rally of dramatic proportions. It is the perfect selling storm! I'm getting long the E-Mini S&P 500 at 1100.00."

Prophetic words indeed. The market that day stabilized, and then a final wave (for now) of selling took the market down nearly 400 points. But in the last few hours, it began clawing its way back from a 400-point deficit and closed down only 98 points on the day. Within three trading days, the S&P was 70 points higher and the Dow 700 points higher than they were at the moment of the Gnome's phone call. Exhibit 10.7 shows a chart of two of the three indicators.

This example culls three popular indicators together in one trade. On that day, each reading on its own would have been a good indicator that the selling had hit its peak and that the market was overdue for a rebound.

RSI, or relative strength, is an overbought or oversold indicator that is carried by most technical analysis packages and vendors. There are short-term (intraday) and longer-term RSI readings. RSI readings of 75 or above indicate the market is getting quite overbought and are usually accompanied by several days of strong market advances. During the final phases of the bull market in 1999–2000, readings of 80 or higher were frequent. RSI readings below 25 to 30 are the opposite and

Exhibit 10.7 Hourly S&P 500 Futures with Bollinger Bands and RSI

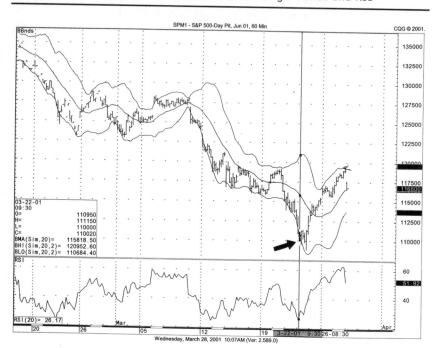

Source: CQG, 2001. Reprinted with permission.

represent weakness in the market. At the extremes—75 and 25 (or 80 and 20 as preferred by some)—the RSI is used as a contrarian indicator. Above 75 or 80 means the market has worked significantly higher and a correction is in order. Below 30 or 25 means the market is oversold and due for a rally, even if it is short term in nature.

CBOE's volatility index, the VIX, normally measures between 18 and 30. As traders become scared that the market may melt down, they run to the options market for protection, usually buying put options (which increase in value when the market declines). The huge demand for puts (and options in general) causes their prices to skyrocket. VIX readings above 35 percent generally indicate some fear in the market. One way to measure this fear is by volatility. Quote vendors and charting packages sometimes offer VIX levels throughout the day. *Barron's Financial* magazine carries it weekly and has some historical VIX data as well. On March 22, the VIX registered 40.65 percent in the late morning—a huge reading and indicative of panicky put buyers. In the past, readings at the 35 to 40 percent level have been excellent indicators of an oversold market on the verge of a rebound. In 1997, 1998 high readings were very accurate. In 2000 we also had good bounces following high readings. March 22, 2001, was the latest high reading that worked quite satisfactorily.

When the Gnome talked about the collapse of the S&P 500, he spoke of the *Bollinger Bands*—which are upper and lower boundaries calculated using statistical standard deviation. Most daily market movements are confined to one or perhaps two standard deviation moves. Bollinger Bands take the current market price and a standard deviation (or two) above and below the current price. Piercing these boundaries is an indicator to some technical analysts of an overbought (if the upper boundary is broke) or oversold (if the lower boundary is broke) condition.

Interestingly, all three of these indicators registered oversold on March 22. To be sure, the market could have continued south, but well placed stop-loss orders would have limited risk. The Gnome's limit was 20 points, for a maximum risk of $1,000 (20 × $50/point = $1,000). Thus, if we declined to 1080.00, he would have been out of the trade.

For those wishing to dig deeper into the world of technical indicators and trading systems that employ them, see the Suggested Reading list at the end of this book.

Strategy 9: Profiting from the "Month-End Bulge": Using the E-Mini S&P 500 or Spiders.

This strategy has proponents and detractors, but the numbers are quite interesting. I first read about it in Yale Hirsch's *Stock Trader's Almanac*, an interesting annual publication loaded with useful statistics. It is referred to as the "Month-End Bulge," with the name deriving from the fact that the market seems to strengthen around the last trading day of the month and into the first few days of the next month. It is a simple long-only mechanical system. You enter the trade at the close of the last trading day of the month. Some use a slight variation and include being in the market on the entire last day. In this variation, you would have to be a buyer at the close on the second to the last day of the month. With either variation, you exit the trade at the close of the fourth trading day of the next month. Exhibit 10.8 shows how the market has behaved over the past few years. In all, there were 26 trades, with 10 losers and 16 winners.

You must be willing to do this over the course of time because there will be times when the strategy fails several months in a row. And like Strategy 8, you must be willing to exit the trade at a predetermined

Exhibit 10.8 Month-End and Beginning-of-the-Month Rallies

	S&P 500 Closing Price, Last day of the Month	S&P 500 Closing Price, Fourth Trading Day of Next Month	Profit/Loss, in Points
January/February	1366.01	1352.22	−13.79
December/January 2001	1320.28	1298.35	−21.93
November/December	1314.95	1351.46	36.51
October/November	1429.40	1432.19	2.79
September/October	1436.51	1436.28	−0.23
August/September	1517.68	1502.51	−15.17
July/August	1430.83	1462.93	32.1
June/July	1454.60	1478.90	24.3
May/June	1420.60	1457.84	37.24
April/May	1452.43	1409.57	−42.86
March/April	1498.58	1501.34	2.76
February/March	1366.42	1391.28	24.86
January/February	1394.46	1424.37	29.91
December/January 2000	1469.25	1403.45	−65.8
November/December	1388.91	1423.33	34.42
October/November	1362.93	1362.64	−0.29
September/October	1282.71	1325.40	42.69
August/September	1320.41	1350.45	30.04
July/August	1341.03	1305.33	−35.7
June/July	1372.71	1395.86	23.15
May/June	1301.84	1327.75	25.91
April/May	1335.00	1332.05	−2.95
March/April	1286.00	1326.89	40.89
February/March	1238.33	1246.64	8.31
January/February	1279.64	1248.49	−31.15
December/January99	1229.23	1269.73	40.5

Note: In the first column, the first month listed is for the month end, and the second is for the beginning of the month.

point (stop-loss order) should a severe decline occur during this time period. Critics complain that the strategy has lost its touch over the past few years and that it has worked only because we have been in a super-bull market and the month-end timing is irrelevant in a major upswing. In my opinion, the strategy is worth at least a look; Exhibit 10.8 shows that it was profitable about two-thirds of the time. As a homework assignment, you could keep an eye on this strategy and map out how it performs in up and down markets. With declines in many of the major averages in early 2001, we could very well see how the system performs in down markets. The nice thing about it is its simplicity, with no need for complex algorithms, spreadsheets, or charts. It would be a great place for a beginner to learn about markets and systems.

SOME TRADING SUGGESTIONS FOR THE NEW E-MINI STOCK INDEX TRADER

Before we move on, a few suggestions are in order. They are the result of hundreds of conversations with traders, large and small, successful and unsuccessful:

- Do your homework. Without the correct facts and thorough analysis, profits will be much more difficult to come by.
- Try not to ask, "Why?" Amateurs ask why the market is moving up or down. Professionals try to profit from the movement and do not care why it is moving.
- Even successful traders are wrong the majority of the time, yet with prudent risk and money management, they can profit handsomely.
- Many traders cannot accept three consecutive losses before losing discipline or giving up.
- "Expert" forecasts are generally not as good as you would think.
- There is not a large correlation between intelligence and success. Brilliant people lose money. It does not take a Mensa-level IQ to profit in this business.
- The vast majority of traders lack discipline and a trading plan.
- Lack of capital, lack of money management, and lack of knowledge are the three top reasons that traders and investors lose money.
- Systematically analyze your past trades. What is the average size of your losing trades? What is the average size of your winning trades? What is the average overall? What is your biggest gain? Biggest loss? You may be able to avoid mistakes by observing your past behaviors.
- Develop mentor relationships if possible. One or two sound principles that you learn from a mentor could be a catalyst for a sound trading plan.
- Learn to trade spreads. They will allow you to profit in up or down markets and also allow you to divorce yourself from the prevailing thought of trying to figure out where the market is heading.

- Keep a diary. You may discover something over time by cataloguing your thoughts and actions.
- Read and filter. Read lots. Much of what you read will prove to be of little use in terms of profitable trading. But every so often you will get an idea that will be a grand slam. I almost never invest or trade off what I read in magazines—and I read many of them. But years ago I read an article on Pfizer's immense pipeline of new drugs. The article made no mention of Viagra at the time. I bought the stock based on a very well-written article. I had doubled my money in a few months—and then Viagra was released, and I doubled it again, all within 18 months. It was one of the single best trades I ever made, and I got the idea from a magazine.
- Keep things on a simple level. Complicated strategies that require too many decisions will be less profitable over time.
- Guard your emotions. Fear and greed are okay to a point. But blind greed caused a lot of people to lose a lot of money during our recent Internet bubble. Fear will cause you to sell out at the bottom or cover shorts at the top. At times this will be unavoidable. But if you make a habit of it, you will not last long in the investing or trading business.

REVIEW QUIZ (PART III)

1. The two main differences between the regular S&P 500 futures and the E-Mini S&P 500 futures are
   a. the underlying index and contract size.
   b. the underlying index and the exchange where they trade.
   c. the contract size and the method or platform of trading.
   d. the number of stocks in the underlying changes from 500 to 100.

2. Futures exchanges play a role in which of the following?
   a. price discovery process   c. stock splits
   b. risk transfer process   d. ETF formation

3. The regular S&P 500 and E-Mini S&P 500 are settled by the
   a. cash-settled process.   c. never settled.
   b. physically delivery process. d. T+3 process.

4. Each day the CME Clearing House pays and collects balances from clearing firms. The firms in turn debit and credit accounts with open futures positions depending on the movement of the futures in question. This process is called

a. initial margin.   c. profit margin.
b. variation margin.   d. loss margin.

5. You can generally trade a futures contract through the same account as you trade stocks. True or false?

6. Which of following applies to the SEC and the CFTC:
   a. SEC regulates securities markets.
   b. CFTC regulates commodities markets.
   c. SEC regulates price levels of commodities.
   d. CFTC regulates price levels of commodities.

7. The regular S&P 500 futures and the E-Mini S&P 500 futures are successful largely because of
   a. a large underlying cash market.
   b. a large pool of speculators.
   c. a large pool of hedgers.
   d. the presence of arbitrage traders and spreaders.

8. Which of the following is true concerning S&P futures and their underlying cash index?
   a. S&P 500 futures generally trade at a premium to the cash index.
   b. S&P 500 futures always trade at a discount to the cash index.
   c. S&P 500 futures do not track the cash index.
   d. S&P 500 futures always trade at parity with the cash index.

9. Which of the following can be said of stock index futures in general?
   a. They trade exactly at their fair value throughout the day.
   b. They trade well above their fair value on holidays.
   c. They trade well below their fair value on holidays.
   d. They trade a little above and below their fair value throughout the day.

10. Which of the following variables will affect the theoretical fair value of a futures contract?
    a. interest rates   c. time to expiration
    b. dividend yields   d. level of cash index

11. Futures contract specifications give information on
    a. delivery or settlement months.
    b. trading hours.
    c. contract and tick size.
    d. how to make money.

12. Convergence in the S&P 500 and E-mini S&P 500 futures usually occurs at
    a. expiration.
    b. election years.
    c. every year.
    d. the end of the age.

13. A trader buys the E-Mini S&P 500 at 1300.00 and sells it 3 weeks later for 1307.00. The trader made a profit of
    a. $1,750.
    b. $1,000.
    c. $350.
    d. $700.

14. The SPY and QQQ trade at the
    a. AMEX.
    b. CBOT.
    c. CME.
    d. DNA.

15. Futures can be used for
    a. hedging and speculating.
    b. arbitrage trading.
    c. spread trading.
    d. all of the above.

16. A trader believes that large-cap value stocks will outperform large-cap growth stocks. Which of the following strategies would be appropriate?
    a. Long S&P MidCap 400 futures and short Russell 2000 futures
    b. Long S&P 500/Barra Value futures and short S&P 500/Growth futures
    c. Long S&P 500/Barra Value iShares and short S&P 500/Growth iShares
    d. Long Russell 1000 Value iShares and short Russell 1000 iShares

Part IV

ADVANCED TOPICS
AND THE ROAD AHEAD

Credit: *Grant's Interest Rate Observer*. Reprinted with permission.

11

LONGER-TERM STRATEGIES: ASSET ALLOCATION WITH ETFS

Given the huge volume in ETFs, especially in the S&P 500 Spiders (SPY) and the Nasdaq-100 Index Tracking Stock (QQQ), it is obvious that short-term traders love these products. Unfortunately, one of their greatest attributes, tax efficiency, is largely offset by actively trading these instruments. In my opinion, their greatest strengths will lie in intermediate- to longer-term strategies. Short-term trading can be very lucrative, but it can also be costly in terms of taxable events and transaction costs. For those who trade mostly on a short-term basis, stock index futures are a superior alternative. They are generally cheaper in terms of transaction costs and receive more favorable tax treatment (futures receive 60/40 treatment—60 percent of the gain is treated as favorable long-term capital gain and 40 percent is taxed as ordinary income).

The previous chapters focused mainly on short- to intermediate-term strategies. Our attention now shifts to the long term, where ETFs can be used to construct indexed portfolios that match the budget, risk appetite, and degree of sophistication of any investor. And no discussion of the long term would be complete without the topic of asset allocation, one of the key disciplines practiced by pension funds, mutual funds, and Wall Street institutions for decades and a cornerstone to building long-term portfolios. In fact, years ago, if an investor wanted to implement an asset allocation portfolio that included the major asset classes as well as subclasses such as style investing (such as value and growth indexes), it would have required volumes of capital and substantial contacts on the Street, including execution and trading, custodial and banking relationships, all of which were obviously out of reach of the average investor. ETFs bring this type of institutional class investing right to the front door of *all investors* and therefore make excellent core holdings for longer-term-oriented accounts such as IRAs and 401(k) accounts.

A PRIMER ON ASSET ALLOCATION

Asset allocation is simply a term used to describe the process of how to combine asset classes with different return and risk characteristics. In the broadest terms, there are three asset classes: stocks, bonds, and cash. Some on the Street include real estate and precious metals as asset classes in themselves. Some add entire baskets of commodities, since they tend to have a negative correlation with equities. Still others subdivide stocks into various capitalization groups, such as large-caps, mid-caps and small-caps (and some go even deeper into the value and growth classifications). The market timers (those who try to predict market tops and bottoms and invest accordingly) have even entered the world of asset allocation and have tried to switch among asset classes depending on their outlook. If stocks look cheap relative to bonds, market timers shift assets out of cash and bonds and into stocks. If stocks are expensive relative to fixed-income securities, they shift back into cash or bonds.

As with any other Wall Street discipline or practice, asset allocation has been the subject of much debate. In 1986, the debate was launched when a controversial study concluded that 93.6 percent of the variation in a portfolio's quarterly performance was attributed to its asset mix of stocks, bonds, and cash.[1] Being a stock or bond picker or a market timer was not likely to add value. However, in 1997 a study by William Jahnke drew a vastly different conclusion. Jahnke's study concluded that asset allocation might determine only about 14.6 percent of returns.[2] The quandary grows when you examine the record of one of the greatest portfolio managers of all time, Peter Lynch, who tended to avoid bonds and stuck mainly with stocks. This rendered the question of how to allocate Magellan's mighty assets moot. Nearly everything at the time went into stocks. Ironically, after Lynch's retirement from portfolio management, his Magellan successor, Jeff Vinik, made a huge bet in bonds. Because of this and other reasons, Magellan began to underperform its benchmark, and Vinik left Fidelity to run his own hedge fund (and did quite well).

With the experts differing so widely, what's an investor to do? At the risk of sounding like an economist, I have to respond by saying, "It depends." In the long run, as we will see, stocks have (operative word is *have*—as in the past) outperformed bonds and cash. But during shorter time windows, the situation changes. In October 1987, while equities were imploding, bonds had an enormous rally, and cash did provide a positive rate of return. If you held equities, you lost a lot of money. Now, in hindsight, we know that the decline was only temporary; the market eventually recovered and went on to record highs. But what if you needed cash at some point and you were forced to sell your stocks at lower levels? The haircut would have been painful. In contrast, the holders of bonds and cash had positive returns. But as investors increase their time horizons to 10, 20, 30 or more years, stocks provide superior returns. The best bond fund and best money market fund manager will probably not beat the S&P 500 over the long term. Why, then, do we find so many pension fund and mutual fund portfolios stuffed with these securities? The answer lies in a four-letter word: *risk*. One thing the Street does not refute is that a mix of the three major assets can provide excellent returns while at the same time reducing volatility or risk.

If you perform a side-by-side comparison of the major asset classes, you can understand how phrases like, "Stocks are the best place to be in the long run," became popular. The 28 percent annualized returns in stock prices during the later 1990s certainly add credibility to that school of thought. And no one could forget the "cash is trash" slogan, which has been repeated thousands of times during the historic bull market that saw its beginnings in 1982 when the Dow Jones Industrials stood at 776. Just how well have the three major asset classes performed over time? Exhibit 11.1 shows the record for the period 1980–1999.

Returns on stocks have beaten those of bonds by a healthy margin. But remember that the 1980s and 1990s were extraordinary decades for investors—one of the greatest bull markets in history. Only the

Exhibit 11.1   Performance of Various
Investment Classes, 1980–1999

Stocks	17.88%
Long-term bonds	10.03
U.S. Treasury Bills	6.89

Source: Stocks, Bonds, Bills and Inflation® 2000 Yearbook, ©2000 Ibbotson Associates, Inc. Based on copyrighted works by Ibbotson and Sinquefield. All rights reserved. Used with permission.

1950s showed superior returns. Thus, 20-year returns, while no doubt qualifying as long term, have been skewed considerably by the outsized gains of this roaring bull market. Perhaps a longer time period would be a better gauge. Go back 50 years, and the returns on stocks drop to about 13.6 percent, bonds to 5.6 percent, and cash about 5.1 percent. If you look at the returns on various investment classes for the past seven decades, you will see stocks return 11.3 percent, bonds, 5.1 percent, and cash about 3.8 percent. Returns diminish dramatically when you use longer time periods—time periods that include wars, depressions, financial calamities, and so on. To get a realistic assessment for investment class returns, you must include a time window that includes several economic cycles, including recessions, bear markets, and economic disruptions.

Unfortunately, many investors have grown accustomed to 17 to 20 percent returns in the market (as it has generously provided since 1982). Surveys conducted in the late 1990s revealed that investors came to expect 20 percent returns as if it was their birthright. I remember one 28-year-old being interviewed in a leading investment magazine. He planned on retiring at age 40. The return assumption that he put into his retirement software was 18 percent. In fact, long-term returns are 500 basis points lower. It could happen, but the odds are slim that the next one or two decades will be as gratifying to investors as the previous two were. In fact, this is the perfect time to give a little investment return guidance.

Many newcomers to futures markets have inflated expectations of returns. Some novice investors and futures traders even believe that 100 percent or greater annualized returns are attainable. When I hear inflated expectations such as these, I offer the following responses:

- Long-term returns in the U.S. stock market are in the 10 to 12 percent per year range over the past 70 or so years. The best year in the U.S. stock market over that time was about 55 percent and the worst year was a decline of 43 percent.
- The very best investors in the world have long-term track records (by long term, I mean 30 years) of about 25 to 30 percent per annum.
- Top commodity trading advisers (CTAs) who manage and trade portfolios of futures contracts (rather than stocks) earn returns in the area of 25 to 35 percent annually over the long run. Some have extraordinary years, with triple-digit gains, but the law of mathematics prevents that from happening over the long run. (At 100 percent gains per annum, you would own the GNP of the planet in 10 to 15 years.)

- A very small subset of unknown or largely inaccessible investors and traders actually can do better, but this is not likely to occur over 30 years. It is unlikely you will ever hear about them or gain access to them. For example, Vinod Khosla, a partner in the Venture Capital firm Kleiner Perkins, has a knack for finding Cisco-like companies long before they become successful. Venture capitalists are in on the ground floor—the incubation or seed stage—long before a company goes public. The returns are in the stratosphere on some of their investments. Remember, too, that for every Cisco, there are dozens and dozens of failures.
- Anyone who promises you extraordinary returns over the long run is probably lying. One cold calling broker practically guaranteed 60 percent returns over the next 10 years if I invested with him. I said, "You are that good?" He said, "Yes, and I want to develop a long-term relationship—one that you can trust." I replied, " You can do twice as good as Peter Lynch and Warren Buffett, two of the greatest of all time?" He repeated, "Yes. Now will you open an account?" I said if he would send me the Schedule D section of his 1040 returns for the past 20 years, proving that he attained 60 percent returns, I'd mortgage my house and open an account and convince friends and relatives to do the same. He promptly hung up.

In 2000 and early 2001, many investors learned the painful lesson of "mean reversion"—that stocks do not always go up but eventually revert to the average. Moreover, a decade-by-decade look will reveal that although stocks offer superior long-term returns, they usually do not provide 18 percent returns consistently. Look at Exhibit 11.2 and study how some of the various asset classes have performed during the past 60 to 70 years.

Despite some awareness of the relative potential of stocks, bonds, and cash, investors, especially those who participate in employer-sponsored defined-contribution plans (i.e., 401(k) plans) more often than not will throw their hands up in frustration when it comes to allocating their payroll deductions to the various asset classes. Compounding the problem is the availability of numerous choices in a typical corporate 401(k) plan. The average such plan at a corporation contains eight choices. On a regular basis, my employer conducts educational seminars for its employees regarding its 401(k) plan as well as general retirement investing. One of the most common questions asked is how contributions and existing balances should be allocated among stocks, bonds, and cash. My approach has been to provide information regarding the relative returns of each asset class and, more important, to generate some awareness on the topic of the risks involved. Exhibit 11.2

Exhibit 11.2　Performance of Various Investment Classes, by Decade

	Stocks[a]	Bonds[b]	T-bills
1930s	−0.1%	4.9%	0.6%
1940s	9.2	3.2	0.4
1950s	19.4	−0.1	1.9
1960s	7.8	1.4	3.9
1970s	5.9	5.5	6.3
1980s	17.5	12.6	8.9
1990s	18.2	8.8	4.9
1950–1999	13.6	5.6	5.1
1960–1999	12.2	7.0	6.0

[a]Measured by S&P 500.
[b]Measured by long-term U.S Treasury bonds.
Source: Stocks, Bonds, Bills and Inflation® 2000 Yearbook, ©2000 Ibbotson Associates, Inc. Based on copyrighted works by Ibbotson and Sinquefield. All rights reserved. Used with permission.

gave the returns of each of the major asset classes over the decades, but it does not show what returns would look like if you blended the different investment choices together in various ratios. For instance, how would a portfolio that contained 80 percent stocks, 15 percent bonds, and 5 percent cash have performed over the long run? Would the addition of bonds alter the returns significantly? Would the addition of bonds and/or cash reduce the risk of the portfolio? For some answers, we'll turn to Exhibit 11.3, which gives some historical perspective on how various asset allocation schemes would have performed.

Obviously, a portfolio with 100 percent stocks outperformed all other asset mixes during the 30-year time period by providing a compounded

Exhibit 11.3　Performance of Various Asset Allocations, 1970–1999

Asset Allocation Assumptions (%)					
Stocks	Bonds	Cash	Average Annual Return	Return Best Year	Return Worst Year
100	0	0	13.7%	37.6%	−26.5%
80	15	5	13.0	36.6	−19.1
60	30	10	12.0	29.8	−12.9
40	45	15	10.8	25.7	−6.5
0	100	0	8.9	31.7	−7.7
0	0	100	6.7	14.7	2.9

Source: Schwab Center for Investment Research.

annualized return of 13.7 percent. The best year in that time frame would have shown a gain of 37.6 percent, and the worst year would have shown a loss of 26.5%. Notice though, what occurs when you modify the mix by adding bonds and cash. If you modified the asset mix to 80 percent stocks, 15 percent bonds, and 5 percent cash, your long-term performance hardly suffered. Your annualized gain of 13 percent would have been about 95 percent of the gain in an all-stock portfolio. The best year would have been a still-gratifying 36.6 percent, and the worst year would have seen a decline of 19.1 percent, substantially less than a portfolio with 100 percent stocks. The addition of bonds and cash did not drastically reduce returns, but did reduce the portfolio's risk as measured by worst one-year return. Similarly, if you doubled the amount of bonds and cash and reduced the amount of equities to 60 percent, your portfolio still would have returned a very respectable 12.0 percent over thirty years. In your best year, you would have seen a 29.8 percent return, but your worst year would have shown only a 12.9 percent decline—less than half the worst decline experienced by the all-stock portfolio.

Prudent investment management boils down to getting the best return possible while taking the least amount of risk. Even a portfolio of 40 percent stocks and 60 percent bonds and cash provided the long-term investor with double-digit returns and a worst-year loss of a mere 6.5 percent—yet many investors show a disdain of fixed-income investments. Given the equity returns over the past 20 years, this attraction to stocks is understandable. One negative of having a stable of bonds and cash is that the income generated from such instruments is taxable as ordinary income. Unless these assets are under a tax-deferred umbrella such as an IRA or 401(k) plan, the investor in the 39.6 percent tax bracket faces the prospect of paying a good chunk of T-bill or T-bond interest in taxes. Yet the numbers are compelling. In summary, by adding bonds and perhaps a smattering of cash (via T-bills or other money market instruments), investors have the potential for solid returns in the long run while reducing risk. Remember, too, that past performance is no guarantee of future returns. Stocks could have a horrible decade, as they did in the 1930s, or provide single-digit gains, as they did in the 1960s and 1970s. It is also possible for both stocks and fixed-income instruments to provide subpar results over a given time frame.

Where can you turn to obtain more information and guidance on asset allocation? For starters, you could study how some of the nation's corporate and government pension systems have allocated the assets of their prospective retirees. Pension funds such as CALPERS (California Public Employees Retirement System) and the IBM retirement fund have an enormous fiduciary responsibility to their clientele; the retirement of millions of Americans is in the hands of these kinds of pension institutions. Certainly, there are a few pension funds that find themselves in the unattractive position of being underfunded, meaning that their long-term liabilities (that is, the amount of future payout to retirees) to pensioners exceed the combination of the fund's assets, investment returns, and contributions. These funds will have to make additional generous contributions to shore up their asset-to-liability mismatch to enable dependable long-term payouts. On the opposite side of the spectrum, some pension funds are overfunded and have plenty of assets to pay out pension benefits to retirees.

No matter how a pension's financial picture looks, it is at least worth examining the asset allocation mix of some U.S. pension funds, if only to serve as a template or starting point for the novice. Exhibit 11.4 lists examples. You can also consult the *Money Market Directories* (MMD), a giant reference guide typically available at local libraries, filled with information on investment managers and corporate and public pension plans. Many of the pension plans list the amount of client assets as well as the asset allocation breakdown. *Pensions and Investments*, a money management newspaper, annually lists the largest pension plans in the United States, along with pension and 401(k) plan assets and asset mixes.

It does not take a seasoned investment pro to notice that none of the institutions in Exhibit 11.4 have 100 percent of their assets in stocks. Recall the previous discussion regarding a portfolio with an allocation of 60 percent stocks, 30 percent bonds, and 10 percent cash. Its 12.0 percent return over the past 40 years came with the bonus of reduced volatility or risk. The worst year resulted in a decline of 12.9 percent—less than half that of an all-stock portfolio. It is no coincidence that these and other giant pension funds have about 50 to 70 percent of assets in stocks. The bonds and cash components yield interest payments that equities generally do not match. You can be sure that a significant portion of the equity allocation is also indexed. With billions under their belts, allocation often includes international equities, fixed-income securities, and real estate as well as cash. Fixed-income securities for pension funds are typically U.S. Treasury bonds and notes, corporate bonds, and mortgage-backed securities of varying maturities. Alternative investments cover a wide swath and include investments in hedge funds, private equity, venture capital, derivatives, and commodity indexes. With regard to real estate, most individual investors in the United States invest through REITs—real estate investment trusts. They may also choose from a number of mutual funds that

Exhibit 11.4 Asset Allocation Mix of Selected Pension Plans

California Public Employees' Retirement System (pension)—$171 billion

U.S. equities	44.4%	Real estate	5.1%
International equities	18.9	Cash	0.8
Fixed income	26.4	Other	4.4

Merck & Co. (pension)—$2.6 billion

U.S. equities	57.2%	Real estate	2.9%
International equities	25.4	Cash	1.6
Fixed income	12.8	Other	0.1

IBM Retirement Fund (pension)—$46 billion

U.S. equities	34.1%	Real estate	5.1%
International equities	20.0	Other	7.5
Fixed income	33.3		

Johnson & Johnson (pension)—$3.5 billion

U.S. equities	56.9%	Real estate	0.2%
International equities	17.5	Cash	0.3
Fixed income	22.6	Other	2.5

New York State Teachers' Retirement System (pension)—$90 billion

U.S equities	61.7%	Cash	1.8%
International equities	9.3	Real estate	3.9
Fixed income	19.0	Other	4.3

SBC Communications (pension)—$45 billion

U.S equities	54%	Cash	2%
International equities	14	Real estate	1
Fixed income	23	Other	6

Motorola Inc. (pension)—$ 4 billion

U.S. equities	61%	Fixed income	24%
International equities	14	Cash	1

United Parcel Service (pension)—$8.5 billion

U.S. equities	52.2%	Cash	5.0%
Foreign equities	20.9	Real estate	4.3
Fixed income	15.0	Other	2.6

Teamsters Pension Trust, Western Conference (pension)—$23.8 billion

U.S. equities	42.3%	Real estate	4.7%
Fixed income	49.1	Other	3.3
Cash	0.6		

Note: Data as of September 30, 2000, except United Parcel Service (June 6, 2000) and Teamsters (July 31, 2000).

Sources: Special Report: The Largest Pension Funds, *Pensions and Investments*, January 22, 2001.

invest in a diversified portfolio of REITs. With pension funds, though, they have huge amounts of capital to invest and often invest directly in real estate. Many large office buildings are owned or financed by pension funds.

The financial press regularly writes on the topic of asset allocation and can be a good source of information on the topic. Indeed, the *Wall Street Journal* frequently catalogues the asset allocation recommendations of all the major firms in the United States and compares their performance with one another, as well as key benchmarks. *Investment Advisor* magazine has devoted portions of issues on the topic and publishes the opinions of many well-known Street strategists. For example, in early 2001, A. Marshall Acuff from Salomon Smith Barney recommended that 65 percent of investors' capital be allocated to stocks, 30 percent to bonds, and 5 percent to cash. Tom Galvin, from Donaldson Lufkin & Jenrette (recently acquired by Credit Suisse First Boston), recommended 90 percent stocks, 0 percent bonds, and 10 percent cash.[3]

Given the results of studies outlined in Exhibit 11.3 and the investment philosophy of pension fund sponsors that control several trillion dollars in assets, there seems to be life beyond stocks. Fixed-income securities, cash, and alternative investments can add diversity that some portfolios lack. When the market lags or even declines, as it did in 2000, bonds and cash clearly add to the total return of a portfolio and provide an income stream that many investors should consider. The reduction in overall portfolio volatility is also another reason for diversity. There are, however, some investors who appear to have only 100 percent stocks *or* only 100 percent bonds or cash. Many individuals who lived through the Great Depression have an understandable aversion to owning stocks, since the severe market decline caused vast amounts of wealth to be wiped out in the 1930s. Some of the progeny of the depression era also have been taught that caution pays, and thus they avoid equities. On the other hand, with markets marching ever upward in the past 20 years, a new generation of investors has learned that stocks are the only way to go and to be anything but fully invested in the stock market will result in a less-than-adequate nest egg 30 or 40 years down the road. In fact, I've spoken to many people in their 30s in recent years, and one of their greatest fears is not having enough to spend when they retire. Given that younger investors have three or four decades of compounding working in their favor, there is a lot of time to make up for those inevitable periods of negative returns and for those with less of an appetite for risk, obtaining good returns is certainly possible without having 100 percent of your nest egg in stocks.

COMBINING ETFS WITH TRADITIONAL MUTUAL FUNDS

To achieve a desired asset allocation, ETFs can play an important foundation. But as of March 2001, there were only three ETFs that covered the real estate sector and only one fixed-income ETF (although more are on the way). Hence, investors will have to combine ETFs (on domestic, global, and international equities) with traditional mutual funds (or other investments) to match some of the strategies employed by pension funds and other investment managers. For example, an investor with $10,000 could allocate an investment as follows: $6,000 invested in S&P 500 SPDRs (SPY), $3,000 invested in Vanguard Long Term Bond fund, and $1,000 invested in 3- or 6-month T-bills or money market funds. This strategy combines 60 percent stock exposure with 30 percent bonds and 10 percent cash, a strategy not unlike that of thousands of pension funds worldwide. It is easy to execute and requires a sum of capital attainable by many investors. It combines one of the most liquid and tax-efficient indexed ETFs with a low-cost bond fund (Vanguard's fixed-income bond funds charge roughly 25 basis points annually) and a money market fund. For investors who are attracted to other fund families such as Fidelity or Janus, almost any asset allocation strategy imaginable can be executed by combining ETFs with funds from these investment companies as well. Many of Wall Street's biggest firms on the full-service and discount sides of the fence also offer fund supermarkets. Hence, your ETF holdings and your mutual fund holdings will be consolidated on one statement for convenience.

CORE-SATELLITE APPROACH TO ASSET ALLOCATION

The one (and the only) drawback to indexing is that the indexed investor will never really hit what I refer to as a grand slam: triple-digit gains in a 12-month period. The only way you'll hit a grand slam is if the index itself has a stellar year. Since the mid-1920s, the S&P 500 has seen calendar returns in the 50 percent area during two years. It has also experienced 30 to 40 percent annual returns in about 20 of the past 75 years. Most pundits in finance regard a 30 percent return for a 12-month period as stellar. The Nasdaq-100 returned 85 percent in 1999, and many sectors showed triple-digit gains over recent years. And some active managers (stock pickers) have attained results several times greater than the S&P 500 in a given year. The 1999 return for Munder Net-Net fund was 176 percent. Returns like this simply do not occur in indexing on a year-to-year basis. And investors, even die-hard indexers, love to pick stocks sometimes. They all want to find the "next Cisco or Microsoft" at least once. Other proponents of active stock picking point to Warren Buffett, the second richest man in the United States, and exclaim that he does not index (although he tells others to index). Can indexing peacefully co-exist with active management under one roof? Or will an ill-fated love affair between passive and active management result?

Investors, especially large institutions, have shown that the two can coexist. The strategy is known as the *core-satellite approach* to investing. Core-satellite is an investment philosophy whose goal is to minimize the risk of lagging the market while at the same time trying to outperform it with a portion of the investor's assets. The strategy attempts to blend the benefits of indexing while retaining the potential of outperforming the market with some strategically placed, actively managed investments. This may seem like a huge contradiction given the arguments I put forth in Chapter 1. In addition, the jury is still out on how well the strategy has done. But large pension funds and endowment funds in the United States have recently implemented core-satellite approaches. The core portion of the strategy consists of indexing. Surrounding the core are satellites of active stock picking, accomplished through mutual funds or investing in individual stocks. Exhibit 11.5 portrays how a typical core-satellite strategy would look.

Exhibit 11.5   Core-Satellite Approach

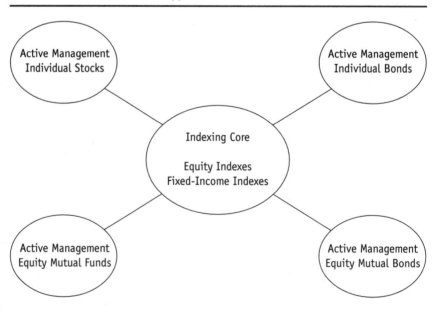

Active Management
Individual Stocks

Active Management
Individual Bonds

Indexing Core

Equity Indexes
Fixed-Income Indexes

Active Management
Equity Mutual Funds

Active Management
Equity Mutual Bonds

How much of a portfolio should consist of core and how much satellite is up to the investment policy guidelines of the pension fund. For individual investors, it all depends on how much risk they are willing to accept and how much they agree with the philosophy of indexing. Some financial institutions advocate indexing for at least 50 percent of assets while allocating the remaining assets to strategically chosen active funds. While *core-satellite* is a term that usually pertains to equity investing, the strategy is perfectly appropriate for fixed-income investing too. Similarly, many investors index a portion of a bond portfolio to one of several well-known bond indexes while investing in individual fixed-income securities or by using a mutual fund that actively picks bonds or other fixed-income instruments.

In short, asset allocation can be accomplished in many ways. The investor can pick individual stocks, bonds, and money market instruments or accomplish the same through actively managed equity and fixed-income mutual funds. But at the heart of many asset allocation schemes lies the powerful tool of indexing. As each year passes, more and more dollars are drawn toward the indexing revolution. With ETFs based on dozens of popular broad-based and style indexes, those dollar flows should continue. Given all the attributes of ETFs and their meteoric rise to date, there is no doubt that ETFs will make their way into the asset allocation strategies of millions of investors' portfolios as either a pure play in indexing or an integral part of a core-satellite strategy.

ASSET ALLOCATION AND REBALANCING

Suppose that at the beginning of the year you had invested $2,000 in stocks and $1,000 in bonds, for an asset mix of 67 percent stocks and 33 percent bonds. Let's further assume that you wanted to maintain approximately that mix (67/33). If during the year stocks provided a total return of 30 percent and bonds provided a total return of zero, your asset mix would be altered. Under this scenario, your $2,000 stock investment would now be worth $2,600, and the bond portion would remain at $1,000. Total assets would stand at $3,600. The appreciation in the equity portfolio lifted the equity percentage to about 72 percent and decreased the fixed-income portion to 28 percent. Although this is not a significant deviation from the previous 67/33 allocation, continued strength in equities relative to bonds would drive the mix out of kilter further. Hence, you might wish to consider rebalancing your asset mix. You would merely have to sell enough equities and use the proceeds to purchase bonds to restore the original mix. Large pension funds keep their asset mix in well-defined target ranges. If a particular asset exceeds its target allocation, rebalancing is required. This is accomplished as a risk management measure so that stocks do not become too large a percentage of the overall portfolio.

ASSET ALLOCATION IN ACTION: SAMPLE PORTFOLIOS

The sample portfolios that follow offer a glimpse into the art of asset allocation. One of the many fabulous advantages of asset allocation is flexibility. A portfolio can be tailor-made according to the amount of investment capital and the risk appetite of the individual or institution. If being 100 percent invested in stocks keeps you awake at night, you merely need to balance your portfolio with less risky assets such as bonds or cash. Given the 100 ETFs in existence, the thousands of mutual funds, as well as access to U.S. Treasury securities, the sheer number of combinations is virtually endless. I have provided a dozen or so here. One of my favorites is shown in Exhibit 11.14: the low cost–low maintenance growth portfolio, with an annual cost under .10 percent. The cost for initial implementation is also low relative to the asset base. In the days of on-line and discounted commissions, the transaction cost on $90,000 worth of S&P 500 iShares (or the SPY version) is minimal and over time would not add appreciably to this low-budget (but high-quality) offering. Even if it was transacted through a full-service broker and held for the long haul, the costs would easily be lower than assembling a basket of large-cap stocks and lower than just about any large-cap mutual fund. Commissions, whether discounted or full service will also be magnified, sometimes dramatically, in smaller portfolios such as the $1,000 example in Exhibit 11.6. Economies of scale apply to the individual as well as the titans on Wall Street. It is likely you will have greater sums to invest in the future as your income and financial situation improve over time. To a 22-year-old college graduate, $1,000 might as well be a billion. But when the first job comes along and the cash starts to come, $1,000 no longer seems like a distant dream. As you invest increasingly larger sums, the transaction costs in creating many of these portfolios drops dramatically. So grab a legal pad and pencils, and start sketching. While concocting your optimum allocation mix, ask yourself a few questions and make a few assumptions.

Let's say you have $10,000 to invest. How much can you afford to lose? Five percent? Ten percent? Twenty percent or more? If the $10,000 was worth only $9,000 in a year, how would you react? (This is exactly what would have occurred if your $10,000 was invested in the

S&P 500 during the year 2000.) And what if your $10,000 was worth $5,500 after two years? This actually happened in 1973–1974 when the Arab oil embargo, recession, and some bad economic policies caused the market to have its worst decline since the Great Depression. Then determine whether you could weather the declines knowing that perhaps over the next 5, 10, or 20 years, the market could be dramatically higher. It has been said that if you do not know yourself, the stock market can be an awfully expensive place to find out who you are. If you loathe losing money or cannot afford to lose money you have, the stock market should not be your prime consideration.

A couple I knew were given $20,000 for a down payment on a house by some well-to-do relatives. They were going to buy the house within six months and asked me if they should park it in the stock market until the closing. I said that would entail taking risks and that they might actually lose money—lots of money—and then not be able to buy their house. The stock market could be higher in three years *and* lower in six months. The husband wanted to put the whole wad in Qualcomm (I cringed!); the wife wanted to put it in CDs or a money fund. I sided with the wife. The husband had little choice (the $20,000 came from the wife's side of the family), so they settled for 6.5 percent risk free. I ran into the couple after their purchase (they seemed happy) and noted that a $20,000 investment in Qualcomm would now be worth less than $10,000 and that it had been a good idea to go with the more conservative investment given their time horizon. They saw it as a valuable lesson in risk versus reward. (Interestingly, if this conversation had taken place in 1999, $20,000 invested in Qualcomm would have grown to $250,000—and I would have looked like a moron.) Similarly, a couple with $500,000 in assets who are two years away from retirement would be foolish to allocate a gigantic portion of their nest egg—one they worked an entire lifetime to accumulate—to a risky asset like stocks.

How do you feel about taxes? Large helpings of bonds and cash throw off interest that is taxed at less-than-favorable rates unless they are part of a portfolio that is under a tax-deferred umbrella such 401(k) accounts, IRAs, or tax-free status such as enjoyed by Roth IRA participants. But on the other hand, they can help reduce risk. Bonds too have had some respectable returns depending on which era you study.

In the stock market and commodity markets there is a practice referred to as *paper trading*—investing hypothetically in a variety of stocks or certain futures contracts. You can try this with asset allocation as well. Put together a portfolio, or a few portfolios, and monitor their performance over the course of a few weeks or months. How did your mix perform in rising markets? In falling markets? Did lower interest rates help or hinder your portfolio? You can even create some friendly competition between you and your spouse (but in the end, when you finally invest, you must both be on the same page—trust me on this one). The only negative with simulated portfolios or paper trading is that no real money is at risk. Losing 10 percent of your invested hypothetical capital is painful only to one's ego. Losing a few thousand of real cash and knowing that the Hawaiian vacation is on hold or canceled is painful mentally and economically.

You cannot get a real handle on your own risk tolerance until you actually invest. At the very least, you will learn a lot. Investing, by either indexing with ETFs or picking your own stocks and funds, will teach you about business and economics. You will learn as much about businesses from a few years of investing in the stock market as you would taking classes at a business school.

When you have asked dozens of questions or perhaps sought out the help of a trusted professional, it will be time to write some checks. This could prove quite revealing. How is your nervous quotient? Did the 35 percent decline in the Nasdaq-100 in 2000 give you an ulcer or serve to drive you and maybe your spouse into depression? Better lighten up on the QQQs then. Did a lack of cash on hand cause you to miss some opportunities during the market decline in 2000? Keeping 5 percent or more cash on hand might help avoid that situation in the future. And remember most of all, no asset allocation is permanently etched in granite. If you are not happy with it, change it! Professional investors change their mix. Some do it frequently; some fine-tune once every year or so. Others, like Warren Buffett, hold their investments for decades. (Buffett has sold some holdings over the years, but his core portfolio remains largely unchanged.) Imagine all the taxes and fees saved by his low-turnover strategy. No wonder the guy is so rich. (See Exhibits 11.6 through 11.17 for sample portfolios.) Also, investors may wish to check out www.foliofn.com. This site offers a service that allows one to build portfolios or stocks in dollar amounts. They currently offer this service with about 50 ETFs.

"Our favorite holding period is forever."

—Warren Buffett

Exhibit 11.6   Asset Allocation: $1,000 Sample Portfolio—Aggressive Growth

Asset Allocation

Stocks 100%

ETF or Other Investment	Sector/Market	Amount Invested	Percentage of Portfolio	Expense Ratio
S&P 500 Depositary Receipts (SPY)	Large-cap	$1,000	100	0.12%
Can substitute: *Russell 1000 iShares*				
Total size of portfolio		$1,000	100	

Overall asset mix		Equity Capitalization Mix	
Stocks	100%	Large-cap	100%
Bonds	0%	Mid-cap	0%
Cash	0%	Small-cap	0%

This simple one-ETF portfolio can be added to over time. It is also very tax efficient. The holder of this portfolio would be exposed to the volatility of the U.S. stock market, but with 30 or more years to retirement, there is plenty of time to make up for any inevitable bear markets. The commission will be a high percentage of the total assets, common in a portfolio with a smaller base. Overtime, the asset base will increase, and annual expenses as a percentage of the portfolio will drop markedly.

Risk (5 = high risk, 0 = T-bills)	4.25
Estimated of tax burden (if not in tax-deferred account)	Very low
Appropriate age bracket for this asset mix	20–35

Exhibit 11.7 Asset Allocation: $5,000 Sample Portfolio—Growth

ETF or Other Investment	Sector/Market	Amount Invested	Percentage of Portfolio	Expense Ratio
S&P 500 Depositary Receipts (SPY)	Large-cap	$2,000	40	0.12%
Russell 2000 iShares (IWM)	Small-cap	2,000	40	0.20%
U.S. Treasury note (5- or 10-year maturity)	Fixed income	1,000	20	0.00%

	Total size of portfolio	$5,000

Overall Asset Mix		Equity Capitalization Mix	
Stocks	80%	Large-cap	40%
Fixed-Income	20%	Mid-cap	0%
Cash	0%	Small-cap	40%

This portfolio is similar to that in Exhibit 11.6 in that long-term growth is the objective. We now add a layer of small-cap exposure as well as a fixed-income component. The 80 percent equity exposure is not overly aggressive but could provide solid returns in a rising market. The 5- or 10-year Treasury notes will provide a good return should interest rates drop and throw off cash flow in terms of interest payments that will help dampen any downside swings in the stock market. U.S. Treasury notes can be bought directly from the U.S. Treasury (Bureau of Public Debt) after setting up a Treasury Direct account. There are no fees or commissions when purchasing U.S. Treasuries through a Treasury Direct account.

Overall risk (5 = high risk, 0 = T-bills)	4.0
Estimated of tax burden (if not in tax-deferred account)	Low
Appropriate age bracket for this asset mix	25–40

Exhibit 11.8   Asset Allocation: $7,500 Sample Portfolio—Very Aggressive Growth

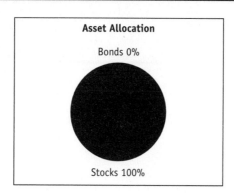

Asset Allocation

Bonds 0%

Stocks 100%

ETF or Other Investment	Sector/Market	Amount Invested	Percentage of Portfolio	Expense Ratio
S&P 500 Depositary Receipts (SPY)	Large-cap	$2,500	33	0.12%
Russell 2000 iShares (IWM)	Small-cap	2,500	33	0.20%
Nasdaq-100 Index Shares (QQQ)	Fixed income	2,500	33	0.18%
Total size of portfolio		$7,500		

Overall asset mix		Equity Capitalization Mix	
Stocks	100%	Large-cap	66%
Bonds	0%	Mid-cap	0%
Cash	0%	Small-cap	33%

This very aggressive portfolio would provide great potential on the upside, but would entail risk. In 2000, this portfolio would have been down significantly, but in the prior five years would have rewarded the investor handsomely. The QQQ shares would give additional large-cap exposure but heavily tilted toward technology, telecom, and biotech. Remember that the S&P 500 SPDRs have a 20 percent weighting in technology too. Not for the timid—but for the individual who believes technology will recover from its 2000-2001 doldrums and lead the way in the future.

Risk (5 = high risk, 0 = T-bills)	4.5
Estimated of tax burden (if not in tax-deferred account)	Very low (depending on Russell Index rebalancing)
Appropriate age bracket for this asset mix	25–35

Exhibit 11.9 Asset Allocation: $7,500 Sample Portfolio—Value Tilt

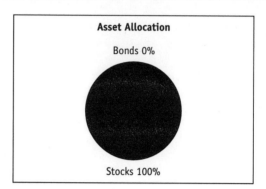

ETF or Other Investment	Sector/Market	Amount Invested	Percentage of Portfolio	Expense Ratio
S&P 500 Depositary Receipts (SPY)	Large-cap	$2,500	33	0.12%
S&P MidCap/Barra Value iShares	Mid-cap value	2,500	33	0.25%
S&P SmallCap/Barra Value iShares	Small-cap value	2,500	33	0.25%
Can substitute Russell 2000 Value iShares for the small cap portion				

Total size of portfolio $7,500

Overall asset Mix		Equity Capitalization Mix	
Stocks	100%	Large-cap	33%
Bonds	0%	Mid-cap	33%
Cash	0%	Small-cap	33%

This portfolio has a tilt toward the value school of investing. If sky-high P.E. ratios and price-to-book ratios give you the shakes, then it's time to load up on value. Value investing provides a nice refuge when storms hit, as they did in 2000. Most value indexes beat their growth counterparts by a wide margin in 2000. The S&P 500, MidCap 400, and SmallCap Value stood more than 20 full percentage points above their growth counterparts in performance.

Risk (5 = high risk, 0 = T-bills)	4.0+
Estimated of tax-burden (if not in tax-deferred account)	Low
Appropriate age bracket for this asset mix	25–35

Exhibit 11.10   Asset Allocation: $10,000 Sample Portfolio—Growth and International

Asset Allocation

Fixed Income 20%

International Stocks 20%

U.S. Stocks 60%

ETF or Other Investment	Sector/Market	Amount Invested	Percentage of Portfolio	Expense Ratio
S&P 500 Depositary Receipts (SPY)	Large-cap	$ 2,000	20	0.12%
S&P MidCap 400 SPDR (MDY)	Mid-cap	2,000	20	0.25%
Russell 2000 iShares (IWM)	Small-cap	2,000	20	0.20%
S&P Europe 350 Large Cap iShares	International	2,000	20	0.60%
U.S. Treasury notes or bonds	fixed income	2,000	20	0.00%

Total size of portfolio	$10,000	

Overall Asset Mix		Equity Capitalization Mix	
U.S. stocks	60%	Large-cap	40%
International stocks	20%	Mid-cap	20%
Fixed income	20%	Small-cap	20%

This is a fairly aggressive portfolio with exposure in large-, mid-, and small-cap stocks. The international component adds two more dimensions of risk: overseas stock markets and currency risk. The rewards of investing internationally have been well documented, but investors must understand the risks involved with crossing the Atlantic.

Risk (5 = high risk, 0 = T-bills)	4.25
Estimated tax burden (if not in tax-deferred account)	Low
Appropriate age bracket for this asset mix	25–35

Exhibit 11.11   Asset Allocation: $10,000 Sample Portfolio—Moderate Growth

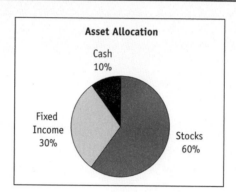

ETF or Other Investment	Sector/Market	Amount Invested	Percentage of Portfolio	Expense Ratio
S&P 500 Depositary Receipts (SPY)	Large-cap	$ 3,000	30	0.12%
Russell 3000 iShares (IWV)	Total Market	3,000	30	0.20%
U.S Treasury notes (5- or 10-year maturity	Fixed income	3,000	30	0.00%
U.S. Treasury bills (3-month to 1-year)	Cash	1,000	10	0.00%

Total size of portfolio $10,000

Overall Asset Mix		Equity Capitalization Mix	
Stocks	60%	Large-cap	30%
Fixed Income	30%	Total Market	30%*
Cash	10%		

*Russell 3000 includes all segments of market capitalization.

This portfolio is for investors not willing to take the risks that accompany a growth or aggressive growth portfolio. On the fixed-income side, investor could potentially boost income by purchasing shares in an indexed corporate/government bond fund such as the Vanguard Total Bond Market Index fund. Its annual management fee is only 20 basis points, and it is designed to track the Lehman Brothers aggregate bond index. With 60 percent exposure to equities, the portfolio should produce good long-term gains without being subject to the violent draw-downs of more aggressive offerings.

Risk (5 = high risk, 0 = T-bills)	3.5
Estimated tax burden (if not in tax-deferred account)	Medium+
Appropriate age bracket for this asset mix	35-50 (or younger if risk averse)

Exhibit 11.12   Asset Allocation: $25,000 Sample Portfolio—Balanced

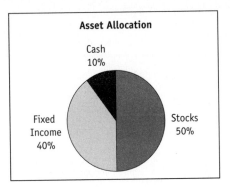

Asset Allocation

Cash 10%

Fixed Income 40%

Stocks 50%

ETF or Other Investment	Sector/Market	Amount Invested	Percentage of Portfolio	Expense Ratio
S&P 500 Depositary Receipts (SPY)	Large-cap	$ 7,500	30	0.12%
iShares Dow Jones U.S. Real Estate Index fund	REIT sector	2,500	10	0.60%
Utilities Select Sector SPDRs	Utilities sector	2,500	10	0.28%
U.S Treasury notes (5- or 10-year maturity)	Fixed Income	10,000	40	0.00%
U.S. Treasury bills (3-month to 1-year)	Cash	2,500	10	0.00%

Total size of portfolio $25,000

Overall Asset Mix		Equity Capitalization Mix	
Stocks	50%	Large-cap	30%
Fixed income	40%	Sector	20%
Cash	10%		

If you have ever invested in a total return or balanced mutual fund and took a close look at the portfolio, you would notice the presence of utility stocks, real estate investment trusts (REITS), bonds, and a dollop of cash. While income generation is significant in this portfolio, exposure to the S&P 500, as well as REITS and utilities, provide the opportunity for longer term gain as well. Beware though: This portfolio will generate taxable income unless it is in a tax-sheltered account. SSGA also offers a REIT ETF, called the street-TRACKS Wilshire REIT Index. BGI recently launched an iShare product based on the Cohen and Steers REIT.

Risk (5 = high risk, 0 = T-bills)	2.5
Estimated tax burden (if not in tax-deferred account)	High
Appropriate age bracket for this asset mix	50+ (as retirement nears percentage of stocks decreases)

Exhibit 11.13 Asset Allocation: $50,000 Sample Portfolio—Growth and Small- and Mid-Cap Tilt

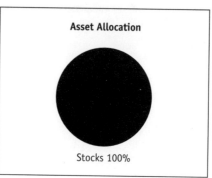

ETF or Other Investment	Sector/Market	Amount Invested	Percentage of Portfolio	Expense Ratio
S&P 500 Depositary Receipts (SPY)	Large-cap	$10,000	20	0.12%
S&P MidCap 400 SPDR (MDY)	Mid-cap	20,000	40	0.25%
Russell 2000 iShares (IWM)	Small-cap	20,000	40	0.20%
	Total size of portfolio	$50,000		

Overall Asset Mix		Equity Capitalization Mix	
Stocks	100%	Large-cap	20%
Fixed income	0%	Mid-cap	40%
Cash	0%	Small-cap	40%

This portfolio is for investors attracted to small and midsize companies. The S&P 500 forms a basic core index that is then overlaid with small- and mid-capitalization exposure. This portfolio should also prove to be tax efficient, although the MidCap SPDRs had some rather large distributions in their history (see Chapter 15.) Although few under the age of 30 have portfolios in the $50,000 range, for who that do, the growth potential of smaller companies and the compounding effect of three or more decades could put this portfolio in the seven-figure club. (If the Russell and MidCap indexes can return 11 percent over the next 30 years, this mix will grow to $1,144,614.)

Risk (5 = high risk, 0 = T-bills)	4.25
Estimated tax burden (if not in tax-deferred account)	Very low to low (depending on Russell index rebalancing)
Appropriate age bracket for this asset mix	25–35

Exhibit 11.14   Asset Allocation: $100,000 Sample Portfolio—Low-Cost and Low-Maintenance Growth

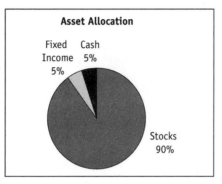

ETF or Other Investment	Sector/Market	Amount Invested	Percentage of Portfolio	Expense Ratio
S&P 500 iShares (IVV)	Large-cap	$90,000	90	0.09%
U.S. Treasury notes or bonds	Fixed income	5,000	5	0.00%
U.S Treasury bills (3-month to 1-year)	Cash	5,000	5	0.00%

Total size of portfolio	$100,000	

Overall Asset Mix		Equity Capitalization Mix	
Stocks	90%	Large-cap	90%
Fixed income	5%	Mid-cap	0%
Cash	5%	Small-cap	0%

This portfolio is designed for the investor who has begun to accumulate some substantial wealth; it is incredibly low cost—as close to free as you will ever see. Nine basis points for the equity portion is a management fee usually available only to institutions. The S&P 500 SPDR is only 3 basis points more expensive. The U.S. Treasury securities can be purchased for free. And if time is money, then you will save even more, as this is a low-maintenance mix that will not require you to scour over research reports; a myriad of statements and the typical paperwork burdens of a $100,000 or greater portfolio.

Risk (5 = high risk, 0 = T-bills)	4.0
Estimated tax burden (if not in tax-deferred account)	Low
Appropriate age bracket for this asset mix	25–35

Exhibit 11.15 Asset Allocation: $100,000 Sample Portfolio—Playing the Age Wave

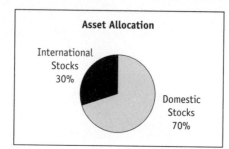

ETF or Other Investment	Sector/Market	Amount Invested	Percentage of Portfolio	Expense Ratio
Pharmaceutical HOLDRS (PPH)	Drugs/health	$20,000	20	NA
Financial Select Sector SPDRs (XLF)	Banks/ brokerage	20,000	20	0.28%
Biotechnology HOLDRS (BBH)	Biotech	20,000	20	NA
Nasdaq 100 Index Shares (QQQ)	Tech	10,000	10	0.18
iShares MSCI Taiwan	Country	10,000	10	0.99
iShares MSCI Singapore	Country	10,000	10	0.84
iShares MSCI Hong Kong	Country	10,000	10	0.84

Total size of portfolio $100,000

Overall Asset Mix		Equity Capitalization Mix	
Domestic stocks	70%	Large-cap	NA
International stocks	30%	Mid-cap	NA
Cash	0%	Small-cap	NA

This is for those who want to play the aging baby boomer market. The theory goes something like this: As the boomers age, they will accumulate more assets, and this benefits the brokerage and banking industry. And the older they become, the more likely they will need drugs and health-care items. Biotechnology, according to the experts, will contribute to the medical advances that the boomers will experience. As for the overseas portion, Asia has a large boomer generation itself, with a population many times the size of that of the United States. This is a very concentrated portfolio that will experience incredible volatility. But if the demographers are correct, the rewards could be huge.

Risk (5 = high risk, 0= T-bills)	5.0 (emerging markets and sectors make it high risk)
Estimated tax burden (if not in tax-deferred account)	Very low
Appropriate age bracket for this asset mix	30+ (as demographics will take decades to play out)

Exhibit 11.16   Asset Allocation: $5,000 Sample Portfolio—Growth and College Savings

Asset Allocation

Stocks 100%

ETF or Other Investment	Sector/Market	Amount Invested	Percentage of Portfolio	Expense Ratio
Russell 3000 iShares (IWV)	Total market	$5,000	100%	0.20%
Or substitute S&P 500 (SPY), Russell 1000 iShares (IWB) or Vanguard's VIPER (VTI)				

	Total size of portfolio	$5,000

Overall Asset Mix		Equity Capitalization Mix	
Stocks	100%	Large-cap	total market
Fixed income	0%	Mid-cap	total market
Cash	0%	Small-cap	total market

If the overall market returns 10 percent over the next eighteen years, this sum could grow to $27,799—not a bad start on paying for college.

Risk (5 = high risk, 0 = T-bills)	4.0
Estimated tax burden (if not in tax-deferred account)	Low (depending on Russell index rebalancing)
Appropriate age bracket for this asset mix	NA (18 years maximum time per child)

Exhibit 11.17 Asset Allocation: $50,000 Sample Portfolio—Core-Satellite
Portfolio

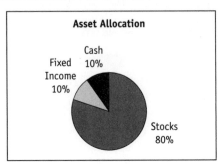

ETF or Other Investment	Sector/Market	Amount Invested	Percentage of Portfolio	Expense Ratio
S&P 500 SPDRs (SPY)	Large-cap	$25,000	50	0.12%
Legg Mason Value Trust	Large-cap (value)	5,000	10	1.68%
Liberty Acorn	Small-cap (growth)	5,000	10	0.85%
Berkshire Hathaway Class B shares	NA	5,000	10	NA
Vanguard Long Term U.S. Treasury Bond Fund	Fixed income	2,500	5	0.28%
Northeast Investors Trust	High-yield bond	2,500	5	0.61%
U.S. Treasury bills (3-month to 1-year)	Cash	5,000	10	0.00%

	Total size of portfolio	$50,000

Overall Asset Mix		Equity Capitalization Mix	
Stocks	80%	Large-cap	70%
Fixed income	10%	Mid-cap	0%
Cash	10%	Small-cap	10%

We all like to try to pick winning stocks and mutual funds. The core-satellite approach gives a taste of both worlds: indexing and active stock and fund picking. The core of this portfolio is the popular benchmark, the S&P 500. Surrounding the core are five active satellites consisting of some of the best management that money can buy (notice the higher annual management fees on the active funds). Bill Miller's Legg Mason fund is one of the few that consistently beats the S&P. Ralph Wanger, who runs the Acorn funds, is one of the premier small-cap investors. And 10 percent of the portfolio is in Warren Buffett's holding company, Berkshire Hathaway. Buffett is the best long-term investor in history. Northeast Investors Trust is a high-yield bond fund that has an excellent long-term record and complements the U.S. Treasury bond fund.

Risk (5 = high risk, 0 = T-bills)	3.75
Estimated tax burden (if not in tax-deferred account)	Medium
Appropriate age bracket for this asset mix	30–40

BUYING FIXED-INCOME SECURITIES ON THE CHEAP

Some of the sample portfolios in Exhibits 11.6 through 11.17 had fixed-income components comprising mainly long-term U.S. Treasury bonds or intermediate-term maturity U.S. Treasury notes. (The cash portion of some portfolios consisted of short-term U.S. Treasury bills, but bank certificates of deposit or money market funds would suffice.) You could substitute bond mutual funds that invest in U.S Treasuries, but it is likely you would be better off investing directly in these instruments, primarily because of costs and safety. Remember that costs have a huge impact on investment performance. With the much lower total returns generally available through bonds, high costs become an even greater burden, along with an already high tax burden, because interest on fixed-income securities is taxed as income and generally not subject to favorable capital gains rates. A quick glance at the Morningstar data on U.S. government bond funds shows that the average expense ratio for U.S. government bond funds is 108 basis points per year, and the average portfolio turnover for U.S. government bond funds is 155 percent per year. With government bond yields in the 5 to 6 percent area as of early 2001, a 108-basis-point cost is simply unacceptable. And after taxes and inflation, much of the return of these funds is exhausted.

In Part I, I discussed at length how difficult it is for the typical actively managed equity mutual fund to beat the S&P 500 over the long run. The same studies have been run on bond funds in the United States, and the results are sobering. The standard benchmark for bond funds in the United States is the Lehman Brothers Aggregate Bond Index, which tracks the performance of U.S. government and corporate bonds. Exhibit 11.18 shows the abysmal performance of active fund

Exhibit 11.18   Fund Performance vs. Benchmarks in Various Equity Asset Classes

Asset	Benchmark	Percentage of Funds Underperforming Benchmark, 10 Years Ending June 2000
U.S. large-cap equity	S&P 500	78%
U.S. mid-cap equity	S&P MidCap	70
U.S. bond funds	Lehman Aggregate	80
European equity	MSCI Europe	71
Global emerging equity	FTSE All-Emerging	78

managers relative to their benchmarks over the past 10 years. Notice in particular bond fund performance relative to its benchmark.

As an alternative, you can buy U.S. Treasuries of varying maturities directly from the U.S. government through the Treasury Department's Bureau of Public Debt. The program is called Treasury Direct. You deal directly with the Treasury's Bureau of Public Debt—no middleman, no broker or banker, and best of all, no commission. The fee for going through the Treasury Direct program is *zero*. You can buy up to $100,000 worth of U.S. Treasuries for free. If and when your account exceeds $100,000, you will be charged a very nominal fee of $25 per year. At the $100,000 level, your $25 fee would translate into fewer than 3 basis points per year, an enormous savings when compared with the 108 basis points of a typical government bond fund. The minimum amount required to buy any U.S. Treasury bill, note, or bond is $1,000. You can purchase them through the mail and over the Internet. I have been doing this for over a decade now and have had a perfect experience. Although the U.S. government may have a reputation for slowness, the Treasury Department has its act together. In ten years, it has never been late on any of my interest payments. My statements have never had any error of any kind. Wire transfers and reinvestment of instruments have been executed flawlessly.

RISK AND RETURN WITH TREASURIES

The main difference among U.S. Treasury bills, Treasury notes, and Treasury bonds is the length of maturity. T-bills come in 3-month, 6-month, and 1-year maturities. Treasury notes are usually 2-year, 5-year, and 10-year maturities. T-bonds generally carry 30-year maturities. Since Treasuries are direct credit obligations of the government and thus backed by the full faith and credit of the U.S. Treasury, they are regarded as one of the safest investments in existence. If held until maturity, there is no way you will lose money.

On the other hand, the longer-dated maturities do carry risk of another kind. The U.S. Treasury guarantees interest payments and return of principle—if the securities are held to maturity. What happens between your initial purchase and final maturity is a different story. If you are holding a 30-year bond with a 5 percent coupon, there is a risk that the value of the bond will decrease should interest rates rise. Think of it this way: If interest rates rose over the next few months on 30-year Treasuries to 7 percent, then newly issued T-bonds would now be carrying 7 percent interest rates (coupons). Your 5 percent T-bond pays significantly less. In the secondary market, Treasuries trade very actively. If you had two bonds, one paying 7 percent interest and the other paying 5 percent interest, which would you pay more for? (This is not a trick question.) You would pay more for the 7 percent T-bond or, conversely, less for the 5 percent bond. Hence, the secondary market would reflect this, and your 5 percent bond would lose value if rates rise. Similarly, if rates declined to 4 percent, your bond would now become more valuable and rise in price. Thus, T-note and T-bond instruments move inversely with interest rates. In addition, the longer the maturity is, the more sensitive a fixed-income security will be to changes in interest rates. If rates rose dramatically, 30-year bonds would lose more value than 10-year notes. If rates declined, the longer-maturity instruments would gain more value than the shorter-maturity notes. In conclusion, the longer maturities tend to carry more risk.

Generally, increasing risk in capital markets means greater return. This generally holds true in the U.S. Treasury market as well. During the past 20 years, a period characterized by a gradual, sustained decline in interest rates, long-term government bonds did outperform intermediate-term treasury notes. But during the 1960s and 1970s, periods of higher inflation and rising rates, notes outperformed bonds. Difficult as it may be to believe, over the past 70 or so years, intermediate government notes have performed almost as well as longer-term government bonds and have done so with decidedly less interest rate risk and lower volatility.

Treasury bills, on the other hand, carry no default risk and no interest rate risk. They are the safest investment in the world. But ultimate safety translates into smaller returns. The phrase *no risk–no reward* is never more apparent than in Treasury bills. CDs and money market funds often carry significantly higher yields than T-bills with virtually no additional risk. You should therefore consider these for the cash portion of your portfolios.

The figures that follow show the Treasury yield curve for March 2, 2001. Witness the yield increase as maturities lengthen from 3-month bills out to 30-year bonds:

Instrument	*Interest Rate*
3-month Treasury bill	4.70 percent
10-year Treasury note	4.95 percent
30-year Treasury bond	5.37 percent

Some investors no doubt will want to shop around for higher rates. Instead of Treasuries, you could choose investment-grade corporate notes and bonds (those rated AAA, AA, A, or BBB by Standard & Poor's). The pickup in yield will be noticeable, but so will the added costs. You would have to purchase corporate bonds through a brokerage firm or invest in them by a mutual fund. Brokers charge a commission, and we have already discussed the high fees associated with government bond funds. Some fund companies like Vanguard keep costs very low. Corporate bond funds, on average, have expense ratios of about 95 basis points. If you insist on buying corporates (or even Treasuries) through a broker or a corporate bond fund, do everything possible to mitigate these costs, as they will make a huge difference in the long run. Exhibit 11.19 compares the various options available for the fixed-income portion of your investment portfolio. It also highlights the risks of various debt instruments and compares the costs of some of these instruments. Exhibit 11.19 is not meant to be inclusive of all fixed-income securities. For lack of space (and time), government agency and mortgage instruments were excluded, as were tax-free debt. Most brokerage firms can provide the basics regarding fixed-income investing. Those who wish to dive further into the subject can check out the Suggested Reading list at the end of this book.

CONCLUSION

Whichever fixed-income vehicle you choose, combining ETFs with Treasuries, investment-grade corporate bonds, or high-quality fixed-income mutual funds, you will have assembled a solid institutional-class portfolio that should stand the test of time and provided a handsome payoff. But the near-zero cost of combining some ETFs with Treasury securities purchased through the Treasury Direct program is difficult to let pass.

Exhibit 11.19 Various Options for the Fixed-Income Portion of an Asset Allocation Portfolio

	Credit Risk	Interest Rate Risk	Maturities	Costs	Yield, March 5, 2001
U.S. Treasury bills	None	No	3 months, 6 months, 1 year	Zero[a]	4.70%
Bank CDs	Extremely low	No	Various	Zero	5.00%[b]
Money market funds	Low (no FDIC)	No	Below 1 year	.2–.8%	5.37%[b]
U.S. Treasury notes	None	Low/medium	2, 5, 10 year	Zero[a]	4.95%[b]
Intermediate-term corporate bonds—investment grade	Low	Low/medium	2–10 year	Commission	5.99%[b]
Intermediate-term corporate bond funds	Very low	Low/medium	Various	.20–1.00%+	6.66%[c]
U.S. Treasury bonds	None	Medium/high	20–30 year	Zero[a]	5.37%[b]
Long-term corporate bonds—investment grade	Low	Medium/high	20+	Commission	6.83%[b]
Long-term corporate bonds—investment grade	Very low to low	Medium/high	Various	.2–1.0%+	6.6%[c]

[a]Treasury Direct Program.
[b]From *Barron's Financial*.
[c]Vanguard Intermediate Corporate Bond fund and Long Term Corporate Bond fund.

12

RISK: THE MOST IGNORED FOUR-LETTER WORD

Suffering, risks, and unscheduled life events are part of life; they may occur today, and they will certainly come tomorrow. When I think of the phrase, "Trouble today, trouble tomorrow," it reminds me of October 19, 1987. There was lots of trouble that day—unless you were short stocks or in cash. Statistically, the crash of 1987 and its 23 percent decline in stock prices in a single day should never have happened. It was a 13-standard-deviation event according to my mathematically gifted colleagues. A move of greater than 1 standard deviation occurs about one time out of three. A move of greater than 2 standard deviations occurs 1 time out of 20, and a greater than 3 standard deviation move occurs less than 1 time out of 100. Beyond 3 standard deviations, the odds are incredibly low. Thirteen standard deviations is off the chart. In the entire recorded history of the universe, a move of that magnitude should never have happened. But it did, and it is one of the best examples of risk (trouble) I can think of.

One of the most important traits separating successful traders and investors from the unsuccessful is an appreciation of risk. We all love returns, especially the outsized gains since 1982. The *Wall Street Journal* is replete with full-page ads showing the glowing returns of the many mutual funds offered by fund companies and investment managers. How many of them talk about risk? We all wonder about how much return we can expect in any investment. We ask, Can I obtain a 20 percent return? Thirty percent? Can I double my money every quarter? How many investors ask themselves, "How much money can I *lose*?" We are so focused on the gain that we often do not realize the inevitable risks. Someone at a seminar once asked, "What really separates the successful professionals from the wannabes?" "First," I replied, "is lack of knowledge. Too many people invest or trade with little or no preparation. Second, sufficient capital is important. Too little capital, and one bad trade forces you out of the game." The third thing I mention is risk management and money management. Amateurs usually ask how much they can profit. Professionals always ask, "What is the risk? How much can I lose, and what is the most I could lose?" They know how much gain is possible, but controlling the downside, a great mystery to beginning investors and traders, is at the heart of every successful investor or trader.

A FEW EXAMPLES OF RISK AND MONEY MANAGEMENT

A friend bought 100 shares of VA Linux after its record-breaking initial public offering. The stock soared nearly 700 percent on its first day of trading to over $300 per share. While she did not pay the all time high price, she did pay more than $275. VA Linux, as well as Red Hat, were part of the Linux movement, a movement that many thought would finally topple Microsoft and its virtual monopoly in the PC operating system software sector. Linux software was part of the "open source" software movement. Open source meant that the software code was widely available. In fact, you could download the Linux code for free off the Internet. The software was supposedly stable, scalable, and rather simple compared to the millions of lines of code embedded in Microsoft's software. Anything remotely related to Linux was considered golden, and the stocks were afforded lofty prices. High prices, however, ultimately bring out sellers. As VA Linux began its descent toward $200, my friend began to worry. "What do you think?" she asked one day.

"Honestly?"

"I'm down $7,000. I need to hear the truth."

"The greatest advances are usually followed by the greatest declines. The laws of gravity apply to the stock market as well."

"So what are you saying? How bad can this get?"

"The company has some potential, but it is insanely overpriced. You could lose half your money in a very brief amount of time."

"No way," she replied.

"Way," I snapped back. "You should think about limiting your losses here; you can control risk to some degree. Set a stop loss [a type of order where if the stock hits a predetermined price, your broker will sell your stock. It works as a sort of forced margin call, although you are not on margin]. "How does $200 grab you? If the stock goes below $200, you are out."

Then she muttered those famous words that kill every novice investor, "I can't sell now. It's only a paper loss. It will come back."

"How would you feel if the stock declined further, to 150? Would you reconsider?"

"Yes, I'd take my losses then."

VA made it to $150, and my friend suffered a loss of about $13,000. Were it not for stop losses and risk management, it would have been substantially worse. A few months later, she found some consolation in the news that VA Linux was trading below 30 (it eventually made it below 10!). She confessed that she knew the risks but did not know how large they could be.

My second story is also about risk or, rather, total ignorance of risk. I overheard a discussion on a train where one fellow was telling another that he should invest his 401(k) account in an index fund because there are no risks in an index fund. I interrupted the conversation and told the man on the receiving end of this advice that he should find another investment adviser because his commuting partner might put him in the poorhouse. I told them that indexes are my business and that I was right in the middle of the trillion-dollar market. That got the attention of both of them. I gave them a 10-minute discourse on how the S&P 500 can and does go down, and thus an index fund that tracks the S&P 500 can also go down. I reminded them that the long run has rewarded index investors but that bear markets like that of 1973–1974 and other less-than-fabulous years do occur regularly.

The third story involves inadequate capital. A caller wanted to trade the E-Mini S&P 500 futures. He had only $3,000 in capital and knew that the exchange minimum for the Mini S&P was about $4,300. Apparently his broker told him that if he day-traded (i.e., offset all his trades before the close and did not carry any positions overnight), he could trade for half the exchange margin, or $2,400. He was not aware that some firms allow this and wanted to know if it were true. I said that it was—but trading the Mini S&P 500 with such a low capital base might lower his chances for success. If he were on the wrong side of a 20-point move in the Mini S&P 500, he would lose one-third of his capital and not be able to trade any further until he came up with additional funds. The S&P 500 has 20-point swings quite regularly. I suggested he build up his funds so he could withstand a few losses and still continue to trade.

I know from experience that undercapitalized traders have a tough time becoming successful traders. Like any new business, you need cash on hand to handle the storms until you are more proficient.

RISK AND RETURN

Now let's examine risk along with its companion, return. In general, individuals who do comprehend risk know that greater returns are available but usually entail taking on greater risk. The more risk you take, the greater your return should be. Unfortunately, this is not always the case. Let's take a hypothetical case of two investment managers: Manager A and Manager B.

Manager A has obtained 7 percent annualized compounded returns over the past 10 years by investing in U.S. Treasury bills. Investor B has obtained the same 7 percent compounded return over the past decade but has done so by speculating in pork belly futures. Would you rather invest your money with Manager A or Manager B? Some would say it does not matter, since both provided 7 percent returns. But an astute investor who considers not only on returns *but also the risks taken to obtain those returns* would choose Manager A. Why? T-bills are risk free. You cannot lose money with them. The U.S. government guarantees the return of your money, and there are no fluctuations or volatility investing in T-bills. The fluctuations in the pork belly market can be quite dramatic. Indeed, pork bellies are one of the more volatile commodity futures in the industry. You would have a dramatically increased chance of a big loss (and a big gain) trading pork bellies. Yet for all the increase in risk and volatility, Manager B could not generate a greater return! Taking greater risks should produce greater profits, but in this case, greater risk did not give the investor a larger gain. The crux of investment management is to obtain the highest possible return on an investment with the least amount of risk. The investment world is rife with investors who are taking absurdly high risks and not being adequately compensated for the increased risk with higher returns.

Now consider Managers A and B with a slightly different comparison. Let's say Manager A returned the same 7 percent while Manager B returned 10 percent. Is this enough additional return to justify the risks? What if A returned 7 percent and B returned 20 percent? At some point, every investor must evaluate the trade-off between risk and return. If we move from the hypothetical example above to the real world, the investor will not have to search far to see that increasing the risk appetite will not always result in better returns. Exhibit 12.1

Exhibit 12.1   Risk and Return in Large- and Small-Cap Stocks over Two Decades

Decade	Cap Level	Compounded Annualized Return	Risk as Measured by Standard Deviation
1990s	Large-caps	18.2%	15.8%
	Small-caps	15.1	20.2
1980s	Large-caps	17.5	19.4
	Small-caps	15.8	22.5

Source: CME Index Products, Ibbotson Associates.

shows returns for large-cap stocks versus small-cap stocks over two decades. In the 1990s, large-caps returned an annualized compounded 18.2 percent versus 15.1 percent for small stocks. Yet risk, as measured by standard deviation, for large-caps was less than small-caps: 15.8 percent versus 20.2 percent.

Although investors in small-cap stocks were exposed to greater risk compared with large stocks, they were not compensated with a greater return. The same thing happened in the previous decade. Small stock investors received about 170 basis points less return per annum but exposed themselves to 300 basis points more risk. You would have to go back to the 1970s to see riskier small stocks outperform their large brethren. One might draw the obvious conclusion that investors should shun smaller, riskier stocks in favor of large-caps. Not necessarily; there are some small-cap fund managers who have provided investors with good "risk-adjusted" returns. Moreover, just because the 1980s and 1990s were less generous to small stocks does not mean that future decades hold the same fate. In addition, there are cycles within decades that are extremely profitable for small (and midsize) issues. In Appendix 2, we cover that topic in more detail and discuss how ETF investors can take advantage of small-cap stocks. And finally, if we return to the long-run measuring stick of 50 to 70 years, we would observe that small stocks do outperform larger stocks. Their risk is higher and the ride will be bumpy, but the rewards can be significant. This is why we have diversification. This is why many of the sample portfolios in Chapter 11 contained mid- and small-cap exposure.

If we move our risk return discussion to overseas investments, a similar pattern exists. Some of the emerging markets have exhibited extraordinary risk but have not rewarded investors accordingly. Exhibit 12.2 lists the risk (standard deviation) of several MSCI country indexes. Remember that individuals or institutions can invest in these indexes via the iShares MSCI ETFs.

Exhibit 12.2   Risk of Selected MSCI Country Indexes

MSCI Country Index	Risk: 5-Year Monthly Standard Deviation	ETF Return: Inception to December 31, 1999
MSCI Malaysia	47.7%	−16.8%
MSCI Singapore	35.0	−5.7
MSCI Mexico	40.4	+19.4
MSCI Switzerland	17.5	+12.0
MSCI U.K.	10.9	+20.9

Source: MSCI and Barclays Global Investors.

The country with the lowest risk in the exhibit, the United Kingdom, has provided the best return since March 1996, the inception date of many of the iShares MSCI funds. Some higher-risk countries have failed to compensate investors for their extra risk. The iShares U.K. ETF took one-fourth the risk of the Mexico ETF and still exceeded its return. This is precisely what an investor needs to be aware of: Taking enormous risks does not always provide an enormous payoff, and usually an investor can obtain a given return while still minimizing or mitigating his or her risk. Investors who master these lessons will enjoy several benefits:

- They will be better informed and thus able to make better investment choices and are less likely to suffer catastrophic losses.
- They will understand that greater risk does not always produce greater returns.
- They will not only appreciate degrees of risk but may be able to quantify risk and match it to their appetite.
- Diversification can pay off. An investment in Malaysia or Singapore would have cost the investor. But if the portfolio of ETFs were spread across a more diverse area, say, Europe, then the situation would have been different. And volatility or risk can also be mitigated by investing across various asset classes, such as bonds, notes, cash, and real estate.

BUFFETT, MERIWETHER, AND THE RISKS UNKNOWN

If you dissect the philosophies and financial maneuverings of Warren Buffett and John Meriwether, you will find some interesting similarities. Meriwether was a fabulously successful trader at Salomon Brothers, in charge of fixed-income trading as well as the all-important bond-arbitrage group. His group was stuffed with quantitative geniuses from MIT and Stanford. They relentlessly plugged reams of data into computers and formulated complex models that could tell whether certain fixed-income instruments were out of line in terms of price or yield. If the 2-year note yield was priced a bit high relative to the 10-year note, they would construct and implement a trade that would profit from this view. They reputedly had all the angles calculated. The bond-arbitrage group knew with fairly good precision how out-of-whack things could get and the odds of their coming back in line. For a time, the group amassed huge profits.

Then the success of the bond-arbitrage group was interrupted during the Salomon Brothers government bond scandal. Although the scandal cost Meriwether his job, it was not long before he raided his former employer's arbitrage group and assembled his own trading group—a hedge fund named Long-Term Capital Management (LTCM). Meriwether brought in other brilliant minds, including a few Nobel Prize winners, and went on to establish one of the most eccentric financial enterprises on Wall Street. In the first few years, profits were large. Before long, the capital base grew, and additional investors, the large institutional variety, were ready to pony up additional billions. Things were going quite well. Their computer models were running like a well-oiled machine, constantly churning out probabilities, risk, and out-of-sync instruments. In addition, most trades were of the hedged type, so the risks turned out to be smaller than forecasted. In a letter to LTCM's investors, these leading academicians reported to fund holders the precise risks of loss. Although they understood and acknowledged risk, they thumbed their noses at uncertainty and calculated that investors may experience a loss of 5 percent or more in about 1 month in 5 and a loss of 10 percent or more in about 1 month in 10. Only 1 year in 50 should it lose at least 20 percent of its portfolio. Apparently, losses beyond 20 percent were unthinkable, as those odds were not discussed. Most investors probably did not give that rash scenario too much thought.

LTCM had anticipated every contingency except one: The models did not account for a Russian debt default crisis. When Russia's and Asia's problems surfaced, all the wheels came off quickly and trades that were executed because things were out of line did not come back into line. In fact, despite the impossible odds, the trades went hopelessly against Meriwether's group. More important, because the rocket scientists were sure of their computers, they made huge leveraged bets. But the soured trades paired with the overwhelming leverage took the firm, its partners, and investors to the brink of extinction. Only a rescue package engineered by the Federal Reserve and this nation's largest banks saved the teetering system from spinning out of control.

Compare LTCM's attitudes about risk with those of Warren Buffett. Many know Buffett as a great investor. The truth is that he is also fanatical about risk. He has to be. After all, he sits atop one of the mightiest risk enterprises in the world. We all know Buffett as the chairman of Berkshire Hathaway. But nestled in Berkshire's portfolio are several very large insurance operations in GEICO Insurance and General Reinsurance (when large insurance companies take on too much risk, they lay it off on other insurance companies) Buffett's insurance operations also extend to *super-cat policies*—policies that insure against catastrophic losses. Because of the extraordinary risks, super-cat business brings in exceedingly large premiums. Read what Buffett's letter to his investors has to say about risk and uncertainty:

> Occasionally, however, the cost of our float (premiums) will spike severely. That will occur because of our heavy involvement in the super-cat business, which by its nature is the most volatile of all insurance lines. In this operation, we sell policies that insurance and reinsurance companies purchase in order to limit their losses when mega-catastrophes strike. Berkshire is often the preferred market for sophisticated buyers: When the "big one" hits, the financial strength of the super-cat writers will be tested, and Berkshire has no peer in this respect.
>
> Since truly major catastrophes are rare occurrences, our super-cat business can be expected to show large profits in most years—and to record a huge loss occasionally. In other words, the attractiveness of our super-cat business will take a great many years to measure.[1] *What you must understand, however, is that a truly terrible year in the super-cat business is not a possibility—it's a certainty. The only question is when it will come.*

Buffett respects risk. He expects and embraces uncertainty. Buffett does not just calculate the odds of a 5 percent loss or a 10 to 20 percent loss. He braces his entire financial foundation for the inevitable by acknowledging that terrible catastrophes will most certainly come knocking. He states, "*When* the big one hits," not, "*If* the big one hits." He dismisses probabilities in favor of certainties. His financial strength is not built on an overleveraged house of cards but rather on an enormous pile of cash and reserves.

I believe that John Meriwether and his partners at LTCM were extraordinary investors. They lost an obscene sum of money, but also made handsome profits before the Russian storm hit and before LTCM while still at Salomon Brothers. In my opinion, these people put too much reliance on computer models (and leverage). Computers are only as good as the people who program them. One thing the computer models cannot quite figure out is the inevitable chaos in Russia or that one day Sadaam Hussein will wake up and decide he wants to own some Kuwait real estate. No supercomputer on earth could forecast the accounting fraud that would reduce the market value of Cendant Corporation by 50 percent in one day. And no model could predict the complete evisceration of the Internet stocks. Human frailty and emotions cannot be tamed by a spreadsheet.

When the storms arrive, I'd rather be in the House of Buffett any day. If you polled smart investors around the globe and offered them the choice between Buffett's cerebrum making investment decisions and a few Ph.Ds with Pentium IVs calling the shots, I think the results would be obvious. As an investor in the markets through either ETFs or E-mini stock index futures, you would be well served to learn a few lessons about risk from both these individuals.

"VAR [Value at Risk] is extremely dangerous.* People look at their computer models and think they are safe. It is much better to have no models and watch your net worth every day. Watching it crumble is what told me to get out."[2]

—Stanley Druckenmiller, Soros Capital Management

---

*Value at Risk is a computer model that helps firms gauge risk by determining how much their positions might lose at a given time. LTCM and dozens of other firms embraced this type of modeling. It was fine if things behaved the way they did in the past. But if some unforeseen event should rock the financial markets, the models fall short.

13

ETFs BEYOND THE UNITED STATES

ETFs within the United States grew at a healthy clip from their introduction in 1993 until about 1998. Then growth skyrocketed as the number of fund offerings multiplied exponentially and existing ETFs became ever more popular. It was only a matter of time before our neighbors to the North and countries across the Atlantic and Pacific would take notice.

Exchanges in Canada, Europe, and Asia had excellent experiences introducing derivative products of their own, and those same products are now among the most actively traded futures and options in the world. Overseas exchanges knew that if they could build on the critical mass already in existence with index futures and options, then ETFs had a very good chance at succeeding outside the United States. They had the know-how, and they had advanced electronic trading systems (the major exchanges in Europe and Asia were already all-electronic). They also had products. Futures contracts on the German DAX 30, the French CAC 40, the European Blue Chip EuroSTOXX 50, and every other major European and Asian index futures contract had average daily dollar turnover exceeding $1 billion, as well as six-figure open interest levels, as Exhibit 13.1 shows.

The only obstacles to success for foreign exchanges were regulatory and infrastructure related. In the United States, one regulatory agency, the Securities and Exchange Commission, oversees all ETF regulation. In Europe, there are 20 regulatory bodies and 16 national

Exhibit 13.1   Selected Global Index Futures Products

Index Future	Country	Daily Turnover	Open Interest Number of Contracts
EuroSTOXX 50	Continental Europe	$2.77 billion	497,902
FTSE 100	United Kingdom	3.01 billion	263,270
CAC 40	France	3.13 billion	362,334
DAX 30	Germany	5.51 billion	177,536
Nikkei 225	Japan	2.70 billion	163,285
Hang Seng	Hong Kong	1.51 billion	34,728

Source: FIA, CME Index Products Marketing.

legislatures that would be involved in these products. In the United States, almost all ETFs trade on the AMEX (the NYSE and CBOE have snatched one ETF apiece). In Europe, over a dozen exchanges are vying for an ETF prize. In fact, because of the structure of licensing agreements overseas, some ETFs are listed on several exchanges. This structural difference promotes healthy competition, but it can also serve to dilute liquidity. Even more important is the clearing issue. The NSCC and DTC (now merged entities) provide a cheap, efficient, and extremely reliable clearing mechanism that is mandatory for ETF settlement and the all-important creation and redemption process. Overseas exchanges no doubt can clear these types of instruments, but can they do it cheaply enough to make ETFs overseas as low cost as they are in the United States?

Despite the regulatory and infrastructure hurdles, other countries have done an excellent job of importing ETF know-how from the United States. They have even leapfrogged us by being first to introduce ETFs on actively managed mutual funds. Some U.S. financial institutions (Nuveen, Vanguard, ProFunds) have expressed a desire to launch ETFs on some of their mutual funds. In fact, on May 31 The Vanguard Group launched their first ETF—The Vanguard Index Participation Equity Receipt (VIPER, ticker VTI). Initial interest is excellent. VIPERs are an ETF that track the Vanguard Total Stock Market Index Fund, which replicates the Wilshire 5000 Index. Look for additional ETFs of this type in the near future.

As of February 2001, there were about 1.5 billion euros ($1.38 billion) of assets under management in European-listed ETFs alone (see Exhibit 13.2). ETFs on the CAC 40, the DAX 30, FTSE 100, and EuroSTOXX 50 have the lions share of assets (66 percent).

Exhibit 13.2 European ETFs: Market Share by Assets

ETF	Exchange	Assets Under Management (in millions of euros)	Market Share
CAC 40	Euronext	360	24%
EuroSTOXX 50 LDRS	Deutsche Borse	345	23
FTSE 100 iShares	LSE	195	13
DAX 30	Deutsche Borse	120	8
STOXX 50 LDRS	Deutsche Borse	105	7
iBloomberg/ Pharmaceuticals	LSE and Euronext	45	3
iBloomberg/Financial	LSE and Euronext	45	3
iBloomberg/Technology	LSE and Euronext	45	3
iBloomberg/Telecom	LSE and Euronext	30	2
iShares TMT	LSE	30	2

Many of the European broad-based and country indexes now have liquid ETFs. Like their American counterparts, index providers are licensing and introducing dozens of sector ETFs, such as the Bloomberg European Investable Indexes. Barclays Global Investors is the manager for the Bloomberg European Index ETFs, and Bloomberg owns and calculates the indexes (hence the moniker iBloomberg). State Street Global Advisors will also launch more than a dozen new street-TRACKS ETFs, including the MSCI Pan-Euro Index, MSCI Europe Small Cap Index, a U.K. and Amsterdam index, as well as several MSCI European sector streetTRACKS.

Recently the bid-offer spread on the DAX 30 ETF traded at the German Exchange, Deutsche Borse, was measured at 6 basis points. This is tighter than any U.S.-based ETF by several basis points. It has been said that the market maker for the product will quote extremely deep markets without widening the bid/offer spread. That Europe and its exchanges want to be major players in ETFs is quite evident. And despite their infancy, they are enjoying major success.

While Europe is off to a great start, ETFs in Canada and Asia are evidently the most successful ever launched outside the United States. In August 1998, the Hong Kong government acquired an enormous portfolio (HK$230 billion, $28 billion USD—7 percent of the value of the Hang Seng Index) of Hong Kong–listed securities as it tried to prop up share prices during the Asian crises of 1997–1998. The securities were mostly shares composing the venerable Hang Seng Stock Index, a cap-weighted index of 33 large Hong Kong corporations. When the Hong Kong financial authorities finally decided to dispose of these shares, the government wanted to do so in a manner that would have as little market impact as possible. Evidently it determined that an ETF structure would be the best way of off-loading the shares into institutional and retail investors without sinking the Hong Kong stock market. In November 1999, under the management of State Street Global Advisors, the Hong Kong government launched the Tracker Fund of Hong Kong (TraHK). The HK$34 billion ($4.3 billion) TraHK initial public offering was Asia's largest ever (excluding Japan). Since then, the government has been able to transfer over HK$60 billion (7.5 billion USD) back into the market using this unique ETF. TraHK now enjoys an asset base of $3.4 billion, with very high turnover.

Canada's iUnits S&P/TSE 60 fund is the standout in terms of assets. With an asset base of nearly $5 billion (U.S. dollars), this ETF would rank number three in the United States after the QQQ and SPY. The S&P/TSE Index consists of 60 of the largest (by capitalization) stocks listed on the Toronto Stock Exchange. BGI is the manager of the Canadian offering. Annual expenses amount to 17 basis points. Canada is also the first to have an ETF based on a fixed-income instrument. iG5 and iG10 are ETFs based on 5- and 10-year Canadian government bonds. They are unique in that they are not based on bond indexes. They contain only the 5-year Canadian government bond or the 10-year version. It would be tantamount to having an ETF on Microsoft—that is, the entire fund would be not an index of stocks but one stock. The Toronto exchange has announced its intention to launch six new iUnits based on a Canadian MidCap index and several Canadian sector indexes.

Although ETFs that are equally accessible to institutional as well as retail investors are relatively new in Europe, a unique institutional-only ETF has existed in Europe nearly as long as the original S&P 500 SPDRs. In April 1993, the investment banking firm of Morgan Stanley introduced OPALS (Optimized Portfolios As Listed Securities) in response to institutional demand for a simpler and less costly way to get exposure to equity markets across the globe. Most OPALS are listed on the Luxembourg Stock Exchange and are available on nearly 60 indexes. OPALS exist on 10 major country indexes and nearly 50 MSCI indexes, including developed and emerging markets, global and regional markets, and European sector indexes. All of the advantages offered by ETFs exist with OPALSs. They are liquid, low cost, trade at very close to net asset value, and offer non-U.S. institutional investors a means to gain exposures to many different global markets. Unfortunately, U.S. investors are not allowed to trade in OPALS; only qualified non-U.S. institutions such as pension funds, asset managers, private banks, insurance companies, and not-for-profit institutions are allowed. But many of the country and regional indexes are available to U.S. investors through the iShares MSCI series.

Restrictions regarding overseas ETFs are not limited to OPALS. Most of the ETFs listed on foreign exchanges are not registered under the U.S. Securities Act of 1933, nor have many of the issuers been registered under the Investment Companies Act of 1940. Hence, these products cannot be sold directly or indirectly in the United States or to an account of a U.S. citizen. Word has it that in the future the SEC may rule that some of these products could be sold to investors in the United States. However, it may be a long time, if ever, before you see some of them sold in the United States.

14

THE FUTURE OF ETFs AND E-MINI STOCK INDEX FUTURES: THE ROAD AHEAD

I began this book in San Francisco, home of Barclays Global Investors, the proprietors of iShares and the largest indexer on earth (as well as the pioneering institution in indexing). It is fitting that I write the final words in Chicago on the day when the E-Mini S&P 500 smashed its previous trading record by trading over 200,000 contracts a day ($10 billion notional) and the E-Mini Nasdaq-100 volume soared to a record 150,000 contracts ($5 billion notional). For those not familiar with the history of futures markets and volume levels, most contracts traded in the world do not trade 100,000 per day. That the Mini S&P 500 accomplished this in 3 years and the Mini Nasdaq-100 in less than 2 years is nothing short of incredible. When the Nasdaq-100 Index shares were launched (3 months before the E-Mini Nasdaq-100 futures), the opening-day volume was 2.6 million shares, also an incredible feat. And since the CME was scheduled to launch the Mini Nasdaq-100 futures in June, the success of the QQQs would be formidable competition. As popular as the QQQs, S&P 500 SPDRs, and some other ETFs have become, the E-mini futures have enjoyed even greater success, certainly in dollar turnover. This success is even more remarkable when you consider that the distribution channel for ETFs—the number of stockbrokers and firms available to push stock exchange products—dwarfs the number of futures brokers and firms that sell E-minis. The CME is in the middle of a concerted effort to open up access to its GLOBEX electronic trading system. When the number of "screens" providing access begins to increase rapidly, it is quite possible that the minis will double their volume again within a few years. They would join the big S&P 500 and the Eurodollar futures contracts as some of the most actively traded instruments in the world. Moreover, it is likely that other E-mini stock index futures would be brought to market too. Some participants have expressed an interest in a mini-Russell 2000 Index future or a Mini S&P MidCap 400 Index future.

Despite the extraordinary success of ETFs to date, their future potential, like E-mini stock index futures, is boundless. Combine all the advantages discussed in Part I with the marketing muscle and infrastructure possessed by BGI, SSGA, BNY, and AMEX, and you have the ingredients for an explosion of activity. Small investors and multibillion-dollar pension funds are doing business in ETFs in increasing numbers. The press has labeled ETFs mostly as investments for the average retail investor. In truth, ETF activity is greatest among institutions. The sheer number of broad-based, style, and sector ETFs helps attract interest since there is literally something for everyone. During the writing of this book, the number of ETFs grew from about 70 to over 100.

Such success has not gone unnoticed. Nuveen Investments filed registration statements with the SEC for seven new exchange-traded municipal bond funds in early January 2001. This would be a totally new class of ETFs. Nuveen is also reportedly working on other equity-based ETFs that should be trading later in 2001 or in early 2002. Also planning to enter the ETF market is Vanguard, which has applied for SEC approval of a series of ETFs called VIPERs (Vanguard Index Participation Equity Receipts). VIPERs will be a share class that tracks Vanguard's five most popular index funds: the Vanguard 500 Index fund, Vanguard Growth Index fund, Vanguard Small-Cap Index Fund, Vanguard Total Stock Market Index Fund,* and the Vanguard Value Index Fund. ProFunds, the Maryland-based investment company, has announced plans to introduce ETFs based on some of its index fund offerings. Even insurance companies, with their large stables of cash and extensive risk and investment management prowess, want to be part of the ETF game. New York Life Investment Management is planning to offer its first ETF, which will track the Pacific Stock Exchange (PSE) Technology 100 index. TECHIES, an acronym for Technology Index Equity Shares, will reportedly trade on the AMEX and the Pacific Stock Exchange.

---

*VIPERs on the Total Stock Market Index Fund were launched on May 31st.

BGI has launched fixed-income ETFs in Canada, and they will likely appear in the United States before long. Fixed-income ETFs would be a valuable tool in constructing asset allocation portfolios using all ETFs

ETFs will grow not only in number but also in accessibility in the world marketplace. While E-mini futures are available around the clock, only now are securities exchanges in the United States making the move toward 24-hour availability. The AMEX has announced agreements with two exchanges, Euronext, the pan-European exchange, and the Singapore exchange to cross-list ETFs. So by late 2001, investors in Europe and Asia will be able to trade SPDRs or DIAMONDs. Initially, only a handful of AMEX ETFs will be listed, with others following later. U.S. investors too should have access to many ETFs listed overseas.

Another catalyst that will promote ETFs will be investment advisers and managed account programs. On the futures side, managed futures accounts harbor assets of well over $30 billion. It is highly probable that asset management firms will pile on in this area, offering clients managed accounts using ETFs. They will invest in a diversified portfolio of ETFs depending on the risk tolerance of the client, and they will be marketed as tax-efficient, low-cost vehicles. As such, certain investors, such as high-net-worth clients would likely be willing to pay a small management fee in addition to the small fees charged by ETF sponsors for good management. Critics will say that active management will only create more taxable events, increase costs, and if the mutual fund industry is any indication, not likely add enough value (beat the market) to justify another layer of fees. Nevertheless, if enough assets migrate toward this kind of product, it will attract some talented managers, some of whom might end up beating the market. After all, the S&P 500 over the long run does beat most managers—but not all of them. The trick will be to identify them in advance.

Several investment management firms have announced their intention to provide clients with programs that actively manage a portfolio of ETFs. Addison Capital Management LLC was the first asset management firm in the United States to offer such services. Addison, with $300 million under management, introduced in September 2000 a product it called Active Index Core Strategy. These actively managed portfolios are made up exclusively of ETFs. In the beginning, Addison used primarily the S&P 500 SPDRs, but accounts now include a broader array of ETFs

Everest Funds Management LLC in Omaha, Nebraska, launched a fund of ETFs in December 2000. This too is the first fund of ETFs (similar to the fund of funds concept, where a manager invests client money in a diversified program of mutual funds). Its goal is to try to attract defined-contribution plan assets—401(k) accounts—as well as retail investors. With the immense amount of dollars in Americans' 401(k) accounts and their love affair with indexing, this fund of ETFs has great potential. However, the fund, named the Everest Cubed Fund, is an SEC-registered regulated investment company. It will thus not be traded throughout the trading day like the ETFs in which it invests. The fund is registered in only two states (Nebraska and Virginia) but plans to expand as demand and assets grow. It will allocate money primarily in the Spiders, DIAMONDs, and QQQs, with quarterly allocation reviews and rebalancing. Depending on the costs and the market-timing expertise of this outfit, this could be yet another intriguing product with great potential.

Finally, the major wirehouses and investment banks have been expanding their presence in the ETFs dramatically. Research as well as trading desks have been strengthened to deal with the dramatic growth in these products.

How much more can ETFs grow? Some estimates I have seen put total assets under management at between $300 billion and $500 billion by 2005. Given that they have doubled in the past 18 months alone, these optimistic forecasts are not outrageous. Will ETFs follow in the steps of their traditional mutual fund cousins and grow in number to more than 8,000? Given the geometric increase in financial products over the past 20 years, this would not be a total surprise. No one thought we would see the proliferation in the fund industry that we have experienced since the 1970s, when only a few hundred were in operation. Some critics say that indexing will lose its allure and active management will make a comeback. I agree. But any comeback will likely be temporary. There have been many periods, sometimes lasting 2 to 4 years, where active managers did outperform, but over the long run, most will not beat the S&P 500. When they do, it is usually because of strong markets in mid- and small-cap issues. When those times come, investors have at their disposal over a dozen small-cap and mid-cap ETFs to turn to. The long-term growth rate of ETFs will also be dependent on market conditions. Bear markets have a way of stalling the growth of the best-laid plans. In 1973–1974, the worst bear market since the depression, the fund industry had problems, as did the Street as a whole. At worst, growth would be postponed—a mere speed bump in the road to what appears to be an extraordinary future.

"In spite of occasional claims to the contrary, indexation today is more center stage than it has ever been before, and is accepted in more and more markets as being a core part of any major long-term fund's strategy. The industry continues to evolve at a rapid rate bringing relevant product to both institutional and retail investors to help them meet their investment objectives. And while indexation cannot ever have the glamour of certain other strategies, the results are far more predictable, something that all of us, and most importantly our clients appreciate."

Alan J. Brown
Group Chief Investment Officer & Chairman,
State Street Global Advisors UK Limited

Speaking at the 2000 World Cup of
Indexing in Barcelona, Spain

15

FREQUENTLY ASKED QUESTIONS (AND ANSWERS) ABOUT ETFS AND E-MINI STOCK INDEX FUTURES

Q: The S&P MidCap 400 SPDR is supposed to trade at one-fifth of the underlying index. On February 9, 2001, the MidCap 400 cash index traded at 522.06. This implied that the MidCap 400 SPDR should have been trading somewhere around 104.40. Yet on that same day, the MidCap SPDRs closed at 95.29 per share. Why does this discount persist with MidCap SPDRs, while the iShares S&P MidCap 400 ETF trades much closer to one-fifth the size of the underlying cash index (for example, on February 9, 2001, the iShares S&P MidCap 400 closed at 103.65)?

A: The answer has to do with distributions and the length of time each fund has been in existence. MidCap SPDRs have been trading since May 1995, and many stocks in the underlying index had undergone significant price appreciation. At the same time, some of these stocks were deleted from the S&P MidCap 400 Index (as they graduated to the S&P 500 Index, a large-cap index). Since the MidCap SPDRs are a unit investment trust, they must fully replicate the underlying index. When a stock in the index is deleted, the trust must also delete or sell the stock from the portfolio and in turn purchase any stock that is added to the index. If it sold shares that had appreciated significantly, the fund would, under SEC regulation, have to distribute those capital gains to fund holders. Usually the fund can offset taxable gains with tax losses from other

259

issues in the portfolio—but not always. The tremendous appreciation along with the number of stocks deleted from the index in recent years have caused some rather large distributions to fund holders. Any time a fund pays out a distribution, the assets of the fund are reduced by the amount of the distribution, and thus the ETF's price also will be reduced. The iShares MidCap fund has been in existence only a short time; thus, years of accumulated gains and changes in the index have not had the same effect.

Q: *Why have the iShares MSCI Sweden fund and Canada fund paid such large capital gains distributions? Aren't ETFs supposed to be tax efficient?*

A: ETFs generally have been and will be more tax efficient than traditional funds; however, some distributions are unavoidable. A few isolated situations have cast a pall on their reputed tax efficiencies. In the case of the iShares MSCI Canada, the fund managers were forced to sell shares in some holdings to meet SEC diversification requirements. The SEC requires that no one position in the fund can amount to more than 25 percent of assets. Nortel Networks, the largest holding in the iShares Canada fund, was near the 25 percent level. Thus, the fund had to trim its holdings. Given Nortel's huge run-up in recent years, there were tax consequences to fund holders. The distribution amounted to over $4 per share. One of the culprits in the iShares MSCI Sweden fund was wireless giant L. M. Ericsson. The iShares Sweden fund paid $5 capital gain distribution. Large and frequent taxable distributions will usually manifest themselves in any ETF where turnover in the underlying index is relatively greater. No ETF fund manager wants high turnover or high taxes; nevertheless, they are forced to play by the SEC's rules. Over the long haul, investors should see greater tax efficiencies.

Q: *Are ETFs good candidates for dollar-cost-averaging programs?*

A: It depends. If you want to invest small amounts, say $50 to $100 per month, probably not. Many ETFs trade above $50 per share, and purchasing fractional shares is tricky, if not impossible, at some firms. But there are some new on-line outfits that do allow purchase of fractional amounts (by small regular dollar amounts) for a small fee. You would have to run the numbers. With one of these firms I am aware of, you could invest $100 a month in three or four issues. Hence, your $100 would be distributed three or four ways, and you would purchase tiny fractions of a portfolio of ETFs. You could slowly accumulate a portfolio over time. Beware, though, and watch those costs. Even small fees can add up if you are making monthly (or quarterly) purchases by dollar-cost averaging.

Q: Why is the Nasdaq-100 Index tracking stock (QQQ) so much more volatile than the S&P 500 SPDRs?

A: An ETF is usually as volatile as its underlying index, and an index is only as volatile as its underlying components. It is true that the Nasdaq-100 is more volatile than the S&P 500. In fact, the Nasdaq-100 is more than twice as volatile as the venerable benchmark. You have only to look at the underlying issues to find the answer. Compare some of the top S&P issues: General Electric, Pfizer, ExxonMobil, and Wal-Mart. These are solid companies with relatively stable earnings and business franchises that have been around in some cases for over a century. Compare these blue chips with Oracle, Sun Microsystems, and Cisco, some of the top Nasdaq-100 issues. None of these companies has an operating history of more than 25 years, and they are clearly more volatile than a General Electric or an ExxonMobil. Moreover, the speculative hot money tends to flow in and out of technology issues at a greater frequency than blue chip stocks. Think of it this way: If you were a day trader, would you focus on Juniper Networks, which frequently moved 20 points per day, or General Electric, which on a volatile day would fluctuate 2 or 3 points? For a look at just how volatile the Nasdaq-100 is, compare the daily percentage price ranges for the Nasdaq-100 index with the S&P 500 daily percentage price ranges in Exhibit 15.1. Almost all the daily price percentage movements in the S&P are under 2.5 percent, but the majority of the daily price range movements for the volatile Nasdaq benchmark are over 3.0 percent. Now that's volatile!

Q: Some ETF transactions are recorded on brokerage trade confirmations as occurring not on the AMEX but on other regional exchanges. Aren't ETFs traded only on AMEX?

A: Although the American Stock Exchange is the primary market for most ETFs, it does not hold a monopoly. Products can be traded at other exchanges such as the Chicago Stock Exchange. In fact, the Chicago Stock Exchange trades quite a large number of SPDRs.

Exhibit 15.1   Daily Percentage Price Range Distribution for Nasdaq-100 (January 1, 2000–December 31, 2000) and S&P 500 Composite (January 29, 1993–December 31, 2000)

	Price Range	Frequency	Percentage of Total
Nasdaq-100 Index	0–1.00%	0	.00%
	1.01–1.50	1	.40
	1.51–2.00	13	5.16
	2.01–2.50	20	7.94
	2.51–3.00	26	10.32
	3.01–3.50	25	9.92
	3.51–4.00	27	10.71
	4.01–5.00	49	19.44
	Over 5.00	91	36.11
S&P 500 Index	0–.25	1	0.05
	.25–.5	237	11.84
	.51–1.0	753	37.63
	1.01–1.5	483	24.14
	1.51–2.0	278	13.89
	2.01–2.5	124	6.20
	2.51–3.0	65	3.25
	3.01–3.5	29	1.45
	Over 3.50	31	1.55

Source: SPDR Trust Prospectus; Nasdaq-100 Trust Prospectus.

In early January, when the QQQs traded over 100 million shares in a day, more than a third of the volume traded on exchanges other than the AMEX. ETFs also trade on ECNs such as Island and Instinet.

Q: Who or what determines if an order goes to the AMEX or another exchange?

A: This is a very controversial issue. Some brokerage houses receive payment for directing an order to a particular exchange. It is legal, according to the SEC, and it occurs quite often. The practice is called *payment-for-order flow.*

Q: What type of investor buys and sells ETFs? It seems as if ETFs were designed with small investors in mind.

A: Although they are attractive to smaller investors, all types of investors, including high-net-worth investors and giant pension funds, buy and sell ETFs. The 13f filings for the S&P 500 SPDRs (SPY) and the Nasdaq-100 Index Shares (QQQ) clearly reveal this (*13f filings* are federal regulatory guidelines that require larger investors to file with the government the number of shares and the percentage of outstanding shares they hold). A short list of some major holders of SPY includes Morgan Stanley, which holds 17.375 million SPY (10.31 percent outstanding), the Regents of the University of California, with 6.78 million SPY (4.03 percent outstanding), and the State Board of Administration of Florida, with 3.85 million (2.28 percent outstanding). Of course, there are lots of individual investors who hold 100 shares or fewer of many ETFs.

Q: Some ETFs have substantial volume, while some hardly trade at all. Will investors be able to get in and out of less actively traded ETFs?

A: Do not always assume that low volume means low liquidity. While some ETFs trade fewer than 20,000 contracts per day, specialists on the AMEX and regional exchanges make good markets in those issues despite the low volume. Do not be fooled into thinking that because an ETF has low activity that the bid-offer spreads will be hundreds of basis points wide. On the other hand, the QQQs, by far the most active ETF (about 30 million shares per day in 2000), are sometimes themselves a victim of wider markets. When markets become volatile, QQQ bid-offer spreads have reached $.75 to $1.00. Usually, though, the spreads are around 10 to 12 cents. Remember that most ETFs have been around for only a year or so. It will take years for some ETFs to develop a noticeable critical mass; some, although they may be useful to some investors, will not ever achieve the critical mass of the more popular ETFs.

Q: How much of a pension fund's assets are indexed?

A: It depends on the pension fund, who is running it, and, to some extent, the pension consultants. Some funds feel they can add value by actively managing the assets (or having outside active managers do the job). Others feel that indexing is a powerful tool and thus have an enormous sum of money indexed. CALPERS, one of the largest pension funds in the United States, indexes about 47 percent of its equity assets (and some fixed income) according to *Money*

Market Directories. Some index only a small portion—perhaps 10 to 15 percent or less. A significant amount of the assets indexed will be to the S&P 500, but there is a contingent of pensions and institutions that use benchmarks such as the Russell 1000. A small-cap manager certainly would want the benchmark to track small-cap stocks. When you have billions in assets in the hands of dozens of active money managers, you cannot help but receive "indexed" returns over time since those managers themselves make up the market.

Q: Will ETFs ever trade 24 hours like stock index futures do?

A: It's hard to say. The trend is toward increasing the length of the trading day, although with the market cooling down in 2000 and 2001, there does not seem to be the same impetus for 24-hour trading anymore. No one knows the answer at this point; still, with the continuing progress on electronic trading systems, it is not difficult to envision 24-hour trading sooner rather than later. The AMEX recently announced alliances with overseas exchanges to list ETFs on these exchanges, effectively opening the door for around-the-clock ETF availability.

Q: Do all ETFs have listed options?

A: No. Options exist for some ETFs but not all. The QQQ has a very active options counterpart. All of the HOLDRS products and a few of the broad-based and sector ETFs have listed options too. The following list identifies ETFs that have options that trade on either the AMEX or the CBOE (as of February 13, 2001). Some ETFs trade on other options exchanges as well.

S&P 100 iShares	CBOE
S&P MidCap 400	AMEX
Nasdaq-100 Index Shares	AMEX
Russell 1000 iShares	AMEX
Russell 2000 iShares	AMEX
Russell 2000 Growth iShares	AMEX
Russell 2000 Value iShares	AMEX
Basic Industries Select Sector SPDR	AMEX
Cyclical/Transportation Select Sector SPDR	AMEX
Cons Staples Select Sector SPDR	AMEX
Energy Select Sector SPDR	AMEX

Financial Select Sector SPDR	AMEX
Industrial Select Sector SPDR	AMEX
Technology Select Sector SPDR	AMEX
Utilities Select Sector SPDR	AMEX
All HOLDRS	CBOE or AMEX or both exchanges depending on HOLDR

Q: *The Barclays S&P 500 iShare (IVV) has an annual expense ratio of .09 percent, while the S&P 500 SPDR (SPY) has an expense ratio of .12 percent. However, the SPY trades about 7 million a day, while the IVV, essentially the same instrument, trades fewer than 250,000 per day. Why doesn't the cheaper alternative garner more volume?*

A: To some people, the 3 basis points is meaningless because they do not hold SPY or IVV for a year. On 100 shares of SPY (about $13,500 worth of ETF), it amounts to about $4 per year. To an institution, it is incredibly important to get every basis point of savings possible. To a trader, liquidity is the prime concern, and annual costs do not matter because they will be in and out of the market. SPY, around since 1993, is the first and thus oldest of all the ETFs, but IVV has been around only since May 2000. The race is not over, although it may seem so at this point. Usually it is difficult to displace a fully dominant product. SPY is quite dominant and has built a loyal following over eight years. The two are also structured a little differently. The SPY is a UIT, while the IVV is a managed investment company.

Q: *How responsive is the SPY to the underlying cash? Are they like futures which are very responsive and sometimes lead the cash market, or is there a long lag time?*

A: Exhibit 15.2 shows the SPY relative to the cash market and the futures market (both mini and regular S&P 500 futures) at several time intervals throughout the day. Because of the close link (via arbitrage) between the underlying indexes, the futures on the indexes, and the ETFs, all tend to move in concert. On occasion, the futures will rise or fall faster than the cash, usually because of some sudden news announcement or a large order hitting the futures pit that does not affect the cash index. The ETF usually tracks the cash index, but I have seen the SPY "jump" track and

Exhibit 15.2 Comparison of Price Levels of ETF, Cash Index, and Index Futures, Various Times Throughout the Day

Time	SPY	SPY × 10	S&P 500 Cash	E-Mini S&P 500 Futures
10:00 A.M.	133.88	1338.80	1336.19	1345.75
10:15	134.00	1340.00	1338.13	1348.00
10:30	134.95	1349.50	1337.32	1347.75
10:45	134.16	1341.60	1338.30	1347.50
11:15	134.13	1341.30	1339.04	1348.75
11:30	134.53	1345.30	1343.23	1353.50
11:45	134.81	1348.10	1344.23	1354.75
12:03 P.M.	134.97	1349.70	1346.04	1357.25
12:17	135.25	1352.50	1349.10	1359.50
12:30	135.16	1351.60	1348.34	1359.75
1:00	135.31	1353.10	1349.26	1360.00
1:15	135.52	1355.20	1352.07	1363.00

follow the futures very closely—especially in the 3:00 to 3:15 central standard time bracket when the cash market is closed or during the day. For all intents and purposes, the three track each other fairly well.

Q: Given the success of ETFs and the eventual introduction of ETFs on actively managed mutual funds, will traditional mutual funds be rendered obsolete?

A: ETFs have skyrocketed from virtually nothing to about $80 billion in assets in a few years. Experts predict that these instruments will have about $500 billion in assets by 2004–2005, but this is still a small sum compared to the trillions stashed away in traditional mutual funds. ETFs have a bright future ahead, but I do not think Fidelity and Vanguard have to worry.

Q: In early January 2001, the assets of the Nasdaq-100 Index Shares (QQQ) overtook the S&P 500 SPDRs to become the largest ETF in terms of assets and average daily volume. How could the assets of the QQQ trust have gone up so much despite the Nasdaq-100's declining by over 50 percent from its highs?

A: The reason probably lies with the creation and redemption process and the mechanics of short selling. First, increasing creation unit activity usually increases the number of shares of the ETF. It is possible for the number of shares to increase enough to overcome the decline in the ETF's price. If there were 200 million QQQ shares outstanding a few months ago when they traded at $80 per share, that would give the trust an asset base of $16 billion ($80 × 200 million = $16 billion). A few months later, in early 2001, roughly 400 million QQQ shares were outstanding because of increased creation activity. Despite the price drop in QQQs, the total value of the trust is now $24 billion, (400 million shares × $60 per share) The increase in shares outstanding was so dramatic that it more than compensated for the decline in the Nasdaq-100 index. (A few weeks later, SPY regained the top slot.)

There are many reasons that creation activity might be on the upswing. One lies with the process of short selling. An investor who wishes to sell short QQQ or SPY or any stock must first borrow shares. Brokerage firms also lend out securities for short selling purposes. Some of the increase in creation activity may be to enable some firms to have enough QQQ shares on hand to lend them out for short selling purposes. This is a common practice on the Street, and entire departments within brokerage houses exist to lend securities (they are referred to as stock loan departments).

Q: *Will decimalization make markets tighter in general?*

A: Tighter for whom? Since the NYSE and AMEX made the conversion to decimal price increments, some markets have narrowed slightly. Tight markets consist not just of narrow bid-offer spreads. How much depth there is in the bid and offer is just as important. If a market is 133.10 bid 133.15 offered, the appearance of a 5 cent market appears on the screen. But how deep is that market? How many shares can you buy at 133.15? 100? 1000? 1,000,000? For an institution that needs to buy a large number of shares, this could be a nightmare. Let's assume the following offers existed in the SPY:

1,000 shares at 133.15
1,000 shares at 133.16
1,400 shares at 133.17
10,000 shares at 133.18
100,000 shares at 133.19

An institution that wanted to buy 500,000 shares might get filled at multiple prices. This can lead to reporting errors and back-office mistakes. For the small investor, however, it could be beneficial.

Q: With regard to ETFs, what is the difference between the fund manager, the custodian, and the depository?

A: We'll use S&P 500 SPDRs to illustrate:

Fund manager: State Street Global Advisors (SSgA) is the investment management division of State Street Bank. The manager is responsible for the actual portfolio of stocks in the ETF. With the S&P 500 SPDRs it manages the 500 stocks that make up the ETF. It is also responsible for any additions or deletions to the index and makes the appropriate transactions to ensure that the ETF fully replicates the S&P 500 composite index.

Custodian: State Street Bank, which holds the assets of the fund. The custodian is also responsible for trade settlement of ETF shares and the underlying baskets. The custodian facilitates movement of the creation and redemption trades to the clearing agent and depository.

Depository: Holder of ETF "certificates" (although the transfer agent keeps records of ETF shares). Investors actually hold shares in book entry form and do not receive certificates as they do in common stocks.

Q: Will there be more HOLDRS products introduced in the future?

A: I think that the number of HOLDRS offerings will be higher 1 to 3 years from now. Like many other ETFs, they have been a huge success and are frequently at the top of the most active list on the AMEX.

Q: Is there a minimum share requirement to purchase ETFs?

A: With HOLDRS, you must purchase at least 100 shares. With most other ETFs, you could conceivably buy just one share.

Q: Are there firms that construct and subsequently invest in portfolios of ETFs?

A: Yes. Many brokerage firms have realized that their customers are huge fans of ETFs and have created new departments dedicated to them.

A few money management firms are also dedicated to the ETF arena and manage money for investors using ETFs. Some of these firms believe that although ETFs are mostly index products, they can add value and outperform the indexes through active management.

Q: The E-mini and regular S&P 500 futures contracts have price limits. Why don't ETFs have those same limits?

A: The answer has to do with the nature of the two instruments. With futures contracts, the sheer size and use of leverage are part of the explanation. If the market were to drop substantially, a leveraged position could present a risk management problem. The limits give the firms and the clearing houses time to request and collect additional performance bond margin from investors, bolstering the entire system. If the market had no limits during a major market decline, the market could conceivably continue downward, and the firms would have to scramble to collect additional funds from investors. The limits enable the back office operations and exchanges to "catch up" in situations that could expose investors and traders (as well as firms) to undue risk. On the other hand, since most investors put up the entire sum of money when investing in ETFs, the firm is not at risk should additional funds be needed; they are already in place. While ETFs themselves do not have limits, the NYSE and AMEX do have circuit breakers to help stem severe market declines. Fortunately for investors, these limits are rarely activated.

Q: Why are the E-mini S&P 500 and E-mini Nasdaq-100 open for $23\frac{1}{2}$ hours? Why not just have them open 24 hours a day like foreign exchange markets?

A: The GLOBEX system is down for 30 minutes per day (3:15 to 3:45 P.M. CST) for two primary reasons: (1) system maintenance and (2) the upload and download of unexecuted pit orders from the regular pit-trading hours onto the electronic system for the regular-size index futures contracts (The regular S&P 500 trades in pit during the day and electronically at night, whereas the Mini S&P 500 trades electronically all the time.)

Q: Will the CME introduce mini stock index futures contracts on other stock indexes such as the Russell 2000 or the S&P MidCap 400?

A: People have suggested that CME consider this, but there can be a long time lag between consideration and actual development of a futures contract. There is a good chance that the CME will have an E-mini Russell 2000 by the end of 2001.

Q: *What is all the hype about fair value and premium as discussed on CNBC and the press. Are they important?*

A: I'll respond with a question: Would you buy a car that did not have a working oil pressure indicator light or temperature indicator light? These critical gauges tell you that something is too low (oil pressure) or too high (engine temperature), respectively. If you drive your car with the oil pressure light on for too long, you will scorch your engine block. Trading without a knowledge of how futures contracts are priced might prove damaging to your net worth. Fair value can (but does not always) help determine whether futures are expensive or cheap relative to the underlying cash index. If the premium (futures over cash) is supposed to be 5 points and it is 8 when you enter a market order to buy, that 3-point difference can be costly. If, after your order hits the market and is executed, the normal premium is reestablished, the premium will shrink from 8 to 5, and you may lose money before the trade has a chance to work. Of course, a major upswing in the market could bail you out of a poorly timed trade. But if the market treads water, the reestablishment of the normal 5 premium might clip 3 points off the futures (or cause cash to rally 3 points).

Buying "expensive" futures can also be a double-edged sword in a declining market, since losses on the declining futures will be exacerbated by the excessive premium you paid for the futures. Professional traders closely monitor factors such as premium and fair value. New or inexperienced traders should do the same.

Q: *Do ETF traders have to monitor futures' fair value?*

A: Probably not, unless you are doing some kind of spread or arbitrage between an ETF and a futures contract. But fair value and premium can sometimes be indicators of short-term market direction, and they can be calculated quickly.

Q: *Why are CNBC's fair value and premium numbers different from other calculations on a given day?*

A: The answer has to do with the inputs to fair value—interest rates, dividends, and so on. If you polled 10 firms on their calculation of fair value, you would probably get 10 different results because borrowing requirements differ from firm to firm. Goldman Sachs does not borrow and lend at the same rates available to you and me. Merrill Lynch's dividend assumptions may differ slightly from Morgan Stanley's. Hence, different inputs to the formula result in differing values from firm to firm. They should, however, be somewhat close to one another. I do not know where CNBC gets its numbers from. There is a Web site that gives estimates of fair value, programtrading.com.

Q: Why does the margin requirement for futures at my firm sometimes differ from CME's margin requirement?

A: CME and other exchanges have minimum performance bond requirements. A brokerage firm, however, can charge more if it feels appropriate (as with extremely risky markets) as long as it meets CME exchange minimum. During the Nasdaq's violent slide during part of 2000, the exchange minimum performance bond margin on the regular Nasdaq was $39,375. However, some firms required several thousand dollars above that figure. Again, it is all part of the risk management and back office process at a firm, which will do everything necessary to ensure the financial integrity of the brokerage firm.

Q: Does the CME have any input regarding the components, construction, and calculation of the S&P 500 cash index or other indexes which it trades futures?

A: None whatsoever. That is the exclusive right of the index providers such as Standard & Poor's, Frank Russell and Nasdaq. CME trades futures contracts on these popular benchmarks, the underlying indexes are not CME property. It is fascinating, though, how many calls we get at CME applauding our decision to add a certain stock to the S&P 500. I have to inform the callers that we had nothing to do with it; that the index committee at Standard & Poor's makes that decision.

Q: Why do the Nasdaq-100 futures and the E-mini Nasdaq futures always trade at a discount to the cash index?

A: The Nasdaq futures (mini and regular size) almost never trade at a discount to the cash. If they do, it is because you are looking at the wrong cash index. Many people mistakenly look at the Nasdaq Composite Index, which is significantly different from the Nasdaq-100, which includes the top 100 nonfinancial stocks in the composite. The value of the composite is always higher than the Nasdaq-100 by approximately 100 to 200 points. On February 14, 2001, the various indexes and futures closed at the following prices:

Nasdaq Composite Index (cash)	2491.41
March Nasdaq-100 futures	2316.00
Nasdaq-100 Index (cash)	2305.82

The futures trade at a premium to the Nasdaq-100 cash index, which tracks the Nasdaq-100, not the Nasdaq Composite.

Q: How can trading in futures occur overnight if the underlying stocks in the cash market are not open for trading?

A: After-hours trading has been significant in the stock market and the futures markets. The Mini S&P 500 and Mini Nasdaq-100 do some fairly good volume after the cash market closes at 3:00 P.M. CST and also in the morning before the cash markets reopen in the United States, especially when unexpected news comes out. When there are news announcements such as earnings or government reports, traders wishing to enter or exit positions have the opportunity to do so. Although stocks generally are closed during the wee hours of the morning (3:00 P.M.–8:30 A.M. CST), there are many areas traders can turn to for information. First, many large-cap stocks on the S&P 500 and Nasdaq-100 trade on overseas markets, and traders can use these movements as navigational tools. In addition, foreign stock markets and their respective indexes also trade around the globe and give traders an additional glimpse of overnight trends. Of course, volume is obviously lower during the night session because spreaders, arbitrageurs, and many other traders are inactive. But during the volatility engendered by the Asian crises of 1997 and 1998, volume on the system was several times higher than normal as traders tried to offset positions or initiate new ones to take advantage of the rapidly moving markets.

Q: What is the difference between program trading and index arbitrage?

A: The NYSE defines *program trading* as portfolio trades or strategies consisting of 15 or more stocks with a value of $1 million or more. *Index arbitrage* is a form of program trading and involves the simultaneous purchase and sale of futures contracts and their underlying cash basket. There are program trades that do not involve stock index futures. For example, a money manager who received an influx of cash—say, $20 million—could index the $20 million to the S&P 500 quite easily. An institutional brokerage firm could facilitate this trade, and within a matter of minutes, the manager would own $20 million worth of the S&P 500—all 500 "names" in the index in their exact proportions. A preprogrammed computer system (thus, the name *program* trading) would execute a list of all 500 stocks in the S&P 500. This would certainly qualify as a program trade since more than 15 stocks and more than $1 million in value are involved, but there is no futures contract in this example. But index arbitrage and plain-vanilla indexing programs are two of the more popular forms of program trading.

Q: *Does CME calculate and disseminate fair value?*

A: No. Because of potential liability issues, CME, as an exchange, does not calculate fair value. CME's Web site has an example of how to calculate fair value, and we are always willing to assist traders and investors of all types on how to arrive at an accurate value.

Q: *But CME does calculate and disseminate fair value. Isn't that what the fair value settlement at the end of the month is all about?*

A: The month-end fair value settlement for all domestic stock index futures is done by survey. We survey some of the largest players in the equity index derivatives arena and derive the fair value from averaging the values obtained in the survey, so it is essentially the firms that do the calculation. The exchange merely assembles the data and then disseminates the results of the survey as soon as possible.

Q: *Why is there a monthly fair value settlement?*

A: Stock index futures are open for 15 minutes longer than the cash index. (Futures close at 3:15 CST and reopen at 3:45 P.M.; the cash index closes at 3:00 P.M. CST.) During this 15-minute window, the futures contracts can sometimes move dramatically higher or lower in relation to the 3:00 P.M. cash close, causing large artificial shifts in the basis. Institutions that practice synthetic indexing (they index using stock index futures instead of the underlying stocks) find that tracking error can be exacerbated during that period. Settling futures to their fair value has mostly eliminated the tracking error.

Q: What are the daily price limits for domestic stock index futures, and how long have they been in effect?

A: Price limits were instituted in 1988 and have evolved since then. The current percentage-based price limit system began on April 15, 1998. The price limits are set on a quarterly basis and are based on percentage movements of 5 percent, 10 percent, 15 percent, and 20 percent. New limits go into effect at the beginning of each calendar quarter. Although the percentages do not change, the actual price limit may change depending on the movement in the underlying index. The average closing price of the lead month futures contract determines the level for the next quarter. For more details and updates on stock index price limits, visit the CME's Web site at www.cme.com.

Q: What is meant by the "roll" or "roll period"?

A: An example will illustrate the roll concept. Assume that a trader or investor is long a December S&P 500 futures contract. Further assume that the quarterly expiration is approaching, but the trader wishes to maintain a long position in futures beyond the December expiration (usually the third Friday of the contract month). He would sell his December futures and at the same time go long (buy) the next quarterly futures contract—in this case, March S&P 500 futures. The process of offsetting the expiring contract and reentering a new position in the following expiration is referred to as *rolling a futures contract forward—rolling* for short. Roll activity begins to increase the week before the quarterly futures expiration and peaks on or around expiration day.

Appendix 1

ELECTRONIC TRADING CONSIDERATIONS

In June 1992 when CME launched the GLOBEX electronic trading system, I was in London at the 24-hour trading desk of BZW, the money management arm of Barclays Bank PLC. It was a bit after midnight there (early evening in Chicago), and the trading desk was staffed by two individuals. For the first time ever, a CME product would trade in cyberspace rather than through roaring trading pits, a Chicago tradition for more than a century. Trading was slow, with 1,000 to 2,000 contracts trading during the ETH (electronic trading hours or GLOBEX) session as compared with 300,000 to 500,000 during the regular trading hours (RTH).

At seminars and conferences, the topic of electronic trading versus open outcry came up with alarming frequency. I would eventually be asked several times per week how long it would be before the pits would close down and the switch to all-electronic trading would occur. In the United States, growth of electronic futures trading was growing at a healthy clip but still had a minuscule fraction of overall trading volume. I kept a close eye on the volume figures and to this day monitor them here as well as overseas. Initially, I thought the two platforms could coexist for at least 5 to 10 years. That turned out to be right, but I also thought that despite the substantial rise in electronic trading overseas, where many exchanges such as DTB (now Eurex), LIFFE, and others were totally electronic, no electronic system in existence could duplicate the liquidity that CME enjoyed in Eurodollar futures. Because of the way the Eurodollar is engineered, hedgers and traders implement strategies that use several quarterly expirations. Therefore, where most futures contracts enjoy liquidity primarily in their front month, the Eurodollar enjoyed huge liquidity several years out—literally quarter after quarter of deferred month futures experienced large volume and open interest. Will it continue its success in the open outcry forum, or will it too succumb to the inevitable? I do not know. What I do know is that you can trade thousands (billions of notional amount) of Eurodollar contracts at a clip with barely a perceptible flutter in the bid-offer spread. Several years ago, CME attempted side-by-side trading, giving the marketplace the opportunity to vote by placing orders for Eurodollar futures in either the pit or the GLOBEX system. The pit won—by a large margin.

As the year 2001 unfolds, the giant Eurodollar continues to set records. Open interest is around 4 million contracts, larger than most other exchanges in the world. On an average day, it trades 700,000 contracts. On a busy day, it breaks 1 million by lunchtime. The market-making capability in the pit—especially in the important back months where synthetic swaps, strips, packs, and bundles trade feverishly—is incredible. There are individual traders as well as huge institutions that will take the other side of just about any size trade you want. Want to do a $5 billion synthetic swap 3 to 5 years out? These market makers will do it with the flick of a wrist and faster than you can punch the Enter key on your PC. But figure out a way to replicate this on the GLOBEX system, and perhaps the shift to electronic trading will accelerate.

On the other hand, if one were to walk a few floors down from the Eurodollar pit to the equity quadrant, where the S&P pit is surrounded by hundreds of E-mini S&P 500 and E-mini Nasdaq-100 terminals, the ambience is decidedly different. The great evolution is clearly obvious. With Eurodollars, everyone, at least for now, prefers the pits. With equity index futures, electronic trading of the two mini products is turning heads and keyboards everywhere. Members, as well as the trading community at large, are clamoring for GLOBEX terminals to trade the Mini S&P and Mini Nasdaq. For all of 1992, average daily volume on the system was under 1,000 per session. Average daily volume for 2000 was 136,000 (see Exhibit A1.1) With the two minis alone doing well over 100,000 per day early in 2001, that number is sure to climb. Too, the total number of GLOBEX terminals recently passed 1,700 and is sure to soar as CME's new CEO, Jim McNulty, has moved forward on an initiative to open up access to the system dramatically. Some CME members say that when this happens, 100,000 mini S&Ps will be a slow day.

Exhibit A1.1   GLOBEX$_2$ Average Daily Volume by Year 1992–2001

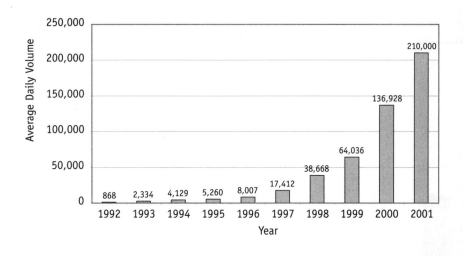

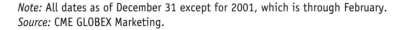

Note: All dates as of December 31 except for 2001, which is through February.
Source: CME GLOBEX Marketing.

Although electronic trading has made quantum leaps in the United States and abroad, it has not come without growing pains. On July 23, 1998, the MATIF exchange in Paris was experiencing one of these pains when huge sell orders suddenly flooded the NSC trading system (the NSC system is the matching engine for the Paris exchange's electronic platform) in the French government bond futures (Notionnel Bond Futures). Buy the time it was over, more than 10,000 contracts had been sold, and the bond got a good whacking from the selling pressure. After an investigation by the MATIF, it turned out that a trader had accidentally leaned on the F12 key on the NSC terminal. That key, when double-clicked, enters trades instantly. Interestingly, a system upgrade that would have eliminated the F12 key problems was due to be installed on that firm's terminals.[1]

A few months later in November, Eurex (German Electronic Exchange) felt the downside of electronic trading on its system. The story, never confirmed, goes like this: Apparently a trader at a small German bank was training on the system and doing simulated trading in German government bonds. It was believed that the trader thought he was on a simulated session that provides training and testing for new trainees. Apparently he was not. The trades were genuine trades, not simulated ones.

The critics of electronic trading had a field day saying that kind of thing could never happen in a pit. They went on to state that so many people mistakenly believe that electronic trading is so superior and these kinds of incidents are the first of many on the horizon. The critics are right in some regard, but again the marketplace is voting. Electronic trading continues to gain in popularity. Despite the inevitable and potentially costly outages, periodic slowdowns, keyboard risk, software risk—despite all these risks—investors and traders see these risks as merely speed bumps in the road and are making the transition. The belief is that systems will improve, outages will largely disappear, software will get better, and speed improvements will occur. It may take longer for some products, perhaps much longer. But with others the transition is already well underway. Currently, 80 percent of the transactions executed by Charles Schwab are done electronically. MATIF, LIFFE and many other exchanges have long since made the transition to an all-electronic system. Following is a review of the pros and cons of open outcry and e-trading:

Open Outcry

Pros	*Cons*
Execution risk reduced	Costly infrastructure and
No outages	maintenance
No slowdowns	Audit trail less precise

E-Trading

Pros	*Cons*
Faster executions	Outages
Execution risk	Slowdowns
Near-perfect audit trail	Keyboard errors

With 24-hour trading, we get more than around-the-clock trading opportunities. We also get price discovery before markets in the United States open and after these markets close for the day. Traders are always looking for tools to gauge the market's tone as they begin the trading day. In the past, professionals would look to see how U.S. stocks performed on overseas exchanges. Scores of large-cap U.S. issues like GE, GM, and IBM are listed on European and Asian markets, and their price behavior there is one indicator of how markets in the United States might open. But with the advent of GLOBEX, which features around-the-clock stock index futures trading, traders have a powerful premarket indicator for the S&P 500 Index. With the regular Nasdaq-100 and the E-mini Nasdaq-100 also trading overnight, investors also have some gauge as to how tech stocks might open the session.

How accurate is the GLOBEX session in determining the market's opening tone? I am not aware of any detailed quantitative studies showing the predictive power of the overnight session, but large overnight moves up or down have been fairly accurate in predicting the market's direction for the first 15 to 30 minutes. After that, it is usually anyone's guess. If the S&P 500 futures on GLOBEX are down 15 to 20 points 30 minutes before the NYSE open, it is quite likely the cash market will open down sharply. It may rally and even close higher on the day, but the opening moments will probably be rough, and traders can plan accordingly.

Extended trading hours also give futures traders the chance to enter or exit positions when news announcements occur after the 4:00 P.M. NYSE close. Since nearly all earnings announcements (or earnings "preannouncements") occur after the market closes, this can be a considerable source of post-close fireworks. In mid-February 2001, Cisco, Dell, and Nortel Networks made such announcements shortly after trading halted at 3:00 P.M. CST. Nasdaq-100 futures quickly provided some "price discovery" (a key attribute of the futures markets) as they were trading 45 to 55 points lower than their 3:00 P.M. price level when the markets normally shut down. Through GLOBEX, traders had not just a few more hours to adjust positions but the entire evening to cover shorts, add to shorts, and initiate new short positions, or, for the contrarian, initiate longs.

Although a few more hours of extended trading were available through ECNs such as Instinet and various brokerage firms, their reach falls well short of the around-the-clock availability that Nasdaq chief Frank Zarb envisions: "In a few years, trading securities will be digital, global, and accessible 24 hours a day. People will be able to instantly get stock-price quotations and instantly execute a trade day or night, anywhere on the globe, with stock markets linked and almost all electronic."[2]

In terms of securities, Zarb's prediction will probably become reality, and traders will be able to buy and sell QQQs, Spiders, or any stock for that matter around the clock. The irony is that many firms such as Schwab and E*Trade have harnessed the power of the Internet and allow on-line trading for their customers. The Internet is 24/7. The

NYSE and AMEX as of now are not. But while the securities industry is moving toward 24-hour or seamless trading, the foreign exchange markets in the United States have been trading that way for decades. Futures have traded around the clock at CME since 1992, with stock index futures following shortly after. Additionally, many exchanges throughout Europe and Asia have begun a massive consolidation or formed powerful alliances. Euronext, a consolidation of the Paris Bourse, Amsterdam, and Brussels exchanges, is a prime example. U.S. stock and futures exchanges have also formed alliances with overseas exchanges. The AMEX recently announced that it will list for trading some of its ETF products on the Euronext platform. The CBOT has linked up with the German Eurex system, and the CME has the potentially powerful Globex Alliance with MATIF (the French derivatives exchange), the Singapore Exchange (SGX), MEFF (Spanish Futures and Options Exchange), and the Montreal Exchange. And in June 2001, the CME and CBOE announced a joint venture to trade single stock futures.

Appendix 2

ETFs AND SMALL- VERSUS LARGE-CAP CYCLES

In some of the sample portfolios in this book, ETFs representing small-cap and mid-cap indexes made several appearances, for a very good reason. In the past 5 or so years, the large-capitalization stocks and technology stocks took center stage at the expense of smaller and mid-size issues. It is extremely important to bring to your attention that large-caps should not be the sole focus of your portfolio. ETF investors (and futures traders) should expand their circle of investments beyond large-caps and technology and consider the long-term implications of owning ETFs that replicate small and midsize stocks as well.

From 1995 until 1999, large-cap stocks as measured by the S&P 500 had a remarkable 5-year performance. This period was the first ever in the history of the index where returns exceeded 20 percent for five years running. Most investors were pleased beyond words, and new investors thought these returns were the norm. Mid-cap and small-cap stocks did well too, but fell short of the amazing performance of the large-caps. The year 2000 brought a sea change in this thinking as the S&P 500 was down 10.14 percent (price return only). The Russell 2000, the primary measure of small-caps, was down only 4 percent and the S&P MidCap 400 index of midsize companies was *up* an astounding 19 percent! This trend of small- and mid-cap outperformance continues as the first half of 2001 comes to a close. The investment community began discussing if this is the start of one of those multiyear trends when small- and midsize stocks trounce the generals. Some experts think so. In the past 50 to 75 years, there were plenty of cycles when the smaller issues seized the day. But before you isolate the various periods or cycles of performance, and just observe the very long term, you will notice something quite unique. From 1926 through 1999, large stocks outperformed all other asset classes. The Ibbotson data in Chapter 11 proved this. But Ibbotson's studies also proved that small stocks outperform large stocks over the long run:

Long-Run Returns, 1926–1999

Small stocks	12.6 percent
Large stocks	11.3 percent

There are many reasons that small- and mid-cap issues might have a powerful jet stream at their backs. First, the advance of large-caps during the past 5 years has driven price-to-earnings (PE) ratios to the stratosphere relative to smaller issues. Stocks like General Electric and Coca Cola were trading at lofty PE ratios of 40 and 60, respectively. True, both of these blue chip companies have enormous worldwide franchises and are superb growth companies, with 13 to 18 percent long-term earnings growth rates. But PE ratios of this magnitude had previously been the exclusive territory of ultra-high-growth tech firms like Cisco and Microsoft (which during the tech bubble of the later 1990s exploded above 100). Some experts think the relative valuations between the larger-caps and small-caps will be resolved partly with a decline in price of large-caps (underway as of the end of February 2001) but mostly with a solid rally in smaller and midsize stocks.

Second, declining interest rates tend to favor small-cap stocks. During the first 45 days of trading in 2001, Federal Reserve chairman Alan Greenspan had loosened the Fed's monetary grip by initiating not one but two 50 basis point rate cuts. The economists and stock market pundits feel that Greenspan tightened too much in previous years, and the early 2001 easing will prove to be merely a prelude to still lower rates as time progresses. With inventories piled high in numerous sectors and layoff announcements becoming a daily occurrence, economic growth certainly seems to be ebbing.

The third reason that smaller-size issues may gain prominence has to do with the Internet. In the past two decades, there were hundreds of sources for information on larger-cap stocks for the typical investor. Value Line, S&P, Moody's, and many other outfits provided excellent coverage of large-cap stocks. Smaller stocks, however, were usually covered only by certain analysts at certain brokerage firms. Hundreds of analysts covered stocks like IBM or General Motors, but with most small firms, coverage was usually totally absent. As research staffs have been beefed up on Wall Street, coverage continues to increase in this sector. But thanks to the Internet, individual investors have tremendous access to information on small stocks. There are plenty of sites dedicated to research, and that includes small stocks too. In addition, nearly all small companies have Web sites that provide at the least some information about their company, including financial statements, historical price information, and news releases.

The Internet has also allowed smaller and sometimes nimbler companies access to business opportunities. Take E*Trade, for example. True, its stock had a tremendous run-up in the dot-com mania and subsequently suffered a mighty fall. But no one can argue the influence that E*Trade has had with regard to on-line investing (not to mention E*Trade's excellent TV commercials). Ten years ago, the investing public would never have guessed that anyone could own 100 shares of any NYSE, AMEX, or Nasdaq stock with the click of a mouse. Although many firms on the Street were slow to join up, most eventually embraced the concept.

Moreover, Amazon.com may take a very long time to become profitable, but this small Seattle-based company changed the bookselling market and attracted the attention of the traditional bricks and mortar book chains. The Internet has changed the way investors trade and do research. It has also given small companies a huge competitive weapon. The Internet cannot directly change sales at a McDonalds franchise or have much of an impact on Coca Cola sales, but to small start-ups, it might just provide the background for an astounding business in the future.

Cycles of Small- and Large-Cap Stocks in Recent History

Below are a few of the major cycles that small- and large-cap stocks have undergone during the past 27 years. The appearance of these cycles is evidence that long-term investors should look beyond large-cap issues.

1995–1999	Large stocks outperform as cash cascades into mutual funds. With huge amounts of cash, managers are forced to go largely with large-caps. Attraction to large-cap tech names exacerbates the situation. The Asian and Russian crises also cause a flight to quality, which favors large blue chips.
1990–1993	The post–Gulf War era has a pronounced positive effect on smaller stocks. Interest rates decline to

the lowest in decades as T-bill rates dip below 3.0 percent in November 1993 and 30-year bond yields drop below the 6 percent level.

1983–1990   As the greatest bull market since the 1950s got its start, large-caps raced ahead of everything else. Strength in foreign currencies versus the U.S. dollar also favored large-caps with tremendous overseas exposure (e.g., Merck, Coke, Philip Morris).

1973–1982   Small issues outperform large-caps by a wide margin as small oil and gas stocks lead the way higher during a decade when gas lines, OPEC, and energy concerns were prominent.

Other factors contribute to smaller issues' racing ahead at certain cycles. Larger growth capacity is an overwhelming contributor. At early stages, it is not uncommon for small companies to exhibit 50 to 75 percent or more revenue and earnings growth. Growth rates always slow, as we have seen with Wal-Mart and Microsoft, but in the early stages it is truly meteoric, and the stock market sometimes takes notice, with the stocks having quite a ride up. The market will always pay up regarding high growth rates. But at the first sign that growth is slowing, you can be sure the market will adjust. Given the small capitalizations of these companies, it takes only a few mutual fund managers with a few million dollars to launch a rocket. Consider a fund manager with $100 million to invest. That $100 million is equivalent to 1.2 million shares of ExxonMobil, the largest oil company in the world and one of the largest companies in the S&P 500. That 1.2 million shares represents only .035 percent of Exxon's 3.4 billion outstanding shares. That same $100 million put into a small-cap or a collection of small-cap equities could represent a substantial percentage. Clearly the potential for large moves in smaller-size stocks is enormous. And as the cycle history shows, when the momentum builds, the fireworks display can go on for years.

Following are abbreviated lists of ETFs and futures that concentrate on small- and mid-cap issues:

Futures

S&P MidCap 400 Futures (CME)
Russell 2000 Futures (CME)
E-mini Russell 2000 Futures (CME launch date TBD)

ETFs

Russell 2000 iShares
Russell 2000 Growth iShares
Russell 2000 Value iShares
S&P SmallCap iShares
S&P SmallCap/Barra Growth iShares
S&P SmallCap/Barra Value iShares
DJ US SmallCap Growth streetTRACKS
DJ US SmallCap Value streetTRACKS
S&P MidCap 400 SPDRs
S&P MidCap 400 iShares
S&P MidCap/Barra Growth iShares
S&P MidCap/Barra Value iShares

Appendix 3

INDEX ARBITRAGE AND PROGRAM TRADING

In Chapter 9, we touched on the notion of fair value and premium and how they serve to link stock index futures contracts and their underlying cash indexes. When the relationship between a stock index futures and the underlying cash index strolls too far from equilibrium (too far above or below the theoretical premium), a powerful force will converge on the market and bring the relationship back toward equilibrium. This powerful force is commonly referred to as *index arbitrage*. Individuals practicing arbitrage are called *arbitrageurs*, or *arbs* for short. Index arbitrage falls under the heading of *program trading*, a strategy involving the purchase (or sale) of a portfolio of 15 stocks or more with a value of $1 million or more. Not all program trading involves futures contracts. But we will start with index arbitrage, which typically does involve baskets or portfolios of stock and stock index futures contracts. The E-mini stock index contracts and ETFs are also used in arbitrage.

Although virtually all investors will never practice the art of arbitrage, a study of the subject will help you gain an understanding of an important practice that plays out in the markets daily. Professional traders in S&P 500 futures and ETFs pay close attention to arbitrage activity since the potential short-term effect can mean the difference between profit and loss for the short-term trader. Knowledge of arbitrage activity will not make you a great trader or even a good trader, but it might make you a better trader. At the very least, you will have a better grasp of the inner workings of the fascinating index markets.

Arbitrage is the simultaneous purchase and sale of similar or identical instruments (often in different geographical locations) to take advantage of short-term price discrepancies. For example, gold trades in several major financial centers around the world—New York, London, Paris, Hong Kong, and Tokyo. If gold were trading in New York for $300 per ounce and in London for $302 per ounce, you could, in effect, buy gold in New York and immediately sell an equal amount in the London market, profiting $2 per ounce. Why would the precious metal be quoted $2 higher in London? The reason is short-term supply and demand fluctuations. Perhaps a European jeweler or metal fabricator placed a large order in the London market. The short-term demand may cause the price to rise in London relative to New York or other financial centers. Throughout the world, a cadre of gold traders watch their screens for hours waiting for such a moment. Armed with lightning-fast reflexes and a few million dollars or so in capital, they pounce. They quickly buy as much gold in New York as possible and simultaneously sell it in London, pocketing the $2 per ounce price differential. Hundreds of worldwide arbs acting in concert have an almost immediate effect: Gold in New York will quickly rise, and in London it will just as quickly fall, until the price differential disappears or is so small that the arb's costs of business would outweigh the now negligible spread.

What is the risk in a trade like this? Virtually zero. Arbitrage seeks to take advantage of short-term price discrepancies. A successful arbitrage trade carries almost no risk. The only real risk is execution risk. Although the trader would buy and sell immediately in both markets, there is a small risk that right in the middle of the trade, the market will move quickly against him and cause him to lock in a lower differential or, worse, lock in a loss. It happens. Traders get hung on one side of a multiple-sided trade all the time. It's part of the business. But over time, a skilled arbitrageur minimizes these events and can look forward to a lucrative business.

Stock index arbitrage (or index arbitrage) is a variation on the same theme, but instead of New York and London gold, the similar instruments are a basket or portfolio of stocks traded largely on the NYSE in the form of the S&P 500 Index, and a futures contract based on the index that trades in Chicago—the S&P 500 futures contract.* While arbitrage occurs with many stock indexes, activity is particularly

---

*Most of the stocks in the S&P 500 trade on the NYSE, but some are listed on the AMEX and some on the Nasdaq stock market.

focused on the S&P 500 cash and futures markets The combination of deep, liquid markets in both the cash index and the futures makes it an ideal candidate for this type of trading. Here we will see, step-by-step, how such a trade is made, taking into account fair value and premium as well as buy and sell programs.

Let us start with a quick review of fair value, using the formula from Chapter 9 and actual data from February 15, 2001:

March S&P 500 futures	1334.70
Cash S&P 500	1330.00
Days to expiration of futures	30 days
Interest rate/financing costs	5.5%
Dividend yield on S&P cash	1.3%
Theoretical fair value of futures	$= \text{cash} (1 + [r - d] [x/365])$
	$= 1330.00 (1 + [.042] [30/365])$
	$= 1330.00 (1.003452)$
	$= 1334.59$

Fair value in itself is not of much use. It is really the premium or basis that matters—the spread between the cash and the futures.

Theoretical premium (or basis)	= Theoretical fair value of futures − actual cash index value
	=1334.59 − 1330.00
	= 4.59 points
Actual premium (or basis)	= Actual level of futures − actual cash index value
	= 1334.70 −1330.00
	= 4.70 points

In this example, the S&P 500 futures should be trading about 4.6 points above the cash index. This does not mean they always will. In fact, for most of the trading session, the futures will trade slightly above and below the theoretical premium due to order flow, supply and demand, volatility, and a whole host of other factors. Exhibit A3.1 traces the cash and futures prices throughout the trading session on February 15.

Only when supply and demand fluctuations cause a large shift away from the theoretical premium level will arb activity start to occur. In the example, the actual premium is 4.7 points, a mere .10 point away from theoretical premium. For arbitrageurs to make a profit, the

Exhibit A3.1 The Spread Between S&P 500 Futures and the S&P 500 Cash Index

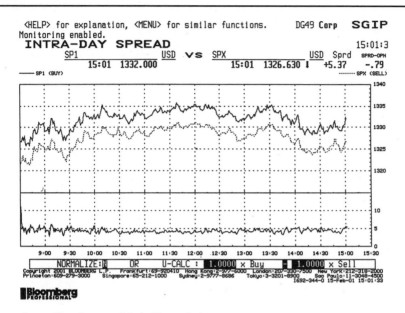

Source: Bloomberg, reprinted with permission.

actual premium has to increase by at least 1 or more points above the theoretical premium to cover fixed costs such as commissions, trader salaries, equipment, and telecom lines. Thus, using our 4.6-point theoretical premium as reference, no arb activity would begin until the premium widened to around 6 or so points. What would cause the premium differential to widen that much? Again, like the New York–London gold example, it is due to short-term supply and demand considerations. What if a large customer of a brokerage firm decided she wanted to gain exposure to the stock market through S&P 500 futures? If she put in a large enough order, say 500 to 1,000 contracts, the short-term demand would cause the S&P futures to begin to climb relative to the cash market. Once the discrepancy climbed to a point where arbs could profit from the differential, an intricately linked set of events is set into motion. (For this illustration, we use 1.4 points as the amount the premium would have to increase above equilibrium or theoretical value to cover all costs and still allow the arbitrageur to profit. In other words, if the theoretical premium is 4.6 points, the arb trader would need the actual premium to widen an additional 1.4 points, to 6.0

points, for an index arb trade to become profitable after costs. This is just an example. In reality, this breakeven figure may be greater or less than 1.4 points.)

After the large customer's order hit the trading floor, here is how the prices in the market might look:

Actual value of S&P 500 futures	1336.00 (CME)
Actual value of S&P 500 cash index	1330.00 (NYSE)
Actual premium or basis	6.00

At this point, some of the best and the brightest on Wall Street will effect index arbitrage. They will purchase the relatively cheap S&P 500 cash index, consisting mostly of NYSE issues, and simultaneously sell the relatively expensive S&P 500 futures contracts at CME. It is very similar to the New York–London example except that instead of buying and selling a yellow metal, they buy and sell baskets of stocks. Many of the larger program trading and index arbitrage players apply their trade in New York, but with computers and modern telecommunications, it could conceivably be done from anywhere. The precision required to pull off this kind of strategy is quite amazing. The futures side can be done rather quickly, as it involves only one instrument. But how do arbs quickly and accurately buy all 500 member stocks since they need to do the cash and futures sides of the trade at the same time? The answer lies with a system referred to as SuperDOT. DOT stands for Designated Order Turnaround System or Direct Order Turnaround System. The DOT system electronically routes orders directly to the specialist's post on the floor of the NYSE. At the press of a button, a firm can send an order to the NYSE for immediate execution. The system can be programmed with customized lists of stocks (also called names) that trade at the NYSE. The DOT system can thus allow a trader to buy or sell all 500 names in the S&P 500 at once. In reality, most firms probably do not buy all 500 names in the index. They have in-house researchers who do mathematical regressions and portfolio optimization and can put together a list of fewer than 500 names that would track (hopefully) the S&P 500 with close precision. If you look at a list of all the components in the S&P 500, you would notice the last 50 to 100 names have a very small weighting on the overall index (the top 40 stocks account for about 50 percent of the capitalization of the index).

How many shares of each component stock and how many futures are bought and sold? This depends largely on the size of the program (remember that index arbitrage falls under the heading of program trading). Most programs are in the $10 million to $15 million range, but some can reach much higher levels. As an example, let's see what is involved in a $10 million index arbitrage buy program. In an index arbitrage buy program, you would be buying the cash basket of stocks and selling the futures. In a sell program, you would be selling the cash basket of stocks and buying the futures. You do not just divide up $10 million in 500 equal installments. You must buy the stocks in their exact proportion to their weighting in the index. For example, GE is the largest stock in the S&P 500 Index and accounts for about 4.01 percent of the overall index. Therefore, you must spend 4.01 percent of your $10 million on General Electric, or $401,000. If GE's current price is $46 per share, that means purchasing approximately 8,717 shares. ExxonMobil is the third largest issue, at about 2.515 percent of the index, and 2.515 percent of $10 million is $251,500 At a price of $82, you would have to buy 3,067 shares of the large oil company. You would continue in a similar fashion with the other 498 stocks in the index. Exhibit A3.2 lists some of the share amounts required in a $10 million index arb program. The list is preprogrammed, and with simple spreadsheets, the entire breakdown for the cash side of the arb trade is calculated in nanoseconds. If the house wanted to do a larger program, the programmed list would automatically adjust the number of shares.

Despite the use of the DOT system to buy the list of stocks in the S&P 500 cash index, the futures side is slightly less cumbersome. If the March futures were priced at 1336.00, the contract size would be $334,000 (1336 × $250—remember this is the standard size S&P futures). If you buy $10 million of the cheap underlying cash basket, you must sell $10 million of the relatively expensive futures contracts to do the arbitrage correctly, and $10 million divided by $334,000 comes out to about 30 contracts.

At the appropriate time, you will enter the order through the DOT system to purchase the basket of stocks in the S&P 500 in a $10 million amount, thereby replicating the cash index. At the same time, the trading desk will instruct the broker in the S&P 500 futures pit to sell 30 futures contracts that are designed to track the cash index closely but at this moment are a bit expensive due to short-term supply and demand factors. In a matter of moments, the arb desk begins receiving reports on the two transactions. As other arb traders execute similar

Exhibit A3.2   Sample Index Arb Program

	Ticker	Percentage of S&P 500	Amount Required in $10 Million Buy Program	Price	Number of Shares Required in $10 Million Buy Program
1 General Electric	GE	4.01	$401,000	46	8,717
2 Microsoft	MSFT	2.63	263,200	57	4,618
3 ExxonMobil	XOM	2.52	251,500	82	3,067
4 Pfizer	PFE	2.46	245,900	45	5,464
5 Citigroup	C	2.34	233,800	52	4,485
6 Wal-Mart	WMT	2.01	201,400	46	4,378
7 Intel Corp	INTC	1.99	199,200	31	6,426
8 AOL Time Warner	AOL	1.80	180,200	46	3,917
9 Cisco Systems	CSCO	1.75	175,100	26	6,735
10 IBM	IBM	1.74	173,700	100	1,737
.					
.					
.					
499 Worthington Ind.	WOR	0.008	800	8	100
500 American Greetings	AM	0.007	700	9.4	74

trades, the act of concerted selling and buying in futures and cash, respectively, will force the rich 6-point premium back toward its equilibrium or theoretical value of 4.6.

Unwinding such a trade takes equal skill. Some of these trades are offset in the future (which could mean minutes, hours, days, or weeks), and some remain on the books until expiration. At expiration, convergence will force the cash and futures contracts to trade at equal values. No matter where the market ends up at expiration, the arbitrageur profits by whatever amount the premium level he sold at (6 points) exceeds the theoretical premium (4.6 points) minus trading costs. When (not if) the premium falls back to normal levels, the entire trade could, in effect, be unwound. If the trader is fortunate and bearish sentiment prevails, the futures could decline below the 4.6 equilibrium point, and

Exhibit A3.3   NYSE Trading Report

Firm	Number of Shares Involved, Index Arbitrage	Number of Shares of All Other Program Strategies
Deutsche Bank/Alex Brown	18.8	255.9
Morgan Stanley	34.8	162.7
Salomon Smith Barney	—	159.7
Interactive Brokers	—	144.6
Merrill Lynch	—	124.8
Goldman Sachs	—	105.0
First Boston	4.4	105.0
RBC Dominion	31.7	102.4
BNP Paribas Brokerage Srvs	—	101.8
Susquehanna Brokerage Srvs	38.0	89.3
Bear Stearns	—	76.4
Spear Leeds	—	68.8
W & D Securities	—	65.0
TLW Securities LLC	4.9	60.8
Nomura Securities	10.0	51.1

Source: NYSE Research, March 2001.

his profit would obviously be greater. Should the premium level drop too far, another type of index arbitrage program might enter the market. If futures become too cheap relative to the cash index, traders will buy the cheap futures and sell the now-expensive stocks. This is called an *index arbitrage sell-program* (*sell-program*, for short).

Exhibit A3.3 lists the more prominent program traders; they can also be found in the NYSE's weekly program trading activity report (available on its Web site). The activity of all program trades is closely monitored by the NYSE. At any given week, program activity can be as high as 20 percent of NYSE volume. The report for the period February 26 through March 2, 2001, shows a breakdown of all program activity, as well as index arbitrage and the number of shares done under each strategy by every major firm. Share amounts are in millions.

How can a trader benefit from a knowledge of fair value, premium, and index arbitrage? I think the greatest benefit lies in gauging the relative cheapness or expensiveness of futures relative to the cash market. For the short-term trader of E-mini S&P 500 futures or regular-size futures, this is critical. A case study will illustrate why knowing how to price futures may improve your trading.

A few months back a trader called me screaming about how "bad" his fill was in the larger S&P 500 futures. His call was routed to me at about 1:30 P.M. Here is how the conversation went:

DL: By any chance, did this bad fill happen about 30 minutes ago?

Caller: Yes. How did you know?

DL: By any chance did you put in a market order to buy futures?

Caller: Yes. Again, nice guess.

DL: Did you know what the theoretical premium was when you placed your order?

Caller: No! I simply put in a market order to buy 1 June S&P 500 futures. What is the point of all this?

DL: Here is the point.

I then explained what had happened. At 1:00 P.M. the following prices were flashing on my screen:

June S&P 500 futures	1410.10
June S&P 500 futures theoretical fair value	1410.00
S&P 500 cash index	1400.00
Cash/futures theoretical basis (Fair value – cash)	10.00
Cash/futures actual basis (Actual futures – cash)	10.10

A few moments later, at about 1:05, a large order to buy then entered the pit and drove futures prices higher relative to the cash market. The following prices were then available:

June S&P 500 futures	1412.00
June S&P 500 theoretical value:	1410.00
S&P 500 cash index	1400.00
Cash/futures theoretical premium (Fair value – cash)	10.00
Cash/futures actual premium (Actual futures – cash)	12.00

The caller's market order to buy S&Ps hit right when the market was trading at 1412.00. He was filled at 1411.80—1.80 points above the theoretical premium level. Within minutes, the market did what it always does: Arbitrageurs and traders came into the market to take advantage of a premium level that took a stroll too far from equilibrium. As you now know from the index arb lesson, skilled arb traders sell expensive futures and buy cheap stock when the basis or premium becomes too large. This type of trading can rapidly force prices back into line. The trader's order hit the pits right when this activity began, at around 1:05 P.M., producing an immediate loss of 1.80 points in the position ($450). Now the question beckons, Is this really a poor fill, or is it due more to bad timing that could have been prevented by knowing a little bit about the pricing mechanisms in stock index futures contracts? In my opinion, it is the latter. If the trader had known that futures were temporarily expensive relative to the cash index, he could have delayed his order by just a few moments; the futures would have returned to their normal fair value, and our conversation would never have taken place. Merely knowing the theoretical value of the futures is not enough. You must know what the premium (or basis) should be trading at and, equally important, where it is trading at the present. In this example, the normal basis is 10. For a brief moment, it was 12 points—2 points too high.

Although cash and futures markets usually return to equilibrium rather quickly, extraordinary events may prevent this. Fed chairman Greenspan's 50 basis point rate cut in January 2001 was a great illustration of one of these extraordinary events. Shortly after the announcement, both regular and Mini S&P 500 futures contracts rocketed higher. Remember that futures are nearly always more responsive than the underlying cash market. As a result, the cash market took a lot longer to play catch-up. The trader who waited for the normal premium to reappear would have missed out on a fabulous rally. Should the market make quick, violent moves up or down, waiting for fair value to reassert itself could prove costly in terms of lost opportunities. But over the long run, consistently buying and selling futures at well above or below theoretical premium is a prescription for poor results.

Aside from arbitrageurs, other market constituents benefit from the price discrepancies between stock index markets and their cash market counterparts. Those lumbering giants, the pension funds, take advantage of arbitrage opportunities. While having cash reserves on hand is consistent with their investment policies, it is also part of those policies to earn every basis point of return possible. Cash management has been elevated to an art form on the Street, and as strange as it may seem, pension funds and other large institutions use index arbitrage as a cash management tool. Think about it for a moment. You have tens or hundreds of millions in idle cash earning T-bill, commercial paper, or CD rates. They receive money market rates with virtually no risk. However, index arbitrage is also largely absent risk. What if a major institutional brokerage firm with index arb expertise could provide a greater return than typical cash instruments but without any additional risk? An index arb program could be offset in a matter of hours or days, but some can be held until expiration. Returns on arb programs held until expiration are greater than returns on money market instruments and are obtained without any additional risk. If a pension fund can gain a risk-free return advantage over money market instruments of several dozen basis points, it would be foolish not to include this in its cash management policy.

ENDNOTES

CHAPTER 1

1. Burton G. Malkiel, *A Random Walk Down Wall Street* (New York: Norton, 1999), p. 170.
2. Barton Waring, "Conclusions from 30 Years of 'Modern Portfolio Theory'" (presented at Barclays Global Investors Chicago Client Conference, November 2, 2000).
3. John C. Bogle, "Success in Investment Management: What Can We Learn from Indexing?" (presented at Investment Analysts Society of Chicago, October 26, 2000).
4. Ibid.
5. Ibid.
6. Burton G. Malkiel, *A Random Walk Down Wall Street* (New York: Norton, 1999), p. 262.
7. John C. Bogle, *John Bogle on Investing—The First 50 Years* (New York: McGraw-Hill, 2001), p. 105.

CHAPTER 2

1. Sabine Schramm, "Index Assets Up 9% in 6 Months," *Pensions and Investments*, September 4, 2000, p. 52.

CHAPTER 3

1. All index statistics in this chapter are from CME Index Products.
2. The general guidelines are from Standard & Poor's *S&P 500 1999/2000 Directory* (New York: Standard & Poor's, 1999), p. 33.
3. Ibid.

CHAPTER 4

1. Lawrence Carrel and Trevor Delaney, "The Smart Money 30," *Smart Money* (December 2000): 148.
2. *Morningstar Mutual Fund 500*, 2000 ed. (Morningstar: Chicago, 2000), p. 36.

CHAPTER 6

1. Berkshire Hathaway Inc., Annual Meeting, Omaha, Nebraska, 1998.

CHAPTER 7

1. ADRs are American depositary receipts, a way for Americans to invest in foreign companies. They are a "receipt" backed by stock certificates in foreign companies. ADRs in their own right have garnered a tremendous amount of interest as Americans discovered some of the potential in overseas markets. Sony ADRs are quite active, as was Tel-Mex (Mexican Telephone Company). Hundreds of ADRs trade on United States exchanges.
2. Annual Mutual Fund Rankings, *Barron's*, January 8, 2001, p. F-31.
3. Shintaro Ishihara, *The Japan That Can Say No. Why Japan Will Be First Among Equals* (New York: Simon & Schuster, 1991).

CHAPTER 10

1. Adam Smith, *The Money Game* (New York: Vintage, 1976), pp. 227–235.

CHAPTER 11

1. Gary P. Brinson, L. Randolph Hood, and Gilbert L. Beebower, "Determinants of Portfolio Performance," *Financial Analysts Journal* (July–August 1986): 39–44.
2. William Jahnke, "The Asset Allocation Hoax," *Journal of Financial Planning* (February 1997), pp. 109–113.
3. William Glasgall, "Allocate, Amigo," *Investment Advisor* (February 2001), pp. 24, 184.

CHAPTER 12

1. Berkshire Hathaway 1997 annual report. Chairman's letter to stockholders, p. 8.
2. "The Taming of the Shrewd," *Economist*, May 6, 2000, p. 75.

APPENDIX 1

1. Patrick Young and Thomas Theys, *Capital Market Revolution* (London: Prentice Hall, 1999), p. 64.
2. Frank Zarb, "Nasdaq's Vision" *Economist*, May 20, 2000.

GLOSSARY

Active Management: The process of actively researching, choosing, and managing a portfolio of investments (stock picking) in order to obtain a return in excess of a particular benchmark.

Alpha: A term used by modern portfolio theory practitioners and money managers that describes the excess returns that a fund exhibits over its benchmark (some practitioners adjust alpha by the fund's beta coefficient). Let's say an active manager whose benchmark is the S&P 500 earns a 25 percent return in a given year while the benchmark S&P 500 returns 20 percent in that same year. Generally it would be said that the manager had an excess return of 5 percentage points. This excess return is called *alpha*. It is one of the single most driving forces on Wall Street. After all, no money manager wants to underperform his benchmark (negative alpha). The formula for alpha that many money managers use is: Alpha = Excess return − (beta × (benchmark return − Treasury bill return). *See also* Beta.

AMEX: Acronym for the American Stock Exchange. Located in New York City, the AMEX is where nearly all ETFs trade in the United States.

Arbitrage: The simultaneous purchase and sale of similar or identical instruments, often in differing geographical locations, to take advantage of short-term price discrepancies. It is a strategy usually practiced by large institutions or highly skilled professional traders. Arbitrage is usually risk free.

Asset Allocation: The process whereby an investor combines asset classes in a portfolio with different return and risk characteristics. Assets such as stocks, bonds, cash, and other types of investments have very different risk-return characteristics and can add value to a portfolio while reducing risk. ETFs alone or in combination with U.S. Treasury securities or other mutual funds are regarded as a solid foundation for a long-term portfolio.

Associated Person: A commodity futures broker—an individual who is registered by the Commodity Futures Trading Commission to solicit orders, customers, and customer funds for a futures broker, introducing broker, or commodity trading adviser. Most associated persons have taken and passed the Series 3 exam, which is also required to be a commodity futures broker.

Authorized Participant (AP):   Usually a large institutional brokerage firm, specialist, or financial entity that can participate in the creation and redemption process of ETFs. APs are capable of transacting, clearing, and set-

299

tling ETFs through connection to the NSCC's (now part of the Depository Trust Clearing Corporation—DTCC) continuous net settlement system.

Bank of New York (BNY):   One of three major banking institutions that provides custodial and fund management services to ETFs. BNY is the manager-custodian for the QQQs, the MidCap SPDRs, and the HOLDRS products.

Barclays Global Investors (BGI):   The money management arm of Barclays Bank. BGI is the largest manager of indexed assets in the world and one of the largest money managers overall.

Basket: A term used to describe the purchase or sale of an entire portfolio of stocks in a particular index. For example, if you purchased all the underlying issues in the S&P 500, you would be buying a group of stocks listed in the S&P 500. The S&P 500 Spiders are essentially made up of a basket of stocks consisting of the issues in the S&P 500.

Basis: The difference between the price of a futures contract and its underlying cash index. Basis occurs because of cost-of-carry factors.

Beta: A measure of a fund's (or stock's) sensitivity to market movements. High beta funds or stocks have larger movements relative to the market. Lower beta issues have smaller movements relative to the market. By definition, the beta of the market (market being the S&P 500) is 1.00. A fund with a beta of 1.20 has performed 20 percent better than the market in an up market (in general) and 20 percent worse than the market in a down market. Beta is another modern portfolio theory calculation. *See also* Alpha.

Capitalization Weighted: A term used in reference to the different methods of calculating an index. For example, the S&P 500 is capitalization weighted, meaning the stocks with the largest capitalization have the greatest weighting in the index. The capitalization of a stock is simply its price multiplied by the number of shares outstanding. Issues such as General Electric have very large capitalizations and a greater weight in the index. Most indexes are capitalization weighted in some form. The Dow Jones Industrial Average, on the other hand, is a price-weighted average.

Cash Drag: The drag on a portfolio's performance in a rising market due to the manager's holding excessive cash reserves. Cash, however, is preferred in a down market, as it provides a positive rate of return and helps to cushion the portfolio during periods of declining markets.

Chicago Mercantile Exchange Inc: The exchange (recently demutualized) where the E-Mini S&P 500 and E-Mini Nasdaq-100 futures trade. CME is a licensed, federally regulated commodity exchange and has a 94 percent market share (in the United States) in stock index futures trading. The regular-sized counterparts to the minis also trade at CME, along with stock index futures on the S&P MidCap 400 Index, S&P 500/Barra Growth and Value Index, Russell 2000 Index, and the Nikkei 225 Stock Index.

Clearing House: The entity through which all futures and options on futures are settled. The clearing house is responsible for setting all performance bond margins, paying, and collecting funds from clearing firms (and their customers). It is the ultimate guarantor of performance on trades executed on a futures exchange.

Commodity Trading Advisor (CTA): An individual registered with the National Futures Association and eligible to trade, on a discretionary basis, a portfolio of futures contracts for a customer. CTAs are like mutual fund managers. Instead of investing in a portfolio of stocks, they manage a client's money through a portfolio of futures contracts.

Core-Satellite Strategy: Strategy whereby an investor combines a core of index investing with a touch of active management. A typical core-satellite may involve indexing 50 percent of assets to a major equity benchmark such as the S&P 500 or the Russell 2000. The remaining assets would be invested in active management strategies.

Creation Unit: The process whereby ETF shares are created. The process involves the deposit of a basket or portfolio of securities with a custodian, who arranges for the issuance of ETF shares (although there are no paper certificates—they are held in book entry form). Creation units are typically done in large block sizes of 50,000 shares.

Cube or Cubes: Generic or nickname for the Nasdaq-100 Index Shares. Also known as QQQs.

Custodian: The custodian of ETFs holds and maintains the assets of the fund and is responsible for trade settlement of ETF shares and the underlying baskets. The custodian also facilitates the processing of creation and redemption trades to the clearing agent and depository. For example, State Street Corporation is the custodian for the S&P Spiders. It holds the assets (basket of S&P 500 components) and helps facilitate creation and redemption in SPY and works in conjunction with the clearing and depository agents.

Deutsche Boerse: One of the largest exchanges in the world, located in Germany. Eurex, the electronic trading platform of Deutsche Boerse, also trades derivatives, and the XTF division is where ETFs such as the DAX 30, EuroSTOXX, and DWS ETFs trade.

DIAMONDS: ETF that tracks the Dow Jones Industrial Average.

Discount/Premium to NAV: Discount occurs when an ETF price trades below the actual net asset value (NAV) per share. If the QQQ had an NAV at the end of the day of 50.00 per share and the QQQs themselves traded at 49.97, they would be trading at a discount to NAV. If they traded above the 50.00 NAV, they would be trading at a premium to the NAV. Institutional arbitrage keeps prices in line with NAVs.

Distributor: Accepts and approves orders for the creation unit and redemption process.

DWS Funds: Launched in November 2000, Deutsche Bank ETFs are the first actively managed ETFs. DWS funds are actually a hybrid that combines a fund run by a manager with shares that trade throughout the day like equities. The 11 DWS funds are available only to investors in select European countries and trade on Germany's Deutsche Boerse. It is thought that ETFs based on actively managed portfolios will eventually trade in the United States.

E-Mini Stock Index Futures: A term used to describe electronically traded, miniature versions of the S&P 500 and Nasdaq-100 futures contracts at the CME. The E-Mini S&P 500 and the E-Mini Nasdaq-100 are one-fifth the size of the regular S&P and Nasdaq contracts. They trade virtually 24 hours a day on CME's GLOBEX electronic trading system.

Equitizing Cash: Fancy name for putting cash to work quickly in the markets. Since stock index futures, mini stock index futures, and ETFs are very liquid, low-cost, and efficient vehicles, it is easy for all types of investors to become quickly invested in the markets through these vehicles.

ETF: Acronym for Exchange Traded Fund. ETFs are uniquely structured investments that usually track broad-based or sector indexes and are traded on regulated securities exchanges throughout the day. In less than seven years, ETF assets in the United States have mushroomed from virtually nothing to $78 billion as of the end of February 2001.

Euronext: European exchange formed from the combination of the Paris Bourse, Amsterdam Exchange, and Brussels Exchange. Trades CAC 40 and LDRS ETFs (based on STOXX 50 and EuroSTOXX 50 Indexes).

Expense Ratio: Number that represents the annual costs or expenses of a fund, usually expressed as a percentage of assets. One of the key attractions of ETFs is their low annual expense ratio.

Expiration: The period or date after which a futures or options contract ceases to exist. For the E-Mini S&P 500 and E-Mini Nasdaq-100, there are four quarterly expirations: in March, June, September, and December.

Fair Value: Where a futures contract should theoretically trade given dividend yields, time to expiration, and financing costs. Obtained using a simple algebraic formula. The actual price of a futures contract often differs (but not by much) from the theoretical price.

Futures Contract: A standardized agreement, traded on a commodity exchange, to buy or sell a commodity at a date in the future. Futures contracts specify the commodity, quality, quantity, delivery date, and delivery point or cash settlement. With stock indexes, the buyer and seller agree to transfer the cash value of the contract at a futures date—the expiration date. All futures contracts are either physically delivered or cash settled. E-mini stock index futures and regular-sized stock index futures at CME are cash settled.

Grantor Trust: One of three main types of ETF structures, Grantor trusts are not investment companies under the SEC Investment Company Act of 1940. They cannot loan out securities or use derivatives, and taxation is basically the same as owning the underlying stocks. Merrill Lynch's HOLDRS are a type of grantor trust.

Hedge: The process of protecting or insuring a financial asset or portfolio against adverse market moves. For a portfolio manager, an adverse market move would be a declining stock market. The manager could hedge using stock index futures contracts or ETFs.

HOLDRS: Acronym for Holding Company Depositary Receipts. Introduced by Merrill Lynch, HOLDRS ETFs are available in several sectors and in broad-based versions. Each holds approximately 20 securities, but a few hold a greater number of issues. HOLDRS must be purchased in 100-share minimums.

Index Arbitrage: A form of program trading; an institution or professional trader buys (sells) a basket of stocks and sells (buys) the corresponding futures contract in an attempt to profit from short-term price discrepancies. Many index arbitrage trades center around the S&P 500 futures and the underlying cash index or basket.

Index Provider: A financial concern that develops, calculates, and maintains indexes, usually broad-based and sector stock indexes. Standard & Poor's, Frank Russell, Dow Jones, Fortune, MSCI, and Wilshire are some of the major index providers.

Index Receipt Agent: Performs many of the services that a custodian does with ETFs. *See* custodian.

Investment Company Act of 1940: The rules and regulations written by the Securities and Exchange Commission that govern investment companies and ETFs.

iShares: ETFs developed and introduced by Barclays Global Investors. Several dozen were launched in spring and summer 2000.

iUnits: ETFs, developed by Barclays Global Investors that trade in Canada, such as the iUnits S&P/TSE 60 ETF that trades in Toronto.

LDRS: Listed diversified return securities—ETFs traded on overseas exchanges such as the Deutsch Boerse and Euronext.

Managed Investment Company/Open-Ended Mutual Fund: Of the three primary ETF structures, managed investment companies (also known as open-ended mutual funds) are overseen by a manager with discretionary power. The underlying index would not have to be perfectly replicated under this ETF structure. The manager is allowed to create an optimized basket of securities that should closely track an index. Dividends are typically reinvested; securities have no lending restrictions, and they can trade derivatives.

Market Capitalization: A broad term used to categorize the size of a particular company such as large capitalization, midsize capitalization, and small capitalization (large-, mid-, and small-caps). There are several indexes available for each capitalization level. The S&P 500 and the Russell 1000 are large-cap stock indexes, for example.

Modern Portfolio Theory (MPT): A standard financial and academic method for assessing the risk of a fund or portfolio relative to the market or some benchmark. Alpha, beta, and R-squared are three key MPT statistics that financial professionals use to evaluate investment portfolios. *See also* Alpha; Beta.

NSCC/DTC: The National Securities Clearing Corporation, which clears nearly all brokerage security transactions. It also clears ETF trades and facilitates the movement of all the securities in an ETF basket during the creation and redemption process. When you "create" an S&P 500 Spider, you must deposit all 500 stocks in the index with the custodian. The custodian then interfaces with the NSCC to clear all the transactions and complete the process of creation or redemption. DTC is the Depository Trust Company and the depository for ETF shares in book entry form. DTC and NSCC have merged to form the Depository Trust and Clearing Corporation.

OPALS: Optimized Portfolios as Listed Securities—ETFs developed and introduced overseas by Morgan Stanley Dean Witter. Only qualified non-U.S. institutional investors can invest in OPALS.

Open Interest: The total number of futures contracts that have not been offset; one measure of liquidity in the marketplace.

Passive Management: Also known as indexing. A strategy that attempts to earn market returns by mimicking a well-known benchmark. Passive managers are able to avoid using costly research and avoid portfolio turnover. The resulting low-cost, low-transaction strategy allows them to maintain the returns of the benchmark, which often outperforms their active management counterparts. Over $1 trillion is indexed in the United States, much of it to the S&P 500.

Performance Bond Margin: The minimum, up-front, good-faith deposit a trader must deposit with a futures broker before entering into futures transactions. Performance bond margins are set by the exchanges and vary according to contract size and the volatility of the futures contract. Performance bonds help ensure the financial integrity of brokers, clearing members, and the exchange as a whole.

Portfolio Composition File (PCF): Published by an ETF fund manager or fund adviser, the PCF file is crucial to the creation-redemption process. It lists all the stocks in a particular index and the exact number of shares required to create a creation unit, along with cash distribution amounts, creation fees, and accrued dividends.

Premium: Sometimes referred to as *basis*, premium is the amount by which a stock index futures contract trades above its underlying cash index. If the S&P 500 futures contract is trading at 1275.00 and the underlying cash index is trading at 1270.00, the futures would be at a 5.00 point premium.

Program Trading: A set of strategies that involves the purchase or sale of a basket of 15 or more stocks with a value of $1 million or greater. Index arbitrage is one form of program trading.

QQQ: Ticker symbol for the Nasdaq-100 Index Shares, the most actively traded ETF in the world. Also known as "cubes."

R-squared (or R²): Ranges from 0 to 100 and reflects the percentage of a fund's movements that are explained by movements in its benchmark index. Index funds will have an R^2 very close to 100.

Random Walk: A term coined by academicians and some on Wall Street that states that short-term fluctuations in the stock market cannot be predicted. Analysts, newsletters, and technical and fundamental analysis are of little or no use in predicting stock prices. Those who coined the term went so far as to state that throwing a dart at the stock pages would be equally effective in choosing stocks as using the average analyst or money manager.

Redemption/Redemption Process: The opposite of the ETF creation process. Shares of the ETF are deposited with the custodian. The authorized participant (usually an institutional investor) then receives the shares of each stock in the underlying basket.

Registered Rep (Stock Broker): A person registered with the SEC and usually licensed via the Series 7 examination to solicit customers and purchase and sell stocks on behalf of a customer for a brokerage firm.

Risk: The potential of losing money according to some; to others, it is the annualized standard deviation of returns. Standard deviations are expressed as a percentage. For example, the standard deviation of the S&P 500 Index in 2000 was 22.23 percent. The standard deviation of the Nasdaq-100 was 56.63 percent, more than twice the S&P 500. Market pundits would say the Nasdaq is riskier than the S&P 500. And given the movements of the Nasdaq from the 1800 level in 1998 to over 5000 in the year 2000 and back down to 1700 in early 2001, the index would certainly qualify as risky.

Sector Indexes, ETFs: A compilation of a narrow group of stocks in a particular sector of the economy such as technology, pharmaceuticals, or utilities. Investment managers usually obtain exposure in many sectors of the economy. Sector ETFs, such as the Select Sector SPDRs, offer an instrument by which an investor, large or small, can add exposure to a particular sector. There are dozens of sector ETFs, many of which have holdings in narrow-based sectors of the economy. The S&P 500 is a collection of the many sectors in the U.S. economy.

Settlement or Settlement Price: A figure determined from the daily closing range that is used to calculate gains and losses in futures markets and accounts and determine the need for performance bond margin calls.

SPDRs: Standard & Poor's Depositary Receipts—a group of ETFs indexed to various Standard & Poor's broad-based and sector indexes.

Special Opening Quotation (SOQ): The procedure for final settlement of many stock index futures contracts in the United States. The SOQ for each index is based on the opening price of each component stock in that index on expiration Friday (most CME index products undergo the SOQ procedure on the third Friday of the contract month—March, June, September, and December). Expiring index futures contracts will be cash settled to final SOQs. Say a trader purchased a March E-Mini S&P 500 futures at 1200.00, and the SOQ for the March expiration was 1242.78. At the final settlement (at expiration), the trader's account would be credited with 42.78 points, or $2,139 (42.78 points × $50 per E-mini point =$2,139) in cash—hence the term *cash settlement*.

Specialist: Specialists who function on the floor of the NYSE and the AMEX (and other exchanges) and mainly provide liquidity for the markets. They are to maintain a fair and orderly market and also maintain a book of public orders to be executed at certain prices.

Spiders: Nickname or generic name for ETFs in general, although usually a reference to the S&P 500 SPDRs or Select Sector SPDRs.

Spreading: The process of buying and selling similar instruments to take advantage of longer-term price disparities such as the outperformance of mid-cap stocks versus large-caps during 2000. It is a common strategy in futures contracts. It can be employed with ETFs but would be more costly.

SPY: Well-known ticker symbol for the oldest and largest ETF, the S&P 500 Depositary Receipts.

SSgA: Abbreviation for State Street Global Advisors, the money management arm of State Street Corporation. SSgA manages many of the underlying indexes that make up an ETF.

Standard Deviation: A statistical measure of the movement of some instrument or index. It is one of the most widely used measurements of variation about a mean and, for many purposes, a suitable proxy for risk and volatility. Higher standard deviations usually indicate greater movement or volatility.

streetTRACKS: A family of ETFs managed by State Street Global Advisors. Many of them trade on the AMEX, and several will be trading on overseas exchanges such as Euronext.

Style Indexes: A subdivision of broad-based indexes that seeks to categorize the components of the index into growth or value issues. For instance, the S&P 500 index has been sliced into growth and value style indexes. The S&P/Barra Growth and S&P/Barra Value Indexes comprise growth and value stocks, respectively. S&P and Barra use book value to price and other criteria to determine a stock's growth or value status.

SuperDOT system: DOT stands for Designated Order Turnaround System or Direct Order Turnaround System—a system that allows firms to route orders directly to the exchange specialist on the trading floor of the NYSE. It facilitates order entry and allows institutions to program trading.

Tracking Error: Sometimes ETF returns may deviate from the returns on the underlying index. ETF returns may also deviate from returns on net asset value of the ETF. (Remember that the underlying basket of stocks and the ETF itself are independent instruments. Although they do closely track one another, they can have small deviations.) This deviation of returns is called *tracking error*. Tracking error with ETFs is very low due to the arbitrage mechanism and the "in-kind" creation and redemption process. For example, in 1999, the

S&P 500 Index was up 21.04 percent. The S&P 500 Spider was up 20.39 percent, a very slight tracking error due in part to imperfect replication of the index, dividend reinvestment policy, index modifications, and fees.

Tracker Fund of Hong Kong (TraHK):   An ETF listed on the Stock Exchange of Hong Kong that approximates the Hang Seng Index, the primary stock index of the Hong Kong Stock Market. TraHK was a unique way for the government of Hong Kong to off-load a massive equity portfolio accumulated during the market downturns of 1997 and 1998 in order to stabilize the Hong Kong markets. The Hong Kong government's holdings ($30 billion) have been slowly and systematically transferred to this ETF.

Treasury Direct (TD):   A program established by the U.S. Treasury Department's Bureau of Public Debt to allow investors to buy U.S. Treasury securities (T-bills, T-notes, and T-bonds) directly from the U.S. government free of charge. TD can be accomplished through the mail or over the Internet. The only charge incurred is if a TD account holdings exceed $100,000. In that case, there is a nominal fee of $25.00 per year.

Trustee: *See* Custodian.

Turnover Rate: A good approximation of a fund's (or an investment manager's) trading activity. It is calculated by taking the fund's purchases (or sales) and dividing by the average monthly assets of the fund. Turnover rates over 100 indicate higher-than-normal trading activity. Turnover rates of 30 percent or below indicate a lack of trading activity. Index mutual funds tend to have extremely low turnover activity. High turnover engenders greater transaction costs as well as taxable events.

Unit Investment Trust: Regulated under the SEC Investment Company Act of 1940, UITs are not allowed to make discretionary investment decisions. They must completely replicate the underlying basket of stocks, remain fully invested, and hold interest and dividends in a non-interest-bearing account until distributed to investors. UITs also are disallowed from using derivatives or lending out securities.

Variation Margin: The daily debiting and crediting of commodity futures accounts due to movements in futures positions in the account. This way, losses and gains are "paid" up daily, and losses cannot accumulate. It is one of the primary risk management operations that gives futures exchange clearing houses a solid financial foundation. Also known as *mark-to-market*.

VIPER (Vanguard Index Participation Equity Receipts):   ETFs that track Vanguard's Index funds, including the massive Vanguard 500 Index fund. Currently the S&P 500 VIPER is tied up in litigation over licensing rights. But on May 31, 2001, Vanguard launched a VIPER product on its total Stock Market Index Fund, which is based on the Wilshire 5000 Index.

SUGGESTED READING

Bernstein, Peter L., *Against the Gods: The Remarkable Story of Risk*, John Wiley & Sons, New York, 1996.

There are only four things that matter in investing: returns, costs, time, and risk. Bernstein examines the history of risk over the past 800 years. The book is filled with incredible facts about risk, probability, and gambling and how they relate to human thought processes and investing. If you want to be a better investor, you should learn about risk. This is a great place to start.

Bogle, John C., *John Bogle on Investing—The First 50 Years*, McGraw-Hill, New York, 2001.

Bogle, John C., *Common Sense on Mutual Funds—New Imperatives for the Intelligent Investor*, John Wiley & Sons, New York, 1999.

Bogle on Investing is a compilation of many key speeches that John Bogle, founder of the Vanguard Group, has given over his career. *Common Sense* is an excellent book that will cause investors to think hard about the advantages of indexing, the costs and risks involved with active investing in both equities and fixed-income instruments. For those trying to figure out the stock market, *Common Sense* will put you on solid ground.

Gidel, Susan Abbott, *Stock Index Futures and Options: The Ins and Outs of Trading Any Index, Anywhere*, John Wiley & Sons, New York, 2000.

Gidel, a seasoned veteran in the futures industry, provides all the basics that a beginner needs to know before opening an account and beginning to trade, with a bit of important history added for good measure. Gidel also talks about stock index futures across the globe, a subject serious traders should at least be aware of, even if their trading activities will be confined within the borders of the United States.

Hill, John, George Pruitt, and Lundy Hill, *The Ultimate Trading Guide*, John Wiley & Sons, New York, 2000.

For those interested in trading systems and technical analysis. This book examines dozens of trading systems, from simple to complex, and covers the important aspects of all successful systems. Good detail on topics such as risk management, drawdowns, and average profit and loss per trade.

Kaufman, Perry, J., *Trading Systems and Methods*, John Wiley & Sons, New York, 1998.

An excellent, comprehensive look at the technical analysis of markets and various trading systems.

Lofton, Todd, *Getting Started in Futures*, John Wiley & Sons, New York, 2001.

For those who want a good grounding in the fundamentals of futures, this is a popular book.

Lowenstein, Roger, *Buffett—The Making of an American Capitalist*, Random House, New York, 1995.

Buffett is the undisputed greatest investor of all time. And more than a great investor, he is a great businessman. Many books have been written on the Oracle of Omaha. This is the best.

Malkiel, Burton G., *A Random Walk Down Wall Street—The Best Investment Advice for the New Century*, Norton, New York, 1999.

One of the great investment classics that should be on everyone's reading list. Do not invest a penny until you read this book. After reading *A Random Walk*, you will be left wondering why you have tried to beat the market all these years.

McMillan, Lawrence, *Options as a Strategic Investment*, Prentice Hall, Upper Saddle River, NJ: 1992.

There are dozens of options texts available, and this is the best for most investors.

Nassar, David, S., *Rules of the Trade: Indispensable Insights for Online Profits*, McGraw-Hill, New York, 2001.

Anyone thinking of trading or investing should have plan. Part of that plan should be rules. This new book could provide valuable insight to any plan.

Natenberg, Sheldon, *Options Volatility and Pricing*, Probus Publishing, Chicago, 1994.

McMillan's book is the best for the masses. Natenberg's is the best for those already familiar with options. It is written for the professional or more advanced options traders. The discussion on volatility is superb. For those who want to do delta-neutral trading and spread trading and get to the heart of options, this is your candidate. To be thorough, you really should read Natenberg and McMillan, the two best books on the subject.

Schwager, Jack D., *Market Wizards: Interviews with Top Traders*, Harper Business, New York, 1993.

Schwager, Jack D., *The New Market Wizards: Conversations with America's Top Traders*, Harper Business, New York, 1994.

Schwager, Jack D., *Stock Market Wizards: Interviews with America's Top Stock Traders*, Harper Business, New York, 2001.

> When new traders ask for a reading list, Schwager's books usually come first. These three have dozens of fascinating interviews with the best in the business. Schwager catalogs the philosophies of market wizards who trade futures, options, stocks, currencies, and anything else. He goes beyond just interviews and discusses what the wizards have in common and what sets them apart.

Young, Patrick, and Thomas Theys, *Capital Market Revolution—The Future of Markets in an Online World*, Pearson Education Limited, England, 1999.

> A great work on where markets, particularly futures and options markets, have been and where they are heading in terms of the traditional trading platforms versus the new on-line electronic platforms. Anyone who trades from a screen or is interested in screen-based trading should pick up a copy of this witty book, written by an ex–floor trader and the founder of one of the largest screen-based front-end software providers in the trading world.

RECOMMENDED WEB SITES

There are hundreds, if not thousands, of sites dedicated to finance and investing. Some sites are excellent in that they provide incredible detail in terms of education, statistics, and data. The following sites are dedicated solely to ETFs or E-mini stock index futures.

www.amex.com

Click on the Exchange Traded Funds tab, and you'll have plenty of information on ETFs. Since nearly all U.S.-based ETFs trade on the AMEX, there will be a large amount of data. For the trader, make sure you visit www.amextrader.com too.

www.cme.com

This is a great web site that has all the information you need if you are considering trading the E-Mini S&P 500 or the E-Mini Nasdaq-100. It contains lots of data and statistics, as well as educational materials. Nearly all the brochures on stock index products are in PDF format for easy downloading. The site contains performance bond margin information as well as GLOBEX information, settlement prices, and a host of other information useful to futures traders.

www.holdrs.com

At their inception, Merrill's HOLDRS were very popular despite the lack of widespread information on these unique ETFs. As popularity swelled, Merrill put out this very good site dedicated to the product line. It has all the components of each of the HOLDRS and their precise share amounts, with plenty of downloadable information.

www.indexfunds.com

An excellent site dedicated to the indexing revolution. Go to the ETF zone, which is filled with data on ETFs as well as traditional index funds. Want to know the 15-year returns on a major index? This site probably has it, as well as discussion boards.

www.iShares.com

Barclays Global Investors' site dedicated to their ETF products. Since mid-2000, BGI has launched over 50 iShares products. You can track prices, download prospectuses, and find lots of additional information. The site also contains features for investment advisers and retail and institutional investors.

www.morningstar.com

The definitive place for detailed mutual fund information. Morningstar also has devoted part of its site to ETFs. Go to the home page, and click on the ETF tab. Great statistics and timely feature articles, as well as links to many other ETF sites.

www.nasdaq.com

Like the AMEX's site, this has an amazing amount of information on all ETFs. Click on the ETF tab. Make sure you check out the ETF Heatmaps—an interesting tool that measures percentage changes in many ETFs throughout the day and color codes them by performance. See also www.nasdaqtrader.com.

www.programtrading.com

Good site for information on fair value, premium, and the material covered in Appendix 3. Careful, though: If you polled 10 firms on their calculation of the premium, you would likely get 10 different answers.

www.russell.com

This is the site to visit for up-to-date information on the Russell indexes.

www.spglobal.com

The Web site for Standard & Poor's indexes. It contains updated information on all S&P indexes.

www.streetTracks.com

The Web site for up-to-date information on SSgA's streetTRACKS product line.

www.traderslibrary.com

Great site for books on the topics of trading and investing.

TIMELINE

1896	Charles Dow and Edward Jones debut the Dow Jones Industrial Average. The original DJIA had only 12 companies. General Electric is the only company of the original 12 that is still a component.
1923–1926	Standard & Poor's develops its first stock market indicators. The new indexes covers 26 industry groups and 233 companies. In 1926, S&P creates 90 Stock Composite Price Index.
1941	The "233" grows to 416.
December 1949	John C. Bogle reads a *Fortune* article entitled, "Big Money in Boston," that discusses a new industry in making: investment companies. It becomes the subject for his senior thesis.
March 1951	Bogle submits his senior thesis, "Economic Role of Investment Companies," to Princeton's Economics Department.
1957	The "416" becomes the S&P 500 Composite Stock Price Index. In order to create a lengthy historical time series, the new 500 is linked to the "90" stock price index, and daily S&P 500 prices become available back to 1928. Thus, the original indexes, the "233" and the "90," evolve into the modern Standard & Poor's 500. It consists of 425 industrials, 60 utilities, and 15 rails.
1971	Wells Fargo Investment Advisors launches the first indexing strategy using the NYSE composite index.
1973	Wells Fargo Investment Advisors launches the first indexing strategy using the S&P 500 index.
1973	The first edition of *A Random Walk Down Wall Street*, by Burton Malkiel, appears. Wall Street is miffed at the "dart board" analogies.
January 1974	John Bogle is fired from his investment management job.
September 1974	John Bogle founds the Vanguard Group.
December 1975	Vanguard creates the first index mutual fund, First Index Investment Trust, with $11 million in assets.

February 1982	The Kansas City Board of Trade launches the first stock index futures contract based on the Value Line Index.
April 1982	The Chicago Mercantile Exchange introduces S&P 500 futures, first-day volume is 3,963 contracts.
1983	CBOE introduces options on the S&P 100 (OEX) and the S&P 500 (SPX) cash indexes.
1984	Frank Russell & Co. establishes the Russell 1000, Russell 2000, and Russell 3000 indexes.
1990	Wells Fargo joins Nikko Securities Co. to become Wells Fargo Nikko Investment Advisors.
June 1991	Standard & Poor's debuts the S&P MidCap 400 Index, providing a benchmark for mid-tier companies.
1992	Vanguard introduces a mutual fund based on the Wilshire 5000 Index.
	Chicago Mercantile Exchange launches S&P Midcap 400 futures and Options.
January 1993	The AMEX launches its first exchange traded fund—Standard & Poor's Depositary Receipts, or SPDRs. State Street Global Advisors is the fund manager.
February 1993	The CME begins trading futures and options on the Russell 2000 Index.
May 1995	Trading begins in MidCap SPDRs at the AMEX.
1996	CME begins trading futures and options on the Nasdaq-100 Index.
	Barclays PLC buys Wells Fargo Nikko Investment Advisors and merges it with its investment management arm—BZW Investment Management—to form Barclays Global Investors. BGI becomes the largest indexer in the world.
March 1996	AMEX launches World Equity Benchmark Shares on 17 countries.
1997	AMEX launches ETF on Dow Jones Industrials called DIAMONDS.
1998	AMEX launches ETFs on S&P Select Sectors called Select Sector SPDRs.
September 1997	CME launches E-mini S&P 500 futures contact—the first all electronically traded futures contract with virtual 24-hour availability. Day 1 volume is 7,494 contracts.
March 1999	AMEX begins trading the Nasdaq-100 Index Shares—the QQQ. Day 1 volume exceeds 2.5 million shares.

June 1999	CME begins trading E-Mini Nasdaq-100 futures. Day 1 volume is 2,136.
November 1999	Vanguard 500 Index Fund reaches $100 billion in assets.
Spring 2000	Barclays Global Investors launches the first ETFs named iShares.
Fall 2000	State Street Global Advisors launches streetTRACKS ETF.
March 2001	E-mini S&P 500 futures trade record 201,555 contracts.
May 2001	Vanguard introduces VIPERs ETF based on its Total Stock Market Index Fund that tracks the Wilshire 5000.
June 2001	ETFs in Europe now number 46. Assets in European ETFs reach $11 billion.
July 2001	NYSE announces it will list the QQQ and other ETFs thereby challenging the AMEX's dominance.

ANSWERS TO QUIZZES

Parts I and II Quiz (page 126)

1. a,b,c,d
2. a
3. Investment management fees, transaction costs, taxes, cash drag
4. c, the Dow Jones Industrials is a price-weighted average
5. d, Nathan Most and Steve Bloom did most of the pioneering work at the AMEX
6. AMEX
7. b
8. d
9. a
10. c
11. c
12. a
13. a
14. Currency risk and political risk
15. d
16. c
17. a. Brazil is an emerging market and has higher volatility
18. d. 100 is the minimum amount of HOLDRS you can deal in
19. c
20. a
21. d
22. d
23. b
24. True
25. b

Part III Quiz (page 202)

1. c	5. false	9. d	13. c
2. a,b	6. a,b	10. a,b,c,d	14. a
3. a	7. a,b,c,d	11. a,b,c	15. d
4. b	8. a	12. a	16. b and/or c

INDEX